Mobil
Travel Guide

Great Plains

2006

Iowa

Kansas

Missouri

Nebraska

Oklahoma

ExxonMobil
Travel Publications

Acknowledgements

We gratefully acknowledge the help of our representatives for their efficient and perceptive inspections of the lodging and dining establishments listed; the establishments' proprietors for their cooperation in showing their facilities and providing information about them; and the many users of previous editions who have taken the time to share their experiences. Mobil Travel Guide is also grateful to all the talented writers who contributed entries to this book.

www.mobiltravelguide.com

Front cover photo: Rockbridge Mill, Missouri

ISBN: 0-7627-3923-1

ISSN: 1550-1930

Manufactured in the United States of America.

10 9 8 7 6 5 4 3 2 1

Contents

MAP SYMBOLS

TRANSPORTATION

CONTROLLED ACCESS HIGHWAYS

Freeway
Tollway
Under Construction
Interchange and Exit Number

OTHER HIGHWAYS

Primary Highway
Secondary Highway
Divided Highway
Other Paved Road
Unpaved Road
Check conditions locally

HIGHWAY MARKERS

Interstate Route
U.S. Route
State or Provincial Route
County or Other Route
Trans-Canada Highway
Canadian Provincial Autoroute
Mexican Federal Route

OTHER SYMBOLS

Distances along Major Highways
Miles in U.S.; kilometers in Canada and Mexico
Tunnel; Pass
Auto Ferry; Passenger Ferry

RECREATION

National Park
National Forest; National Grassland
Other Large Park or Recreation Area
Small State Park
with and without Camping
Military Lands
Indian Reservation
Trail
Ski Area
Point of Interest

CITIES AND TOWNS

National Capital
State or Provincial Capital
Cities, Towns, and Populated Places
Type size indicates relative importance
Urban Area
State and province maps only
Large Incorporated Cities
City maps only

OTHER MAP FEATURES

Time Zone Boundary
Mt. Olympus
7,965
Mountain Peak; Elevation
in Feet
Perennial; Intermittent River

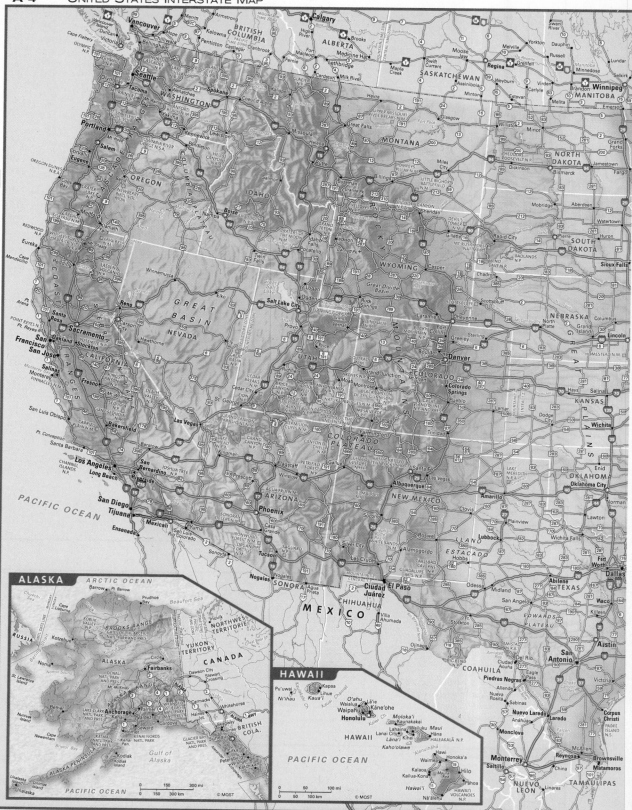

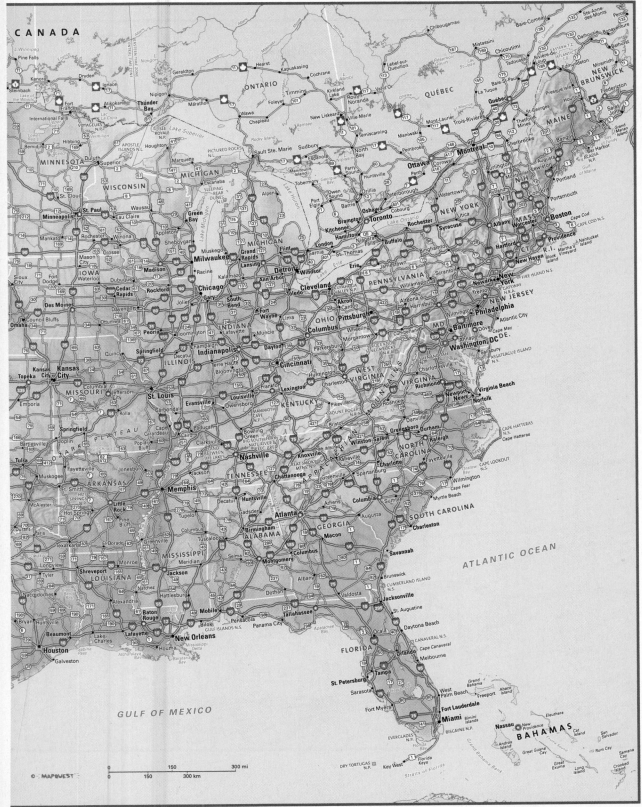

© MAPQUEST

| 0 | 150 | 300 mi |
| 0 | 150 | 300 km |

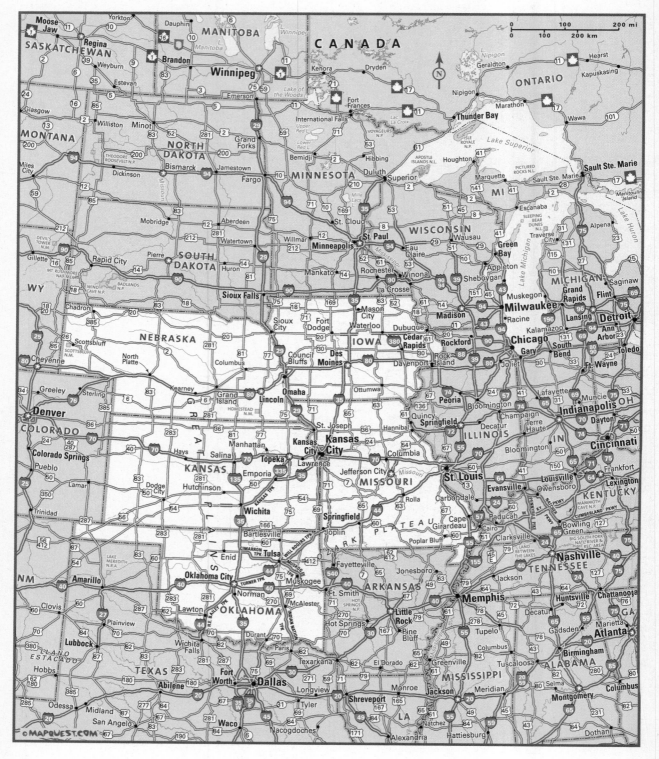

©MAPQUEST.COM

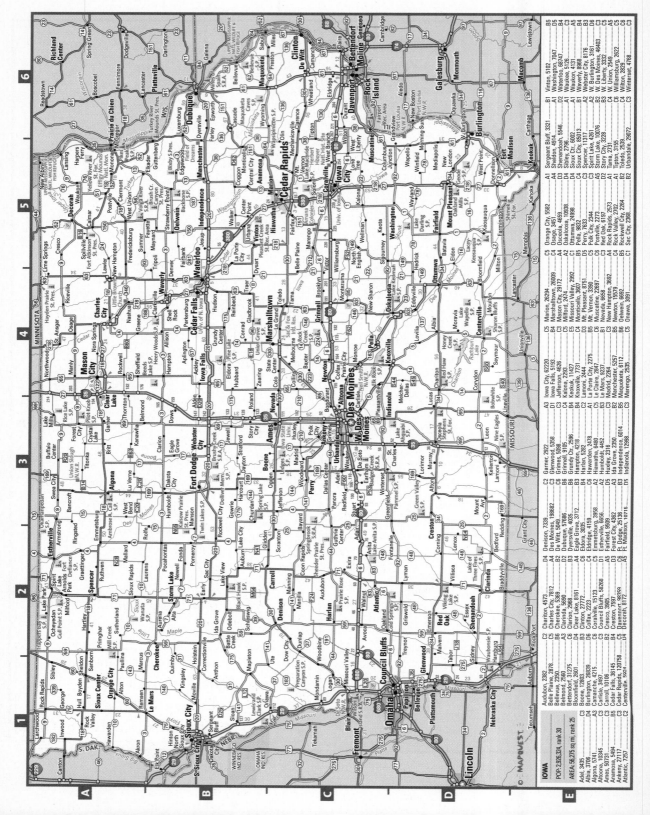

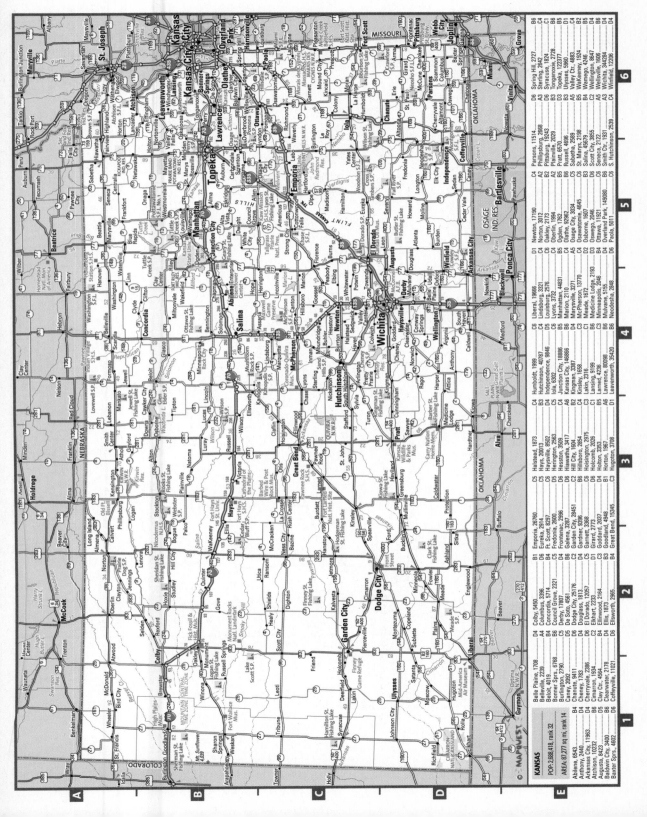

KANSAS

POP. 2,688,418, rank 32

AREA: 87,277 sq. mi., rank 14

Abilene, 6543	B4		Parsons, 11514	B6
Anthony, 2440	D4		Newton, 17190	C4
Arkansas City, 11963	D5		Norton, 3012	A3
Atchison, 10232	B6		Oakley, 2173	C6
Augusta, 8423	C5		Oberlin, 1994	A2
Baldwin City, 3400	B6		Olathe, 92962	B6
Baxter Sprs., 4602	D6		Osage City, 3034	C5
Belle Plaine, 1708	D4		Osawatomie, 4645	B6
Belleville, 2239	A4		McPherson, 13770	C4
Beloit, 4019	B4		Osborne, 1607	B3
Bonner Sprs., 6768	B6		Osborne, 1607	B3
Burlington, 2790	C6		Oswego, 2046	B6
Caney, 2092	D5		Overland Park, 149080	B6
Chanute, 9411	C6		Paola, 5011	C6
Cheney, 1783	D4		Phillipsburg, 2668	A3
Clay Ctr., 4564	B4		Pittsburg, 19243	D6
Clearwater, 2178	D4		Plainville, 2029	B3
Coffeyville, 11021	D6		Pratt, 6570	C3
Colby, 5450	C2		Russell, 4696	B3
Columbus, 3396	A4		Sabetha, 2589	A5
Concordia, 5714	B4		St. Marys, 2198	B5
Council Grove, 2321	B5		Salina, 45679	C4
Derby, 17807	D4		Scott City, 3855	C2
De Soto, 4561	A6		Seneca, 2122	A5
Dodge City, 25176	D2		Smith Ctr., 1931	A3
Douglass, 1813	D5		S. Hutchinson, 2539	C4
El Dorado, 12057	C5		Spring Hill, 2727	B6
Elkhart, 2233	D1		Sterling, 2642	C4
Ellinwood, 2164	C3		Syracuse, 1824	D1
Ellis, 1873	B3		Tonganoxie, 2728	B6
Ellsworth, 2965	C4		Topeka, 122377	B5
Emporia, 26760	C5		Ulysses, 5960	D1
Eureka, 2914	C5		Valley Ctr., 4883	C4
Ft. Scott, 8297	C6		Wakeeney, 1924	B2
Fredonia, 2600	D5		Wamego, 4246	B5
Frontenac, 2996	D6		Wellington, 8647	D4
Galena, 3287	D6		Wellsville, 1606	B6
Garden City, 28451	D2		Wichita, 344284	D4
Gardner, 9396	B6		Winfield, 12206	D4
Garnett, 3368	C6			
Girard, 2773	D6			
Goddard, 2037	C4			
Goodland, 4948	C1			
Great Bend, 15345	B4			
Halstead, 1873	C4			
Hays, 20013	B3			
Haysville, 8502	D6			
Herington, 2563	B5			
Hesston, 3509	A1			
Hiawatha, 2996	A6			
Hill City, 1617	B3			
Hillsboro, 2854	C3			
Hoisington, 2975	B3			
Holcomb, 2026	D2			
Holton, 3353	B5			
Horton, 1967	A6			
Hugoton, 3708	C3			
Humboldt, 1999	C4			
Hutchinson, 40787	B3			
Independence, 9846	D5			
Iola, 6302	B5			
Junction City, 18886	B5			
Kansas City, 146866	A6			
Kingman, 3387	C3			
Kinsley, 1658	C3			
Lakin, 2316	C1			
Lansing, 9199	C1			
Larned, 4236	D3			
Lawrence, 80098	B5			
Leavenworth, 35420	D1			
Liberal, 19666	C6			
Lindsborg, 3321	D1			
Louisburg, 2576	D5			
Lyons, 3732	C6			
Manhattan, 44831	B5			
Marion, 2110	C3			
Marysville, 3271	A5			
Meade, 1672	C1			
Medicine Lodge, 2193	D3			
Minneapolis, 2046	B4			
Mulvane, 5155	B6			
Neodesha, 2848	C6			

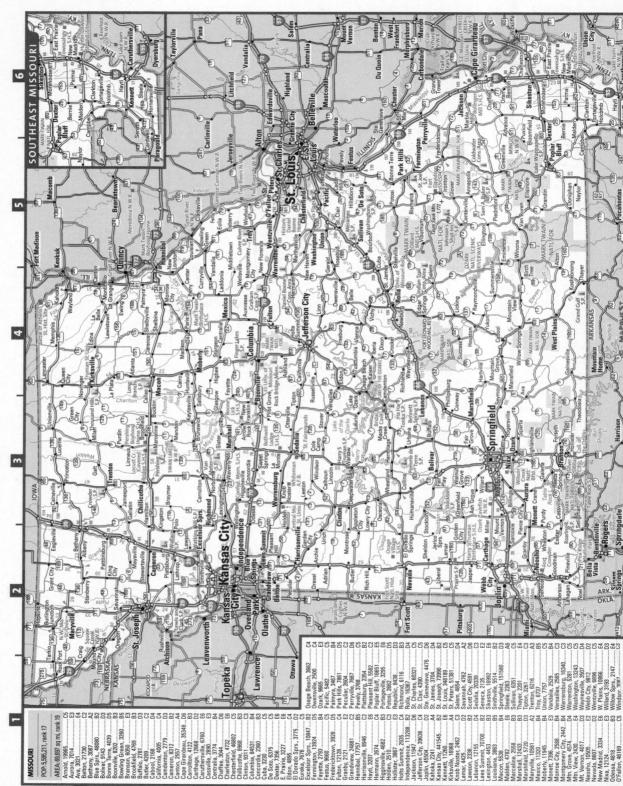

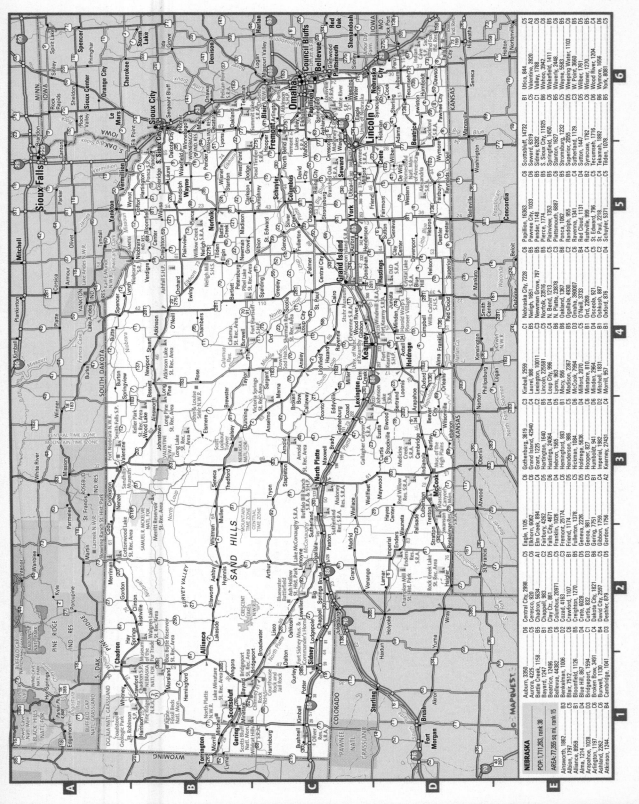

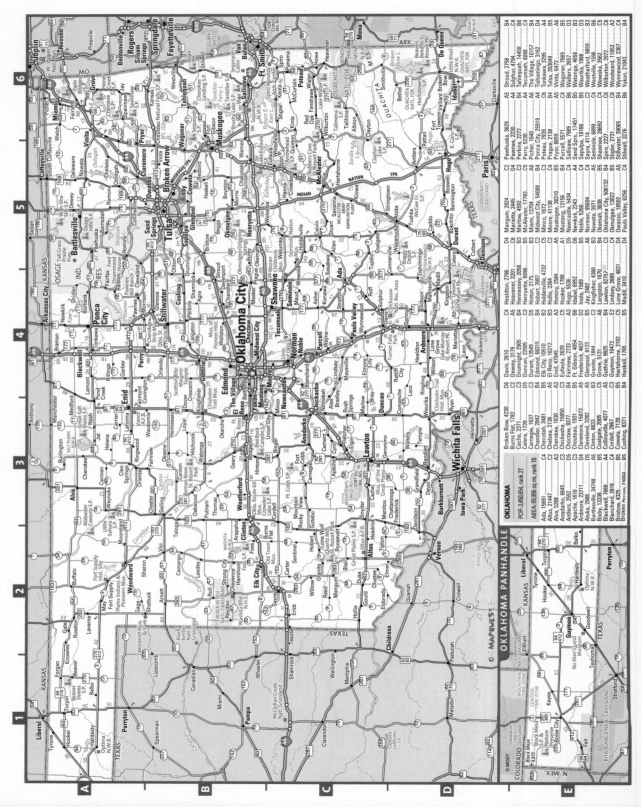

Distances in chart are in miles.
To convert miles to kilometers, multiply the distance in miles by 1.609

Example:
New York, NY to Boston, MA = 215 miles or 346 kilometers (215 x 1.609)

Cities listed (top-to-bottom along the right edge and left-to-right along the bottom):

WICHITA, KS · WASHINGTON, DC · VANCOUVER, BC · TORONTO, ON · TAMPA, FL · SEATTLE, WA · SAN FRANCISCO, CA · SAN DIEGO, CA · SAN ANTONIO, TX · SALT LAKE CITY, UT · ST. LOUIS, MO · RICHMOND, VA · RENO, NV · RAPID CITY, SD · PORTLAND, OR · PORTLAND, ME · PITTSBURGH, PA · PHOENIX, AZ · PHILADELPHIA, PA · ORLANDO, FL · OMAHA, NE · OKLAHOMA CITY, OK · NEW YORK, NY · NEW ORLEANS, LA · NASHVILLE, TN · MONTRÉAL, QC · MINNEAPOLIS, MN · MILWAUKEE, WI · MIAMI, FL · MEMPHIS, TN · LOUISVILLE, KY · LOS ANGELES, CA · LITTLE ROCK, AR · LAS VEGAS, NV · KANSAS CITY, MO · JACKSON, MS · INDIANAPOLIS, IN · HOUSTON, TX · EL PASO, TX · DETROIT, MI · DES MOINES, IA · DENVER, CO · DALLAS, TX · CLEVELAND, OH · CINCINNATI, OH · CHICAGO, IL · CHEYENNE, WY · CHARLOTTE, NC · CHARLESTON, WV · CHARLESTON, SC · BURLINGTON, VT · BUFFALO, NY · BOSTON, MA · BOISE, ID · BISMARCK, ND · BIRMINGHAM, AL · BILLINGS, MT · BALTIMORE, MD · ATLANTA, GA · ALBUQUERQUE, NM

© MapQuest.com, Inc.

Welcome

Dear Traveler,

Since its inception in 1958, Mobil Travel Guide has served as a trusted advisor to auto travelers in search of value in lodging, dining, and destinations. Now in its 48th year, the Mobil Travel Guide is the hallmark of our ExxonMobil family of travel publications, and we're proud to offer an array of products and services from our Mobil, Exxon, and Esso brands in North America to facilitate life on the road.

Whether you're looking for business or pleasure venues, our nationwide network of independent, professional evaluators offers their expertise on thousands of travel options, allowing you to plan a quick family getaway, a full-service business meeting, or an unforgettable Mobil Five-Star celebration.

Your feedback is important to us as we strive to improve our product offerings and better meet today's travel needs. Whether you travel once a week or once a year, please take the time to contact us at www.mobiltravelguide.com. We hope to hear from you soon.

Best wishes for safe and enjoyable travels.

Lee R Raymond

Lee R. Raymond
Chairman and CEO
Exxon Mobil Corporation

A Word to Our Readers

Travelers are on the roads in great numbers these days. They're exploring the country on day trips, weekend getaways, business trips, and extended family vacations, visiting major cities and small towns along the way. Because time is precious and the travel industry is ever-changing, having accurate, reliable travel information at your fingertips is critical. Mobil Travel Guide has been providing invaluable insight to travelers for more than 45 years, and we are committed to continuing this service well into the future.

The Mobil Corporation (known as Exxon Mobil Corporation since a 1999 merger) began producing the Mobil Travel Guide books in 1958, following the introduction of the US interstate highway system in 1956. The first edition covered only five Southwestern states. Since then, our books have become the premier travel guides in North America, covering all 50 states and Canada.

Since its founding, Mobil Travel Guide has served as an advocate for travelers seeking knowledge about hotels, restaurants, and places to visit. Based on an objective process, we make recommendations to our customers that we believe will enhance the quality and value of their travel experiences. Our trusted Mobil One- to Five-Star rating system is the oldest and most respected lodging and restaurant inspection and rating program in North America. Most hoteliers, restaurateurs, and industry observers favorably regard the rigor of our inspection program and understand the prestige and benefits that come with receiving a Mobil Star rating.

The Mobil Travel Guide process of rating each establishment includes:

○ Unannounced facility inspections

○ Incognito service evaluations for Mobil Four-Star and Mobil Five-Star properties

○ A review of unsolicited comments from the general public

○ Senior management oversight

For each property, more than 450 attributes, including cleanliness, physical facilities, and employee attitude and courtesy, are measured and evaluated to produce a mathematically derived score, which is then blended with the other elements to form an overall score. These quantifiable scores allow comparative analysis among properties and form the basis that we use to assign our Mobil One- to Five-Star ratings.

This process focuses largely on guest expectations, guest experience, and consistency of service, not just physical facilities and amenities. It is fundamentally a relative rating system that rewards those properties that continually strive for and achieve excellence each year. Indeed, the very best properties are consistently raising the bar for those that wish to compete with them. These properties proactively respond to consumers' needs even in today's uncertain times.

Only facilities that meet Mobil Travel Guide's standards earn the privilege of being listed in the guide. Deteriorating, poorly managed establishments are deleted. A Mobil Travel Guide listing constitutes a positive quality recommendation; every listing is an accolade, a recognition of achievement. Our Mobil One- to Five-Star rating system highlights its level of service. Extensive in-house research is constantly underway to determine new additions to our lists.

○ The Mobil Five-Star Award indicates that a property is one of the very best in the country and consistently provides gracious and courteous service, superlative quality in its facility, and a unique ambience. The lodgings and restaurants at the Mobil Five-Star level consistently and proactively respond to consumers' needs and continue their commitment to excellence, doing so with grace and perseverance.

○ Also highly regarded is the Mobil Four-Star Award, which honors properties for outstanding achievement in overall facility and for providing very strong service levels in all areas. These award winners provide a distinctive experience for the ever-demanding and sophisticated consumer.

- The Mobil Three-Star Award recognizes an excellent property that provides full services and amenities. This category ranges from exceptional hotels with limited services to elegant restaurants with a less-formal atmosphere.

- A Mobil Two-Star property is a clean and comfortable establishment that has expanded amenities or a distinctive environment. A Mobil Two-Star property is an excellent place to stay or dine.

- A Mobil One-Star property is limited in its amenities and services but focuses on providing a value experience while meeting travelers' expectations. The property can be expected to be clean, comfortable, and convenient.

Allow us to emphasize that we do not charge establishments for inclusion in our guides. We have no relationship with any of the businesses and attractions we list and act only as a consumer advocate. In essence, we do the investigative legwork so that you won't have to.

Keep in mind, too, that the hospitality business is ever-changing. Restaurants and lodgings—particularly small chains and stand-alone establish-ments—change management or even go out of business with surprising quickness. Although we make every effort to double-check information during our annual updates, we nevertheless recommend that you call ahead to make sure the place you've selected is still open and offers all the amenities you're looking for. We've provided phone numbers; when available, we also list fax numbers and Web site addresses.

We hope that your travels are enjoyable and relaxing and that our books help you get the most out of every trip you take. If any aspect of your accommodation, dining, or sightseeing experience motivates you to comment, please drop us a line. We depend a great deal on our readers' remarks, so you can be assured that we will read your comments and assimilate them into our research. General comments about our books are also welcome. You can write to us at Mobil Travel Guide, 7373 N Cicero Ave, Lincolnwoood, IL 60712, or send an e-mail to info@mobiltravelguide.com.

Take your Mobil Travel Guide books along on every trip you take. We're confident that you'll be pleased with their convenience, ease of use, and breadth of dependable coverage.

Happy travels!

How to Use This Book

The Mobil Travel Guide Regional Travel Planners are designed for ease of use. Each state has its own chapter, beginning with a general introduction that provides a geographical and historical orientation to the state and gives basic statewide tourist information, from climate to calendar highlights to seatbelt laws. The remainder of each chapter is devoted to travel destinations within the state—mainly cities and towns, but also national parks and tourist areas—which, like the states, are arranged in alphabetical order.

The following sections explain the wealth of information you'll find about those travel destinations: information about the area, things to see and do there, and where to stay and eat.

Maps and Map Coordinates

At the front of this book in the full-color section, we have provided state maps as well as maps of selected larger cities to help you find your way around once you leave the highway. You'll find a key to the map symbols on the Contents page at the beginning of the map section.

Next to most cities and towns throughout the book, you'll find a set of map coordinates, such as C-2. These coordinates reference the maps at the front of this book and help you find the location you're looking for quickly and easily.

Destination Information

Because many travel destinations are close to other cities and towns where travelers might find additional attractions, accommodations, and restaurants, we've included cross-references to those cities and towns when it makes sense to do so. We also list addresses, phone numbers, and Web sites for travel information resources—usually the local chamber of commerce or office of tourism—as well as pertinent statistics and, in many cases, a brief introduction to the area.

Information about airports, ground transportation, and suburbs is included for large cities.

Driving Tours and Walking Tours

The driving tours that we include for many states are usually day trips that make for interesting side excursions, although they can be longer. They offer you a way to get off the beaten path and visit an area that travelers often overlook. These trips frequently cover areas of natural beauty or historical significance.

Each walking tour focuses on a particularly interesting area of a city or town. Again, these tours can provide a break from everyday tourist attractions. The tours often include places to stop for meals or snacks.

What to See and Do

Mobil Travel Guide offers information about nearly 20,000 museums, art galleries, amusement parks, historic sites, national and state parks, ski areas, and many other types of attractions. A white star on a black background ★ signals that the attraction is a must-see—one of the best in the area. Because municipal parks, public tennis courts, swimming pools, and small educational institutions are common to most towns, they generally are not mentioned.

Following an attraction's description, you'll find the months, days, and, in some cases, hours of operation; the address/directions, telephone number, and Web site (if there is one); and the admission price category. The following are the ranges we use for admission fees, based on one adult:

✪ **FREE**

✪ **$** = Up to $5

✪ **$$** = $5.01-$10

✪ **$$$** = $10.01-$15

✪ **$$$$** = Over $15

Special Events

Special events are either annual events that last only a short time, such as festivals and fairs, or longer, seasonal events such as horse racing, theater, and summer concerts. Our Special Events listings also include infrequently occurring occasions that mark certain dates or events, such as a centennial or other commemorative celebration.

Side Trips

We recognize that your travels don't always end where state lines fall, so we've included some side trips that fall outside the states covered in this book but that travelers frequently visit when they're in the region. Nearby national parks, major cities, and other prime tourist draws fall into this category. You'll find side trips for a particular state at the end of that state's section.

Listings

Lodgings, spas, and restaurants are usually listed under the city or town in which they're located. Make sure to check the related cities and towns that appear right beneath a city's heading for additional options, especially if you're traveling to a major metropolitan area that includes many suburbs. If a property is located in a town that doesn't have its own heading, the listing appears under the town nearest it, with the address and town given immediately after the establishment's name. In large cities, lodgings located within 5 miles of major commercial airports may be listed under a separate "Airport Area" heading that follows the city section.

LODGINGS

Travelers have different wants and needs when it comes to accommodations. To help you pinpoint properties that meet your particular needs, Mobil Travel Guide classifies each lodging by type according to the following characteristics.

Mobil Rated Lodgings

- **Limited-Service Hotel.** A limited-service hotel is traditionally a Mobil One-Star or Mobil Two-Star property. At a Mobil One-Star hotel, guests can expect to find a clean, comfortable property that commonly serves a complimentary continental breakfast. A Mobil Two-Star hotel is also clean and comfortable but has expanded amenities, such as a full-service restaurant, business

center, and fitness center. These services may have limited staffing and/or restricted hours of use.

- **Full-Service Hotel.** A full-service hotel traditionally enjoys a Mobil Three-Star, Mobil Four-Star, or Mobil Five-Star rating. Guests can expect these hotels to offer at least one full-service restaurant in addition to amenities such as valet parking, luggage assistance, 24-hour room service, concierge service, laundry and/or dry-cleaning services, and turndown service.

- **Full-Service Resort.** A resort is traditionally a full-service hotel that is geared toward recreation and represents a vacation and holiday destination. A resort's guest rooms are typically furnished to accommodate longer stays. The property may offer a full-service spa, golf, tennis, and fitness facilities or other leisure activities. Resorts are expected to offer a full-service restaurant and expanded amenities, such as luggage assistance, room service, meal plans, concierge service, and turndown service.

- **Full-Service Inn.** An inn is traditionally a Mobil Three-Star, Mobil Four-Star, or Mobil Five-Star property. Inns are similar to bed-and-breakfasts (see below) but offer a wider range of services, most significantly a full-service restaurant that serves at least breakfast and dinner.

Specialty Lodgings

Mobil Travel Guide recognizes the unique and individualized nature of many different types of lodging establishments, including bed-and-breakfasts, limited-service inns, and guest ranches. For that reason, we have chosen to place our stamp of approval on the properties that fall into these two categories in lieu of applying our traditional Mobil Star ratings.

- **B&B/Limited-Service Inn.** A bed-and-breakfast (B&B) or limited-service inn is traditionally an owner-occupied home or residence found in a residential area or vacation destination. It may be a structure of historic significance. Rooms are often individually decorated, but telephones, televisions, and private bathrooms may not be available in every room. A B&B typically serves only breakfast to its overnight guests, which is included in the room rate. Cocktails and refreshments may be served in the late afternoon or evening.

○ **Guest Ranch.** A guest ranch is traditionally a rustic, Western-themed property that specializes in stays of three or more days. Horseback riding is often a feature, with stables and trails found on the property. Facilities can range from clean, comfortable establishments to more luxurious facilities.

Mobil Star Rating Definitions for Lodgings

○ ★ ★ ★ ★ ★ : A Mobil Five-Star lodging provides consistently superlative service in an exceptionally distinctive luxury environment, with expanded services. Attention to detail is evident throughout the hotel, resort, or inn, from bed linens to staff uniforms.

○ ★ ★ ★ ★ : A Mobil Four-Star lodging provides a luxury experience with expanded amenities in a distinctive environment. Services may include, but are not limited to, automatic turndown service, 24-hour room service, and valet parking.

○ ★ ★ ★ : A Mobil Three-Star lodging is well appointed, with a full-service restaurant and expanded amenities, such as a fitness center, golf course, tennis courts, 24-hour room service, and optional turndown service.

○ ★ ★ : A Mobil Two-Star lodging is considered a clean, comfortable, and reliable establishment that has expanded amenities, such as a full-service restaurant on the premises.

○ ★ : A Mobil One-Star lodging is a limited-service hotel, motel, or inn that is considered a clean, comfortable, and reliable establishment.

Information Found in the Lodging Listings

Each lodging listing gives the name, address/location (when no street address is available), neighborhood and/or directions from downtown (in major cities), phone number(s), fax number, total number of guest rooms, and seasons open (if not year-round). Also included are details on business, luxury, recreational, and dining facilities at the property or nearby. A key to the symbols at the end of each listing can be found on the page following the "A Word to Our Readers" section.

For every property, we also provide pricing information. Because lodging rates change frequently, we list a pricing category rather than specific prices. The pricing categories break down as follows:

○ **$** = Up to $150

○ **$$** = $151-$250

○ **$$$** = $251-$350

○ **$$$$** = $351 and up

All prices quoted are in effect at the time of publication; however, prices cannot be guaranteed. In some locations, short-term price variations may exist because of special events, holidays, or seasonality. Certain resorts have complicated rate structures that vary with the time of year; always confirm rates when making your plans.

Because most lodgings offer the following features and services, information about them does not appear in the listings:

○ Year-round operation

○ Bathroom with tub and/or shower in each room

○ Cable television in each room

○ In-room telephones

○ Cots and cribs available

○ Daily maid service

○ Elevators

○ Major credit cards accepted

Although we recommend every lodging we list in this book, a few stand out—they offer noteworthy amenities or stand above the others in their category in terms of quality, value, or historical significance. To draw your attention to these special spots, we've included the magnifying glass icon to the left of the listing, as you see here.

SPAS

Mobil Travel Guide is pleased to announce its newest category: hotel and resort spas. Until now, hotel and resort spas have not been formally rated or inspected by any organization. Every spa selected for inclusion in this book underwent a rigorous inspection process similar to the one Mobil Travel Guide has been applying to lodgings and restaurants for more than four decades. After spending a year and a half researching more than 300 spas and performing exhaustive incognito inspections of more than 200 properties, we narrowed our list to the 48 best spas in the United States and Canada.

Mobil Travel Guide's spa ratings are based on objective evaluations of more than 450 attributes. Approximately half of these criteria assess basic expectations, such as staff courtesy, the technical proficiency and skill of the employees, and whether the facility is maintained properly and hygienically. Several standards address issues that impact a guest's physical comfort and convenience, as well as the staff's ability to impart a sense of personalized service and anticipate clients' needs. Additional criteria measure the spa's ability to create a completely calming ambience.

The Mobil Star ratings focus on much more than the facilities available at a spa and the treatments it offers. Each Mobil Star rating is a cumulative score achieved from multiple inspections that reflects the spa management's attention to detail and commitment to consumers' needs.

Mobil Star Rating Definitions for Spas

✪ ★ ★ ★ ★ ★ : A Mobil Five-Star spa provides consistently superlative service in an exceptionally distinctive luxury environment with extensive amenities. The staff at a Mobil Five-Star spa provides extraordinary service above and beyond the traditional spa experience, allowing guests to achieve the highest level of relaxation and pampering. A Mobil Five-Star spa offers an extensive array of treatments, often incorporating international themes and products. Attention to detail is evident throughout the spa, from arrival to departure.

✪ ★ ★ ★ ★ : A Mobil Four-Star spa provides a luxurious experience with expanded amenities in an elegant and serene environment. Throughout the spa facility, guests experience personalized service. Amenities might include, but are not limited to, single-sex relaxation rooms where guests wait for their treatments, plunge pools and whirlpools in both men's and women's locker rooms, and an array of treatments, including at a minimum a selection of massages, body therapies, facials, and a variety of salon services.

✪ ★ ★ ★ : A Mobil Three-Star spa is physically well appointed and has a full complement of staff to ensure that guests' needs are met. It has some expanded amenities, such as, but not limited to, a well-equipped fitness center, separate men's and women's locker rooms, a sauna or steam room, and a designated relaxation area. It also offers a menu of services that at a minimum includes massages, facial treatments, and at least one other type of body treatment, such as scrubs or wraps.

RESTAURANTS

All Mobil Star rated dining establishments listed in this book have a full kitchen and offer seating at tables; most offer table service.

Mobil Star Rating Definitions for Restaurants

✪ ★ ★ ★ ★ ★ : A Mobil Five-Star restaurant offers one of few flawless dining experiences in the country. These establishments consistently provide their guests with exceptional food, superlative service, elegant décor, and exquisite presentations of each detail surrounding a meal.

✪ ★ ★ ★ ★ : A Mobil Four-Star restaurant provides professional service, distinctive presentations, and wonderful food.

✪ ★ ★ ★ : A Mobil Three-Star restaurant has good food, warm and skillful service, and enjoyable décor.

✪ ★ ★ : A Mobil Two-Star restaurant serves fresh food in a clean setting with efficient service. Value is considered in this category, as is family friendliness.

✪ ★ : A Mobil One-Star restaurant provides a distinctive experience through culinary specialty, local flair, or individual atmosphere.

Information Found in the Restaurant Listings

Each restaurant listing gives the cuisine type, street address (or directions if no address is available), phone and fax numbers, Web site (if available), meals served, days of operation (if not open daily year-round), and pricing category. Information about appropriate attire is provided, although it's always a good idea to call ahead and ask if you're unsure; the meaning of "casual" or "business casual" varies widely in different parts of the country. We also indicate whether the restaurant has a bar, whether a children's menu is offered, and whether outdoor seating is available. If reservations are recommended, we note that fact in the listing. When valet parking is available, it is noted in the description. In many cases, self-parking is available at the restaurant or nearby.

Because menu prices can fluctuate, we list a pricing category rather than specific prices. The pricing categories are defined as follows, per diner, and assume that you order an appetizer or dessert, an entrée, and one drink:

☺ **$** = $15 and under

☺ **$$** = $16-$35

☺ **$$$** = $36-$85

☺ **$$$$** = $86 and up

Again, all prices quoted are in effect at the time of publication, but prices cannot be guaranteed.

🔍 Although we recommend every restaurant we list in this book, a few stand out—they offer noteworthy local specialties or stand above the others in their category in terms of quality, value, or experience. To draw your attention to these special spots, we've included the magnifying glass icon to the left of the listing, as you see here.

SPECIAL INFORMATION FOR TRAVELERS WITH DISABILITIES

The Mobil Travel Guide 🚫 symbol indicates that an establishment is not at least partially accessible to people with mobility problems. When the 🚫 symbol follows a listing, the establishment is not equipped with facilities to accommodate people using wheelchairs or crutches or otherwise needing easy access to doorways and rest rooms. Travelers with severe mobility problems or with hearing or visual impairments may or may not find the facilities they need. Always phone ahead to make sure that an establishment can meet your needs.

AMERICA'S BYWAYS™

Mobil Travel Guide is pleased to announce a new partnership with the National Scenic Byways Program. Under this program, the US Secretary of Transportation recognizes certain roads as National Scenic Byways or All-American Roads based on their archaeological, cultural, historic, natural, recreational, and scenic qualities. To be designated a National Scenic Byway, a road must possess at least one of these six intrinsic qualities. To receive an All-American Road designation, a road must possess multiple intrinsic qualities that are nationally significant and contain one-of-a-kind features that do not exist elsewhere. The road or highway also must be considered a destination unto itself.

America's Byways are a great way to explore the country. From the mighty Mississippi to the towering Rockies to the Historic National Road, these routes take you past America's most treasured scenery and enable you to get in touch with America's past, present, and future. Bringing together all the nationally designated Byways in the Great Plains, this bonus section of the book is a handy reference whether you're planning to hop in the car tomorrow or you're simply looking for inspiration for future trips. Look for it at the end of the front section, before page 1.

Understanding the Symbols

What to See and Do

⭐ = One of the top attractions in the area

$ = Up to $5

$$ = $5.01 to $10

$$$ = $10.01 to $15

$$$$ = Over $15

Lodgings

$ = Up to $150

$$ = $151 to $250

$$$ = $251 to $350

$$$$ = Over $350

Restaurants

$ = Up to $15

$$ = $16 to $35

$$$ = $36 to $85

$$$$ = Over $85

Lodging Star Definitions

★ ★ ★ ★ ★ A Mobil Five-Star lodging establishment provides consistently superlative service in an exceptionally distinctive luxury environment with expanded services. Attention to detail is evident throughout the hotel/resort/inn from the bed linens to the staff uniforms.

★ ★ ★ ★ A Mobil Four-Star lodging establishment is a hotel/resort/inn that provides a luxury experience with expanded amenities in a distinctive environment. Services may include, but are not limited to, automatic turndown service, 24-hour room service, and valet parking.

★ ★ ★ A Mobil Three-Star lodging establishment is a hotel/resort/inn that is well appointed, with a full-service restaurant and expanded amenities, such as, but not limited to, a fitness center, golf course, tennis courts, 24-hour room service, and optional turndown service.

★ ★ A Mobil Two-Star lodging establishment is a hotel/resort/inn that is considered a clean, comfortable, and reliable establishment, but also has expanded amenities, such as a full-service restaurant on the premises.

★ A Mobil One-Star lodging establishment is a limited-service hotel or inn that is considered a clean, comfortable, and reliable establishment.

Restaurant Star Definitions

★ ★ ★ ★ ★ A Mobil Five-Star restaurant is one of few flawless dining experiences in the country. These restaurants consistently provide their guests with exceptional food, superlative service, elegant décor, and exquisite presentations of each detail surrounding the meal.

★ ★ ★ ★ A Mobil Four-Star restaurant provides professional service, distinctive presentations, and wonderful food.

★ ★ ★ A Mobil Three-Star restaurant has good food, warm and skillful service, and enjoyable décor.

★ ★ A Mobil Two-Star restaurant serves fresh food in a clean setting with efficient service. Value is considered in this category, as is family friendliness.

★ A Mobil One-Star restaurant provides a distinctive experience through culinary specialty, local flair, or individual atmosphere.

Symbols at End of Listings

🚫 Facilities for people with disabilities not available

🐾 Pets allowed

⛷ Ski in/ski out access

⛳ Golf on premises

🎾 Tennis court(s) on premises

🏊 Indoor or outdoor pool

🏋 Fitness room

✈ Major commercial airport within 5 miles

🏃 Business center

Making the Most of Your Trip

A few hardy souls might look back with fondness on a trip during which the car broke down, leaving them stranded for three days, or a vacation that cost twice what it was supposed to. For most travelers, though, the best trips are those that are safe, smooth, and within budget. To help you make your trip the best it can be, we've assembled a few tips and resources.

Saving Money

ON LODGING

Many hotels and motels offer discounts—for senior citizens, business travelers, families, you name it. It never hurts to ask—politely, that is. Sometimes, especially in the late afternoon, desk clerks are instructed to fill beds, and you might be offered a lower rate or a nicer room to entice you to stay. Simply ask the reservation agent for the best rate available. Also, make sure to try both the toll-free number and the local number. You may be able to get a lower rate from one than from the other.

Timing your trip right can cut your lodging costs as well. Look for bargains on stays over multiple nights, in the off-season, and on weekdays or weekends, depending on the location. Many hotels in major metropolitan areas, for example, have special weekend packages that offer leisure travelers considerable savings on rooms; they may include breakfast, cocktails, and/or dinner discounts.

Another way to save money is to choose accommodations that give you more than just a standard room. Rooms with kitchen facilities enable you to cook some meals yourself, reducing your restaurant costs. A suite might save money for two couples traveling together. Even hotel luxury levels can provide good value, as many include breakfast or cocktails in the price of a room.

State and city taxes, as well as special room taxes, can increase your room rate by as much as 25 percent per day. We are unable to include information about taxes in our listings, but we strongly urge you to ask about taxes when making reservations so that you understand the total cost of your lodgings before you book them.

Watch out for telephone-usage charges that hotels frequently impose on long-distance, credit-card, and other calls. Before phoning from your room, read the information given to you at check-in, and then be sure to review your bill carefully when checking out. You won't be expected to pay for charges that the hotel didn't spell out. Consider using your cell phone if you have one; or, if public telephones are available in the hotel lobby, your cost savings may outweigh the inconvenience of using them.

Here are some additional ways to save on lodgings:

- Stay in B&B accommodations. They're generally less expensive than standard hotel rooms, and the complimentary breakfast cuts down on food costs.

- If you're traveling with children, find lodgings at which kids stay free.

- When visiting a major city, stay just outside the city limits; these rooms are usually less expensive than those in downtown locations.

- Consider visiting national parks during the low season, when prices of lodgings near the parks drop by 25 percent or more.

- When calling a hotel, ask whether it is running any special promotions or if any discounts are available; many times reservationists are told not to volunteer these deals unless they're specifically asked about them.

- Check for hotel packages; some offer nightly rates that include a rental car or discounts on major attractions.

- Search the Internet for travel bargains. Web sites that allow for online booking of hotel rooms and travel planning, such as *www.mobiltravelguide .com,* often deliver lower rates than are available through telephone reservations.

ON DINING

There are several ways to get a less expensive meal at an expensive restaurant. Early-bird dinners are popular in many parts of the country and offer considerable savings. If you're interested in visiting a Mobil Four- or Five-Star establishment, consider going at lunchtime. Although the prices are probably still relatively high at midday, they may be half of those at dinner, and you'll experience the same ambience, service, and cuisine.

ON ENTERTAINMENT

Although many national parks, monuments, seashores, historic sites, and recreation areas may be visited free of charge, others charge an entrance fee and/or a usage fee for special services and facilities. If you plan to make several visits to national recreation areas, consider one of the following money-saving programs offered by the National Park Service:

- **National Parks Pass.** This annual pass is good for entrance to any national park that charges an entrance fee. If the park charges a per-vehicle fee, the pass holder and any accompanying passengers in a private noncommercial vehicle may enter. If the park charges a per-person fee, the pass applies to the holder's spouse, children, and parents as well as the holder. It is valid for entrance fees only; it does not cover parking, camping, or other fees. You can purchase a National Parks Pass in person at any national park where an entrance fee is charged; by mail from the National Park Foundation, PO Box 34108, Washington, DC 20043-4108; by calling toll-free 888/467-2757; or at www.nationalparks .org. The cost is $50.

- **Golden Eagle Sticker.** When affixed to a National Parks Pass, this hologram sticker, available to people who are between 17 and 61 years of age, extends coverage to sites managed by the US Fish and Wildlife Service, the US Forest Service, and the Bureau of Land Management. It is good until the National Parks Pass to which it is affixed expires and does not cover usage fees. You can purchase one at the National Park Service, the Fish and Wildlife Service, or the Bureau of Land Management fee stations. The cost is $15.

- **Golden Age Passport.** Available to citizens and permanent US residents 62 and older, this passport is a lifetime entrance permit to fee-charging national recreation areas. The fee exemption extends to those accompanying the permit holder in a private noncommercial vehicle or, in the case of walk-in facilities, to the holder's spouse and children. The passport also entitles the holder to a 50 percent discount on federal usage fees charged in park areas, but not on concessions. Golden Age Passports must be obtained in person and are available at most National Park Service units that charge an entrance fee. The applicant must show proof of age, such as a driver's license or birth certificate (Medicare cards are not acceptable proof). The cost is $10.

- **Golden Access Passport.** Issued to citizens and permanent US residents who are physically disabled or visually impaired, this passport is a free lifetime entrance permit to fee-charging national recreation areas. The fee exemption extends to those accompanying the permit holder in a private noncommercial vehicle or, in the case of walk-in facilities, to the holder's spouse and children. The passport also entitles the holder to a 50 percent discount on usage fees charged in park areas, but not on concessions. Golden Access Passports must be obtained in person and are available at most National Park Service units that charge an entrance fee. Proof of eligibility to receive federal benefits (under programs such as Disability Retirement, Compensation for Military Service-Connected Disability, and the Coal Mine Safety and Health Act) is required, or an affidavit must be signed attesting to eligibility.

A money-saving move in several large cities is to purchase a **CityPass.** If you plan to visit several museums and other major attractions, CityPass is a terrific option because it gets you into several sites for one substantially reduced price. Currently, CityPass is available in Boston, Chicago, Hollywood, New York, Philadelphia, San Francisco, Seattle, southern California (which includes Disneyland, SeaWorld, and the San Diego Zoo), and Toronto. For more information or to buy one, call toll-free 888/330-5008 or visit www. citypass.net. You can also buy a CityPass from any participating CityPass attraction.

Here are some additional ways to save on entertainment and shopping:

- Check with your hotel's concierge for various coupons and special offers; they often have two-for-one tickets for area attractions and coupons for discounts at area stores and restaurants.

- Purchase same-day concert or theater tickets for half-price through the local cheap-tickets outlet, such as TKTS in New York or Hot Tix in Chicago.

- Visit museums on their free or "by donation" days, when you can pay what you wish rather than a specific admission fee.

ON TRANSPORTATION

Transportation is a big part of any vacation budget. Here are some ways to reduce your costs:

- If you're renting a car, shop early over the Internet; you can book a car during the low season for less, even if you'll be using it in the high season.

- Rental car discounts are often available if you rent for one week or longer and reserve in advance.

- Get the best gas mileage out of your vehicle by making sure that it's properly tuned up and keeping your tires properly inflated.

- Travel at moderate speeds on the open road; higher speeds require more gasoline.

- Fill the tank before you return your rental car; rental companies charge to refill the tank and do so at prices of up to 50 percent more than at local gas stations.

- Make a checklist of travel essentials and purchase them before you leave; don't get stuck buying expensive sunscreen at your hotel or overpriced film at the airport.

FOR SENIOR CITIZENS

Always call ahead to ask if a discount is being offered, and be sure to carry proof of age. Additional information for mature travelers is available from the American Association of Retired Persons (AARP), 601 E St NW, Washington, DC 20049; phone 202/434-2277; www.aarp.org.

Tipping

Tips are expressions of appreciation for good service. However, you are never obligated to tip if you receive poor service.

IN HOTELS

- Door attendants usually get $1 for hailing a cab.

- Bell staff expect $2 per bag.

- Concierges are tipped according to the service they perform. Tipping is not mandatory when you've asked for suggestions on sightseeing or restaurants or for help in making dining reservations. However, a tip of $5 is appropriate when a concierge books you a table at a restaurant known to be difficult to get into. For obtaining theater or sporting event tickets, $5 to $10 is expected.

- Maids should be tipped $1 to $2 per day. Hand your tip directly to the maid, or leave it with a note saying that the money has been left expressly for the maid.

IN RESTAURANTS

Before tipping, carefully review your check for any gratuity or service charge that is already included in your bill. If you're in doubt, ask your server.

- Coffee shop and counter service waitstaff usually receive 15 percent of the bill, before sales tax.

- In full-service restaurants, tip 18 percent of the bill, before sales tax.

- In fine restaurants, where gratuities are shared among a larger staff, 18 to 20 percent is appropriate.

- In most cases, the maitre d' is tipped only if the service has been extraordinary, and only on the way out. At upscale properties in major metropolitan areas, $20 is the minimum.

- If there is a wine steward, tip $20 for exemplary service and beyond, or more if the wine was decanted or the bottle was very expensive.

- Tip $1 to $2 per coat at the coat check.

AT AIRPORTS

Curbside luggage handlers expect $1 per bag. Car-rental shuttle drivers who help with your luggage appreciate a $1 or $2 tip.

Staying Safe

The best way to deal with emergencies is to avoid them in the first place. However, unforeseen situations do happen, so you should be prepared for them.

IN YOUR CAR

Before you head out on a road trip, make sure that your car has been serviced and is in good working order. Change the oil, check the battery and belts, make sure that your windshield washer fluid is full and your tires are properly inflated (which can also improve your gas mileage). Other inspections recommended by the vehicle's manufacturer should also be made.

Next, be sure you have the tools and equipment needed to deal with a routine breakdown:

- Jack
- Spare tire
- Lug wrench
- Repair kit
- Emergency tools
- Jumper cables
- Spare fan belt
- Fuses
- Flares and/or reflectors
- Flashlight
- First-aid kit
- In winter, a windshield scraper and snow shovel

Many emergency supplies are sold in special packages that include the essentials you need to stay safe in the event of a breakdown.

Also bring all appropriate and up-to-date documentation—licenses, registration, and insurance cards—and know what your insurance covers. Bring an extra set of keys, too, just in case.

En route, always buckle up! In most states, wearing a seatbelt is required by law.

If your car does break down, do the following:

- Get out of traffic as soon as possible—pull well off the road.
- Raise the hood and turn on your emergency flashers or tie a white cloth to the roadside door handle or antenna.
- Stay in your car.
- Use flares or reflectors to keep your vehicle from being hit.

IN YOUR HOTEL

Chances are slim that you will encounter a hotel or motel fire, but you can protect yourself by doing the following:

- Once you've checked in, make sure that the smoke detector in your room is working properly.
- Find the property's fire safety instructions, usually posted on the inside of the room door.
- Locate the fire extinguishers and at least two fire exits.
- Never use an elevator in a fire.

For personal security, use the peephole in your room door and make sure that anyone claiming to be a hotel employee can show proper identification. Call the front desk if you feel threatened at any time.

PROTECTING AGAINST THEFT

To guard against theft wherever you go:

- Don't bring anything of more value than you need.
- If you do bring valuables, leave them at your hotel rather than in your car.
- If you bring something very expensive, lock it in a safe. Many hotels put one in each room; others will store your valuables in the hotel's safe.
- Don't carry more money than you need. Use traveler's checks and credit cards or visit cash machines to withdraw more cash when you run out.

For Travelers with Disabilities

To get the kind of service you need and have a right to expect, don't hesitate when making a reservation to question the management about the availability of accessible rooms, parking, entrances, restaurants, lounges, or any other facilities that are important to you, and confirm what is meant by "accessible."

The Mobil Travel Guide ⊞ symbol indicates establishments that are not at least partially accessible to people with special mobility needs (people using wheelchairs or crutches or otherwise needing easy access to buildings and rooms). Further information about these criteria can be found in the earlier section "How to Use This Book."

A thorough listing of published material for travelers with disabilities is available from the Disability Bookshop, Twin Peaks Press, Box 129, Vancouver, WA 98666; phone 360/694-2462; disabilitybookshop.virtualave.net. Another reliable organization is the Society for Accessible Travel & Hospitality (SATH), 347 Fifth Ave, Suite 610, New York, NY 10016; phone 212/447-7284; www.sath.org.

Important Toll-Free Numbers and Online Information

Hotels

Adams Mark 800/444-2326
www.adamsmark.com

AmericInn 800/634-3444
www.americinn.com

AmeriHost Inn 800/434-5800
www.amerihostinn.com

Amerisuites 800/833-1516
www.amerisuites.com

Baymont Inns 877/229-6667
www.baymontinns.com

Best Inns & Suites 800/237-8466
www.bestinn.com

Best Value Inn 888/315-2378
www.bestvalueinn.com

Best Western 800/780-7234
www.bestwestern.com

Budget Host Inn 800/283-4678
www.budgethost.com

Candlewood Suites 888/226-3539
www.candlewoodsuites.com

Clarion Hotels 800/252-7466
www.choicehotels.com

Comfort Inns and Suites 800/252-7466
www.comfortinn.com

Country Hearth Inns 800/848-5767
www.countryhearth.com

Country Inns & Suites 800/456-4000
www.countryinns.com

Courtyard by Marriott 800/321-2211
www.courtyard.com

Cross Country Inns (KY and OH) 800/621-1429
www.crosscountryinns.com

Crowne Plaza Hotels and Resorts 800/227-6963
www.crowneplaza.com

Days Inn 800/544-8313
www.daysinn.com

Delta Hotels 800/268-1133
www.deltahotels.com

Destination Hotels & Resorts 800/434-7347
www.destinationhotels.com

Doubletree Hotels 800/222-8733
www.doubletree.com

Drury Inn 800/378-7946
www.druryinn.com

Econolodge 800/553-2666
www.econolodge.com

Embassy Suites 800/362-2779
www.embassysuites.com

ExelInns of America 800/367-3935
www.exelinns.com

Extended StayAmerica 800/398-7829
www.extendedstayhotels.com

Fairfield Inn by Marriott 800/228-2800
www.fairfieldinn.com

Fairmont Hotels 800/441-1414
www.fairmont.com

Four Points by Sheraton 888/625-5144
www.fourpoints.com

Four Seasons 800/819-5053
www.fourseasons.com

Hampton Inn 800/426-7866
www.hamptoninn.com

Hard Rock Hotels, Resorts, and Casinos 800/473-7625
www.hardrock.com

Harrah's Entertainment 800/427-7247
www.harrahs.com

Hawthorn Suites 800/527-1133
www.hawthorn.com

Hilton Hotels and Resorts (US) 800/774-1500
www.hilton.com

Holiday Inn Express 800/465-4329
www.hiexpress.com

Holiday Inn Hotels and Resorts 800/465-4329
www.holiday-inn.com

Homestead Studio Suites 888/782-9473
www.homesteadhotels.com

Homewood Suites 800/225-5466
www.homewoodsuites.com

Howard Johnson 800/406-1411
www.hojo.com

Hyatt 800/633-7313
www.hyatt.com

Inns of America 800/826-0778
www.innsofamerica.com

InterContinental 888/567-8725
www.intercontinental.com

Joie de Vivre 800/738-7477
www.jdvhospitality.com

Kimpton Hotels 888/546-7866
www.kimptongroup.com

Knights Inn 800/843-5644
www.knightsinn.com

La Quinta 800/531-5900
www.laquinta.com

Le Meridien 800/543-4300
www.lemeridien.com

Leading Hotels of the World 800/223-6800
www.lhw.com

Loews Hotels 800/235-6397
www.loewshotels.com

MainStay Suites 800/660-6246
www.mainstaysuites.com

Mandarin Oriental 800/526-6566
www.mandarin-oriental.com

Marriott Hotels, Resorts, and Suites 800/228-9290
www.marriott.com

Microtel Inns & Suites 800/771-7171
www.microtelinn.com

Millennium & Copthorne Hotels 866/866-8086
www.millenniumhotels.com

Motel 6 . . . . 800/466-8356
www.motel6.com

Omni Hotels 800/843-6664
www.omnihotels.com

Pan Pacific Hotels and Resorts 800/327-8585
www.panpac.com

Park Inn & Park Plaza 888/201-1801
www.parkinn.com

The Peninsula Group . . . . Contact individual hotel
www.peninsula.com

Preferred Hotels & Resorts Worldwide 800/323-7500
www.preferredhotels.com

Quality Inn 800/228-5151
www.qualityinn.com

Radisson Hotels 800/333-3333
www.radisson.com

Raffles International Hotels and Resorts . . . 800/637-9477
www.raffles.com

Ramada Plazas, Limiteds, and Inns 800/272-6232
www.ramada.com

Red Lion Inns 800/733-5466
www.redlion.com

Red Roof Inns 800/733-7663
www.redroof.com

Regent International 800/545-4000
www.regenthotels.com

Relais & Chateaux 800/735-2478
www.relaischateaux.com

Renaissance Hotels 888/236-2427
www.renaissancehotels.com

Residence Inn 800/331-3131
www.residenceinn.com

Ritz-Carlton 800/241-3333
www.ritzcarlton.com

RockResorts 888/367-7625
www.rockresorts.com

Rodeway Inn 800/228-2000
www.rodeway.com

Rosewood Hotels & Resorts 888/767-3966
www.rosewoodhotels.com

Select Inn 800/641-1000
www.selectinn.com

Sheraton 888/625-5144
www.sheraton.com

Shilo Inns 800/222-2244
www.shiloinns.com

Shoney's Inn 800/552-4667
www.shoneysinn.com

Signature/Jameson Inns 800/822-5252
www.jamesoninns.com

Sleep Inn 877/424-6423
www.sleepinn.com

Small Luxury Hotels of the World 800/525-4800
www.slh.com

Sofitel 800/763-4835
www.sofitel.com

SpringHill Suites 888/236-2427
www.springhillsuites.com

St. Regis Luxury Collection 888/625-5144
www.stregis.com

Staybridge Suites 800/238-8000
www.staybridge.com

Summerfield Suites by Wyndham 800/833-4353
www.summerfieldsuites.com

Summit International 800/457-4000
www.summithotels.com

Super 8 Motels 800/800-8000
www.super8.com

The Sutton Place Hotels 866/378-8866
www.suttonplace.com

Swissôtel 800/637-9477
www.swissotel.com

TownePlace Suites 888/236-2427
www.towneplace.com

Travelodge 800/578-7878
www.travelodge.com

Vagabond Inns 800/522-1555
www.vagabondinns.com

W Hotels 888/625-5144
www.whotels.com

Wellesley Inn and Suites 800/444-8888
www.wellesleyinnandsuites.com

WestCoast Hotels 800/325-4000
www.westcoasthotels.com

Westin Hotels & Resorts 800/937-8461
www.westin.com

Wingate Inns..........................800/228-1000
www.wingateinns.com
Woodfin Suite Hotels..................800/966-3346
www.woodfinsuitehotels.com
WorldHotels 800/223-5652
www.worldhotels.com
Wyndham Hotels & Resorts 800/996-3426
www.wyndham.com

Airlines

Air Canada..........................888/247-2262
www.aircanada.ca
AirTran..............................800/247-8726
www.airtran.com
Alaska Airlines 800/252-7522
www.alaskaair.com
American Airlines.....................800/433-7300
www.aa.com
America West 800/235-9292
www.americawest.com
ATA..................................800/435-9282
www.ata.com
Continental Airlines 800/523-3273
www.continental.com
Delta Air Lines 800/221-1212
www.delta.com
Frontier Airlines 800/432-1359
www.frontierairlines.com
Hawaiian Airways 800/367-5320
www.hawaiianair.com
Jet Blue Airlines 800/538-2583
www.jetblue.com
Midwest Express 800/452-2022
www.midwestexpress.com

Northwest Airlines....................800/225-2525
www.nwa.com
Southwest Airlines....................800/435-9792
www.southwest.com
Spirit Airlines 800/772-7117
www.spiritair.com
United Airlines 800/241-6522
www.united.com
US Airways 800/428-4322
www.usairways.com

Car Rentals

Advantage 800/777-5500
www.arac.com
Alamo................................800/327-9633
www.goalamo.com
Avis 800/831-2847
www.avis.com
Budget 800/527-0700
www.budget.com
Dollar 800/800-4000
www.dollarcar.com
Enterprise 800/325-8007
www.enterprise.com
Hertz 800/654-3131
www.hertz.com
National..............................800/227-7368
www.nationalcar.com
Payless 800/729-5377
www.paylesscarrental.com
Rent-A-Wreck.com 800/535-1391
www.rent-a-wreck.com
Thrifty 800/847-4389
www.thrifty.com

Meet The Stars

Mobil Travel Guide 2006 *Five-Star* Award Winners

CALIFORNIA
Lodgings
The Beverly Hills Hotel, *Beverly Hills*
Chateau du Sureau, *Oakhurst*
Four Seasons Hotel San Francisco,
   San Francisco
Hotel Bel-Air, *Los Angeles*
The Peninsula Beverly Hills, *Beverly Hills*
Raffles L'Ermitage Beverly Hills, *Beverly Hills*
The Ritz-Carlton, San Francisco, *San Francisco*

Restaurants
Bastide, *Los Angeles*
The Dining Room, *San Francisco*
The French Laundry, *Yountville*
Gary Danko, *San Francisco*

COLORADO
Lodgings
The Broadmoor, *Colorado Springs*
The Little Nell, *Aspen*

CONNECTICUT
Lodging
The Mayflower Inn, *Washington*

DISTRICT OF COLUMBIA
Lodging
Four Seasons Hotel Washington, DC
   Washington

FLORIDA
Lodgings
Four Seasons Resort Palm Beach, *Palm Beach*
The Ritz-Carlton Naples, *Naples*
The Ritz-Carlton, Palm Beach, *Manalapan*

GEORGIA
Lodgings
Four Seasons Hotel Atlanta, *Atlanta*
The Lodge at Sea Island Golf Club,
   St. Simons Island

Restaurants
The Dining Room, *Atlanta*
Seeger's, *Atlanta*

HAWAII
Lodging
Four Seasons Resort Maui at Wailea, *Wailea,
   Maui*

ILLINOIS
Lodgings
Four Seasons Hotel Chicago, *Chicago*
The Peninsula Chicago, *Chicago*
The Ritz-Carlton, A Four Seasons Hotel, *Chicago*

Restaurant
Charlie Trotter's, *Chicago*

MAINE
Restaurant
The White Barn Inn, *Kennebunkport*

MASSACHUSETTS
Lodgings
Blantyre, *Lenox*
Four Seasons Hotel Boston, *Boston*

NEW YORK
Lodgings
Four Seasons, Hotel New York, *New York*
The Point, *Saranac Lake*
The Ritz-Carlton New York, Central Park,
   New York
The St. Regis, *New York*

Restaurants
Alain Ducasse, *New York*
Jean Georges, *New York*
Masa, *New York*
per se, *New York*

NORTH CAROLINA
Lodging
The Fearrington House Country Inn, *Pittsboro*

PENNSYLVANIA
Restaurant
Le Bec-Fin, *Philadelphia*

SOUTH CAROLINA
Lodging
Woodlands Resort & Inn, *Summerville*

Restaurant
Dining Room at the Woodlands, *Summerville*

TEXAS
Lodging
The Mansion on Turtle Creek, *Dallas*

VERMONT
Lodging
Twin Farms, *Barnard*

VIRGINIA
Lodgings
The Inn at Little Washington, *Washington*
The Jefferson Hotel, *Richmond*

Restaurant
The Inn at Little Washington, *Washington*

Mobil Travel Guide has been rating establishments with its Mobil One- to Five-Star system since 1958. Each establishment awarded the Mobil Five-Star rating is one of the best in the country. Detailed information on each award winner can be found in the corresponding regional edition listed on the back cover of this book.

Four- and Five-Star Establishments in Great Plains

Missouri

★ ★ ★ ★ Lodging

The Ritz-Carlton, St. Louis, *Clayton*

★ ★ ★ ★ Restaurants

American, *Kansas City*
Tony's, *St. Louis*

America's Byways™ are a distinctive collection of American roads, their stories, and treasured places. They are roads to the heart and soul of America. In this section, you'll find the nationally designated Byways in Iowa and Missouri.

The Great River Road

IOWA

"**T**he Mississippi is in all ways remarkable," said the famous writer Mark Twain. Join travelers from around the world to discover dramatic vistas of Old Man River during all seasons. View soaring eagles and 100,000 migrating geese and ducks. Experience Midwest hospitality on the main streets of river towns and cities or visit sacred sites and landscape effigies of Native Americans. You can also experience the Mississippi River on steamboats, commercial barges, and recreational crafts. This 326-mile Byway provides a look into America's past, present, and future.

The Byway's story begins with the landscape: abrupt and dramatic limestone bluffs cut by glacial meltwater in the north contrast with broad sandy floodplains in the south. For thousands of years, Native Americans knew the importance of the continent's largest river. Later, its meandering course marked the political boundaries of territories, towns, cities, states, and counties of the advancing society. Today, the Upper Mississippi River and the Great River Road are national repositories of geological wonders, unparalleled scenic beauty, wildlife, native vegetation, and the miracles of hydrology. The river and road are also milestones to the expansion and development of the United States and the Midwest.

The Byway Story

The Great River Road tells archaeological, historical, natural, recreational, and scenic stories that make it a unique and treasured Byway.

ARCHAEOLOGICAL

Regionally and nationally significant archaeological resources of the Iowa Great River Road are numerous and continue to be the focus of research and interpretation. A primary site on the Great River Road is the Effigy Mounds National Monument, the site of 200 mounds. Of these 200 mounds, 29 are effigy outlines of mammals, birds, or reptiles. Eastern Woodland Indian culture built these sites between 500 BC and AD 1300. They are preserved and interpreted for the public. Additional property is being added to the monument site to expand its protection of these unique resources. Other important sites are found at the Mines of Spain State Recreation Area and the Toolesboro Indian Mounds National Historic Landmark.

QUICK FACTS

Length: 326 miles.

Time to Allow: 2 days.

Best Time to Drive: Any time of the year brings dynamic and beautiful views of the river and the surrounding landscape. Fall is a particularly popular time with its beautiful foliage displays.

Byway Travel Information: Iowa Department of Tourism: phone 515/242-4705; Byway local Web site: www.mississippi-river.com/mrpc/fiaframe.htm.

Restrictions: Short portions of the road may be closed once every few years due to winter snowstorms. Such interruptions usually last less than 36 hours.

Bicycle/Pedestrian Facilities: In Iowa, bicyclists enjoy the same rights as motorists and are not prohibited from using any portion of the Iowa Great River Road. The majority of the roadway includes improved shoulders that are available for use by bicyclists. Numerous separated and multi-use recreation trails intersect and parallel the Great River Road as well. Frequent roadside stops provide parking areas, trails, walkways, public rest rooms, and other service amenities.

HISTORICAL

The history of the Great River Road is found in its buildings and towns. People who live along the river can't think of a better combination than historic buildings set in the land of a great river. Ideas and dreams of a moving, bustling riverboat society surface over and over in restored cathedrals and forts or in riverboat casinos.

Although most of Iowa was settled in the mid-1800s, the Mississippi River made it an accessible territory long before the United States became a nation. Natives and explorers alike saw the raw, unharnessed power of this beautiful passageway. One of the first outposts was Fort Madison, where history is still re-created today. Like much of the United States, the Great River Road was under Spanish and French rule until the time of the Louisiana Purchase in 1802.

Soon after, settlers and industry came to Iowa. Bustling river towns created cultural landmarks like Snake Alley—the curviest road in the United States. Little towns along the road grew and became the cities they are today, full of identity as Mississippi River towns. During the booming days of river trade, writer Samuel Langhorn Clemens (better known as Mark Twain) captured the atmosphere and the time period in his novels.

When the Civil War came to Iowa, most of the people living there fought for the Union. Civil War memorials are now found in several of the towns on the Byway.

NATURAL

Geology, the hydrologic cycle, and erosion are among the big stories that the Mississippi River and the Great River Road tell in Iowa. The forces of nature can be seen in how the river has cut a deep channel in ancient limestone layers in the northern reaches. The ever-changing channel of the river, the deposition of sediments, and the broad floodplain of the Mississippi River in the southern part of the state speak of a different natural dynamic. The Upper Mississippi River National Wildlife and Fish Refuge is the nation's oldest, longest, and most popular wildlife refuge. Many other state, county, and city parks provide opportunities for spotting and watching wildlife.

RECREATIONAL

Nationally and regionally important recreational opportunities abound along the Iowa Great River Road. Abundant water recreation activities include boating, sailing, fishing, waterfowl hunting, and swimming. For decades, the Iowa Great River Road and its side roads have been popular pleasure routes for sightseeing. Although fall is a particularly popular time due to the beautiful foliage displays, any time of the year brings dynamic and beautiful views of the river and its attendant landscape. Numerous multipurpose trails and support facilities are available along the road as well.

SCENIC

The magnificent scenery of the Great River Road is centered around the Mississippi River, the landscape it has created, and the cultural expressions that are rooted in the landscape. The river is almost continuously visible from the Great River Road (or is within a few miles of the Byway). Dams along the river create large pools of open water upstream. Along the northern part of the river, steep limestone bluffs descend directly to the bank of the river. Downstream, the floodplain opens to afford long, uninterrupted views of the valley. Collections of stops allow travelers to discover the mix of scenic qualities. Roadside spots, shady parks, and locks and dams of the Mississippi River all offer places for you to stop and take in the scenic beauty of the Great River Road and the Mississippi River.

The four seasons of the upper Midwest provide continually dynamic backgrounds and changes in the vegetation and activity on the water. Culturally, the rural landscape provides a multitude of settings for small farms, protected wetlands, streams and rivers, and intermittent woodlots and forests. The residential and main street architecture of small towns and river cities offers much interest and contrast to the rural images. Many efforts exist to protect the countryside landscape character.

Highlights

Not sure where to begin? Consider taking this Lansing to Guttenberg tour of Iowa's Great River Road.

- The tour begins in **Lansing,** home of Mount Hosmer Park, with a panoramic view of the river. Also of interest is the **Fish Farm Mound** (an Indian burial site) and the nearby **Our Lady of the Wayside** shrine.

- The next stop, **Harper's Ferry,** is 15 miles past Lansing. The town is built on a concentrated area of Native American mounds and was an important river town after the introduction of the steamboat. The Mississippi backwaters behind the town still attract hunters, trappers, and commercial fishing.

- Just south of Harper's Ferry lies the **Yellow River Forest State Recreation Area.** This 8,000-acre forest contains some of Iowa's greatest terrain, with high scenic bluffs and cold streams. The Iowa Department of Natural Resources harvests the Yellow River Forest timber for use all over the state. The Paint Rock unit of the forest houses most recreational opportunities, including camping, canoeing, snowmobiling, hunting and fishing, and hiking and equestrian trails.

- **Effigy Mounds National Monument,** the next stop, is just 2 miles south of Yellow River Forest. Prehistoric mounds are common from the plains of the Midwest to the Atlantic seaboard, but only in this area were they constructed in an effigy outline of mammals, birds, or reptiles. The monument contains 1,481 acres with 200 mounds, of which 29 are effigies; the others are conical, linear, and compound. Eastern Woodland Indian cultures built these mounds from about 500 BC to AD 1300. Natural features in the monument include forests, tallgrass prairies, wetlands, and rivers.

- The Effigy Mounds National Monument Visitor Center, located in **Marquette,** includes displays of local Woodland and Mississippian cultures, artifacts, and a herbarium. Riverboat casino gambling is available on the Miss Marquette Riverboat Casino.

- **Pike's Peak State Park** is 5 miles south of Marquette. This park boasts one of Iowa's most spectacular views across the Mississippi on the highest bluff along the river. It was named for Zebulon Pike, who was sent in 1805 to scout placement of military posts along the river. A fort was never built on this land, and it went into private ownership. Because settlers were not able to build on this property, the peak remains as Pike saw it 200 years ago.

- The tour terminates in **Guttenberg,** 15 miles south of Pike's Peak State Park. Guttenberg boasts two scenic overlooks and a mile-long landscaped park along the river. A copy of the Gutenberg Bible is on display at the local library. The city offers blocks and blocks of historic buildings.

Loess Hills Scenic Byway

IOWA

The Loess Hills Scenic Byway weaves through a landform of windblown silt deposits along the eastern edge of the Missouri River Valley. This unique American treasure possesses natural features that are found in only two places in the world: western Iowa and the Yellow River Valley of China. Travelers are intrigued by the extraordinary landscape of prairies and forest-covered bluffs.

The loess (pronounced LUSS) soil deposits were initially left by glacial melt waters on the floodplain of the Missouri River. These deposits were then blown upward by strong winds. The steep, sharply ridged topography of this area was formed over thousands of years by the deposition and erosion of the wind-blown silt. Today, the rugged landscape and strong local contrasts in weather and soil conditions provide refuge for a number of rare plants and animals, many of which can be found only in the Loess Hills.

As you drive the western edge of Iowa, you pass through dozens of prairie towns. Larger cities like Council Bluffs and Sioux City offer venues of recreation, culture, and history. Learn a little about some of the people who passed through the area on a trek west and discover more about the people who stayed here.

You will want to enjoy the many nature areas along the way as well. The Dorothy Pecaut Nature Center, the Hitchcock Nature Area, and the Loess Hills State Forest are just a few of the many places on the Byway that are dedicated to preserving and restoring the native prairies of western Iowa.

QUICK FACTS

Length: 220 miles.

Time to Allow: 7 hours.

Best Time to Drive: Spring through fall.

Byway Travel Information: Loess Hills Scenic Byway Council: phone 712/482-3029; Western Iowa Tourism Region: phone toll-free 888/623-4232; Byway local Web site: www.loesshillstours.com.

Restrictions: Occasionally, winter weather may necessitate a slower rate of travel. Also, the gravel roads on some of the excursion loops may also become somewhat degraded during periods of high rainfall.

Bicycle/Pedestrian Facilities: With the addition of the Wabash Trace Bicycle and Pedestrian Trail, the Byway now includes opportunities for biking and walking. There are many smaller trails that bicyclists and pedestrians can travel on throughout the corridor as well, but the Wabash Trace was specifically created for biking and walking.

The Byway Story

The Loess Hills Scenic Byway tells archaeological, cultural, historical, natural, recreational, and scenic stories that make it a unique and treasured Byway.

ARCHAEOLOGICAL

As scientists and archaeologists continue to prod the hills for clues to the past, the hills are still revealing artifacts and remnants that point to cultures from many thousands of years ago. Archaeological studies reveal places in the Loess Hills that have been continuously occupied for 12,000 years. Cultures from 12,000 years ago until recent times have been studied and cataloged in order to provide an idea of what human existence has been like in the Loess Hills. Hints of past civilizations are enough to make the Loess Hills an archaeologically significant area.

Evidence of a nomadic culture of hunters and gatherers was found in Turin (which is on the Byway) in the middle of the last century. The site yielded some of the oldest human remains in North America. The bones date back nearly 8,000 years and provided an inside look into life during that time period. In the city of Glenwood, stop at the Mills County Historical Museum to explore a reconstructed earth lodge and artifacts that were discovered in the area. The structure and artifacts are remnants of a culture more recent than that of Turin. You may also want to stop at Blood Run National Historic Landmark, where there was once a center of commerce and society for the Oneota Indians. During the period of AD 1200 to 1700, these people constructed buildings, homes, and effigy mounds in the area. The collection of resources from Loess Hills is informative to both archaeologists and visitors to the Byway wanting to catch a glimpse at life on the Byway thousands of years ago.

CULTURAL

Predominantly agricultural, the cultures on the Byway have influenced one another over the years and evolved with the rest of the nation. Many of the first European settlers of the Loess Hills of Iowa came from Danish, German, or Swedish cultures that settled in the United States nearly 200 years ago to create a unique heritage. These people learned to live among each other, creating a diverse culture characteristic of the United States.

The Byway culture today is a blend of the old and new living side by side. Urban centers like Sioux City and Council Bluffs give way to hidden corners of agricultural hamlets.

From cities to villages, cultural events occur regularly on the Byway. While some visitors may choose to attend theatrical events and tour museums, others may want to taste some of the local flavor at a farmers' market, county fair, or heritage celebration. When travelers come to the Loess Hills Scenic Byway, many of them take part in activities like the rodeo or apple harvest festivals. To learn more about the people of the Loess Hills, visit the Moorhead Cultural Center, which has displays and activities that tell the story of people and culture on the Byway.

HISTORICAL

To complement the area's fascinating natural history, the Loess Hills have another history to tell. The history of human settlement in the Loess Hills has left many stories behind in old buildings and sacred places. A home and hunting ground to some of the continent's earliest people, human habitation in the Loess Hills has been developing for many years. The people native to this land had a great respect for the Loess Hills and recognized them for the natural anomaly that they are. The land was greatly honored until the early 1800s; when explorers began to wind their way through this land in the 1700s, it was the end of an old way of life around the Loess Hills.

Significant historical treasures are located within the Loess Hills from the period of European settlement as well. To see pieces of this history, follow the Lewis and Clark Trail north and south along the hills or prepare for a trip along one of the many trails that traveled to the West. The Oregon Trail, Mormon Trail, and California Trail all traversed the Loess Hills in their route westward. In fact, the Mormon Trail had a stopover point in the hills called the Great Encampment that was used during the winter months. At this point, permanent settlement in the Loess Hills became an option for pioneers crossing the plains.

The places left behind are protected as designated historic sites. You will find National Historic Landmarks, places on the National Register of Historic Places, and National Historic Trails. Museums and information centers along the Byway allow visitors to study the history that surrounds the hills. Buildings like the General Dodge House and the Woodbury County Courthouse display styles of architecture from another time. Many sites in the Loess Hills were also used on the Underground Railroad to transport escaped slaves to the north. And you will find monuments to the first explorers, including Sergeant Floyd of the Lewis and Clark expedition, who was the only explorer to die during the journey. Museums cover everything from Civil War history to prehistoric life in this part of Iowa.

NATURAL

Along the Loess Hills Scenic Byway, the rare kind of soil known as loess has been formed into hills that allow a different kind of ecosystem to develop. This ecosystem features plants and animals that are rarely found anywhere else. Not only do the hills represent a rare kind of soil, but they are also a slice of the once vast prairie lands of the United States. The hills contain most of Iowa's remaining native prairie, making the Byway a site that preserves natural history.

The area of the Loess Hills has been dubbed a National Natural Landmark in order to further promote its protection. There are also four Iowa State Preserves in the Loess Hills. You may want to stop at

Five Ridge Prairie Preserve, Mount Talbot Preserve, Turin Hills Preserve, or Sylvan Runkel Preserve to observe the untouched habitat of the prairie. When you drive through places like Broken Kettle Grassland on the Byway, you may see unique plants like the ten-petal Blazing Star or hear a fat prairie rattlesnake shaking its tail in the distance.

Because many of the creatures along the Byway are threatened or endangered, you will also find wildlife refuges along the Byway. The De Soto National Wildlife Refuge is maintained by the US Fish and Wildlife Service; you may be able to glimpse migratory waterfowl nesting and feeding in the area. About 350,000 snow geese stop here in the fall as they travel south. Many other species of birds and geese stop and stay at the wildlife refuge. The Loess Ridge Nature Center is an excellent place to find out more about the habitat and ecosystem of the Loess Hills. The center provides many engaging exhibits, including live animal displays and a butterfly garden. Other preserves and parks along the Byway have their own information centers where visitors can find out more about a particular place or part of the Loess Hills. After you have stopped at the centers and preserves, the unique traits of the Loess Hills will be apparent.

RECREATIONAL

During a drive on the Loess Hills Scenic Byway, you will want to get out of the car and stretch. And there are several places along the Byway that are perfect for more than just stretching. Opportunities for outdoor recreation are around every corner. Between preserves and state parks, you will have an excellent chance to view unique wildlife. De Soto National Wildlife Refuge is a home and hotel to many waterfowl and migratory birds. Wildlife watching is a popular activity on the Byway's four preserves. At Stone State Park, try camping or tour the trails in your own way. Whether you love hiking, biking, or horseback riding, all these modes of transportation are welcomed. Even snowmobilers ride through these wooded trails onto the white prairie in the wintertime. Stop at an orchard or Small's Fruit Farm to pick your own apples.

If outdoor recreation isn't a priority, try touring historical sites and monuments. Historical museums are located throughout the Byway, along with many unusual buildings and historic districts. Gaming is also a popular activity on the Byway at the casinos in the Byway communities. Visitors will find slot machines, table games, and nightlife. In addition, the

best antique shopping in Iowa is rumored to be found in the communities along the Byway. Cross the river from Council Bluffs to Omaha, Nebraska, to explore this busy city full of distractions. Or simply settle down at a quiet restaurant for a bite to eat and time to look at the map.

SCENIC

The rolling hills created by the loess soil of the Loess Hills make driving this Byway a pleasant experience from any angle. The hills themselves are in the setting of the Missouri River Flood Plain, where they create a view of a unique landform that is characteristic of the Byway. Visitors who drive the Loess Hills Scenic Byway enjoy the scenic overlooks and the sight of the hills rolling on and on. Viewing the unique formations of the Loess Hills creates a sensation of continuity as you see the prairie as a whole. Because of the unique properties of loess soil, you can enjoy "cat steps" in the hills where the loess has slumped off, creating a unified ledge. In the distance, you may catch a glimpse of the Missouri River as it meanders beside the hills.

Throughout the year, the prairie rolls through the seasons. Fall is one of the favorites of travelers who come to see the hardwood forests and prairie vegetation change to rich hues of red and orange. Pieces of an agricultural lifestyle form a patchwork of fields and historic communities along the Byway. Pioneer cemeteries next to country churches tell the story of earlier settlers who came through this place and the hardships they had to face. Travelers also experience the sights of the cities on the Byway, like Sioux City and Council Bluffs, that remain great stopping points at any time of year. Parks, museums, and historic buildings offer a taste of the Byway cities.

Highlights

When driving this Byway, consider using this Loess Hills prairie tour as your itinerary.

○ The tour starts in the **Broken Kettle Grasslands,** just south of Akron. The preserve is half prairie and constitutes the largest remaining section of the vast prairie that once covered most of Iowa. The preserve contains some flora and fauna not found in any other part of the Loess Hills to the south or the state of Iowa; these include the prairie rattlesnake and the ten-petal Blazing Star.

○ **Five Ridge Prairie,** located on the Ridge Road Loop, about 5 miles south of Broken Kettle Grasslands, is a combination of prairie and woodlands. This is one of the best sites of unbroken prairie remnants in Iowa. You'll notice the climate changes between open grasslands, which are warmed by the sun and dry prairie breezes, and the shadowy woods, which remain cooler and more humid. Expect to find some rugged hiking trails at this site.

○ The **Dorothy Pecaut Nature Center** is on the Stone Park Loop just south of the Highway 12 entrance to Stone State Park. The center is devoted wholly to Iowa's Loess Hills. The center has live animal displays, hands-on exhibits, a butterfly garden, and a walk-through exhibit showing life under the prairie.

○ Your final stop, **Stone State Park,** is located on Sioux City's interpretive northwest side. It has 1,069 acres of prairie-topped ridges and dense woodlands. Dakota Point and Elk Point provide scenic overlooks of Nebraska, South Dakota, and Iowa. The multi-use trails handle hikers, bicyclists, horseback riders, and snowmobilers, and campsites with showers are available. This park is a site on the Lewis and Clark National Historic Trail.

Crowley's Ridge Parkway

MISSOURI

Part of a multistate Byway that continues in AR.

C rowley's Ridge, characterized by sand, gravel, and deep gullies, has formed a primary route of transport and commerce for the people of this region for several centuries. During different time periods, the various inhabitants of different nationalities used the ridge to escape the swamps and wetlands. A combination of land travel on the ridge and connecting rivers provided a means of subsistence over a vast corridor of time and place.

The Byway Story

Crowley's Ridge Parkway tells archaeological, historical, and natural stories that make it a unique and treasured Byway.

ARCHAEOLOGICAL

The earliest recorded cemetery in the New World is found in Greene County on Crowley's Ridge. Excavated in 1974, the Sloan Site was both home and burial ground for a small group of Native Americans who lived here approximately 10,500 years ago. Living in small bands and in semi-permanent villages, they established the earliest documented cemetery in North America.

QUICK FACTS

Length: 14.2 miles.

Time to Allow: 30 minutes or more.

Best Time to Drive: Each season offers unique opportunities along the Byway, which makes a for a pleasant visit year-round. High season is summer.

Byway Travel Information: Tourism Advisory Council: phone 573/334-4142.

Special Considerations: Plenty of services are available along the route for any special needs; however, watch your engine temperature so that you notice if it begins to increase.

Bicycle/Pedestrian Facilities: This route was originally designed to be used primarily by vehicles; little thought was given to pedestrians or bicyclists. Many trails are now under development to provide better access for hikers and bikers.

The Mississippian site of Parkin is now the Parkin Archaeological State Park in Cross County and provides a museum, visitor center, walking tour, and research station. This site features a rectangular planned village of 400 houses, with a plaza surrounding mounds and evidence of a large population that experienced interaction with the de Soto expedition.

HISTORICAL

Crowley's Ridge, with its heavy clay and gravel, proved to be a focal point for the historical and cultural events that shaped the region around it. From the unique plant life of the ridge to the lowland swamps, this region is a story waiting to be told. The earliest people in this region were Native Americans, and they were always few in number.

The first known Native Americans were named the Mound Builders. They date from AD 900 to 1500 and were agriculturists who lived in permanent villages. As permanent residents, they made ceramic pots and various utensils, some of which remain on and below the landscape surface today. Sizable collections of these artifacts can be found in the small museums throughout this region. Huge collections also exist at Arkansas State University and Southeast Missouri State University, some large collections are in private hands, and many artifacts exist in the hundreds of mounds that can still be found. However, these mounds are being challenged by the migration of the rice-planting culture and the disastrous raids of illegal collectors and artifact thieves. So the story of the Native Americans in this region continues as a largely untold story.

The early European immigrants to this region were German, Scottish-Irish, and English. Many of them came from Virginia, Tennessee, Kentucky, and Mississippi, and they brought African-American slaves with them. The Byway intersects many of these ethnic islands that have shaped the history and culture of the region. The migration of the cotton culture brought a lifestyle that continues to influence local food, religion, architecture, family values, and religion. Midwestern barns and Southern homes and churches can be found as well.

There continues to exist in this region what the residents call the Chalk Bluff Trail. This trail extends from Cape Girardeau, Missouri, to Helena, Arkansas, and runs along the high ground of the ridge. The trail was originally used by Native Americans as they moved through the region on hunting expeditions. European settlers used the trail as they migrated to the West: it was the only safe way to travel through the swamps in order to capitalize on the 19th-century opportunities that existed in what is now the great American Southwest. Crowley's Ridge was the only all-weather access for settlers to transport trade items. In the 1850s, a plank road was built from Gideon to Portageville, providing the first east-west avenue to Mississippi River ports. The ridge became a vital highway during the Civil War, used by both Union and Confederate troops. On April 30, 1863, an engagement known as the Battle of Chalk Bluff occurred on the banks of the St. Francis River where it crosses Crowley's Ridge in a narrow gap. Small by most Civil War measures, the event was nevertheless significant to people in this region. Local cemeteries contain graves of both Union and Confederate soldiers.

Following the Civil War, many changes occurred in this area, including a restructuring of agriculture and technology that provided for increased farm size. New plows, threshers, seeders, and shellers allowed farmers to work more acres and increase yields per acre. This put more pressure on transportation and further changed the region. The importation of cotton added to the region's transformation. Cotton farmers from the deep South came into the region as they tried to escape the boll weevil, which had temporarily devastated their lands and crops. Droughts in the 1930s withered those crops, however, and brought government programs to the area. In 1933, Congress passed the Agricultural Adjustment Act, which sought to stabilize agriculture. Soil conservation acts also impacted the region and reflected the changing nature of the times. Those benefits that came into the area generally went to the large planters, while little went to the growing number of sharecroppers and tenant farmers.

The land on and around Crowley's Ridge was generally worked well into the 20th century by sharecroppers who lived at the poverty level. The Southern way of life that existed in this area meant that there was little in the way of a middle class. African Americans in the region were almost entirely in the sharecropper class. This system was widespread across the South in the aftermath of the Civil War, but was especially rigid in the new cotton lands of southeast Missouri. This situation lead to one of the greatest stories to come out of Missouri in the 20th century, the story of the sharecropper strike of 1939.

The problems that plagued farmers in this region are still the same today in southeast Missouri. The large farm operator, through increased mechanization, has been able to survive and prosper, while the small farmer (and there are many in this area) has had little economic success. As farms continue to grow larger, owners of small farms have been forced to abandon both their land and their hope. Many have moved to larger cities or taken employment outside the farm. The area around the ridge continues to decline in population while land values increase.

NATURAL
Crowley's Ridge, characterized by sand, gravel, and deep gullies, has formed a primary route of transport and commerce for the people of this region over the past several centuries. The inhabitants used the ridge to escape the swamps and wetlands. A combination of land travel on the ridge and connecting rivers provided a means of subsistence over a vast corridor of time and place.

The ridge begins south of Cape Girardeau near Commerce, Missouri. It moves west in a great arc, coming back to the great river near Helena, Arkansas. The land period of glaciation, some 15,000 years ago, caused massive buildup and melting of the glaciers that resulted in great floodwaters beyond modern imagination and created the Ohio and Mississippi rivers as ice marginal streams. The Mississippi was west of Crowley's Ridge, the Ohio River to the east. The old route of the Mississippi may have followed the course of what is now the St. Francis River. Following the last ice melt, the Ohio joined the Mississippi River just south of the Thebes Gap at Cairo, Illinois. The narrow band of uplands known as Crowley's Ridge is the only remaining remnant of this story. The current river system moved to the east and left Crowley's Ridge.

Crowley's Ridge is a unique landform that is effectively isolated like an island in the middle of a small ocean of land. Plants and animals that inhabited the ridge were isolated and cut off from their natural migratory patterns, so a number of rare or endangered plants and animals are indigenous to the ridge. Of the various natural communities on the ridge, the rarest are the plants that occur along the seeps, runs, and springs. Nettled chain fern, yellow fringed orchid, umbrella sedge, black chokeberry, and marsh blue violet are some examples of these rare and exquisite plants.

The natural changes that happened in the landscape affected not only plants and animals but humans as well. Some historians contend that Hernando de Soto was the first white explorer to reach Crowley's Ridge. If he did so, it remains unclear exactly where he made his first entrance into what is now Missouri. If and when he crossed the Mississippi River above Memphis, it is likely that he and at least some of his men followed Indian and animal trails to the high ridge into present-day Dunklin County, Missouri.

As other immigrants from all parts of northern Europe moved west, they generally moved down the Ohio, crossed the Mississippi, and landed on the Missouri shoreline. This landing usually occurred at Norfolk Landing, located south of Cairo, Illinois. From there, immigrants would cross the alluvial "prairie" swamps and head to the high ground of

Crowley's Ridge. As early as the 1850s, there was discussion and even plans to drain the great wetlands. However, it was not until the early 20th century that the Little River Drainage District was formed and systematic and extensive drainage occurred.

Lumber companies moved into the region after 1913 when the massive log drives on the Mississippi were stopped by the Keokuk Dam. Soon, the region was a timberless, uninhabitable swamp. The Little River Drainage District did the rest. In what is the greatest land transformation in human history, southeast Missouri was moved from natural wetland to field and farm in less than half a century.

Highlights

The following is a suggested itinerary for traveling Crowley's Ridge Parkway in Missouri.

⊘ **Malden:** Start your Byway tour in Malden. Downtown, you can visit the free **Malden Historical Museum** and enjoy the exhibits, which include the history of Malden and the Denis Collection of Egyptian Antiquities. Or spend some time at Malden's **Bootheel Youth Museum,** where adults and kids can both enjoy activities that explore the worlds of math, science, the arts, and more. Interactive exhibits include making (and standing inside!) a giant soap bubble, freezing shadows on the wall, and making music on sewer pipes. When you are ready to continue your drive, leave Malden on County Route J to the west. Enjoy the rural scenery. You may even spot the Military Road, but the easiest place to see the Military Road is at the next stop.

⊘ **Jim Morris State Park and the Military Road:** Shortly after you turn south on County Route WW, you find **Jim Morris State Park.** In addition to showcasing many varieties of trees and other vegetation unique to the ridge, the park is the most practical way to see the **Military Road.** Access the road by the bicycle or pedestrian paths here. This road was used by military troops in the Civil War and by settlers as they moved across the Missouri bootheel. The entire road runs from 1 mile north of Campbell to the intersection of Routes J and WW, with a total length of approximately 6 miles, and can be reached at various points along the route.

⊘ **Peach orchards:** As you drive south on County Route WW, keep an eye out for the more than 800 acres of peach orchards. In the spring, the scent of peach blossoms fills the air. If you are lucky enough to be driving this tour in the summer, be sure to stop at one of the peach stands and buy a tasty treat for the drive ahead.

⊘ **Billy DeMitt Grave:** About 3 miles from the junction of Routes J and WW is the famous site where 10-year-old Billy DeMitt was killed during the Civil War for refusing to tell a group of guerrillas where his father was. A marker at the spot commemorates this tragic story, a true legend in southeast Missouri.

⊘ **Beachwell Gullies:** Also in this area are the visible remnants of erosional forces that scoured the ridge about 200 feet deep from the top of the ridge to the bottom of the gully. The sand here is pure ocean sand (in a landlocked state!), and saltwater shells have been found in this area, evidence that this area was once part of a vast ocean. The gullies can be accessed by a pedestrian trail that is approximately 1 mile long.

⊘ **Campbell:** Next, visit the historic city of Campbell, which has roots dating back to before the Civil War. Several buildings in the Historic District, many of which are on the National Historic Register, are open to visitors. Dine in the quaint local restaurants and visit the antique shops in the Historic District.

⊘ **Chalk Bluff Park:** As you leave Campbell, turn southeast onto Hwy 62. Shortly before the St. Francis River and the Arkansas border, stop and visit the **Chalk Bluff Conservation Area.** This area is full of Civil War history. The Military Road and trenches from the Civil War can still be seen today, especially along the river. Continue on across into the tip of Arkansas to see a related Civil War historical site, Chalk Bluff Battlefield.

⊘ **Chalk Bluff Battlefield Park:** This park will be of interest if you are seeking Civil War history. It is located at a Civil War battlefield site where several skirmishes were fought. The history of the area is interpreted on plaques along a walking trail. Picnic tables are available as well.

Little Dixie Highway of the Great River Road
MISSOURI

The Little Dixie Highway (also called the Mississippi Flyway Byway) is home to a culture expressing a unique Southern flair. Accents of the South are revealed in the area's Victorian-era streetscapes and plantation-era mansions. This touch of the South has earned the region its nickname, Little Dixie. The area reminds travelers of the far-reaching effects of slavery, the Civil War, and the nation's reconstruction.

The Mississippi River played an enormous role in the shaping of the physical and cultural features of the area. The Little Dixie Highway stretches out alongside the river. Limestone bluffs along the route offer stunning views of the mighty Mississippi, and the towns of Clarksville and Louisiana allow access to the river. The Little Dixie Highway is part of the Great River Road, a path of highway that runs alongside the river through several states.

The Byway Story

The Little Dixie Highway of the Great River Road tells cultural, historical, natural, recreational, and scenic stories that make it a unique and treasured Byway.

CULTURAL

As you may expect from a region with such a diverse history, the Little Dixie Highway can boast equally varied and rich cultural qualities. Although the issue of slavery and the Civil War divided the nation, the cultural heritage of the United States proved remarkably resilient. The same can be said about Pike County, where churches and fraternal organizations helped to create a close-knit society that rebuilt itself after the war.

QUICK FACTS

Length: 30 miles.

Time to Allow: 1 hour or more.

Best Time to Drive: Spring through autumn.

Restrictions: Snowfall in January and February can close the highway until snow plowing can occur.

Bicycle/Pedestrian Facilities: Bicycle lanes connecting Clarksville and Louisiana (10 miles) offer travelers the opportunity to see the Byway via means other than the automobile. Both communities have also developed pedestrian facilities, and hiking trails exist in several parks and refuge areas along the Byway.

In his novels, Mark Twain describes a lifestyle that so many people recognize as an essential part of the American historical experience. For many of the residents who grew up along the Little Dixie Highway, Twain's portrait of the Mississippi River corridor is part of their own life experiences. Because the Mississippi River enjoys an essential and dominant role in life along the Little Dixie Highway, its influence is celebrated during the Big River Days festival in Clarksville. Storytelling, music, and displays of the type of craftwork essential to life along the river offer an accompaniment to the festival's main attractions: a giant aquarium filled with the underwater life of the river and the opportunity to travel on the muddy waters of the Mississippi on a majestic riverboat.

Clarksville's craftsmen have taken an active role in preserving this town's cultural heritage by restoring its historic commercial district, which is listed on the National Register of Historic Places. These artisans have constructed the signs, forged the sign brackets, restored the storefronts, and performed the general contracting work necessary for the historically accurate restoration of this Victorian era commercial district. A 50-mile network of artists, artisans, and galleries, called the Provenance Project, also takes an active role in promoting towns from Clarksville north to Hannibal. These artists not only enrich the area aesthetically, but also attract visitors and new resident artists.

HISTORICAL

The Little Dixie Highway travels through an area bursting with history. The Mississippi River played an important and influential role in the area's history, both as a natural resource and as a geographical feature. In addition, the state of Missouri's geographical location between the North and the South left it in a volatile yet influential position.

For centuries, the Mississippi River has provided extremely fertile ground: wildlife for furs and food, an endless supply of water, and transportation. The flowing waters of the Great River have carried canoes, rafts, 19th-century steamboats, tugboats, and barges both to and from the markets of this nation, and to ships that sail to the rest of the world. But perhaps more than anything else, the Mississippi River has provided this entire nation with stories. Mark Twain probably would have agreed that no single geological feature in the country can claim to be the father of an historical and cultural offspring as rich and colorful as the Mississippi River. During the early 1800s, the river served as the edge of the West, the barrier dividing civilization from the wild frontier. As the young nation continued its growth and expansion, clashes continued between new settlers and the native peoples. Eventually, the river proved no longer to be a barrier to the frontier, but a starting line for settlers' hopes and dreams.

Slavery left marks on the history of the region traversed by the Little Dixie Highway. Missouri was a state whose role in the slavery debate proved pivotal. Within the state lay a region that came to be known as Little Dixie because of its links to the cultures and institutions of the American South. Pike County, home of the Little Dixie Highway, was one of eight counties within Little Dixie. The plantation homes and Southern-style architecture that marks the landscape throughout the length of the Byway stands as a testament to that time. As travelers look out over

the Mississippi River and see the shores of Illinois just across the mighty river, they are also reminded of the fact that freedom for the slaves always lay tantalizingly close. Little wonder, then, that the region also included several stops on the Underground Railroad.

The stories of the struggle for justice and freedom soon turned into tales of triumph and renewal. New struggles for a new kind of justice and freedom accompanied the hope ushered in by the Emancipation Proclamation. As the nation attempted to rebuild, so, too, did the residents of Pike County work to repair the damage caused by slavery and the Civil War. The Freedmen's Bureau opened in the town of Louisiana and began fulfilling its mission to uplift the region's ex-slaves. Newly opened schools sought to fulfill the same mission for the children of these former slaves. Fraternal organizations and houses of worship dotted the social landscape, and many of the buildings built by these organizations still influence the physical landscape along this Byway today. These buildings provide evidence of the prosperous society that overcame the ravages of division.

NATURAL

There is nothing quite like strolling along the banks of the Mississippi. The calm waters of the giant stream seem to stretch across for miles and provide habitat for an abundance of plant life and wildlife. These living treasures of the river can be witnessed from the Byway itself, or from many parks and observation points along the Byway, which offer exceptional closeness with the river and its resources. This particular region of the river is an important bird habitat.

A flyway is simply a path for migrating birds. The Mississippi River provides a flight corridor for approximately 40 percent of all North American waterfowl, making this a prime spot for bird-watching. In addition, the Missouri Audubon Society has documented about 39 species of migratory shorebirds in the area, such as the killdeer and the sandpiper. As if that weren't enough, the area also serves as habitat for eagles. Walter Crawford, executive director of the World Bird Sanctuary in St. Louis, has called Clarksville the eagle-viewing capital of the United States. This "fowl" life along the Little Dixie Highway is celebrated with a number of annual festivals. The biggest and best of these festivals, Eagle Days, pays tribute to the area's most notable wildlife resident and brings nearly 10,000 visitors to Clarksville the last weekend of each January. The weekend prior to Eagle

Days, the region's other raptors take center stage at Clarksville's Masters of the Sky festival.

The landscape surrounding the Little Dixie Highway reflects the impact made not only by the river itself, but also by the progression and retreat of two ice advances. The Byway is marked by steeply sloping uplands and prominent knobs and ridges dotted with limestone and shale outcroppings. Deciduous vegetation dominates the landscape in those areas not being used for agriculture.

Because this part of the country experiences the effects of four distinct seasonal changes, nature paints an ever-changing picture. The fall colors are particularly significant to local residents, who justifiably take pride in the beauty the fall brings to the region.

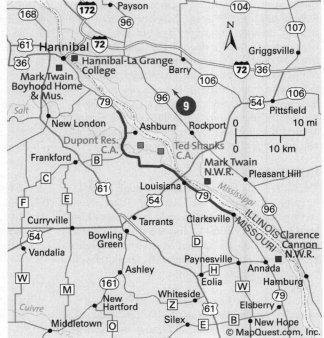

RECREATIONAL

The Little Dixie Highway runs parallel to the area's major source of recreation, the Mississippi River. Recreational opportunities related to the river include some river islands open to the public; great opportunities for fishing, hiking, and cycling; a few wildlife reserves; two boat launches; the Eagle Center in Clarksville; a pair of riverfront municipal parks; Lock and Dam 24 at Clarksville; and a variety of scenic overlooks.

Upon traveling the Little Dixie Highway, some travelers may get the overwhelming urge to kick off their shoes, roll up their pants or overalls, pull out a corncob pipe, and set off down the river on a log raft for some remote camping site. Well, this Byway allows you to relieve that urge. The river contains many small islands, several of which are accessible to the public by log raft, canoe, or any other boat. Many recreationalists canoe over to an island for peaceful camping and great fishing, from launching points such as Silo Park. The Army Corps of Engineers manages the islands and should be contacted to determine which of the islands in Pike County are open to the public.

The Mississippi River has long been a prominent source of fish—catfish and crappie are the most common types found in the river. The parks and other points along the Byway offer great opportunities to land that 20-pound Mississippi River catfish. The reserves along the Byway also offer exceptional fishing. Clarksville and Louisiana each have a boat dock.

The Little Dixie Highway features bike trails or wide shoulders for cyclists and hikers. Cycling along the Byway offers you a chance to really take in the serenity and uniqueness of the Byway and adjacent river. Additionally, the parks and conservation areas along the Byway allow for leisurely walks right next to the river.

SCENIC

You need only capture a view from one of the many scenic overlooks along the Byway to understand a little better why the Mississippi has played such an important role in the lives of Americans. The scenic overlooks from high bluffs north of Louisiana and at the Louisiana Cemetery, in particular, offer a bird's-eye view of the river and of the lush Mississippi Valley. The valley is a deep shade of green most of the time, full of dark, fertile soil that has provided food for Americans for centuries. The Pinnacle, at 850 feet above sea level, is the highest point on the Mississippi River. Barges, other boats, and occasionally even riverboats can often be seen from these various overlooks, reminding you of the important role the river has played in transportation and commerce. For those who simply want an aesthetic treat, autumn provides an abundance of colors to please the eye.

Iowa

Iowa, the heartland of American agriculture, is also a growing center of industry. Iowa is a leader in corn and soybean production, but Iowa industry generates about three and a half times the revenue of agriculture. The 3,600 manufacturing firms in the state produce more than 3,000 different products, ranging from motor homes to microwave ovens. Major appliances, farm implements, and plastics are exported all over the world. Iowa is the only state bordered by two navigable rivers, with the Mississippi River forming its eastern boundary and the Missouri River most of its western boundary. The Sioux called Iowa the "beautiful land."

Iowa's countryside offers tourists a wide range of recreational activities, from boating and fishing on lakes, rivers, and reservoirs to hiking and picnicking at the many state parks and forests. Iowa also offers medium-sized cities with cultural activities, including performing arts, historic sites, and art museums. This is the land of Native American warrior Black Hawk and the birthplace of Buffalo Bill Cody, John Wayne, Herbert Hoover, Meredith Willson, and Dr. James Van Allen.

Four glacial epochs and centuries of untouched wilderness fertilized the soil of Iowa before Marquette and Jolliet came in 1673. A favorite Native American hunting ground, Iowa was part of the Louisiana Purchase. Lewis and Clark passed through in 1804 on their arduous trip to find out what the United States had bought. Treaties with the Native Americans in 1832, 1837, and 1842 opened the area to European settlers. Pioneer settlements were made in Lee County in 1820, at Burlington in 1832, and at Dubuque in 1833. The Territory of Iowa was created from the Territory of Wisconsin in 1838.

Population: 2,926,324
Area: 55,965 square miles
Elevation: 480-1,670 feet
Peak: Near Ocheyedan (Osceola County)
Entered Union: December 28, 1846 (29th state)
Capital: Des Moines
Motto: Our Liberties We Prize And Our Rights We Will Maintain
Nickname: Hawkeye State
Flower: Wild Rose
Bird: Eastern Goldfinch
Tree: Oak
Fair: August in Des Moines
Time Zone: Central
Web Site: www.traveliowa.com

In its 300-mile east-west sweep and 210-mile north-south stretch, Iowa has nearly 56,000 acres of natural and man-made lakes, 19,000 miles of interior fishing streams, and 72 state parks and recreation areas.

When to Go/Climate

Typical Midwestern weather is the norm in Iowa. Summers are hot and humid, and winters are cold and harsh. Long Indian summers can stretch into November, while spring is usually short and rainy.

AVERAGE HIGH/LOW TEMPERATURES (° F)

Des Moines

Jan 28/11	**May** 73/52	**Sept** 76/55
Feb 34/16	**June** 82/67	**Oct** 64/43
Mar 47/28	**July** 87/67	**Nov** 48/30
Apr 62/40	**Aug** 84/64	**Dec** 33/16

Dubuque

Jan 24/8	**May** 69/48	**Sept** 72/52
Feb 30/13	**June** 78/62	**Oct** 61/40
Mar 43/25	**July** 82/62	**Nov** 45/28
Apr 58/37	**Aug** 80/60	**Dec** 29/14

Calendar Highlights

MARCH

St. Patrick's Day Celebration *(Emmetsburg). Phone 712/852-4326.* Parade, pageant, and cultural exhibits. Irish stew dinner, dances, and a guest member of Irish Parliament.

APRIL

Veishea Spring Festival *(Ames). Iowa State University campus. Phone 515/294-1026.* Parade, sports, theatrical events, and academic open houses.

MAY

Snake Alley Criterium Bicycle Races *(Burlington). Phone 319/752-0015.* Olympic-style racing. Memorial Day weekend.

JUNE

All-Iowa Fair *(Cedar Rapids). Hawkeye Downs. Phone Cedar Rapids Area Convention and Visitors Bureau, 319/365-8656.* Stock car races, fine arts, exhibits, and entertainment.

Burlington Steamboat Days & the American Music Festival *(Burlington). Downtown riverfront. Phone 319/754-4334.* Athletic competitions, fireworks, midway, parade, and entertainment.

Glenn Miller Festival *(Clarinda). Phone 712/542-2461.* Musical event in honor of Glenn Miller and his birthplace.

My Waterloo Days Festival *(Waterloo). Phone 319/233-8431.* This citywide festival features an air show, balloon rallies, a parade, a laser and fireworks show, music, a renaissance fair, and food.

JUNE/JULY

Freedom Festival *(Cedar Rapids). Phone 319/365-8313.* Eighty events for all ages are held citywide, topped off by a large fireworks display.

AUGUST

Iowa State Fair *(Des Moines). Fairgrounds. Phone 515/262-3111.* One of the oldest and largest in the country; includes 20 acres of farm machinery, fine arts, grandstand stage and track events, free entertainment, exhibits, demonstrations, contests, and camping.

SEPTEMBER

Midwest Old Threshers Reunion *(Mount Pleasant). Phone 319/385-8937.* Iowa's largest working craft show, antique car show; steam and gas engines, vintage tractors; Midwest Village, log village, narrow-gauge steam railroad, and electric trolley cars; entertainment.

OCTOBER

Covered Bridge Festival *(Winterset). Phone 515/462-1185.* Late 19th-century crafts, entertainment; parade, bus tour of covered bridges.

Parks and Recreation

Water-related activities, hiking, riding, various other sports, picnicking and visitor centers, as well as camping, are available in many of Iowa's state parks. Swimming fees at supervised beaches (bathhouse included) vary. Camping is limited to two weeks; and no reservations are accepted: $9-$11 per night per site (electricity $5 additional; sewer and water $3 additional). Cabins (no bedding, linens): $25-$100 per day or $150-$600 per week; cot, where available, $1 per cot per day; deposit $50. Pets are permitted on leash only. State properties are open daily. At most parks, water facilities are unavailable mid-October-mid-April. For further information, contact the Department of Natural Resources, Wallace State Office Building, Des Moines, 50319; phone 515/281-5145 (automated system).

FISHING AND HUNTING

Fishing for walleye, muskellunge, northern pike, perch, bluegill, smallmouth bass, catfish, and bullhead is good in the natural lakes of northern Iowa. The man-made lakes in the southern part of the state are abundant with largemouth bass, catfish, crappie, and bluegill. There are 87,000 farm ponds in the state, 50 spring-fed trout streams in the northeastern section, and more than 56,000 acres of natural and man-made lakes. Public access to fishing water is furnished at more than 200 state-owned areas, 19,000 miles of meandering inland streams, and 600 miles of boundary streams.

A resident or nonresident aged 16 to 64 who is required to have a fishing license shall not fish unless the person has paid a fish habitat fee ($3.50). A resident or nonresident, when fishing in a privately owned farm pond or lake, is exempt from the fish habitat fee.

Ring-necked pheasant is a popular target of hunters, with all counties open for a 50-plus-day season. Quail hunting, primarily in the southern half of the state, has a season that lasts for approximately 90 days. Ruffed grouse provide a challenge to hunters in northeastern hills, while gray partridges offer good hunting opportunities in the north and north-central counties. Raccoons, rabbits, foxes, and gray squirrels are numerous.

Nonresident season hunting license, $80; duck stamp, $8.50 more. Nonresident season fishing license, $36; seven-day license, $27; trout stamp, $13 more. Required for all hunters and fur harvesters: state habitat stamp, $8.50. Nonresident fur harvester license $200. Nonresident deer tag, $309.50; nonresident turkey tag, $100.50; both require a habitat stamp. For further information, contact the Department of Natural Resources, Wallace State Office Building, Des Moines, 50319-0034; phone 515/281-5918.

Driving Information

Safety belts are mandatory for all persons in the front seat of a vehicle. Children under age 6 must be in approved passenger restraints anywhere in a vehicle; children ages 3-6 may use regulation safety belts; children under age 3 must use approved safety seats. For more information, phone 515/281-3907.

INTERSTATE HIGHWAY SYSTEM

The following alphabetical listing of Iowa towns in this book shows that these cities are within 10 miles of the indicated interstate highways. Check a highway map for the nearest exit.

Highway Number	Cities/Towns within 10 Miles
Interstate 29	Council Bluffs, Missouri Valley, Onawa, Sioux City.
Interstate 35	Ames, Clear Lake, Des Moines, Mason City, Osceola.
Interstate 80	Atlantic, Avoca, Council Bluffs, Davenport, Des Moines, Grinnell, Iowa City, Newton.

Additional Visitor Information

The Department of Economic Development, Iowa Division of Tourism, 200 E Grand Ave, Des Moines 50309, has further information, including an Iowa travel guide, camping and outdoor guide, and calendar of events; phone 515/242-4705 or toll-free 888/472-6035.

Two periodicals worth looking at are *Annals of Iowa,* quarterly, State Historical Society of Iowa, 402 Iowa Ave, Iowa City, 52240 and *The Iowan,* quarterly, Mid-America Publishing Corp, Box 130, Shenandoah, 51601.

There are 22 welcome centers in Iowa; visitors will find information and brochures most helpful in planning stops at points of interest. They are located near the following cities: Amana, Bloomfield, Burlington, Clear Lake, Davis City, Des Moines, Dows, Dubuque, Elk Horn, Elkader, Emmetsburg, Lamoni, LeClaire, Missouri Valley, Sergeant Bluff, Sioux City, Underwood, Victor, and Wilton.

FROM THE BRIDGES OF MADISON COUNTY TO THE LOESS HILLS

This route begins at Interstate 80, exit 110 at De Soto, west of Des Moines. Follow Highway 169 south to Winterset. Surrounded by wooded hills, Winterset—originally a Quaker settlement—is the hub of several short side trips to the six covered bridges made famous by Robert Waller's novel The Bridges of Madison County. If you want to make the full circuit, pick up a free brochure and map to all the bridges from local businesses (most are on remote county roads). If you don't have time for the full tour, one of the bridges is now preserved in Winterset's city park. The Madison County Historical Complex is an 18-acre park with a number of historic buildings, including a limestone barn and the old Winterset train depot.

Quaker-founded Winterset was a station along the Underground Railroad, along which slaves traveled north to freedom from the Confederate states, such as neighboring Missouri. A painted brick house, now in the Winterset Art Center, served as a temporary home for hundreds of displaced slaves during the 1850s and 1860s, including scholar George Washington Carver, who lived here after experiencing discrimination elsewhere in the Midwest. Winterset is also the birthplace of actor John Wayne—born Marion Robert Morrison. His family home is open to visitors.

Continue south on Highway 169 and turn west on Highway 34 to Creston, an old railroading center with an impressive core of late Victorian homes and storefronts. The town's McKinley Park houses the Union County Historical Museum, with remnants of Creston's heyday in the 1880s. Continue on Highway 34 to the village of Corning, once home to the Icarian Colony, the longest operating nonreligious utopian community in the United States. Founded in 1850, the 80-member community disbanded in 1900 after establishing vineyards, lilac hedges, and stands of rhubarb in the area. (Rhubarb pie is still a favorite in local cafés.) The town's original jail is now the Adams County House of History, which preserves relics from the disbanded agrarian commune.

Follow Highway 34 across the prairies to Red Oak, and then go south on Highway 59 to Shenandoah, originally a Mormon settlement during that group's westward migration. Today, the fertile soil that surrounds the town supports three national seed nurseries. From Shenandoah, turn west on Highway 2 toward Sidney, a village in Iowa's famous Loess Hills. These green, heavily eroded hills were formed at the end of the last Ice Age. The Missouri River brought silt-rich waters from the north, where massive glaciers were busy grinding rock into till. As the silt deposits dried, winds blew the fine sand into dunes hundreds of feet high. Now covered with virgin prairie grasslands and upland forests, the Loess Hills are home to wildlife such as coyotes, deer, bald eagles, and prairie dogs and were considered for national park status during the Clinton administration.

While in Sidney, be sure to stop at the Penn Drug Store. Built in 1865, the store is still operated by the Penn family—it's the oldest family-owned business in the state-and features an old-fashioned soda fountain. From Sidney, two scenic backroads, the Pleasant Overview Loop and the Spring Valley Loop, wind into the Loess Hills. South along Highway 2 is Waubonsie State Park, which features hiking and biking trails into the hills. To see more of this curious landscape, continue north on Highway 275 toward Glenwood and Council Bluffs. **(Approximately 205 miles)**

THE DES MOINES RIVER VALLEY

This route travels through picture-perfect farming communities founded by European settlers, then along the lower Des Moines River, where historic towns have changed little since the great riverboat era. From Des Moines, drive east on Highway 163 toward Pella. Founded in 1847 by Dutch settlers who came to this valley to escape religious persecution in Holland, Pella retains a sense of Dutch orderliness and is filled with trim historic homes and tulip-filled public parks. The Pella Historical Village Museum features a number of the town's original structures clustered around a central flower-filled courtyard. The downtown area is filled with

Dutch-style bakeries, gift shops, and restaurants featuring Dutch fare.

East on Highway 163 through rolling hills is Oskaloosa, a farming town settled by Quakers. The town's past is retold at Nelson Pioneer Farm and Craft Museum, which preserves a farm community from the 1850s. The 21-building site includes farm structures, a one-room schoolhouse, a Friends Meeting Room, and a country store. From Oskaloosa, follow Highway 163 to Ottumwa, a busy industrial center. The John Deere Factory here is open for tours.

Continuing on, turn east on Highway 34, then turn south on Highway 16, which closely follows the Des Moines River. One of the earliest settled regions of Iowa, this section of the Des Moines valley is lined with tiny towns founded in the 1830s when the river was the only avenue for travel. Bypassed by the rail lines and the freeway system, these towns were forgotten by the forward rush of time. Today, they are beautifully preserved testaments to a long-passed era, with handsome period architecture, newly refurbished small hotels and inns, historical museums, and antique stores.

The town of Eldon contains one of the most archetypical structures in the Midwest: at the corner of Gothic and Burton streets is the house painted by Grant Wood as the backdrop to his famous portrait American Gothic. The rustic couple in the painting were the painter's sister and his dentist. Fronting onto the Des Moines River, Keosauqua is home to the oldest courthouse in the state, as well as the imposing Manning Hotel, 150 years old and still in operation. Farther downstream, the entire village of Bentonsport—once a sizable river port—is a National Historic District. The Mason House Hotel, built by Mormon craftsmen in the 1840s, is open both for tours and for paying guests. At the town of Bonaparte, the original grist and woolen mills are preserved. A number of artisans work out of historic storefronts.

From Bonaparte, follow Highway 81 south to Farmington, with the oldest Congregational church west of the Mississippi (1848) and a stone carriage factory. Continue east to Highway 218 and turn south to Keokuk, at the confluence of the Des Moines and Mississippi rivers. Keokuk was head of steamboat navigation on the Mississippi before Lock Number 19—the largest on the river system—was built in 1913. The lock is part of Keokuk Dam, which was the world's largest hydroelectric dam until the 1930s. Fittingly, the sternwheeler George M. Verity houses the Keokuk River Museum. Also here is the Keokuk National Cemetery, established after the Civil War as a place of interment for soldiers killed on both sides of the conflict. **(Approximately 185 miles)**

Algona (A-3)

See also Emmetsburg, West Bend

Settled 1854
Population 6,015
Elevation 1,200 ft
Area Code 515
Zip 50511
Information Chamber of Commerce, 123 E State St; phone 515/295-7201
Web Site www.algona.org

Originally known as Call's Grove, the town later chose its present name, a shortened form of "Algonquin." In 1857, a fort enclosed the town hall; after the frontier hostilities abated, this fort was torn down and the wood used for a plank road. On the wide bend of the east fork of the Des Moines River, Algona is the seat and crossroads city of Kossuth County.

What to See and Do

Ambrose A. Call State Park. *2007 Call Park Dr, Algona (50511). 1 1/2 miles S on Hwy 169, then W on paved road. Phone 515/295-3669. www.state.ia.us/dnr/organiza/ppd/ambrose.htm.* These 130 acres of rolling timbered hills include hiking trails, a Frisbee golf course, picnic areas, a playground, 16 campsites (13 with electric hookups), and a log cabin-style lodge. (Daily 4 am-10:30 pm)

Smith Lake Park. *2407 Hwy 169, Algona (50511). 3 miles N on Hwy 169. Phone 515/295-2138.* The 124 acres of this park include the 53-acre Smith Lake. Recreational opportunities include swimming, fishing, boating (electric motors only), picnicking, playgrounds, a hiking trail, and a tree garden. Camping (fee; dump station additional). (Daily during daylight hours)

Limited-Service Hotel

★ **BURR OAK MOTEL.** *Hwy 169 S, Algona (50511). Phone 515/295-7213; toll-free 877/745-6315; fax 515/295-2979. www.burroakmotel.com.* 40 rooms. Pets accepted; fee. Complimentary continental breakfast. Check-out 10 am. **$**

[🔁]

Restaurant

★ ★ **SISTER SARAH'S.** *Hwy 18, Algona (50511).* *Phone 515/295-7757.* American menu. Breakfast, lunch, dinner. Closed Sun-Mon, Thanksgiving, Dec 25. Bar. Children's menu. Outdoor seating. **$**

Amana Colonies (C-5)

See also Cedar Rapids, Iowa City

Settled 1855
Population 71,640
Elevation 715 ft
Area Code 319
Zip 52203
Information Amana Colonies Convention & Visitors Bureau, 39-38th Ave, Suite 100, Amana; phone 319/622-7622 or toll-free 800/579-2294
Web Site www.amanacolonies.com

A religiously motivated community, the Amana Colonies produce smoked meats, woolen goods, bakery products, furniture, ovens and microwaves, refrigerators, food freezers, and air conditioners. The history of the community goes back to the 1714 founding in Germany of the Inspirationists, a Lutheran separatist group. Members migrated to America and settled near Buffalo, New York. Later they bought 25,000 acres of prairie land in Iowa and moved west. Their first Iowa village was called Amana, a Biblical name meaning "remain faithful." Five more villages were built (West, High, Middle, East, and South Amana). The village of Homestead was purchased outright to acquire use of its railroad terminal.

At first, the members of the Amana Colonies lived a simple, communal life. Families were assigned living quarters with common kitchen and dining facilities; everything was shared equally. Farming was and still is a mainstay of the group. The community finally yielded to the pressures of the 20th century. In 1932, common property was dissolved and redistributed on a stock corporation basis. The new corporation, encouraging individual skills and vigor, prospered mostly because of the quality work of its artisans. Today, nearly every family owns its own house.

What to See and Do

⭐ **Amana Heritage Sites.** *Hwy 151 and Hwy 220, Amana (52203). Phone 319/622-3567. www.amanaheritage.org.* This community has a furniture factory that offers tours of the production area; a woolen mill with salesroom (daily); woodworking shops, meat shop, general store, brewery, wineries, restaurants, and shops. The residence of the late Christian Metz, former leader of Amana Colonies, is here. Also here is

Amana Heritage Museum. *4310 220th Trail, Amana (52203). Phone 319/622-3567.* Exhibits include a schoolhouse, crafts and trades, lithographs, and documents. An audiovisual presentation explains the history of the Amanas. (Apr-Nov: Mon-Sat 10 am-5 pm, Sun noon-5 pm) **$$**

High Amana. *1308 G St, Amana (52203). 2 miles W of Middle Amana on Hwy 220.* Amana Arts Guild Center and an old-fashioned general store.

Homestead. *4119 V St, Homestead (52236). 5 miles E of South Amana on Hwy 6.* Meat shop; winery.

Middle Amana. *2 miles W of Amana on Hwy 220.* Restored original Amana communal kitchen, hearth-oven bakery; coopers shop; Amana Refrigeration, includes Amana Lily Lake.

Old Creamery Theatre Company. *Price Creek Stage, 39 38th Ave, Amana (52203). Phone 319/622-6194; toll-free 800/352-6262. www.oldcreamery.com.* Professional theater company performs a variety of productions. (Apr-mid-Dec, Wed-Sun; closed Thanksgiving) **$$$$**

South Amana. *2 miles S of West Amana on IA 220.* Winery, miniature-barn museum, furniture factory and refinishing shops; agricultural museum with displays of early farm equipment.

West Amana. *511 F St, Amana (52203). 1 mile W of High Amana on Hwy 220.* General store, basket, and antique shops.

Limited-Service Hotels

★ ★ **HOLIDAY INN.** *2111 U Ave, Williamsburg (52361). Phone 319/668-1175; toll-free 800/633-9244; fax 319/668-2853. www.amanaholidayinn.com.* 155 rooms, 2 story. Pets accepted. Check-out 11 am. Restaurant, bar. Fitness room. Indoor pool, children's pool, whirlpool. Little Amana complex is adjacent with an old-time general store and winery. **$**
🅳 🔌 🧍 🌊

★ **SUPER 8.** *1708 N Highland St, Williamsburg (52361). Phone 319/668-9718; fax 319/668-9770.* 33 rooms, 2 story. Pets accepted; fee. Complimentary continental breakfast. Fitness room. Indoor pool, outdoor pool, whirlpool. **$**
🔌 🧍 🌊

Restaurants

★ ★ **THE AMANA BARN RESTAURANT.** *4709 220th Trail, Amana (52203). Phone 563/622-3214; toll-free 800/325-2045; fax 319/622-6378. www.amanabarn.com.* German, American menu. Lunch, dinner. Bar. Children's menu. **$$**

★ ★ **BRICK HAUS.** *728 47th Ave, Amana (52203). Phone 319/622-3278; fax 319/622-6294.* German, American menu. Breakfast, lunch, dinner, brunch. Closed Jan 1, Dec 25. Children's menu. Valet parking. Photos on the wall detail the history of village. **$$**

★ ★ **OX YOKE INN.** *4420 220th Trail, Amana (52203). Phone 319/622-3441. www.oxyokeinn.com.* German, American menu. Lunch, dinner. Bar. Children's menu. **$$**
🅳

★ ★ **RONNEBURG.** *4408 220th Trail, Amana (52203). Phone 319/622-3641; fax 319/622-6183.* German, American menu. Breakfast, brunch. Closed Jan 1, Dec 25. Bar. **$$**
🅳

★ ★ **ZUBER'S.** *2206 V St, Amana Colonies (52236). Phone 319/622-3911; fax 319/622-3741.* American menu. Lunch, dinner, late-night, brunch. Children's menu. Restored century-old inn. Baseball memorabilia. **$$**

Ames (C-3)

See also Boone

Settled 1864
Population 47,198
Elevation 921 ft
Area Code 515
Zip 50010
Information Convention & Visitors Bureau, 1601 Golden Aspen Dr, #110; phone 515/232-4032 or toll-free 800/288-7470
Web Site www.ames.ia.us

Located near the geographical center of the state, Ames's economy beats to the pulse of Iowa State University. There are 38 small factories and a regional medical center complex but no major industrial activity. Ames has 500 clubs and organizations. A municipal band performs weekly during the summer. The town is named in honor of a Massachusetts congressman, Oakes Ames, who was financially interested in a local railroad project.

What to See and Do

Iowa Arboretum. *1875 Peach Ave, Madrid (50156). 18 miles SW via Hwy 30, Hwy 17, and County E-57. Phone 515/795-3216.* Arboretum includes 340 acres of trees, shrubs, and gardens. Trails, horticultural plantings, scenic overlooks, ravines, streams. Guided and self-guided tours; educational programs. (Daily) **$**

Iowa State University. *117 Beardshear Hall, Ames (50010). N of Hwy 30. Phone 515/294-4777. www.iastate.edu.* (1858) (27,800 students) One of the oldest land grant universities in the United States, ISU is known for its spacious, green central campus with sculptures and fountains by artist Christian Petersen, and for its many historic buildings. The school is also the birthplace of the electronic digital computer, built by John V. Atanasoff in the basement of the Physics Building in the late 1930s. Major places of interest are

Campanile. *Ames. On central campus.* (1899) The 50-bell carillon is played during the academic year (Mon-Fri) and also played on special occasions.

Christian Petersen Sculptures. *Ames.* Works, executed in the 1930s and 1940s when Petersen was artist-in-residence at ISU, are on display at Memorial Union fountain, State Gym, Dairy Industry Building, MacKay Hall, and several other locations.

Farm House. *290 Farm House Lane, Ames (50010). Near Dairy Industry Building, off Union Dr. Phone 515/294-3342.* (1860) Restored original residence on the Iowa State Agricultural College farm; period furnishings. (Sept-May; closed holidays) **FREE**

Grant Wood Murals. *Ames (50011). In the Parks Library, on Morrill Rd.* Considered among the best works of this Iowa artist, the nine murals began as a WPA project during the Great Depression. They depict various academic divisions of the school as well as the breaking of the sod by pioneer farmers.

Iowa State Center. *Ames (50011). Phone 515/294-3347.* Complex of four buildings includes an auditorium, coliseum, two theaters; Brunnier Museum and Art Gallery. (Tues-Sun; closed holidays)

Reiman Gardens. *1407 Elwood Dr, Ames (50010). Teaching garden on NE edge of campus. Phone 515/294-2710.* Peonies, irises, geraniums, many varieties of roses.

Special Event

Veishea Spring Festival. *40 Iowa State Memorial Union, Ames (50011). Phone 515/294-1026.* Held on Iowa State campus, it features a parade, sports, theatrical events, and academic open houses. Mid-late Apr.

Limited-Service Hotels

★ **BAYMONT INN.** *2500 Elwood Dr, Ames (50010). Phone 515/296-2500; toll-free 866/999-1111; fax 515/296-2874. www.baymontinns.com.* 89 rooms, 2 story. Pets accepted. Complimentary continental breakfast. Check-out noon. Indoor pool, whirlpool. **$**
🅳 🐾 ≋

★ ★ **THE HOTEL AT GATEWAY CENTER.** *Hwy 30 and Elwood Dr, Ames (50010). Phone 515/292-8600; toll-free 800/367-2637; fax 515/268-2224. www.thegatewayames.com.* 188 rooms, 8 story. Pets accepted. Check-out noon. Restaurant, bar. Fitness room. Indoor pool, whirlpool. Airport transportation available. Business center. **$**
🐾 🏋 ≋ 🏃

Restaurants

★ ★ **BROILER STEAKHOUSE.** *6008 Lincoln Way, Ames (50014). Phone 515/292-2516. www.broilersteakhouse.com.* Steak menu. Dinner. Closed Thanksgiving, Dec 25. Bar. Children's menu. **$$$**

★ **HICKORY PARK.** *1404 S Duss, Ames (50010). Phone 515/232-8940; fax 515/232-7275. www.hickorypark-bbq.com.* Barbecue menu. Lunch, dinner. Closed Easter, Thanksgiving, Dec 25. Children's menu. **$$**

★ **LUCULLANS.** *400 Main St, Ames (50010). Phone 515/232-8484.* Italian menu. Lunch, dinner, brunch. Closed holidays. Bar. Children's menu. **$$**

Atlantic (C-2)

See also Avoca

Population 7,432
Elevation 1,215 ft
Area Code 712

Zip 50022
Information Chamber of Commerce, 614 Chestnut St;
phone 712/243-3017 or toll-free 877/283-2124
Web Site www.atlanticiowa.com

What to See and Do

Danish Windmill. *4038 Main St, Elk Horn (51531). 15
miles N via Hwy 173; 7 miles N of I-80 Exit 54. Phone
712/764-7472.* Built in Denmark (1848), this 60-foot-
high working windmill was dismantled and shipped
to Elk Horn where it was reassembled by community
volunteers. (Daily; closed Jan 1, Dec 25) **$**

Limited-Service Hotel

★ **SUPER 8.** *1902 E 7th St, Atlantic (50022). Phone
712/243-4723; toll-free 888/243-2378; fax 712/243-
2864. www.super8.com.* 59 rooms. Complimentary
continental breakfast. Check-out 11 am. **$**

Specialty Lodging

The following lodging establishment is approved
by Mobil Travel Guide, but due to its unique and
individualized nature has not been given a traditional
Mobil Star rating. Included in this listing you may
find bed-and-breakfasts, limited-service inns, guest
ranches, and other unique hotel properties.

CHESTNUT CHARM BED & BREAKFAST. *1409
Chestnut St, Atlantic (50022). Phone 712/243-5652.
chestnutcharm.org.* At this romantic Victorian inn,
built in 1898, there are beautiful guest rooms as well
as cozy carriage houses. With a country setting and
intimate atmosphere, it makes for a serene weekend
getaway. 9 rooms. No children allowed. Complimentary full breakfast. Check-in 4 pm, check-out 11 am. **$**

Avoca (C-2)

See also Atlantic

Population 1,497
Elevation 1,138 ft
Area Code 712
Zip 51521

What to See and Do

Prairie Rose State Park. *680 Rd M47, Harlan (51537).
2 miles N via Hwy 59, then 6 miles E on I-80, exit 46,
then 9 miles N on paved road. Phone 712/773-2701.*
More than 650 acres of wind-formed hills surround

a 204-acre lake. Swimming, fishing, boating (ramp);
snowmobiling, picnicking, camping (electricity, dump
station). Standard hours, fees.

Bettendorf (C-6)

See also Clinton, Davenport

Population 28,132
Elevation 565 ft
Area Code 563
Zip 52722
Information Quad Cities Convention & Visitors
Bureau, 102 S Harrison St, Davenport 52801; phone
563/322-3911 or toll-free 800/747-7800. Chamber of
Commerce, 2117 State St; phone 563/355-4753
Web Site www.quadcities.com

Bettendorf began as a quiet rural village called Gilbert.
In 1903, the town's future changed with the arrival of
the Bettendorf Axle and Wagon Company, which
became the largest manufacturer of railroad cars west
of the Mississippi. The growing city changed its name
in honor of the company. Today Bettendorf, on the
Mississippi River, is part of the Quad Cities metropolitan area that includes Davenport, Iowa, and Moline
and Rock Island, Illinois.

What to See and Do

Buffalo Bill Cody Homestead. *28050 230th Ave,
Princeton (52768). 3 miles N on Hwy 67, then W on
280th/Bluff Rd near McCausland. Phone 563/225-2981.*
Restored boyhood home of Buffalo Bill Cody, built by
his father in 1847. Buffalo are on the grounds. (Apr-
Oct, daily).

Family Museum of Arts & Science. *2900 Learning
Campus Dr, Bettendorf (52722). Phone 563/344-4106.*
Hands-on exhibits; Rhythm Alley, Heartland, The
Homestead, Kinder Garten; also traveling exhibit gal-
lery, children's program area. (Daily; closed holidays)
$

Isle of Capri. *1777 Isle Parkway, Bettendorf (52722).
Riverfront, just E of I-74. Phone 563/359-7280; toll-free
800/724-5825.* Casino gambling; restaurant, gift shop,
lodging. Valet parking.

Limited-Service Hotels

★ ★ **HOLIDAY INN.** *909 Middle Rd, Bettendorf
(52722). Phone 563/355-4761; toll-free 800/626-0780;*

fax 563/355-5572. www.holiday-inn.com. 150 rooms, 2 story. Check-out noon. Restaurant, bar. Fitness room. Indoor pool. Airport transportation available. **$**

★ ★ **THE LODGE.** *900 Spruce Hills Dr, Bettendorf (52722). Phone 563/359-7141; toll-free 800/285-8637; fax 563/355-0670. www.jumers.com.* At this hotel, guests will find surroundings adorned with rich tapestries, fine antiques, and grand elegance. Guest rooms have four-poster beds and will please guests with luxurious comfort. The award-winning restaurant serves both American and German cuisine. 210 rooms. Pets accepted, some restrictions; fee. Check-out noon. Restaurant, bar. Fitness room. Indoor pool, outdoor pool, whirlpool. Airport transportation available. **$**

★ **SIGNATURE INN DAVENPORT/ BETTENDORF.** *3020 Utica Ridge Rd, Bettendorf (52722). Phone 563/355-7575; toll-free 800/822-5252; fax 563/355-1305. www.signatureinn.com.* 119 rooms, 3 story. Complimentary full breakfast. Check-out noon. Fitness room. Outdoor pool. Airport transportation available. Business center. **$**

Specialty Lodging

The following lodging establishment is approved by Mobil Travel Guide, but due to its unique and individualized nature has not been given a traditional Mobil Star rating. Included in this listing you may find bed-and-breakfasts, limited-service inns, guest ranches, and other unique hotel properties.

ABBEY HOTEL. *1401 Central Ave, Bettendorf (52722). Phone 563/355-0291; toll-free 800/438-7535; fax 563/355-7647. www.theabbeyhotel.com.* This breathtaking Romanesque hotel, once a monastery, overlooks the Mississippi River and is surrounded by beautiful gardens and landscaping. With luxurious guest suites and top-rated service, guests can indulge in fine elegance and simple serenity. 19 rooms, 3 story. Complimentary full breakfast. Check-in 2 pm, check-out noon. Bar. Fitness room. Outdoor pool. Airport transportation available. **$**

Restaurants

★ ★ ★ **THE LODGE.** *900 Spruce Hills Dr, Bettendorf (52722). Phone 563/359-1607. www.jumers.com.* Located inside of The Lodge (see), this restaurant features an American, German menu. Such specialties include regensburg goulash, chicken von jumer, and rack of lamb. With a German décor throughout, the restaurant is a true dining experience. American, German menu. Lunch, dinner. Bar. Children's menu. **$$**

★ ★ **STUBBS EDDY RESTAURANT/PUB.** *1716 State St, Bettendorf (52722). Phone 563/355-0073.* Seafood menu. Breakfast, lunch, dinner, late-night. Bar. Children's menu. **$$$**

Boone (B-3)

See also Ames

Founded 1865
Population 12,392
Elevation 960 ft
Area Code 515
Zip 50036
Information Chamber of Commerce, 806 7th St; phone 515/432-3342 or toll-free 800/266-6312
Web Site www.booneiowa.com

In the fertile Des Moines River Valley, Boone is a farming center with several factories. There are a number of summer camps for children in the surrounding area.

What to See and Do

Boone and Scenic Valley Railroad. *225 10th St, Boone (50036). Phone 515/432-4249.* The ride on this short-line railroad includes a scenic, 12-mile, round-trip tour (1 3/4 hour) in vintage 1920s cars pulled by a steam engine (weekends, holidays; three trips daily) or diesel (weekdays; one trip daily); steam locomotive, made in China, is the only engine of its class in the United States; train crosses the highest "single-track, interurban bridge" in the United States. Depot has a snack bar and **Iowa Railroad Museum** with railroad history exhibits. (Memorial Day weekend-Oct, daily) **$$$**

Ledges State Park. *1519 250th St, Madrid (50156). 6 miles S on Hwy 164. Phone 515/432-1852.* More than 1,200 acres with foot trails, streams, and 25 150-foot-high sandstone ledges. Fishing; hiking, snowmobiling, picnicking, camping (electric hookups, dump station).

Mamie Doud Eisenhower Birthplace. *709 Carroll St, Boone (50036). Phone 515/432-1896.* One-story frame house restored to original Victorian style includes such period furnishings as the bed in which Mamie Eisenhower was born. Summer kitchen, library, museum. (June-Oct: daily; Apr-May: Tues-Sun afternoons; also by appointment) **$$**

Special Event

Pufferbilly Days. *903 Story St, Boone (50036). Phone 515/432-3342.* Features train rides, model railroad display, handcar races, spike driving contest; antique car show; parade, entertainment, food, bike races. Weekend after Labor Day.

Full-Service Hotel

★ ★ ★ **HOTEL PATTEE.** *1112 Willis Ave, Perry (50220). Phone 515/465-3511; fax 515/465-3017.* This historic boutique hotel, with just 40 rooms, offers guests a uniquely Midwestern experience. Arts and Crafts style pervades the interior of the building, which is listed on the National Historic Register, while the individually themed guest rooms celebrate the individuals and ethnic groups that settled this region of Iowa. For example, the Bill Bell Room honors one of the world's most famous tuba players who is now buried at a local cemetery, while the Japanese Room, with its king-size futon on a tatami mat, was designed by a Japanese-American descendent of Perry's founder. Accommodations come complete with pillowtop beds and nightly turndown service; some have spa tubs and wood-burning fireplaces as well. There's even a 1913 bowling alley to provide entertainment. The hotel's charming restaurant, David's Milwaukee Diner, serves both simple comfort foods and contemporary cuisine that draws upon the Iowa harvest. 40 rooms, 3 story. Check-out noon. High-speed Internet access. Restaurant. Fitness room. **$**
🖵 🏃

Burlington (D-6)

See also Fort Madison

Settled 1832
Population 27,208
Elevation 540 ft
Area Code 319
Zip 52601
Information Convention & Tourism Bureau, 807 Jefferson St; phone 319/752-6365 or toll-free 800/827-4837
Web Site www.visit.burlington.ia.us

Burlington, a river port, is a shopping, industrial, and farm center. It traces its history back to the days when it was called Flint Hills by Native Americans and served as neutral ground where tribes hunted flint for implements. Zebulon Pike raised the Stars and Stripes here in 1805, and a trading post was built in 1808. The city became capital of the Wisconsin Territory in 1837, then capital of the Iowa Territory from 1838 to 1840. Its retail trade draws shoppers from three states; factories turn out tractors, chemicals, electronic instruments, furniture, and other products.

Burlington Fun Fact

Ripley's Believe It or Not has dubbed Burlington's Snake Alley the "most crooked street in the world."

What to See and Do

Apple Trees Historical Museum. *Perkins Park, 1616 Dill St, Burlington (52601). Phone 319/753-2449.* The museum, a remaining wing of railroad magnate Charles E. Perkins's mansion, contains Victorian furnishings; antique tools, costumes, dolls, toys, buttons, glass, china; Native American artifacts; changing exhibits. Maintained by the Des Moines County Historical Society. Guided tours (May-Oct: Sat-Sun 1:30-4:30 pm; by appointment Mon-Fri) The society also maintains

> **Hawkeye Log Cabin.** *2915 S Main St, Burlington (52601). On bluff in Crapo Park. Phone 319/753-2449.* Replica (1910) of pioneer cabin; antique furnishings and tools. Guided tours (May-Sept, by appointment Mon-Fri; Sat-Sun 1:30-4:30 pm; fee) **FREE**

> **Phelps House.** *521 Columbia St, Burlington (52601). Phone 319/753-2449.* (1850) Mansard-roofed, Italianate Victorian mansion with original furnishings used by three generations of the Phelps family; extensive collection of rare china; family portraits. Guided tours (May-Oct, by appointment Mon-Fri; Sat-Sun 1:30-4:30 pm) **$**

Crapo and Dankwardt Parks. *2700 and 2900 S Main sts, Burlington (52601). On Great River Rd at SE corner of city. Phone 319/753-8110.* The parks (approximately 175 acres) are situated along the Mississippi on the site where the American flag first flew over Iowa soil (1805); includes illuminated fountain, arboretum, formal flower garden. Swimming. Black Hawk Spring Indian trail; tennis, archery range, ice skating. Picnicking; playground. (Daily) **FREE**

Geode State Park. *3249 Racine Dr, Danville (52623). 6 miles W on Hwy 34, then 6 miles W on Hwy 79 and County J20.* Phone 319/392-4601. More than 1,600 heavily wooded acres along limestone bluffs rising out of a 187-acre lake. Swimming, supervised beach, fishing, boating (ramps, rentals); hiking trails, snowmobiling, picnicking, camping (electricity, dump station). Standard hours, fees.

Heritage Hill National Historic District. *Washington and High sts, Burlington. N of downtown.* This 29-square-block area contains churches, mansions, and houses in a wide variety of architectural styles, including a full range of Victorian buildings from the 1870s to the turn of the century. Walking tours, auto cassette tours, and brochures available. Contact the Convention & Tourism Bureau. Also here is

Snake Alley. *Sixth St, Burlington (52601). Between Washington and Columbia sts.* The zigzagging brick-paved street, built in 1894, is, according to *Ripley's Believe It or Not*, the "crookedest street in the world."

Mosquito Park. *3rd and Franklin sts, Burlington (52601).* Located on a bluff overlooking the city and the Mississippi River, just north of downtown.

Special Events

Burlington Steamboat Days & the American Music Festival. *200 N Front St, Burlington (52601). Phone 319/754-4334. Downtown riverfront.* Athletic competitions, fireworks, midway, parade, name entertainment. Six days ending Father's Day, mid-June.

Dan Beid Memorial Jazz Fest. *Burlington Memorial Auditorium Arena, Front St, Burlington. Phone 319/752-6365.* Nationally known jazz ensembles. Mid-June.

Snake Alley Criterium Bicycle Races. *241 N 4th St # 3C, Burlington (52601). Phone 319/752-0015.* Olympic-style racing. Memorial Day weekend.

Limited-Service Hotels

★ ★ **BEST WESTERN PZAZZ MOTOR INN.** *3001 Winegard Dr, Burlington (52601). Phone 319/753-2223; toll-free 800/373-1223; fax 319/753-2224. www.bestwestern.com.* 151 rooms, 3 story. Pets

accepted. Check-out noon. Restaurant, bar. Fitness room. Indoor pool, whirlpool. Airport transportation available. **$**

★ **COMFORT INN.** *3051 Kirkwood, Burlington (52601). Phone 319/753-0000; fax 319/753-0000.* 52 rooms, 2 story. Pets accepted, some restrictions; fee. Complimentary continental breakfast. Check-out 11 am. Outdoor pool. **$**

Carroll (B-2)

Population 9,579
Elevation 1,261 ft
Area Code 712
Zip 51401
Information Chamber of Commerce, 223 W 5th St, PO Box 307; phone 712/792-4383 or toll-free 866/586-4383
Web Site www.carrolliowa.com

This town is named for Charles Carroll, a signer of the Declaration of Independence.

What to See and Do

Black Hawk State Park. *227 S Blossom St, Lake View (51450). 23 miles NW on Hwy 71 in Lake View. Phone 712/657-8712.* Park consists of 86 acres along 925-acre Black Hawk Lake. Swimming, fishing, boating (ramps); snowmobiling, picnicking, camping (electricity, dump station). Standard hours, fees.

Swan Lake Park. *22811 Swan Lake Dr, Carroll (51401). 2 miles S, then 1/2 mile E. Phone 712/792-4614.* The 510 acres includes 115-acre Swan Lake. Swimming, fishing. Nature trails, wildlife exhibit. Access to Sauk Rail Trail. Winter activities. Picnicking. Camping (fee). (Daily)

War Memorial Monuments. *Carroll. E 1st St, S of Grant Rd.* Monument for each war beginning with the Civil War and the latest monument for Desert Storm.

Special Events

Great Raccoon River Fun Float. *Carroll.* Float down the Raccoon River; rest stops on several beaches. Second Sat in July.

Holiday Animated Lighting Extravaganza. *22811 Swan Lake Dr, Carroll (51401). Phone 712/792-1335. In Swan Lake Park.* Campground full of lighted scenes. Thanksgiving-Jan 1.

Limited-Service Hotel

★ ★ **CARROLLTON INN.** *1730 Hwy 71 N, Carroll (51401). Phone 712/792-5600; toll-free 877/798-3535. www.carrolltoninn.com.* Whether traveling for business or a family vacation, guests can expect comfort at very affordable rates. 86 rooms, 2 story. Check-out noon. Restaurant, bar. Indoor pool, whirlpool. **$**

Restaurant

★ ★ **TONY'S.** *1012 Hwy 71 N, Carroll (51401). Phone 712/792-3792.* American menu. Breakfast, lunch, dinner, Sun brunch. Closed Easter, Thanksgiving, Dec 25. Children's menu. **$$**

Cedar Falls (B-4)

See also Waterloo, Waverly

Settled 1845
Population 34,298
Elevation 900 ft
Area Code 319
Zip 50613
Information Tourism & Visitors Bureau, 10 Main St; phone 319/268-4266 or toll-free 800/845-1955
Web Site www.cedarfallstourism.org

Once one of the most important milling centers in the state, today Cedar Falls is a university town and home to a diverse industrial base.

What to See and Do

Black Hawk Park. *2410 W Lone Tree Rd, Cedar Falls (50613). 3 miles N on Hwy 218, then 1 mile W on Lone Tree Rd. Phone 319/266-6813.* Fishing, boating; hiking, shooting and archery ranges, cross-country skiing, ice skating, snowshoeing, ice fishing, picnicking, camping (fee). (Daily)

Cedar Falls Historical Society Victorian Home Museum. *308 W 3rd, Cedar Falls (50613). Phone 319/266-5149.* Civil War-era Victorian house furnished in 1890s-period style. **Carriage House Museum** contains library, archives, fashions, Lenoir

train exhibit, memorabilia of the first permanent settlement in Black Hawk County (1845). (Wed-Sat 10 am-4 pm, Sun 1-4 pm) **FREE**

George Wyth House. *303 Franklin St, Cedar Falls (50613). Phone 319/266-5149.* The residence of George Wyth, founder of the Viking Pump Company, was built in 1907; now furnished in the Art Deco style of the 1920s, it includes pieces by Gilbert Rhode. The Viking Pump Company museum is housed on the third floor. Tours (May-Sept, Sun afternoons, also by appointment). **FREE**

Icehouse Museum. *1st and Franklin sts, Cedar Falls. Enter off Clay St. Phone 319/266-5149.* This round structure, 100 feet in diameter, was once used for storing up to 8,000 tons of ice from the Cedar River. The icehouse now displays antique tools for the harvesting, storing, selling, and use of natural ice; also antique farm equipment; early American kitchen; military memorabilia. (May-Oct, Wed and Sat-Sun afternoons; closed holidays) **FREE**

Little Red School. *1st and Clay sts, Cedar Falls (50613). Phone 319/266-5149.* Country school (1909) has been authentically furnished to reflect turn-of-the-century education. (May-Oct, Wed and Sat-Sun afternoons; closed holidays)

University of Northern Iowa. *1222 W 27th St, Cedar Falls (50614). College St between 23rd St and University Ave. Phone 319/273-2311.* (1876) (14,000 students) Campanile in Italian Renaissance style, 100 feet high; chimes played daily. UNI-Dome, Iowa's first and only multipurpose domed coliseum. Also on campus is a museum (daily; closed holidays) with exhibits on geology and natural history. Campus includes

Gallery of Art. *Kamerick Art Building-South, 27th St and Hudson Rd, Cedar Falls (50614). Phone 319/273-2077.* Permanent collection and changing exhibits. (Daily; closed school holidays and between exhibits) **FREE**

Special Events

Band concerts. *Overman Park, 2nd and Franklin sts, Cedar Falls (50613). Phone 319/266-1253. www.cedar net.org/cfband.* The Cedar Falls Municipal Band, the oldest concert band in the state, entertains crowds of visitors each summer at its outdoor concerts in its modern band shell. Bring a lawn chair or blanket and relax as these forty-five musicians present several light and traditional pieces. Tues evenings in June-Aug. **$**

College Hill Arts Festival. *23rd and College sts, Cedar Falls. Phone 319/266-7304.* Juried arts festival showcasing more than 75 Midwest artists. Third weekend in July.

Sturgis Falls Days Celebration. *Sturgis Falls (50613). www.strugisfalls.org. Overman and Island parks.* Dixieland jazz festival, parade, street fair, arts and crafts. Last full weekend of June.

Limited-Service Hotel

★ ★ **HOLIDAY INN.** *5826 University Ave, Cedar Falls (50613). Phone 319/277-2230; fax 319/277-0364. www.holiday-inn.com.* 181 rooms, 2 story. Check-out noon. High-speed Internet access. Restaurant, bar. Fitness room. Indoor pool, outdoor pool, whirlpool. Airport transportation available. **$**
🆔 🚹 ⛴

Restaurant

★ ★ **OLDE BROOM FACTORY.** *125 W First St, Cedar Falls (50613). Phone 319/268-0877; fax 319/268-1598.* American menu. Lunch, dinner, Sun brunch. Closed Dec 25. Bar. Children's menu. Structure built in 1862. Valet parking. **$$**

Cedar Rapids (C-5)

See also Amana Colonies, Iowa City

Settled 1838
Population 108,751
Elevation 730 ft
Area Code 319
Information Cedar Rapids Area Convention & Visitors Bureau, 119 1st Ave SE, PO Box 5339, 52406-5339; phone 319/398-5009 or toll-free 800/735-5557
Web Site www.cedar-rapids.com

Cedar Rapids, located at the rapids of the Cedar River, is the industrial leader of the state. More than $475 million worth of cereals, corn products, milk processing machinery, farm hardware, stock feeds, and electronic material are exported to worldwide markets.

What to See and Do

Brucemore. *2160 Linden Dr SE, Cedar Rapids (52403). Phone 319/362-7375.* (1886) Queen Anne-style 21-room mansion with visitor center, gift and flower shops, formal gardens, lawns, orchard, and pond; the sunroom was decorated by native artist Grant Wood. The estate serves as a community cultural center. (Feb-Dec: Tues-Sat 10 am-3 pm; Sun noon-3 pm; closed holidays) **$$**

Cedar Rapids Museum of Art. *410 3rd Ave SE, Cedar Rapids (52401). Phone 319/366-7503.* Extensive collection of work by Grant Wood, Marvin Cone, and Mauricio Lasansky; changing exhibits. Gift shop. Children 7 and under free. (Tues-Sun; closed holidays) **$$**

⭐ **Czech Village.** *48 16th Ave SW, Cedar Rapids (52404). On 16th Ave SW near downtown. Phone 319/362-2846.* Bakery, meat market, gift shops, restaurants, historic structures preserving Czech heritage. (See SPECIAL EVENTS) In the village is the

> **National Czech and Slovak Museum & Library.** *30 16th Ave SW, Cedar Rapids (52404). Phone 319/362-8500.* Houses a large collection of folk costumes. Permanent and changing exhibits; museum grounds include restored immigrant home. Tours. (Daily; closed holidays) **$$**

Indian Creek Nature Center. *6665 Otis Rd SE, Cedar Rapids (52403). Phone 319/362-0664.* On this 210-acre nature preserve is an observatory/museum offering changing exhibits in a remodeled dairy barn. Hiking trails. (Mon-Fri; closed holidays) **$**

Masonic Library. *813 1st Ave SE, Cedar Rapids (52401). Grand Lodge Office Building. Phone 319/365-1438.* (1844) Houses the most complete Masonic collection in the United States; also three museum rooms in this late-modern, Vermont-marble structure with bas-relief decoration and stained-glass windows. Tours. (Mon-Fri; closed holidays) **FREE**

Palisades-Kepler State Park. *Cedar Rapids. 12 miles E via Hwy 30. Phone 319/895-6039.* This 970-acre park includes limestone palisades that rise 75 feet above the Cedar River; timbered valleys, wildflowers. Fishing, boating (ramps); nature and hiking trails, snowmobiling, picnicking, lodge, camping (electricity, dump station), cabins. Standard hours, fees.

Paramount Theatre. *123 3rd Ave SE, Cedar Rapids (52401). Phone 319/398-5211. www.uscellularcenter.com.* Restored theater (circa 1925). Stage productions, films, Broadway series, community concert series; home of the Cedar Rapids Symphony.

Science Station. *427 1st St SE, Cedar Rapids (52401). Phone 319/366-0968.* Science and technology museum features unusual hands-on exhibits including a working hot air balloon and giant kaleidoscope. In a historic fire station. (Tues-Sun; closed holidays) **$$**

US Cellular Center. *370 1st Ave NE, Cedar Rapids (52401). Phone 319/398-5211. www.uscellularcenter .com.* This 10,000-seat entertainment center features sports events, concerts, exhibits, rodeos, ice shows, and events.

Wapsipinicon State Park. *Anamosa. 27 miles NE, off Hwy 151. Phone 319/462-2761.* This 251-acre park is along the west bank of the Wapsipinicon River and includes high rock cliffs, open meadows, wooded hills, caves, wildflowers. Fishing, boating (ramp); nine-hole golf course, hiking trails, snowmobiling, picnicking, lodge, camping (electric hook-ups). Standard hours, fees.

Special Events

Freedom Festival. *226 2nd St SE, Cedar Rapids (52401). Phone 319/365-8313.* Eighty events for all ages held citywide, topped off by large fireworks display. Two weeks preceding and including July 4.

Hawkeye Downs. *4400 6th St SW, Cedar Rapids (52404). Phone toll-free 800/279-2823.* Stock car races, fine arts, exhibits, name entertainment. June.

Houby Days. *48 16th Ave SW, Cedar Rapids (52404). Phone 319/362-8500. Czech Village.* Features Czech fine arts, folk arts and customs, music, dancing, food; mushroom hunt contests, races. Weekend after Mother's Day.

Limited-Service Hotels

★ ★ **BEST WESTERN COOPER'S MILL HOTEL.** *100 F Ave NW, Cedar Rapids (52405). Phone 319/366-5323; toll-free 800/858-5511; fax 319/366-5323. www.bestwestern.com.* 86 rooms, 4 story. Pets accepted; fee. Check-out noon. Restaurant, bar. **$**

★ **COMFORT INN.** *5055 Rockwell Dr, Cedar Rapids (52402). Phone 319/393-8247; toll-free 800/228-5150; fax 319/393-8247. www.comfortinn.com.* 59 rooms, 2 story. Pets accepted, some restrictions. Complimentary continental breakfast. Check-out 11 am. **$**

★ **COMFORT INN.** *390 33rd Ave SW, Cedar Rapids (52404). Phone 319/363-7934; toll-free 800/228-5150; fax 319/363-7934. www.comfortinn.com.* 60 rooms, 3 story. Pets accepted, some restrictions. Complimentary continental breakfast. Check-out 11 am. **$**

★ **HAMPTON INN.** *3265 6th St SW, Cedar Rapids (52404). Phone 319/364-8144; toll-free 800/426-7866; fax 319/399-1877. www.hamptoninn.com.* 106 rooms, 3 story. Complimentary continental breakfast. Check-out noon. Bar. Fitness room. Indoor pool, whirlpool. **$**

★ ★ **MARRIOTT CEDAR RAPIDS.** *1200 Collins Rd NE, Cedar Rapids (52402). Phone 319/393-6600; fax 319/393-2308.* A tree-filled atrium and cascading waterfalls are the setting outside the guest rooms. With more than 17,000 square feet of meeting space, a heated indoor pool, and a great Sunday brunch, this hotel is packed with convenient amenities. 221 rooms, 7 story. Check-out noon. Restaurant, bar. Fitness room. Indoor pool, whirlpool. Airport transportation available. Business center. **$**

Full-Service Hotel

★ ★ ★ **CROWNE PLAZA.** *350 First Ave NE, Cedar Rapids (52401). Phone 319/363-8161; toll-free 800/227-6963; fax 319/363-3804. www.crowneplaza.com.* Perfectly located in the heart of downtown Cedar Rapids, this hotel is near fine shopping, restaurants, and entertainment. Amenities include a rooftop restaurant, an indoor pool, fitness center, and more than 25,000 square feet of flexible meeting facilities. 275 rooms, 16 story. Check-out noon. Restaurant, bar. Fitness room. Indoor pool, whirlpool. Airport transportation available. Business center. **$**

Centerville (D-4)

Founded 1846
Population 5,936
Elevation 1,010 ft
Area Code 641
Zip 52544
Information Chamber of Commerce, 128 N 12th St; phone 641/437-4102 or toll-free 800/611-3800
Web Site www.centervilleia.com

Once an important ferry point for Chariton River traffic, Centerville today is an agricultural, industrial, and retail center.

What to See and Do

Rathbun Lake. *Centerville. 7 miles NW. Phone 641/647-2464.* Offers swimming, bathhouse, fishing, boating (ramps, two marinas); picnicking, camping (electricity, dump station May-Sept; fee). On the north shore is

> **Honey Creek State Park.** *12194 Honey Creek Pl, Moravia (52571). 12 miles N on Hwy 5, then 9 1/2 miles W on Hwy 142, 3 miles SE on unnumbered road. Phone 641/724-3739.* On 828 acres. Swimming, fishing, boating; hiking trails, snowmobiling, picnicking, camping (electric hook-ups, dump station). Scenic overlook. Standard hours, fees.

Sharon Bluffs Park. *25100 500th and 20th sts, Centerville (52544). 3 miles E on Hwy 2, then 1 mile S. Phone 641/856-8528.* More than 140 acres on the Chariton River; scenic view from high bluffs of clay and shale. Boating (ramp). Hiking trails. Picnicking, shelter. Camping (hookups, fee). (Daily)

Special Events

Croatian Fest. *Knights of Columbus Hall, 922 W State St, Centerville. Phone 641/856-3391.* Courthouse lawn on city square. Ethnic festival featuring entertainment, dancing, and food. Last Sat in July.

Pancake Day. *Centerville.* Entertainment, parade, craft show, free pancakes. Last Sat in Sept.

Limited-Service Hotel

★ **SUPER 8.** *1021 18th Hwy 5 N, Centerville (52544). Phone 641/856-8888; toll-free 800/800-8000; fax 641/856-8888. www.super8.com.* 41 rooms, 2 story. Complimentary continental breakfast. Check-in 3 pm, check-out 11 am. **$**

Restaurant

★ **GREEN CIRCLE INN.** *22984 Hwy 55, Centerville (52544). Phone 641/437-4472.* Seafood, steak menu. Dinner, brunch. Bar. **$$**

Chariton (D-4)

See also Osceola

Population 4,616
Elevation 1,041 ft
Area Code 641
Zip 50049
Information Chariton Chamber and Development Corp, 104 N Grand, PO Box 488; phone 641/774-4059
Web Site www.chariton.org

The site of this town was recorded as Chariton by Lewis and Clark after the French corrupted the Native American word "thier-aton," meaning "two rivers."

What to See and Do

John L. Lewis Museum of Mining and Labor. *102 Division St, Lucas (50151). Approximately 10 miles W on Hwy 34, junction Hwy 65. Phone 641/766-6831.* Exhibits, library, theater, mining tools collection. (Mid-Apr-mid-Oct, Tues-Sat; also by appointment) **$**

Lucas County Historical Museum. *123 17th St N, Chariton (50049). At Braden Ave. Phone 641/774-4464.* Restored and furnished 1907 home; rural Puckerbrush school and Otterbein church; John L. Lewis building with library, replica of a mine, and antique farm machinery. (Memorial Day-Oct, Tues-Fri and Sun, also by appointment) **FREE**

Red Haw State Park. *Hwy 34, Chariton (50049). 1 mile E on Hwy 34. Phone 641/774-5632.* Approximately 420 acres with a 72-acre lake. Swimming beach; fishing; boating (electric motors only; ramps, rentals). Snowmobiling. Picnicking. Camping (electricity, dump station). Standard hours, fees.

Stephens State Forest. *8th St and Mitchell Ave, Chariton (50049). 10 miles W on Hwy 34 to Lucas, then 2 miles S on Hwy 65, then W on county road. Phone 641/774-4559.* Five units totaling 8,466 acres of evergreens and hardwoods, with a pond. Fishing; boating (electric motors only). Hiking, bridle trails. Hunting. Snowmobiling. Picnicking. Primitive camping. Standard hours, fees.

Wayne County Historical Museum. *515 E Jefferson St, Corydon (50060). Approximately 18 miles S via Hwy 14 to Hwy 2. Phone 641/872-2211.* More than 80,000 artifacts from the county's history; replicas of 17 buildings including a doctor's office, bank, jail, toy shop, and music room; Jesse James exhibit including the safe he robbed in Corydon; bird and animal exhibits; old machinery and vehicles; genealogy section; Mormon exhibit; collection of 150 creche figures from Italy and Germany. (Mid-Apr-mid-Oct, daily) **$$**

Charles City (A-4)

See also Mason City, Waverly

Settled 1852
Population 7,878
Elevation 1,000 ft
Area Code 641
Zip 50616
Information Charles City Area Chamber of Commerce, 610 S Grand Ave; phone 641/228-4234
Web Site www.charlescitychamber.com

One of the first gasoline tractor engines for agricultural and industrial use was produced here.

What to See and Do

Floyd County Historical Society Museum. *500 Gilbert St, Charles City (50616). On Hwy 218 and 18. Phone 641/228-1099.* Includes an authentic 1873 drugstore, model railroad display, Native American artifacts, farm equipment. (June-Aug: daily; rest of year: Mon-Fri) **$**

Special Event

Art-a-Fest. *Central Park, Main St, Charles City (50616). Phone 641/228-6284.* Fine arts festival with art and craft displays, ethnic foods, music, drama, dance performances. Third weekend in Aug.

Limited-Service Hotel

★ **HARTWOOD INN.** *1312 Gilbert St, Charles City (50616). Phone 641/228-4352; toll-free 800/972-2335; fax 641/257-2488.* 35 rooms, 2 story. Complimentary continental breakfast. Check-out 11 am. **$**

Restaurant

★ **BROOKS.** *102 Cedar Mall, Charles City (50616). Phone 515/228-7162.* Steak menu. Breakfast, lunch, dinner. Bar. **$$**

Cherokee (B-2)

See also Storm Lake

Population 6,026
Area Code 712
Zip 51012
Information Chamber of Commerce, 228 W Main St; phone 712/225-6414
Web Site www.cherokeeiowa.net

Center of one of the heaviest cattle feeding and hog raising areas of Iowa, Cherokee is home to many processing and manufacturing plants. The Cherokee Community Center houses a symphony orchestra and an active community theater.

What to See and Do

City Parks. Wescott. *530 W Bluff St, Cherokee (51012). S 2nd St on Little Sioux River. Phone 712/225-2715.* Canoeing; picnicking, playgrounds, sand volleyball courts. **Spring Lake.** *S 2nd St.* Fishing; ice skating, picnicking, camping (hook-ups, dump station; fee). **Gillette.** *W Bluff St.* Swimming pool (Memorial Day-Aug, daily; fee).

Sanford Museum and Planetarium. *117 E Willow St, Cherokee (51012). Phone 712/225-3922.* Natural history, science, and changing exhibits. Classes (by appointment); planetarium programs (last Sun of month; also by appointment). (Daily; closed holidays) **FREE**

Special Events

Cherokee County Fair. *Cherokee County Fairgrounds, Cherokee. Phone 712/225-6414.* Features a demolition derby and team dance competition. Early July.

Cherokee Rodeo. *228 W Main, Cherokee (51012). Phone 721/225-6414.* PRCA sanctioned. Weekend after Memorial Day weekend.

Limited-Service Hotel

★ ★ **BEST WESTERN LA GRANDE HACIENDA.** *1401 N 2nd St, Cherokee (51012). Phone 712/225-5701; toll-free 800/924-3765; fax 712/225-3926. www.bestwestern.com.* 55 rooms, 2 story. Complimentary full breakfast. Check-out 11 am. Restaurant. Indoor pool, whirlpool. **$**
🏊

Clarinda (D-2)

See also Shenandoah

Settled 1853
Population 5,104
Area Code 712
Zip 51632
Information Chamber of Commerce, 200 S 15th St; phone 712/542-2166
Web Site www.clarinda.org

Clarinda is the birthplace of Big Band-era legend Glenn Miller. It's also where, at the turn of the century, rural school teacher Jessie Field Shambaugh started the Boys' Corn Clubs and Girls' Home Clubs, which later became the 4-H movement.

What to See and Do

Lake of Three Fires State Park. *2303 Hwy 49, Bedford (50833). 18 miles E on Hwy 2 to Bedford, then 3 miles NE on Hwy 49. Phone 712/523-2700.* The park has 691 acres with a 97-acre lake. Swimming; fishing; electric boating (ramps, rentals). Hiking, bridle trails. Snowmobiling. Picnicking. Camping (electricity, dump station), cabins. Standard hours, fees.

Nodaway Valley Historical Museum. *1600 S 16th St, Clarinda (51632). Phone 712/542-3073.* Exhibits on the history of the Nodaway River area includes agricultural displays, artifacts from the early days of the 4-H movement, and Glenn Miller memorabilia. Visits to the nearby Glenn Miller Birthplace Home (by appointment only; additional fee) can be arranged through the museum. (Tues-Sun afternoons) **$**

Special Events

Glenn Miller Festival. *122 W Garfield, Clarinda (51632). Phone 712/542-2461.* Honoring his music and birthplace. Second weekend in June.

Page County Fair. *S 6th St, Clarinda (51632). Phone 712/542-5171.* Offers 4-H and FFA livestock and agricultural competitions and entertainment. Last week in July.

Southwest Iowa Band Jamboree. *115 E Main St, Clarinda (51632). Phone 712/542-2166.* High school bands from three states participate. First Sat in Oct.

Restaurant

★ ★ **J. BRUNER'S.** *1100 E Washington, Clarinda (51632). Phone 712/542-3364.* Steak menu. Dinner. Closed Easter, Thanksgiving, Dec 25. Bar. Children's menu. **$$$**

Clear Lake (A-4)

See also Garner, Mason City

Settled 1851
Population 8,183
Elevation 1,236 ft
Area Code 641
Zip 50428
Information Chamber of Commerce, 205 Main Ave, PO Box 188; phone 641/357-2159 or toll-free 800/285-5338
Web Site www.clearlakeiowa.com

Scene of a Native American uprising in 1854, Clear Lake rivaled Mason City (see) for honors as the county seat, but lost out because it was not in the geographic center of the area. Taking its name from the nearby lake, Clear Lake is an ancient Native American fishing and hunting ground. Today it is a popular, modern resort town.

What to See and Do

Clear Lake State Park. *2730 S Lakeview Dr, Clear Lake (50428). Phone 641/357-4212.* Swimming, fishing, boating (ramps); snowmobiling, picnicking, camping (electric hook-ups).

Clear Lake. *2730 S Lakeview Dr, Clear Lake (50428). 2 miles S on Hwy 107. Phone 641/357-4212.* The park has 102 acres with a 3,684-acre lake. Picnicking. Dump station.

McIntosh Woods. *1200 E Lake St, Clear Lake (50482). On N shore of lake, off Hwy 18. Phone 641/829-3847.* There are nature trails in this 62-acre park.

Main Street Trolley. *205 Main Ave, Clear Lake (50428). Phone toll-free 800/285-5338.* Vintage-style trolley available, charters and special events. (Thurs-Sun, Memorial Day-Sept) **$$$**

⊠ **Surf Ballroom.** *460 North Shore Dr, Clear Lake (50428). Phone 641/357-6151.* Site of Buddy Holly's last concert before Holly, Ritchie Valens, and

J. P. Richardson (the Big Bopper) died in a local plane crash on February 2, 1959. Ballroom features varied entertainment weekends; plaque and monument outside commemorate the musicians; museum of musical history. Tours available.

Special Event

Buddy Holly Tribute. *Surf Ballroom, 460 North Shore Dr, Clear Lake (50428). Phone 641/357-6151.* Event commemorates Holly's last concert with local and national entertainers. First weekend in Feb.

Limited-Service Hotel

★ ★ **BEST WESTERN HOLIDAY LODGE.** *I-35 S and Hwy 18, Clear Lake (50428). Phone 641/357-5253; toll-free 800/606-3552; fax 641/357-8153. www.bestwestern.com.* 138 rooms, 5 story. Pets accepted, some restrictions; fee. Complimentary full breakfast. Check-out 11 am. Restaurant. Indoor pool, whirlpool. Airport transportation available. **$**

Clinton (C-6)

See also Bettendorf

Founded 1855
Population 29,201
Elevation 600 ft
Area Code 563
Zip 52732
Information Clinton Area Chamber of Commerce, 333 4th Ave S, PO Box 1024; phone 563/242-5702 or toll-free 800/828-5702
Web Site www.clintonia.com

Agriculture, industry, and business are blended in this city of wide streets and modern buildings on the Mississippi River. First called New York, it was later renamed after DeWitt Clinton, former governor of New York. Once the largest lumber-producing city in the world, Clinton today is the home of a diverse group of industries. It is also the seat of a county famous for its prime beef production.

What to See and Do

Eagle Point Park. *N 3rd St and Stockwell Ln, Clinton (52732). On Hwy 67 at N city limits, overlooking the Mississippi. Phone 563/243-1260.* Flower gardens; picnicking (shelters), lodge; playground, observation tower; children's nature center; petting zoo. (Mid-Apr-late Oct, daily) **FREE**

Riverview Park. *6th Ave N and Riverview, Clinton (52732). On the Mississippi. Phone 563/243-1260.* Swimming pool (Memorial Day-Labor Day); marina, boat ramp; lighted tennis courts, fountain; playground, recreational trail, baseball stadium, picnicking; RV parking (fee). (Daily) **FREE** Also here are

Lillian Russell Theatre. *311 Riverview Dr, Clinton (52732). Phone 563/242-6760.* Aboard the paddlewheel showboat *The City of Clinton.* Musicals and comedies. (June-Aug)

Mississippi Belle II. Showboat Landing, 311 Riverview Dr, Clinton (52732). Phone 563/243-9000; toll-free 800/457-9975. Offers year-round casino gambling along the Mississippi River. Entertainment. Concession.

Special Events

Civil War Reenactment. *Eagle Point Park, 1401 11th Ave N, Clinton (52732). Phone 563/243-5368.* Battle for Burnside Bridge; Military Ball with period music and costumes. May.

Riverboat Days. *115 4th Ave S, Clinton (52732). Phone toll-free 800/395-7277.* Pageant, events, tractor pulls, entertainment, shows, carnival. July 4 weekend.

Symphony of Lights. *Eagle Point Park, 115 4th Ave S, Clinton (52732). Phone 563/243-3442. www.symphonyoflights.org.* More than 800,000 individual lights; Babes in Toyland, medieval castles, illuminated arches, animated snowball throwers (fee per vehicle). Dec.

Limited-Service Hotels

★ ★ **BEST WESTERN FRONTIER MOTOR INN.** *2300 Lincoln Way St, Clinton (52732). Phone 563/242-7112; toll-free 800/728-7112; fax 563/242-7117. www.bestwestern.com.* A tree-lined atrium houses a swimming pool, plus plenty of tables and chairs for a game of cards while the kids splash away. If you'd like a change of scene from the dining room, bring in a heaping plate from the hot breakfast buffet and linger over coffee with your newspaper. There's broad family appeal at the Frontier, whether you're looking for a whirlpool room or a men's public rest room with diaper-changing facilities. 113 rooms, 2 story. Pets accepted, some restrictions; fee. Complimentary full breakfast. Check-in 3 pm, check-out noon. High-speed Internet access. Restaurant, bar.

Fitness room. Indoor pool, whirlpool. Airport transportation available. **$$**

🐾 🏃 ≈

★ **COUNTRY INN & SUITES.** *2224 Lincoln Way, Clinton (52732). Phone 563/244-9922; toll-free 888/ 201-1746; fax 563/243-0967. www.countryinns.com.* If the white-picket-fence front porch doesn't tell you that something's down home here, the lobby will—country wreathes and candles above a fireplace, cushy couches and chairs to sink into, and knotty pine furniture. And if that's not a dead giveaway, the fresh-baked chocolate chip cookies on the reception desk (and 24/7 availability of milk and coffee) sure are. The Clinton Country Inn and Suites, which offers a choice of standard rooms or two-room suites, prides itself on its small touches, such as high-speed Internet access and even a lending library. 63 rooms. Pets accepted, some restrictions; fee. Complimentary continental breakfast. Check-in 3 pm, check-out noon. High-speed Internet access. Indoor pool, whirlpool. Airport transportation available. **$**

🐾 ≈

Council Bluffs (D-1)

See also Missouri Valley; also see Omaha, NE

Settled 1824
Population 54,315
Elevation 986 ft
Area Code 712
Information Convention & Visitors Bureau, 7 N 6th St, PO Box 1565, 51502; phone 712/325-1000 or toll-free 800/228-6878
Web Site www.councilbluffsiowa.com

The Lewis and Clark expedition stopped in Council Bluffs in 1804 to rest and hold their first "council bluff" with local Native American tribes. Council Bluffs was settled in 1846 by Mormons who were fleeing religious persecution. They called the town "Kanesville"; but the city officially took the name Council Bluffs in 1853. The town subsequently became a booming hub of commerce as the nation's fifth-largest rail center. Today the Loess Hills Scenic Byway (see MISSOURI VALLEY) passes through the area. A mix of insurance, gaming, telecommunications, agriculture, and manufacturing industries have created a diverse employment base.

What to See and Do

Golden Spike Monument. *S 21st St and 9th Ave, Council Bluffs (51501).* Erected in 1939, this 56-foot golden concrete spike commemorates the junction of the Union Pacific and Central Pacific railroads in Council Bluffs.

Historic General Dodge House. *605 3rd St, Council Bluffs (57503). Phone 712/322-2406.* (1869) Restored Victorian home built by Grenville M. Dodge, chief construction engineer for the Union Pacific Railroad and a general in the Civil War. Guided tours (Tues-Sun; closed holidays; also Jan). **$$**

Historic Pottawattamie County Jail. *226 Pearl St, Council Bluffs (51503). Phone 712/323-2509.* (1885) This unique three-story rotary jail is sometimes referred to as the "human squirrel cage" or "lazy Susan jail." (May and Sept: Sat-Sun; June-Aug: Wed-Sun, or by appointment; closed holidays) **$$**

Lake Manawa State Park. *1100 S Shore Dr, Council Bluffs (51501). 1 mile S on Hwy 92/275. Phone 712/ 366-0220.* A more than 1,500-acre park with a 660-acre lake. "Dream Playground" designed by and for children. Swimming, supervised beach, fishing, boating (ramps, rentals); hiking trails, bicycle trails, snowmobiling, picnicking, camping (electricity). Standard hours, fees.

Lewis and Clark Monument. *19962 Monument Rd, Council Bluffs (51503). Rainbow Point, N on 8th St. Phone 712/328-4650.* Shaft of native stone on bluffs depicts Lewis and Clark holding council with Oto and Missouri.

Lincoln Monument. *323 Lafayette Ave, Council Bluffs (51503).* Granite shaft marks the spot from which Lincoln designated the town as the eastern terminus of the Union Pacific Railroad. Erected in 1911.

Mormon Trail Memorial. *Council Bluffs (51503). Bayliss Park, Pearl St and 1st Ave.* A huge boulder marks the passage of Mormons out of the city on the trek to Utah.

RailsWest Railroad Museum. *16th Ave and S Main St, Council Bluffs (51503). Phone 712/323-5182.* Historic Rock Island depot (1899); railroad memorabilia, HO gauge model trains on display. (Mar-Dec, Wed-Mon; closed holidays) **$$**

Ruth Anne Dodge Memorial. *N 2nd and Lafayette aves, Council Bluffs (51503). Phone 712/328-4992.* Commissioned by the daughters of G. M. Dodge in memory of their mother, this bronze statue of an angel is the work of Daniel Chester French.

Western Historic Trails Center. *3434 Richard Downing Ave, Council Bluffs (51501). Phone 712/366-4900.* Explore preserved and restored sites along Lewis and Clark, Mormon Pioneer, California, and Oregon trails. Discover history of Native American tribes and trails heritage in the region. Guided group tours. (Daily; closed holidays) **FREE**

Special Event

Renaissance Faire of the Midlands. *Westfair Fairgrounds, 22984 Hwy 6, Council Bluffs. Phone 712/328-4992. www.faire.org.* Renaissance period crafts, entertainment, concessions; jousting contests, street performers. June.

Limited-Service Hotels

★ ★ **AMERISTAR CASINO.** *2200 River Rd, Council Bluffs (51501). Phone 712/328-8888; toll-free 877/462-7827; fax 712/328-8882. www.ameristarcasinos .com.* The only gaming riverboat and hotel in the area, guests will experience the excitement of the casinos along with several restaurants, live entertainment, and much more. The courteous staff and comfortable guest suites are an added pleasure. 160 rooms, 5 story. Check-out 11 am. Restaurant, bar. Fitness room. Indoor pool, whirlpool. **$**
🏃 ⊠

★ **FAIRFIELD INN.** *520 30th Ave, Council Bluffs (51501). Phone 712/366-1330; toll-free 800/228-2800; fax 712/366-1330. www.fairfieldinn.com.* 62 rooms, 3 story. Complimentary continental breakfast. Check-out noon. Indoor pool, whirlpool. **$**
⊠

★ **HEARTLAND INN COUNCIL BLUFFS.** *1000 Woodbury Ave, Council Bluffs (51503). Phone 712/322-8400; toll-free 800/334-3277; fax 712/322-4022. www.heartlandinns.com.* 87 rooms, 2 story. Pets accepted, some restrictions; fee. Complimentary continental breakfast. Check-in 3 pm, check-out noon. High-speed Internet access. Indoor pool. Business center. **$**
🐾 ⊠ 🏃

Restaurants

★ **CHRISTY CREME.** *2853 N Broadway, Council Bluffs (51503). Phone 712/322-2778; fax 712/322-5422.*

American menu. Breakfast, lunch, dinner. Closed July 4; also Dec-Jan. Children's menu. Outdoor seating. **$**

★ **PINK POODLE RESTAURANT.** *633 N Old Lincoln Hwy, Crescent (51526). Phone 712/545-3744.* A quaint small-town favorite known for prime rib. American menu. Breakfast, lunch, dinner. **$**

Creston

Founded 1869
Population 7,911
Elevation 1,314 ft
Area Code 641
Zip 50801
Information Chamber of Commerce, 208 W Taylor, PO Box 471; phone 641/782-7021
Web Site www.crestoniowachamber.com

In the heart of Iowa's High Lakes country, Creston has long been a railroad town and a shopping, medical, and educational hub for southwest Iowa.

What to See and Do

Green Valley State Park. *1480 130th St, Creston (50801). 2 1/2 miles N off Hwy 25. Phone 641/782-5131.* The 991-acre park amid rolling hills has a 390-acre lake. Swimming, fishing, boating (ramps, rentals); snowmobiling, picnicking, camping (electricity, dump station), cabin rentals. Standard hours, fees.

Special Event

Creston Hot Air Balloon Days. *Municipal Airport, 1945 Cherry St Rd, Creston (50801). Phone 641/782-2383.* Three balloon races; parade, marching band contest, and art and book fairs. Mid-Sept.

Limited-Service Hotel

★ **SUPER 8.** *804 W Taylor St, Creston (50801). Phone 641/782-6541; toll-free 800/800-8000; fax 641/782-6541. www.super8.com.* 83 rooms, 2 story. Check-in 3 pm, check-out 11 am. **$**

Davenport (C-6)

See also Bettendorf, Muscatine

Founded 1808
Population 95,333

Davenport and Mississippi River Islands

Davenport is one of the Quad Cities, a four-city metropolitan area that straddles the Mississippi and includes Moline and Rock Island in Illinois, plus Bettendorf, just upriver from Davenport. This hike explores the old waterfront of Davenport, as well as two park islands in the Mississippi between Illinois and Iowa. Begin on Credit Island Park, the site of a turn-of-the-century amusement park. Scenic trails loop around the island, which is now a community park with a playground area and a municipal golf course. A number of public art pieces are also found here, part of the Quad Cities' Art in the Park project.

Cross over to the Iowa mainland from the east end of Credit Island Park, and walk along the Mississippi through two more riverside parks. Centennial Park features riverside walkways past sports fields and stadiums. Atop the bluff on Division Street is Museum Hill, home of the Putnam Museum of Science and Natural History (1717 W 12th St) and the Davenport Museum of Art (1737 W 12th St). The Putnam houses two permanent exhibits about the Mississippi River; the art museum's permanent collection includes works by Midwestern painters, such as Thomas Hart Benton and Grant Wood, an Iowa native famous for his painting *American Gothic*. Just to the east is LeClaire Park, home to summer outdoor events and concerts.

The Davenport Downtown Levee includes a riverboat casino, restaurants, nightclubs, and the renovated Union Station railroad depot, which houses the Quad Cities Convention and Visitors Center. A local Farmers' Market is also held here on Wednesday and Saturday mornings from May through October.

Just downstream from the historic Government Bridge, Dam 15 provides a navigational pool for commercial shipping on the Mississippi. Lock 15 allows boats to transfer between the river's pools. Cross Government Bridge to Arsenal Island, which was acquired by the US Government in 1804 under a treaty with the Sauk and Fox Indians. Fort Armstrong was established in 1816 on the tip of the island, where a replica now stands. Manufacturing began on the island in 1840, and in 1869 it became home to the Rock Island Arsenal, a major military manufacturing facility. The island contains a number of historic homes and structures, including the Rock Island Arsenal Museum; the restored Colonel George Davenport Mansion, filled with furnishings from the mid-1800s; and the Mississippi River Visitors Center, with exhibits about the history of navigation on the river. A Confederate Soldiers' Cemetery and National Military Cemetery date back to the 1800s. Hikers and bikers can enjoy a 5-mile trail around the island.

Elevation 589 ft
Area Code 563
Information Quad Cities Convention & Visitors Bureau, 102 S Harrison St, 52801; phone 563/322-3911 or toll-free 800/747-7800
Web Site www.quadcities.com

Stretching 5 miles along the Mississippi River, Davenport is part of the Quad Cities metropolitan area, which also includes Bettendorf, Iowa, and Moline and Rock Island, Illinois. Principally a regional retail center, Davenport also produces machinery, agricultural goods, and food products. Davenport's Palmer College of Chiropractic is the fountainhead of that practice in the United States. The city is named for its founder, a former US Army officer who explored this bank of the river while stationed on Rock Island. The state's first railroad came here when tracks were put across the Mississippi at this point in 1854. In pre-Civil War days, Dred Scott claimed the town as his home, and John Brown provisioned here before his attack on Harpers Ferry.

What to See and Do

Dan Nagle Walnut Grove Pioneer Village. *18817 290th St, Long Grove (52756). 8 miles N on Hwy 61. Phone 563/328-3283.* Three-acre walk-through site contains 18 historic buildings moved from various locations in the county. Visitors can explore a blacksmith shop, schoolhouse, pioneer family home; also St. Anne's Church. (Apr-Oct, daily) **DONATION**

Fejevary Park. *1800 W 12th St, Davenport (52804). Phone 563/326-7812.* Swimming pool, picnic areas, playground (Apr-Oct). A zoo in the park features North American animals. (Late May-early Sept, Tues-Sun)

Figge Art Museum. *1737 W 12th St, Davenport (52804). Phone 563/326-7804.* Rotating displays from permanent collection of 19th- and 20th-century paintings, Mexican Colonial, Asian, native Haitian art collections; works by regional artists Grant Wood and Thomas Hart Benton. (Tues-Sun; closed holidays) **DONATION**

Putnam Museum of History & Natural Science. *1717 W 12th St, Davenport (52804). Phone 563/324-1933. www.putnam.org.* Permanent and changing exhibits of regional history, natural science, and world cultures. (Daily; closed holidays) **$$**

Rhythm City Casino. *101 W River Dr, Davenport (52801). Phone toll-free 800/262-8711. www.rhythm citycasino.com.* Departs from River Drive, between Centennial and Government bridges.

Scott County Park. *19251 290th St, Long Grove (52756). 8 miles N on Hwy 61, follow signs. Phone 563/285-9656.* More than 1,000 acres with a pioneer village and nature center. Swimming (fee), fishing; ball fields, 18-hole golf, skiing, tobogganing, ice skating, picnicking, camping, trailer sites (fee; electricity additional). (Daily)

Special Event

Bix Beiderbecke Memorial Jazz Festival. *Riverfront at LeClaire Park, 311 N Ripley St, Davenport (52801). Phone 563/324-7170. www.bixsociety.org.* Honors the Davenport-born musician. Includes three indoor venues: Davenport Holiday Inn, Col Ballroom, Danceland Ballroom. Mid-July.

Limited-Service Hotels

★ **HAMPTON INN.** *3330 E Kimberly Rd, Davenport (52807). Phone 319/359-3921; toll-free 800/426-7866; fax 319/359-1912. www.hamptoninn.com.* 132 rooms, 2 story. Pets accepted, some restrictions; fee. Complimentary continental breakfast. Check-out noon. Fitness room. Indoor pool. Airport transportation available. **$**

★★ **HOLIDAY INN.** *5202 N Brady St, Davenport (52806). Phone 563/391-1230; toll-free 800/465-4329; fax 563/391-6715. www.holiday-inn.com.* 294 rooms, 3 story. Check-out noon. Restaurant, bar. Fitness room. Indoor pool. Airport transportation available. **$**

★★ **PRESIDENTS CASINO BLACKHAWK.** *200 E 3rd St, Davenport (52801). Phone 319/328-6000; toll-free 800/553-1173; fax 319/328-6047.* 189 rooms, 11 story. Check-out noon. Restaurant, bar. Fitness room. Airport transportation available. **$**

★ **SUPER 8.** *410 E 65th St, Davenport (52807). Phone 563/388-9810; toll-free 800/800-8000; fax 563/388-4705. www.super8.com.* 61 rooms, 2 story. Pets accepted, some restrictions; fee. Complimentary continental breakfast. Check-out 11 am. **$**

Restaurants

★ **IOWA MACHINE SHED.** *7250 NW Blvd, Davenport (52806). Phone 563/391-2427; fax 563/391-8652. www.machineshed.com.* American menu. Breakfast, lunch, dinner, brunch. Closed Thanksgiving, Dec 25. Bar. Children's menu. **$$**

★★ **THUNDER BAY GRILLE.** *6511 Brady St, Davenport (52806). Phone 563/386-2722. www.hoari.com.* American menu. Lunch, dinner. Closed Jan 1, Thanksgiving, Dec 25. Bar. Children's menu. Bilevel dining. **$$**

Decorah (A-5)

Population 8,063
Elevation 904 ft
Area Code 563
Zip 52101
Information Decorah Area Chamber of Commerce, 300 W Water; phone 563/382-3990 or toll-free 800/463-4692
Web Site www.decorah-iowa.com

A center of Norwegian culture in the United States, Decorah is the seat of Winneshiek County, one of the state's most picturesque areas. Within a short distance are Siewers and Twin Springs and towering spires of limestone along the Upper Iowa River. The town is named for a Native American chief who aided settlers during the Black Hawk War.

What to See and Do

Antonin Dvorak Memorial. *Spillville (52168).* The tablet on a huge boulder is a monument to famed the Czech composer who lived here one summer. Titles of some of his outstanding works are inscribed on the base of the monument.

Bily Clocks. *323 N Main St, Spillville (52168). Phone 563/562-3569.* Collection of elaborately carved musical clocks with moving figures, some 9 feet tall. (May-Oct, daily) **$$**

Fort Atkinson State Preserve. *16 miles SW via Hwy 52, Hwy 24. Phone 563/425-4161.* Fort built in 1840 as federal protection for the Winnebago from the Sac, Fox, and Sioux. Restored buildings include barracks, blockhouse, magazine. Museum exhibits Native American and pioneer relics. (Mid-May-mid-Oct, daily) **FREE**

Seed Savers Heritage Farm. *3094 N Winn Rd, Decorah (52101). 6 miles N of town off Hwy 52. Phone 563/382-5990.* This 173-acre farm features displays of endangered vegetables, apples, grapes, and ancient White Park cattle. Preservation Gardens house 15,000 rare vegetable varieties; Cultural History Garden displays old-time flowers and vegetables. Historic Orchard has 650 19th-century apples and 160 hardy grapes. Meeting center; gift shop. (Daily) **$**

Upper Iowa River. *College Dr and Water St, Decorah (52101). Phone toll-free 800/463-4692 (canoe, tube rental information).* Popular for canoeing and tubing.

★ **Vesterheim Norwegian-American Museum.** *523 W Water St, Decorah (52101). Phone 563/382-9681.* Extensive exhibits relate history of Norwegians in America and Norway. Pioneer objects, handicrafts, ship gallery, arts displayed in a complex of 13 historic buildings with a restored mill. (Daily; closed holidays) **$$**

Special Event

Nordic Fest. *300 W Water St, Decorah (52101). Phone toll-free 800/382-3378.* Parades, dancing, pioneer tool display; demonstrations of cooking, needlework, and rosemaling. Last full weekend in July.

Limited-Service Hotel

★ **SUPER 8.** *810 Hwy 9 E, Decorah (52101). Phone 563/382-8771; toll-free 800/800-8000; fax 563/382-1118. www.super8.com.* Surprisingly quiet for a hotel just off a highway (9), the Super 8 is 2 miles from the Vesterheim and Porter House museums, 4 miles from Luther College, and an easy drive into the center of town. The hotel is family-friendly, with the definition of "family" extending all the way down to pets. 60 rooms, 2 story. Pets accepted. Complimentary continental breakfast. Check-in 2 pm, check-out 11 am. Fitness room. Whirlpool. **$**

Full-Service Hotel

★ ★ ★ **HOTEL WINNESHIEK.** *104 E Water St, Decorah (52101). Phone 563/382-4164; fax 563/382-4189.* The Hotel Winneshiek is a rare gem: an elegantly restored 1905 hotel in the heart of downtown. Guests are greeted at a concierge desk in an entryway decorated with fresh flowers and displays of antique glassware and porcelain figurines. The entryway opens onto a lobby with an octagonal three-story atrium, set under a large stained-glass skylight. A marble fireplace, Waterford crystal chandelier, and antique furnishings make you long for a delay during check-in, but it's not to be; the service is as efficient as it is friendly. 31 rooms. Complimentary continental breakfast. Check-in 4 pm, check-out noon. Restaurant, bar. **$**

Specialty Lodgings

The following lodging establishments are approved by Mobil Travel Guide, but due to their unique and individualized nature have not been given a traditional Mobil Star rating. Included in this listing you may find bed-and-breakfasts, limited-service inns, guest ranches, and other unique hotel properties.

SUZANNE'S BED & BREAKFAST. *120 N 3rd St, Lansing (52151). Phone 563/538-3040.* This beautiful Victorian-era bed-and-breakfast was built in 1865. 4 rooms, 3 story. **$**

THORNTON HOUSE. *371 Diagonal St, Lansing (52151). Phone 563/www.thorntonhouse.net.* This brick mansion has over 3,300 square feet of living space with a two-story enclosed deck. 4 rooms, 3 story. **$$$$**

Restaurants

★ **MILTY'S.** *200 Main St, Lansing (52151). Phone 563/538-4585.* This family-style eatery is a local favorite. American menu. Lunch, dinner. Closed Sun. **$**

★ **STONE HEARTH INN.** *811 Commerce Dr, Hwy 9, Decorah (52101). Phone 563/382-4614.* American menu. Lunch, dinner. Closed Jan 1, Thanksgiving, Dec 25. Bar. Children's menu. **$$**

Denison (C-2)

Founded 1855
Population 6,604
Area Code 712
Zip 51442
Information Chamber of Commerce, 109 N 14th St; phone 712/263-5621
Web Site www.denisonia.com

J. W. Denison, an agent for the Providence Western Land Company and a Baptist minister, came to this area in 1855 and gave the new town his name. The following year the town survived raids by Native Americans. In 1933, Denison survived martial law brought about when farmers nearly rioted during land foreclosures triggered by the Great Depression. Denison is the seat of Crawford County.

What to See and Do

Yellow Smoke Park. *2237 Yellow Smoke Rd, Denison (51442). 1 mile E on Hwy 30, then 1/2 mile N on county road. Phone 712/263-2070.* A 320-acre recreation area with swimming beach; fishing; boating (no power boats). Hiking. Winter sports. Picknicking. Camping (fee). (Daily) **FREE**

Special Event

Donna Reed Festival for the Performing Arts. *1305 Broadway, Denison (51442). Phone 712/263-3334.* Special workshops in the performing arts conducted by professionals from around the nation. Parade. Golf tourney. 10K run. Sat night gala. Street fair. Third full week in June.

Limited-Service Hotel

★ **SUPER 8.** *502 Boyer Valley Rd, Denison (51442). Phone 712/263-5081; toll-free 800/800-8000; fax 712/263-8123. www.super8.com.* 40 rooms, 2 story. Complimentary continental breakfast. Check-out 11 am. **$**

Restaurant

★ **CRONK'S.** *812 4th Ave S, Denison (51442). Phone 712/263-4191.* Steak menu. Breakfast, lunch, dinner, late-night, brunch. Closed Dec 25. Bar. **$**

Des Moines (C-3)

See also Indianola

Founded 1843
Population 193,187
Elevation 803 ft
Area Code 515
Information Greater Des Moines Convention & Visitors Bureau, 405 Sixth Ave, Suite 201, 50309; phone 515/286-4960 or toll-free 800/451-2625
Web Site www.desmoinesia.com

Des Moines (De-MOYN) is the capital and largest city in the state. This metropolis is the industrial, retail, financial, and political hub of Iowa. A military garrison established Fort Des Moines at a point on the Raccoon and Des Moines rivers in 1843. Two years later the territory was opened to settlers and the town of Fort Des Moines was chosen as the county seat. The word "fort" was abandoned when the community became a city in 1857; the next year it became the state capital. Today more than 60 insurance companies have their home offices here.

Additional Visitor Information

The Greater Des Moines Convention & Visitors Bureau, Two Ruan Center, Suite 222, 601 Locust St, 50309, has tourist guidebooks, maps, and brochures, as well as a guide to events; phone 515/286-4960 or toll-free 800/451-2625. There is a visitor information center located at the Des Moines International Airport, Fleur Dr, phone 515/287-4396 (Mon-Fri, Sun).

Public Transportation

Buses (Metropolitan Transit Authority), phone 515/283-8100

Airport Des Moines International Airport, weather 515/270-2614; cash machines, Terminal Building.

Information Phone 515/256-5100

Lost and found Phone 515/256-5000

What to See and Do

Adventureland Park. *305 34th Ave NW, Altoona*

(50009). Phone 515/266-2121. www.adevntureland-usa.com. Amusement park with more than 100 rides, shows, and attractions. Features the Dragon, Spaceshot double-looping, Tornado, and Outlaw roller coasters; Raging River, whitewater rapids; live musical entertainment. (June-late Aug: daily; May and Sept: weekends) **$$$$**

Blank Park Zoo. *7401 SW 9th St, Des Moines (50315). Phone 515/285-4722. www.blankparkzoo.com.* Animal and bird areas designed for close viewing; Australian and African walk-through displays; farm animal contact area; camel rides and Old West train ride; concession. (Daily) **$$**

Civic Center. *221 Walnut St, Des Moines (50309). Phone 515/243-1120 (recording). www.civiccenter.org.* Varied musical and theatrical entertainment, symphony concerts, and ballet performances all year. Free tours by appointment.

Des Moines Art Center. *4700 Grand Ave, Des Moines (50312). In Greenwood Park. Phone 515/277-4405.* Exhibits of 19th- and 20th-century paintings and sculptures in a striking contemporary building, original building by Eliel Saarinen, additions by Meier and Pei; changing exhibits; library, museum shop, restaurant. (Tues-Sun; closed Jan 1, Dec 25, Dec 31) **FREE**

Des Moines Botanical Center. *909 Robert D. Ray Dr, Des Moines (50316). Phone 515/323-6290.* Displays of nearly 1,500 species from all over the world; seasonal floral displays. (Daily; closed holidays) **$**

Drake University. *2507 University Ave, Des Moines (50311). Phone 515/271-2011.* (1881) (6,500 students) Six colleges and schools. Many buildings designed by distinguished architects, including Eliel and Eero Saarinen; Harry Weese & Associates; Brooks, Borg & Skiles; Ludwig Mies van der Rohe. Campus tours. (See SPECIAL EVENTS)

Heritage Village. *State Fairgrounds, E 30th and University Ave, Des Moines (50317). 12 blocks E of I-235 on E University. Phone 515/262-3111.* Century-old barn, exposition hall (1886) with display of early farm machinery; authentically furnished country school; replicas of 1834 church, Fort Madison block-house, turn-of-the-century pharmacy, general store, telephone building, totem pole; state fair museum, barber shop, and railroad station. Tours (mid-Apr-mid-Oct, by appointment) **$**

Hoyt Sherman Place. *1501 Woodland Ave, Des Moines (50309). Phone 515/244-0507.* (1877) Once home of

General Sherman's brother. Now features the city's oldest art gallery, including artifacts, antique furniture, and art collection. Tours (by appointment; fee). Theater (1,200 seats) added in 1922. (Mon-Fri)

Iowa Historical Building. *Capitol Complex, 600 E Locust, Des Moines (50309). Phone 515/281-5111.* Modern cultural center houses state historical museum; displays portray Iowa history and heritage. Library contains county, state, and family history materials; rare books and manuscripts about Iowa; census records; and newspapers. Museum (Daily). **FREE**

⭐ **Living History Farms.** *2600 111th St, Urbandale (50322). W via I-35, I-80 exit 125, to Hickman Rd (Hwy 6). Phone 515/278-5286. www.lhf.org.* Complex has four farms and town on 600 acres: Native American settlement of 1700 includes gardens, shelters, crafts of Ioway tribe; pioneer farm of 1850 features log cabin and outbuildings, demonstrations of early farming methods; horse-powered farm of 1900 depicts farm and household chores typical of period; crop center emphasizes modern agriculture and crops. The 1875 town of Walnut Hill includes a Victorian mansion; schoolhouse; pottery, blacksmith and carpentry shops; veterinary infirmary; church, law, bank, newspaper and doctor's offices; there is also a general store. (May-mid-Oct, daily) **$$$**

Polk County Heritage Gallery. *111 Court Ave, Des Moines (50309). Phone 515/286-3215.* Formerly the city's main post office (1908), the building's lobby was restored to its original Beaux Arts classical architecture. The gallery houses changing art exhibits, including brass writing desks. (Mon-Fri; closed between exhibits) **FREE**

Prairie Meadows Racetrack & Casino. *1 Prairie Meadows Dr, Altoona (50009). 10 miles E on I-80, exit 142. Phone toll-free 800/325-9015.* Live Thoroughbred, quarter horse, and harness racing (late Apr-Oct); simulcasts of Thoroughbred and greyhound racing (daily); 24-hour casino with more than 1,500 slots, poker room, and video poker machines. (Daily) **FREE**

Salisbury House. *4025 Tonawanda Dr, Des Moines (50312). Phone 515/274-1777.* A 42-room replica of King's House in Salisbury, England, on 11 acres of woodland. Houses authentic furnishings of Tudor age; classic paintings and sculpture; tapestries; 80 Oriental rugs; stained-glass windows; huge fireplaces; collector's library contains a leaf from the Gutenberg Bible. Guided tours only. **$$**

Science Center of Iowa. *4500 Grand Ave, Des Moines (50312). In Greenwood Park. Phone 515/274-4138.* Natural and physical science exhibits, live demonstrations; Digistar planetarium shows; laser shows (fee). (Daily; closed Thanksgiving, Dec 25) **$$$**

State Capitol. *1005 Grand Ave, Des Moines (50309). Phone 515/281-5591.* (1871) Towering central dome covered with 23-carat gold leaf; four smaller domes have golden seam marks. State offices and the Supreme Court are on the first floor. House and Senate chamber, and law library are on the second floor. Paintings, mosaics, collection of war flags. Building (daily; closed holidays). Call for tour times Mon-Sat. **FREE**

⭐ **Terrace Hill.** *2300 Grand Ave, Des Moines (50312). Phone 515/281-3604.* (1869) Extravagant Italianate/Second Empire mansion, now residence of Iowa governors, is situated on a commanding knoll above downtown. The restored house is an outstanding example of Victorian residential architecture. Tours include first and second floors, carriage house, and gardens. (Open Mar-Dec, Tues-Sat 10 am-1:30 pm; closed holidays) **$$**

White Water University. *5401 E University, Des Moines (50327). E on I-235, then 3 1/2 miles E on E University. Phone 515/265-4904.* Water park featuring wave pool, slides, tubing, hot tub; children's pool; picnicking, refreshments. (Memorial Day-Labor Day, daily) Miniature golf, go-karts (also open weekends spring and fall; additional fee) **$$$$**

Special Events

Drake Relays. *2507 University Ave, Des Moines (50311). Phone 515/271-3647. Drake University.* One of the most prestigious intercollegiate track and field events in the country; more than 5,000 athletes compete. Last week in Apr.

Iowa State Fair. *Fairgrounds, E 30th and University Ave, Des Moines (50317). Phone 515/262-3111.* One of the oldest and largest fairs in the country, it includes 20 acres of farm machinery, fine arts, a giant midway, grandstand stage and track events, free entertainment, exhibits, demonstrations, contests; camping. Aug.

Limited-Service Hotels

★ ★ **ADVENTURELAND INN.** *I-80 and Hwy 65, Altoona (50009). Phone 515/265-7321; toll-free 800/910-5382; fax 515/265-3506. www.adventureland-usa.com.* Located next to Adventureland Park, this newly renovated inn provides complimentary shuttle service to and from the park. Guests can enjoy the fun of Adventureland then return to the comforts of the inn, with a tropical pool and live entertainment. 130 rooms, 2 story. Check-out 11 am. Restaurant, bar. Indoor pool. **$**
🏊

★ **BEST INN.** *5050 Merle Hay Rd, Johnston (50131). Phone 515/270-1111; toll-free 800/237-8466; fax 515/331-2142. www.bestinn.com.* 91 rooms, 2 story. Pets accepted; fee. Complimentary continental breakfast. Check-out 1 pm. Indoor pool, whirlpool. **$**
🐾🏊

★ ★ **EMBASSY SUITES.** *101 E Locust St, Des Moines (50309). Phone 515/244-1700; toll-free 800/362-2779; fax 515/244-2537. www.embassysuites.com.* Located on the Des Moines River, the large, two-room suites here keep guests coming back time and time again. The conference meeting facilities attract business clientele, a complimentary airport shuttle is available, and guests can enjoy nearby entertainment, shopping, and restaurants. 234 rooms, 8 story, all suites. Complimentary full breakfast. Check-out noon. Restaurant, bar. Fitness room. Indoor pool, whirlpool. Airport transportation available. **$$**
🏃🏊

★ ★ **FOUR POINTS BY SHERATON.** *1810 Army Post Rd, Des Moines (50321). Phone 515/287-6464; toll-free 800/368-7764; fax 515/287-5818. www.fourpoints.com.* 141 rooms. Complimentary continental breakfast. Check-out noon. Restaurant, bar. Indoor pool. Airport transportation available. **$**
🏊

★ **HAMPTON INN.** *5001 Fleur Dr, Des Moines (50321). Phone 515/287-7300; toll-free 800/426-7866; fax 515/287-6343. www.hampton-inn.com.* 122 rooms, 4 story. Complimentary continental breakfast. Check-out 11 am. Fitness room. Outdoor pool. Airport transportation available. **$**
🏃🏊

★ **HEARTLAND INN DES MOINES WEST.** *11414 Forest Ave, Des Moines (50325). Phone 515/226-0414; toll-free 800/334-3277; fax 515/226-9769. www.heartlandinns.com.* 85 rooms, 2 story. Pets accepted, some restrictions; fee. Complimentary continental breakfast. Check-in 3 pm, check-out 11 am.

High-speed Internet access. Whirlpool. Business center. **$**

★ ★ **HOLIDAY INN.** *6111 Fleur Dr, Des Moines (50321). Phone 515/287-2400; toll-free 800/248-4013; fax 515/287-4811. www.holiday-inn.com.* 227 rooms, 3 story. Check-out noon. Restaurant, bar. Fitness room. Indoor pool, whirlpool. Airport transportation available. Business center. **$**

★ ★ **HOTEL FORT DES MOINES.** *1000 Walnut St, Des Moines (50309). Phone 515/243-1161; toll-free 800/532-1466; fax 515/243-4317. www.hotelfortdes moines.com.* This historic hotel, restored to its original beauty, has always been popular in Des Moines. With beautiful facilities for both meetings and social events, the grand style here captures its rich history and architectural wonder. 242 rooms, 11 story. Pets accepted. Check-out noon. Restaurant, bar. Fitness room. Indoor pool, whirlpool. Airport transportation available. **$**

★ **WILDWOOD LODGE.** *11431 Forest Ave, Clive (50325). Phone 515/222-9876; toll-free 800/728-1223; fax 515/276-8969. www.thewildwoodlodge.com.* 100 rooms, 3 story. Complimentary continental breakfast. Check-out noon. Bar. Fitness room. Indoor pool, whirlpool. **$**

Full-Service Hotel

★ ★ ★ **MARRIOTT DES MOINES.** *700 Grand Ave, Des Moines (50309). Phone 515/245-5500; toll-free 800/228-9290; fax 515/245-5567. www.marriott.com.* Busy travelers have come to rely on this modern hotel suited to meet every need. Conveniently located in the financial district, guests will find spacious guest rooms. 415 rooms, 33 story. Pets accepted, some restrictions. Check-out noon. Restaurant, bar. Fitness room. Indoor pool, whirlpool. Airport transportation available. **$**

Restaurants

★ **A TASTE OF THAILAND.** *215 E Walnut St, Des Moines (50309). Phone 515/243-9521; fax 515/282-0094.* Thai menu. Lunch, dinner. Closed Sun; holidays. **$**

★ ★ ★ **CHRISTOPHER'S.** *2816 Beaver Ave, Des Moines (50310). Phone 515/274-3694.* Honest, Italian-American food, including pastas, steaks, and seafood, and a friendly, casual atmosphere have made this dining room a local favorite for many years. The restaurant's banquet space is a popular choice for special events. American, Italian menu. Dinner. Closed Sun; holidays. Bar. Children's menu. **$$**

★ ★ ★ **GREENBRIER.** *5810 Merle Hay Rd, Johnston (50131). Phone 515/253-0124; fax 515/253-0920.* The American menu at this main-street restaurant has offered a broad selection of seafood, chicken, pasta, and specialty prime rib since 1987. The white-tablecloth dining room has a handsome waiting area with a brass-accented, mahogany bar. Seafood menu. Lunch, dinner. Closed Sun; holidays. Children's menu. Outdoor seating. **$$**

★ **HOUSE OF HUNAN.** *6810 Douglas Ave, Des Moines (50322). Phone 515/276-5556.* Chinese menu. Lunch, dinner. Bar. **$**

★ **JESSE'S EMBERS.** *3301 Ingersoll, Des Moines (50312). Phone 515/255-6011. www.jessesembers.com.* Seafood, steak menu. Lunch, dinner. Closed Sun; holidays. Bar. **$$$**

★ **THE MACHINE SHED.** *11151 Hickman Rd, Urbandale (50322). Phone 515/270-6818; fax 515/270-0832. www.hoari.com.* American menu. Breakfast, lunch, dinner. Closed Jan 1, Thanksgiving, Dec 25. Bar. Children's menu. Farm implements on display. **$$**

★ **SPAGHETTI WORKS.** *310 Court Ave, Des Moines (50309). Phone 515/243-2195; fax 515/243-2204.* American, Italian menu. Dinner. Closed Thanksgiving, Dec 25. Bar. Children's menu. Outdoor seating. **$$**

Dubuque (B-6)

See also Strawberry Point

Settled 1833
Population 57,546
Elevation 650 ft
Area Code 563
Information Convention and Visitors Bureau, 300 Main St, Suite 200, PO Box 705, 52004-0705; phone 563/557-9200 or toll-free 800/798-8844
Web Site www.traveldubuque.com

Facing both Wisconsin and Illinois across the broad Mississippi River, Dubuque became the first known European settlement in Iowa when Julien Dubuque, a French Canadian, came from Québec in 1788 and leased land from the Native Americans to mine lead. After his death, Native Americans barred settlement until 1833 when the territory was opened under a treaty with Chief Black Hawk. Once a boisterous river and mining town, Dubuque had the first bank and the first newspaper in what is now Iowa. Dubuque prospers as a center of more than 300 industries, including publishing, software development, and manufacturing.

What to See and Do

Bellevue State Park. *24668 Hwy 52, Dubuque (52031). 26 miles S on Hwy 52, 67. Phone 563/872-3243.* Approximately 540 acres on a high bluff; river view. Native American mounds, rugged woodlands. Hiking trails, snowmobiling, picnicking, camping (electricity, dump station). Nature center. Standard hours, fees.

Cathedral Square. *2nd and Bluff sts, Dubuque (52001). Phone 563/582-7646.* Surrounding the square are stylized figures of a lead miner, farmer, farmer's wife, priest, and river hand; opposite the square is the architecturally and historically significant St. Raphael's Cathedral.

Clarke College. *1550 Clarke Dr, Dubuque (52001). At W Locust St. Phone 563/588-6300.* (1843) (1,000 students) Music performance hall, art gallery, library, and chapel open from 56-foot-high glass atrium plaza. Tours (by appointment).

Crystal Lake Cave. *7699 Crystal Lake Cave Dr, Dubuque (52003). 3 miles S off Hwy 52. Phone 563/556-6451.* Network of passageways carved by underground streams; surrounding the lake with glittering stalactites and stalagmites. Guided tours. (Memorial Day-late Oct: daily; May: Sat-Sun) **$$$**

Diamond Jo Casino. *Ice Harbor, 400 E 3rd St, Dubuque (52001). Phone 563/583-7005; toll-free 800/582-5956.* Casino gambling on the river.

Dubuque Arboretum and Botanical Gardens. *3800 Arboretum Dr, Dubuque (52001). Phone 563/556-2100. www.dubuquearboretum.com.* Features annual and perennial gardens, rose, water, formal gardens; ornamental trees, woodland, and prairie wildflower walk. (Daily) **FREE**

Dubuque County Courthouse. *720 Central Ave, Dubuque (52001). Phone 563/589-4445.* This gold-domed courthouse is on the National Historic Register of Places. (Mon-Fri; closed holidays) **FREE** Adjacent is

Dubuque Museum of Art/Old County Jail. *701 Locust St, Dubuque (52001). Phone 563/557-1851.* Museum is housed in a brand-new facility; gallery is an example of Egyptian Revival architecture. (Tues-Fri, weekend afternoons)

Eagle Point Park. *2200 Bunker Hill Rd, Dubuque (52001). Off Shiras Ave, NE corner of city. Phone 563/589-4263.* On a high bluff above the Mississippi, the 164-acre park overlooks three states. A WPA project, the park's Prairie School pavilions and naturalistic landscaping were designed by Alfred Caldwell, who studied under Frank Lloyd Wright. Floral displays. Tennis. Picnicking (shelters), playgrounds. (Mid-May-mid-Oct, daily) **$**

Fenelon Place Elevator. *512 Fenelon Pl, Dubuque (52001). Phone 563/582-6496.* One of world's shortest, steepest incline railways; connects Fenelon Place with 4th Street, providing a three-state view. In operation since 1882. (Apr-Nov, daily 8 am-10 pm) **$**

⭐ ***Field of Dreams* Movie Site.** *28963 Lansing Rd, Dyersville (52040). 25 miles W on Hwy 20, on Lansing Rd. Phone 563/875-8404.* Background set of the movie *Field of Dreams,* includes baseball diamond. (Daily) Gift shop (early Apr-early Nov, daily). **FREE**

Five Flags Theater. *405 Main St, Dubuque (52001). Phone 563/589-4254. www.fiveflagscenter.com.* (1910) Designed by Rapp and Rapp, premier theater architects of their day, the Five Flags was modeled after Parisian music halls. Tours (by appointment). (Daily)

General Zebulon Pike Lock and Dam. *3000 Lock and Dam Road, Dubuque (52001). Can be seen from Eagle Point Park. Phone 563/582-1204.* Steady stream of barges and other river traffic moves through lock.

Grand Opera House. *135 8th St, Dubuque (52001). Phone 563/588-1305.* Century-old opera house offers a variety of entertainment throughout the year.

Heritage Trail. *13606 Swiss Valley Rd, Dubuque (52068). 2 miles N on Hwy 52. Phone 563/556-6745.* Trail provides 26 miles of scenic hiking, biking, and cross-country skiing on an old railroad along rugged Little Maquoketa River valley. Level, surfaced trail crosses from wooded, hilly, "driftless" area to rolling prairie near Dyersville. Self-guided tour identifies railroad landmarks, includes water-powered mill sites. (Daily) **$**

Iowa Welcome Center. *300 Main St, Suite 100, Dubuque (52001). 3rd St, Ice Harbor. Phone 563/556-4372; toll-free 800/798-8844.*

Julien Dubuque Monument. *Grandview Ave and Julien Dubuque Dr, Dubuque (52001). 1/2 mile from end of Julien Dubuque Dr. Phone 563/556-0620.* Tower built in 1897 at the site of Dubuque's mine and the spot where Native Americans buried him in 1810. Provides an excellent view of the Mississippi River. On 18 acres.

Loras College. *1450 Alta Vista St, Dubuque (52004). Phone 563/588-7100; toll-free 800/245-6727. www.loras.edu.* (1839) (1,900 students) Liberal arts. On campus is Heitkamp Planetarium (academic year, Fri evenings; also by appointment). Wahlert Memorial Library has a collection of 2,200 rare books, many printed before 1500.

Mathias Ham House Historic Site. *2241 Lincoln Ave, Dubuque (52001). Below Eagle Point Park. Phone 563/583-2812.* (1857) Italianate villa/Victorian mansion (32 rooms) with a cupola, offering spectacular views of the Mississippi River. Built by lead miner Mathias Ham. Also Iowa's oldest log cabin and one-room schoolhouse. (June-Oct: daily; May: weekends only) **$$**

Mines of Spain Recreation Area. *8999 Bellevue Heights, Dubuque (52003). Phone 563/556-0620.* This 1,380-acre park features nature trails, limestone quarry, wetlands, prairie. (Daily)

⭐ **Mississippi River Museum.** *400 E 3rd St, Dubuque (52001). Ice Harbor, downtown. Phone 563/557-9545.* Complex of six Dubuque County Historical Society museums, all emphasizing the city's river history. (Daily) **$$$** Two-day pass includes

Boatyard. *400 E 3rd St, Dubuque. Phone 563/5579545.* Exhibits and replicas of small craft that plied the Mississippi; boat building and restoration demonstrations.

Dubuque Heritage Center. *400 E 3rd St, Dubuque. Phone 563/556-4372.* Changing exhibits on riverboating and other local history.

National Rivers Hall of Fame. *400 E 3rd St, Dubuque. Phone 563/556-4672.* Museum celebrating the nation's river heroes—Samuel Clemens, Lewis and Clark, Robert Fulton, and others.

Paddlewheel Towboat *Logsdon*. *Dubuque.* One of the last wooden-hulled paddlewheel towboats on inland waterways; first operated in 1940.

"River of Dreams". *400 E 3rd St, Dubuque (52001). Phone 563/556-4372.* Interactive film (15 minutes) on the history of the Mississippi River. (Daily) Shown in the Iowa Welcome Center.

Sidewheeler *William M. Black*. *400 E 3rd St, Dubuque.* One of the last steam-powered sidewheelers. Tour the main deck, boiler, hurricane decks, pilothouse with speaking tubes and brass gauges, and engine room. (May-Oct)

Woodward Riverboat Museum. *3rd St Ice Harbor, Dubuque (52004).* Dramatizes 300 years of Mississippi River history: Native Americans, explorers, lead miners, boat builders, and steamboat captains; lead mines; pilothouse and log raft displays.

National Farm Toy Museum. *1100 16th Ave SE, Dyersville (52040). Phone 563/875-2727.* A wide array of farm toys are displayed amid agricultural scenes. Theater has a ten-minute film called "Toys to Treasure." Annual toy show held in early June. (Daily; closed holidays) Children 5 and under admitted free. **$$**

Old Shot Tower. *River and Tower sts, Dubuque (52001).* (1856) Tower, 140 feet high, produced three tons of shot daily during the Civil War; lead melted on ninth floor was dropped through screens into water at bottom as finished shot.

Redstone Inn. *504 Bluff St, Dubuque (52001). Phone 563/582-1894.* (1894) Red sandstone Queen Anne/Victorian mansion built by a prominent Dubuque industrialist as a wedding present for his daughter. Overnight stays available (see THE REDSTONE INN), restaurant; open all year.

Rustic Hills Carriage Tours. *4th and Bluff sts, Dubuque (52003).* Half-hour or hour narrated tours; horse-drawn carriage. Sleigh and hay rides. (Daily) **$$$**

Spirit of Dubuque. *400 E 3rd St, Dubuque (52001). Ice Harbor, in the Port of Dubuque. Phone 563/583-8093; toll-free 800/747-8093.* Sightseeing and dinner cruises (1 1/2-hour) on the Mississippi River aboard this paddlewheeler (May-Oct). **$$$$**

Storybook Hill Children's Zoo. *12345 N Cascade Rd, Dubuque (52003). Phone 563/588-2195.* Recreation area and petting zoo; playground; concession; train ride. (Memorial Day-Labor Day, daily)

Sundown Mountain Ski Area. *16991 Asbury Rd, Dubuque (52002). Phone 563/556-6676; toll-free*

888/786-3696 (except Dubuque). www.sundownmtn.com. Five chairlifts, tow rope; patrol, school, rentals; snowmaking; cafeteria, concession, bar. Twenty-one runs; longest run 1/2 mile; vertical drop 475 feet. (Late Nov-mid-Mar, daily; closed Dec 25) **$$$$**

Trolleys of Dubuque, Inc. *Dubuque (52001). Depart from Iowa Welcome Center, 3rd St, Ice Harbor. Phone toll-free 800/408-0077.* One-hour narrated tours explore the history of the town and offer panoramic views of Dubuque, the Mississippi River, Wisconsin, and Illinois. (Apr-Oct, daily) **$$$**

University of Dubuque. *2000 University Ave, Dubuque (52001). Phone 563/589-3000. www.dbq.edu.* (1852) (1,200 students) Liberal arts; theological seminary. Historic Alumni Hall (1907), a replica of a 15th-century English structure, features changing art exhibits; Blades Hall has impressive stained-glass windows; Steffens Arcade serves as the doorway to the campus. Carillon on campus plays concerts. Tours (Mon-Fri, by appointment)

Special Events

Dubuque Catfish Festival. *Hawthorne St, Dubuque. Phone 563/583-8535.* Catfish tournament; carnival; music; craft show; food and entertainment. Late June.

Dubuque County Fair. *Dubuque County Fairgrounds, 14569 Olde Hwy Rd, Dubuque (52002). Phone 563/ 588-1406.* Late July.

Mighty Summer Farm Toy Show. *1100 16th Ave Ct SE, Dyersville (52040). Phone 563/875-2311.* Antique tractors and farm machinery; city-wide garage sales; indoor/outdoor farm toy show. First full weekend in June.

Limited-Service Hotels

★ ★ **BEST WESTERN DUBUQUE INN.** *3434 Dodge St (Hwy 20W), Dubuque (52003). Phone 563/ 556-7760; toll-free 800/747-7760; fax 563/556-4003. www.dubuqueinn.com.* Check your e-mail with the high-speed wireless Internet access in the lobby and then go for a dip in the pool, spend time in the sauna, or sit on the sundeck while the kids play Ms. Pac Man or Attack from Mars. Even Fido is welcome at this hotel that has a little something for everyone—just put him on a diet if he weighs more than 25 pounds. 156 rooms, 3 story. Pets accepted, some restrictions; fee. Complimentary full breakfast. Check-in 2 pm,

check-out 11 am. Restaurant, bar. Indoor pool, whirlpool. Airport transportation available. **$**

★ ★ **BEST WESTERN MIDWAY HOTEL.** *3100 Dodge St, Dubuque (52003). Phone 563/557-8000; toll-free 800/336-4392; fax 563/557-7692. www.midway hoteldubuque.com.* The rooms of this hotel open onto an expansive glass-domed atrium that holds a pool, whirlpool, sauna, billiards, ping-pong table, and video game area, plus a small fitness room with rest room/ changing area. Situated just off Highway 20, the hotel is less than 2 miles from the Mississippi and 3 miles from the center of downtown. 148 rooms, 4 story. Pets accepted, some restrictions. Complimentary full breakfast. Check-in 3 pm, check-out 1 pm. High-speed Internet access. Restaurant, bar. Children's activity center. Fitness room. Indoor pool, whirlpool. Airport transportation available. **$**

★ **COMFORT INN.** *4055 McDonald Dr, Dubuque (52003). Phone 563/556-3006; toll-free 800/228-5150; fax 563/556-3006. www.choicehotels.com.* This comfortable hotel sits off Highway 20, not far from Diamond Jo's Riverboat Gambling. If you're not trying your luck at the slot machines, grab a cup of coffee (available 24 hours) and relax at the hotel's pool or watch an in-room movie. If you've tried your luck and won, e-mail your friends from your in-room dataport. The Comfort Inn is located 25 miles from the Chestnut Ski Resort and just 3 miles from Sundown. 52 rooms, 3 story. Pets accepted, some restrictions; fee. Complimentary continental breakfast. Check-in 2 pm, check-out 11 am. Indoor pool, whirlpool. Airport transportation available. **$**

★ ★ **DAYS INN.** *1111 Dodge St, Dubuque (52003). Phone 563/583-3297; toll-free 800/772-3297; fax 563/583-5900. www.daysinn.com.* If you're heading to Dubuque for a little riverboat gambling, you might want to gamble on the Days Inn first. Located 20 minutes from Sundown Mountain and 30 minutes from the Field of Dreams (located in Dyersville), the Days Inn Dubuque is just five to ten minutes from the riverboat gambling cruises and offers free transportation for all guests. 155 rooms, 2 story. Pets accepted; fee. Complimentary continental breakfast. Check-in 2 pm, check-out 11 am. Restaurant, bar. Fitness room. Outdoor pool. **$**

★ ★ THE GRAND HARBOR RESORT & WATERPARK.

350 Bell St, Dubuque (52001). Phone 563/690-4000; toll-free 888/690-4006; fax 563/690-0558. www.grandharborresort.com. Ah, to be a kid in a water park—lunging down a chute, slipping through a spout, sliding along an indoor/outdoor tube, when suddenly a giant bucket dumps 800 gallons of water on you, making your 25,000-square-foot swimming pool of adventure go "sploosh!" Massive squirt guns, high-powered water cannons, a lazy river to float down...and when all that fun makes you hungry, squish on over to the Water Park Café for a snack to fuel you up. Families love The Grand Harbor Resort and Water Park, not just for its attached, one-of-a-kind watery theme park, but also for its video arcade (approximately 150 games keep kids busy), weekend children's programs, and family-friendly room service menu of buckets of chicken and pizza. There's also plenty of fun for grown-ups, including two giant hot tubs and a fitness room. And in case you want more water, every room has a view of the Mississippi River. 193 rooms. Check-in 4 pm, check-out 11 am. Restaurant, bar. Children's activity center. Fitness room. Indoor pool, outdoor pool, children's pool, whirlpool. Airport transportation available. **$$**

★ HEARTLAND INN DUBUQUE WEST.

4025 McDonald Dr, Dubuque (52003). Phone 563/582-3752; toll-free 800/334-3277; fax 563/582-0113. www.heartlandinns.com. A quiet motel off well-traveled Highway 20, which here becomes Dodge, the Heartland will appeal to those who enjoy homemade holiday decorations in the lobby and a bountiful continental breakfast in the morning. 85 rooms, 2 story. Pets accepted, some restrictions; fee. Complimentary continental breakfast. Check-in 3 pm, check-out 11 am. Indoor pool. Airport transportation available. **$**

★ ★ HOLIDAY INN.

450 Main St, Dubuque (52001). Phone 563/556-2000; toll-free 800/465-4329; fax 563/556-2303. www.holiday-inn.com. A beautiful, airy lobby greets guests in this family-friendly downtown hotel. High ceilings, pillars, and lush flower arrangements provide a feeling of grandeur, but several conversation areas of small wooden coffee tables, sofas, and curved chairs make the open space seem cozy and interesting. Porter's Restaurant, tucked behind closed doors, has a "patio" that spills out onto the lobby. 193 rooms, 5 story. Pets accepted. Check-in 3 pm, check-out noon. High-speed Internet access, wireless Internet access. Restaurant, bar. Fitness room.

Indoor pool, whirlpool. Airport transportation available. Business center. **$**

★ ★ JULIEN INN.

200 Main St, Dubuque (52004). Phone 563/556-4200; toll-free 800/798-7098; fax 563/582-5023. www.julieninn.com. If Matt Dillon and Miss Kitty were living in Dubuque, they'd be hanging out at the Julien, probably sitting by the barber chair in the lobby of this historic hostelry. Its site has housed a hotel since 1839; the present hotel was built in 1914, after a fire ravaged the hotel that had been there since 1854. The Julien has an auspicious history; not only did Al Capone escape here when things in Chicago got hot, but he owned the Julien during Prohibition and even built an underground garage to hide his car. The hotel retains the atmosphere of days of old. Even the Riverboat Lounge, with its piano bar and ornamental iron work, is designed to replicate the saloons of the Mississippi steamers of yesteryear. 137 rooms, 8 story. Check-in 2 pm, check-out 11 am. Restaurant, bar. Fitness room. Airport transportation available. **$**

★ ★ TIMMERMAN'S HOTEL & RESORT.

7777 Timmerman Dr, East Dubuque (61025). Phone 815/747-3181; toll-free 800/336-3181; fax 815/747-6556. www.timmermanhotel.com. 74 rooms, 3 story. Pets accepted, some restrictions; fee. Complimentary continental breakfast. Check-out noon. Restaurant, bar. Indoor pool, whirlpool. **$**

Specialty Lodgings

The following lodging establishments are approved by Mobil Travel Guide, but due to their unique and individualized nature have not been given a traditional Mobil Star rating. Included in this listing you may find bed-and-breakfasts, limited-service inns, guest ranches, and other unique hotel properties.

THE LANDING. *703 S River Park Dr, Guttenberg (52151). Phone 563/252-1615. www.thelanding615.com.* This German-built limestone structure was erected in the late 1800s and features great views of the Mississippi River. 5 rooms, 3 story. **$$**

THE REDSTONE INN. *504 Bluff St, Dubuque (52001). Phone 563/582-1894; fax 563/582-1893. www.theredstoneinn.com.* The Redstone Inn is a modern-day oxymoron: a beautiful 1890s Victorian mansion with high-speed wireless Internet access. Built by an 1800s businessman named Cooper who made his considerable fortune in wagons before being ruined by the Studebaker, the Redstone opened as a bed-and-breakfast in 1984 and has undergone a series of updates. Today, you'll enjoy a full breakfast in a cozy nook off the entryway, perhaps return to the inn for afternoon tea in the antique-filled parlor, and then warp-speed to your room to watch cable TV or check your e-mail. You'll see the marble fireplaces and stained glass, but not the fax machine. The rooms are filled with old-fashioned, gleaming wood furniture, and many suites have whirlpool tubs. Enjoy whatever ambience you like; just don't forget to say hello to Maddy, the gentle house dog, who doesn't care what century it is as long as you pet her. 14 rooms, 3 story. Pets accepted. Complimentary full breakfast. Check-in 3 pm, check-out 11 am. High-speed Internet access, wireless Internet access. **$$$**

Restaurants

★ ★ **CAFE MISSISSIPPI.** *431 S River Park Dr, Guttenberg (52052). Phone 563/252-4405.* Located along the Mississippi River Lock and Dam 10. American menu. Lunch, dinner. **$$**

★ **MARIO'S.** *1298 Main St, Dubuque (52001). Phone 563/556-9424.* Italian, American menu. Lunch, dinner. Closed holidays. Bar. **$$**

★ **YEN CHING.** *926 Main St, Dubuque (52001). Phone 563/556-2574.* Chinese menu. Lunch, dinner. Closed Sun; holidays. **$**

Emmetsburg (A-2)

See also Algona, Spencer, West Bend

Settled 1858
Population 3,940
Elevation 1,234 ft
Area Code 712
Zip 50536
Information Chamber of Commerce & Iowa Welcome Center, 1013 Broadway; phone 712/852-2283
Web Site www.emmetsburg.com

In the Des Moines River valley, flanked by Kearney Park, Emmetsburg is the seat of Palo Alto County. A colony of Irish families built the first settlement here and named the community in honor of Irish patriot Robert Emmet. A statue of Emmet stands in the courthouse square. The town is the official "Sister City" of Dublin, Ireland.

What to See and Do

Kearney Park. *N Lawler St, Emmetsburg (50536). NW edge of town. Phone 712/852-4030.* Forty-five acres on Five Island Lake, which covers 945 acres. Boating, fishing; golf, picnicking, camping (fee).

Special Event

St. Patrick's Day Celebration. *1001 Broadway, Emmetsburg (50536). Phone 712/852-4326.* Features a guest member of Irish Parliament. Parade, pageant, cultural exhibits, Irish stew dinner, dances. Three days around Mar 17.

Estherville (A-2)

See also Okoboji, Spirit Lake

Settled 1857
Population 6,720
Area Code 712
Zip 51334
Information Chamber of Commerce, 804 Central Ave, PO Box 435; phone 712/362-3541
Web Site www.estherville.org

What to See and Do

Fort Defiance State Park. *Estherville. 1 mile W on Hwy 9, then 1 1/2 miles S on County N 26. Phone 712/362-2078.* Memorial to a fort erected during the Civil War to protect settlers from attacks by Native Americans. 181 acres; picnic area surrounded by wooded hills, wildflowers. Bridle, hiking trails. Snowmobiling. Picnicking, lodge. Primitive camping.

Special Event

Sweet Corn Days. *804 Central Ave, Estherville (51334). Phone 712/362-3541.* Parade, craft show, carnival, street dance. First week in Aug.

Fairfield (D-5)

See also Mount Pleasant, Ottumwa

Settled 1839
Population 9,768
Elevation 778 ft

Area Code 641
Zip 52556
Information Fairfield Area Chamber of Commerce, 204 W Broadway; phone 641/472-2111
Web Site www.fairfieldiowa.com

What to See and Do

⭐ **Bentonsport-National Historic District.** *21964 Hawk Dr, Keosauqua (52565). 20 miles S on Hwy 1, then 5 miles E on County J40. Phone 319/592-3579.* Preserved 1840s village with 13 original buildings; Mason House Inn (1846) with original furnishings offers lodging and tours (fee); churches, stately brick houses; antique and craftshops; lodging. Canoeing. Special events. Village (Apr-Oct, daily).

Jefferson County Park. *2003 Libertyville Rd, Fairfield (52556). 1/2 mile SW on County H33 (Libertyville Rd). Phone 641/472-4421.* This 191-acre area is mostly oak and hickory timberland, which provides an excellent wildlife habitat; three ponds stocked with bass, bluegill, and catfish. Hiking, bicycle trails. Cross-country skiing. Picnicking, playground. Camping (fee; electricity additional). **FREE**

Lacey-Keosauqua State Park. *Hwy 1, Keosauqua (52565). 23 miles S on Hwy 1. Phone 319/293-3502.* Approximately 1,500 acres includes Ely's Ford, famous Mormon crossing. Heavily wooded; scenic views; 22-acre lake. Swimming, beach; fishing; boating (ramp, rentals). Hiking trails. Snowmobiling. Picnicking, lodge. Camping (electricity, dump station), cabins. Standard hours, fees.

Old Settlers Park. *Fairfield. B St, N edge of town.* An 11-acre park; Bonnifield Cabin (1838); the grave of the first settler.

Limited-Service Hotel

★ ★ **BEST WESTERN FAIRFIELD INN.** *2200 W Burlington Ave, Fairfield (52556). Phone 641/472-2200; toll-free 800/780-7234; fax 641/472-7642. www.bestwestern.com.* 52 rooms, 2 story. Pets accepted. Complimentary continental breakfast. Check-out noon. Restaurant. Indoor pool, whirlpool. **$**

Fort Dodge (B-3)

See also Humboldt, Webster City

Founded 1853

Population 25,894
Elevation 1,030 ft
Area Code 515
Zip 50501
Information Chamber of Commerce, 1406 Central Ave, PO Box T; phone 515/955-5500 or toll-free 800/765-1438
Web Site www.fortdodgechamber.com

Astride the Des Moines River, atop a gypsum bed that covers nearly 30 square miles and nestled amid fertile farms, Fort Dodge has every ingredient for prosperity. Major industries are veterinary pharmaceuticals, gypsum products, pet food, and aluminum cans.

Fort Dodge was established to protect settlers. Its commander, Major William Williams, was given a large tract of land as part of his compensation, and here the town was laid out. Fort Dodge was an innocent party to a scientific hoax when a huge slab of gypsum cut here was freighted to Chicago and carved into the celebrated Cardiff Giant, falsely claimed to be a petrified prehistoric man (now at the Farmer's Museum, Cooperstown, New York).

What to See and Do

Blanden Memorial Art Museum. *920 3rd Ave S, Fort Dodge (50501). Phone 515/573-2316.* American and European paintings and sculpture; Asian paintings and decorative arts; African, Pre-Columbian art, graphic art; photography; changing exhibits. (Tues-Sat) **FREE**

Dolliver Memorial State Park. *2757 Dolliver Park Ave, Fort Dodge (50557). 8 miles S on Hwy 169, then 5 miles E on Hwy 50, then 1 mile N. Phone 515/359-2539. www.state.ia.us/dnr/organiza/ppd/dolliver.htm.* This 572-acre park features deep ravines, 75-foot limestone walls, Native American mounds, and a scenic overlook. Fishing, boating (ramp); hiking trails, picnicking, camping (electricity, dump station), cabins, lodges. Standard hours.

⭐ **Fort Dodge Historical Foundation, Fort Museum, and Frontier Village.** *South Kenyon and Museum Rd, Fort Dodge (50501). At junction Hwy 20 Business. Phone 515/573-4231.* Replica of 1862 fort houses museum, trading post, blacksmith shop, general store, log home, drugstore, cabinet shop, newspaper office, church, jail, and one-room school. A replica of the "Cardiff Giant" is on display at the Fort Museum. (May-Oct: daily; rest of year: by appointment)

John F. Kennedy Memorial Park. *1415 Nelson Ave, Fort Dodge (50501). 5 miles N on County P56. Phone 515/576-4258.* Swimming, fishing, boating (ramp; no motors); picnicking, shelter; "children's forest," playground; golfing, tent and trailer sites (mid-Apr-Oct; fee). (Daily) **FREE**

Kalsow Prairie. *Manson. 15 miles W on Hwy 7 to Manson, then 2 miles N on county road.* Approximately 160 acres preserving untouched Iowa prairie.

Site of Old Fort Dodge. *1st Ave N and N 4th St, Fort Dodge (50501).* Boulder with bronze tablet marks the spot where the fort stood.

Twin Lakes State Park. *227 S Blossom St, Lake View (51450). 26 miles W on Hwy 7, then 3 miles S on Hwy 4, then E on Hwy 124. Phone 712/657-8712.* Approximately 15 acres adjacent to N Twin Lake. Swimming; fishing; boating (ramps). Picnicking. Standard hours.

Limited-Service Hotel

★ ★ **HOLIDAY INN.** *2001 Hwy 169 S, Fort Dodge (50501). Phone 515/955-3621; toll-free 800/465-4329; fax 515/955-3643. www.holiday-inn.com.* 102 rooms, 2 story. Pets accepted. Check-out 1 pm. High-speed Internet access. Restaurant, bar. Fitness room. Indoor pool, children's pool. **$**

⬛🕴⬛

Fort Madison (D-5)

See also Burlington, Keokuk

Settled 1808
Population 11,618
Elevation 536 ft
Area Code 319
Zip 52627
Information Convention & Visitors Bureau, 614 9th St, PO Box 425; phone 319/372-5472 or toll-free 800/210-8687
Web Site www.visitfortmadison.com

Fort Madison began as the first military outpost (1808-1813) on the upper Mississippi River. Settlers established the town in the early 1830s; steamboats and logging were important early industries. Fort Madison entered an era of prosperity when the Sante Fe Railroad arrived in the 1880s. Today, the manufacture of pens and paints is important to the economy. Fort Madison is also home to the state's only maximum-security prison.

What to See and Do

Lee County Courthouse. *701 Ave F, Fort Madison (52627). Phone 319/372-3523.* (1841) Oldest courthouse in continuous use in the state. (Mon-Fri; closed holidays) **FREE**

Riverview Park. *Hwy 61 and 6th St, Fort Madison (52627). Between river and business section at E end of town. Phone 319/372-7700.* Approximately 35 landscaped acres. Marina; flower garden; picnicking. Reflecting pool and fountain. (May-Sept, daily). **$$** Also here is

> **Old Fort Madison.** *Riverview Park, 716 Madison Fort, Fort Madison (52627). Phone 319/372-6318.* Full-scale replica of the fort that existed from 1808-1813. Complete living history experience including uniformed soldiers loading and firing muskets. (Memorial Day-Aug: daily; May and Sept-Oct: weekends) **$$**

Rodeo Park. *811 Ave E, Fort Madison (52627). 1 mile N on Hwy 88. Phone 319/372-7700.* 234 acres. Picnicking; camping (Apr-Oct, fee); nature trails. (Daily) **FREE**

Santa Fe Railway Bridge. *2nd St, Fort Madison. E edge of town.* The largest double-track, double-decked railroad swing-span bridge in the world.

Sante Fe Depot Historic Museum and Complex. *9th and Ave H, Fort Madison (52627). Phone 319/372-7661.* Local historical displays, old fire engine; replica of old icehouse; prison and railroad displays. (Memorial Day-Labor Day, Wed-Sat 12:30-4:30 pm)

Shimek State Forest. *25 miles W on Hwy 2, E of Farmington. Phone 319/878-3811.* Park has 7,940 acres with 20-acre lake. Fishing, boating (electric motors only); hunting, hiking, and bridle trails, snowmobiling, picnicking, primitive camping. Standard hours, fees.

Special Event

Tri-State Rodeo. *Rodeo Arena, 2046 303rd Ave, Fort Madison (52627). N on County X32, at Old Denmark Rd. Phone 319/372-2550.* Rated one of top ten PRCA rodeos in the United States. Preceded by a week of festivities. Wed-Sat following Labor Day.

Limited-Service Hotel

★ **MADISON INN.** *3440 Ave L, Fort Madison (52627). Phone 319/372-7740; toll-free 800/728-7316; fax 319/372-1315. www.madisoninnmotel.com.* 20

rooms. Pets accepted, some restrictions; fee. Check-out 11 am. **$**
🐾

Garner (A-3)

See also Clear Lake, Mason City

Population 2,916
Elevation 1,216 ft
Area Code 641
Zip 50438
Information Chamber of Commerce, 415 State St; phone 641/923-3993
Web Site www.garnerchamber.net

What to See and Do

Pilot Knob State Park. *2148 340th St, Garner (50436). 3 miles W via Hwy 18, then 10 miles N on Hwy 69, then 6 miles E on Hwy 9, then 1 mile S on Hwy 332. Phone 641/581-4835.* Glacial formation rising to one of the highest points in the state. More than 700 heavily wooded acres with a 15-acre lake. Fishing, boating (electric motors only), bridle and hiking trails, snowmobiling, picnicking. Observation tower. Camping (electricity, dump station). Standard hours, fees.

Rice Lake State Park. *Lake Mills. 3 miles W via Hwy 18, then 24 miles NE on Hwy 69, then S on unnumbered road. Phone 641/581-4835.* Park has 47 acres on a 612-acre lake. Fishing; picnicking.

Grinnell (C-4)

See also Marshalltown, Newton

Founded 1854
Population 8,902
Elevation 1,016 ft
Area Code 641
Zip 50112
Information Chamber of Commerce, 833 Fourth Ave, PO Box 538; phone 641/236-6555
Web Site www.grinnellchamber.org

When Horace Greeley said, "Go west, young man, go west and grow up with the country!" he was talking to Josiah Bushnell Grinnell, who took the advice, went west to a bit of prairie between the Iowa and Skunk rivers, and established the town of Grinnell. Today, Grinnell is a thriving college town prospering on the fruits of the surrounding farmland and its more than 20 factories and processing plants.

What to See and Do

Grinnell College. *1121 Park St, Grinnell (50112). On Hwy 6, NE of business district. Phone 641/269-3400. www.grinnell.edu.* (1846) (1,243 students) Considered one of the top coeducational, liberal arts colleges in the United States. Tours (by appointment).

Grinnell Historical Museum. *1125 Broad St, Grinnell (50112).* Historical furnishings; relics, documents of J. B. Grinnell and aviator Billy Robinson in a late Victorian house. (June-Aug: Tues-Sun afternoons; rest of year: Sat afternoons or by appointment) **DONATION**

Rock Creek State Park. *5628 E Rock Creek, Kellogg (50135). 7 miles W on Hwy 6, then 3 miles N on Hwy 224. Phone 641/236-3722.* More than 1,260 acres on a 602-acre lake. Swimming, fishing, boating (ramp, rentals); hiking trails, snowmobiling, picnicking, camping (electricity, dump station). Standard hours, fees.

Wells Fargo Bank of Iowa–Poweshiek County. *Grinnell. Downtown, on corner opposite town square.* (1914) The second in the series of "jewel box" banks that architect Louis Henri Sullivan designed late in his career. This unique structure, one of the more important designs in the series, has been restored within the confines of a working bank environment. (Mon-Fri)

Limited-Service Hotel

★ **SUPER 8.** *2111 West St S, Grinnell (50112). Phone 641/236-7888; toll-free 800/800-8000; fax 641/236-7888. www.super8.com.* 53 rooms, 2 story. Pets accepted, some restrictions; fee. Complimentary continental breakfast. Check-in 3 pm, check-out 11 am. **$**
🐾

Hampton (B-4)

Founded 1856
Population 4,133
Elevation 1,145 ft
Area Code 641
Zip 50441
Information Chamber of Commerce, 5 First St SW; phone 614/456-5668
Web Site www.hamptoniowa.org

What to See and Do

Beed's Lake State Park. *1422 165th St, Hampton (50441). 3 miles NW near junction Hwy 65, Hwy 3.* Phone 641/456-2047. Park of 319 acres; dam creates 100-acre lake. Swimming, beach, fishing, boating (ramps); hiking, snowmobiling, picnicking, camping (electricity, dump station). Standard hours, fees.

Limited-Service Hotel

★ **GOLD KEY.** *1570 B Hwy 65N, Hampton (50441). Phone 641/456-2566; fax 641/456-3622.* 20 rooms. Pets accepted, some restrictions. Check-out 11 am. **$**
🐾

Humboldt (B-3)

See also Fort Dodge, Pocahontas

Population 4,438
Elevation 1,089 ft
Area Code 515
Zip 50548
Information Humboldt/Dakota City Chamber of Commerce, 29 S 5th St, PO Box 247; phone 515/332-1481
Web Site www.ci.humboldt.ia.us

A small religious sect led by the Rev. S. H. Taft came to this site on the West Fork of the Des Moines River and founded the community of Springvale, later renamed Humboldt in honor of the German scientist.

What to See and Do

Frank A. Gotch Park. *2568 Gotch Park Rd, Humboldt (50548). 3 miles SE off Hwy 169. Phone 515/332-4087.* A 67-acre park at the confluence of the east and west forks of the Des Moines River. Fishing, boating; picnicking, camping (fee).

Humboldt County Historical Museum. *905 1st Ave N, Humboldt (50548). E edge of Dakota City, S of Hwy 3 and County P 56. Phone 515/332-5280.* Housed in eight buildings; Mill Farm House (1879), a handmade two-story brick house with summer kitchen, enclosed summer porch, Victorian furnishings, doll and toy collections; Red Barn exhibits include Native American artifacts, farm equipment, tools, carpenter and blacksmith shops, and old-time post office; Willow School (1883), restored as a one-room 1890s schoolhouse. Also an authentically furnished log

cabin, kettle shed, jail (circa 1907), church (circa 1900) with stained-glass windows, and chicken house (circa 1875). (May-Sept, Thurs-Tues) **$**

Joe Sheldon Park. *407 2nd Ave N, Humboldt (50529). 2 miles W of Hwy 169, S of Hwy 3. Phone 515/332-4087.* An 81-acre park with fishing, boating (ramp); camping (fee), picnicking.

Indianola (C-3)

See also Des Moines, Winterset

Population 11,340
Elevation 970 ft
Area Code 515
Zip 50125
Information Chamber of Commerce, 515 N Jefferson, Suite D; phone 515/961-6269
Web Site www.cityofindianola.com

What to See and Do

Lake Ahquabi State Park. *1650 118th Ave, Indianola (50125). 5 miles S off Hwy 69. Phone 515/961-7101.* More than 770 acres with a 114-acre lake. Swimming, beach, fishing, boating (ramps, rentals); hiking trail, snowmobiling, picnicking, lodge, camping (electricity, dump station). Standard hours, fees.

National Balloon Museum. *1601 N Jefferson, Indianola (50125). N edge of town on Hwy 65/69. Phone 515/961-3714.* Ballooning artifacts and history spanning more than 200 years. (Daily; closed holidays) **FREE**

Simpson College. *701 N C St, Indianola (50125). N Buxton St and W Clinton Ave. Phone 515/961-6251. www.simpson.edu.* (1860) (1,700 students.) On campus are George Washington Carver Science Building, Dunn Library with historic exhibit, Blank Performing Arts Center, and Amy Robertson Music Center. Tours.

Special Events

Des Moines Metro Opera Summer Festival. *Blank Performing Arts Center, Simpson College, 106 W Boston Ave, Indianola (50125). Phone 515/961-6221.* Three operas performed in repertory by the Des Moines Metro Opera Company. Mid-June-mid-July.

National Balloon Classic. *1601 N Jefferson St, Indianola (50125). 2 miles E on Hwy 92. Phone 515/961-8415. www.nationalballoonclassic.com.* Hot air balloons is the main event here but there is a lot more things to see and do like an arts and craft show, parades, and fireworks. Late July or early Aug.

Iowa City (C-5)

See also Amana Colonies, Cedar Rapids, Washington

Founded 1839
Population 59,738
Elevation 698 ft
Area Code 319
Information Iowa City/Coralville Convention & Visitors Bureau, 408 First Ave, Riverview Square, Coralville, 52241; phone 319/337-6592 or toll-free 800/283-6592
Web Site www.icccvb.org

Fondly referred to as "the river city," Iowa City is the home of the University of Iowa and the state's first capital. Founded to become Iowa's territorial capital, Iowa City boomed as a backwoods metropolis, with the Territorial Legislative Assembly meeting here for the first time in 1841. A Doric stone capitol was erected, but with the shift of population, the legislators moved to Des Moines in 1857. As a conciliatory gesture to Iowa City, they selected it as the site of the new university. The university was given then "Old Capitol" and 10 acres of land for its use.

The university is the major enterprise, but the community is also important as one of the top medical centers in the country, the key city of hog, cattle, and grain-raising in Johnson County, and an industrial center.

What to See and Do

Coralville Lake. *2850 Prairie du Chien Rd, Iowa City (52240). 3 1/2 miles N of I-80. Phone 319/338-3543.* A 5,400-acre lake; swimming; boating (marinas, ramps); off-road biking; fishing, hunting. Picnicking. Improved camping (eight areas, fees). Flooding that occurred during the summer of 1993 eroded a 15-foot-deep channel exposing the underlying bedrock. Now called Devonian Fossil Gorge, it offers a rare opportunity to view Iowa's geological past. An Army Corps of Engineers project. (Daily)

Herbert Hoover National Historic Site. *110 Parkside Dr, West Branch (52358). 10 miles E on I-80, exit 254. Phone 319/643-2541.* The 187-acre park includes the restored house in which President Hoover was born; the Quaker meeting house where he worshiped as a

boy; a school; a blacksmith shop; and the graves of President and Lou Henry Hoover. (Daily; buildings closed Jan 1, Thanksgiving, Dec 25) **$** Also in the park is

Herbert Hoover Presidential Library-Museum. *210 Parkside Drive, West Branch (52358). Phone 319/ 643-5301.* (1962) Administered by the National Archives and Records Administration. Features a museum with re-created historic settings in China, Belgium, Washington, and other places prominent in Hoover's 50 years of public service. Changing exhibits, film. Research library (by appointment). (Daily; closed Jan 1, Thanksgiving, Dec 25) **$**

Iowa Children's Museum. *1451 Coral Ridge Ave, Coralville (52241). I-80 exit 240. Phone 319/625-5500.* Interactive exhibits for the young and young at heart. (Tues-Sun) **$$**

★ **Kalona Historical Village.** *411 9th St, Kalona (52247). Approximately 18 miles SW via Hwy 1. Phone 319/656-2519.* Amish traditions and lifestyle are preserved in this village containing the Wahl Museum, the Mennonite Museum and Archives, and an implement building; restored 110-year-old depot, log house (1842), one-room school, country store, outdoor bake oven, Victorian house, working windmill, post office (1880), and church (1869). (Mon-Sat) **$$**

Lake Macbride State Park. *3525 Hwy 382 NE, Solon (52333). 11 miles N on Hwy 1, then 4 miles W on Hwy 382. Phone 319/624-2200.* More than 2,150 acres with a 812-acre lake. Swimming, bathhouse, supervised beach; fishing; boating (ramps, rentals). Hiking. Snowmobile trails. Picnicking, concession. Improved and primitive camping (electricity, dump station; fee). Standard hours, fees.

Plum Grove. *1030 Carroll St, Iowa City (52240). Phone 319/337-6846.* (1844) Residence of the territory's first governor, Robert Lucas; restored and furnished. (Memorial Day-Oct, Wed-Sun 1-5 pm) **$**

University of Iowa. *IMU Madison and Jefferson sts, Iowa City (52242). In the central section of city on both sides of Iowa River. Phone 319/335-0557. www. uiowa.edu.* (1847) (28,000 students) More than 100 major buildings on 1,900 acres; 11 colleges, 6 schools, 82 departments. On campus are

Carver-Hawkeye Arena. *Elliott Dr and Newton Rd, Iowa City (52242).* Seats 15,500. Big Ten basketball games, wrestling meets, gymnastics, volleyball; also concerts and special events.

Iowa Hall. *Iowa City.* An exhibit gallery showing the state's geological, cultural, and environmental history. **FREE**

Medical Museum. *200 Hawkins Dr, Iowa City (52242). On W campus at the University of Iowa Hospitals and Clinics, Patient and Visitor Activities Center, eighth floor. Phone 319/356-7106.* Photographs, artifacts, and hands-on displays focusing on the history of medicine and patient care in Iowa. Changing exhibits. (Daily) **FREE**

Museum of Art. *100 Museum of Art, Iowa City (52242). W bank of Iowa River. Phone 319/335-1727.* Paintings, prints, lithographs; sculpture; silver; African art. (Wed-Sun; closed holidays) **FREE**

Museum of Natural History. *10 Macbride Hall, Iowa City. On east campus. Phone 319/335-0481.* Habitat dioramas; mounted mammals, fish, reptiles, birds. (Daily; closed holidays) **FREE**

Special Events

Iowa Arts Festival. *408 S 1st Ave, Iowa City (52245). Phone 319/337-7944.* Celebration of the arts. Mid-June.

Kalona Fall Festival. *Kalona Historical Village, 9th and D Ave, Kalona (52247). Phone 319/656-3232.* Amish food, crafts, and displays. Last weekend in Sept.

Limited-Service Hotels

★ ★ **HAMPTON INN.** *1200 1st Ave, Coralville (52241). Phone 319/351-6600; toll-free 800/426-7666; fax 319/351-3928. www.hamptoninn.com.* 115 rooms, 4 story. Complimentary continental breakfast. Check-out noon. Restaurant. Fitness room. Indoor pool, whirlpool. Airport transportation available. Business center. **$**
🏃 ⌛ 🏃

★ ★ **HOLIDAY INN.** *1220 1st Ave, Coralville (52241). Phone 319/351-5049; toll-free 800/252-7466; fax 319/354-4214. www.holiday-inn.com.* 96 rooms, 4 story. Complimentary continental breakfast. Check-out noon. Restaurant. Fitness room. Indoor pool. **$**
🏃 ⌛

Full-Service Hotel

★ ★ ★ **SHERATON IOWA CITY HOTEL.** *210 S Dubuque St, Iowa City (52240). Phone 319/337-4058; toll-free 800/848-1335; fax 319/337-9045.*

www.sheraton.com. Located just one block from the University of Iowa, this hotel caters to business and leisure travelers alike. 236 rooms, 9 story. Check-out noon. Restaurant, bar. Fitness room. Indoor pool, whirlpool. Airport transportation available. **$$**
🏃 ⌛

Restaurant

★ ★ **IOWA RIVER POWER COMPANY.** *501 First Ave, Coralville (52241). Phone 319/351-1904; fax 319/354-3518.* Seafood menu. Dinner, Sun brunch. Closed Dec 24-25. Bar. Children's menu. Multi-tiered dining in former power generating building. **$$$**

Keokuk (E-5)

See also Fort Madison

Settled 1820
Population 12,451
Elevation 550 ft
Area Code 319
Zip 52632
Information Keokuk Area Convention & Tourism Bureau, 329 Main St; phone 319/524-5599 or toll-free 800/383-1219
Web Site www.keokuk.com

At the foot of the Des Moines rapids on the Mississippi, Keokuk served as a gateway to the West and North and a manufacturing center for the pioneer frontier. The town was named for a Native American chief and developed as a fur trading center. Manufacturing and agricultural industries are its mainstays now.

What to See and Do

Keokuk Dam. *End of N Water St at the riverfront. Phone 319/524-4091.* (1910-1913) Ameren-Union Electric Power Plant with a mile-long dam across the Mississippi River to Hamilton, Illinois. Lock 19 operated by Army Corps of Engineers. **FREE**

Keokuk River Museum. *101 Mississippi Dr, Keokuk (52632). Victory Park, foot of Johnson St. Phone 319/524-4765.* Sternwheel towboat *George M. Verity* houses historical items of the upper Mississippi River valley. (May-Oct, daily) **$**

National Cemetery. *S 18th and Ridge sts, Keokuk (52632).* Unknown Soldier monument, Civil War graves. **FREE**

Rand Park. *Orleans Ave and N 14th St, Keokuk (52632).* Statue and grave of Chief Keokuk. Flower gardens, picnic area. (Daily) **FREE**

Samuel F. Miller House and Museum. *318 N 5th St, Keokuk.* Phone 319/524-5599. Restored home of US Supreme Court Justice appointed by Abraham Lincoln. (Fri-Sun afternoons) **$**

Special Events

Bald Eagle Appreciation Days. *Keosippi Mall, 300 Main St, Keokuk (52632). Keosippi Mall and the riverfront, with a shuttle between the two locations. Phone 319/524-5599; toll-free 800/383-1219. www.keokuk-ia.com/tourism/bald.htm.* You can find Bald Eagles in Keokuk from November through March. Every January, Bald Eagle Appreciation Days features several programs about Bald Eagles including seminars, exhibits, films, and other educational events. Third weekend in Jan.

Civil War Reenactment. *Rand Park, 17th and Orleans sts, Keokuk (52632). Phone 319/524-5599; toll-free 800/383-1219. www.keokuktourism.com/New_Site/reenactment.htm.* The weekend includes two historical reenactments (one Saturday and one Sunday) of the Battle of Pea Ridge as well as a Military Memorial and Salute at the National Cemetery in Keokuk. Visitors may also attend the Military Ball on Saturday night or the Ladies Tea and Lecture Program on Sunday morning (fee). Last full weekend in Apr.

Limited-Service Hotel

★ **HOLIDAY INN EXPRESS.** *4th and Main sts, Keokuk (52632). Phone 319/524-8000; toll-free 800/465-4329; fax 319/524-4114. www.holiday-inn.com.* 80 rooms, 5 story. Complimentary continental breakfast. Check-out noon. Fitness room. Indoor pool, whirlpool. **$**
🛅 ⛱

Le Claire (C-6)

Restaurant

★ ★ **THE FAITHFUL PILOT CAFÉ.** *117 N Cody Rd, Le Claire (53753). Phone 563/289-4156. www.faithfulpilotcafe.com.* Featuring progressive American cuisine in an elegant, modern dining room. American menu. Dinner. **$$**

Le Mars (B-1)

See also Sioux City

Settled 1869
Population 8,454
Elevation 1,231 ft
Area Code 712
Zip 51031
Information Chamber of Commerce, 50 Central Ave SE; phone 712/546-8821
Web Site www.lemarsiowa.com

A young English gentleman sought opportunities in this part of Iowa, formed a land company, and induced a colony of Englishmen to settle here. A training farm, cricket and polo fields, and a tavern called "The House of Lords" soon blossomed. Le Mars was well-known in Great Britain and was advertised there as a training ground for second sons in the areas of farming and stock raising. However, as the young Englishmen preferred horse racing, pubs, and sports to working the soil, the Germans, Irish, Luxembourgers, and Scandinavians took over the serious business of farming.

Today, Le Mars is the financial, educational, and recreational center for the area. As home to Wells Dairy, Inc, it has earned the name "Ice Cream Capital of the World."

What to See and Do

Plymouth County Historical Museum. *355 1st Ave SW, Le Mars (51031). Phone 712/546-7002.* More than 100 antique musical instruments; antique farm machinery, tools and furnishings; Native American artifacts; restored log cabin; four 1900-period rooms. (Tues-Sun; closed holidays) **FREE**

Special Events

Ice Cream Days. *50 Central Ave SE # 101, Le Mars (51031). Phone 712/546-4090.* Citywide event includes Art in the Park, children's learning fair, parade, street dance, fireworks. Mid-July.

Plymouth County Fair. *335 1st Ave SW, Le Mars (51031). Phone 712/546-4525.* Pioneer village and historic round barn; exhibits, arts and crafts; entertainment. Last week in July.

Limited-Service Hotel

★ **SUPER 8.** *Hwy 75 S, Lemans (51031). Phone 712/546-8800; toll-free 800/800-8000; fax 712/546-8800. www.super8.com.* 61 rooms, 3 story. Complimentary continental breakfast. Check-in 3 pm, check-out 11 am. **$**

Maquoketa (B-6)

Founded 1838
Population 6,111
Elevation 700 ft
Information Chamber of Commerce, 117 S Main St, 52060; phone 563/652-4602 or toll-free 800/989-4602
Web Site www.maquoketaia.com

From 1840 to 1870, this town was a stopping point for wagon trains before they ferried across the Maquoketa River heading west. Today Maquoketa is a beef and dairy production center and the home of several diversified industries.

What to See and Do

Costello's Old Mill Gallery. *22095 Hwy 64, Maquoketa (52060). 1 mile E on Hwy 64. Phone 563/652-3351.* Restored stone mill with waterwheel, built in 1867; inside constructed entirely of oak. Art gallery. (Apr-Dec: daily; rest of year: Wed-Sun) **FREE**

Jackson County Historical Museum. *1212 Quarry St, Maquoketa (52060). Fairgrounds. Phone 563/652-5020.* Replicas of general store and one-room country school; 19th-century bedroom, living room, and kitchen; old fire equipment, log cabin, buggies; barn with antique machinery, blacksmith shop; church; medical center; entertainment center, tent show; toy shop; wildlife display. Changing exhibits; exhibits by local artists. (Tues-Sun; closed holidays) **FREE**

Maquoketa Caves State Park. *10756 98th St, Maquoketa (52060). 7 miles NW on Hwy 428. Phone 563/652-5833.* Park of 272 acres. Large limestone caves; natural bridge rises 50 feet above the valley floor; 17-ton rock balanced on a cliff. Hiking trail, picnicking, camping. Standard hours, fees.

Marquette (A-5)

Settled 1779
Population 479
Elevation 627 ft
Area Code 563
Zip 52158
Information McGregor/Marquette Chamber of Commerce, 146 Main St, PO Box 105, 52157; phone 563/873-2186 or toll-free 800/895-0910

First known as North McGregor, this town was later renamed for Father Jacques Marquette; he and Louis Jolliet were the first to see Iowa territory from the mouth of the Wisconsin River in 1673. Within a 15-mile radius of the town are hundreds of effigy mounds, fortifications, and earthworks.

What to See and Do

★ **Effigy Mounds National Monument.** *151 Hwy 76, Harpers Ferry (52146). 3 miles N on Hwy 76. Phone 563/873-3491.* Preserves traces of indigenous civilization from 2,500 years ago. Mounds built in shapes of animals, birds, and other forms. Area divided by Yellow River; Great Bear Mound is the largest known bear effigy in the state, 70 feet across the shoulders, 137 feet long, and 5 feet high. Footpath leads from headquarters to Fire Point Mound Group, to scenic viewpoints overlooking the Mississippi and Yellow rivers. Guided walks (Memorial Day-Labor Day, daily). Visitor center has museum, 15-minute film. (Daily; closed Jan 1, Thanksgiving, Dec 25) **$**

Pikes Peak State Park. *15316 Great River Rd, McGregor (52157). 5 miles SE on Hwy 340. Phone 563/873-2341.* Park of 970 acres on bluffs overlooking the Mississippi River. Native American mounds, colored sandstone outcroppings, woods, and wild-flowers. A trail leads across rugged terrain to Bridal Veil Falls. Hiking. Picnicking. Camping (electricity, dump station). Observation point. Boardwalks. Views of river. Standard hours, fees.

Spook Cave and Campground. *13299 Spook Cave Rd, McGregor (52157). 5 miles SW on Hwy 18, then 2 miles N on unnumbered road. Phone 563/873-2144.* Guided 35-minute tour of underground cavern via power boat. Campground has swimming beach; lake fishing; hiking trails; picnic areas. (May-Oct, daily) **$$$**

Limited-Service Hotel

★ **HOLIDAY SHORES.** *110 Front St, McGregor (52157). Phone 563/873-3449; fax 563/873-3328.* 33 rooms, 3 story. Check-out 10:30 am. Indoor pool, whirlpool. Overlooks the Mississippi River. **$**

Marshalltown (C-4)

See also Grinnell

Founded 1853
Population 25,178
Elevation 938 ft
Area Code 641
Zip 50158
Information Convention & Visitors Bureau, 709 S Center St, PO Box 1000; phone 641/753-6645 or toll-free 800/697-3155
Web Site www.marshalltown.org

The business center of Marshall County prides itself on its symbols of the "good life" in the Midwest—the historic courthouse, pleasant parks, and numerous churches. Perhaps its most famous son is "Cap" Anson, son of the founder, who is enshrined in the Baseball Hall of Fame in Cooperstown, New York.

What to See and Do

Fisher Community Center Art Gallery. *709 S Center St, Marshalltown (50158). Phone 641/753-9013.* Art collection including paintings by Sisley, Utrillo, and Cassatt. (Daily; closed holidays) Contact the Central Iowa Art Association. **FREE**

Glick-Sower Historical Homestead. *201 E State St, Marshalltown (50158). Phone 641/752-6664.* Contains original furnishings of post-Civil War era; also furnished one-room country school with world maps of 1880. (Apr-Oct, Sat; groups by appointment year-round) **FREE**

Riverview Park. *803 N 3rd Ave, Marshalltown (50158). N 3rd Ave and Woodland. Phone 641/754-5715.* Camping. Picnicking, playground, ballfields. Park (Apr-Oct, daily). Some fees.

Limited-Service Hotel

★ ★ **BEST WESTERN REGENCY INN.** *3303 S Center St, Marshalltown (50158). Phone 641/752-6321; toll-free 800/780-7234; fax 641/752-4412. www.bestwestern.com.* 105 rooms, 2 story. Check-out noon. Restaurant, bar. Indoor pool, whirlpool. **$**
⌨

Mason City (A-4)

See also Charles City, Clear Lake, Garner

Settled 1853
Population 29,040
Elevation 1,138 ft
Area Code 641
Zip 50401
Information Convention & Visitors Bureau, 15 W State St, PO Box 1128, 50402-1128; phone 641/422-1663 or toll-free 800/423-5724
Web Site www.masoncityia.com

Mason City, a trading, manufacturing, farming, and transportation hub, is a major producer of cement; it also processes meat and dairy products. A Native American uprising slowed growth of the city after the first settlement, but pioneers, many of whom were Masons, gradually returned. The town was first known as Shibboleth, later as Masonic Grove. This is the seat of Cerro Gordo County and was the inspiration for the classic musical *The Music Man*.

What to See and Do

Charles H. MacNider Museum. *303 2nd St SE, Mason City (50401). Phone 641/421-3666.* Art Center features changing and permanent exhibits with emphasis on American art; gallery featuring "Bil Baird: World of Puppets," films, music, lectures, classes. (Tues-Sun; closed legal holidays). **FREE** Just east of the museum is

> **Meredith Wilson Footbridge.** *2nd St SE, Mason City.* Formerly called the Willow Creek Bridge, based on the movie *The Music Man*.

Frank Lloyd Wright Stockman House. *530 1st St NE, Mason City (50401). Phone 641/421-3666.* (1908) The only Prairie School house in Iowa designed by Frank Lloyd Wright; one of few houses built by Wright during this period to address middle-class housing needs. Tours. (June-Aug: Thurs-Sun; Sept-Oct: weekends) **$$**

Kinney Pioneer Museum. *Hwy 18 W, Mason City (50401). 7 miles W on Hwy 18, at entrance to Municipal Airport. Phone 641/423-1258.* Local history, pioneer, military exhibits; antique cars; original log cabin (circa 1854); one-room schoolhouse; old farm machinery, railroad caboose; artifacts, fossils. (May-Sept, Tues-Sun) **$$**

Lime Creek Nature Center. *3501 Lime Creek Rd, Mason City (50401). Phone 641/423-5309.* On limestone bluffs in the Lime Creek Conservation Area, center includes plant, bird, mammal, insect, and fish displays. More than 8 miles of trail wind throughout 400 acres of forest, field, prairie, pond, and river. (Daily; closed holidays) **FREE**

Margaret M. MacNider/East Park. *841 Birch Dr, Mason City (50401). At Kentucky Ave NE. Phone 641/421-3673.* The Winnebago River divides this park into two areas. Swimming pool; fishing. Hiking trails. Picnicking facilities, playground. Improved camping (fees). (Apr-Oct, daily)

Meredith Wilson Boyhood Home. *314 S Pennsylvania Ave, Mason City (50401). Phone 641/423-3534.* Birthplace of the author of *The Music Man.* (May-Oct: daily; Nov-Apr: Sat-Sun) **$$**

Special Events

North Iowa Band Festival. *East Park, 841 Birch Dr, Mason City (50401). Phone 641/423-5724.* Music, entertainment. Memorial Day weekend.

North Iowa Fair. *3700 4th St SW, Mason City (50401). Phone 641/423-3811.* Fairgrounds, Hwy 18 W. Nine-county area fair; carnival; food, wine and livestock exhibits; crafts; concessions, entertainment. Late July.

Limited-Service Hotel

★ **COMFORT INN.** *410 5th St SW, Mason City (50401). Phone 641/423-4444; toll-free 800/228-5150; fax 641/424-5358. www.comfortinn.com.* 60 rooms, 3 story. Complimentary continental breakfast. Check-out 11 am. Indoor pool, whirlpool. **$**

🏊

Missouri Valley (C-1)

See also Council Bluffs; also see Blair, NE

Settled 1858
Population 2,888
Elevation 1,019 ft
Area Code 712
Zip 51555
Information Chamber of Commerce, 100 S 4th St, PO Box 130; phone 712/642-2553
Web Site www.missourivalley.com

A town rich in Native American history, this was the site of the first settler's cabin in the Missouri Valley along the Willow River.

What to See and Do

DeSoto National Wildlife Refuge. *1434 316th Ln, Missouri Valley (51555). 6 miles W on Hwy 30. Phone 712/642-4121.* Partly in Nebraska and partly in Iowa, this approximately 7,800-acre refuge surrounds DeSoto Lake, once a bend in the Missouri River. In spring and fall thousands of geese and ducks may be found here. Self-guided auto tours (Mid-Oct-Nov). Excavation site of the *Bertrand*, a steamboat sunk in 1865. Visitor center (daily; closed holidays) houses the steamboat's artifacts and displays wildlife exhibits. Fishing, hunting; boating. Nature trails. Picnicking. **$$**

Harrison County Historical Village/Welcome Center. *2931 Monroe Ave, Missouri Valley (51555). 3 miles NE on Hwy 30. Phone 712/642-2114.* Includes a two-story log display building. The village consists of a school (1868), log cabin (1853), harness shop, print shop, and chapel. Contains relics of pioneer period. Museum (mid-Apr-mid-Nov, daily). Welcome center (daily; closed holidays) **$**

Loess Hills Scenic Byway. *400 E Erie St, Missouri Valley (51555). Phone 712/642-2553.* This 220-mile paved byway takes travelers through the Loess Hills region of western Iowa, traversing seven counties and revealing beautiful geologic formations along the way. For a map and information, contact the Chamber of Commerce. **FREE**

Missouri Valley Antique and Craft Malls. *1931 Hwy 30, Missouri Valley (51555). Phone 712/642-2125.* Sixty antique dealers in the mall; more than 40 booths in craft mall. (Daily; closed holidays).

Wilson Island State Recreation Area. *32801 Camp Ground Ln, Missouri Valley (51555). Hwy 30 to I-29 S, exit Loveland, then 7 miles W on Hwy 362. Phone 712/642-2069.* More than 550 acres. Fishing, boating (ramps); hunting, hiking, cross-country skiing, snow-mobiling, picnicking, playground, camping (electricity additional; dump station). Standard hours, fees.

Mount Pleasant (D-5)

See also Fairfield

Settled 1834

Population 8,027
Elevation 725 ft
Area Code 319
Zip 52641
Information Henry County Tourism Association, 502 W Washington; phone 319/385-2460 or toll-free 800/421-4282; Chamber of Commerce, 124 S Main, PO Box 109; phone 319/385-3101 or toll-free 800/436-7619
Web Site www.henrycountytourism.org

The first courthouse in Iowa was constructed here. One of the first roads in the state was a plank road between Burlington and Mount Pleasant.

What to See and Do

Iowa Wesleyan College. *601 N Main St, Mount Pleasant (52641).* (1842) (550 students.) Harlan-Lincoln Home is on campus (open by appointment at IWC Chadwick Library). **FREE**

⭐ **Midwest Old Threshers Heritage Museum.** *405 E Thresher Rd, Mount Pleasant (52641). S of town. Phone 319/385-8937.* Houses one of the nation's largest collections of steam engines, steam-powered farm machines; agricultural artifacts; turn-of-the-century farmhouse and barn; women's exhibit. **The Theatre Museum** has memorabilia of early tent, folk, and repertory theater (Sept-May: Mon-Fri; rest of year: Tues-Sun; fee). Camping (fee). (Memorial Day-Labor Day: daily; mid-Apr-Memorial Day and after Labor Day-Oct: Mon-Fri) **$$**

Oakland Mills Park. *2593 Nature Center Dr, Mount Pleasant (52641). 4 miles S, off Hwy 34. Phone 319/986-5067.* Approximately 104 wooded acres with a picnic area overlooking the Skunk River. Fishing, boating; hiking trails, camping (electrical hookups; fee). **FREE**

Special Event

Midwest Old Threshers Reunion. *405 E Thresher Rd, Mount Pleasant (52641). Phone 319/385-8937.* Iowa's largest working craft show, antique car show; steam and gas engines, vintage tractors; Midwest Village, log village, narrow-gauge steam railroad and electric trolley cars; entertainment. Five days ending Labor Day.

Limited-Service Hotel

★ **HEARTLAND INN MOUNT PLEASANT.** *810 N Grand Ave, Mount Pleasant (52641). Phone 319/385-2102; toll-free 800/334-3277; fax 319/385-*

3223. www.heartlandinns.com. 58 rooms, 2 story. Pets accepted; some restrictions; fee. Complimentary continental breakfast. Check-in 3 pm, check-out 11 am. High-speed Internet access. Indoor pool, whirlpool. Business center. **$**
🐾 🏊 🏃

Muscatine (C-6)

See also Davenport

Founded 1836
Population 22,881
Elevation 550 ft
Area Code 563
Zip 52761
Information Convention & Visitors Bureau, 319 E 2nd St, PO Box 297; phone 563/263-8895 or toll-free 800/257-3275
Web Site www.muscatine.com

Famous Muscatine cantaloupes and watermelons, as well as plastics, grain handling, food processing, and manufacturing are the major industries of this city. Samuel Clemens, who once lived here, declared Muscatine's summer sunsets unsurpassed.

What to See and Do

Mark Twain Overlook. *Lombard and 2nd sts, Muscatine (52761).* Three acres with a panoramic view of Mississippi River Valley and downtown Muscatine; picnicking.

Muscatine Art Center. *1314 Mulberry Ave, Muscatine (52761). Phone 563/263-8282.* Consists of the Laura Musser Museum and the Stanley Gallery. The museum is housed in an Edwardian mansion; changing art exhibits, special events, Estey player pipe organ with 731 pipes, antiques, and historical displays; Oriental carpets, furniture, paintings, drawings, prints, sculpture, graphics in permanent collection. (Tues-Sun; closed holidays) **FREE**

Pearl Button Museum. *Iowa Ave and 2nd St, Muscatine (52761).* Dedicated to the pearl button industry. Exhibits on making buttons from Mississippi River mussel shells. (Tues-Sat) **FREE**

Saulsbury Bridge Recreation Area. *2007 Saulsbury Rd, Muscatine (52761). W on Hwy 22.* Approximately 675 acres. Fishing, canoeing; picnicking, playground, nature trails and center, cross-country skiing, camping (hook-ups mid-Apr-mid-Oct only; fee). Park (daily). **FREE**

Shady Creek Recreation Area. *3550 Hwy 22, Muscatine (52761). 7 miles E on Hwy 22, on Mississippi River. Phone 563/263-7913.* 15 acres. Boat ramp. Picnicking, playground, shelter. Improved camping (May-Oct; fee). Park (daily). **$$$**

Wildcat Den State Park. *1884 Wildcat Den Rd, Muscatine (52761). 12 miles E on Hwy 22. Phone 563/263-4337.* A 321-acre park with historic mid-19th-century gristmill, one-room schoolhouse, Pine Creek Bridge; scenic overlook. Hiking trails, working mill, picnicking, primitive camping. Standard hours, fees.

Limited-Service Hotel

★ ★ **HOLIDAY INN.** *2915 N Hwy 61, Muscatine (52761). Phone 563/264-5550; toll-free 800/465-4329; fax 563/264-0451. www.holiday-inn.com.* 112 rooms, 3 story. Pets accepted; fee. Check-out noon. Restaurant, bar. Fitness room. Indoor pool, children's pool, whirlpool. Business center. **$**

Newton (C-4)

See also Grinnell

Population 14,789
Elevation 950 ft
Area Code 641
Zip 50208
Information Convention & Visitors Bureau, 113 1st Ave W; phone 641/792-0299 or toll-free 800/798-0299
Web Site www.visitnewton.com

The washing machine industry was born here in 1898, and the Maytag Company continues to make Newton the "home laundry appliance center of the world."

What to See and Do

Fred Maytag Park. *301 S 11th Ave W, Newton (50208). Phone 641/792-1470.* Donated by the founder of the Maytag Company. Tennis, picnicking, playground, amphitheater, log cabin, concession. Pool and water slide (June-Aug, daily; fee). Park (daily). **FREE**

Jasper County Historical Museum. *1700 S 15th Ave W, Newton (50208). Phone 641/792-9118.* Local historical displays include bas-relief sculpture of the natural history of the county, Victorian home, schoolroom,

chapel, tool and farm equipment collections, sound film of early county scenes. Also the Maytag historical display of washing machines. (May-Sept, afternoons) **$**

Trainland, USA. *3135 Hwy 117 N, Colfax (50054). 12 miles W via I-80, then 2 1/2 miles N on Hwy 117. Phone 515/674-3813.* Toy train museum exhibits depict development of the railroad across the United States in three eras: frontier, steam, and diesel; original railroad memorabilia and toy trains dating from 1916 to the present. (Memorial Day-Labor Day: daily; Labor Day-late Oct: by appoinment) **$$**

Limited-Service Hotels

★ ★ **BEST WESTERN NEWTON INN.** *I-80 and Hwy 14, Newton (50208). Phone 641/792-4200; toll-free 800/373-6350; fax 641/792-0108. www.bestwestern.com.* 118 rooms, 2 story. Pets accepted, some restrictions. Complimentary full breakfast. Check-out noon. Restaurant, bar. Fitness room. Indoor pool, whirlpool. **$**

★ **SUPER 8.** *1635 S 12th Ave W, Newton (50208). Phone 641/792-8868; toll-free 800/800-8000; fax 641/792-8868. www.super8.com.* 43 rooms, 2 story. Complimentary continental breakfast. Check-out 11 am. **$**

Full-Service Inn

★ ★ ★ **LA CORSETTE MAISON INN.** *629 1st Ave E (Hwy 6), Newton (50208). Phone 641/792-6833. www.lacorsette.com.* This historic 1909 mission-style mansion is beautifully decorated with stained glass and oak. Guest suites have French furnishings and a cozy comfort to them. Guests will find the wood-burning fireplaces peaceful and relaxing. A full complimentary breakfast is also served. 9 rooms, 2 story. Complimentary full breakfast. Check-in 4-6 pm, check-out 11:30 am. Restaurant. **$$**

Restaurant

★ ★ ★ **LA CORSETTE MAISON INN.** *629 1st Ave E (Hwy 6), Newton (50208). Phone 641/792-6833. www.lacorsette.com.* Located inside La Corsette Maison Inn, guests are served by tuxedoed waiters and entertained with music from the baby grand piano. American, French menu. Lunch, dinner. Closed Thanksgiving, Dec 25. Three sets of floral patterned

leaded glass French doors lead to the enclosed, mosaic-tiled atrium. Reservations recommended. **$$$**
🄳

Okoboji (A-2)

See also Estherville, Spencer, Spirit Lake

Founded 1855
Population 775
Elevation 1,450 ft
Area Code 712
Zip 51355
Information Tourism, 243 W Broadway, PO Box 215; phone 712/332-2209 or toll-free 800/270-2574
Web Site www.vacationokoboji.com

Lake Okoboji and the surrounding area are among the most popular resort areas in Iowa.

What to See and Do

Arnolds Park Amusement Park. *37 Lake St, Arnolds Park (51331).* Phone 712/332-2183. Century-old amusement park with classic old rides and newer favorites, plus entertainment and games. (Mid-June-mid-Aug: daily; May-mid-June and late Aug: weekends; hours vary)

Boji Bay. *Jct Hwys 71 and 86, Okoboji. N of town.* Family water park features water slides, wave pool, tube rides, sand volleyball courts, arcades, and games. Concessions. (Mid June-Labor Day)

Gardner Cabin. *94 Monument Dr, Arnolds Park (51331). 3 miles SW on Hwy 71, one block W of Arnolds Park Amusement Park.* Phone 712/332-7248. (1856) Restored; period furnishings; displays on pioneer life and the history of the region. (Memorial Day-Labor Day) **FREE**

Gull Point State Park. *1500 Harpen St, Wahpeton (51351). Approximately 6 miles SW off Hwy 71.* Phone 712/337-3211. On 165 acres and on West Okoboji Lake. Swimming, fishing, boating, snowmobiling. Hiking trails. Picnicking, lodge. Camping (electricity, dump station).

Higgins Museum. *1507 Sanborn Ave, Okoboji (51355).* Phone 712/332-5859. Displays notes and artifacts of the National Banks. (Memorial Day-Labor Day: Tues-Sun; May and Sept: weekends) **FREE**

Okoboji Queen II. *37 Lake St, Arnolds Park (51331). Docks at Arnolds Park Amusement Park (see).* Phone 712/332-5159. 1 1/4-hour steamship cruises on West Okoboji Lake. Schedule varies; call ahead. (Several cruises daily in summer) **$$$**

Special Event

Okoboji Summer Theater. *Okoboji. 1 mile N on Hwy 71.* Phone 712/332-7773. New play each week; operated by Stephens College of Columbia, Missouri. Performances Tues-Sun. Also children's theater. Mid-June-mid-Aug.

Limited-Service Hotel

★ ★ **INN AT OKOBOJI.** *3301 Lakeshore Dr, Okoboji (51355).* Phone 712/332-2113; fax 712/332-2714. www.theinnatokoboji.com. An inviting place for rest and relaxation, this inn is located on Lake Okoboji. It has two pools, a golf course, and a recreation area for kids. Guests can enjoy live entertainment, a café, and much more. 152 rooms, 2 story. Closed Oct-Apr. Check-out noon. Restaurant, bar. Children's activity center. Indoor pool, outdoor pool. Golf. Tennis. **$**
🛏️ 🎿 🏊

Full-Service Resort

★ ★ ★ **ARROWWOOD RESORT AND CONFERENCE CENTER BY CLUBHOUSE.** *1405 Hwy 71 N, Okoboji (51355).* Phone 712/332-2161; fax 712/332-7727. This spacious resort and conference center provides guests with a relaxed environment and a host of activities to choose from. Guests can enjoy tennis, swimming, or simply taking in the beautiful scenery. 99 rooms, 2 story. Pets accepted, some restrictions. Check-out 11 am. Restaurant, bar. Fitness room. Two outdoor pools, whirlpool. Golf. Tennis. **$**
🐾 🎿 🛏️ 🏊

Onawa (C-1)

Population 2,936
Elevation 1,052 ft
Area Code 712
Zip 51040
Information Chamber of Commerce, 1009 Iowa Ave; phone 712/423-1801
Web Site www.onawa.com

What to See and Do

Lewis and Clark State Park. *21914 Park Loop, Onawa (51040). 3 miles NW via Hwy 175, 324. Phone 712/423-2829.* Park of 176 acres on 250-acre lake. Swimming; fishing; boating (ramp). Hiking trails. Snowmobiling. Picnicking. Replica of Lewis and Clark keelboat *Discovery.* Camping (electricity, dump station). Standard hours, fees.

Limited-Service Hotel

★ **SUPER 8.** *22868 Filbert Ave, Onawa (51040). Phone 712/423-2101; toll-free 800/800-8000; fax 712/423-3480. www.super8.com.* 80 rooms. Pets accepted, some restrictions; fee. Check-out 11 am. **$**
🐾

Osceola (D-3)

See also Chariton

Settled 1850
Population 4,164
Elevation 1,139 ft
Area Code 641
Zip 50213
Information Chamber of Commerce, 100 S Fillmore St, PO Box 1; phone 641/342-4200

The seat of Clarke County is named for a Seminole warrior; a 30-foot figure of Osceola, carved from a cedar tree trunk, stands on the west side of the city. The town was settled by pioneers from Indiana and Ohio.

What to See and Do

Nine Eagles State Park. *County Rd J-66 and Hwy 69, Davis City (50065). 29 miles S on Hwy 69, then 6 miles SE on county road. Phone 641/442-2855.* Timbered 1,119-acre park with 67-acre lake. Swimming, supervised beach; fishing; electric boating (ramps, rentals). Hiking. Snowmobiling. Picnicking. Camping (electricity, dump station). Standard hours, fees.

Oskaloosa (D-4)

See also Ottumwa, Pella

Settled 1843
Population 10,632
Elevation 845 ft
Area Code 641

Zip 52577
Information Chamber of Commerce & Development Group, 124 N Market St; phone 641/672-2591
Web Site www.oacdg.org

Native American tribes lived here when the site was picked for the county seat, and the name of a Native American maiden ("last of the beautiful") was chosen as the name of the new community. Oskaloosa has a thriving retail trade and is the home of several manufacturers. It is also a center of production of corn, hay, hogs, cattle, and soybeans.

What to See and Do

Lake Keomah State Park. *Oskaloosa. 5 miles E off Hwy 92. Phone 641/673-6975.* More than 370 acres with a 84-acre lake. Swimming, beach; fishing; electric boating (ramps, rentals). Hiking trails. Snowmobiling. Picnicking, lodge. Camping (electricity, dump station).

Nelson Pioneer Farm Museum. *2294 Oxford Ave, Oskaloosa (52577). 2 miles NE of Penn College on Glendale Rd. Phone 641/672-2989.* Family farm of 1800s includes house, barn, one-room schoolhouse, log cabin, quilt collection, Friends Meeting House; post office and country store (1900); museum with historical exhibits; mule cemetery. (Mid-May-mid-Oct, Tues-Sat) **$$**

Special Events

Art on the Square. *Downtown, Oskaloosa. Phone 641/672-2591.* Arts and crafts demonstrations and workshops; children's activities. Second Sat in June.

Southern Iowa Fair. *700 N I St, Oskaloosa (52577). Phone 641/673-7004.* Classic county fair. Late July.

Limited-Service Hotel

★ **SUPER 8.** *306 S 17th St, Oskaloosa (52577). Phone 641/673-8481; toll-free 800/800-8000; fax 641/673-8481. www.super8.com.* 51 rooms, 2 story. Check-out 11 am. **$**

Ottumwa (D-4)

See also Fairfield, Oskaloosa

Settled 1843
Population 24,488
Elevation 650 ft
Area Code 641

Zip 52501
Information Ottumwa Area Convention & Visitors Bureau, 217 E Main St; phone 641/682-3465
Web Site www.ottumwa.com/cvb/index.html

A major Iowa trade center, Ottumwa is an industrial and agricultural city. The city was born in a land rush as settlers staked out this site on both sides of the Des Moines River. The name Ottumwa comes from a Native American word meaning "swift rapids" and later "perseverance." A historical marker east of town marks the site of the 1842 Indian Council, which resulted in the purchase of much of Iowa from the Sac and Fox.

What to See and Do

Beach Ottumwa. *101 Church St, Ottumwa (52501). Phone 641/682-7873. www.beachottumwa.com.* Water recreation park featuring 22,000-square-feet wave pool, 340-foot body slide, 200-foot speed slide, and 4-acre lagoon with kayak and paddleboats. Children's activity pool. Sand volleyball courts. Concessions. Some indoor recreational facilities operate year-round. **$$$**

John Deere Ottumwa Works. *928 E Vine St, Ottumwa (52501). Phone 641/683-2493 (call one day in advance).* Hay, forage implements; 90-minute guided tour (Mon-Fri; no tours the last week in July-early Aug, Dec 25-Jan). Over 12 years only; no sandals or tennis shoes. **FREE**

Lake Wapello State Park. *15248 Campground Rd, Drakesville (52552). 16 miles S on Hwy 63, then 10 miles W on Hwy 273. Phone 641/722-3371.* A 1,168-acre park with 289-acre lake. Swimming beach; fishing; boating (ramp). Hiking trails. Snowmobiling. Picnicking. Camping (electricity, dump station), cabins. Standard hours, fees.

Ottumwa Park. *105 E 3rd St, Ottumwa (52501). At junction Hwy 34, 63. Phone 641/682-1307.* A 365-acre recreation area in the center of the city includes camping (fee), fishing, tennis, volleyball, basketball courts, baseball diamond, horseshoes, bocce. (Apr-mid-Oct, daily)

Special Events

Octoberfest. *Ottumwa (52501). Phone 641/682-3465.* Downtown. Parade. Beer tent. Nightly entertainment. Late Sept-early Oct.

Ottumwa Pro Balloon Races. *Ottumwa Park, 105 E 3rd St, Ottumwa (52501). Phone 641/682-3465.* Balloon flights, races; concessions, fireworks. Last weekend in June.

Limited-Service Hotel

★ **HEARTLAND INN OTTUMWA.** *125 W Joseph Ave, Ottumwa (52501). Phone 641/682-8526; toll-free 800/334-3277; fax 641/682-7124. www.heartlandinns.com.* 85 rooms. Pets accepted, some restrictions; fee. Complimentary continental breakfast. Check-in 3 pm, check-out noon. High-speed Internet access. Indoor pool, whirlpool. Business center. **$**
⬛ ⬛ ⬛ ⬛

Restaurant

★ **FISHERMAN'S BAY.** *221 N Wapello St, Ottumwa (52501). Phone 641/682-6325.* Seafood menu. Lunch, dinner. Closed Thanksgiving, Dec 25. Bar. Children's menu. Casual attire. **$$**

Pella (C-4)

See also Oskaloosa

Settled 1847
Population 9,270
Elevation 878 ft
Area Code 641
Zip 50219
Information Chamber of Commerce, 518 Franklin St; phone 641/628-2626 or toll-free 888/746-3882
Web Site www.pella.org

Dutch refugees from religious intolerance first settled Pella, and the town retains many Dutch customs. Dutch influence can be seen in the architectural design of the business district and in the many tulip gardens in the area. Pella was the boyhood home of Wyatt Earp. It is the headquarters of the Pella Corporation, a major manufacturer of prefabricated windows.

What to See and Do

Central College. *812 University St, Pella (50219). Phone 641/628-9000.* (1853) (1,700 students) Liberal arts. Mills Gallery with changing exhibits. Tours.

Klokkenspel at Franklin Place. *Franklin St, Pella. 1/2 block E of town square.* A 147-bell carillon in the

Franklin Place Arch with figurines representing Pella's early history, town founders, Wyatt Earp, and others; Sinterklaas and his faithful companion, Black Piet, during the Christmas season. Courtyard on south side of arch has scenes of Holland in Dutch tiles. Concerts (five times daily). **FREE**

⭐ **Pella Historical Village Museum.** *507 Franklin St, Pella (50219). Phone 641/628-4311.* Restoration project of 21 buildings housing exhibits and antiques; working grinding windmill, pottery and blacksmith shops, pioneer log cabin, Wyatt Earp Boyhood Home, Heritage Hall, Dutch museum and bakery; gristmill in garden. (Apr-Dec: Mon-Sat; rest of year: Mon-Fri; closed holidays) **$$$**

Red Rock Lake. *1105 Hwy 215, Knoxville (50138). 4 1/2 miles SW. Phone 641/828-7522.* A 19,000-acre lake formed by Army Corps of Engineers dam impounding the Des Moines River. Swimming, boating, fishing; picnicking. Approximately 400 developed campsites (mid-Apr-mid-Oct; fee).

Scholte House. *728 Washington, Pella (50219). Phone 641/628-3684.* Oldest permanent dwelling in Pella built by town founder H. P. Scholte; many original furnishings and possessions; gardens with more than 25,000 tulips. (Mon-Sat afternoons; also by appointment; closed Jan-Feb, Easter, Dec 25) **$$**

Special Event

Tulip Time Festival. *507 Franklin, Pella (50219). Phone 641/628-4311.* Citizens dress in Dutch costumes; scrubbing the streets is a colorful and traditional feature; Dutch dancers; stage performances, parades. Early May.

Pocahontas (B-2)

See also Humboldt, Storm Lake

Population 2,085
Elevation 1,227 ft
Area Code 712
Zip 50574
Information Chamber of Commerce, PO Box 125; phone 712/335-3864
Web Site www.pocahontasiowa.com

Named in honor of the famous daughter of Powhatan, this town, in pheasant-hunting country, is also the seat of Pocahontas County.

Limited-Service Hotel

★ **CHIEF MOTEL.** *801 W Elm Ave, Pocahontas (50574). Phone 712/335-3395.* 34 rooms, 2 story. Check-out 11 am. **$**
🅳

Red Oak (D-2)

See also Shenandoah

Population 6,264
Elevation 1,077 ft
Area Code 712
Zip 51566
Information Chamber of Commerce, 405 Reed St; phone 712/623-4821
Web Site www.redoakiowa.com

What to See and Do

Viking Lake State Park. *2780 Viking Lake Rd, Stanton (51573). 12 miles E off Hwy 34. Phone 712/829-2235.* More than 950 acres on a 137-acre lake. Swimming, fishing, boating (ramp, rentals); hiking trail, snowmobiling, picnicking, camping (electricity, dump station). Standard hours, fees.

Limited-Service Hotel

★ **RED COACH INN.** *1200 Senate Ave, Red Oak (51566). Phone 712/623-4864; toll-free 800/544-6002; fax 712/623-2389.* 74 rooms, 2 story. Check-out noon. Bar. Outdoor pool. **$**
🏊

Shenandoah (D-2)

See also Clarinda, Red Oak

Founded 1870
Population 5,572
Elevation 981 ft
Area Code 712
Zip 51601
Information Chamber and Industry Association, 301 S Maple, PO Box 38; phone 712/246-3455

Mormons settled here, moving in from Manti (Fisher's Grove). Other early settlers fought with General Sheridan in the Shenandoah Valley of Virginia and brought the name back with them. The town is now the home of three large seed and nursery companies, a truck transmissions plant, and a windows and doors plant.

Limited-Service Hotel

★ ★ **COUNTRY INN.** *1503 Sheridan Ave, Shenandoah (51601). Phone 712/246-1550; fax 712/246-4773.* 65 rooms, 2 story. Pets accepted, some restrictions. Check-out 11 am. Restaurant, bar. Airport transportation available. **$**

🅿 ➦

Sioux City (B-1)

See also Le Mars, South Sioux City, Vermillion

Settled 1854
Population 80,505
Elevation 1,117 ft
Area Code 712
Information Sioux City Convention Center/Tourism Bureau, 801 4th St, PO Box 3183, 51102; phone 712/279-4800 or toll-free 800/593-2228
Web Site www.siouxcitytourismconvention.com

At the heart of a tri-state region bordered by the Sioux and Missouri rivers, Sioux City has historically been a hub for shipping, transportation, and agriculture. The Lewis and Clark expedition followed the Missouri River; the only fatality of that historic march is commemorated here with the Sergeant Floyd Monument, the first registered historic landmark in the United States.

Today, the Missouri River is important to the city from a recreational standpoint. A developed riverfront with parks, a dance pavilion, and a riverboat casino greet visitors. Sioux City has also grown to be a cultural and historical destination with many theaters, parks, an art center, nature center, historical attractions, and festivals and events throughout the year.

What to See and Do

Argosy **Casino.** *100 Larsen Park Rd, Sioux City (51103). Phone toll-free 800/424-0080.* Tri-level riverboat casino. (May-Oct, daily)

Morningside College. *1501 Morningside Ave, Sioux City (51106). Phone 712/274-5000. www.morningside.edu.* (1894) (1,400 students) Liberal arts. The Fine Arts Building contains a lobby art gallery. Tours.

Sergeant Floyd Monument. *Glenn Ave and Hwy 75, Sioux City (51106). On E bank of Missouri River.* First registered national historic landmark in the United States. The 100-foot obelisk marks the burial place of Sergeant Charles Floyd, the only casualty of the Lewis and Clark expedition.

Sergeant Floyd Welcome Center and Museum. *1000 S Larson Park Rd, Sioux City (51103). Exit 149 off I-29, Hamilton Blvd to S Larsen Park Rd. Phone 712/279-0198.* Former Missouri River inspection ship now houses a museum, information center, and gift shop. (Daily) **FREE**

Sioux City Art Center. *225 Nebraska St, Sioux City (51103). Phone 712/279-6272.* Contemporary traveling exhibits and permanent collection. Three-story glass atrium. Special programs. (Tues-Sat, Sun afternoon; closed holidays) **FREE**

Sioux City Public Museum. *2901 Jackson, Sioux City (51103). Phone 712/279-6174.* Exhibits show Sioux City history and life in pioneer days; geological, archaeological, and Native American materials. Located in a Romanesque 23-room mansion. Museum store. (Tues-Sun; holidays) **FREE**

Stone State Park. *4800 Sioux River Rd, Sioux City (51103). I-29 exit 151. Phone 712/255-4698.* On 1,069 acres. The park overlooks the Missouri and Big Sioux river valleys; view of three states from Dakota Point Lookout near Big Sioux River. Fishing; bridle and hiking trails, snowmobiling, picnicking, camping. Standard hours, fees. Ten-acre **Dorothy Pecant Nature Center** (Tues-Sun; closed holidays).

Trinity Heights. *33rd and Floyd Blvd, Sioux City (51103). Phone 712/239-8670.* A 30-foot stainless steel statue of the Immaculate Heart of Mary, Queen of Peace. Life-size carving of the Last Supper. Outdoor cathedral with a 33-foot statue of Christ. (Daily) **FREE**

Woodbury County Courthouse. *620 Douglas St, Sioux City (51104). Between 7th and Douglas sts. Phone 712/279-6624.* (1916-1918) This courthouse was the largest structure ever completed in the architectural style of Chicago's Prairie School. Designed by Purcell and Elmslie, long-time associates of Louis Sullivan, the city-block-long building is constructed of Roman brick, ornamented with massive pieces of Sullivanesque terra-cotta, stained glass, and relief sculpture by Alfonso Ianelli, who also worked with Frank Lloyd Wright. Both the exterior and highly detailed interior are in near-pristine condition; courtrooms still contain original architect-designed furniture, and lighting fixtures. (Mon-Fri)

Special Events

River-Cade Festival. *1201 Council Oak Dr, Sioux City (51103). Phone 712/277-4226.* Features fireworks, antique show, entertainment, midway, baseball, bowling, "fun run." Mid-July.

Saturday in the Park. *Granview Park, Sioux City. Phone 712/277-2575.* Day-long music festival. Early July.

Limited-Service Hotels

★ **BEST WESTERN CITY CENTRE.** *130 Nebraska St, Sioux City (51101). Phone 712/277-1550; toll-free 800/780-7234; fax 712/277-1120. www.bestwestern.com.* 114 rooms, 2 story. Pets accepted, some restrictions; fee. Check-out noon. Bar. Outdoor pool. Airport transportation available. **$**

★ ★ **SIOUX CITY PLAZA HOTEL.** *707 4th St, Sioux City (51101). Phone 712/277-4101; toll-free 800/593-0555; fax 712/277-3168.* Conveniently located downtown on the river, this hotel will happily accommodate both corporate and leisure travelers. A heated indoor pool, more than 12,000 square feet of meeting space, and easy access to shopping and entertainment make this hotel popular. 193 rooms, 12 story. Pets accepted, some restrictions; fee. Check-out noon. Restaurant, bar. Fitness room. Indoor pool. Airport transportation available. **$**

★ **SUPER 8.** *4307 Stone Ave, Sioux City (51106). Phone 712/274-1520; toll-free 800/800-8000; fax 712/274-1820. www.super8.com.* 60 rooms, 2 story. Pets accepted, some restrictions; fee. Check-out 11 am. **$**

Specialty Lodging

The following lodging establishment is approved by Mobil Travel Guide, but due to its unique and individualized nature has not been given a traditional Mobil Star rating. Included in this listing you may find bed-and-breakfasts, limited-service inns, guest ranches, and other unique hotel properties.

THE INNS OF ROSE HILL. *1525 Douglass St, Sioux City (51105). Phone 712/277-1386. www.innsof rosehill.com.* Featuring luxury private rooms and amenities in two restored English mansions in the Rose Hill Historic District. 11 rooms, 3 story. **$$**

Restaurants

★ **GREEN GABLES.** *1800 Pierce St, Sioux City (51105). Phone 712/258-4246.* Steak menu. Lunch, dinner, late-night. Closed Dec 25. Children's menu. **$$**

★ **HUNAN PALACE.** *4280 Sergeant Rd, Sioux City (51106). Phone 712/274-2336.* Chinese menu. Lunch, dinner. Bar. **$**

★ ★ **MINERVA'S RESTAURANT & BAR.** *2901 Hamilton Blvd, Sioux City (51104). Phone 712/252-0994.* This comfortable, family-style establishment features steaks and seafood. American menu. Lunch, dinner. **$**

★ ★ ★ **THE VICTORIAN OPERA COMPANY.** *1021 4th St, Sioux City (51104). Phone 712/255-4821.* Known for interesting sandwiches and desserts. American menu. Lunch. Closed Sun-Mon. **$**

Spencer (A-2)

See also Emmetsburg, Okoboji, Spirit Lake

Founded 1859
Population 11,066
Elevation 1,321 ft
Area Code 712
Zip 51301
Information Chamber of Commerce, 122 W 5th St, PO Box 7937; phone 712/262-5680
Web Site www.spenceriowachamber.org

In 1859, George E. Spencer gave his name to this city. In 1878, the first railroad was built through the black, fertile prairie, and in less than a year the settlement, known as Spencer, grew from 300 to a bustling town of 1,000. Its growth has continued, and due to its location in the middle of a large agricultural area, the town is now a prosperous business center serving surrounding farm communities.

What to See and Do

East Leach Park Campground. *305 4th St SE, Spencer (51301). Phone 712/264-7265.* Campground with tent and trailer sites (dump station); aquatic center, fishing; playground. Campground (mid-Apr-mid-Oct, daily). **$$$**

Gull Point State Park. *1500 Harpen St, Milford, Spencer (51351). Phone 712/337-3211.* The park has 160 wooded acres overlooking the scenic Little Sioux River valley. Hiking, picnicking.

Wanata State Park. *16 miles S on Hwy 71, then 10 miles W on Hwy 10. Phone 712/337-3211.* This Park's 160 wooded acres overlook the scenic Little Sioux River Valley. Hiking. Picnicking.

Special Events

Clay County Fair. *Fairgrounds, 1404 W 4th Ave, Spencer (51301). Phone 712/262-4740. www.claycountyfair.com.* Headliners like Kenny Chesney, Clay Aiken, and The Righteous Brothers have taken the stage to entertain crowds at the Clay County Fair in recent years. Daily attractions include an art barn, classic car show, vintage tractor display, and 4-H exhibits. Nine days in Sept. **$**

Flagfest Summer Festival. *122 W 5th St, Spencer (51301). Phone 712/262-5680.* Art festival, craft fair, parade, air show, dance, talent contest, entertainment. Early June.

Limited-Service Hotel

★ **DAYS INN.** *102 11th St SW Plz; jct Hwys 18 and 71 S, Spencer (51301). Phone 712/262-6100; toll-free 800/329-7466; fax 712/262-5742. www.daysinn.com.* 58 rooms, 2 story. Complimentary continental breakfast. Check-in noon, check-out 11 am. **$**

Spirit Lake (A-2)

See also Estherville, Okoboji, Spencer

Settled 1856
Population 3,871
Elevation 1,450 ft
Area Code 712
Zip 51360
Information Okoboji Tourism, 243 W Broadway, PO Box 215; phone 712/332-2209 or toll-free 800/270-2574
Web Site www.vacationokoboji.com

Spirit Lake serves tourists in the resort region and farming community flanking it. This area was a popular Native American meeting ground, visited by French explorers around 1700. The so-called Indian Massacre of Spirit Lake actually took place on the shores of three lakes—Spirit, East Okoboji, and West Okoboji. This is the scene of McKinlay Kantor's book *Spirit Lake.*

What to See and Do

Mini-Wakan State Park. *Off Hwy 276, on N shore of Spirit Lake. Phone 712/337-3211.* On 20 acres. Swimming, fishing, boating (ramp); snowmobiling, picnicking.

Spirit Lake. *Access area at Marble Beach, 3 miles NW on Hwy 276.* On 4,169 acres; largest glacier-carved lake in the state. Swimming, fishing, boating (ramp); camping (fee).

Storm Lake (B-2)

See also Cherokee, Pocahontas

Population 8,769
Elevation 1,435 ft
Area Code 712
Zip 50588
Information Chamber of Commerce, 119 W 6th St, PO Box 584; phone 712/732-3780 or toll-free 888/752-4692
Web Site www.stormlake.org

A college town—Buena Vista University is located here—and county seat on the north shore of Storm Lake, this community is also a meat and poultry center for the surrounding farms.

What to See and Do

Buena Vista County Historical Museum. *214 W 5th St, Storm Lake (50588). Annex at 214 W 5th St. Phone 712/732-4955.* Exhibits on early county history; changing displays; genealogy library. Changing exhibits and video presentations. (Mon-Fri afternoons, also by appointment) **DONATION**

Living Heritage Tree Museum. *Sunset Park, W Lakeshore Dr, Storm Lake (50588).* Seedlings and cuttings of more than 30 noteworthy trees, including the Charter Oak Tree and the NASA seedling sent into space with *Apollo 14.* Descriptive plaques; pamphlets available at Chamber of Commerce. Illuminated at night. (Daily) **FREE**

Storm Lake. *1001 Sunrise Rd, Storm Lake (50588). Phone 712/732-8023.* Fourth-largest natural lake in Iowa with water surface of more than 3,000 acres, Storm Lake offers swimming on the north, east, and south shores; fishing for bullhead, walleye, crappie, catfish, northern, and bass. Along the shore are 135 acres of state and municipal parks with boating (docks, ramps). Golf. Camping at Sunrise Campground (Apr-Oct, daily; hook-ups; fee).

Special Events

Santa's Castle. *5th and Erie sts, Storm Lake. Phone 712/732-3780.* More than 70 detailed animated characters, some dating to the early 1900s. Thanksgiving-Dec 25.

Star-Spangled Spectacular. *Storm Lake (50588). North side of lake. Phone 712/732-3780; toll-free 888/752-4692. www.stormlakeonline.com/spectacular.html.* More than 10,000 people visit the small town of Storm Lake each year for its annual Star-Spangled Spectacular. Fireworks, kiddie rides, and canoe races are at Chautauqua Park; musical entertainment, a kiddie parade, and an art fair are at Sunset Park. July 4.

Strawberry Point (B-5)

See also Dubuque

Population 1,357
Elevation 1,200 ft
Area Code 563
Zip 52076
Web Site www.strawberrypt.com

This town took its name from the wild strawberries that once grew nearby.

Strawberry Point Fun Fact

Strawberry Point is the home of the world's largest strawberry.

What to See and Do

Backbone State Park. *1347 129th St, Strawberry Point (52038). 4 miles SW on Hwy 410. Phone 563/924-2527.* Approximately 2,000 acres with limestone bluffs rising 140 feet from the Maquoketa River, scenic overlook, and 100-acre lake. Swimming, beach; fishing on stocked trout stream; boating (ramps, rentals). Hiking trails. Snowmobiling. Picnicking. Improved and primitive camping (electricity, dump station), cabins. Civilian Conservation Corps museum. Standard hours.

Brush Creek Canyon State Park. *6 miles W on Hwy 3, then 5 miles N on Hwy 187 to Arlington, then 2 miles N. Phone 563/425-4161.* More than 210 acres featuring a gorge with steep limestone walls that cut through 100 feet of bedrock; diversity of wildlife; state preserve. Hiking trails. Picnicking.

Wilder Memorial Museum. *123 W Mission St, Strawberry Point (52076). Phone 563/933-4615.* More than 900 dolls and eight dollhouses; many rooms furnished in late 1800s style; art glassware, porcelain; oil paintings; rare Queen Anne doll; model of Iowa farm; display of Norwegian rosemaling; spinning wheels; forty lighted hanging Victorian lamps. (Memorial Day-Labor Day, daily) **$$**

Walcott (C-6)

Web Site www.cityofwalcott.com

Restaurant

★ **GRAMMA'S KITCHEN.** *I-80, exit 284, Walcott (52773). Phone 563/284-5055; fax 563/284-6503. www.hoari.com/grammas.* American menu. Breakfast, lunch, dinner. Closed Jan 1, Thanksgiving, Dec 25. Valet parking. **$**

Washington (D-5)

See also Iowa City

Population 7,074
Elevation 762 ft
Area Code 319
Zip 52353
Information Chamber of Commerce, 212 N Iowa Ave; phone 319/653-3272
Web Site www.washingtoniowachamber.com

What to See and Do

Lake Darling State Park. *111 Lake Darling Rd, Washington (52540). 12 miles SW on Hwy 1, then 3 miles W on Hwy 78. Phone 319/694-2323.* A 1,387-acre park with a 299-acre lake. Swimming; fishing; boating (ramps, rentals). Hiking trail. Snowmobiling. Picnicking. Camping (electricity, dump station). Standard hours, fees.

Waterloo (B-4)

See also Cedar Falls, Waverly

Settled 1845
Population 66,467
Elevation 867 ft
Area Code 319
Information Convention & Visitors Bureau, 215 E 4th St, PO Box 1587, 50704; phone 319/233-8350 or toll-free 800/728-8431
Web Site www.waterloocvb.org

One of the largest tractor production facilities in the world is located here and contributes to the area's production of more than $1 billion worth of goods per year. On both banks of the wide Cedar River, Waterloo has established park and picnic areas, docks, and boating facilities along the shoreline.

What to See and Do

George Wyth Memorial State Park. *2659 Wyth Rd, Waterloo (50703). Between Cedar River and Hwy 20. Phone 319/232-5505.* The 1200-acre park includes several lakes. Swimming, fishing, boating (ramp); nature, hiking, and bicycle trails, snowmobiling, picnicking, camping (electricity, dump station). Standard hours.

Grout Museum of History and Science. *503 South St, Waterloo (50701). W Park Ave and South St, on Hwy 218. Phone 319/234-6357.* Permanent and changing exhibits on regional history and science; Discovery Zone offers many hands-on activities. Pioneer Hall, photo history area, industrial hall; genealogy library. Planetarium shows. (Tues-Sat; closed holidays). **$$**

John Deere Waterloo Works. *3500 E Donald St, Waterloo (50703). Phone 319/292-7668.* Guided 1 1/2-hour tours of farm tractor facility (Mon-Fri; closed holidays). Over 12 years only; low-heeled shoes advised; no open-toed sandals. Also tours of John Deere Component Works and John Deere Engine Works. Reservations required. **FREE**

Rensselaer Russell House Museum. *520 W 3rd St, Waterloo (50701). Phone 319/233-0262 (seasonal).* (1861) Guided tours of restored Victorian mansion; period furnishings. (Apr-Oct, Tues-Sat) **$$**

Waterloo Community Playhouse. *224 Commercial St, Waterloo (50701). Phone 319/235-0367.* Since 1916; offers seven productions yearly including comedies, dramas, mysteries, and classics. **$$$$**

Waterloo Museum of Art. *225 Commercial St, Waterloo (50701). Phone 319/291-4490.* Permanent collections include Haitian, American, and regional art; Grant Wood drawings. Changing exhibits. Gift shop offers works by Midwest artists. (Tues-Sun; closed Jan 1, Thanksgiving, Dec 25) **FREE**

Special Event

My Waterloo Days Festival. *215 E 4th St, Waterloo (50701). Phone 319/233-8431.* Citywide festival features air show, balloon rallies, parade, laser and fireworks show, music, renaissance fair, food. Four days beginning the Thurs after Memorial Day.

Limited-Service Hotels

★ ★ **BEST WESTERN STARLITE VILLAGE.** *214 Washington St, Waterloo (50701). Phone 319/235-0321; toll-free 800/903-0009; fax 319/235-6343. www.bestwestern.com.* 219 rooms, 11 story. Pets accepted; fee. Check-out noon. Restaurant, bar. Indoor pool. Airport transportation available. **$**

★ **HEARTLAND INN WATERLOO CROSSROADS.** *1809 LaPorte Rd, Waterloo (50702). Phone 319/235-4461; toll-free 800/334-3277; fax 319/235-0907. www.heartlandinns.com.* 113 rooms, 2 story. Pets accepted, some restrictions; fee. Complimentary continental breakfast. Check-in 3 pm, check-out noon. High-speed Internet access. Fitness room. Indoor pool. Business center. **$**

★ **HEARTLAND INN WATERLOO GREYHOUND PARK.** *3052 Marnie Ave, Waterloo (50701). Phone 319/232-7467; toll-free 800/334-3277; fax 319/232-0403. www.heartlandinns.com.* 54 rooms, 2 story. Pets accepted, some restrictions; fee. Complimentary continental breakfast. Check-in 3 pm, check-out noon. High-speed Internet access. Indoor pool, whirlpool. Business center. **$**

Waverly (B-4)

See also Cedar Falls, Charles City, Waterloo

Population 8,539
Elevation 919 ft
Area Code 319
Zip 50677
Information Chamber of Commerce, 118 W Bremer Ave, Suite A; phone 319/352-4526 or toll-free 800/251-0360
Web Site www.waverlyia.com

Astride the Cedar River, Waverly serves a rich farm area as a major retail and industrial center.

What to See and Do

***Iowa Star Clipper* Dinner Train.** *Departs from Waverly depot for afternoon or evening trips. Phone 319/352-5467.* Scenic round-trip, four-course dining excursions (three hours) through Cedar River Valley in 1950s-era dining cars. (Year-round, days vary) **$$$$**

Wartburg College. *100 Wartburg Blvd, Waverly (50677). 9th St NW and Bremer Ave. Phone 319/352-8200.* (1852) (1,450 students) Liberal arts. The Becker Hall of Science has a collection of New Guinea artifacts (daily; closed Sun in June-Aug, holidays). Also Schield International Museum (fee), a planetarium and art gallery. The Wartburg College Lageschulte Prairie is 3 miles NE. (Sept-May, Mon-Fri; closed holidays)

Webster City (B-3)

See also Fort Dodge

Settled 1850
Population 7,894
Area Code 515
Zip 50595
Information Area Association of Business & Industry, 628 2nd St, PO Box 310; phone 515/832-2564
Web Site www.webstercity.com

What to See and Do

Depot Museum Complex. *Ohio and Superior sts, Webster City (50595).* Log cabin, original courthouse, other historic buildings. (May-Sept, daily) **FREE**

Limited-Service Hotel

★ **BEST WESTERN NORSEMAN INN.** *I-35, exit 144, Williams (50271). Phone 515/854-2281; toll-free 800/780-7234; fax 515/854-2447. www.bestwestern.com.* 33 rooms. Pets accepted, some restrictions. Complimentary continental breakfast. Check-out noon. Bar. **$**
🐾

West Bend (A-3)

See also Algona, Emmetsburg

Founded 1880
Population 862
Elevation 1,203 ft
Area Code 515
Zip 50597
Information Chamber of Commerce, PO Box 366; phone 515/887-4721
Web Site www.westbendiowa.com

The large bend in the West Fork of the Des Moines River gives this town its name.

What to See and Do

Grotto of the Redemption. *300 N Broadway Ave, West Bend (50597). 2 blocks off Hwy 15 at north end of town. Phone 515/887-2371.* Begun in 1912 by Reverend P. M. Dobberstein, the grotto, which covers an entire city block, tells the story of the fall and redemption of man. Constructed of ornamental stones from many states and countries, the shrine is reputed to be the largest collection of shells, minerals, fossils, and other petrified material in the world. Illuminated at night. Camping (hookups, dump station). (Daily; guided tours May-Oct; also by appointment) **DONATION**

West Des Moines (C-3)

Web Site www.wdm-ia.com

Restaurants

★ ★ **CHINA PALACE.** *2800 University Ave, West Des Moines (50266). Phone 515/225-2800; fax 512/225-2800.* Chinese menu. Lunch, dinner. Closed holidays. Bar. **$$**

★ ★ **CHINA WOK.** *1960 Grand Ave, Suite 23, West Des Moines (50265). Phone 515/223-8408; fax 515/223-3839.* Chinese menu. Lunch, dinner. Bar. **$$**

★ **MAXIE'S.** *1311 Grand Ave, West Des Moines (50265). Phone 515/223-1463.* Steak menu. Lunch, dinner. Closed Sun, holidays. Bar. Children's menu. **$$**

★ **OHANA STEAKHOUSE.** *2900 University Ave, West Des Moines (50266). Phone 515/225-3325; fax 515/225-1135. www.ohanasteakhouse.com.* Japanese menu. Dinner. Closed holidays. Bar. Children's menu. **$$**

★ **WATERFRONT SEAFOOD MARKET.** *2900 University Ave, West Des Moines (50266). Phone 515/223-5106; fax 515/224-9665.* Seafood menu. Lunch, dinner. Bar. Children's menu. **$$**

West Union (A-5)

Population 2,490
Elevation 1,107 ft
Area Code 563
Zip 52175
Information Chamber of Commerce, 101 N Vine St, PO Box 71; phone 563/422-3070
Web Site www.westunion.com

What to See and Do

Montauk. *26223 Harding Rd, Clermont (52135). 9 miles NE on Hwy 18, near Clermont. Phone 563/423-7173.* (1874) Former home of William Larrabee, Iowa's 12th governor. Original furnishings; art objects; personal memorabilia; 40-acre grounds. Tours (late May-Oct: daily; early May: by appointment) **FREE**

Volga River State Recreation Area. *10225 Ivy Rd, West Union (52142). 6 miles S via Hwy 150. Phone 563/425-4161.* A 5,500-acre wooded area with lake; boating, fishing; hunting, hiking, horseback riding, cross-country skiing, snowmobiling, camping. Standard hours.

Limited-Service Hotel

★ **LILAC MOTEL.** *310 Hwy 150 N, West Union (52175). Phone 319/422-3861.* 27 rooms. Check-out 11 am. **$**
🄳

Williamsburg (C-5)

Web Site www.williamsburgiowa.org

Restaurant

★ ★ **COLONY VILLAGE.** *2224 U Ave, Williamsburg (52361). Phone 319/668-1223; fax 319/668-1595. www.colonyvillage.com.* American, German menu. Breakfast, lunch, dinner. Bar. Children's menu. **$$**

Winterset (C-3)

See also Indianola

Settled 1846
Population 4,196
Elevation 1,100 ft
Area Code 515
Zip 50273
Information Madison County Chamber of Commerce, 73 Jefferson St; phone 515/462-1185 or toll-free 800/298-6119
Web Site www.madisoncounty.com

What to See and Do

✪ **Covered Bridges.** *Phone 515/462-1185.* Six remain in Madison County; for leaflet, map, and information on guided tours, contact the Chamber of Commerce.

John Wayne Birthplace. *216 S 2nd St, Winterset (50273). Phone 515/462-1044.* House where the actor was born on May 26, 1907; front parlor and kitchen restored to the era when he lived here; other rooms contain memorabilia. Visitor center. (Daily; closed Jan 1, Thanksgiving, Dec 25) **$**

Madison County Museum and Complex. *815 S 2nd Ave, Winterset (50273). Phone 515/462-2134.* Twelve buildings and restored Bevington Mansion (1856). Fossils, Native American artifacts, memorabilia; old barn with live poultry display, log cabin school, log post office, 1881 church, general store, train depot. (May-Oct, daily; also by appointment) **$$**

Special Events

Covered Bridge Festival. *Phone 515/462-1185.* Late 19th-century crafts, entertainment; parade, bus tour of two covered bridges. Second full weekend in Oct.

Madison County Fair. *Fairgrounds. Phone 515/462-1295.* July.

National Skillet-Throwing Contest. *15 miles SW via Hwy 169 and CO G61 in Macksburg.* Contestants throw skillets at stuffed dummies. Second full weekend in June.

Kansas

Native Americans inhabited Kansas thousands of years before Spanish conquistador Francisco Vasquez de Coronado explored the territory in 1541. Though looking for gold and the fabled Land of Quivira, Coronado instead found what he called "the best country I have ever seen for producing all the products of Spain." Other early explorers of Kansas were partners Meriwether Lewis and William Clark. Army Captain Zebulon Pike also explored the area, continuing westward to discover what is now Pikes Peak in Colorado.

By the 1840s, traders and immigrants had established the Santa Fe and Chisholm Trails across the region. Kansas's pre-Civil War activities included the exploits of John Brown, who operated part of the Underground Railroad for slaves escaping through Kansas. Many clashes occurred between antislavery and proslavery forces as Kansas was being admitted to the Union. As railroads expanded westward, the era of cattle drives made such towns as Abilene, Hays, Wichita, and Dodge City centers of the legendary Old West, as did such men as Bat Masterson, Wyatt Earp, "Wild Bill" Hickock, and the Dalton Gang.

Eastern Kansas is green, fertile, and hilly, with woods, streams, and lakes. Western Kansas is a part of the Great Plains, once the grass-covered haunt of the buffalo. In 1874, Mennonite immigrants from Russia introduced their Turkey Red wheat seed to Kansas soil, helping to establish Kansas as the "breadbasket of the nation." Today agriculture has expanded to include a wide range of crops, cattle, and other livestock. Other leading industries include the manufacturing of airplanes and farm equipment, salt mining, and oil refining.

Population: 2,477,574
Area: 82,280 square miles
Elevation: 680-4,039 feet
Peak: Mount Sunflower (Wallace County)
Entered Union: January 29, 1861 (34th state)
Capital: Topeka
Motto: To The Stars Through Difficulties
Nickname: The Sunflower State
Flower: Native Sunflower
Bird: Western Meadowlark
Tree: Cottonwood
Fair: September in Hutchinson
Time Zone: Central and Mountain
Web Site: www.travelks.com
Fun Facts:
- A ball of twine in Cawker City measures more than 38 feet in circumference, weighs more than 16,750 pounds, and is still growing.
- At one time it was against the law to serve ice cream on cherry pie in Kansas.

Crappie, walleye, bass, and channel catfish abound in many lakes and streams to lure the fishing enthusiast. Deer, quail, pheasant, ducks, geese, and many other species of game attract the hunter.

When to Go/Climate

Expect to encounter typical Midwestern temperatures in Kansas—hot summers, with more humidity in the eastern part of the state; cold, sometimes harsh, winters; and a propensity for tornadoes, thunderstorms, and blizzards. Tornadoes are most likely from May-June; half the annual precipitation falls from May-August. Summer, despite the heat, is the most popular time to visit.

Calendar Highlights

FEBRUARY

International Pancake Race *(Liberal)*. Women compete simultaneously with women in Olney, England, running a 415-yard S-shaped course with a pancake in a skillet, flipping it en route.

MARCH

National Junior College Basketball Tournament *(Hutchinson)*. Sports Arena.

MAY

Wichita River Festival *(Wichita)*. Phone 316/267-2817. Includes twilight pop concert and fireworks; antique bathtub races; hotair balloon launch; athletic events; entertainment.

JUNE

Washburn Sunflower Music Festival *(Topeka)*. Phone 785/231-1010. International symphonic musicians perform nightly.

JULY

Indian Powwow *(Wichita)*. Phone 316/262-5221. Tribes gather from all over the country and Canada. Traditional dances; crafts; ethnic food.

AUGUST

Central Kansas Free Fair & PRCA Wild Bill Hickock Rodeo *(Abilene)*. Phone 785/263-4570.

National Baseball Congress World Series *(Wichita)*. Lawrence Stadium. Phone 316/267-3372. Amateur Series.

SEPTEMBER

Historic Fort Hays Days *(Hays)*. Phone 785/625-6812, 785/628-8202, or toll-free 800/569-4505. Two full days of living history including demonstrations of butter churning, tatting, ropemaking, rug weaving, whittling, and stonepost cutting.

Kansas State Fair *(Hutchinson)*. Fairgrounds. Phone 316/669-3600. Exhibits, carnival, entertainment, car racing, etc.

Renaissance Festival *(Kansas City)(Bonner Springs)*. Phone toll-free 800/373-0357. Seven weekends of festivities. Begins Labor Day weekend.

AVERAGE HIGH/LOW TEMPERATURES (° F)

Topeka

Jan 37/16	May 76/53	Sept 80/56
Feb 43/22	June 84/63	Oct 69/44
Mar 55/32	July 89/68	Nov 54/32
Apr 67/43	Aug 88/65	Dec 41/21

Wichita

Jan 40/19	May 77/54	Sept 81/59
Feb 46/24	June 87/65	Oct 71/47
Mar 57/34	July 93/70	Nov 55/34
Apr 68/45	Aug 91/68	Dec 43/23

Parks and Recreation

Water-related activities, hiking, riding, various other sports, picnicking and visitor centers, as well as camping, are available in many areas. Annual vehicle permit is $35; daily vehicle permit is $5.

There is camping at most areas (two-week maximum). Daily camping permit is $6.50; electricity, water, trailer utility hookup is $5-$8. Pets on hand-held leash or in cage only; no pets on bathing beaches. A camping guide is published by the Kansas Department of Wildlife and Parks, Public Information, 512 SE 25th Ave, Pratt, 67124-8174; phone 620/672-5911.

FISHING AND HUNTING

The state maintains more than 35 state fishing lakes and 48 wildlife management and public hunting areas.

Nonresident fishing license: annual $40.50; five-day $20.50; 24-hour $5.50. Nonresident hunting license: annual $70.50; 48-hour nonresident waterfowl license $25.50; Kansas migratory habitat stamp

$5.25; handling fee on all licenses $1. Hunters born on or after July 1, 1957, must have a hunter's education course certificate card in order to purchase a license.

For digests of hunting and fishing regulations, contact Kansas Department of Wildlife and Parks, Public Information, 512 SE 25th Ave, Pratt, 67124; phone 620/672-5911. The department also publishes hunting and fishing guides.

Driving Information

Safety belts are mandatory for all persons in the front seat of a vehicle. Children under the age of 5 must be in approved safety seats anywhere in a vehicle. Children ages 5-13 must wear safety belts anywhere in a vehicle. Phone toll-free 800/416-2522.

INTERSTATE HIGHWAY SYSTEM

The following alphabetical listing of Kansas towns in this book shows that these cities are within 10 miles of the indicated interstate highways. Check a highway map for the nearest exit.

Highway Number	Cities/Towns within 10 Miles
Interstate 35	El Dorado, Emporia, Kansas City, Ottawa, Witchita.
Interstate 70	Abilene, Colby, Goodland, Hays, Junction City, Kansas City, Lawrence, Manhattan, Oakley, Russell, Salina, Topeka, WaKeeney.
Interstate 135	Lindsborg, McPherson, Newton, Salina, Wichita.

Additional Visitor Information

The Kansas Department of Commerce and Housing, Travel and Tourism Development Division, 700 SW Harrison St, Suite 1300, Topeka 66603-3712, phone 785/296-2009 or toll-free 800/252-6727, distributes the *Kansas Attractions Guide*, Kansas transportation map, and calendar of events.

Visitors to Kansas will find welcome centers on Interstate 70W, just west of Goodland; at the Kansas City exit on Interstate 70E (milepost 415); at the southern entrance into Kansas on the turnpike in Belle Plaine; at 229 E Pancake Boulevard in Liberal; at 231 East Wall Street in Fort Scott; at the Civic Center Depot in Abilene; at the Santa Fe Depot/Chamber in Atchison; at the Brown Mansion on Highway 169 in Coffeeville; on Highway 81 near North Belleville; and at the State Capitol in Topeka. Visitors will find information and brochures helpful in planning stops at points of interest.

ACROSS THE PRAIRIE LANDSCAPE

This loop trail passes through prairie landscapes and across the Kansas of past, present, and future. Begin in Witchita, the state's largest city and a prosperous oil and agricultural center. Three of the city's best attractions are found in the Arthur Sim Memorial Park, along a bend of the Arkansas River. The city's historic role as a "cow capital" along the Chisholm Trail is preserved at the Old Cowtown Museum, a historic village with 40 buildings from the city's early boom years in the 1870s. Nearby is the Witchita Art Museum, with a fine collection of American Impressionists and a grand outdoor sculpture garden. Gardeners will enjoy Botanica, The Witchita Garden, with a number of theme gardens.

Drive northeast on Interstate 35 to Cassoday, home to several good antique stores, and join Highway 177 northbound. Known as the Flint Hills Scenic Byway, this route passes through a rugged landscape of rolling hills, mesas, and virgin prairie. At the town of Cottonwood Falls, stop to visit the Chase County Courthouse, the oldest in Kansas. The building was constructed from local limestone in a striking French Renaissance style.

Just north is the Tallgrass Prairie National Preserve, which protects 11,000 acres of native prairie grassland that is home to 40 species of grasses, 200 species of birds, 30 species of mammals, and up to 10 million insects per acre. A number of trails lead across the plains, which in spring are carpeted with wildflowers. The preserve's headquarters are located at the Z Bar Ranch, an imposing stone ranch house cum mansion from the 1880s.

Council Grove is one of Kansas's most historic towns; in fact, the entire settlement has been designated a National Historic Landmark. Council Grove was the last provisioning stop on the old Sante Fe Trail between the Missouri River and Sante Fe, and the town is filled with landmarks of the frontier West. The Council Oak marks the site of the signing of an 1825 peace treaty between the Osage and the United States. The nearby Post Office Oak served as a drop box for letters written by travelers along the Sante Fe Trail. The Last Chance Store and the Hays House Restaurant have both been in business since 1857—the latter is the oldest continuously operating restaurant west of the Mississippi.

Continue north on Highway 57 to Junction City, located at the confluence of the Republican and Smoky Hill rivers. The town owes its existence to Fort Riley, founded in 1853 to protect pioneers traveling along the Sante Fe and Oregon trails. The fort, just north of town along Highway 57, contains a number of historic sites, including the state's first territorial capital, an early home of General George Custer, and the US Cavalry Museum, which chronicles the history of the mounted horse soldier from the Revolutionary War to 1950.

Continue east on Interstate 70 to Abilene, famous as an Old West cow town and as the boyhood home of President Dwight D. Eisenhower. In addition to the frontier and presidential museums you would expect, Abilene offers a couple of unusual attractions, including dinner excursions in an antique train and the American Indian Art Center, which represents 90 artists from 30 Native American nations.

From Abilene, travel north on Highway 15 and north on Highway 106 to visit Rock City, where hiking trails wind through a curious wonderland of house-sized sandstone concretions scattered across a prairie meadow. It's easy to imagine these formations as a prehistoric town turned to stone!

Return to Highway 18, and head east to join Interstate 135 southbound. At McPherson, turn southwest on Highway 61 at exit 58. Hutchinson offers travelers two unusual attractions. The Dillon Nature Center comprises 100 acres of trail-linked prairie and ponds containing 150 plains animal species. The Kansas Cosmosphere and Space Center is one of the nation's foremost museums dedicated to the exploration of space. Displays include rockets and capsules from both the United States and Soviet space programs, plus spy planes, space equipment, and an IMAX Theater. Return to Wichita on Interstate 96. **(Approximately 350 miles)**

WILDLIFE ON THE PRAIRIE

East Central Kansas boasts beautiful tallgrass prairies, some of the few remaining in the United States. Take this drive in early spring, when the old grass is burned to make way for spring growth, or in early summer, when wildflowers are abundant. Head west from Topeka on Interstate 70 to Manhattan. Nearby, the Konza Prairie is a major site for prairie research, with hiking and wildlife-watching. Continue south on Highway 177 to the Tallgrass Prairie National Preserve near Strong Falls. Covered-wagon train trips are offered at El Dorado, northeast of Wichita on Highway 177. From Wichita, take Interstate 135 north to McPherson and visit the McPherson-Maxwell Game Preserve, with one of the state's largest bison herds, as well as elk, deer, and buffalo. Return to Interstate 70 at Salina, then head back east to your starting point. If possible, stop en route in Abilene to visit the Eisenhower Center, featuring the president's boyhood home, museum, and gravesite. **(Approximately 380 miles)**

Abilene (B-4)

See also Junction City, Salina

Founded 1858
Population 6,242
Elevation 1,153 ft
Area Code 785
Zip 67410
Information Convention & Visitors Bureau, 201 NW 2nd St, PO Box 146; phone 785/263-2231 or toll-free 800/569-5915
Web Site www.abileneks.com

Once famous as a Kansas "cow town," Abilene in 1867 was the terminal point of the Kansas Pacific (later Union Pacific) Railroad and the nearest railhead for the shipment of cattle brought north over the Chisholm Trail. The number of cattle shipped east from here between 1867 and 1871 has been estimated at more than a million, and often 500 cowboys were paid off at a time. City marshals Tom Smith and "Wild Bill" Hickock brought in law and order in the 1870s. Today, Abilene is a wheat center, perhaps best known as the boyhood home of Dwight D. Eisenhower.

What to See and Do

Abilene Smoky Valley Excursion Train. *200 S 5th, Abilene (67410). Phone 785/263-1077. www.asvrr.org.* One hundred-year-old wooden coach/diner makes trips through historic countryside. (Memorial Day-Labor Day, Tues-Sun) **$$$**

Dickinson County Historical Museum. *412 S Campbell St, Abilene (67410). Phone 785/263-2681.* Exhibits depict life in early pioneer days, the Native Americans and the buffalo; antique toys and household items used at the turn of the century; cowboys and cattle trails; Heritage Center, carousel, log cabin. Teaching tours for children by appointment. (Daily) Admission includes

Museum of Independent Telephony. *412 S Campbell St, Abilene (67410). Phone 785/263-2681.* More than a century of telephones from 1876 to present; insulators, cables, pay stations. Exhibits include an old switchboard and crank-type phones. (Daily)

★ **Eisenhower Center.** *200 SE 4th St, Abilene (67410). E of Hwy 15. Phone 785/263-4751.* This house, built in 1887, where Dwight D. Eisenhower and his five brothers were raised, was purchased by the family in 1898. Interior and most furnishings are original. The museum houses changing exhibits of mementos, souvenirs and gifts received during Dwight D. Eisenhower's career; murals in the lobby depict his life. Thirty-minute orientation film shown in visitor center. The library contains presidential papers. President and Mrs. Eisenhower are buried in the Meditation Chapel. (Daily; closed Jan 1, Thanksgiving, Dec 25) **$$**

Greyhound Hall of Fame. *407 S Buckeye St, Abilene (67410). Phone 785/263-3000.* Exhibits, twelve-minute film on history and heart of the sport. (Daily; closed Jan 1, Thanksgiving, Dec 25) **FREE**

Lebold Mansion. *106 N Vine, Abilene (67410). Phone 785/263-4356.* Restored Victorian mansion with period furnishings, built in 1880 by C. H. Lebold. Tours (Tues-Sun 10 am-4 pm) Call for special tours and group discounts. **$$**

Seelye Mansion and Museum. *1105 N Buckeye, Abilene (67410). Phone 785/263-1084. www.seelyemansion.com.* Twenty-five-room Georgian mansion listed on the National Register of Historic Places. Built in 1905 by A. B. Seelye, patent medicine entrepreneur. The museum depicts a turn-of-the-century medicine business. Tours (daily; closed Dec 25). **$$$**

Special Events

Central Kansas Free Fair & PRCA Wild Bill Hickock Rodeo. *619 N Rogers St, Abilene (67410). Phone 785/263-4570.* Early Aug.

Chisholm Trail Festival. *412 S Campbell St, Abilene (67410). Phone 785/263-2681.* First Sat in Oct.

Garden Tour. *Abilene. Phone 785/263-1884.* June.

National Greyhound Association Spring Meet. *, Abilene. Phone 785/263-4660. 1 1/2 miles W on Hwy 40 at the Greyhound Association.* Greyhound racing in the hometown of the National Greyhound Association. Last week of Apr and second week of Oct.

Limited-Service Hotel

★ **SUPER 8.** *2207 N Buckeye Ave, Abilene (67410). Phone 785/263-4545; toll-free 800/800-8000; fax 785/263-7448. www.super8.com.* 62 rooms, 3 story. Pets accepted; fee. Check-out 11 am. **$**

Restaurants

★ ★ **BROOKVILLE HOTEL DINING ROOM.** *105 E Lafayette, Abilene (67410). Phone 785/263-2244. www.brookvillehotel.com.* American menu. Lunch, dinner. Closed Mon. In historic frontier hostelry; period décor. **$$$**

★ ★ ★ **KIRBY HOUSE.** *205 NE 3rd St, Abilene (67410). Phone 785/263-7336; fax 785/263-1885. www.kirby-house.com.* Built as a home by banker Thomas Kirby in 1885, this Victorian-style restaurant has a friendly atmosphere popular with large groups and anyone celebrating a special occasion. The American menu is enjoyed in multiple, antique-filled dining rooms during lunch, dinner, and Sunday brunch. American menu. Lunch, dinner, Sun brunch. Closed Jan 1, Dec 25. Bar. Children's menu. **$$**

Arkansas City (D-4)

See also Winfield; also see Ponca City, OK

Founded 1870
Population 12,762
Elevation 1,120 ft
Area Code 620
Zip 67005
Information Chamber of Commerce, 106 S Summit, PO Box 795; phone 620/442-0230
Web Site www.arkcityks.org

Situated near the Oklahoma border, Arkansas City is home to meat packing, oil refining, and aircraft-related industries. Approximately 100,000 homesteaders started the run for the Cherokee Strip on September 16, 1893, from here. The run was a race held by the US government as a means to give away land for settlement in what was then the Oklahoma Territory.

What to See and Do

Chaplin Nature Center. *27814 27th Dr, Arkansas City (67005). 3 miles W on Hwy 166, then 2 miles N on gravel road (follow signs). Phone 620/442-4133.* More than 200 acres of woodland, prairie, and streams along the Arkansas River; visitor center, nature center, self-guided trails. (Daily; guided tours by appointment) **FREE**

Cherokee Strip Land Rush Museum. *31639 Hwy 77, Arkansas City (67005). Phone 620/442-6750.* Articles related to the Cherokee Strip Run; reference library on Run, Native Americans, genealogy. (Tues-Sat; closed holidays) **$$**

Special Events

Arkalalah Celebration. *Downtown, Arkansas City (67005). Phone 620/442-6077.* Last weekend in Oct.

Last Run Car Show. *Agri-Business Building, 712 W Washington, Arkansas City (67005). Phone 620/442-0230.* Fourth weekend in Sept.

PrairieFest. *Wilson Park, Arkansas City (67005). Phone 620/442-5895.* More than 80 juried artists display and sell their works. Entertainment, international foods. Early June.

Limited-Service Hotel

★ ★ **REGENCY COURT INN.** *3232 N Summit St, Arkansas City (67005). Phone 620/442-7700; toll-free 800/325-9151; fax 620/442-1218.* 87 rooms. Check-out 11 am. Restaurant, bar. Indoor pool, whirlpool. **$**
🏊

Atchison (B-6)

See also Hiawatha, Leavenworth; also see St. Joseph, MO

Founded 1854
Population 10,656
Elevation 810 ft
Area Code 913
Zip 66002
Information Atchison Area Chamber of Commerce, 200 S 10th St, PO Box 126; phone 913/367-2427 or toll-free 800/234-1854
Web Site www.atchisonkansas.net

Atchison grew up around a desirable landing site on the Missouri River—an important factor in its crowded history. Lewis and Clark camped here in 1804; so did Major Stephen Longstreet's Yellowstone Expedition in 1819; French explorers from the colony of Louisiana preceded both. In the 1850s and 1860s steamboat and wagon traffic to the West was bustling; mail coaches left daily on the 17-day round trip to Denver. A railroad from St. Joseph, Missouri, established in 1859 by means of an Atchison city bond issue, was the first direct rail connection eastward from a point this far west. Another Atchison bond issue the same year made the Atchison, Topeka, and Santa Fe Railroad possible, although the first lines were not opened until 1872. The town's position in the Missouri-Kansas border struggles of the 1850s caused it to be named for US Senator David Rice Atchison of Missouri (who, it is claimed, was president of the United States from noon, March 4 to noon, March 5, 1849). Today, Atchison is a manufacturing and wholesale center producing flour, feeds, alcohol, and steel castings. It is also the birthplace of aviatrix Amelia Earhart. A 1-acre "earthwork" portrait by crop artist Stan Herd pays tribute to this accomplished pilot.

What to See and Do

Amelia Earhart Birthplace Museum. *223 N Terrace St, Atchison (66002). Phone 913/367-4217. www.amelia earhartmuseum.org.* House built in 1861 by Judge Alfred Otis, Amelia Earhart's grandfather. Earhart was born here on July 24, 1897, and lived her early years here. The museum includes exhibits of her life and flying accomplishments. (Daily; closed holidays) **$**

Atchison County Historical Society Museum. *200 S 10th St, Atchison (66002). Phone 913/367-6238.* Amelia Earhart exhibit; World War I collection; gun collection; pictures, local historical items. (Daily) **$**

Atchison Trolley. *Santa Fe Depot, 200 S 10th St, Atchison (66002). Phone 913/367-2427.* One-hour tours of city history and visitor highlights. (May: Thurs-Sun; Aug-Oct: Fri-Sun; June-July: Wed-Sun) **$$**

Evah C. Cray Historical Home Museum. *805 N 5th St, Atchison (66002). Phone 913/367-3046.* Nineteenth-century period rooms and country store, children's display. (May-Oct: daily; Jan-Feb: Sat-Sun; rest of year: by appointment) Children only with adult. **$**

Independence Park. *Atchison. Near downtown.* Five-acre park with boat landing on Missouri River; Lewis and Clark Trail landmark. **FREE**

International Forest of Friendship. *274th and Price Blvd, Atchison (66002). 2 miles SW, just S of Warnock Lake. Phone 913/367-2427.* A bicentennial gift to the United States from the city and the Ninety Nines Inc, an international organization of women pilots. The forest includes trees from all 50 states and from 33 countries. A concrete walkway (wheelchair accessible) winds through the forest; embedded in the walkway are granite plaques honoring those people who have contributed to the advancement of aviation and the exploration of space; statue of Amelia Earhart; NASA astronaut memorial. (Daily) **FREE**

Jackson Park. *1500 S 6th St, Atchison (66002).* Covers 115 acres with iris-bordered drives; scenic view of the Missouri River valley from Guerrier Hill. Pavilion (fee), picnicking (May-Oct, daily) **FREE**

Warnock Lake Recreation Area. *274th and Prince Blvd, Atchison (66002). 2 miles SW.* Camping (fee), fishing, swimming, beach; picnicking. (Daily) **FREE**

Special Events

Amelia Earhart Festival. *200 S 10th St, Atchison (66002). Phone 913/367-2427.* Mid-July.

Antique Airplane Fly-In. *Amelia Earhart Airport, 16701 286th Rd, Atchison (66002). Phone 913/367-2427.* Memorial Day weekend.

Atchison County Fair. *Fairgrounds, 405 Main St, Atchison (66002). Phone 913/833-5450.* Mid-Aug.

Haunted Home Tours. *Santa Fe Depot, Atchison (66002). Phone 913/367-2427.* Halloween week.

Oktoberfest. *Main St, Atchison (66002). Phone 913/367-2427.* First weekend in Oct.

Limited-Service Hotel

★ **COMFORT INN.** *509 S 9th St, Atchison (66002). Phone 913/367-7666; toll-free 800/228-5150; fax 913/367-7566. www.comfortinn.com.* 45 rooms, 3 story. Complimentary continental breakfast. Check-out 11 am. Bar. **$**

Restaurant

★ **TIME OUT FAMILY RESTAURANT.** *337 S 10th St, Atchison (66002). Phone 913/367-3372.* American menu. Breakfast, lunch, dinner, late-night, brunch. Closed holidays. Children's menu. **$**

Belleville (A-4)

See also Concordia, Mankato

Population 2,517
Elevation 1,550 ft
Area Code 785
Zip 66935
Information Chamber of Commerce, 1819 L St; phone 785/527-2310 or toll-free 866/527-2355
Web Site www.bellevilleks.org

Belleville's Rocky Pond was used in early railroad days to provide water for steam engines and supply ice for refrigerated cars. Fishing, picnicking, and camping are allowed in Rocky Pond Park.

A Sandzen mural from WPA days hangs in the post office at 18th and L streets.

What to See and Do

Crossroads of Yesteryear Museum. *2726 Hwy 36, Belleville (66935). Phone 785/527-5971.* Log cabin (built in 1870), rural school, church (built in 1900), and museum on 5 acres. Exhibits feature artifacts of the county, the history of agriculture, and the Bertil Olson Tool Collection. (Mon-Fri, Sun; closed Thanksgiving, Dec 25) **FREE**

Pawnee Indian Village State Historical Site. *Hwy 266, Belleville. 13 miles W on Hwy 36, then 8 miles N on Hwy 266. Phone 785/361-2255.* Built on the site of a Pawnee village (circa 1820); excavated earthlodge floor; displays depicting Pawnee culture. (Wed-Sun; closed holidays) **FREE**

Special Event

North Central Kansas Free Fair. *Belleville. Phone 785/527-5544.* Features Midget Nationals car races. First weekend in Aug.

Limited-Service Hotel

★ **BEST WESTERN BEL VILLA MOTEL.** *215 W Hwy 36, Belleville (66935). Phone 785/527-2231; toll-free 800/780-7234; fax 785/527-2572. www.bestwestern.com.* 40 rooms. Pets accepted, some restrictions. Check-out 11 am. Outdoor pool. **$**

Beloit (B-4)

See also Concordia, Mankato

Population 4,066
Elevation 1,386 ft
Area Code 785
Zip 67420
Information Chamber of Commerce, 123 N Mill, PO Box 582; phone 785/738-2717
Web Site www.beloitks.org

What to See and Do

Glen Elder State Park. *Beloit. 12 miles W on Hwy 24. Phone 785/545-3345.* A 1,250-acre park on a 12,600-acre lake. An early Native American historical site. It was here that Margaret Hill McCarter wrote some of her well-loved tales of Kansas. Swimming beach; fishing; boating (ramp, marina). Picnicking. More than 300 primitive and improved campsites (dump station). Amphitheater. (Daily) **$$**

Chanute (D-6)

See also Iola, Parsons, Yates Center

Founded 1873
Population 9,488
Elevation 943 ft
Area Code 620
Zip 66720
Information Chamber of Commerce, 21 N Lincoln Ave, PO Box 747; phone 620/431-3350
Web Site www.chanute.org

What to See and Do

Chanute Art Gallery. *17 N Lincoln Ave, Chanute (66720). Phone 620/431-7807.* Houses permanent collection of more than 500 works. Changing exhibits. (Tues-Sat) **FREE**

Martin and Osa Johnson Safari Museum. *111 N Lincoln Ave, Chanute (66720). Located in a renovated Santa Fe train depot. Phone 620/431-2730.* Contains artifacts and photographs of the South Seas, Borneo, and African trips of photo-explorers Martin and Osa Johnson (she was born in Chanute); exhibits illustrating West African village life including ceremonial artifacts and musical instruments; ten-minute film shown upon request. Wildlife paintings and sketches, other art objects displayed in the Selsor Gallery. Stott Explorers Library houses expedition journals, monographs, and books on exploration. (Daily; closed holidays) **$$**

Special Events

Artist Alley and Fall Festival. *Main St, Chanute (66720). Phone 620/431-0056.* Includes parade, art booths. Fourth weekend in Sept.

Mexican Fiesta. *Siesta Grounds, Chanute. Phone 620/431-3350.* Celebration of Mexican independence from Spain. Second weekend in Sept.

Coffeyville (D-6)

See also Independence, Parsons

Founded 1869
Population 12,917
Elevation 736 ft
Area Code 620
Zip 67337
Information Chamber of Commerce, 807 Walnut, PO Box 457; phone 620/251-2550 or toll-free 800/626-3357
Web Site www.coffeyville.com

Named for Colonel James A. Coffey, who in 1869 built a house and trading post near the Verdigris River. With the coming of the railroad shortly after its settlement, Coffeyville followed the usual pattern of cow towns. The famous Dalton raid occurred here October 5, 1892, when the three Dalton brothers and two confederates attempted to rob two banks at once and fought a running battle with armed citizens. Several of the defenders were killed or wounded; of the gang, only Emmett Dalton survived.

The town prospered with the development of natural gas and oil fields in 1903. Today its chief industries are oil refineries, smelters, oil field equipment, lawn mowers, power transmissions, and foundries. Wendell Willkie, the Republican presidential candidate in 1940, lived and taught school here.

What to See and Do

Brown Mansion. *2019 Walnut St, Coffeyville (67337). Phone 620/251-0431.* (1904) Designed by proteges of Stanford White; original furniture, hand-painted canvas wall coverings; Tiffany chandelier in dining room. (June-Aug, Tues-Sun; hours vary rest of year; closed holidays) **$$**

Dalton Defenders Museum. *113 E 8th St, Coffeyville (67337). Phone 620/251-5944.* Dalton raid souvenirs; mementos of Wendell Willkie and Walter Johnson. (Daily) **$$**

Special Events

Dalton Defenders Day. *113 E 8th St, Coffeyville (67337). Phone toll-free 800/626-3357.* Commemorates the Dalton raid on Coffeyville. Sat closest to Oct 5.

Inter-State Fair and Rodeo. *Walter Johnson Park, Coffeyville (67337). Phone toll-free 800/626-3357.* Second full week in Aug.

Intertribal Powwow. *8th and Roosevelt, Coffeyville (67337). Phone 620/252-6819.* First weekend in Nov.

New Beginning Festival. *Downtown, Coffeyville (67337). Phone toll-free 800/626-3357.* Last weekend in Apr.

Limited-Service Hotel

★ **APPLE TREE INN.** *820 E 11th St, Coffeyville (67337). Phone 620/251-0002; fax 620/251-1615.* 64 rooms, 2 story. Pets accepted, some restrictions; fee. Complimentary continental breakfast. Check-out noon. Indoor pool, whirlpool. **$**

Colby (B-1)

See also Goodland, Oakley

Founded 1885
Population 5,396
Elevation 3,160 ft
Area Code 785
Zip 67701
Information Convention & Visitors Bureau, 350 S Range, PO Box 572; phone 785/462-7643 or toll-free 800/611-8835
Web Site www.colbychamber.com

This town is the hub of northwest Kansas due to its cultural, shopping, and hospitality facilities. Agribusiness drives the economy.

What to See and Do

Northwest Research Extension Center. *105 Experiment Farm Rd, Colby (67701). W of city, 1/4 mile S of Hwy 24. Phone 785/462-7575.* Branch of Kansas State University. Crop, soil, irrigation, and horticulture research. (Mon-Fri) **FREE**

Prairie Museum of Art & History. *1905 S Franklin St, Colby (67701). Adjacent to I-70 between exits 53 and 54.* Museum complex is located on a 24-acre site. On exhibit are rare bisque and china dolls; Meissen, Tiffany, Sèvres, Capo de Monte, Royal Vienna, Satsuma, Ridgway, Wedgwood, and Limoges; glass and crystal, such as Redford, Stiegel, Steuben, Gallé; Chinese and Japanese artifacts; textiles; furniture. On the museum site are a sod house, restored 1930s farmstead, one-room schoolhouse, a country church, and one of the largest barns in Kansas. (Daily; closed holidays) **$$**

Special Events

Pickin' on the Plains Bluegrass 'n' Folk Festival. *350 Range St, Colby (67701). Phone toll-free 800/611-8835.* Third weekend in July.

Prairie Heritage Day. *1905 S Franklin Ave, Colby (67701). Phone toll-free 800/611-8835.* Third Sat in June.

Thomas County Fair. *350 S Range St, Colby (67701). Phone toll-free 800/611-8835.* Last week in July.

Limited-Service Hotel

★ ★ **QUALITY INN.** *1950 S Range Ave, Colby (67701). Phone 785/462-3933; toll-free 800/228-5151; fax 785/462-7255. www.qualityinn.com.* 117 rooms, 2 story. Check-out noon. Restaurant, bar. Indoor pool. **$**

Concordia (B-4)

See also Belleville, Beloit

Population 6,167
Elevation 1,369 ft
Area Code 785
Zip 66901
Information Chamber of Commerce, 606 Washington St; phone 785/243-4290 or toll-free 800/343-4290
Web Site www.dustdevil.com/towns/concordia

What to See and Do

⭐ **Brown Grand Theatre.** *310 W 6th St, Concordia (66901). Phone 785/243-2553. www.browngrand.org.* Built in 1907 by Colonel Napoleon Bonaparte Brown at a cost of $40,000, the restored 650-seat theater has two balconies and features a grand drape which is a reproduction of a Horace Vernet painting entitled *Napoleon at Austerlitz.* The theater currently hosts plays, concerts, and shows. Guided tours (Tues-Fri, limited hours; fee).

Special Events

Cloud County Fair. *E 6th St and Industrial Rd, Concordia (66901). Phone 785/243-4290.* Mid-July.

Fall Fest. *6th St, Concordia (66901). Phone 785/243-4290.* Last Sat in Sept.

North Central Kansas Rodeo. *Rodeo Arena Fair Ground, E 6th St, Concordia (66901). Phone 785/243-1313.* Mid-Aug.

Limited-Service Hotel

★ **ECONO LODGE.** *89 Lincoln St, Concordia*

A Walk through the Old West

Forget Dodge City. If you're looking for an authentic Old West town, journey to Council Grove, a bustling trading center on the Sante Fe Trail during the 1840s and 1850s—and largely unchanged since. Council Grove contains some of the best-preserved frontier-era architecture in Kansas, and many of the buildings are still used for their original commercial purpose.

Begin your tour at the Kaw Mission State Historic Site, at 500 North Mission Street. Methodist missionaries built this school for native Kaw children in 1851. Today the structure contains a museum dedicated to the Kaw, the Sante Fe Trail, and early Council Grove. From here, walk south on Mission Street to Main Street, which follows the route of the Sante Fe Trail through town. The Cottage House Hotel (25 N Neosho) is a beautifully maintained Victorian hotel with wraparound porches and striking Queen Anne turrets and gazebos. Still in operation, this is a marvelous place to spend the night in period splendor. Across Main Street, the Farmers and Drovers Bank (201 W Main), is a handsome landmark of redbrick and limestone, with eclectic architectural features like Romanesque arches, stained-glass windows, and a Byzantine dome.

One block east on Main Street is another historic structure, which is still in operation. The Hays House Restaurant (112 W Main) is the oldest continuously operating restaurant west of the Mississippi. Since it was constructed in 1857, the restaurant has served the likes of General George Custer and Jesse James. Although the ambience is frontier-era, the food is up-to-date and delicious—stop by for a piece of peach pie. Also on this block of Main Street is the stone Last Chance Store (in operation since 1857 as well) and the Council Grove National Bank Building.

Before crossing the Neosho River Bridge, turn south two blocks to the Seth Hays Home. Built in 1867, this home has been preserved in period condition and is open to visitors on Sundays and by appointment. Cross the Neosho River on Main Street. In a shelter along the riverbank is the remains of the Council Oak, a once-vast oak tree under which representatives of the United States and the Osage tribe signed a treaty in 1825 that guaranteed settlers safe passage across Indian territory. On the north corner of Main and Union streets is a small park containing the *Madonna of the Trail,* a statue of a pioneer mother and children erected in 1925 by the Daughters of the American Revolution. Along with a museum of frontier history, the park is home to the Post Office Oak, a 300-year-old bur oak that served as an unofficial post depository for travelers along the Sante Fe Trail. Continue east on Main to Durland Park (at 5th St) where Council Grove's first jail, constructed in 1849, still stands. Also in Durland Park are two 19th-century train depots.

(66901). Phone 785/243-4545; toll-free 877/424-6423; fax 785/243-4545. www.econolodge.com. 48 rooms. Pets accepted, some restrictions; fee. Check-out 11 am. Outdoor pool. **$**

🔲 🦮 🌄

Council Grove (C-5)

See also Emporia, Junction City

Founded 1858
Population 2,228
Elevation 1,233 ft
Area Code 316, 620

Zip 66846
Information Convention & Visitors Bureau, 212 W Main St; phone 316/767-5882 or toll-free 800/732-9211
Web Site www.councilgrove.com

As the last outfitting place on the Santa Fe Trail between the Missouri River and Santa Fe, Council Grove, now a National Historic Landmark, holds historic significance in the development of the West. The town grew up around a Native American campground in a grove of oaks near the Neosho River and is now an agricultural and merchandising center. The town also has many lovely turn-of-the-century buildings, several parks, and two lakes.

What to See and Do

Council Grove Federal Lake. *945 Lake Rd, Council Grove (66846). 1 mile N on Hwy 177. Phone 620/767-5195.* Covers 3,200 acres. Fishing, boating, marina (seasonal); hunting, camping (some fees/night). (Daily) **$**

Council Oak Shrine. *313 E Main St, Council Grove (66846).* Here the treaty of 1825 was signed between US government commissioners and the Osage.

Custer's Elm Shrine. *S Neosho St, Council Grove (66846). 6 blocks S of Main St.* Elm trunk stands as a shrine to the tree that was 100 feet tall, 16 feet in circumference, and reputedly sheltered the camp of General George Custer in 1867 when he was leading an expedition to western Kansas.

Hays House. *112 W Main St, Council Grove (66846). Phone 620/767-5911.* (1857) This National Registered Historic Landmark houses a restaurant.

Madonna of the Trail Monument. *Union and Main sts, Council Grove (66846).* One of 12 statues erected in each of the states through which the National Old Trails Roads passed. The Madonna pays tribute to pioneer mothers and commemorates the trails that opened the West.

Old Calaboose. *502 E Main St, Council Grove (66846). On Hwy 56.* (1849) The only pioneer jail on Santa Fe Trail in the early days.

Post Office Oak. *E Main and Union sts, Council Grove (66846).* Mammoth oak tree with a cache at its base served as an unofficial post office for pack trains and caravans on the Santa Fe Trail from 1825 to 1847.

Special Event

Wah-Shun-Gah Days. *212 W Main St, Council Grove (66846). Phone 620/767-5041.* Kaw Intertribal Pow-wow, Santa Fe Trail ride and supper, antique tractor pull, street dance. Third weekend in June.

Restaurant

★ ★ **HAYS HOUSE 1857.** *112 W Main St (Hwy 56), Council Grove (66846). Phone 620/767-5911. www.hayshouse.com.* American menu. Breakfast, lunch, dinner, Sun brunch. Closed Dec 24-25. Bar.

Children's menu. National Register of Historic Landmarks on Santa Fe Trail. **$$**

Dodge City (C-2)

Settled 1872
Population 21,129
Elevation 2,530 ft
Area Code 620
Zip 67801
Information Convention & Visitors Bureau, 400 W Wyatt Earp Blvd, PO Box 1474; phone 620/225-8186 or toll-free 800/653-9378
Web Site www.visitdodgecity.org

Memorable for buffalo hunts, longhorn cattle, and frontier marshals, Dodge City was laid out by construction crews of the Santa Fe Railroad and named for nearby Fort Dodge. Vast herds of buffalo—estimated at 24 million or more—which then covered the surrounding plains, had been hunted for years. But the railroad provided transportation to make the hides commercially profitable. A skilled hunter could earn $100 in a day at the industry's height; by 1875 the herds were nearly exterminated. Cattle drives, also stimulated by the railroad, took the buffalo's place in the town's economy. In the 1870s, Dodge City became the cowboy capital of the region. Among its notable peace officers were Bat Masterson and Wyatt Earp. The prevalence of sudden and violent death resulted in the establishment of Boot Hill cemetery. In the mid-1880s the era of the cattle drives ended; by 1890 much of the grazing land had been plowed for crops. Dodge City is now the hub of one of the nation's greatest wheat-producing areas and a growing production and marketing center for cattle.

What to See and Do

Dodge City Trolley. *400 W Wyatt Earp Blvd, Dodge City (67801). 4th and W Wyatt Earp Blvd. Phone 620/225-8186.* Narrated tour of city's history and folklore. (Memorial Day-early Aug: daily; rest of year: by appointment) **$$**

Ford County's Home of Stone/Mueler-Schmidt House. *112 E Vine St, Dodge City (67801). Phone 620/227-6791.* (1881) Preserved Victorian home with many original furnishings; occupied until 1964. Guided tours (Memorial Day-late Aug, daily).

⭐ **Historic Front Street.** *Dodge City.* Reconstruction of two blocks of main street of the 1870s: Long Branch Saloon, Saratoga Saloon, general store, blacksmith, saddle shop, drugstore, many other businesses. Beeson Gallery contains exhibits, many objects of historical significance from the Southwest and Dodge City; Hardesty House, home of an early cattle baron, has been restored and furnished with original pieces; exhibits of early banking.

> **Boot Hill Museum.** *Front and Fifth sts, Dodge City (67801). Phone 620/227-8188.* Museum and cemetery are on the site of the original Boot Hill Cemetery; depot, locomotive, "Boot Hill Special." Old Fort Dodge Jail; gun collection. Stagecoach rides in summer. (Daily; closed Jan 1, Thanksgiving, Dec 25) **$$$**

Special Events

Dodge City Days. *Dodge City. Phone 620/227-9501.* Parades; PRCA rodeo features cowboy competition in several events. Last week in July-first weekend in Aug.

Long Branch Saloon. *121 N Main St, Dodge City (67428).* Variety show, nightly (fee). Stagecoach rides; reenacted gunfights, daily. Late May-Labor Day.

El Dorado (C-5)

See also Eureka, Newton, Wichita

Population 11,504
Elevation 1,291 ft
Area Code 316
Zip 67042
Information Chamber of Commerce, 383 E Central, PO Box 509; phone 316/321-3150
Web Site www.eldoradochamber.com

El Dorado, the seat of Butler County, is located on the western edge of the Flint Hills. The city's growth can be attributed to oil; two refineries are here. Stapleton # 1, the area's first gusher (1915), is commemorated by a marker at the northwestern edge of the town.

What to See and Do

El Dorado State Park. *618 NE Bluestem Rd, El Dorado (67042). 5 miles NE on Hwy 177. Phone 316/321-7180.* The largest of Kansas's state parks, El Dorado is made up of four areas totaling 4,000 acres. Rolling hills, wooded valleys, and open prairie make up the natural

environment of the park. El Dorado Lake, 8,000 acres, is also within the park. Swimming beaches; fishing (with license); boating (ramps, marina). Hiking trails. Picnicking, concession. More than 1,100 primitive and improved campsites (hook-ups, dump stations). (Daily) **$$**

Kansas Oil Museum. *383 E Central Ave, El Dorado (67042). Phone 316/321-9333. skyways.lib.ks.us/ museums/kom.* Interpretive displays here depict oil, ranching, and agricultural history, including a model rotary drilling rig; outdoor historic oil field exhibits include a restored cable-tool drilling rig, shotgun lease house, and antique engines. In all, more than 20 pieces of antique oil drilling equipment and exhibits explain Kansas's place in the US oil industry. In conjunction with the Prairie Port Festival in late July, the museum is open for free to those with a Prairie Port button, with demonstrations of oil drilling equipment beginning at 2:30 pm. Library, archives. Walking tour, nature trail. (Mon-Sat 9 am-5 pm, Sun 1-5 pm; closed holidays) **$**

Limited-Service Hotel

★ ★ **BEST WESTERN RED COACH INN.** *2525 W Central St, El Dorado (67042). Phone 316/ 321-6900; toll-free 800/780-7234; fax 316/322-0057. www.bestwestern.com.* 73 rooms, 2 story. Pets accepted. Check-out 11 am. Restaurant. Fitness room. Indoor pool, whirlpool. Airport transportation available. **$**
🅱️ 🐾 👤 🛏️

Emporia (C-5)

See also Council Grove

Founded 1857
Population 25,512
Elevation 1,150 ft
Area Code 620
Zip 66801
Information Convention & Visitors Bureau, 719 Commercial St, PO Box 703; phone 620/342-1803 or toll-free 800/279-3730.
Web Site www.emporiakschamber.org

This was the home of one of America's most famous newspaper editors, William Allen White. His *Emporia Gazette* editorials attracted nationwide attention. The seat of Lyon County and "front porch" to the Flint Hills, Emporia is a center of education, industry, agriculture, and outdoor recreation.

What to See and Do

All Veterans Memorial. *933 S Commercial St, Emporia (66801). Phone 620/342-1803.* The first memorial in the nation to honor all veterans from all wars. Dedicated May 26, 1991.

Eisenhower State Park. *75 Sodens Rd, Emporia (66801). 20 miles E on I-35, 7 miles N on Hwy 75. Phone 785/528-4102.* A 1,785-acre park on a 6,900-acre lake. Crappie, walleye, catfish, and bass. Beach, bathhouse; fishing; boating (ramp). Picnicking; walking trail. Camping (electricity, dump station). (Daily)

Emporia Gazette Building. *517 Merchant St, Emporia (66801). Phone 620/342-4800.* Houses White's widely-quoted newspaper; small one-room museum displays newspaper machinery used in White's time. (Mon-Fri; weekends by appointment; closed holidays) **FREE**

Flint Hills National Wildlife Refuge. *310 W Maple Ave, Hartford (66854). 10 miles E on I-35, then 8 miles S on Hwy 130. Phone 620/392-5553.* Consists of 18,500 acres located on the upstream portion of John Redmond River. Hiking, camping. Wild food gathering is permitted. Bald eagles present in fall and winter. Fishing and hunting in legal seasons. (Daily; some portions closed during fall migration of waterfowl) **FREE**

Jones Aquatic Park. *W 18th Ave, Emporia (66801).* Water slides, lazy river ride, sand volleyball courts, playground equipment, picnic shelter, competition pool, zero-depth entry pool, and children's water activities.

Lyon County Historical Museum. *118 E 6th Ave, Emporia (66801). Phone 620/340-6310.* In the Carnegie Library Building (1904). Rotating exhibits, gift gallery with locally made items. (Tues-Sat; closed holidays) **FREE** Opposite is

> **Research Center and Archives.** *225 E 6th Ave, Emporia (66801). Phone 620/340-6320.* Valuable collection of city directories, newspapers dating from 1857 on microfilm; a complete file of the *Emporia Gazette*; genealogy collection for Lyon County, including marriage and cemetery records. (Tues-Sat; closed holidays) **FREE**

National Teachers Hall of Fame. *1320 C of E Dr, Emporia (66801). Phone 620/341-5660; toll-free 800/968-3224. www.nthf.org.* Committed to drawing the public's attention to exceptional teachers through a museum, teacher's resource center, and an induction ceremony that recognizes five of the nation's most outstanding Pre-Kindergarten through Grade 12 educators each year. (Mon-Sat; closed holidays). **DONATION**

Peter Pan Park. *75 Soden Rd, Emporia (66801). Phone 620/342-6558.* Approximately 50 acres given to the city by the White family; bust of William Allen White by Jo Davidson. Wading pool (June-Aug, daily); lake (children under age 14 and senior citizens may fish here). Softball fields. Picnic grounds. (Daily) **FREE**

Prairie Passage. *W Hwy 50 and Industrial Rd, Emporia (66801).* Eight massive limestone sculptures reflecting Emporia's heritage, each weighing from 5-9 tons and standing 10-15 feet high. (Daily) **FREE**

Soden's Grove Park. *S Commercial and Soden Rd, Emporia (66801).* Thirty acres bordered by the Cottonwood River; baseball field, picnic area; miniature train (seasonal, evenings). Located in the park is

> **Emporia Zoo.** *75 Soden Rd, Emporia (66801). Phone 620/342-6558.* Nearly 400 specimens of birds, mammals, and reptiles representing more than 80 species are housed in natural habitats. Drive or walk through. (Daily; closed Jan 1, Thanksgiving, Dec 25) **FREE**

Special Events

Lyon County Free Fair. *Fairgrounds, W Hwy 50, Emporia (66801). Phone 620/342-5014.* Exhibits, entertainment, carnival, rodeos. Late July-early Aug.

Mexican-American Fiesta. *Fairgrounds, 719 Commercial St, Emporia (66801).* Celebration of Emporia's Hispanic heritage. Entertainment, food, dance. Weekend after Labor Day.

Limited-Service Hotel

★ ★ **BEST WESTERN HOSPITALITY HOUSE.** *3021 W Hwy 50, Emporia (66801). Phone 620/342-7587; toll-free 800/362-2036; fax 620/342-9271. www.bestwestern.com.* 143 rooms. Pets accepted, some restrictions. Complimentary continental breakfast. Check-out noon. Restaurant, bar. Fitness room. Indoor pool, whirlpool. Business center. **$**
🐾 🏋 🏊 🏃

Eureka (C-5)

See also El Dorado, Yates Center

Population 2,974

Elevation 1,084 ft
Area Code 316
Zip 67045
Information Eureka Area Chamber of Commerce, 112 N Main; phone 316/583-5452
Web Site www.eurekakansas.com

What to See and Do

Fall River State Park. *144 Hwy 105, Toronto (66777). 17 miles SE, just off Hwy 96.* Phone 620/637-2213. Park encompasses 917 acres that overlook a 2,500-acre reservoir. Rolling uplands forested by native oak adjoining native tallgrass prairies. Beach, bathhouse; fishing; boating (ramps, docks). Trails. Picnicking. Tent and trailer camping (electricity, dump station). (Daily) **$$**

Greenwood County Historical Society and Museum. *120 W 4th St, Eureka (67045).* Phone 620/583-6682. Collection of historical artifacts; 19th-century kitchen and farm display; county newspapers from 1868 to 1986; genealogy section. (Mon-Fri; closed holidays) **FREE**

Hawthorne Ranch Trail Rides. *Eureka.* Phone 620/583-5887. View the beautiful Flint Hills from horseback. Trail rides twice daily (reservations required; must be age 10 or over). This 960-acre ranch also has a wilderness campsite, fishing, hiking. (Apr-Nov, daily) **$$$$**

Special Event

Quarter horse racing. *Eureka Downs, 210 N Jefferson, Eureka (67045).* Phone 620/583-5381. May-July 4.

Limited-Service Hotel

★ **BLUE STEM LODGE.** *1314 E River St, Eureka (67045).* Phone 620/583-5531. 27 rooms. Check-out 11 am. Outdoor pool. **$**
🏊

Fort Scott (C-6)

See also Pittsburg; also see Nevada, MO

Founded 1842
Population 8,362
Elevation 846 ft
Area Code 620
Zip 66701
Information Visitor Information Center, 231 E Wall St, PO Box 205; phone 620/223-3566 or toll-free 800/245-3678

Web Site www.fortscott.com

Named for General Winfield Scott and established as a military post between Fort Leavenworth and lands designated for the displaced Cherokee, Fort Scott was manned by troops in 1842. Although the fort was abandoned in 1853 and its buildings sold at auction in 1855, the town survived. Located only 5 miles from the Missouri border, it became a center for pre-Civil War agitation by those for, as well as those against, slavery. Rival groups had headquarters on the Plaza—the former parade ground—in the Free State Hotel and the Western Hotel. John Brown and James Montgomery were among the antislavery leaders who met here. During the Civil War, the fort was again active as a supply center for Union troops. Today the town is a livestock center, with an economy based on service and manufacturing.

What to See and Do

Fort Scott National Cemetery. *900 E National Cemetery, Fort Scott (66701).* Designated by President Abraham Lincoln in 1862. (Daily)

Fort Scott National Historic Site. *Old Fort Blvd at business jct Hwy 69 and 54, Fort Scott (66701).* Phone 620/223-0310. Established in 1842, the fort was the base for infantry and dragoons protecting the permanent Indian frontier. The buildings have been restored and reconstructed to represent the fort (circa 1842-1853). Visitor center located in restored post hospital; officers' quarters, powder magazine, dragoon stable, guardhouse, bakery, quartermaster's storehouse, post headquarters, and barracks; museum exhibits, audiovisual programs (daily). Some special events. Living history and interpretive programs (June-Aug, weekends). (Daily; closed Jan 1, Thanksgiving, Dec 25) **$**

Gunn Park. *1010 Park Ave, Fort Scott (66701). W edge of town, along the Marmaton River.* Phone 620/223-0550. Covers 135 acres, two lakes. Fishing (fee). Picnicking, playground. Camping (fee). (Daily) **FREE**

Historic Trolley Tour. *231 E Wall, Fort Scott (66701). Phone toll-free 800/245-3678.* Narrated trolley tours pass the historic 1840s fort, one of the country's oldest national cemeteries, and several miles of Victorian architecture. (Mid-Mar-early Dec, daily) Contact visitor information center for schedule. **$$**

Special Events

Bourbon County Fair. *County Fairgrounds, Horton St,*

Fort Scott (66701). Phone toll-free 800/245-3678. Third week in July.

Good Ol' Days Celebration. *Main St, Fort Scott (66701). Phone toll-free 800/245-3678.* First weekend in June.

Pioneer Harvest Fiesta. *County Fairgrounds, Horton St, Fort Scott (66701). Phone toll-free 800/245-3678.* Steam, gas engine, and tractor show; demonstrations of farm activities. Late Sept.

Limited-Service Hotel

★ **BEST WESTERN FORT SCOTT INN.** *1st and State sts, Fort Scott (66701). Phone 620/223-0100; toll-free 888/800-3175; fax 620/223-1746. www.bestwestern.com.* 76 rooms, 2 story. Pets accepted, some restrictions; fee. Complimentary continental breakfast. Check-out 11 am. Fitness room. Outdoor pool, whirlpool. **$**

Garden City (C-2)

Founded 1878
Population 24,097
Elevation 2,839 ft
Area Code 620
Zip 67846
Information Chamber of Commerce, Finney County Convention & Tourism Bureau, 1511 E Fulton Terrace; phone 620/276-3264 or toll-free 800/879-9803
Web Site www.gcnet.com

This is the center for raising and processing much of the state's beef for shipment throughout the world. The city is also the heart of the state's irrigation operations, which are important to wheat, alfalfa, and corn crops in the area. It is home to one of the oldest known state-owned bison herds.

What to See and Do

Finney Game Refuge. *1511 E Fulton Terrace, Garden City (67846). Phone 620/276-3264.* Some 3,670 acres of sandsage prairie biome, which is home to more than 100 head of bison, lesser prairie chickens, jack-rabbits, quail, deer, and other wildlife. Wildflowers are abundant, and the lake is stocked with trout in the spring and fall.

Finnup Park and Lee Richardson Zoo. *312 Finnup Dr, Garden City (67846). S city limits, on Hwy 83. Phone 620/276-1250 (zoo).* More than 300 mammals and birds can be found in the zoo including the Wild Asia Exhibit. Picnic area, playgrounds; food and gift shop (fee for vehicles; closed Jan 1, Thanksgiving, Dec 25). Swimming pool (Mar-Nov, daily). Museum with memorabilia of early settlers (daily) **FREE**

Special Events

Beef Empire Days. *Garden City (67846). Phone 620/275-6807.* Early June.

Finney County Fair. *501 S 9th St, Garden City (67846). Phone 620/272-3670.* Early Aug.

Mexican Fiesta. *9th and Isabel sts, Garden City (67847). Phone 620/276-7207.* Second weekend in Sept.

Tumbleweed Festival. *Finnup Park, 401 S 4th St, Garden City (67846). Phone 620/275-8621.* Late Aug.

Limited-Service Hotel

★ ★ **GARDEN CITY PLAZA INN.** *1911 E Kansas, Garden City (67846). Phone 620/275-7471; toll-free 800/875-5201; fax 620/275-4028.* 109 rooms, 2 story. Pets accepted; fee. Check-out noon. Restaurant, bar. Indoor pool, whirlpool. Airport transportation available. **$**

Goodland (B-1)

See also Colby

Population 4,983
Elevation 3,683 ft
Area Code 785
Zip 67735
Information Convention and Visitors Bureau, 104 W 11th St, PO Box 628; phone 785/899-3515 or toll-free 888/824-4222
Web Site www.goodlandnet.com/cvb

What to See and Do

High Plains Museum. *1717 Cherry St, Goodland (67735). Phone 785/899-4595.* Houses a replica of the first patented American helicopter (built in 1910). Also contains displays of Native American artifacts; farm implements, 19th-century clothing and household goods; miniature local history dioramas. (June-Aug, daily; closed holidays) **FREE**

Special Events

Flatlander Fall Festival. *Goodland. Phone toll-free 888/824-4222.* IMCA race. Last Sat in Sept.

Northwest Kansas District Free Fair. *Sherman County Fairgrounds, 417 N Main St, Goodland (67735). Phone toll-free 888/824-4222.* First week in Aug.

Sunflower Festival. *Fairgrounds, Goodland. Phone 785/899-7130; toll-free 888/824-4222.* Second weekend in Aug.

Limited-Service Hotel

★ **BEST WESTERN BUFFALO INN.** *830 W Hwy 24, Goodland (67735). Phone 785/899-3621; toll-free 800/433-3621; fax 785/899-5072. www.bestwestern.com.* 93 rooms, 2 story. Pets accepted. Complimentary full breakfast. Check-out 11 am. Bar. Indoor pool, children's pool, whirlpool. Airport transportation available. Business center. **$**

Great Bend (C-3)

See also Larned

Founded 1871
Population 15,427
Elevation 1,849 ft
Area Code 620
Zip 67530
Information Convention & Visitors Bureau, 3111 10th St, PO Box 274; phone 620/792-2750
Web Site www.greatbend.com

Great Bend, named for its location on the Arkansas River, was an early railhead on the Santa Fe Trail.

What to See and Do

Barton County Historical Society Museum and Village. *85 S Hwy 281, Great Bend (67530). Phone 620/793-5125.* The village contains a church (circa 1895), a schoolhouse (circa 1915), agricultural buildings, a native stone blacksmith shop, a Dodge homestead, a depot, and a post office. The museum's exhibits include local Native American history, furniture, and clothing; an antique doll collection; farm machinery; and a firetruck. (Apr-mid-Nov: Tues-Sun; rest of year:

by appointment).

Brit Spaugh Park and Zoo. *N Main St, Great Bend (67530). Phone 620/793-4160.* Swimming pool (fee). Zoo. Picnicking, playground. (Daily) **FREE**

Cheyenne Bottoms. *56 NE 40 Rd, Great Bend (67530). Phone 620/793-7730.* Migratory waterfowl refuge, public hunting area, and bird-watching area. The water area is about 13,000 acres. Fishing from shoreline in all pools (catfish, bullhead, carp). (Daily) **FREE**

Quivira National Wildlife Refuge. *Great Bend. Phone 620/486-2393.* This 22,135-acre refuge includes 5,000 acres of managed wetlands and 15,000 acres of tall grass prairie. It was established in 1955 to provide a feeding and resting area for migratory waterfowl during spring and fall migrations. Auto tour route and wildlife drive (daily). Hunting and fishing permitted some seasons. **FREE**

Special Event

Barton County Fair. *Expo Complex, G St, Great Bend (67530). Phone 620/797-3247.* Mid-July.

Limited-Service Hotel

★ ★ **HOLIDAY INN.** *3017 W 10th St, Great Bend (67530). Phone 620/792-2431; toll-free 800/465-4329; fax 620/792-5561. www.holiday-inn.com.* 172 rooms, 2 story. Pets accepted. Check-out noon. Restaurant, bar. Fitness room. Indoor pool, whirlpool. Airport transportation available. **$**

Greensburg (D-3)

See also Pratt

Population 1,792
Elevation 2,230 ft
Area Code 620
Zip 67054
Information Chamber of Commerce, 315 S Sycamore; phone 620/723-2261 or toll-free 800/207-7369
Web Site www.bigwell.org

Incorporated in 1886, Greensburg is named for pioneer stagecoach driver "Cannonball" Green. This community came to life in 1884, when two railroads extended their lines here and brought settlers. In 1885, the railroads began construction of what has been called the world's largest hand-dug well; it is still in good condition today.

What to See and Do

Big Well. *315 S Sycamore St, Greensburg (67054). Three blocks S of Hwy 54. Phone 620/723-2261.* The well is 32 feet wide and 109 feet deep; steps lead downward to water level (fee). Gift shop contains 1,000-pound pallasite meteorite found on a nearby farm and said to be the largest of its type ever discovered. (Daily; closed Thanksgiving, Dec 25) **$**

Limited-Service Hotel

★ **BEST WESTERN J-HAWK MOTEL.** *515 W Kansas Ave, Greensburg (67054). Phone 620/723-2121; toll-free 800/780-7234; fax 620/723-2650. www.bestwestern.com.* 30 rooms. Pets accepted, some restrictions. Complimentary continental breakfast. Check-out 11 am. Fitness room. Indoor pool, whirlpool. Airport transportation available. **$**

Hays (B-3)

See also Russell, WaKeeney

Founded 1867
Population 17,767
Elevation 1,997 ft
Area Code 785
Zip 67601
Information Convention & Visitors Bureau, 1301 Pine, Suite B; phone 785/628-8202 or toll-free 800/569-4505
Web Site www.haysusa.com

Fort Hays, military post on the old frontier, gave this railroad town its name. Oil, grain, cattle, educational and medical facilities, tourism, and light industry are important to the area.

What to See and Do

Ellis County Historical Society and Museum. *100 W 7th St, Hays (67601). Phone 785/628-2624.* More than 26,000 items are on display in the museum; including antique toys and games, musical instruments; rotating exhibits including quilts from the 1800s-present (selected days Apr-June). Also here are a one-room schoolhouse and the oldest stone church in Ellis County. (June-Aug: Tues-Fri; also Sat afternoons; rest of year: Tues-Fri; closed holidays)

Historic Fort Hays. *1472 Hwy 183, Hays (67601). Phone 785/625-6812.* Parade grounds, small buffalo herd. Museums in original guardhouse, officers' quarters, and blockhouse; visitor center. (Daily; closed holidays) **DONATION**

Sternberg Museum of Natural History. *3000 Sternberg Drive, Hays (67601). Phone 785/628-4286.* Natural history, paleontological, and geological collections. (Tues-Sun; closed Jan 1, Thanksgiving, Dec 25) **$$**

Special Events

Ellis County Fair. *Ellis County Fairground, 1301 Pine St # B, Hays (67601). Phone 785/628-8202.* Entertainment, activities, tractor pull, arts and crafts. Mid-late July.

Oktoberfest. *Frontier Park and S Main, Hays (67601). Phone 785/628-8202.* Arts and crafts, entertainment. Early Oct.

Pioneer Days at Historic Fort Hays. *1472 Hwy 183 Alt, Hays (67601). Phone 785/625-6812.* Two full days of living history including demonstrations of butter churning, tatting, ropemaking, rug weaving, whittling, and stonepost cutting. Sept.

Wild West Festival. *Frontier Park, 1301 Pine St, Hays (67601). Phone 785/628-8202.* Family oriented activities; concerts, food booths, fireworks display. Early July.

Limited-Service Hotels

★ **HAMPTON INN.** *3801 Vine St, Hays (67601). Phone 785/625-8103; toll-free 800/426-7866; fax 785/625-3006. www.hamptoninn.com.* 117 rooms, 2 story. Pets accepted, some restrictions. Complimentary continental breakfast. Check-out noon. Airport transportation available. **$**

★ ★ **HOLIDAY INN.** *3603 Vine St, Hays (67601). Phone 785/625-7371; toll-free 800/465-4329; fax 785/625-7250. www.holiday-inn.com.* 191 rooms, 2 story. Check-out noon. Restaurant, bar. Fitness room. Indoor pool, whirlpool. Airport transportation available. **$**

Restaurant

★ **GUTIERREZ.** *1106 E 27th, Hays (67601). Phone 785/625-4402; fax 785/625-4417.* Mexican, American menu. Lunch, dinner. Closed Easter, Thanksgiving, Dec 25. Bar. Children's menu. **$$**

Hiawatha (A-6)

See also Atchison, Seneca; also see St. Joseph, MO

Population 3,603
Elevation 1,136 ft
Area Code 785
Zip 66434
Information Chamber of Commerce, 602 Oregon St; phone 785/742-7136
Web Site www.cityofhiawatha.org

What to See and Do

Brown County AG Museum. *RR 2, Hiawatha (66434). E Iowa St. Phone 785/742-3702.* Features display of windmills, the Old Barn, Ernie's cabinet shop, blacksmith shop, horsedrawn implement building, antique tractor and car display. (Tues-Sat) **$$**

⭐ **Davis Memorial.** *Hiawatha. 1/2 mile E on Iowa St in Mt Hope Cemetery.* Eccentric half-million-dollar tomb features 11 life-size Italian marble statues depicting John Davis and his wife in various periods of their lives. Completed in 1937.

Special Event

Halloween Parade. *Oregon St, Hiawatha (66434). Phone 785/742-7136.* Afternoon and evening parade held every year since 1914. The Sat nearest Oct 31.

Limited-Service Hotel

★ ★ **HIAWATHA INN.** *101 Lodge Rd, Hiawatha (66434). Phone 785/742-7401; fax 785/742-3334.* 40 rooms, 2 story. Check-out 11 am. Restaurant. Outdoor pool. **$**
🏊

Restaurant

★ **HEARTLAND.** *101 Lodge Rd, Hiawatha (66434). Phone 785/742-7401; fax 785/742-3334.* American menu. Breakfast, lunch, dinner. Closed Dec 25. Bar. Children's menu. **$**

Hutchinson (C-4)

See also McPherson, Newton, Wichita

Founded 1872
Population 39,308
Elevation 1,538 ft
Area Code 620
Information Greater Hutchinson Convention & Visitors Bureau, 117 N Walnut, PO Box 519, 67504; phone 620/662-3391 or toll-free 800/691-4262
Web Site www.hutchchamber.com

In 1887, drillers for natural gas discovered some of the world's richest rock salt deposits under the town of Hutchinson. The industry was promptly established; today the town is a major salt-producing center, with a mine and processing plants. Hutchinson, the principal city and county seat of Reno County, also is a wholesale and retail trade center for central and western Kansas.

What to See and Do

Dillon Nature Center. *3002 E 30th St, Hutchinson (67502). Phone 620/663-7411.* More than 150 species of birds, along with deer, coyote, and other animals can be spotted at the 100-acre center, which includes special gardens, nature trails, a discovery building, and two ponds for fishing and canoeing. Guided nature tours (by appointment), discovery building (Mon-Fri). Grounds (daily). **FREE**

Historic Fox Theatre. *18 E 1st Ave, Hutchinson (67501). Phone 620/663-5861.* Restored in 1931, the theater exemplifies Art Deco architecture. Named the "state movie palace of Kansas," the theater is on the National Register of Historic Places. Professional entertainment for all ages; classic and independent film; arts education programs. Guided tours (daily, by appointment).

Kansas Cosmosphere and Space Center. *1100 N Plum, Hutchinson (67501). Phone 620/662-2305; toll-free 800/397-0330. www.cosmo.org.* Major space science center for the Midwest, featuring Hall of Space Museum exhibits from the US and Soviet space programs. Displays include a full-scale space shuttle replica, the actual *Apollo 13* command module "Odyssey," a Northrup T-38 jet used for pilot training, and an SR71 Blackbird spy plane—one of only 29 in the world. Cosmosphere with planetarium (fee) and Omnimax (70 mm) projectors. Cosmosphere shows (daily). (Daily; closed Dec 25) **$$$$**

Reno County Museum. *100 S Walnut St, Hutchinson (67501). Phone 620/662-1184.* Features four rotating exhibit galleries; two interactive areas for children (101 and 102 Children's Place), along with several temporary exhibits. An educational program offers lectures, classes, and workshops. (Tues-Sun; closed holidays) **FREE**

Special Events

Kansas State Fair. *Fairgrounds, 2000 N Poplar St, Hutchinson (67502). Phone 620/669-3600. www.kansas statefair.com.* Twins contest, celebrity goat milking contest, and nostalgic car show are some of the events found at the Kansas State Fair. Sept.

NJCAA Men's National Basketball Tournament. *Sports Arena, 730 W 4th Ave, Hutchinson (67501). Phone 620/662-0573.* Mid-Mar.

Limited-Service Hotel

★ ★ **HUTCHINSON PLAZA HOTEL.** *1400 N Lorraine St, Hutchinson (67501). Phone 620/669-9311; fax 620/669-9830.* 220 rooms, 2 story. Check-out noon. Restaurant. Indoor pool, whirlpool. **$**

Independence (D-5)

See also Coffeyville, Kansas City, Parsons

Founded 1870
Population 9,942
Elevation 826 ft
Area Code 620
Zip 67301
Information Convention & Visitors Bureau, 322 N Penn, PO Box 386; phone 620/331-1890 or toll-free 800/882-3606
Web Site www.indkschamber.org

Montgomery County, of which Independence is the seat, was part of the Osage Indian Reservation. In 1869 the Independent Town Company from Oswego, Kansas, obtained 640 acres from the tribe. When the Osage moved to Oklahoma following a treaty in 1870, the entire reservation was opened to settlement. The discovery of natural gas in 1881 and of oil in 1903 caused temporary booms. Today leading industrial products are cement, electrical and electronic parts and equipment, wood products, small aircraft, truck bodies, and gas heaters. Farming in the area produces beef cattle, dairy products, hogs, wheat, beans, alfalfa, corn, and grain sorghums.

Alfred M. Landon, presidential candidate in 1936; playwright William Inge; author Laura Ingalls Wilder; oilman Harry F. Sinclair; and actress Vivian Vance lived here.

What to See and Do

Elk City State Park. *4825 Squaw Creek Rd, Independence (67301). 7 miles NW off Hwy 160. Phone 620/331-6295.* An 857-acre park on a 4,500-acre lake. Nearby is Table Mound, overlooking Elk River Valley, site of one of the last Osage villages. Arrowheads and other artifacts are still found here. Beach; fishing; boating (ramp, dock). Hiking, nature trails. Picnicking. Camping (electricity, dump station). (Daily) **$$**

Independence Historical Museum. *123 N 8th St, Independence (67301). 8th and Myrtle sts. Phone 620/331-3515.* Miscellaneous collections on display; period rooms and monthly exhibits. (Wed-Sun) **$**

Independence Science & Technology Center. *125 S Pennsylvania St, Independence (67301). Phone 620/331-1999.* Hands-on museum; anti-gravity simulator; Van de Graaff generator. (Daily; closed holidays) **$$**

Little House on the Prairie. *Independence. 13 miles SW on Hwy 75. Phone toll-free 800/882-3606.* Reproduction of log cabin occupied by Laura Ingalls Wilder's family from 1869 to 1870. Also a one-room schoolhouse (circa 1870) and old post office. (Mid-Mar-late Oct, daily) **DONATION**

Montgomery State Fishing Lake. *Independence. 5 miles S via 10th St Rd, then 1 mile E. Phone 620/431-0380.* Fishing; boating. Picnicking. Primitive camping.

Riverside Park. *Oak St and Park Blvd, Independence (67301). Phone 620/331-1890; toll-free 800/882-3606.* Covers 124 acres. Ralph Mitchell Zoo, Kiddy Land, miniature train (fee), merry-go-round (fee), and miniature golf (fee) (May-Labor Day, daily; rest of year, hours vary). Swimming pool (Memorial Day-Labor Day, daily; fee). Tennis courts; playground; picnic grounds, shelter houses. Park (daily). **FREE**

Special Event

Neewollah. *Independence. Phone 620/331-1890; toll-free 800/882-3606.* Week-long Halloween festival. Musical entertainment. Last full week in Oct.

Limited-Service Hotel

★ **APPLETREE INN.** *201 N 8th St, Independence (67301). Phone 620/331-5500; fax 620/331-0641.* 64 rooms, 2 story. Pets accepted, some restrictions. Complimentary continental breakfast. Check-out noon. Indoor pool, whirlpool. **$**

Iola (C-6)

See also Chanute, Yates Center

Population 6,351
Elevation 960 ft
Area Code 620
Zip 66749
Information Chamber of Commerce, 208 W Madison, PO Box 722; phone 620/365-5252
Web Site www.iola.com/guide.html

What to See and Do

Allen County Historical Society & Museum Gallery. *20 S Washington, Iola (66749). Phone 620/365-3051.* Display of historical artifacts and memorabilia. (May-Sept, Tues-Sat also by appointment) **FREE** Adjacent is

> **Old Jail Museum.** *207 N Jefferson, Iola (66749).* Historic building; downstairs is the solitary confinement cell (1869) and cell cage (1891); upper floor is a re-creation of the sheriff's living quarters (1869-1904). (Schedule same as Museum Gallery) **FREE**

Bowlus Fine Arts Center. *205 E Madison, Iola (66749). Phone 620/365-4765.* Hosts a number of cultural attractions in the 750-seat capacity auditorium.

Boyhood Home of Major General Frederick Funston. *207 N Jefferson, Iola (66749). Phone 620/365-3051.* Built in 1860; originally located on a homestead about 5 miles north of Iola. Restored according to the Victorian décor of the 1880s and 1890s. Many original family items on display. (May-Sept, Wed-Sat). **FREE**

Special Events

Allen County Fair. *Riverside Park, 600 S State St, Iola (66749). Phone 620/365-5252.* First week in Aug.

Buster Keaton Festival. *Bowlus Fine Arts Center, 205 E Madison, Iola (66749). Phone 620/365-4765.* Last weekend in Sept.

Farm City Days. *Town Square, 1 N Washington, Iola (66749). Phone 620/365-5252.* Third weekend in Oct.

Limited-Service Hotel

★ ★ **BEST WESTERN INN.** *1315 N State St, Iola (66749). Phone 620/365-5161; toll-free 800/769-0007; fax 620/365-6808. www.bestwestern.com.* 59 rooms. Pets accepted, some restrictions. Check-out noon. Restaurant. Outdoor pool. **$**

Junction City (B-5)

See also Abilene, Council Grove, Manhattan

Settled 1855
Population 20,604
Elevation 1,107 ft
Area Code 785
Zip 66441
Information Geary County Convention & Visitors Bureau, 425 N Washington St, PO Box 1846; phone 785/238-2885 or toll-free 800/528-2489
Web Site www.junctioncity.org

Its situation at the junction of the Republican and Smoky Hill rivers gave the town its name. The seat of Geary County, it has long been a trading point for soldiers from Fort Riley.

What to See and Do

Fort Riley. *Holbrook and Pershing Pl, Junction City (66441). Phone 785/239-6727.* (1853). A 101,000-acre military reservation; once a frontier outpost and former home of the US Cavalry School. Marked tour. (Daily) Here are

> **1st Infantry Division Museum.** *Fort Riley.* Division history and memorabilia. (Tues-Sat; closed Jan 1, Thanksgiving, Dec 25) **FREE**

> **Custer House.** *Junction City.* The George Armstrong Custers lived in quarters similar to this house. (Memorial Day-Labor Day, daily; hours vary rest of year) **FREE**

> **First Territorial Capitol.** *Junction City.* "Permanent" capitol July 2-6, 1855, before Free Staters won legislative majority. (Thurs-Sun; closed holidays) **FREE**

St Mary's Chapel. *Junction City.* (1855) Kansas's first native limestone church; still in use.

US Cavalry Museum. *Fort Riley.* Army memorabilia and local history. (Daily; closed holidays) **FREE**

Geary County Historical Museum. *530 N Adams, Junction City (66441). Phone 785/238-1666.* Three-story native limestone building is an example of the stonecutter's art and houses the first Junction City High School. Galleries feature changing and rotating exhibits portraying the Native American Indian period to present day. (Tues-Sat; closed holidays) **FREE**

Milford Lake. *Junction City (66441). 4 miles NW via Hwy 77, Hwy 57. Phone 785/238-5714.* A 15,700-acre reservoir with a 163-mile shoreline; arboretum, fish hatchery, and nature center. Swimming; fishing, boating (marinas). Picnicking. Camping (fee). (Daily) **$$**

Milford State Park. *8811 State Park Rd, Milford (66514). 5 miles NW on Hwy 57. Phone 785/238-3014.* A 1,084-acre park on a 16,200-acre lake; it is the largest man-made lake in Kansas. Native red cedars border the shoreline. Nearby is Fort Riley, a major military reservation. Beach, bathhouse; fishing; boating (rentals, ramps, docks, marina). Concession. Tent and trailer camping (electricity, dump station). (Daily)

Limited-Service Hotel

★ **DAYS INN.** *1024 S Washington St, Junction City (66441). Phone 785/762-2727; toll-free 800/329-7466; fax 785/762-2751. www.daysinn.com.* 108 rooms, 2 story. Pets accepted. Complimentary continental breakfast. Check-out noon. Bar. Indoor pool, outdoor pool, whirlpool. **$**

Kansas City (B-6)

See also Independence, Lawrence, Leavenworth, Overland Park, Topeka; also see Kansas City, MO

Settled 1843
Population 149,767
Elevation 744 ft
Area Code 913
Information Kansas City, Kansas Area Convention & Visitors Bureau, 727 Minnesota Ave, PO Box 171517, 66117; phone 913/371-3070 or toll-free 800/264-1563
Web Site www.kckcvb.org

Kansas City, as it is today, was formed by the consolidation of eight individual towns. The earliest of these, Wyandot City, was settled in 1843 by the Wyandot, an emigrant tribe from Ohio, who bought part of the Delaware tribe's land. This cultured group brought government, schools, churches, business, and agricultural methods to the area. In 1849, alarmed at the influx of settlers on their way to seek California gold, the Wyandot took measures to dispose of their property at a good price. Their successors created a boomtown and changed the spelling to "Wyandotte." Other towns arose nearby, especially as the meat packing industry developed. Eventually they all merged into the present city, which took the name of one of the earliest towns.

Kansas City has several grain elevators, in addition to fabricating steel mills, automobile manufacturers, soap factories, railway yards, and various other industries.

What to See and Do

Children's Museum of Kansas City. *4601 State Ave, Kansas City (66102). In the Indian Springs Shopping Center. Phone 913/287-8888.* Learning museum for children ages 4-12 has more than 40 hands-on exhibits dealing with science, history, art and technology. Exhibits include a shadow retention wall, grocery store, a slice of city streets, a crawl-around salt water aquarium, chain reaction demonstrations, and simple machines. (June-Aug: daily; Sept-May: Tues-Sun) **$$**

Grinter House. *1420 S 78th St, Kansas City (66111). Phone 913/299-0373.* (1860) Home of Moses and Anna Grinter, built on the Delaware Indian Reservation. (Wed-Sat, also Sun afternoons; closed holidays) Maintained by the Kansas State Historical Society. **DONATION**

Huron Indian Cemetery. *7th and Ann sts, Kansas City. In Huron Park, Center City Plaza. Phone 785/321-5800.* The tribal burial ground of the Wyandots; an estimated 400 burials (1844-1855).

Lakeside Speedway. *5615 Wolcott Dr, Kansas City (66109). Phone 913/299-2040. www.lakesidespeedway.net.* Lakeside Speedway is a 1/2-mile oval that was converted from asphalt to dirt in 2000. Lakeside hosts the NASCAR Dodge Weekly Series on Friday nights from April to mid-September. **FREE**

National Agricultural Center and Hall of Fame. *630 Hall of Fame Dr, Bonner Springs (66012). 18 miles W on I-70. Phone 913/721-1075.* National Farmer's

Memorial; history and development of agriculture; library/archives, gallery of rural art; Museum of Farming; "Farm-town USA" exhibit; 1-mile nature trail. (Mid-Mar-Nov, daily; closed holidays) **$$**

The Woodlands. *9700 Leavenworth Rd, Kansas City (66109). Phone 913/299-9797; toll-free 800/695-7223. www.woodlandskc.com.* Check out greyhound racing year-round and thoroughbred and quarterhorse racing in late summer and autumn. At the Weiner Dog Nationals, 64 randomly chosen dachshunds compete for the Grand Champion title. RV parking and camping available (fee; phone 913/596-5978; shuttle runs from campgrounds to Kansas Speedway). Call for race dates and post times. **FREE**

Village West. *1601 Village West Pkwy, Kansas City (66111). villagewest.us.* The Village West retail complex, located across the street from the Kansas Speedway, opened in 2003 and continues to grow. Cabela's, one of the largest sporting goods retailers in the world, offers a wide array of camping gear and accessories. Nebraska Furniture Mart sprawls over 712,000 square feet and offers hundreds of electronic products.

Wyandotte County Historical Society and Museum. *631 N 126th St, Bonner Springs (66012). 15 miles W on I-70, Bonner Springs exit. Phone 913/721-1078.* Native American artifacts, horse-drawn fire engine, pioneer furniture, costumes, county history; research library, archives. (Mon-Sat; closed mid-Dec-Jan 2) **FREE**

Special Event

Renaissance Festival. *Kansas City. Phone toll-free 800/373-0357. www.kcrenfest.com.* Adjacent to the Agricultural Hall of Fame in Bonner Springs. Seven weekends beginning Labor Day weekend.

Larned (C-3)

See also Great Bend

Founded 1872
Population 4,490
Elevation 2,004 ft
Area Code 620
Zip 67550
Information Chamber of Commerce, 502 Broadway, PO Box 240; phone 620/285-6916 or toll-free 800/747-6919
Web Site www.larned.org

What to See and Do

Fort Larned National Historic Site. *US 156, Larned. 6 miles W on Hwy 156. Phone 620/285-6911.* (1859-1878). Considered one of the best-preserved frontier military posts along the Santa Fe Trail; quadrangle of nine original stone buildings plus reconstructed blockhouse. Includes officers' quarters, enlisted men's barracks, blacksmith and carpenter shops, post bakery, hospital, quartermaster and commissary storehouses. The visitor center contains a museum, orientation program, and bookstore. Conducted tours (Mon-Fri in summer). Living history programs, demonstrations and special events (most summer weekends). One-mile history/nature trail. Picnic area. (Daily; closed Jan 1, Thanksgiving, Dec 25) **$$**

Santa Fe Trail Center. *2 miles W on Hwy 156. Phone 620/285-2054.* Museum and library with exhibits explaining exploration, transportation, settlement, and cultural development along the Santa Fe Trail. On the grounds are a sod house, frontier schoolhouse, limestone cooling house, dugout, and depot. (Memorial Day-Labor Day: daily; rest of year: Tues-Sun; closed Jan 1, Thanksgiving, Dec 25) **$$**

Limited-Service Hotel

★ **BEST WESTERN TOWNSMAN MOTEL.** *123 E 14th St, Larned (67550). Phone 620/285-3114; toll-free 800/780-7234; fax 620/285-7139. www.bestwestern.com.* 44 rooms. Pets accepted. Check-out noon. Outdoor pool. **$**
🐾 ⛱

Lawrence (B-6)

See also Kansas City, Leavenworth, Ottawa, Topeka

Founded 1854
Population 65,608
Elevation 850 ft
Area Code 785
Information Convention & Visitors Bureau, 734 Vermont, Suite 101, PO Box 586, 66044; phone 785/865-4411 or toll-free 800/529-5267
Web Site www.visitlawrence.com

Lawrence had a stormy history in the territorial years. It was founded by the New England Emigrant Aid Company and named for one of its prominent members. The center of Free State activities, the town was close to a state of war from 1855 until the Free Staters triumphed in 1859. The Confederate guerrilla leader, William Quantrill, made one of his most spectacular raids on Lawrence in 1863, burning the town and killing 150 citizens. After the Civil War, the town experienced a gradual and peaceful growth as an educational, cultural, trading, and shipping point, and developed a variety of industries.

What to See and Do

Baker University. *606 8th St, Baldwin City (66006). 13 miles S on Hwy 59, then 5 miles E on Hwy 56. Phone 785/594-6451. www.baker.edu.* (1858) (950 students) Oldest university in the state. Original building is now Old Castle Museum and Complex, housing pioneer relics and Native American artifacts (Tues-Sun; closed holidays); Quayle Bible collection (daily), reservations required at Collins Library. Campus tours.

Clinton State Park. *798 N 1415 Rd, Lawrence (66049). 4 miles W off Hwy 40. Phone 785/842-8562.* A 1,485-acre park on a 7,000-acre lake. High, heavily wooded hills and grassland on the north shore. Beach, bathhouse; fishing; boating (ramps, docks). Nature trails. Picnicking, concession. Camping (electricity, dump station). (Daily) **$$**

Haskell Indian Nations University. *155 Indian Ave, Lawrence (66044). Phone 785/749-8450.* (1884) (1,000 students.) A 320-acre campus. More than 120 tribes are represented among the students. The campus is a registered historic landmark; cultural activities; American Indian Athletic Hall of Fame. (Mon-Fri)

Lawrence Arts Center. *940 New Hampshire St, Lawrence (66044). Phone 785/843-2787.* Galleries featuring the work of local artists and craftspeople; performance hall for theater, dance, and music; art classes and workshops for all ages. (Mon-Sat) **FREE**

Old West Lawrence Historic District. *402 N 2nd St, Lawrence (66044). 2 blocks W of downtown on Tennessee and Missouri sts. Phone 785/865-4499.* Self-guided tour through area of notable 19th-century homes. (Daily) **FREE**

University of Kansas. *Corner of 15th and Iowa sts, Lawrence (66044). Phone 785/864-3131. www.ku.edu.* (1866) (26,000 students) A 1,000-acre campus. Some of the campus attractions are the Campanile Bell Tower; Museum of Natural History (daily; phone 785/864-4450); Museum of Anthropology (daily; phone 785/864-4245); and Spencer Museum of Art (Tues-Sun; phone 785/864-4710). (All buildings are closed holidays) Tours of campus.

Watkins Community Museum. *1047 Massachusetts St, Lawrence (66044). Phone 785/841-4109.* Museum housed in an 1888 bank building; Victorian era children's playhouse; 1920 Milburn Light Electric car; Quantrill Raid artifacts; permanent and changing exhibits pertaining to the history of Lawrence and Douglas County. (Tues-Sun; closed holidays) **FREE**

Special Events

Douglas County Free Fair. *2120 Harper St, Lawrence (66046). Phone 785/865-4499.* Early Aug.

Lawrence Indian Arts Show. *University of Kansas Museum of Anthropology, 1340 Jayhawk Blvd, Lawrence (66044). Phone 785/864-2700.* Juried exhibit featuring work by contemporary American Indian artists from across the United States. Sept-Oct.

Limited-Service Hotels

★ **DAYS INN.** *2309 Iowa St, Lawrence (66047). Phone 785/843-9100; fax 785/843-1572.* 101 rooms, 3 story. Pets accepted, some restrictions. Complimentary continental breakfast. Check-out noon. Bar. Fitness room. Indoor pool, whirlpool. **$**

★ ★ **HOLIDAY INN.** *200 McDonald Dr, Lawrence (66044). Phone 785/841-7077; toll-free 800/465-4329; fax 785/841-2799. www.holiday-inn.com.* 192 rooms, 4 story. Check-out noon. Restaurant, bar. Fitness room. Indoor pool, whirlpool. **$**

Full-Service Hotel

★ ★ ★ **ELDRIDGE HOTEL.** *7th and Massachusetts sts, Lawrence (66044). Phone 785/749-5011; toll-free 800/527-0909; fax 785/749-4512. www.eldridgehotel.com.* This historic inn, with its unique history dating to the Civil War, is located near the University of Kansas. Built in 1855 as a Free State hostelry for abolitionists, many fights during the Civil War took place here. 48 rooms, 5 story. Check-in 3 pm, check-out noon. Wireless Internet access. Restaurant, bar. **$**

Specialty Lodging

The following lodging establishment is approved by Mobil Travel Guide, but due to its unique and individualized nature has not been given a traditional Mobil Star rating. Included in this listing you may find bed-and-breakfasts, limited-service inns, guest ranches, and other unique hotel properties.

HALCYON HOUSE BED & BREAKFAST.
1000 Ohio St, Lawrence (66044). Phone 785/841-0314; toll-free 888/441-0314; fax 785/843-7273. www.thehalcyonhouse.com. 9 rooms, 3 story. Children over 12 years only. Complimentary full breakfast. Check-in 1 pm, check-out 11:30 am. High-speed Internet access. Victorian inn built in 1885. **$**

Leavenworth (B-6)

See also Atchison, Kansas City, Lawrence; also see Kansas City, MO and St. Joseph, MO

Founded 1854
Population 38,495
Elevation 800 ft
Area Code 913
Zip 66048
Information Leavenworth Convention & Visitors Bureau, 518 Shawnee St, PO Box 44; phone 913/682-4113 or toll-free 800/844-4114
Web Site www.lvarea.com

Leavenworth was the first incorporated town in Kansas Territory. At first strongly pro-slavery, Leavenworth had many border conflicts, but during the Civil War it was loyal to the Union. In the years just before the war, the town was the headquarters for a huge overland transportation and supply operation sending wagons and stagecoaches northwest on the Oregon Trail and southwest on the Santa Fe Trail. Fort Leavenworth, adjoining the city, is the oldest military post west of the Mississippi River that has been in continuous operation (since 1827). A federal penitentiary is on the grounds adjacent to the fort. Industries in the city of Leavenworth include the Hallmark Card Company and the production of flour, milling machinery, and agricultural chemicals.

What to See and Do

Carroll Mansion. *1128 5th Ave, Leavenworth (66048). Phone 913/682-7759.* Victorian home (1867) and furnishings; school room; local mementos. Gift shop. (Tues-Sat; closed holidays, also Jan) **$$**

Fort Leavenworth. *600 Thomas Ave, Fort Leavenworth (66027). 3 miles N on Hwy 73. Phone 913/684-5604.* Features of interest are US Army Command and General Staff College, US Disciplinary Barracks, National Cemetery, Buffalo Soldier Monument, and branches of the Oregon and Santa Fe trails. Frontier Army Museum features artifacts of pioneer history and the Army of the West. (Daily; closed holidays) Fort (daily). Obtain self-guided Historical Wayside Tour brochure at the information center inside the fort entrance on Grant Avenue. **FREE**

Frontier Army Museum. *Fort Leavenworth, 100 Reynolds Dr, Leavenworth (66048). Phone 913/684-3191.* Discover the history of Fort Leavenworth and the United States Regular Army on the Frontier. See historic army uniforms, weapons, and equipment, including a 1917 JN4D Jenny biplane and the carriage that Abraham Lincoln traveled in when he visited in 1859. (Mon-Fri 9 am-4 pm, Sat 10 am-4 pm; closed holidays)

Parker Carousel. *Downtown Historic Riverfront Area, Leavenworth.* Restored 1913 carousel features hand-carved, one-of-a-kind horses, ponies, and rabbits. (Daily) **$**

Special Events

Fort Leavenworth Homes Tour and Frontier Army Encampment. *Leavenworth. Phone 913/684-3767.* Mid-Apr.

Lansing Daze. *220 Lion Ln, Lansing (66043). Phone 913/727-3233.* Community-wide festival. Early June.

Leavenworth River Fest. *Historic Riverfront Downtown, 501 Delaware St, Leavenworth (66048). Phone 913/682-3924.* Mid-Sept.

Limited-Service Hotel

★ **DAYS INN.** *3211 S 4th St, Leavenworth (66048). Phone 913/651-6000; toll-free 888/540-4020; fax 913/651-7722. www.daysinn.com.* 52 rooms, 2 story. Complimentary continental breakfast. Check-out noon. Outdoor pool. **$**

Restaurant

★ ★ **SKYVIEW.** *504 Grand Ave, Leavenworth (66048). Phone 913/682-2653. www.skyviewrestaurant.net.* Seafood, steak menu. Dinner. Closed Easter, Thanksgiving, Dec 25. Bar. Victorian house (1892); antique tile fireplaces, hand-woven portieres (circa 1850). Gazebo and herb garden. **$$**

Leawood (B-6)

Web Site www.leawood.org

Restaurants

★ **GATES BAR-B-QUE.** *2001 W 103 Rd, Leawood (66206). Phone 913/383-1752; fax 913/923-3922. www.gatesbbq.com.* Barbecue menu. Lunch, dinner, late-night. Closed Thanksgiving, Dec 25. **$$**

★ ★ ★ **HEREFORD HOUSE.** *5001 Town Center Dr, Leawood (66211). Phone 913/327-0800; fax 913/ 327-0881. www.herefordhouse.com.* Jack Webb founded the original branch of this steakhouse in Kansas City in 1957. Now, this Town Center Plaza location is one of three, and is becoming a statewide favorite for charcoal-grilled steaks and friendly, no-hassle service. Steak menu. Breakfast, dinner. Closed holidays. Bar. Children's menu. Outdoor seating. **$$$**

★ ★ **YAHOOZ.** *4701 Town Center Dr, Leawood (66211). Phone 913/451-8888; fax 913/451-1504. www.eatpbj.com.* Yahooz offers "contemporary cowboy cuisine." The wood-burning fireplaces and leather furniture create a cozy atmosphere, and the lively menu, with kids' choices, makes this a unique steakhouse. American, steak menu. Lunch, dinner, Sun brunch. Closed Dec 25. Bar. Children's menu. Reservations recommended. Outdoor seating. No credit cards accepted. **$$$**

Lenexa (B-6)

Web Site ci.lenexa.ks.us

What to See and Do

Great Mall of the Great Plains. *20700 W 151st St, Olathe (66061). I-35, exit 215. Phone 913/829-6277. www.greatmallgreatplains.com.* Kansas's largest outlet mall offers entertainment for children and adults, great food, great shopping, and more. (Mon-Sat 10 am-9 pm, Sun noon-6 pm)

Restaurants

★ ★ **EL CARIBE.** *12112 W 87th St, Lenexa (66215). Phone 913/599-2270.* Caribbean menu. Lunch, dinner, late-night. Closed Thanksgiving, Dec 25. Bar. Children's menu. **$$**

★ ★ **THE WOKS.** *8615 Hauser Dr, Lenexa (66215). Phone 913/541-1777; fax 913/541-9179.* Chinese menu. Breakfast, lunch, dinner. Closed Thanksgiving, Dec 25. Bar. Children's menu. **$$**

Liberal (D-1)

Founded 1888
Population 16,573
Elevation 2,836 ft
Area Code 620
Zip 67901
Information Tourist Information Center, 1 Yellow Brick Rd; phone 620/626-0170
Web Site www.liberal.net

Liberal's name comes from the generosity of one of its first settlers, Mr. S. S. Rogers. Although water was scarce in southwestern Kansas, Mr. Rogers never charged parched and weary travelers for the use of his well—a "liberal" fee.

Liberal, on the eastern edge of the Hugoton-Oklahoma-Texas Panhandle natural gas field, has many gas and oil company offices. Its agricultural products have become more diversified through irrigation. Beef processing and health care are also important.

What to See and Do

Coronado Museum. *567 E Cedar St, Liberal (67901). Phone 620/624-7624.* Displays depict early life of the town; some exhibits trace Francisco Coronado's route through Kansas. Also included are Dorothy's House from *The Wizard of Oz* and an animated display of the story. (Daily; winter, Tues-Sun; closed holidays) **FREE**

Mid-America Air Museum. *2000 W Second St, Liberal (67901). Phone 620/624-5263.* Aviation collection of 99 aircraft including civilian aircraft, military aircraft from World War II, and planes of the Korean and Vietnam era. Also here is the Liberal Army Airfield exhibit. Theater, library, special events, and guest speakers. (Daily; closed Jan 1, Thanksgiving, Dec 25)

Special Events

Five-State Free Fair. *Fairgrounds, 8th and Western, Liberal (67901). Phone 620/624-3743.* Early-mid-Aug.

International Pancake Race. *Downtown, 6th and Kansas, Liberal (67901). Phone 620/626-0171.* Women compete simultaneously with women in Olney, England, running a 415-yard S-shaped course with a pancake in a skillet, flipping it en route. Day prior to Ash Wednesday.

Oztoberfest. *567 E Cedar St, Liberal (67901). Phone 620/624-7624.* Munchkin parade, carnival. Second weekend in Oct.

Restaurant

★ **KING'S PIT BAR-B-Q.** *355 E Pancake Blvd (Hwy 54), Liberal (67901). Phone 620/624-2451.* Barbecue menu. Lunch, dinner. Children's menu. No credit cards accepted. **$$**

Lindsborg (C-4)

See also McPherson, Salina

Founded 1869
Population 3,076
Elevation 1,333 ft
Area Code 785
Zip 67456
Information Chamber of Commerce, 104 E Lincoln; phone 785/227-3706 or toll-free 888/227-2227
Web Site www.lindsborg.org

Lindsborg was founded by Swedish immigrants who pioneered cooperative farming in Kansas. The Swedish heritage of Lindsborg is evident in the Old World motifs of its business district, Bethany College, and in its cultural life, which includes many ethnic festivals.

What to See and Do

Birger Sandzen Memorial Art Gallery. *401 N 1st St, Lindsborg (67456). On Bethany College campus. Phone 785/227-2220.* Paintings and prints by Birger Sandzen and other artists; fountain by Carl Milles. (Tues-Sun afternoons; closed holidays) **DONATION**

Kanopolis State Park. *200 Horsethief Rd, Lindsborg (67456). 19 miles W on Hwy 4, then N on Hwy 141. Phone 785/546-2565.* A 1,585-acre park on a 3,550-acre lake. Excellent fishing for white bass, crappie, walleye, catfish, and largemouth bass. Hiking and bridle trails in rugged Horsethief Canyon, site of the 150-foot-high Inscription Rock, with petroglyphs representing three Native American cultures covering the face of the cliff. North of the reservoir is the Mushroom Rock area, containing unique sandstone formations shaped like giant toadstools. Beach, bathhouse; fishing; boating (ramp, dock, marina). Picnicking, concession. Tent and trailer camping (electricity, dump station). (Daily) **$$**

McPherson County Old Mill Museum and Park. *120 Mill St, Lindsborg (67456). On the Smoky Hill River. Phone 785/227-3595.* The museum features Native American history, natural history, and collections on pioneer and Swedish culture. The Smoky Valley Roller Mill and Swedish Pavilion (1904) have been restored. (Daily; closed holidays) **$**

Special Events

Lucia Fest. *Lincoln and Main St, Lindsborg (67456). Phone 785/227-3706.* Christmas season ushered in according to 18th-century Swedish tradition. Second Sat in Dec.

Messiah Festival. *421 N 1st St, Lindsborg (67456). Phone 785/227-3311. Presser Hall, Bethany College campus.* Special art shows, concerts, and recitals, including oratorios of Handel and Bach; presented annually since 1882. Eight days, Palm Sunday-Easter.

Midsummer's Day Festival. *Lincoln and Main St, Lindsborg (67456). Phone 785/227-3706.* Swedish ethnic celebration. Folk dancing, arts and crafts. Third Sat in June.

Limited-Service Hotel

★ **VIKING MOTEL.** *446 Harrison, Lindsborg (67456). Phone 785/227-3336; toll-free 800/326-8390.* 24 rooms, 2 story. Complimentary continental breakfast. Check-out 11 am. Outdoor pool. **$**

Restaurant

★ ★ **SWEDISH CROWN.** *121 N Main St, Lindsborg (67456). Phone 785/227-2076.* Swedish, American menu. Lunch, dinner. Closed Mon. Children's menu. **$$**

Manhattan (B-5)

See also Junction City

Founded 1857

Population 37,712
Elevation 1,056 ft
Area Code 785
Zip 66502
Information Convention & Visitors Bureau, 501
Poyntz Ave; phone 785/776-8829 or toll-free 800/759-0134
Web Site www.manhattan.org

Several early settlements were combined to form
Manhattan. Lying in a limestone bowl-shaped depression resulting from glacial action, the town developed
as a trading center for farm products. Later, when
the Rock Island Railroad extended a branch here, it
became a shipping point. Kansas State University is in
Manhattan; its forerunner, Bluemont Central College,
opened in 1863.

What to See and Do

City Park. *1101 Freemont, Manhattan (66502). Poyntz
Ave between 11th and 14th sts.* Phone 785/587-2757.
Picnicking, tennis, playground, games; swimming
(Memorial Day-Labor Day); rose garden with 400
varieties of roses (spring-summer). Also here is a
pioneer log cabin with farm and shop tools on display
(Apr-Oct, Sun; also by appointment; phone 785/565-6490). Historic cast-iron fountain, monument to
Quivera. (Daily) **FREE**

Goodnow House Museum. *2309 Claflin Rd, Manhattan
(66502). In Pioneer Park.* Phone 785/565-6490. (Circa
1860) Original limestone home of Isaac T. Goodnow,
pioneer educator; period furnishings. (Tues-Sun;
closed holidays) **FREE**

Hartford House. *2309 Claflin Rd, Manhattan (66502).
In Pioneer Park.* Phone 785/565-6490. (Circa 1855)
Period furnishings in a restored prefabricated house.
One of ten buildings brought to Manhattan in 1855
on a riverboat by a group of Free Staters (those who
wished to establish Kansas as anti-slavery territory).
(Tues-Sun; closed holidays) **FREE**

Kansas State University. *17th and Anderson sts,
Manhattan (66502). Center of town.* Phone 785/532-6250. www.ksu.edu. (Circa 1863) (21,500 students)
Buildings constructed of native limestone on a 664-acre campus. Geological displays in Thompson Hall
(Mon-Fri). Tours, Anderson Hall (Mon-Fri).

Riley County Historical Museum. *2309 Claflin Rd,
Manhattan (66502). In Pioneer Park.* Phone 785/565-6490. Changing exhibits depict the history of Riley
County; the lifestyle of early Kansas settlers; farm,
household, and Native American tools; clothing,
musical instruments, furniture. Archives and library.
(Tues-Sun; closed holidays) **FREE**

Sunset Zoo. *2333 Oak St, Manhattan (66502). At
Summit Ave, SW edge of city off Hwy 24, Hwy 18.*
Phone 785/587-2737. Houses more than 300 animals,
including snow leopards and red pandas. Includes
the Australian Outback, with wallabies and kangaroos, Primate Building, Asian Forest Preserve, and a
children's petting zoo. (Daily) **$$**

Tuttle Creek State Park. *5020 Tuttle Creek Blvd,
Manhattan (66502). 5 miles N on Hwy 24.* Phone
785/539-7941. A 1,156-acre park on a 13,350-acre
lake. Special observation area with distant views of the
Blue River Valley and Randolph Bridge, the largest in
Kansas. Beach, bathhouse; fishing; boating (marina).
Picnicking, concession. Tent and trailer camping
(electricity, dump station). **$$**

Limited-Service Hotels

★ **ECONO LODGE.** *1501 Tuttle Creek Blvd,
Manhattan (66502).* Phone 785/539-5391; toll-free
800/553-2666; fax 785/539-0847. www.econolodge.com.
119 rooms, 2 story. Pets accepted, some restrictions;
fee. Complimentary continental breakfast. Check-out
noon. Outdoor pool. **$**

★ ★ **HOLIDAY INN.** *530 Richards Dr, Manhattan
(66502).* Phone 785/539-5311; toll-free 800/465-4329;
fax 785/539-8368. www.holiday-inn.com. 197 rooms,
3 story. Pets accepted, some restrictions. Check-out
noon. Restaurant, bar. Indoor pool, children's pool,
whirlpool. **$**

★ ★ **RAMADA PLAZA HOTEL.** *1641 Anderson
Ave, Manhattan (66502).* Phone 785/539-7531; toll-free
800/298-2054; fax 785/539-3909. www.ramada.com.
116 rooms, 6 story. Pets accepted; fee. Check-out
noon. Restaurant, bar. Fitness room. Outdoor pool.
Airport transportation available. **$**

Restaurant

★ ★ **HARRY'S UPTOWN SUPPER CLUB.** *418
Poyntz, Manhattan (66502).* Phone 785/537-1300; fax
785/537-6800. American menu. Lunch, dinner. Closed
Sun; Easter, Thanksgiving, Dec 25. **$**

Mankato (A-4)

See also Belleville, Beloit, Smith Center

Population 1,037
Elevation 1,776 ft
Area Code 785
Zip 66956
Information Chamber of Commerce, 703 N West; phone 785/378-3652

What to See and Do

Lovewell State Park. *Lovewell. 20 miles NE via Hwy 36, Hwy 14, unnumbered road in Lovewell. Phone 785/753-4971.* A 1,100-acre park on a 3,000-acre lake shaded by dense growth of cedar and bur oak. The State Historical Society's Pawnee Indian Village and Archaeological Museum is nearby, east of Lovewell Dam. Beach, bathhouse; boating (ramps, dock, marina). Picnicking, playground, concession. Camping (electricity, dump station). Interpretive center. (Daily) **$$**

Limited-Service Hotel

★ **CREST-VUE MOTEL.** *E Hwy 36, Mankato (66956). Phone 785/378-3515.* 12 rooms. Pets accepted, some restrictions; fee. Check-out 11 am. **$**
🔊 🐾

Marysville (A-5)

See also Seneca

Founded 1854
Population 3,359
Elevation 1,202 ft
Area Code 785
Zip 66508
Information Chamber of Commerce, 101 N 10th St; phone 785/562-3101 or toll-free 800/752-3965
Web Site skyways.lib.ks.us/Kansas/towns/Marysville/

This was the first home station out of St. Joseph, Missouri, on the Pony Express route. Many emigrant parties camped near here in the 1840s-1850s, including the ill-fated Donner Party, for which Donner Pass in California is named.

What to See and Do

Hollenberg Station State Historic Site. *2889 23rd Rd, Hanover (66945). N on Hwy 148, E on Hwy 243. Phone 785/337-2635.* Built in 1857; believed to be the first house in Washington County. Six-room frame structure served as a family house, neighborhood store, and tavern, as well as a station on the Pony Express. (Wed-Sat, also Sun afternoons; closed holidays) **DONATION**

Koester House Museum. *919 Broadway, Marysville (66508). Phone 785/562-2417.* Restored Victorian home of 1876; original furnishings, costumes. (Daily; closed holidays) **$$**

Pony Express Barn Museum. *106 S 8th St, Marysville (66508). Phone 785/562-3901.* Original Pony Express barn (circa 1859), home station #1; houses Native American artifacts, Pony Express memorabilia; doll collection, displays of old tools, and harness equipment. (May-Oct, daily) **DONATION**

Limited-Service Hotel

★ **BEST WESTERN SURF.** *2105 Center St, Marysville (66508). Phone 785/562-2354; toll-free 800/780-7234; fax 785/562-2354. www.bestwestern.com.* 52 rooms, 2 story. Pets accepted, some restrictions; fee. Complimentary continental breakfast. Check-out 11 am. Fitness room. **$**
🐾 👤

McPherson (C-4)

See also Hutchinson, Lindsborg, Newton, Salina

Population 12,422
Elevation 1,495 ft
Area Code 316
Zip 67460
Information Convention & Visitors Bureau, 306 N Main, PO Box 616; phone 316/241-3340 or toll-free 800/324-8022
Web Site www.mcphersonks.org

Both the city and the county bear the name of Civil War hero General James Birdseye McPherson, who was killed in the Battle of Atlanta in 1864. Today the center of a diversified agricultural region, McPherson also has a large oil refinery and manufactures plastic pipe, RVs, pharmaceutical products, fiberglass insulation, and other products.

What to See and Do

Maxwell Wildlife Refuge. *101 N Main St, Canton (67428). 14 miles NE via Hwy 56, Canton exit.* A 2,650-acre prairie provides a natural environment for elk, deer, and buffalo. Observation tower; 46-acre fishing lake, boat ramp; nature trail. Primitive campsites. Tram tours (Memorial Day-Oct, weekends). (Daily) **$$$**

Special Events

Prairie Day Celebration. *Maxwell Wildlife Refuge, Canton (67428).* June.

Scottish Festival and Highland Games. *E Lakeside and Kansas Ave, McPherson (67460).* Fourth weekend in Sept.

Limited-Service Hotel

★ ★ **BEST WESTERN HOLIDAY MANOR.** *2211 E Kansas Ave, McPherson (67640). Phone 620/241-5343; toll-free 888/841-0038; fax 620/241-8086. www.bestwestern.com.* 110 rooms, 2 story. Pets accepted, some restrictions; fee. Check-out noon. Restaurant. Indoor pool, outdoor pool, whirlpool. **$**
🐾 🏊

Meade (D-2)

Population 1,526
Elevation 2,497 ft
Area Code 620
Zip 67864
Information Chamber of Commerce, 200 E Carthage, PO Box 376; phone 620/873-2359
Web Site skyways.lib.ks.us/Kansas/towns/meade/

What to See and Do

Meade County Historical Society. *200 E Carthage, Meade (67864). Phone 620/873-2359.* History of Meade County through exhibits of furnished rooms. (Daily; closed holidays) **DONATION**

Meade State Park. *13051 V Rd, Meade (67864). 13 miles SW on Hwy 23. Phone 620/873-2572.* Originally carved out of the Turkey Track Ranch, this 443-acre park has a varied terrain of prairie, rolling hills, bogs, and a small lake. Beach, bathhouse; fishing; boating (ramps, dock). Picnicking. Camping (electricity, dump station; fee). (Daily) **$$**

Medicine Lodge (D-3)

See also Pratt

Founded 1873
Population 2,453
Elevation 1,510 ft
Area Code 316
Zip 67104
Information Chamber of Commerce, 108 W First St; phone 316/886-3417
Web Site www.cyberlodg.com/mlchamber

Long before settlers came to Kansas, Native Americans of all the Plains tribes peacefully shared the use of a "medicine lodge" on the Medicine River in a spot they regarded as sacred. In 1867, when the US Government planned a peace council to end the Indian wars, the site of the present town was chosen by the tribes for the meeting. Two weeks of negotiations, with 15,000 Native Americans and 600 government commissioners present, resulted in a treaty that fixed the Kansas southern boundary and opened the area to settlement. The town was officially chartered in 1879. Today the town of Medicine Lodge is a shipping point for cattle and wheat and has a large gypsum plant. It was the home of the hatchet-wielding temperance crusader Carry Nation.

What to See and Do

Carry A. Nation Home Memorial. *211 W Fowler Ave, Medicine Lodge (67104). At Oak St.* WCTU shrine and museum; original furnishings. (Daily) **$** Admission includes

> **Medicine Lodge Stockade.** *209 W Fowler, Medicine Lodge (67104).* Replica of the 1874 stockade. Log house with authentic 1800s furnishings; museum with pioneer relics. (Daily)

Gypsum Hills. *103 E Kansas Ave, Medicine Lodge (67104). 4 miles W on Hwy 160.* Deep canyons in hills carved by erosion.

Limited-Service Hotel

★ **BUDGET HOST INN.** *401 W Fowler Ave, Medicine Lodge (67104). Phone 620/886-5673; toll-free 800/316-2673; fax 620/886-5241. www.budgethost.com.* 54 rooms, 2 story. Pets accepted; fee. Check-out 11 am. **$**
🅳 🐾

Newton (C-4)

See also El Dorado, Hutchinson, McPherson, Wichita

Founded 1871
Population 16,700
Elevation 1,448 ft
Area Code 316
Zip 67114
Information Convention & Visitors Bureau, 500 N Main St, Suite 101; phone 316/283-7555 or toll-free 800/899-0455
Web Site www.infonewtonks.com

When the Santa Fe Railroad extended its line to Newton in 1871, the town succeeded Abilene as the terminus of the Chisholm Cattle Trail and the meeting place of cowboys, gamblers, and gunmen.

Mennonites migrating from Russia settled in this area in the 1870s, bringing the Turkey Red hard winter wheat they had developed on the steppes. This revolutionized Kansas agriculture and made it one of the world's greatest wheat areas. Newton still has a large Mennonite population with the oldest educational institution of the sect, Bethel College. Active in historic preservation, Newton has adapted such buildings as the Old Mill, 500 Main Place, and Newton Station into interesting shopping, eating, and business sites.

What to See and Do

Kansas Learning Center for Health. *505 Main St, Halstead (67056). 10 miles W on Hwy 50, then 2 miles S on Hwy 89. Phone 316/835-2662.* Exhibits on the human body; transparent "talking" model. (Mon-Fri; closed holidays) **$**

Kauffman Museum. *27th and Main sts, North Newton (67117). 1 mile N via Hwy 15, opposite entrance to Bethel College. Phone 316/283-1612.* A Mennonite museum devoted to the environment and people of the plains. Exhibits include prairie animals and birds, and the cultural history of the Cheyenne and the central Kansas Mennonites. Log cabin, 1880s farmhouse, barn, and windmill. (Tues-Sun) **$**

Warkentin House. *211 E 1st St, Newton (67114). Phone 316/283-7555.* (Circa 1887) Victorian mansion with original furnishings; also carriage house and gazebo (June-Aug: Tues-Sun afternoons; Apr-May and Sept-Dec: Sat-Sun only). For tours contact the Convention & Visitors Bureau. **$$**

Special Events

Bethel College Fall Festival. *300 E 27th St, Newton (67114). Phone 316/284-5252.* Second weekend in Oct.

Chisholm Trail Festival. *Athletic Park, Newton (67114). Phone 316/282-0308.* Late June-July 4.

Limited-Service Hotel

★ **BEST WESTERN RED COACH INN.** *1301 E 1st St, Newton (67114). Phone 316/283-9120; toll-free 800/780-7234; fax 316/283-4105. www.bestwestern.com.* 81 rooms, 2 story. Pets accepted, some restrictions. Check-out 11 am. Fitness room. Indoor pool, whirlpool. **$**
🔾 🖾 🖼

Norton (A-2)

See also Oberlin, Phillipsburg

Founded 1871
Population 3,017
Elevation 2,339 ft
Area Code 785
Zip 67654
Information Chamber of Commerce, 100 S State St, PO Box 97; phone 785/877-2501
Web Site www.us36.net/nortonkansas

What to See and Do

Gallery of Also-Rans. *105 W Main, Norton (67654). Phone 785/877-3341. www.firststatebank.com.* What do Rufus King, Horatio Seymour, and Charles Pinckney have in common? They all ran for President of the United States but lost. Most "also-rans" slide into obscurity following their loss in the race to the White House, but a Kansas bank attempts to bring a little notice to these presidential losers. On the mezzanine of the First State Bank in Norton, KS, the Gallery of Also-Rans has photos and biographies detailing the political life and downfall of every presidential runner-up. (Mon-Fri; closed holidays) **FREE**

Prairie Dog State Park. *RR 3, Norton. 4 miles W via Hwy 36 to Hwy 261, S 1 mile. Phone 785/877-2953.* A 1,000-acre park on a 600-acre lake. Site of a restored sod house furnished with articles of the homestead era and an original old schoolhouse (circa 1880). Wildlife observation. Beach, bathhouse; fishing; boating (ramps, dock). Picnicking. Camping (electricity, dump station). (Daily) **$$**

Station 15. *Wayside Park, Hwy 36, Norton (67654).* *Phone 785/877-2501.* "Look in" building; 1859 stage-coach depot replica; costumed figures. (Daily) **FREE**

Limited-Service Hotel

★ **HILLCREST MOTEL.** *W Hwy 36, Norton (67654). Phone 785/877-3343; toll-free 800/283-4678; fax 785/877-3377.* 25 rooms. Check-out 11 am. Outdoor pool. Airport transportation available. City park adjacent. **$**

Oakley (B-2)

See also Colby

Population 2,045
Elevation 3,029 ft
Area Code 785
Zip 67748
Information Oakley Area Chamber of Commerce, 313 Center; phone 785/672-4862
Web Site www.oakley-kansas.com

What to See and Do

Fick Fossil and History Museum. *700 W 3rd St, Oakley (67748). Phone 785/672-4839.* Fossils, rocks, minerals; shark tooth collection (11,000 teeth); unique fossil paintings, photographs; general store, sod house, depot replica. Changing exhibits. Tours. (May-Labor Day, Mon-Sat; also Sun afternoons; closed holidays) **DONATION**

Limited-Service Hotel

★ **BEST WESTERN GOLDEN PLAINS MOTEL.** *3506 Hwy 40, Oakley (67748). Phone 785/ 672-3254; toll-free 800/780-7234; fax 785/672-3200. www.bestwestern.com.* 26 rooms, 2 story. Pets accepted, some restrictions. Complimentary continental breakfast. Check-out 11 am. Outdoor pool. **$**

Restaurant

★ ★ **COLONIAL STEAK HOUSE.** *464 Hwy 83, Oakley (67748). Phone 785/672-4720; fax 785/672-4687.* Steak menu. Breakfast, lunch, dinner, brunch. Closed Thanksgiving, Dec 25. Children's menu. **$$**

Oberlin (A-2)

See also Norton

Founded 1873
Population 2,197
Elevation 2,562 ft
Area Code 785
Zip 67749
Information Decatur County Area Chamber of Commerce, 132 S Penn; phone 785/475-3441

What to See and Do

Decatur County Museum. *258 S Penn Ave, Oberlin (67749). Phone 785/475-2712.* Native American artifacts, tools, sod house, church, school, doctor's office, 19th-century depot, jail. (Apr-Nov, Tues-Sat; closed holidays) **$$**

Special Events

Decatur County Fair. *W Hwy 36, Oberlin (67749). Phone 785/475-3441.* 4-H exhibits, parade, carnival, theater production. First full week in Aug.

Mini-Sapa Days. *Decatur County Museum, W Hwy 36, Oberlin (67749). Phone 785/475-3441.* Two-day fall festival honors those killed in the Northern Cheyenne Native American Raid of 1878. First weekend in Oct.

Osawatomie (C-6)

See also Ottawa

Founded 1855
Population 4,590
Elevation 865 ft
Area Code 913
Zip 66064
Information Chamber of Commerce, 526 Main St, PO Box 338; phone 913/755-4114

Osawatomie is chiefly associated with John Brown (1800-1859), most famous of the militant abolitionists. In the 1856 Battle of Osawatomie, five of his men were killed. He was later executed in Charles Town, West Virginia, and buried at his home in North Elba, New York.

What to See and Do

Driving tour. One-hour driving tour includes six sites on the National Register of Historic Places. Contact Chamber of Commerce for details.

Fishing. *City Lake, 4 miles NW.* Marais des Cygnes Wildlife Refuge and Pottawatomie River.

John Brown Memorial Park. *10th and Main sts, Osawatomie (66064). W side of town. Phone 913/755-4384.* Site of one of the first battles of the Civil War. Contains a life-size statue of Brown; also a log cabin he used (now a state museum) with period furnishings. (Wed-Sun; closed Jan 1, Thanksgiving, Dec 25) Picnic facilities. Campsites (hook-ups; fee). Park (daily). **FREE**

Special Event

John Brown Jamboree. *11th and Main St, Osawatomie (66064). Phone 913/755-4114.* Parade, carnival, and entertainment. Mid-June.

Ottawa (C-6)

See also Lawrence, Osawatomie

Founded 1837
Population 10,667
Area Code 785
Zip 66067
Information Franklin County Tourism Bureau, 109 E 2nd St, PO Box 580; phone 785/242-1411
Web Site www.visitottawakansas.com

In 1832, the Ottawa were given land in this area in exchange for their Ohio lands. In 1837, the Reverend Jotham Meeker established the Ottawa Indian Baptist Mission. During the border warfare it was the headquarters for Free State men, including John Brown. Today the town is a trading and manufacturing center.

What to See and Do

Dietrich Cabin Museum. *City Park, Main and 5th sts, Ottawa (66067). Phone 785/242-4097.* In Pioneer log cabin (circa 1859); restored, period furnishings. (June-Aug, Sun, or by appointment) **FREE**

Old Depot Museum. *135 Tecumseh St, Ottawa (66067). 1/2 block S of Hwy 68. Phone 785/242-4097.* Historical museum housing relics of the area; model railroad room; general store; period rooms. (Tues-Sun, daily) **$$**

Ottawa Indian Burial Grounds. *NE of city.* Jotham Meeker is buried here.

Pomona Lake. *5260 Pomona Dam Rd, Ottawa (66067). 20 miles W on Hwy 68, 268. Phone 785/453-2201.* A 4,000-acre lake; eight developed public use areas, one access area. Swimming; fishing, hunting; boating. Nature trails. Picnicking. Primitive camping (free); improved camping, group camping (fee). (Daily) **FREE** Also on the reservoir is

> **Pomona State Park.** *22900 Hwy 368, Ottawa (66543). 15 miles W on Hwy 68, 5 miles W on Hwy 268, then N on Hwy 368. Phone 785/828-4933.* A 490-acre park on a 4,000-acre lake. Beach, bathhouse; fishing; boating (rentals, ramps, docks, marina). Picnicking, shelters. Nature trail. Tent and trailer camping (hook-ups, dump station). Interpretive programs. (Daily) **$$**

Special Events

Franklin County Fair. *Fairgrounds, 208 W 17th St, Ottawa (66067). Phone 785/242-1411.* Rodeo. Third week in July.

Yule Feast Weekend. *1001 S Cedar St, Ottawa (66067). Phone 785/242-1411.* Parade, Christmas homes tours, craft fair. Reservations required for madrigal dinner. First weekend in Dec.

Limited-Service Hotel

★ **TRAVELODGE.** *2209 S Princeton St, Ottawa (66067). Phone 785/242-7000; toll-free 888/540-4024; fax 785/242-8572. www.travelodge.com.* 60 rooms, 2 story. Pets accepted; fee. Complimentary continental breakfast. Check-out 11 am. Outdoor pool. **$**
🔁 ⌷

Overland Park (B-6)

See also Kansas City

Population 111,790
Elevation 950 ft
Area Code 913
Information Convention & Visitors Bureau, 9001 W 110th St, Suite 100, 66210; phone 913/491-0123 or toll-free 800/262-7275
Web Site www.opcvb.org

The suburb Overland Park is located directly south of Kansas City.

What to See and Do

Deanna Rose Children's Farmstead. *138th St and Switzer Rd, Overland Park (66221). Phone 913/897-2360. www.deannarosefarmstead.org.* Feed and pet farm animals (fee), hop on a horse-drawn wagon (fee), and walk through a replica of an early 1900s Kansas farmhouse. Playground equipment. (Memorial Day-Labor Day: daily 9 am-8 pm; Apr-Memorial Day and Labor Day-Oct: daily 9 am-5 pm) **FREE**

Old Shawnee Town. *11501 W 57th St, Shawnee (66203). N on I-35 to Johnson Dr, then W to 57th and Cody. Phone 913/248-2360.* Re-creation of a typical Midwestern pioneer town of the 1800s-early 1900s. The collection of buildings and structures includes both originals and replicas; all are authentically furnished. (Mar-Oct, Tues-Sat; closed holidays) **$**

Overland Park Arboretum and Botanical Gardens. *8909 W 179th St, Overland Park (66221). Phone 913/685-3604.* Three hundred acres including 3 miles of hiking trails (some wheelchair accessible) through gardens; picnic facilities. Naturalized areas feature a Meadow Garden, Butterfly Garden, and Woodland Garden. Continuous development occurring. Guided tours (by appointment). (Daily, weather permitting) **FREE**

Limited-Service Hotels

★ **CLUBHOUSE INN.** *10610 Marty St, Overland Park (66212). Phone 913/648-5555; fax 913/648-7130. www.clubhouseinn.com.* 143 rooms, 3 story. Complimentary full breakfast. Check-out noon. Fitness room. Outdoor pool, whirlpool. **$**

★ ★ **COURTYARD BY MARRIOTT.** *11001 Woodsen St, Overland Park (66211). Phone 913/317-8500; toll-free 800/321-2211; fax 913/317-8585. www.courtyard.com.* 168 rooms, 6 story. Check-in 3 pm, check-out noon. Restaurant, bar. Fitness room. Indoor pool. **$**

★ ★ **DOUBLETREE HOTEL.** *10100 College Blvd, Overland Park (66210). Phone 913/451-6100; toll-free 800/222-8733; fax 913/451-3873. www.doubletree.com.* Located near riverboat casinos, shopping, and entertainment areas. 356 rooms, 18 story. Check-out noon. Restaurant, bar. Fitness room. Indoor pool, whirlpool. Airport transportation available. Business center. **$$**

★ ★ **EMBASSY SUITES.** *10601 Metcalf Ave, Overland Park (66212). Phone 913/649-7060; toll-free 800/362-2779; fax 913/649-9382. www.embassysuites.com.* This hotel is located in the heart of the south Kansas City business district. 199 rooms, 7 story, all suites. Complimentary full breakfast. Check-in 3 pm, check-out noon. Restaurant, bar. Fitness room. Indoor pool, whirlpool. Business center. **$**

★ **HAMPTON INN.** *10591 Metcalf Frontage Rd, Overland Park (66212). Phone 913/341-1551; toll-free 800/426-7866; fax 913/341-8668. www.hamptoninn.com.* 134 rooms, 5 story. Complimentary continental breakfast. Check-out noon. Outdoor pool, whirlpool. **$**

★ ★ **HOLIDAY INN.** *8787 Reeder Rd, Overland Park (66214). Phone 913/888-8440; toll-free 888/825-7538; fax 913/888-3438. www.holiday-inn.com.* This hotel resides at a quiet location in the suburbs with restaurants and taverns nearby. 191 rooms, 7 story. Check-in 3 pm, check-out noon. Restaurant, bar. Fitness room. Indoor pool, outdoor pool, whirlpool. Business center. **$**

Full-Service Hotel

★ ★ ★ **MARRIOTT OVERLAND PARK.** *10800 Metcalf Ave, Overland Park (66210). Phone 913/451-8000; toll-free 800/228-9290; fax 913/451-5914. www.marriott.com.* This full-service hotel is located in suburban Kansas City, near a large office park and about a mile from the shopping at Metcalf South Mall. 390 rooms, 11 story. Check-in 3 pm, check-out noon. Restaurant, bar. Fitness room. Indoor pool, outdoor pool, whirlpool. Airport transportation available. Business center. **$$**

Restaurants

★ ★ **COYOTE GRILL.** *4843 Johnson Dr, Mission (66205). Phone 913/362-3333; fax 913/362-3362. www.eatpbj.com.* Southwestern menu. Lunch, dinner, Sun brunch. Bar. **$$$**

★ **DICK CLARK'S AMERICAN BANDSTAND GRILL.** *10975 Metcalf Ave, Overland Park (66210). Phone 913/451-1600; fax 913/451-4783. www.crghospitality.com/abgrill.* The pictures and memorabilia on the walls depict eras of rock and roll. American menu. Lunch, dinner, late-night. Closed Thanksgiving, Dec 25. Bar. Children's menu. Casual attire. **$$**

★ **DON CHILITO'S.** *7017 Johnson Dr, Mission (66202). Phone 913/432-4615. www.donchilitos.com.* Mexican menu. Lunch, dinner. Closed Thanksgiving, Dec 25. **$**

★ ★ **FIORELLA'S JACK STACK BARBECUE.** *9520 Metcalf Ave, Overland Park (66212). Phone 913/385-7427; fax 913/385-5020. www.jackstackbbq.com.* Barbecue menu. Lunch, dinner. Closed Dec 25. Children's menu. **$$$**

★ ★ **IL TRULLO.** *9056 Metcalf Ave, Overland Park (66212). Phone 913/341-3773; fax 913/341-0138.* Italian menu. Lunch, dinner. Closed Thanksgiving, Dec 25. Bar. **$$**

★ ★ **INDIA PALACE.** *9918 W 87th St, Overland Park (66212). Phone 913/381-1680; fax 913/381-5060.* Indian menu. Lunch, dinner. Closed Jan 1, Thanksgiving, Dec 25. **$$**

★ ★ ★ **J. GILBERT'S WOOD FIRED STEAKS.** *8901 Metcalf Ave, Overland Park (66212). Phone 913/642-8070; fax 913/642-1843. www.jgilberts.com.* Intimate dining room. Steak menu. Dinner. Closed Dec 25. Bar. Children's menu. **$$$**

★ ★ **JOHNNY CASCONE'S.** *6863 W 91st St, Overland Park (66212). Phone 913/381-6837.* American, Italian menu. Lunch, dinner. Closed Thanksgiving, Dec 25. Bar. Children's menu. **$$**
🅳

★ **JUN'S JAPANESE RESTAURANT.** *7660 State Line Rd, Prairie Village (66208). Phone 913/341-4924; fax 913/341-4924.* Japanese menu. Breakfast, lunch, dinner. Closed Thanksgiving, Dec 25. Bar. **$$**
🅳

★ ★ **K. C. MASTERPIECE.** *10985 Metcalf Ave, Overland Park (66210). Phone 913/345-1199; fax 913/345-1854. www.kcmrestaurants.com.* Barbecue menu. Lunch, dinner, brunch. Closed Thanksgiving, Dec 25. Bar. Children's menu. Casual attire. **$$**

★ ★ ★ **NIKKO.** *10800 Metcalf Rd, Overland Park (66210). Phone 913/451-8000; fax 913/451-5914.* Japanese steakhouse with tableside teppanyaki chefs. Entrées include soup, salad, shrimp, steamed rice, and vegetables. Japanese menu. Dinner. Children's menu. Valet parking. **$$**

★ ★ **RAOUL'S VELVET ROOM.** *7222 W 119th St, Overland Park (66213). Phone 913/469-0466; fax 913/469-0091. www.raoulsvelvetroom.com.* American menu. Dinner, late-night. Closed Jan 1, Dec 24. Bar. **$$**

★ **SUSHI GIN.** *9559 Nall Ave, Overland Park (66207). Phone 913/649-8488; fax 913/649-4317. www.sushigin.com.* Japanese menu. Lunch, dinner. Closed Sun; holidays. Children's menu. **$$**

★ ★ ★ **TATSU'S.** *4603 W 90th St, Prairie Village (66207). Phone 913/383-9801; fax 913/383-1770. www.tatsus.com.* French menu. Lunch, dinner. Closed holidays. Bar. **$$**

★ ★ **YIAYIAS EUROBISTRO.** *4701 W 119th St, Overland Park (66209). Phone 913/345-1111; fax 913/345-9930. www.yiayias.com.* Mediterranean menu. Lunch, dinner. Closed Dec 25. Bar. Outdoor seating. **$$**

Parsons (D-6)

See also Chanute, Coffeyville, Independence, Pittsburg

Founded 1871
Population 11,924
Elevation 907 ft
Area Code 620
Zip 67357
Information Chamber of Commerce, 1715 Corning, PO Box 737; phone 620/421-6500 or toll-free 800/280-6401
Web Site www.parsonsks.com

Parsons's economy is based on industry and agriculture. The Union Pacific Railroad is here as well as assorted industries. Dairying, beef cattle, and cereal grains are important.

What to See and Do

Neosho County State Fishing Lake. *200 Heacock Ave, Parsons (67357). Phone 620/421-7093.* 5 miles N on Hwy 59, then 3 miles E on unnumbered road. E Main St. Parsons Lake. Beach, bathhouses. Camping, electrical hook-ups (fee). Camping, electrical hook-ups. (Daily) **FREE**

Pearson-Skubitz Big Hill Lake. *19065 Cherryvale Pkwy, Cherryvale (67335). 9 miles W on Hwy 160, then 5 miles S on unnumbered road, then 3 miles W on unnumbered road.* Phone 620/336-2741. Swimming; fishing; boating (ramps). Hiking. Picnic area. Camping (fee). (Apr-Oct, daily) **FREE**

Oakwood Cemetery. *Parsons. S Leawood.* Contains Civil War graves and monuments.

Parsons Historical Museum. *401 S 18th St, Parsons (67357).* Phone 620/421-7030. Display of items dating from 1871; memorabilia related to Missouri-Kansas-Texas Railroad. (May-Oct, Fri-Sun, also by appointment) **FREE**

Limited-Service Hotel

★ ★ **GUESTHOUSE INTERNATIONAL.** *400 E Main St, Parsons (67357).* Phone 620/421-5000; toll-free 800/214-8378; fax 620/421-9123. 75 rooms, 5 story. Complimentary continental breakfast. Checkout 11 am. Restaurant. Outdoor pool. **$**
🅟 ⌴

Phillipsburg (A-3)

See also Norton, Smith Center, Stockton

Population 2,828
Elevation 1,951 ft
Area Code 785
Zip 67661
Information Phillipsburg Area Chamber of Commerce, 270 State St, PO Box 326; phone 785/543-2321 or toll-free 800/543-2321
Web Site www.phillipsburgks.us

What to See and Do

Kirwin National Wildlife Refuge. *702 E Xavier Rd, Phillipsburg (67661). 5 miles S on Hwy 183, then 6 miles E on Hwy 9, near Kirwin.* Phone 785/543-6673. An overlay project on a flood control reservoir. Auto tour route, nature trail, bird-watching, fishing, hunting. (Daily) **FREE**

Old Fort Bissell. *Phillipsburg. City Park, W edge of town, on Hwy 36.* Phone 785/543-6212. Replicas of fort and sod house; authentic log cabin; one-room schoolhouse (circa 1870); depot; store; old gun collection. (Late Apr-Sept, Tues-Sun). **DONATION**

Special Events

Phillips County Fair. *Phillips County Fairgrounds, Phillipsburg (67661).* Phone 785/543-6845. Early Aug.

Rodeo. *Phillipsburg Rodeo Grounds, Phillipsburg.* Phone 785/543-2321. One of the largest in the state. Early Aug.

Pittsburg (D-6)

See also Fort Scott, Parsons

Founded 1876
Population 17,775
Elevation 944 ft
Area Code 620
Zip 66762
Information Crawford County Convention & Visitors Bureau, 117 W 4th St, PO Box 1115; phone 620/231-1212 or toll-free 800/879-1112
Web Site www.morningsun.net/cvb

Rich in natural resources, this coal center of Kansas began as a mining camp and was named for Pittsburgh, Pennsylvania. Surviving depressions and strikes, today it is a prosperous consumer, industrial, and educational center.

What to See and Do

Crawford County Historical Museum. *651 S Hwy 69, Pittsburg (66762). N of 20th St on Bypass 69.* Phone 620/231-1440. Artifacts related to coal industry of area; also old schoolhouse and store. (Thurs-Sun afternoons; closed holidays) **FREE**

Crawford State Park. *1 Lake Rd, Farlington (66734). 7 miles N on Hwy 69, then 7 miles W on Hwy 57, then 9 miles N on Hwy 7.* Phone 316/362-3671. In the heart of the strip coal mining area, here is a tiny piece of the Ozarks with redbuds and flowering trees in the spring and brilliant autumn colors in the fall. Located on a small lake. Beach, bathhouse; fishing; boating (rentals, ramps, dock, marina). Picnicking, concession. Camping (electricity, dump station). (Daily) **$**

Lincoln Park. *Memorial Dr and Hwy 69 Bypass, Pittsburg (66762).* Phone 620/231-8310. Pittsburg Family Aquatic Center (late May-Aug, daily); wading pool, picnic area and campgrounds, tennis courts, batting cage, playground, kiddie rides. Park (mid-Apr-mid-Oct). Eighteen-hole golf, driving range, miniature golf (all year). Fee for activities. (Daily)

Limited-Service Hotel

★ **HOLIDAY INN EXPRESS.** *4020 Parkview Dr, Pittsburg (66762). Phone 620/231-8700; toll-free 800/465-4329; fax 620/230-0154. www.holiday-inn.com.* 100 rooms, 2 story. Complimentary continental breakfast. Check-out noon. Bar. Fitness room. Outdoor pool, whirlpool. **$**
🏃 🏞

Pratt (D-3)

See also Greensburg, Medicine Lodge

Founded 1884
Population 6,687
Elevation 1,891 ft
Area Code 620
Zip 67124
Information Chamber of Commerce, 114 N Main, PO Box 469; phone 620/672-5501
Web Site www.prattkan.com

What to See and Do

Kansas State Fish Hatchery/Nature Center. *512 SE 25th Ave, Pratt (67124). 2 miles E on Hwy 54, then 1 mile S on Hwy 64. Phone 620/672-5911.* Covers 187 acres and has more than 90 brood ponds, a nature center, aquarium; picnicking. One of the first channel catfish hatcheries. (Spring: daily; rest of year: Mon-Fri) Operations headquarters of the Department of Wildlife and Parks are located on the grounds. **FREE**

Pratt County Historical Society Museum. *208 S Ninnescah, Pratt (67124). Phone 620/672-7874.* Pioneer Room settings include a complete dentist's office, 1890s kitchen, blacksmith shop, gun collection, artifacts, and an old-time Main Street. (Tues-Sun afternoons, also by appointment) **FREE**

Special Events

Miss Kansas Pageant. *Pratt Community College, 114 N Main St, Pratt (67124). Phone 620/672-5501.* First full weekend in June.

Pratt County Fair. *Fairgrounds, 300 S Ninnescah St, Pratt (67124). S of town. Phone 620/672-6121.* Late July.

Limited-Service Hotel

★ **BEST WESTERN HILLCREST.** *1336 E 1st, Pratt (67124). Phone 620/672-6407; toll-free 800/336-2279; fax 620/672-6707. www.bestwestern.com.* 40 rooms. Pets accepted, some restrictions; fee. Complimentary continental breakfast. Check-out 11 am. Outdoor pool. **$**
🐾 🏞

Russell (B-3)

See also Hays

Population 4,781
Elevation 1,826 ft
Area Code 785
Zip 67665
Information Russell County Convention & Visitors Bureau, 610 Main St; phone 785/483-6960 or toll-free 800/658-4686
Web Site www.russellks.org

Russell is located in the heart of an oil district.

What to See and Do

Deines Cultural Center. *820 N Main St, Russell (67665). Phone 785/483-3742.* Houses permanent and traveling art exhibits; also a collection of wood engravings by E. Hubert Deines. (Tues-Sun afternoons) **FREE**

Fossil Station Museum. *331 N Kansas St, Russell (67665). Phone 785/483-3637.* History of Russell County. Also houses furniture and artifacts of settlers in a building made of hand-hewn post rock. (Memorial Day-Labor Day: daily; rest of year: by appointment) **FREE**

Oil Patch Museum. *100 E Edward Ave, Russell (67665). Jct I-70 and Hwy 281. Phone 785/483-6640.* History of the oil industry in Russell County. Outdoor displays of oil equipment are also included. (May-Labor Day, daily) Guided tours. **FREE**

Wilson Dam and Reservoir. *21 miles E on I-70 to Wilson, then 8 miles N on Hwy 232.* Swimming; fishing; boating. Camping (fee) (daily). On the southern shore is

    Wilson State Park. *State Park Rd 1, Sylvan Grove (67481). 21 miles E on I-70, then 5 miles N on Hwy 232. Phone 785/658-2465.* A 927-acre park on a

9,000-acre lake. An area of unique beauty with deep canyons and steep hills devoid of trees and brush. Rugged chimney rocks and arches rim the lake on Hell Creek Canyon. Home to thousands of migratory water fowl. Beach, bathhouse; fishing; boating (rentals, ramps, dock, marina). Hiking trails. Picnicking, concession. Camping (electricity, dump station). (Daily) **$$**

Salina (B-4)

See also Abilene, Lindsborg, McPherson

Founded 1858
Population 42,303
Elevation 1,220 ft
Area Code 785
Information Chamber of Commerce, 120 W Ash, PO Box 586, 67402; phone 785/827-9301
Web Site www.salinakansas.org

The Salina site was chosen by a New York newspaper correspondent who established a store to trade with Native American hunting parties. Business improved in 1860 when gold hunters stocked up on their way to Pikes Peak. The arrival of the Union Pacific Railroad in 1867 brought new growth, and the wheat crops in the 1870s established a permanent economy. Alfalfa, now one of the state's major crops, was first introduced in Kansas by a Salina resident in 1874. The city was rebuilt in 1903 after the Smoky Hill flood destroyed most of the community. Today it is a leading agricultural, regional trade, and medical center. Manufacturing also contributes to its economic base.

What to See and Do

Bicentennial Center. *800 The Midway, Salina (67401).* Phone 785/826-7200. Concerts; trade shows and expositions; athletic events; special events.

Central Kansas Flywheels Inc. *1100 W Diamond Rd, Salina (67401).* Phone 785/825-8473. Museum features antique farm machinery and other artifacts. Bygone Days demonstration (Apr). Antique engine show and tractor pull (Oct). (Mon-Fri or by appointment; closed holidays) **$$**

Salina Art Center. *242 S Santa Fe, Salina (67401).* Phone 785/827-1431. Features art exhibits; also hands-on art laboratory for children. (Tues-Sun afternoons; closed holidays) **FREE**

Smoky Hill Museum. *211 W Iron Ave, Salina (67401).* Phone 785/309-5776. Area history represented by photos and artifacts; changing exhibits; general store period room. (Tues-Sun; closed holidays) **FREE**

Special Events

Smoky Hill River Festival. *Oakdale Park, Salina (67401).* Phone 785/309-5770. Mid-June.

Tri-Rivers Fair and Rodeo. *Kenwood Park, Salina (67401).* Phone 785/826-6532. Early Aug.

Limited-Service Hotel

★ ★ **HOLIDAY INN.** *1616 W Crawford St, Salina (67401).* Phone 785/823-1739; toll-free 800/465-4329; fax 785/823-1791. www.holiday-inn.com. 195 rooms, 3 story. Check-out noon. Restaurant, bar. Fitness room. Indoor pool, outdoor pool, whirlpool. Airport transportation available. **$**
🏃 ⛳

Restaurant

★ **GUTIERREZ.** *1935 S Ohio, Salina (67401).* Phone 785/825-1649. www.gutzsalina.com. Mexican, American menu. Lunch, dinner. Closed Thanksgiving, Dec 25. Children's menu. **$**

Scott City (C-2)

Population 3,785
Elevation 2,978 ft
Area Code 620
Zip 67871
Information Chamber of Commerce, 221 W 5th St; phone 620/872-3525
Web Site www.scottcity.com

What to See and Do

Lake Scott State Park. *520 W Scott Lake Dr, Scott City (67871). 10 miles N on Hwy 83, N on Hwy 95.* Phone 620/872-2061. A memorial marker notes the 17th-century pueblo ruins of El Cuartelejo; the old Steele home is open for viewing. Spring-fed lake is bordered by willow, cedar, elm, pine, and cottonwood trees. Beach, bathhouse; boats (rentals, ramp, dock). Picnicking, concession. Camping (electricity, dump station). (Daily) **$$**

Seneca (A-5)

See also Hiawatha, Marysville

Population 2,027
Elevation 1,131 ft
Area Code 785
Zip 66538
Information Chamber of Commerce, PO Box 135; phone 785/336-2294

What to See and Do

Fort Markley and Indian Village. *5260 Pomona Dam Rd, Seneca (66538). 1/2 mile W on Hwy 36. Phone 785/336-2285.* Old Western town, museum, antique shop; fishing; tent and trailer sites (fee); restaurant. (Daily) **$**

Nemaha County Historical Museum. *113 N 6th St, Seneca (66538). Phone 785/336-6366.* Old county jail with a resident sheriff; memorabilia from a local farmer; variety of items used over a century ago. (May-Sept: Mon-Fri, Sun afternoons; holidays and rest of year: by appointment).

Shawnee (B-6)

Web Site www.cityofshawnee.org

Restaurants

★ ★ **LEONA YARBROUGH'S.** *10310 W 63rd St, Shawnee (66203). Phone 913/248-0500; fax 913/248-1070. www.yarbroughsrestaurant.com.* American menu. Lunch, dinner. Children's menu. **$$**

★ ★ **PAULO & BILL.** *16501 Midland Dr, Shawnee (66217). Phone 913/962-9900; fax 913/962-9377.* Italian, American menu. Breakfast, lunch, dinner. Closed holidays. Bar. Children's menu. Outdoor seating. **$$**

Smith Center (A-3)

See also Mankato, Phillipsburg

Population 2,016
Elevation 1,804 ft
Area Code 785
Zip 66967
Information Smith Center Area Chamber of Commerce, 219 S Main St; phone 785/282-3895
Web Site www.smithcenterks.com

What to See and Do

Home on the Range Cabin. *Smith Center. 8 miles W on Hwy 36, then 8 miles N on Hwy 8, then 3/4 miles W. Phone 785/282-6258.* Restored cabin where homesteader Dr. Brewster M. Higley wrote the words to the song "Home on the Range" in 1872. (Daily) **FREE**

Old Dutch Mill. *Wagner Park, 3rd and Main sts, Smith Center (66967). Phone 785/456-7344.* (May-Sept, daily) **FREE**

Stockton (B-3)

See also Phillipsburg

Population 1,507
Elevation 1,792 ft
Area Code 785
Zip 67669
Information City of Stockton, 115 S Walnut, PO Box 512; phone 785/425-6162
Web Site www.stocktonkansas.net

What to See and Do

Frank Walker Museum. *921 S Cedar, Stockton (67669). Phone 785/425-7217.* Houses artifacts related to Rooks County history; records, old newspapers, photographs, family heirlooms; horse-drawn buggy; displays include old-time general store, schoolroom, and doctor's office. (Tues-Sat; other times by appointment) **FREE**

Log Hotel. *Hwy 24 and Cypress sts, Stockton (67669).* Replica of the first log hotel.

Webster State Park. *1285 11 Rd, Stockton (67669). 9 miles W on Hwy 24. Phone 785/425-6775.* An 880-acre park located on Webster Reservoir on the south fork of the Solomon River, with 1,400 acres of water. Walleye, catfish, bass, crappie, and bullhead. Beach, bathhouse; fishing; boating (ramps, dock). Trails. Picnicking. Camping (electricity, dump station). (Daily) **$$**

Topeka (B-5)

See also Kansas City, Lawrence

Founded 1854
Population 119,883

Elevation 951 ft
Area Code 785
Information Convention & Visitors Bureau, 1275 SW Topeka Blvd, 66612; phone 785/234-1030 or toll-free 800/235-1030
Web Site www.topekacvb.org

The capital city of Kansas was born because a young Pennsylvanian, Colonel Cyrus K. Holliday, wanted to build a railroad. The present Topeka site on the Kansas River (familiarly the Kaw) was chosen as a suitable terminus, and a town company was formed in 1854. It flourished, becoming the Shawnee county seat in 1857; in 1861 when Kansas became a state, Topeka was designated state capital. Colonel Holliday's railroad, the Atchison, Topeka, and Santa Fe, began to build westward from Topeka in 1869; its general offices and machine shops were established there in 1878 and are still important to the city. Other industries today include tires, steel products, cellophane, printing, insurance, grain milling, and meat packing. World-famous psychiatric clinic and research center, the Menninger Foundation, is in Topeka. Herbert Hoover's vice president, Charles Curtis, who was part Kaw and a descendant of one of Topeka's earliest settlers, was born here.

What to See and Do

Brown v. Board of Education National Historic Site. *424 S Kansas Ave, Topeka (66603). Phone 785/354-4273. www.nps.gov/brvb/.* This site commemorates the US Supreme Court's ground-breaking 1954 finding that segregation in public schools is unconstitutional. Here you'll find Monroe Elementary School, one of Topeka's four formerly segregated elementary schools for African-American children, along with interpretive exhibits and educational programs. (Mon-Fri 8 am-4 pm; closed federal holidays)

Combat Air Museum. *J St Hangars #602 and #604, Topeka. Forbes Field, 5 miles S on Hwy 75. Phone 785/862-3303.* Jets, cargo transports, fighters, and trainers from 1917 to 1980 are displayed here, as well as military artifacts. Guided tours (by appointment). (Daily; closed holidays) **$$**

Gage Park. *9635 SW Gage Blvd, Topeka (66603). Phone 785/368-3700.* Tennis, swimming, softball, and volleyball facilities are available here, along with playground equipment for different ages and abilities. The newly restored carousel was built in 1908 and operates from 10 am to 8 pm (75 cents) during the summer and on weekends only in September and October. A mini-train ($) runs along the park for a pretty view. Home to the Topeka Zoo (phone 785/368-9180; daily 10 am-5 pm). (Daily sunrise-sunset) **FREE**

Governor's Mansion (Cedar Crest). *Fairlawn Rd and I-70, Topeka (66603). 1 mile N. Phone 785/296-3636.* Period architecture with Loire Valley overtones on 244 acres. Built in 1928, bequeathed to the state in 1955, it became the governor's residence in 1962. Guided tours (Mon afternoons). **FREE**

Heartland Park Topeka. *7530 SW Hwy 75, Topeka (66619). Phone 785/862-4781; toll-free 800/437-2237.* Motorsports complex featuring professional and amateur race events. (Daily)

Historic Ward-Meade Historical Park. *124 NW Fillmore, Topeka (66606). Phone 785/368-3888.* Historical Ward-Meade house, restored rock livery stable, log cabin, depot, general store, caboose, and one-room schoolhouse (Mar-Oct: Mon-Fri; Nov-Feb: weekends by appointment; two tours daily). Botanical gardens (free). Gift shop. **$$**

Kansas Museum of History. *6425 SW 6th St, Topeka (66615). Phone 785/272-8681.* Contains displays relating to the history of Kansas and the plains. Museum, changing exhibits, hands-on Discovery Place. (Tues-Sun; closed holidays) **DONATION**

Kansas State Historical Society. *Center for Historical Research, 6425 SW 6th St, Topeka (66615). Phone 785/272-8681.* Library of Kansas, Native American, and Western history and genealogy; one of the largest newspaper collections in the nation; manuscript, photograph, and map collections. State Historic Preservation Office; State Archaeology Office. (Tues-Sat; closed holidays) **FREE**

Lake Shawnee Recreational Area. *3131 SE 29th St, Topeka (66605). SE 29th St and West Edge Rd. Phone 785/267-1156.* Lake Shawnee, covering more than 400 acres, offers fishing, boating, sailing, and swimming and is surrounded by more than 1,500 acres of parkland with foot trails, a golf course, a marina, tennis courts, shelter houses, ball diamonds, and gardens. (Daily sunrise-sunset) **FREE**

Perry State Park. *5441 Westlake Rd, Topeka (66070). 16 miles E via Hwy 24, 4 miles N on Hwy 237. Phone 785/246-3449.* A 1,600-acre park on 12,200-acre lake. Beach, bathhouse; fishing; boating (ramps, docks). Trails. Picnicking. Camping (electricity, dump station). (Daily) **$$**

⭐ **Potwin Place.** *400 Woodlawn, Topeka (66606). Between 1st and 4th sts on Woodlawn and Greenwood sts.* Phone 785/234-1030. A community of stately homes, towering trees, and distinctive circular parks on 70 acres. Begun in 1869, the area is a landmark of Topeka's heritage. Self-conducted walking and driving tours. **FREE**

State Capitol. *300 W 10th St, Topeka (66603). On 20-acre square in center of city.* Phone 785/296-3966. Design based on US Capitol. On the grounds are statues of Lincoln and Pioneer Woman, both by Topeka-born sculptor Merrell Gage; murals on second floor by John Steuart Curry; those on the first floor are by David H. Overmeyer; second floor statuary by Pete Felten, Jr. Guide service (Mon-Fri; closed Jan 1, Thanksgiving, Dec 25). **FREE**

Topeka Zoo. *6th St, Topeka (66603). 6th and 10th St entrances, inside Gage Park on Gage Blvd.* Phone 785/272-5821. Discovering Apes Building with orangutans and gorillas exhibit; Black Bear exhibit; Lions Pride exhibit; tropical rain forest under geodesic dome with plants and free-roaming animals. (Daily 10 am-5 pm; closed Dec 25) **$$**

Washburn University of Topeka. *1700 SW College Ave, Topeka (66621).* Phone 785/231-1010. (1865) (6,100 students) Liberal arts college. Tours, including Mulvane Art Center, Petro Allied Health Center, an observatory, and a planetarium.

Special Events

Huff 'n Puff Balloon Rally. *Lake Shawnee, Topeka (66605).* Phone 785/234-1030. Hot air balloons. Sept.

Washburn Sunflower Music Festival. *1700 SW College Ave, Topeka (66621).* Phone 785/231-1010. International symphonic musicians perform nightly. First two weeks in June.

Limited-Service Hotels

★ **CLUBHOUSE INN.** *924 SW Henderson Rd, Topeka (66615). Phone 785/273-8888; toll-free 800/258-2466; fax 785/273-5809. www.clubhouseinn.com.* 121 rooms, 2 story. Complimentary full breakfast. Check-out 11 am. Outdoor pool, whirlpool. **$** 🏊

★ **DAYS INN.** *1510 SW Wanamaker Rd, Topeka (66604). Phone 785/272-8538; toll-free 800/329-7466; fax 785/272-8538. www.daysinn.com.* 62 rooms, 2

story. Pets accepted; fee. Complimentary continental breakfast. Check-out 11 am. Indoor pool, whirlpool. **$** 🐾 🏊

★ ★ **RAMADA INN.** *420 E 6th St, Topeka (66607). Phone 785/234-5400; toll-free 800/272-6232; fax 785/233-0460. www.ramada.com.* 360 rooms, 11 story. Pets accepted. Check-out noon. Restaurant, bar. Indoor pool, outdoor pool. **$** 🐾 🏊

Restaurants

★ **CARLOS O'KELLY'S.** *3425 S Kansas Ave, Topeka (66611). Phone 785/266-3457; fax 785/266-2563. www.carloskellys.com.* Mexican, American menu. Lunch, dinner. Closed holidays. Bar. Children's menu. **$$**

★ ★ **MCFARLAND'S.** *4133 W Gage Center Dr, Topeka (66604). Phone 785/272-6909.* American menu. Lunch, dinner. Closed Mon, holidays. Bar. Children's menu. **$$**

WaKeeney (B-2)

See also Hays

Founded 1877
Population 2,161
Elevation 2,465 ft
Area Code 785
Zip 67672
Information Chamber of Commerce, 216 Main St; phone 785/743-2077

This county seat, halfway between Denver and Kansas City, produces extra-high-protein wheat. It is known as the "Christmas City of the High Plains."

What to See and Do

Cedar Bluff State Park. *8 miles SE on I-70, then 13 miles S on Hwy 147, exit 135.* Phone 785/726-3212. A 1,700-acre park on a 6,800-acre lake. Channel catfish, bass, crappie and walleye. Dam is 12,500 feet long and rises 134 feet above the stream bed. Sweeping view of the Smoky Hill River Valley as it winds through prehistoric, fossil-rich chalk beds. Beach, bathhouse; fishing; boating (ramps, docks). Trails. Picnicking. Tent and trailer camping (electricity, dump station). (Daily) **$$**

Chalk beds. *In Smoky Hill River Valley. W of town.* Rich in fossils.

Special Events

The Gatherin'. *Eisenhower Park, Cedar Bluff, WaKeeney (67672). Phone 785/743-2077.* Highland games, Celtic music, and storytelling. First Sat in May.

Trego County Free Fair. *County fairgrounds, WaKeeney (67672). Phone 785/743-5806.* Late July.

Specialty Lodging

The following lodging establishment is approved by Mobil Travel Guide, but due to its unique and individualized nature has not been given a traditional Mobil Star rating. Included in this listing you may find bed-and-breakfasts, limited-service inns, guest ranches, and other unique hotel properties.

THISTLE HILL BED & BREAKFAST. *RR 1, WaKeeney (67672). Phone 785/743-2644; fax 785/ 734-2644. www.thistlehillonline.com.* 3 rooms, 2 story. Complimentary full breakfast. Check-in 4 pm, check-out 11 am. On a 320-acre farm with a 60-acre wildflower preserve. **$**
🅱

Wichita (D-4)

See also El Dorado, Hutchinson, Newton

Settled 1864
Population 304,011
Elevation 1,305 ft
Area Code 316
Information Convention & Visitors Bureau, 100 S Main, Suite 100, 67202; phone 316/265-2800 or toll-free 800/288-9424
Web Site www.visitwichita.com

The largest city in Kansas has a definite metropolitan flavor, with its tall buildings, wide streets, and bustling tempo. Still a major marketing point for agricultural products, it is now best known as an aircraft production center. McConnell Air Force Base is here. Wichita is the petroleum capital of Kansas, with many independent oil companies represented. Some of the nation's largest grain elevators for wheat storage are here.

The town's first settlers were the Wichita, who built a village of grass lodges on the site. The following year James R. Mead set up a trading post and in 1865 sent his assistant, Jesse Chisholm, on a trading expedition to the Southwest. His route became famous as the Chisholm Trail, over which longhorn cattle were driven through Wichita to the Union Pacific at Abilene. As the railroad advanced to the southwest, Wichita had its turn as the "cow capital" in the early 1870s. By 1880, farmers drawn by the land boom had run fences across the trail and the cattle drives were shifted west to Dodge City. The interrupted prosperity was restored by wheat crops of the next two decades and the discovery of oil after World War I.

What to See and Do

Allen-Lambe House Museum and Study Center. *255 N Roosevelt St, Wichita (67208). Phone 316/687-1027.* Designed in 1915 by Frank Lloyd Wright as a private residence, it is considered the last of Wright's prairie houses. Living and dining room surround a sunken garden; furniture designed by Wright in collaboration with interior designer George M. Niedecken. Visitor center, bookstore. Guided tours (by appointment only, minimum of five people). **$$$**

Botanica, The Wichita Gardens. *701 Amidon, Wichita (67203). Phone 316/264-9799 (recording).* Display of exotic flowers as well as plants native to Kansas. Among the gardens are the Butterfly Garden, Shakespearean Garden, Aquatic Collection, and Xeriscape Demonstration Garden. (Apr-Dec: daily; rest of year: Mon-Fri) **$$**

Century II Convention Center. *225 W Douglas, Wichita (67202). Phone 316/264-9121.* Circular structure houses convention and exhibition halls, meeting rooms, theater, concert hall. For ticket information, phone 316/263-4717.

Cheney State Park. *16000 NE 50 St, Cheney (67025). 20 miles W on Hwy 54, then 4 miles N on Hwy 251. Phone 316/542-3664.* A 1,913-acre park on a 9,537-acre lake. Popular with sailboat and windsurfing enthusiasts. Large-scale regattas are a featured part of the many lake activities. Beach, bathhouse; fishing; boating (ramps, docks, marina). Picnicking, concession. Camping (electricity, dump station). (Daily) **$$**

Clifton Square Shopping Village. *3700 E Douglas, Wichita (67028). At Clifton, in the historic College Hill neighborhood. Phone 316/686-2177.* Nineteenth-century houses converted into shops; brick walkways and old-fashioned lampposts. (Daily)

Edwin A. Ulrich Museum of Art. *On Wichita State University campus, in the McKnight Art Center, 1845 Fairmount, Witchita (67203). Phone 316/978-3664.* Exhibitions of contemporary art; also outdoor mosaic mural by Joan Miró. (Tues-Sun) Tours by appointment. Also on campus are

>   **Corbin Education Center.** *1845 Fairmount, Wichita (67203). Near Yale and 21st sts.* Designed by Frank Lloyd Wright. (Mon-Fri)

>   **Martin H. Bush Outdoor Sculpture Collection.** *129 McKnight Art Center E, Wichita (67260).* Boasts a 60-piece collection of 20th-century sculpture by internationally known artists.

Indian Center Museum. *650 N Seneca, Wichita (67203). Phone 316/262-5221.* Changing exhibits of past and present Native American art. (Tues-Sun; closed holidays) **$$$**

Lake Afton Public Observatory. *25000 W 39th St S, Wichita (67260). 15 miles SW via Hwy 54, Viola Rd exit. Phone 316/978-7827.* Public programs (two hours) offer the opportunity to view a variety of celestial objects through a 16-inch reflecting telescope; astronomy computer games; exhibits and displays. Programs begin 1/2 hour after sunset. (Sept-May: Fri-Sat; June-Aug: Fri-Sun; closed Dec 23-Jan 1) **$$**

O. J. Watson Park. *3055 S Lawrence Rd, Wichita (67217). S Lawrence Rd at Carp St, just S of Arkansas River. Phone 316/529-9940.* Covers 119 acres; fishing, boats; miniature golf; pony, train, and hayrack rides (fees). Picnic area, concession. (Mar-Nov) **FREE**

Old Cowtown Museum. *1871 Sim Park Dr, Wichita (67203). Phone 316/264-0671.* A 40-building historic village museum depicting Wichita life in the 1870s; restaurant, shops. (Apr-Oct, daily) (See SPECIAL EVENTS) **$$$**

Omnisphere and Science Center. *220 S Main St, Wichita (67202). Phone 316/337-9178.* Planetarium and hands-on science center. (Tues-Sat; closed holidays) **$$**

Sedgwick County Zoo. *5555 Zoo Blvd, Wichita (67212). Phone 316/660-9453. www.scz.org.* Animals in their natural habitat; African veldt; herpetarium; jungle; pampas; prairie; outback; boat and train rides (summer). (Daily) **$$$**

Wichita Art Museum. *1400 Museum Blvd, Wichita (67203). Phone 316/268-4921.* Traveling exhibits; collection of American art; paintings and sculpture by Charles M. Russell; pre-Columbian art; works by contemporary and historic Kansas artists. (Tues-Sun; closed holidays) **FREE**

Wichita Center for the Arts. *9112 E Central, Wichita (67206). Phone 316/634-2787.* Changing and permanent exhibits. (Tues-Sun; closed holidays) Also School of Art for adults and children, theater with concerts, plays, and recitals. **FREE**

Wichita-Sedgwick County Historical Museum. *204 S Main St, Wichita (67202). Phone 316/265-9314.* Local history, Native American artifacts, period rooms, costume collection, 1917 Jones Auto display. (Tues-Sun; closed holidays) **$$**

Special Events

Indian Powww. *Indian Center Museum, 650 N Seneca St, Wichita (67203). Phone 316/262-5221.* Tribes gather from all over the country and Canada. Traditional dances; crafts; ethnic food. Sep.

Jazz Festival. *Wichita State University, 1318 W 18th St N, Wichita (67203). Phone 316/262-2351.* Jazz clinic; entertainment. Apr.

National Baseball Congress World Series. *Lawrence Stadium, 300 S Sycamore St, Wichita (67213). Phone 316/267-3372.* (Amateur) Late July-early Aug.

Old Sedgwick County Fair. *Old Cowtown Museum, 1871 Sim Park Dr, Wichita (67203). Phone 316/264-0671.* Re-creation of 1870s fair; crafts, livestock, demonstrations, music, food, games. First full weekend in Oct.

Wichita River Festival. *1820 E Douglas Ave, Wichita (67214). Phone 316/267-2817.* Includes twilight pop concert and fireworks; antique bathtub races; hot air balloon launch; athletic events; entertainment. Mid-May.

Limited-Service Hotels

★ **CLUBHOUSE INN.** *515 S Webb Rd, Wichita (67207). Phone 316/684-1111; fax 316/684-0538. www.clubhouseinn.com.* 120 rooms, 2 story. Complimentary full breakfast. Check-out noon. Outdoor pool, whirlpool. **$**

★ **COMFORT SUITES AIRPORT.** *658 Westdale Dr, Wichita (67209). Phone 316/945-2600; fax 316/945-5033.* 50 rooms, 3 story. Pets accepted, some restrictions; fee. Complimentary full breakfast. Check-out noon. Bar. Fitness room. Outdoor pool. Airport transportation available. **$**

★ **DAYS INN.** *550 S Florence St, Wichita (67209). Phone 316/942-1717; toll-free 800/329-7466; fax 316/942-1717. www.daysinn.com.* 42 rooms, 2 story. Complimentary continental breakfast. Check-out 11 am. **$**

★ ★ **HOLIDAY INN.** *549 S Rock Rd, Wichita (67207). Phone 316/686-7131; toll-free 800/465-4329; fax 316/686-0018. www.holiday-inn.com.* 238 rooms, 9 story. Pets accepted; fee. Check-out noon. Restaurant, bar. Indoor pool, outdoor pool. Business center. **$**

Full-Service Hotels

★ ★ ★ **HYATT REGENCY WICHITA.** *400 W Waterman, Wichita (67202). Phone 316/293-1234; toll-free 800/633-7313; fax 316/293-1200. www.hyatt.com.* 303 rooms, 18 story. Check-out noon. Restaurant, bar. Fitness room. Indoor pool. Business center. **$**

★ ★ **MARRIOTT WICHITA.** *9100 E Corporate Hills Dr, Wichita (67207). Phone 316/651-0333; toll-free 800/610-0673; fax 316/651-0990. www.marriott.com.* 294 rooms, 11 story. Check-out noon. Restaurant, bar. Fitness room. Indoor pool, outdoor pool, whirlpool. Airport transportation available. Business center. **$$**

Specialty Lodging

The following lodging establishment is approved by Mobil Travel Guide, but due to its unique and individualized nature has not been given a traditional Mobil Star rating. Included in this listing you may find bed-and-breakfasts, limited-service inns, guest ranches, and other unique hotel properties.

INN AT THE PARK. *3751 E Douglas, Wichita (67218). Phone 316/652-0500; toll-free 800/258-1951; fax 316/652-0525. www.innathepark.com.* Built in 1909, with luscious landscaping, rich hardwood floors, and eight fireplaces, this 7,400 square foot mansion calms the senses and warms the spirit. Guests can enjoy fresh muffins and specially brewed coffee in the morning, then go for a horse-drawn carriage ride. 12 rooms, 3 story. Complimentary full breakfast. Check-in 4 pm, check-out 11 am. High-speed Internet access. **$**

Restaurants

★ ★ **GRAPE.** *550 N Rock Rd, Wichita (67206). Phone 316/634-0113.* Steak menu. Lunch, dinner. Closed Sun; holidays. Bar. Outdoor seating. **$$**

★ ★ ★ **OLIVE TREE.** *2949 N Rock Rd, Wichita (67226). Phone 316/636-1100; fax 316/636-1158. www.olivetreebistro.com.* There is a good blend between comfort and sophistication, both on the plate and in the dining-room décor, at this European-style bistro with its extensive wine list. Carryout, catered banquets, Sunday brunch. American menu. Lunch, dinner, late-night, Sun brunch. Closed Jan 1, Dec 25. **$$**

Winfield (D-4)

See also Arkansas City

Founded 1870
Population 11,931
Elevation 1,127 ft
Area Code 620
Zip 67156
Information Chamber of Commerce, 205 E 9th, PO Box 640; phone 620/221-2420
Web Site www.winfieldchamber.org

Settled on land leased from Osage Chief Chetopah for $6, Winfield manufactures crayons, water coolers, and ice chests, and has oil and gas wells.

What to See and Do

City Lake. *Winfield. 10 miles NE. Phone 620/221-5635.* A 2,400-acre recreation area including reservoir with a 21-mile shoreline. Swimming; fishing; boating (launching ramp). Tent and trailer camping. (Daily) **$$**

Cowley County Historical Museum. *1011 Mansfield, Winfield (67156). Phone 620/221-4811.* Glass collection, period rooms, early artifacts, library, archives. (Tues-Sun) **FREE**

Fairgrounds and Pecan Grove. *Winfield (67156). W end of North Ave.* Surrounded by Walnut River. Fishing. Picnicking, playground. (Daily) **FREE**

Limited-Service Hotel

★ **BEST VALUE INN.** *1710 Main St, Winfield (67156). Phone 620/221-9050; fax 620/221-7062.* 29 rooms, 2 story. Check-out 11 am. **$**
🅳

Yates Center (C-5)

See also Chanute, Eureka, Iola

Population 1,815
Elevation 1,136 ft
Area Code 620
Zip 66783
Information Woodson County Chamber of Commerce, 108 S Main St, PO Box 211; phone 620/625-3235
Web Site www.woodsoncounty.net

What to See and Do

Toronto State Park. *144 Hwy 105, Toronto (66777). 12 miles W on Hwy 54, then S on Hwy 105. Phone 620/637-2213.* A 1,075-acre park at a 2,800-acre lake. Located in the Chautauqua Hills region, the forested uplands of Black Jack and Post Oak overlook the reservoir nestled in the Verdigris Valley. Beach, bathhouse; fishing; boating (ramps, docks). Trails. Picnicking, concession. Tent and trailer camping (fee; reservations accepted; hook-ups, dump station). (Daily) **$$**

For a change of scenery, leave the flatlands of Kansas behind and spend the weekend exploring the mountain vistas of Denver. The Mile-High City, about three hours from the Kansas border on I-70, has something to offer just about every traveler, from cultural events to outdoor activities to distinctive boutiques to relaxing gardens.

Denver, CO

3 hours, 197 miles from Goodland, KS

Settled 1858
Population 544,636
Elevation 5,280 ft
Area Code 303
Information Denver Metro Convention & Visitors Bureau, 1555 California St, Suite 300, 80202; phone 303/892-1112 or toll-free 800/233-6837
Web Site www.denver.org

The Mile High City, capital of Colorado, began as a settlement of gold seekers, many of them unsuccessful. In its early years, Denver almost lost out to several booming mountain mining centers in becoming the state's major city. In 1858, the community consisted of some 60 raffish cabins, plus Colorado's first saloon. With the onset of the silver rush in the 1870s, Denver came into its own. By 1890, the population had topped 100,000. Nourished by the wealth that poured in from the rich mines in the Rockies, Denver rapidly became Colorado's economic and cultural center. It boomed again after World War II and in the 1990s; there were a few financial busts along the way as well.

Today, with the Great Plains sweeping away to the east, the foothills of the Rocky Mountains immediately to the west, and a dry, mild climate, Denver is a growing city with 2.5 million people in the metropolitan area. A building boom in the 1990s resulted in a new airport, a downtown

baseball park surrounded by a lively nightlife district dubbed LoDo ("lower downtown"), new football and basketball/hockey stadiums, and a redeveloped river valley just west of downtown with an aquarium, amusement park, and shopping district. Once economically hitched to the ebb and flow of the market for Colorado's natural resources, Denver now boasts one of the most diverse economies in the United States and is entrenched as a hub for the cable and telecom industries.

Parks have long been a point of civic pride in Denver, and the Denver Mountain Park System is a unique land-management arrangement in the Rocky Mountain foothills (beyond the city limits). It covers 13,448 acres, scattered over 380 square miles. The chain begins 15 miles west of the city at Red Rocks Park (the site of a renowned musical venue) and extends to Summit Lake (perched 12,740 feet above sea level), 60 miles to the west.

What to See and Do

16th Street Mall. *16th St, Denver (80202). Between Market St and Broadway. Phone 303/534-6161.* This tree-lined pedestrian promenade of red-and-gray granite runs through the center of Denver's downtown shopping district; outdoor cafés, shops, restaurants, hotels, fountains, and plazas line its mile-long walk. European-built shuttle buses offer transportation from either end of the promenade. Along the mall are

    Larimer Square. *Larimer and 14th sts, Denver (80202). Phone 303/534-2367. www.larimersquare.com.* Restoration of the first street in Denver, this collection of shops, galleries, nightclubs, and restaurants is set among Victorian courtyards, gaslights, arcades, and buildings; carriage rides around square. (Daily)

    Tabor Center. *1201 16th St, Denver (80202). Between Arapahoe and Larimer sts. Phone 303/628-1000. www.taborcenter.com.* Tabor Center is a sophisticated urban shopping, dining, and lodging center in the heart of downtown Denver's retail district. Though smaller than outlying malls, Tabor Center nevertheless provides a full array of name-brand men's and women's apparel, gift and jewelry stores, a food court, and three full-service restaurants: The Cheesecake Factory, Big Bowl, and ESPN Zone. The center recently underwent a $26 million renovation. (Mon-Sat 10 am-7 pm; closed Jan 1, Dec 25)

Antique Row. *400-2000 S Broadway, Denver (80210). Phone 303/765-1372. www.antiques-internet.com/colorado/antiquerow.* Denver's largest concentration of antique dealers can be found along a 14-block stretch of South Broadway. More than 400 shops sell everything old, from books to music, vintage Western wear to museum-quality furniture. Take the light rail to Broadway and I-25 to begin your antiquing tour. Most dealers are located between the 400 and 2000 blocks of South Broadway and 25 and 27 blocks of East Dakota Avenue. (Daily)

Arvada Center for the Arts & Humanities. *6901 Wadsworth Blvd, Arvada (80003). Phone 303/431-3080. www.arvadacenter.org.* Performing arts center with concerts, plays, classes, demonstrations, art galleries, banquet hall. Amphitheater seats 1,200 (June-early Sept). Historical museum with old cabin and pioneer artifacts. Museum and gallery (Mon-Fri 9 am-6 pm, Sat 9 am-5 pm, Sun 1-5 pm). **FREE**

⭐ **The Brown Palace Hotel.** *321 17th St, Denver (80202). One block from the 16th St pedestrian mall. Phone 303/297-3111; toll-free 800/321-2599. www.brownpalace.com.* Located in the heart of downtown Denver, this stunning landmark hotel has played gracious host to presidents, princesses, and countless celebrities in the 110 years since it was built by noted Colorado architect Frank E. Edbrooke. With its unique triangle shape and nine-story atrium lobby, it is worth a visit, if only to experience the sheer opulence of its interior details and lush décor. For a real taste of turn-of-the-century elegance, stay for afternoon tea, served daily from noon to 4 pm in the atrium lobby. Reservations are recommended.

Byers-Evans House Museum. *1310 Bannock St, Denver (80204). Phone 303/620-4933.* Restored Victorian house featuring the history of two noted Colorado pioneer families. Guided tours available. (Tues-Sun 11 am-3 pm; closed holidays) **$**

Chatfield State Park. *11500 N Roxborough Park Rd, Littleton (80125). 1 mile S of C-470 on Wadsworth St, near Littleton. Phone 303/791-7275. parks.state.co.us.* Swimming beach, bathhouse, water-skiing, fishing, boating (rentals, dock), marina; hiking, biking, bridle trails; picnicking, snack bar, camping (electrical hook-ups, dump station). Nature center; interpretive programs. (Daily) **$**

Cherry Creek State Park. *4201 S Parker Rd, Aurora (80014). 1 mile S of I-225 on Parker Rd (Hwy 83), near south Denver. Phone 303/699-3860. www.parks.state.co.us.* Swimming, bathhouse, water-skiing, fishing, boating (ramps, rentals); horseback riding, picnicking (shelters), concession, camping. Model airplane field, shooting range. (Daily) **$**

The Children's Museum of Denver. *2121 Children's Museum Dr, Denver (80211). Off I-25, exit 211. Phone 303/433-7444. www.cmdenver.org.* This 24,000-square-foot, two-story hands-on environment allows children to learn and explore the world around them. Exhibits include a room with thousands of plastic balls; Kidslope, a year-round ski slope; science center; and a grocery store. (Mon-Fri 9 am-4 pm, Sat-Sun 10 am-5 pm; closed holidays) Children's Museum Theater (weekends) and special events. **$$**

Civic Center. *100 W 14th Ave Pkwy, Denver (80209). W of Capitol Complex.* Includes

Denver Art Museum. *100 W 14th Ave Pkwy, Denver (80204). S side of Civic Center. Phone 720/865-5000. www.denverartmuseum.org.* Houses a collection of art objects representing almost every culture and period, including a fine collection of Native American arts; changing exhibits. Free admission Sat for Colorado residents. (Tues-Sat 10 am-5 pm, Sun noon-5 pm; closed holidays) **$$**

Denver City and County Buildings. *100 W 14th Ave Pkwy, Denver (80209). W side of Civic Center. Phone 303/866-2604.* Courts, municipal council, and administrative offices.

Denver Public Library. *10 W 14th Ave Pkwy, Denver (80204). Phone 720/865-1111. www.denver.lib.co.us.* First phase of new library opened in 1995; it encompasses the old library. Largest public library in Rocky Mountain region with nearly 4 million items; outstanding Western History collection, Patent Depository Library, genealogy collections, and branch library system. Programs, exhibits. (Mon-Tues 10 am-9 pm, Thurs-Sat 10 am-5:30 pm, Sun 1-5 pm; closed holidays) **FREE**

Greek Theater. *100 W 14th Ave Pkwy, Denver (80209). S side of Civic Center.* Outdoor amphitheater, summer folk dancing.

Colorado's Ocean Journey. *Qwest Park, 700 Water St, Denver (80211). Located in the Central Platte Valley on the NE corner of I-25 and 23rd Ave. Phone 303/561-4450; toll-free 888/561-4450.* This world-class, 106,500-square-foot aquarium brings visitors face to face with more than 300 species of fish, birds, mammals, and invertebrates from around the world. Exhibits follow the re-creation of water's journey from river to ocean, showcasing the varied and often exotic variety of habitats and creatures found along the way. Several areas encourage hands-on encounters between visitors and animals, including the Critters Up Close demonstrations, the Tide Pool Treasures touchable tide pool display, and the Parade of Rays pool stocked with pettable stingrays. Additional attractions include the Seafoam Fun Zone play area for young children and the "AquaPod" virtual aquatic adventure ride. Upon your arrival, check out the daily presentation notice for times and locations of special exhibits. (Late May-early Sept: daily 10 am-6 pm; early Sept-late May: daily 10 am-5 pm, hours are subject to change without notice). **$$$**

Colorado Avalanche (NHL). *Pepsi Center, 1000 Chopper Cir, Denver (80204). Phone 303/405-1100. www.colorado avalanche.com.* Professional hockey team.

Colorado History Museum. *1300 Broadway, Denver (80203). Phone 303/866-3682.* Permanent and rotating exhibits on people and history of the Colorado. Dioramas, full-scale mining equipment, Native American artifacts, photographs; sodhouse. Head-quarters of Colorado Historical Society. (Mon-Sat 10 am-5 pm, Sun noon-5 pm; closed Jan 1, Thanksgiving, Dec 25) **$**

Colorado History Tours. *Phone 303/866-4686.* Two-hour guided walking tours; three-hour guided step-on bus tours. Reservations required; ten people mini-mum. Prices and schedules vary.

Colorado Rapids (MLS). *Invesco Field at Mile High, 1701 Bryant St, Denver (80204). Phone 720/258-3888. www.coloradorapids.com.* Professional soccer team. Tours (fee) (Thurs-Sat 10 am-3 pm, every 30 minutes).

Colorado Rockies (MLB). *Coors Field, 2001 Blake St, Denver (80205). Phone 303/292-0200; toll-free 800/ 388-7625 (tickets). www.colorado.rockies.mlb.com.* Pro-fessional baseball team. Tours of Coors Field available; call for fees and schedule.

Comanche Crossing Museum. *56060 E Colfax Ave, Strasburg (80136). 30 miles E. Phone 303/622-4322.* Memorabilia of the completion of the transcontinen-tal railway, artifacts pertaining to area history; two buildings with period rooms; restored schoolhouse (circa 1891); Strasburg Union Pacific Depot; caboose,

wood-vaned windmill (circa 1880), and homestead on landscaped grounds. (May-Aug: daily 1-4 pm) **DONATION**

Denver Botanic Gardens. *1005 York St, Denver (80206). Phone 720/865-3500; fax 720/865-3713. www.botanicgardens.org.* This tropical paradise in the middle of the Rockies is home to more than 15,000 plant species from around the world. Located ten minutes east of downtown Denver, the Denver Botanic Gardens beckons visitors to explore its 23 acres of beautiful outdoor and indoor displays. The Conservatory, with more than 850 tropical and subtropical plants in an enclosed rain forest setting, is a soothing retreat for midwinter guests. A newer exhibit is the 20-by-40-foot Cloud Forest Tree covered with hundreds of orchids and rare tropical plants. Other gardens include alpine, herb, Japanese, shade, and wildflower displays. Children particularly enjoy navigating the mazes in the Secret Path garden and climbing the resident banyan tree. (Mid-Sept-Apr: daily 9 am-5 pm; May-mid-Sept: Sat-Tues 9 am-8 pm, Wed-Fri 9 am-5 pm; closed Thanksgiving) **$$**

Denver Broncos (NFL). *Invesco Field at Mile High, 1701 Bryant St, Denver (80204). Phone 720/258-3888 (tours). www.denverbroncos.com.* Professional football team. Tours are available; call for fees and schedule.

Denver Firefighters Museum. *1326 Tremont Pl, Denver (80204). Phone 303/892-1436. www.denverfirefighters museum.org.* Housed in Fire House No. 1; maintains the atmosphere of a working firehouse; firefighting equipment from the mid-1800s. (Mon-Sat 10 am-4 pm; closed holidays) **$**

Denver Museum of Nature and Science. *City Park, 2001 Colorado Blvd, Denver (80205). Phone 303/322-7009; toll-free 800/925-2250. www.dmns.org.* Ninety habitat exhibits from four continents are displayed against natural backgrounds. The Prehistoric Journey exhibit displays dinosaurs in re-created environments. There's also an earth sciences lab, gems and minerals, and a Native American collection. (Daily 9 am-5 pm; closed Dec 25) **$$$$** Combination tickets are available for

Charles C. Gates Planetarium. *2001 Colorado Blvd, Denver (80205). Phone 303/322-7009 (schedule and fees). www.dmns.org.* Contains a Minolta Series IV star projector; presents a variety of star and laser light shows daily. The **Phipps IMAX Theater** has an immense motion picture system projecting images on screen 4 1/2 stories tall and 6 1/2 stories wide. Located in the Denver Museum of Nature & Science. Daily showings. **$$$$**

Hall of Life. *2001 Colorado Blvd, Denver (80205). Phone 303/370-6453.* Health education center has permanent exhibits on genetics, fitness, nutrition, and the five senses. Part of the Denver Museum of Nature & Science. Classes and workshops (fee). (Daily 9am-5pm) **$$**

Denver Nuggets (NBA). *Pepsi Center, 1000 Chopper Cir, Denver (80204). Phone 303/405-1212. www.nba.com/nuggets.* Professional basketball team. Tours of the arena are available; phone 303/405-8556 for information.

Denver Performing Arts Complex. *950 13th St, Denver (80204). Phone 303/640-2862. www.artscomplex.com.* One of the most innovative and comprehensive performing arts centers in the country. With the addition of the Temple Hoyne Buell Theatre, the complex is the largest art center under one roof in the nation. The complex also contains shops and restaurants.

   Auditorium Theatre. *Denver (80204). Phone 303/640-2862. www.denvercenter.org.* (1908) Past host to grand opera, political conventions, minstrel shows, revivalist meetings, and military maneuvers; now hosts touring Broadway productions and the Colorado Ballet. Home of Colorado Contemporary Dance.

   Boettcher Concert Hall. *Denver Performing Arts Complex, 950 13th St, Denver (80204). Phone 303/640-2862.* The first fully "surround" symphonic hall in the US; all of its 2,630 seats are within 75 feet of the stage. Home of the Colorado Symphony Orchestra (Sept-early June) and Opera Colorado with performances "in the round" (May).

   Temple Hoyne Buell Theatre. *950 13th St, Denver (80204). Phone 303/640-2862.* The most recent addition to the complex. The 2,800-seat theater has a glass facade and Colorado sandstone walls. It is host to Opera Colorado and Broadway plays and home of the Colorado Ballet.

   The Galleria. *Denver Performing Arts Complex, Denver (80204).* A walkway covered by an 80-foot-high arched glass canopy. It connects all the theaters in the complex.

   The Helen Bonfils Theatre Complex. *Denver (80204). Phone 303/893-4000 (tours).* Home of the Denver Center Theatre Company. Contains three theaters: the Stage, seating 547 in a circle around

a thrust platform; the Space, a theater-in-the-round seating 450; and the Source, a small theater presenting plays by American playwrights. Also contains the **Frank Ricketson Theatre,** a 195-seat theater available for rental for community activities, classes, and festivals.

★ **Denver Zoo.** *City Park, 2300 Steele St, Denver (80205). Phone 303/376-4800; fax 303/376-4801. www.denverzoo.org.* Among Colorado's most popular city attractions is the Denver Zoo. Located in City Park just east of downtown, this 80-acre zoological wonderland is home to more than 4,000 animals representing 700 species. Founded in 1896, the zoo has evolved into one of the nation's premiere animal exhibits, noted for its beautiful grounds, innovative combination of outdoor and enclosed habitats, and world-class conservation and breeding programs. Don't miss the Primate Panorama, a seven-acre showcase of rare monkeys and apes. Visit the 22,000-square-foot, glass-enclosed Tropical Discovery and feel what it's like to walk into a tropical rain forest complete with caves, cliffs, waterfalls, and some of the zoo's most exotic (and dangerous!) creatures. Equally popular is the Northern Shores Arctic wildlife habitat, which provides a nose-to-nose underwater look at swimming polar bears and sea lions. Be sure to check out the feeding schedule posted just inside the zoo's entrance. During the evenings throughout December, millions of sparkling lights and holiday music transform the zoo as part of the traditional "Wonderlights" festival. (Apr-Sept: daily 9 am-6 pm; Oct-Mar: daily 10 am-5 pm) **$$$**

Forney Museum of Transportation. *4303 Brighton Blvd, Denver (80216). Phone 303/297-1113. www.forneymuseum.com.* The museum's collection houses more than 300 antique cars, carriages, cycles, sleighs, steam locomotives and coaches; many with costumed figures. One of the most notable permanent exhibits is that of Union Pacific "Big Boy" locomotive X4005, which was involved in a horiffic crash in 1953, but has been restored and sits on the museum's grounds. The "Gold Bug" Kissel automobile owned by Amelia Earhart and Crown Prince Aly Khan's Rolls Royce are also here. If it has wheels, chances are the Forney Museum has something like it! (Mon-Sat 9 am-5 pm) **$$**

Four Mile Historic Park. *715 S Forest St, Denver (80246). Located east of Colorado Boulevard between Cherry Creek Dr S and Alameda. Phone 303/399-1859. www.fourmilehistoricpark.org.* Take a stroll through Denver history at Four Mile Historic Park. Once a stage stop, this 14-acre living history museum encompasses the oldest house still standing in Denver (circa 1859), plus other outbuildings and farm equipment from the late 1800s. Guides in period costume reenact life on a farmstead. It's a great place for a picnic. Kids particularly enjoy chasing the chickens, visiting with the draft horses, and riding on a real stagecoach (weekends only). (Apr-Sept: Wed-Fri noon-4 pm, Sat-Sun 10 am-4 pm; Oct-Mar: Sat-Sun noon-4 pm) **$**

Gray Line bus tours. *5855 E 56th Ave, Commerce City (80217). Phone 303/289-2841; toll-free 800/348-6877. www.coloradograyline.com.* Call or visit Web site for schedule and tour information.

Hyland Hills Adventure Golf. *9650 N Sheridan Blvd, Westminster (80030). Phone 303/650-7587. www.hylandhills.org/adventuregolf.html.* It's miniature golf on a mega scale. Located 15 minutes north of downtown Denver, Hyland Hills Adventure Golf puts your putting skills and your imagination to the test with 54 stunningly landscaped holes in a fantasy setting of cliffs, caves, and waterfalls. (Mid-May-Sept, daily) **$$**

⭐ **Hyland Hills Water World.** *88th Ave and Pecos St, Federal Heights (80260). 15 minutes N of downtown Denver. Phone 303/427-7873. www.waterworldcolorado .com.* Ranked among the nation's largest water parks, this 64-acre aquatic extravaganza is not a place for the faint of heart, but it's a great spot for the young at heart and a terrific good time for all ages. One admission fee provides unlimited access to 40 amusement and water thrill rides. Water World's beautifully landscaped grounds include a wave pool the size of a football field, 16 water slides, nine inner-tube rides, and a splash pool for tots. Older kids won't want to miss the Lost River of the Pharaohs, a whitewater rafting trip through a mummy-filled pyramid and down a spiraling slide. Younger visitors will enjoy Voyage to the Center of the Earth, a gentler ride featuring close encounters with animatronic dinosaurs. Hours vary according to season and weather, so be sure to call ahead. (Late May-early Sept: daily 10 am-6 pm) **$$$$**

Molly Brown House Museum. *1340 Pennsylvania St, Denver (80203). Phone 303/832-4092. www.molly brown.org.* The Molly Brown House Museum stands as an enduring tribute to one of Denver's most prominent architects, William Lang, and one of its most colorful characters, Margaret "Molly" Brown. A spectacular example of Colorado Victorian design, the fully restored 1880s sandstone and lava stone man-

sion now serves as a museum, filled with many of the lavish furnishings and personal possessions of its most famous occupant. Anyone interested in the story of the *Titanic* and the heroics of its "Unsinkable" survivor should take a moment to step back in time and enjoy a tour of her home. (Sept-May: Tues-Sat 10 am-3:30 pm; Sun noon-3:30 pm. June-Aug: Mon-Sat 10 am-3:30 pm; Sun noon-3:30 pm) **$$**

Park system. *Denver (80202).* More than 200 parks within the city provide approximately 4,400 acres of facilities for boating, fishing, and other sports. The system includes six golf courses. There are also 27 mountain parks within 72 miles of the city, covering 13,448 acres of land in the Rocky Mountain foothills. Parks of special interest are

Cheesman Park. *E 8th Ave and Franklin St, Denver (80206).* This park has excellent views of nearby mountain peaks with aid of dial and pointers. Congress Park swimming pool (fee) is adjacent. Located between Cheesman and Congress parks is the Denver Botanic Gardens (fee), with the Boettcher Memorial Conservatory.

City Park. *Colorado Blvd and York St, Denver (80205). Runs between 17th and 26th aves. Phone 303/331-4113.* Contains the Denver Museum of Nature and Science, an 18-hole golf course, and the **Denver Zoo** (see). Animals in natural habitats; primates, felines, and giraffes; aviary, children's zoo, miniature railroad. (Daily) Children under 16 must be accompanied by adult at zoo. **FREE**

Washington Park. *Denver (80209). Runs between S Downing and S Franklin sts, E Louisiana and E Virginia aves. Phone 303/698-4930.* This 165-acre park features a large recreation center with an indoor pool (fee). Floral displays include a replica of George Washington's gardens at Mount Vernon.

Pearce-McAllister Cottage. *1880 Gaylord St, Denver (80206). Phone 303/322-1053.* (1899) Dutch Colonial Revival house contains original furnishings. Guided tours give insight into upper middle-class lifestyle of the 1920s. Second floor houses the Denver Museum of Dolls, Toys, and Miniatures. (Tues-Sat 10 am-4 pm, Sun 1-4 pm) **$**

Sakura Square. *Between 19th and 20th Streets, Denver (80202). Lawrence to Larimer sts.* Denver's Japanese Cultural and Trade Center features Asian restaurants, shops, businesses; authentic Japanese gardens. Site of a famed Buddhist Temple.

Six Flags Elitch Gardens. *2000 Elitch Cir, Denver (80204). Phone 303/595-4386. www.sixflags.com/parks/elitchgardens/index.asp.* If you're into adrenaline overload, then Six Flags Elitch Gardens is your kind of place. This granddaddy of amusement parks in downtown Denver features more than 45 rides sure to satisfy even the most experienced coasterhead. The park is best known for its extreme roller coaster rides; other favorites include a 22-story freefall in the Tower of Doom, Disaster Canyon whitewater rafting, and the new Flying Coaster, which simulates the experience of flying. Six Flags includes a kiddie park for younger children, the popular Island Kingdom water park, and live entertainment nightly. (June-Aug 10 am-10 pm; limited and weekend hours May and Sept) **$$$$**

Ski Train. *Union Station, 555 17th St, Suite 2400, Denver (80202). Phone 303/296-4754. www.skitrain.com.* A ride on the Ski Train from downtown Denver to Winter Mountain Ski Resort in Winter Park has been a favorite day trip for skiers, hikers, bikers, and family vacationers since 1940. Operating on weekends year-round, the 14-car train takes its passengers on a spectacular 60-mile wilderness ride through the Rockies and across the Continental Divide, climbing 4,000 feet and passing through 28 tunnels, and then drops them off at the front entrance of beautiful Winter Park Resort. Tickets are for round-trip, same-day rides only, and reservations are highly recommended to assure a seat. (Winter: Sat-Sun; June-Aug: Sat) **$$$$**

State Capitol. *200 E Colfax Ave, Denver (80203). Phone 303/866-2604. www.milehighcity.com/capitol.* This magnificent edifice overlooking Civic Center Park is a glorious reminder of Denver's opulent past. Today, it serves as Colorado's legislative center. Designed by architect Elijah Myers in the classical Corinthian style, it was 18 years in the making before its official dedication in 1908. The building is renowned for its exquisite interior details and use of native materials such as gray granite, white marble, pink Colorado onyx, and, of course, the gold that covers its dome. Tours include a climb to the dome, 272 feet up, for a spectacular view of the surrounding mountains. Make sure that the kids find the special marker on the steps outside noting that they are, indeed, a mile high. (Mon-Fri 7 am-5:30 pm) **FREE**

University of Denver. *Denver (80210). S University Blvd and E Evans Ave. Phone 303/871-2000. www.du.edu.* (1864) (8,500 students) Handsome 125-acre main campus with Penrose Library, Harper Humanities Gardens, Shwayder Art Building, Seely G. Mudd Building (science), William T. Driscoll University Center, and historic buildings dating from the 1800s. The 33-acre Park Hill campus at Montview Boulevard and Quebec Street is the site of the University of Denver Law School (Lowell Thomas Law Building) and the Lamont School of Music (Houston Fine Arts Center. For a schedule of performances, phone 303/871-6400. Campus tours. The university maintains

Chamberlin Observatory. *2930 E Warren Ave, Denver (80210). Observatory Park. Phone 303/871-5172. www.du.edu/~rstencel/Chamberlin.* Houses a 20-inch aperture Clark-Saegmuller refractor in use since 1894; lectures. Tours (Tues and Thurs; closed holidays, Christmas week; reservations required). **$**

Special Events

Cherry Creek Arts Festival. *Denver (80206). In Denver's Cherry Creek North, on Second and Third aves between Clayton and Steele sts. www.cherryarts.org.* Features works by 200 national artists; culinary, visual, and performing arts. July 4 weekend.

Denver Film Festival. *Starz FilmCenter at the Tivoli, 900 Auraria Pkwy, Denver (80204). Phone 303/595-3456. www.denverfilm.org.* Movie junkies will get more than their fill of flicks at the ten-day Denver International Film Festival in the fall. Showcasing 175 films while playing host to many of their stars, the festival includes international feature releases, independent fiction and documentaries, experimental productions, and children's programs. All films are shown at the Starz FilmCenter at the Tivoli. It's best to order tickets ahead of time, as many of the features sell out. Fall. **$$**

Denver Lights and Parade of Lights. *Downtown, starting at Civic Center Park in front of the City and County Building. Phone 303/478-7878. www.denverparadeoflights.com.* From early December through January, downtown Denver is ablaze with what is very possibly the largest holiday light show in the world. Locals and tourists alike drift down to Civic Center Park after dark to view the incredible rainbow display covering the buildings. A spectacular Parade of Lights that winds for 2 miles through Denver's downtown kicks off the holiday season.

Furry Scurry. *Washington Park, Louisiana Ave and Downing St, Denver (80209). Phone 303/964-2522. www.ddfl.org/furryscurry.* The Furry Scurry is a 2-mile walk and fun run through Denver's Washington Park. Featuring a 2.6-mile jogging trail, several picnic areas, large flower gardens, and two lakes, the park is the perfect spot for an outdoor-loving family to spend the day. The race is a fundraiser for the Denver Dumb Friends League, and most participants bring their dogs as racing companions. The event typically attracts more than 6,000 two- and four-legged participants and raises $400,000 for the league. Early May. **$**

Greyhound racing. *Mile High Greyhound Park, 6200 Dahlia St, Commerce City (80022). 7 miles NE at junction I-270 and Vasquez Blvd. Phone 303/288-1591.* Pari-mutuels. Mid-June-mid-Feb: nightly Tues-Sat; matinee racing Mon, Fri-Sat. Satellite "off-track" betting all year.

The International at Castle Pines Golf Club. *29 miles south of Denver, 1000 Hummingbird Ln, Castle Rock (80104). Phone 303/688-6000. www.golfintl.com.* The International is a week-long, world-class golf event that attracts some of the top professional golfers. The Jack Nicklaus-designed course is renowned for the beauty of its pine-strewn mountain setting and the challenge of its terrain. The tournament begins in earnest on Thursday, but spectators are welcome to watch practice rounds as well as the junior and pro-am tournaments held earlier in the week. One week in August. **$$$$**

National Western Livestock Show, Horse Show, & Rodeo. *National Western Complex, 4655 Humboldt St, Denver (80216). Located E of I-25 on I-70. Phone 303/297-1166; toll-free 888/551-5004 (tickets). www.nationalwestern.com.* If you are in Denver in the middle of January, you'd better hang onto your Stetson, because that's when the National Western Stock Show and Rodeo comes to town, along with 600,000 rootin' tootin' exhibitors and spectators. Billed as the largest livestock exhibition in the world, this two-week extravaganza is packed with nonstop shows and demonstrations, from sheep shearing to steer wrestling. Daily rodeos showcase the horse and bull-riding skills of some of the best riders in the country before cheering, sellout crowds in the National Western Complex. Other favorites include barrel races, show-horse contests, a junior rodeo (where some of the riders are 3 years old!), Wild West shows, and the colorful Mexican Rodeo Extravaganza. Take a break from the action and tour the exhibition hall for demonstrations in wool spinning and goat milking, or walk the grounds to see what a yak looks like up close. Mid-Jan. **$$**

Limited-Service Hotels

★ **COMFORT INN.** *401 17th St, Denver (80202). Phone 303/296-0400; toll-free 800/252-7466; fax 303/312-5941. www.comfortinndenver.com.* Clean, comfortable, and pet-friendly, with a bountiful complimentary continental breakfast and high-speed Internet access in every guest room, this Comfort Inn offers a rare bonus: access to the facilities of its next-door neighbor, the Mobil Four-Star Brown Palace Hotel. This includes a spectacular health club, laundry service, and dining at all of the Brown Palace's restaurants (with a 15 percent discount). And when the Brown Palace upgrades, the Comfort Inn has been known to tag along. Witness the "book mark" TV feature, which allows guests to take advantage of pay-per-view, pause a movie in the middle to go for dinner, and then pick up where they left off, at no additional cost. 241 rooms, 22 story. Pets accepted. Complimentary continental breakfast. Check-in 3 pm, check-out noon. High-speed Internet access. Fitness room. Airport transportation available. Business center. **$$**
🐾🏃🚶

★ ★ **FOUR POINTS DENVER CHERRY CREEK.** *600 S Colorado Blvd, Denver (80246). Phone 303/757-3341; toll-free 800/359-7234; fax 303/756-6670. www.fourpoints.com/denvercherrycreek.* 210 rooms. Pets accepted; fee. Check-in 3 pm, check-out noon. Restaurant, bar. **$**
🐾

★ ★ **HOLIDAY INN.** *10 E 120th Ave, Northglenn (80233). Phone 303/452-4100; fax 303/457-1741. www.holiday-inn.com.* 235 rooms, 6 story. Pets accepted; fee. Check-out noon. Restaurant, bar. Fitness room. Indoor pool, whirlpool. **$**
🐾🏃🏊

Full-Service Hotels

★ ★ ★ ★ **THE BROWN PALACE HOTEL.** *321 17th St, Denver (80202). Phone 303/297-3111; toll-free 800/321-2599; fax 303/312-5900. www.brownpalace.com.* This historical landmark has been hosting visitors since 1892, and many presidents, monarchs, and celebrities have graced its halls. In the lobby, a magnificent stained-glass ceiling tops off six levels of cast-iron balconies. The award winning Palace Arms restaurant (see) features signature favorites like rack of lamb and pan-roasted veal. Cigar aficionados flock to the library ambience of the

Churchill Bar, while the Ship Tavern appeals to lovers of the sea. Ellygnton's Sunday brunch is legendary. 231 rooms, 10 story. Pets accepted, some restrictions. Check-in 4 pm, check-out noon. High-speed Internet access. Restaurant, bar. Fitness room. Airport transportation available. Business center. **$$$**

★ ★ ★ **GRAND HYATT.** *1750 Welton St, Denver (80202). Phone 303/295-1234; toll-free 800/233-1234; fax 303/292-2472. www.granddenver.hyatt.com.* The beautiful lobby of this centrally located hotel boasts a 20-foot sandstone fireplace and cozy seating areas with touches of mahogany, granite, and wrought iron, a tip of the hat to the Rocky Mountains. The hotel's restaurant is called 1876, which is the year Colorado became a state. But that's where the antiquity ends. The Hyatt is all about step-to-it service and modern conveniences, even providing guests with rooftop tennis courts surrounded by a jogging track, plus an indoor swimming pool and a health club with free weights, exercise cycles, treadmills, and stair climbers. 511 rooms, 26 story. Check-in 3 pm, check-out noon. Restaurant, bar. Fitness room. Indoor pool, whirlpool. Tennis. Airport transportation available. Business center. **$$**

★ ★ ★ **HOTEL MONACO DENVER.** *1717 Champa St, Denver (80202). Phone 303/296-1717; toll-free 800/990-1303; fax 303/296-1818. www.monaco-denver.com.* Just how much fun can sophistication be? To find out, check in to the Hotel Monaco. When you enter the lobby, you'll feel like you're in an elegant, somewhat exotic living room—did they mean to call it the Hotel Morocco?—with cushy couches, recessed bookshelves, and potted palms. Then you look up and see that you're sitting under what the Monaco's designer calls a Russian Circus Tent. The domed ceiling is all about wide stripes and diamonds, blues and golds, a theme that carries through to the subtly striped wall coverings in the halls and meeting rooms, the softly colored guest room doors, and the stripes-on-wood chests of drawers. Yet the plush duvet covers, bathroom phones, 24-hour room service, terrycloth shower curtains, and automatic turndown service remind you that the Monaco is as serious about service as it is about fun. Even your dog will think so when he is presented with his own bowl and a bag of gourmet treats. Don't forget to buy a yo-yo from your mini-bar. 184 rooms, 7 story. Pets accepted. Check-in 3 pm, check-out noon. High-speed Internet access.

Restaurant, bar. Fitness room. Airport transportation available. Business center. **$$$**

★ ★ ★ **HOTEL TEATRO.** *1100 Fourteenth St, Denver (80202). Phone 303/228-1100; toll-free 888/727-1200; fax 303/228-1101. www.hotelteatro.com.* Located across from the Denver Center for the Performing Arts, the Hotel Teatro inspires its guests with creative design and contemporary flair. Costumes and photographs from the Denver Center Theatre Company line the walls of the public and private spaces, and the mood is decidedly artistic. Gold and sage tones are used in the guest rooms and suites to create seductively soothing environments, while 12-foot ceilings lend a dramatic air. Tucked inside the original Denver Tramway Building dating to 1911, this boutique hotel manages to respect its heritage while providing guests with a thoroughly modern experience. If you want someone to draw you an aromatherapy bath with your turndown service, this is the hotel for you. The Teatro prides itself on the extras it offers its guests, and the automatic bath is just one. An in-room laser printer and fax machine is another. How about customizing your mini-bar when you check in? If you don't want the temptation of chips or Twizzlers, ask for fresh fruit and mineral water instead (and it will be waiting for you the next time you check in, too). Guest rooms include niceties like down comforters, Frette linens, Aveda bath products, and Starbucks coffee. The hotel even has Range Rovers to transport you around the downtown area. Chef Kevin Taylor is something of a local sensation, and his two restaurants here are a feast for the senses. And don't think you're the only one who will be pampered here. Not only does the Teatro not charge a pet deposit for Fido, but the hotel will provide a customized doggie dish with his name on it and present him with a bowl of Fiji water to lap. 111 rooms, 9 story. Pet accepted, some restrictions. Check-in 3 pm, check-out noon. High-speed Internet access. Two restaurants, bar. Fitness room, fitness classes available. Airport transportation available. Business center. **$$$**

★ ★ ★ **JW MARRIOTT DENVER AT CHERRY CREEK.** *150 Clayton Ln, Denver (80206). Phone 303/316-2700; toll-free 800/468-9571; fax 303/316-4697. www.marriott.com.* 196 rooms. Pets accepted. Check-in 3 pm, check-out noon. Restaurant, bar. **$$**

★ ★ ★ **LOEWS DENVER HOTEL.** *4150 E Mississippi Ave, Denver (80246). Phone 303/782-9300; toll-free 800/345-9172; fax 303/758-6542. www.loewshotels.com.* Saying Loews is pet friendly is like calling Denver a village. Not only does Fido get his own bed, toy, and even a video, but he gets a room service menu of veterinarian-approved items. Fortunately, the kids won't be jealous, since Loews offers Frisbees, backpacks, and games for kids of all ages. And the hotel has a plethora of amenities for the littlest ones, from baby tubs and electric bottle warmers to tub faucet guards, rattles, and invisible outlet plugs. For mom and dad, there's a menu of "comfort items" like chenille throws, different sleeping pillows, and CDs and a player. 183 rooms, 11 story. Pets accepted. Check-in 3 pm, check-out 11 am. High-speed Internet access. Two restaurants, bar. Fitness room. Airport transportation available. Business center. **$**

★ ★ ★ **LUNA HOTEL.** *1612 Wazee St, Denver (80202). Phone 303/572-3300; toll-free 866/724-5862; fax 303/623-0773. www.thelunahotel.com.* The phrase "ultramodern" was invented for the Luna. Retrofitted in the tall, narrow space of a former apartment building, the dimly lit lobby of this boutique hotel gives you an idea of what you're in for. To the right are the tables and open counter of Velocity, where guests are served crepes and organic coffee each morning. To the left, stretching almost the entire length of the lobby is the futuristic Flow Bar, backlit in soft colors that change every few minutes. Guests step around a handful of tall, round cocktail tables to get to the inconspicuous reception desk. There are just 19 rooms in the Luna, in which standard amenities are anything but. No coffeemakers here; just French plunge pots. No ice buckets; just funky, round, insulated pitchers. No clock radios; instead, each room has a CD alarm clock with a library of CDs and a flat-screen TV. Throughout the hotel, the lighting is soft and low, even in the small fitness room and the two wireless workstations. The Luna is a study in sleek. 19 rooms. Complimentary continental breakfast. Check-in 3 pm, check-out 11 am. High-speed Internet access, wireless Internet access. Restaurant, bar. Fitness room. Airport transportation available. **$$**

★ ★ ★ **THE MAGNOLIA HOTEL.** *818 Seventeenth St, Denver (80202). Phone 303/607-9000; toll-free 888/915-1110; fax 303/607-0101. www.magnoliahotels.com.* Many visitors to Denver make the Magnolia their home for extended stays, and it's easy to see why. Set back from busy 17th Street, its double-door entrance framed by potted evergreens, the Magnolia says "cozy" from the wingback chairs in its lobby to the full-size kitchens in its suites. Access to a snazzy health club is included with your stay—state-of-the-art machines set in a hexagonal pattern, lit with a bluish light "to simulate the outdoors." A men's and women's steam room is tucked into each changing room. For a few dollars more, guests can use the Magnolia Club, which offers wireless Internet access, a nightly cocktail reception, continental breakfast, and late-night cookies and milk. Just the thing after a day of high-powered business meetings. 246 rooms, 10 story. Pets accepted; fee. Complimentary continental breakfast. Check-in 3 pm, check-out 11 am. High-speed Internet access, wireless Internet access. Bar. Airport transportation available. **$$**

★ ★ ★ **MARRIOTT DENVER CITY CENTER.** *1701 California St, Denver (80202). Phone 303/297-1300; toll-free 800/444-2206; fax 303/298-7474. www.denvermarriott.com.* A better health club in an urban hotel may not exist. Bench press, free weights, treadmills, stair climbers, recumbent and upright bicycles, rowing machines, a personal trainer, massages, body treatments...and, of course, a swimming pool and whirlpool. And you may need the workout facilities after you've put in a long day of business since this hotel has the facilities for that, too. There is high-speed Internet access in every guest room, wireless Internet access in the lobby, and a business center if you need it. Located in downtown Denver, this property is within walking distance of Coors Field, as well as several restaurants and shops. 613 rooms, 19 story. Check-in 3 pm, check-out noon. High-speed Internet access. Two restaurants, bar. Fitness room. Indoor pool, whirlpool. Airport transportation available. Business center. **$$**

★ ★ ★ **OMNI INTERLOCKEN RESORT.** *500 Interlocken Blvd, Broomfield (80021). Phone 303/438-6600; toll-free 800/843-6664; fax 303/438-7224. www.omnihotels.com.* Metropolitan Denver is home to the wonderful Omni Interlocken Resort. Situated midway between Denver and Boulder in the area's technology corridor, the resort is part of the Interlocken Advanced Technology Park. Sharing space with leading businesses and the FlatIron Crossings shopping center, this all-season resort is a premier recreational destination. Set against the backdrop of the Rocky Mountains, the 300-acre property has something for everyone. Golfers needing to brush up on their game head for the L. A. W.'s Academy of Golf for its celebrated instruction before hitting the three 9-hole courses. The well-equipped fitness center and pool keep guests active, while the full-service spa attends to every need. Indigenous Colorado materials are used throughout the resort, enhancing the local flavor of the design. The guest rooms are comfortably elegant and include 21st-century amenities like WebTV and high-speed Internet connections. Three restaurants run the gamut from traditional to pub style. 390 rooms, 11 story. Pets accepted, some restrictions. Check-in 3 pm, check-out noon. High-speed Internet access. Restaurant, bar. Fitness room, fitness classes available, spa. Indoor pool, outdoor pool, whirlpool. Golf. Airport transportation available. Business center. **$$**

★ ★ ★ **OXFORD HOTEL.** *1600 17th St, Denver (80202). Phone 303/628-5400; toll-free 800/228-5838; fax 303/628-5413. www.theoxfordhotel.com.* Built in 1891 and located next to Union Station, this luxurious restored hotel has become a landmark in Denver, touted as the city's "oldest grand hotel." Centrally located, it is near many attractions, including Coors Field, the 16th Street Mall, Larimer Square, and many shops and galleries. 80 rooms, 5 story. Pets accepted; fee. Check-in 3 pm, check-out noon. High-speed Internet access, wireless Internet access. Three restaurants, bar. Fitness room. Airport transportation available. Business center. **$$**

★ ★ ★ **RENAISSANCE DENVER HOTEL.** *3801 Quebec St, Denver (80207). Phone 303/399-7500; toll-free 800/468-9571; fax 303/321-1966. www.marriott.com.* This atrium hotel boasts breathtaking Rocky Mountain views. With indoor and outdoor swimming pools, a well-equipped fitness center, an on-premise restaurant providing room service, and large guest rooms that include standard amenities plus mini-refrigerators, the Renaissance Denver is a good choice for families looking for a full-service hotel while trying to stay within a budget. The sights and attractions of downtown Denver are about a ten-minute drive away. 400 rooms, 12 story. Check-in 3 pm, check-out 1 pm. Restaurant, bar. Fitness room. Indoor pool, outdoor pool, whirlpool. Airport transportation available. Business center. **$**

★ ★ ★ **THE WESTIN TABOR CENTER.** *1672 Lawrence St, Denver (80202). Phone 303/572-9100; toll-free 800/937-8461; fax 303/572-7288. www.westin.com/taborcenter.* The Starbucks in the lobby might be enough for some. Others may like the whirlpool, the sauna, the outstanding fitness center (with a personal flat-screen TV on each piece of cardio equipment), or the indoor half-basketball court. And the Westin's in-room high-speed Internet access and business center make this hotel a good choice for those who want to work as well as work out or play. Centrally located to downtown Denver and adjacent to the 16th Street Mall, this hotel boasts some of the largest guest rooms in the city, many with views of the Rocky Mountains. The Westin's signature Heavenly Beds ensure a good night's sleep. 430 rooms, 19 story. Pets accepted, some restrictions. Check-in 3 pm, check-out noon. High-speed Internet access. Two restaurants, bar. Fitness room, fitness classes available. Indoor pool, outdoor pool, whirlpool. Airport transportation available. Business center. **$$$**

★ ★ ★ **THE WESTIN WESTMINSTER.** *10600 Westminster Blvd, Westminster (80020). Phone 303/410-5000; toll-free 800/937-8461; fax 303/410-5005. www.westin.com.* Located halfway between Boulder and Denver, just off Hwy 36, the business-friendly Westin Westminster is an oasis in the High Plains. Found along Westminster's promenade, it's surrounded by shops, restaurants, a movie theater, and the country's largest ice arena. Rustic but modern décor defines the public and private spaces here, which celebrate the beauty of Colorado. The Westin's signature Heavenly Beds, Heavenly Cribs, and Heavenly Dog Beds ensure that all guests get a good night's rest. 369 rooms, 14 story. Pets accepted; fee. Check-in 3 pm, check-out noon. High-speed Internet access. Restaurant, bar. Children's activity center. Fitness room. Indoor pool, whirlpool. Business center. **$**

Specialty Lodgings

The following lodging establishments are approved by Mobil Travel Guide, but due to their unique and individualized nature have not been given a traditional Mobil Star rating. Included in this listing you may find bed-and-breakfasts, limited-service inns, guest ranches, and other unique hotel properties.

CAPITOL HILL MANSION BED & BREAKFAST. *1207 Pennsylvania St, Denver (80203).*

Phone 303/839-5221; toll-free 800/839-9329; fax 303/839-9046. www.capitolhillmansion.com. With its ruby sandstone exterior and dramatic entrance, this charming 1891 mansion offers a romantic getaway for couples. Still, it's close to downtown, with a free shuttle that transports guests to the 16th Street Mall. The richly decorated inn features original stained-glass windows and woodwork and a number of fireplaces. In the guest rooms, expect to find fresh flowers, soft lighting, and antique furniture, as well as refrigerators stocked with complimentary water and soft drinks (there's an open kitchen policy, too). In the evening, the owners offer a reception with samples of Colorado wines. For a special treat, ask them to arrange a horse-drawn carriage ride for you. 8 rooms, 3 story. Complimentary full breakfast. Check-in 3 pm, check-out noon. High-speed Internet access, wireless Internet access. **$$**

HISTORIC CASTLE MARNE INN. 1572 Race St, Denver (80206). Phone 303/331-0621; toll-free 800/ 926-2763; fax 303/331-0623. www.castlemarne.com. This lovely bed-and-breakfast, which does indeed resemble a castle, was built in 1889 by well-known Denver architect William Lang. It is on the National Register of Historic Structures and is as beautiful inside as outside: period antiques, family heirlooms, hand-rubbed wood, stained-glass windows, and personal warmth from the proprietors that translates into well-cared-for guests. The Marne has nine rooms of varying sizes, some with whirlpools for one or two, one with an 18-foot cathedral ceiling, and others with beds with feather ticks or pedestal sinks and clawfoot tubs. Melissa Feher-Peiker serves her guests afternoon tea in the parlor (or, weather permitting, in the garden) and will even serve a private candlelight dinner if you make reservations. 9 rooms, 3 story. Complimentary full breakfast. Check-in 4 pm, check-out 11 am. **$$**

THE LUMBER BARON INN. 2555 W 37th Ave, Denver (80211). Phone 303/477-8205. www.lumber baron.com. This place is big—and there are only five guest rooms. The ground floor consists of a parlor, huge dining room, kitchen, and entertainment room with a 61-inch TV. The entire third floor is a big old ballroom. Doesn't every B&B have one? The Lumber Baron Inn was built in 1890 by an immigrant who made his considerable fortune in, yes, lumber, and each room of this mansion consists of a different wood—cherry, sycamore, oak, maple, poplar, and walnut. Every guest room has a different theme, but they all have ceilings covered with wallpaper that replicates old Victorian prints, created especially for the inn. Rooms also have separate showers and whirlpool tubs. And that third-floor ballroom, with its 20-foot vaulted ceiling, small kitchen, and bathroom? It's used for anything from a romantic dinner for two to the weekly murder mystery dinner hosted by the inn. 5 rooms, 3 story. Pets accepted, some restrictions. Complimentary full breakfast. Check-in 4-6 pm, check-out 11 am. **$$**

QUEEN ANNE BED AND BREAKFAST. 2147-51 Tremont Pl, Denver (80205). Phone 303/ 296-6666; toll-free 800/432-4667; fax 303/296-2151. www.queenannebnb.com. Built in the 1800s, this bed-and-breakfast faces the Benedict Fountain Park in the Clement Historic District of downtown Denver. Four of the two-room gallery suites are named for famous painters and display samples of their work. The Aspen Room is spectacular, with a mural of an aspen forest that covers both the walls and the ceiling that rises to the top of the Victorian turret. 14 rooms, 3 story. Check-in 3 pm, check-out noon. Wireless Internet access. **$$**

Restaurants

★ **ANNIE'S CAFE.** 4012 E 8th Ave, Denver (80220). Phone 303/355-8197. If you're looking for pure fun with your French toast, look no further. Annie's, which serves breakfast all day, boasts an authentic, old-fashioned soda fountain where you can get real root beer floats and even egg creams. Sit in a vinyl booth, eat off a Formica table, listen to oldies on the sound system, and savor the sights of walls covered with old movie posters and vintage toys. And when was the last time you had a jar of peanut butter sitting on your table along with ketchup and mustard? American menu. Breakfast, lunch, dinner. Closed holidays. Bar. Children's menu. **$**

★ ★ **BAROLO GRILL.** 3030 E 6th Ave, Denver (80206). Phone 303/393-1040; fax 303/333-9240. If you can't get to the Barolo region of Italy by dinnertime, come to this upscale Italian farmhouse. The interior is both romantic and rustic, with grapevines covering one corner of the stuccolike walls, hand-painted porcelain on display throughout, and hundreds of dried flowers set in baskets and brass urns. The lighting is low, the fireplace crackles, the food is decidedly northern Italian—be sure to ask about the daily tasting menu—and the wine list is extensive. When the weather permits, ask for a table outside. Italian menu. Dinner. Closed Sun-Mon; holidays. Bar. Children's menu. Valet parking. Outdoor seating. **$$**

★ ★ **BENNY'S.** *301 E Seventh Ave, Denver (80203). Phone 303/894-0788; fax 303/839-5488. www.bennys restaurant.com.* This Capitol Hill hangout offers the "fastest service in town"—that is, if you can snag a table. (Don't be put off by the crowd waiting out front on most nights, as diners are usually seated fairly quickly.) Popular margaritas, a wide selection of tequilas, and a lovely setting for outdoor dining in spring, summer, and fall draw hordes of locals to this Mexican hotspot. Mexican menu. Breakfast, lunch, dinner. Closed Thanksgiving, Dec 25. Bar. Casual attire. Outdoor seating. **$**

★ **BRITTANY HILL.** *9350 Grant, Thornton (80229). Phone 303/451-5151; fax 303/451-1013.* American menu. Lunch, dinner, Sun brunch. Bar. Patio deck. **$$**

★ ★ ★ **THE BROKER RESTAURANT.** *821 17th St, Denver (80202). Phone 303/292-5065; fax 303/292-2652. www.restauranteur.com/thebrokerrestaurantcom.* If you're looking for "unique," look no further. The Broker, once part of the Denver National Bank, is now a place where private parties can dine in one of several old board rooms or in rooms where the wealthy once viewed the contents of their safety deposit boxes. The restaurant's centerpiece is a huge bank vault, now its own dining room-within-a-dining room. But go down a few stairs, make a turn here and there, descend another flight, and go through what seems like it might have been a secret passageway, and suddenly you're in another private dining room—the restaurant's massive wine cellar, which has a dining table amid its volumes of nesting bottles. Although the lone table can seat up to 20, it once sat just two. That was when a lucky lady received a very romantic marriage proposal, complete with 80 dozen roses. Steakhouse. Lunch, dinner. Closed Dec 25. Bar. **$$$**
🄳

★ ★ **BUCKHORN EXCHANGE.** *1000 Osage St, Denver (80204). Phone 303/534-9505; fax 303/534-2814. www.buckhorn.com.* Built in 1893, The Buckhorn Exchange, Denver's oldest (and most famous) restaurant, is part dining establishment, part saloon, and part museum. It's worth a visit, if only to marvel at the collection of more than 500 wall-mounted big-game hunting trophies, as well as photos and artifacts from the many dignitaries who have dined here. Its casual Western charm has been honed through 100 years of continuous service. Take the opportunity to sample buffalo sausage, fried alligator tail, or marinated rattlesnake before digging into one of Buckhorn's famous steaks. On weekends, live music and dancing liven up the Lounge. Lunch, dinner. Closed holidays. Bar. Outdoor seating. **$$$**
🄳

★ ★ **DENVER CHOPHOUSE & BREWERY.** *1735 19th St #100, Denver (80202). Phone 303/296-0800; fax 303/296-2800. www.chophouse.com.* There are always seven fresh hand-crafted ales, along with two seasonal beers, on tap at this microbrewery, where small-batch bourbons and single-malt scotches join premium pours to make for a rollicking bar business. A menu heavy on steaks, chops, and surf-and-turf turns this restaurant into a classic American steakhouse. The décor, set among wooden tables and exposed brick, is a combination of beer paraphernalia and old railroad photos, since Denver's historic Union Station is just around the corner. American menu. Lunch, dinner. Bar. Outdoor seating. **$$**

★ **EMPRESS SEAFOOD.** *2825 W Alameda Ave, Denver (80219). Phone 303/922-2822; fax 303/922-2810.* Come here for Denver's best dim sum, the tapas of the Asian world. Federal Boulevard is considered the city's United Nations, and tucked in among the Mexican, Vietnamese, Thai, and other ethnic eateries is this little place with a huge dining room. Servers dash from crowded table to crowded table with wheeled carts, dishing out offerings that include everything from roast pork croissants to rolled sesame balls. The sharing is fun, the atmosphere is chaotic, and there is even musical entertainment for those brave souls who might like a little karaoke with their duck feet. Chinese menu. Lunch, dinner. Bar. **$$**

★ ★ **FOURTH STORY RESTAURANT & BAR.** *2955 E 1st Ave, Denver (80206). Phone 303/322-1824; fax 303/399-2279. www.fourthstory.com.* In this light-filled restaurant, you can take your pick of what to digest: soup, pasta, roasted sea bass, or the latest bestseller. The Fourth Story is, indeed, the fourth story of Denver's famous Tattered Cover bookstore. Not only are you welcome to peruse while you eat, but you can leave the books at your table and the servers will reshelve them after you leave. The restaurant itself is filled with bookshelves; grab the latest biography, political discourse, cookbook, or volume of poems, and if you decide to purchase it, it can be added to your lunch or dinner tab. Depending on what day you're visiting, you might run into a monthly tea tasting or wine dinner, a jazz brunch or a food writer book signing. American menu. Lunch, dinner, Sun brunch. Closed holidays. Bar. Children's menu. **$$**

★ ★ ★ **HIGHLANDS GARDEN CAFE.** *3927 W 32nd Ave, Denver (80212). Phone 303/458-5920; fax 303/477-6695. www.highlandsgardencafe.com.* Take two side-by-side circa 1890 Victorian houses, join them, renovate, and surround them with lush foliage and flower gardens and you have this unique Denver mainstay. The "eclectic American" menu takes advantage of seasonal ingredients. The main dining room is all exposed brick, polished hardwood floors, and crisp white tablecloths, but other rooms have a different ambience; the French Country Room, for instance, is painted white and has double French doors leading out to the gardens. American menu. Lunch, dinner, Sun brunch. Closed Mon; holidays. Outdoor seating. **$$$**

★ ★ **IL FORNAIO.** *1631 Wazee St, Denver (80202). Phone 303/573-5050. www.ilfornaio.com.* This Italian chain, which began as a baking school outside of Milan in 1972, has grown to more than 2,500 locations in Italy. It came to America in 1981 but retains its Italian ties: dried pasta is imported from Italy and hand-made breads are baked according to traditional methods. The restaurant offers a menu highlighting a different region of Italy as its special for the first two weeks of the month. The atmosphere feels like a taste of Tuscany, with clean, light wood; a large stone fireplace; and an open cooking area in back. The bar offers a well-stocked Italian wine list. Italian menu. Lunch, dinner. Closed July 4, Thanksgiving, Dec 25. Bar. Children's menu. Valet parking. Outdoor seating. **$$**

★ ★ ★ **IMPERIAL CHINESE.** *431 S Broadway, Denver (80209). Phone 303/698-2800; fax 303/698-2820. www.imperialchinese.com.* From the giant, mesmerizing fish tank at the entrance to the impressively inventive Szechwan, Cantonese, and Mandarin menu, Imperial Chinese dazzles with its sophistication and creativity. The large dining room is segmented with partitions, which, along with soft lighting, provide a sense of privacy. The service is unobtrusive, and the word is that the Imperial is the "only Chinese restaurant where the dish looks exactly like the picture." And the pictures are gorgeous indeed. Chinese menu. Lunch, dinner. Closed July 4, Thanksgiving, Dec 25. Bar. Casual attire. **$$**

★ ★ **INDIA'S RESTAURANT.** *3333 S Tamarac, Denver (80231). Phone 303/755-4284; toll-free 888/640-8995; fax 303/752-9814. www.indiasrestaurant.com.* This authentic little restaurant is tucked away in Tamarac Square, just off I-25 and I-225. In this funny location, adjacent to stores like Gap, Starbucks, and Denver's largest Ace Hardware, India's Restaurant has the staying power that most Indian restaurants here have lacked. This place opened in the late 1980s and is still thriving, its golden Buddha-cluttered dining room packed with people ordering India's renowned chicken shahi korma and coconut-thickened rice pudding. Couples wanting a romantic dinner for two, families, and groups all find what they want here, including what most say is the best Indian food in Denver County. Indian menu. Lunch, dinner. Bar. **$$**

★ **JAPON RESTAURANT.** *1028 S Gaylord St, Denver (80209). Phone 303/744-0330; fax 303/715-0336. www.japonsushi.com.* Why is it that so many great ethnic restaurants are tucked into strip malls? From the outside, Japon, which has a reputation as the best sushi restaurant in Denver, looks like a dull storefront. But inside this colorful restaurant, the sea urchin, calamari steak, teriyaki chicken, and homemade soy sauce pack in the crowds as tightly as the avocado, crab, and seven types of raw fish are packed into the Hawaiian rolls. The owner, who is usually behind the bar, keeps a watchful eye on the fast, friendly service. Taste, taste, taste—but don't fill up until you top it all off with a slice of mango cheesecake. Japanese menu. Lunch, dinner. Closed July 4, Thanksgiving, Dec 25. **$$** D

★ **LAS DELICIAS.** *439 E 19th Ave, Denver (80203). Phone 303/839-5675; fax 303/839-5859. www.lasdelicias.net.* This popular, family-run Mexican restaurant is shaped like a rectangle—an entire block long and about as wide as a pair of maracas. Its popularity is a testament to the no-frills ethnic restaurant that serves up great, authentic meals. Food is brought by servers who bustle with efficiency, particularly amazing at lunch when the crowds are greatest. Regulars swear by the breakfast burrito, served Friday through Sunday. The restaurant has a trio of musicians who rotate among Las Delicias' four locations (also at 4301 E Kentucky Ave, 51 Del Norte St, and 10109 E Colfax Ave in Aurora). Breakfast, lunch, dinner. Closed Thanksgiving, Dec 25. **$**

★ ★ **LE CENTRAL.** *112 E 8th Ave, Denver (80203). Phone 303/863-8094; fax 303/863-0219. www.lecentral.com.* French menu. Lunch, dinner, brunch. Closed Dec 25. Bar. Casual attire. **$**

★ ★ **MEL'S RESTAURANT AND BAR.** *235 Fillmore St, Denver (80206). Phone 303/333-3979; fax 303/355-7005. www.melsbarandgrill.com.* Set in a tiny area of art galleries and handcrafted jewelry, where art glass and funky clothing compete for window space, Mel's is a surprisingly calm oasis for shoppers and non-shoppers alike. It is bright and cheery with a polished bistro look. Seating can be on zebra-striped chairs pushed up to linen-lined tables or in one of the restaurant's cozy alcoves. In nice weather, the windows open out to patio seating and a parade of always-interesting shoppers. American menu. Lunch, dinner. Closed Easter, Thanksgiving, Dec 25. Bar. Outdoor seating. **$$$**

★ ★ ★ **MORTON'S, THE STEAKHOUSE.** *1710 Wynkoop St, Denver (80202). Phone 303/825-3353; fax 303/825-1248. www.mortons.com.* One of the few places left where one can light up a cigar without interference, this national chain fits right into the up-scale Denver meat-and-potatoes scene. The martinis are top-notch (as is the beef, naturally). Steak menu. Dinner. Closed holidays. Bar. Valet parking. Menu recited. **$$$**

★ ★ ★ **PALACE ARMS.** *321 17th St, Denver (80202). Phone 303/297-3111; fax 303/297-3928. www.brownpalace.com.* The Palace Arms opened its doors in 1892. Granted, 111 years is a long time to carry on culinary excellence, but the task is achieved gracefully and winningly here. This century-old restaurant is a treasure of history and gastronomy. Located in the Brown Palace Hotel (see), the majestic Palace Arms dining room has a unique western charisma, with rich wood, brocade-upholstered seating, and 17th-century antiques. Just as refined as the atmosphere is the delicious contemporary French cuisine, prepared with regional accents and served with impeccable care. The Palace Arms offers guests a rare opportunity to dine in historically opulent surroundings on a menu of magnificent fare. American menu. Dinner. Closed holidays. Jacket required. Reservations recommended. Valet parking. **$$$**

★ ★ ★ ★ **RESTAURANT KEVIN TAYLOR.** *1106 14th St, Denver (80202). Phone 303/820-2600; fax 303/893-1293. www.restaurantkevintaylor.com.* How many uber-chefs are creative enough to design their restaurants? Denver's much-acclaimed Kevin Taylor scoured France for the perfect ingredients, not just for his kitchen, but for the restaurant décor. At Restaurant Kevin Taylor, vaulted ceilings are offset with Versailles mirrors, alabaster chandeliers, chairs covered in green-and-yellow-striped Scalamandré silk fabric, yellow Frette table linens, Bernadaud china, and Christofle silver. Located inside the stylish Hotel Teatro and across from the Denver Center for Performing Arts, the 70-seat Restaurant Kevin Taylor brings French style to downtown Denver. Kevin Taylor earns the applause for his unpretentious contemporary cuisine in French-American style: classic starters such as seared Grade A French foie gras, signature dishes including butter poached Atlantic salmon, pancetta roasted pork loin, Colorado lamb sirloin, and killer dessert of caramelized pineapple Napoleon. Restaurant Kevin Taylor features seasonal menus that change every two months, four- and five-course tasting menus, a prix fixe pre-theatre menu, 900 vintages, and private dining in the 5,000-bottle wine cellar. American, French menu. Dinner. Closed Sun; Jan 1, Thanksgiving, Dec 25. **$$$**

★ **ROCKY MOUNTAIN DINER.** *800 18th St, Denver (80202). Phone 303/293-8383. www.rocky mountaindiner.com.* Bare wood tables, red checkered napkins, and a large buffalo head on the wall tell you that this place is perfectly named. Buffalo meatloaf, hot roast turkey, fried catfish, and even a blue-plate special are among the entrées you'll choose among before looking at a menu of desserts that includes—yes—apple pie. It's a typical diner, except that the restaurant has a well-stocked bar and purports to have one of the largest selections of bourbons in the city. American menu. Lunch, dinner. Closed holidays. Bar. Children's menu. Outdoor seating. **$$**

★ ★ ★ **STRINGS.** *1700 Humboldt St, Denver (80218). Phone 303/831-7310; fax 303/860-8812. www. stringsrestaurant.com.* Light and airy, mostly white with a red wall here and a brick one there, a bar that has remnants of the 1950s, a kitchen open to view, and servers who seem unperturbed no matter what the request, Strings is like no other restaurant in Denver. The locals know it. So do scores of celebrities visiting the city, many of whom have left autographed pictures on the wall. Some love it for the unusual "eclectic American/Continental/Italian" cuisine. Others are admirers of owner Noel Cunningham, a well-known humanitarian who constantly holds fundraisers at the restaurant to help fight illiteracy and hunger. Even when he is not on the premises, servers say his philosophy is in evidence as they point to a huge mural of lines and squiggles over a line from Robert Frost's poem *The Road Not Taken*: "I took the one less traveled by, and that has made all the difference." Lunch, dinner. Closed holidays. Bar. Children's menu. Valet parking. Outdoor seating. **$$$**

★ ★ ★ **TANTE LOUISE.** *4900 E Colfax Ave, Denver (80220). Phone 303/355-4488; fax 303/321-6312. www.tantelouise.com.* If you have a romantic evening in Denver planned, there's little reason to dine anywhere other than Tante Louise. This country inn-style restaurant, equipped with a blazing fire and vintage wall coverings, is the ideal spot for soft, intimate conversations and long, luxurious dinners. Even if you are not in love with your dinner companion when you get there, the mood here is so perfect that you'll leave enamored, if not with each other, then at least with the food and the tranquil, charming setting. The artistic cuisine at Tante Louise features playful and surprising twists on classic French dishes prepared with impressive local ingredients. To match the ambience and the cuisine, the wine list boasts an incredible selection of 600 domestic and imported wines and sparkling wines, perfect for keeping the romance going. French menu. Dinner. Closed Sun. Bar. Business casual attire. Reservations recommended. Valet parking. Outdoor seating. **$$$**

★ ★ **THREE SONS.** *2915 W 44th Ave, Denver (80211). Phone 303/455-4366; fax 303/433-2664. www.threesons.net.* Only Lissa, a bottled water from Italy, is served at this Italian restaurant, which gives you an idea of how seriously they take their mission. Small shelves protruding from the walls hold olive oil bottles and dried flowers, and crystal wineglasses on crisp white tablecloths stand ready to be filled with the restaurant's latest Italian vintage. Of course, you can always order a white Burgundy from France or a Pinot Grigio from California—but what better to go with your chicken cacciatore than a good Chianti? Italian menu. Lunch, dinner. Closed holidays. Bar. Children's menu. **$$**

★ ★ ★ **TUSCANY.** *4150 E Mississippi Ave, Denver (80246). Phone 303/782-9300; fax 303/758-6542.* This Italian restaurant is located in the Loews Hotel (see). It's somewhat too elegant, however, for a family who might have chosen the hotel for its pet-friendly and kid-friendly atmosphere. Tuscany is decorated in creamy earth tones and luxurious fabrics, with lighting that's quiet and calming. Pen-and-ink drawings and paintings of the Tuscan countryside dot the walls. A central, marble fireplace serves to divide the room into areas for quiet conversation at booths and round tables. The feeling is contemporary and comfortable, but the service is so unobtrusive it's easy to forget the surroundings and focus on the company at hand. Italian menu. Breakfast, lunch, dinner. Bar. Children's menu. Reservations recommended. Valet parking. Outdoor seating. **$$**

★ **WAZEE SUPPER CLUB.** *1600 15th St, Denver (80202). Phone 303/623-9518. www.wazeesupperclub.com.* The Wazee Supper Club is a throwback to a different time and place. In this converted plumbing supply house, now packed with students and professionals who come for what is reputed to be the city's best made-from-scratch pizza, you'll find no-pretense décor that includes a 1937 garage door opener converted to a dumbwaiter, a classic 1930s Art Deco bar, and tables and Naugahyde chairs that look like they came straight from the 1950s. American menu. Lunch, dinner. Closed Jan 1, Dec 25. Bar. **$$**

★ ★ ★ **WELLSHIRE INN.** *3333 S Colorado Blvd, Denver (80222). Phone 303/759-3333; fax 303/759-3487. www.wellshireinn.com.* Flowers and latticework in rose, cobalt blue, and gold adorn the china atop the crisp white tablecloths at the Wellshire Inn. You won't see the pattern anywhere else; it was created exclusively for the Wellshire and based on the splendor of England's Tudor period, a theme that is richly executed in this elegant restaurant. Built in 1926 as a clubhouse for the exclusive Wellshire Country Club, the castle-like building fell into disrepair until the late 1970s, when it underwent a painstaking renovation by new owners. Today it boasts four intimate dining rooms. The elegance is not without whimsy: stained-glass windows, intimate seating nooks, high beamed ceilings, and a pair of century-old hand-painted windows share space with a Victorian croquet set, an antique leather hat box, and weathered signs from ancient taverns. American menu. Lunch, dinner, Sun brunch. Closed Jan 1, Memorial Day, Labor Day. Bar. Outdoor seating. **$$$**

★ **ZAIDY'S DELI.** *121 Adams St, Denver (80206). Phone 303/333-5336; fax 303/333-4118. www.zaidysdeli.com.* There's nothing elegant about Zaidy's. In fact, if you're looking for something that even comes close to calm, you may want to look elsewhere. But if you're looking for a typical Jewish deli reputed to serve the best deli food in all of Grand County, treat yourself to this commotion. Try to find a parking spot—good luck—and then sit down at a comfy booth, listen to servers ask the regulars about their lives, and watch them carry a dozen plates up their arms for four different tables without a single written reminder of what goes where. Try real—not canned—corned beef hash for breakfast, chicken soup and a kosher hot dog for lunch, and a brisket plate for dinner. When was the last time you had a box lunch complete with cole slaw, pickle, and a cookie? Deli menu. Breakfast, lunch. Closed Thanksgiving, Rosh Hashanah, Yom Kippur. Bar. Children's menu. Outdoor seating. **$**

Missouri

Since the migration and settlement of Missouri followed the Mississippi and Missouri rivers, the eastern border and the northern and central areas have many points of historic interest. When the first French explorers came down the Mississippi in the late 17th century, Missouri was included in the vast territory claimed for the French king and named Louisiana in his honor. The transfer to Spanish dominion in 1770 made little lasting impression; French names and traditions have remained throughout the state, especially south of St. Louis along the Mississippi. When the United States purchased all of Louisiana in 1803, Missouri, with its strategic waterways and the already-thriving town of St. Louis, became a gateway to the West and remained one throughout the entire westward expansion period. The Pony Express began in St. Joseph in the northwestern corner of the state. The extreme northeast, along the Mississippi, is the land of Mark Twain. The central area north of the Missouri River was the stomping ground of Daniel Boone, and to the west, the Santa Fe, Oregon, and California trails crossed the land. Missouri's southeastern section contains some of the oldest settlements in the state. Settlers came here from the South and New England; later Germans and other Europeans arrived. Consequently, traditions are as varied as the state's topography. Missouri's admission to the Union in 1821 resulted from a famous compromise between free and slave-holding states; in the Civil War its people were sharply divided.

Topographically, Missouri is divided into four regions: the northeastern glacial terrain, the central and northwestern prairie, the Ozark highlands in most of the southern portion, and the southeastern alluvial plain. Indicative of the northeastern section

Population: 5,117,073

Area: 68,945 square miles

Elevation: 230-1,772 feet

Peak: Taum Sauk Mountain (Iron County)

Entered Union: August 10, 1821 (24th state)

Capital: Jefferson City

Motto: Let The Welfare of the People Be the Supreme Law

Nickname: The Show-Me State

Flower: Hawthorn

Bird: Bluebird

Tree: Dogwood

Fair: August in Sedalia

Time Zone: Central

Web Site: www.missouritourism.org

Fun Fact: At the St. Louis World's Fair in 1904, Richard Blechyden served tea with ice and invented iced tea.

are picturesque river scenery, souvenirs of steamboat days, prosperous farmlands, and fine saddle horses. Westward along the Iowa border is rich, prairie farm country. Long-staple cotton is an important crop in the fertile alluvial plain of the Mississippi River. Southwest of St. Louis is Meramec Valley, a forested rural area. It stretches to the northern edge of the Ozarks, which extend south and west to the state borders and afford varied and beautiful mountain scenery. Lakes of all sizes, including Lake of the Ozarks, one of the largest man-made lakes in the United States, and swift-flowing streams where fish are plentiful abound in this area. The southeastern section of the state has large springs and caves.

Missouri's diverse farm economy includes the production of corn, soybeans, wheat, fruit, cotton, and livestock. Missouri's lead mines provide more than three-quarters of the nation's supply. Other mineral products include zinc, coal, limestone, iron ores, and clays. The variety of manufactured

Calendar Highlights

APRIL

World Fest *(Branson). In Silver Dollar City. Contact Chamber of Commerce, phone 417/334-4136 or toll-free 800/952-6626.*

MAY

Apple Blossom Parade and Festival *(St. Joseph). Contact Convention & Visitors Bureau, phone 816/233-6688 or toll-free 800/785-0360. Originally a celebration of area apple growers. Parade with more than 200 entries; food, music, crafts.*

Gypsy Caravan *(St. Louis). One of the largest flea markets in the Midwest, with more than 600 vendors; arts and crafts, entertainment, concessions.*

JULY

Boone County Fair *(Columbia). Contact Convention & Visitors Bureau, phone 573/875-1231. First held in 1835, earliest fair west of the Mississippi; include exhibits, horse show.*

Kansas City Blues and Jazz Festival *(Kansas City). Penn Valley Park, Liberty Memorial Area. Phone 816/753-3378.*

National Tom Sawyer Days *(Hannibal). Contact Chamber of Commerce, phone 573/221-2477.*

National fence painting championship, Tom and Becky contest, entertainment.

AUGUST

Missouri State Fair *(Sedalia). Fairgrounds, 16th St and Limit Ave. Phone 660/530-5600. One of the country's leading state fairs; held here since 1901. Stage shows, rodeo, competitive exhibits, livestock, auto races.*

SEPTEMBER

National Festival of Craftsmen *(Branson). In Silver Dollar City. Contact Chamber of Commerce, phone 417/334-4136. Fiddle making, mule-powered sorghum molasses making, wood carving, barrel making, and dozens of other crafts.*

OCTOBER

American Royal Livestock, Horse Show, and Rodeo *(Kansas City). At the American Royal Center. Phone 816/221-9800.*

Octoberfest *(Hermann). Contact Historic Hermann Information Center, phone 573/486-2017. Area wineries. Wine cellar tours, wine samples; craft demonstrations; German music, food.*

products is almost endless: shoes, clothing, beer, transportation equipment, and foundry and machine shop products are among the most important. St. Louis, on Missouri's eastern border, and Kansas City, on the western side, provide the state's metropolitan areas.

When to Go/Climate

Missouri enjoys four distinct seasons. Summers can be oppressively hot, although it remains the most popular time to visit; winters are cold; and April-June is the wettest period. The state lies in Tornado Alley and experiences an average of 27 twisters a year, peak season running from May through early June. Snowfall is generally light—4 to 6 inches in January is the norm.

AVERAGE HIGH/LOW TEMPERATURES (° F)

Springfield
Jan 42/20	**May** 76/53	**Sept** 80/58
Feb 46/25	**June** 84/62	**Oct** 70/46
Mar 57/34	**July** 90/67	**Nov** 57/36
Apr 68/44	**Aug** 89/65	**Dec** 45/25

St. Louis
Jan 38/21	**May** 76/56	**Sept** 80/61
Feb 43/25	**June** 85/66	**Oct** 69/48
Mar 55/36	**July** 89/70	**Nov** 55/38
Apr 67/46	**Aug** 87/68	**Dec** 42/26

Parks and Recreation

Water-related activities, hiking, riding, various other sports, picnicking and visitor centers, as well as camping, are available in many of these areas. Tent, trailer sites: April-October, $8/day/basic, $14-$17/day/improved; November-March, $7/day/basic, $12-$13/day/improved; limit 15 consecutive days; water and sanitary facilities April-October only in most parks; reservations accepted at some parks. Lodging reservation: one-day deposit (two-day minimum Memorial Day-Labor Day), contact concessionaire in park. Most cabins and dining lodges are open mid-April-October. Parks are open daily, year-round. Senior citizen discounts. Pets on leash only. For further information, contact the Missouri Department of Natural Resources, Division of State Parks; PO Box 176, Jefferson City 65102; phone 573/751-2479, toll-free 800/334-6946 or 800/379-2419 (TDD).

FISHING AND HUNTING

Float trips combine scenic river floating with fishing. Trips vary from half-day to one week. Anglers can bring their own canoes, rent canoes, or hire professional guides to manipulate johnboats (flat-bottomed boats suited to shallow waters). Some outfitters provide equipment and food. About 35 Ozark rivers have black bass, goggle-eye, wall-eye, sunfish, or trout. *Missouri Ozark Waterways* provides information on float fishing and may be purchased from the Missouri Department of Conservation.

Squirrel, rabbit, and quail hunting are fair to good in most areas. Deer, doves, and wild turkeys are relatively plentiful. The larger lakes and rivers are used by migrating ducks, geese, and other water-fowl. Contact the Department of Conservation for outdoor maps.

Nonresident fishing permit: $35; one-day $5; trout permit $7. Nonresident hunting permit: deer $145; turkey $145; small game $65. Nonresident archer's hunting permit $120. Nonresident furbearer hunting and trapping permit: $80. To purchase permits and obtain regulations, contact Missouri Department of Conservation, PO Box 180, Jefferson City, 65102.

Driving Information

Safety belts are mandatory for all persons in the front seats of passenger vehicles. Children under 4 years must be in approved child passenger restraint systems. For further information, phone 573/526-6115.

INTERSTATE HIGHWAY SYSTEM

The following alphabetical listing of Missouri towns shows that these cities are within 10 miles of the indicated interstate highways.

Highway Number	Cities/Towns within 10 Miles
Interstate 29	Kansas City, Mound City, St. Joseph, Weston.
Interstate 35	Bethany, Cameron, Excelsior Springs, Kansas City.
Interstate 44	Carthage, Clayton, Joplin, Lebanon, Mount Vernon, Rolla, St. Louis, Springfield, Sullivan, Waynesville.
Interstate 55	Cape Girardeau, Ste. Genevieve, St. Louis, Sikeston.
Interstate 70	Blue Springs, Columbia, Fulton, Independence, Kansas City, St. Charles, St. Louis, Wentzville.

Additional Visitor Information

For general information, contact the Missouri Division of Tourism, 301 W High St, Box 1055, Jefferson City, 65102; phone 573/751-4133. For a Missouri travel information packet, phone toll-free 800/877-1234. An official state highway map may be obtained from Highway Maps, Department of Transportation, Box 270, Jefferson City, 65102. Another good source of information on Missouri is *The Ozarks Mountaineer,* bimonthly, PO Box 20, Kirbyville, 65679.

Visitor centers are located in St. Louis, Interstate 270 at Riverview Dr; Joplin, Interstate 44 at state line; Kansas City, Interstate 70 at the Truman Sports Complex; Hannibal, Highway 61, 2 miles S of the junction with Highway 36; Rock Port, Interstate 29, just S of the junction with Highway 136; and New Madrid, Interstate 55, at the Marston rest area. They are open year-round; hours vary.

COUNTRY MUSIC AND THE DUCKS

The beautiful Ozark hills drew people to southwest Missouri long before Branson became famous for its country music theaters. From Springfield, drive 41 miles south on Highway 65 to Branson. Touring options here include a railroad that travels through the Ozarks to Arkansas, and "the Ducks," amphibious vehicles that roll around town and onto Table Rock Lake. Other area attractions—beyond the music theaters packing Highway 76 (Country Boulevard)—include the Shepherd of the Hills homestead and outdoor theater and Silver Dollar City theme park. Once you've had your fill of Branson, head east out of town on Highway 76, a scenic stretch through part of the Mark Twain National Forest, then take Highway 5 north. Stop at Mansfield to see the Laura Ingalls Wilder farm, where the author wrote the Little House books. Return to Springfield via Highway 60 west. **(Approximately 150 miles)**

MISSOURI'S EL CAMINO REAL

This driving tour follows a transportation route with its beginnings in prehistory. Originally an Indian trail, this route became the El Camino Real, laid out during the late 18th century when Spain ruled the North American territory west of the Mississippi.

Leave St. Louis on Interstate 55 south to exit 186, then drive east to Highway 61. Head south on Highway 61 to Kimmswick, a little town on the Mississippi that thrived from the 1860s to the end of the 19th century, when it was a busy center for riverboat traffic. Shortly thereafter, time and traffic bypassed the village and it fell into a deep slumber for almost 70 years. Lucianna Gladney Ross, daughter of the founder of the 7-Up soft-drink company, discovered the handsome but dilapidated town and spearheaded a movement to restore the town to its original condition. Today, Kimmswick is part open-air museum, part shopping boutique. Many of the older buildings contain restaurants, antique stores, and other specialty retail shops. The Old House Restaurant, at 2nd and Elm, was once a stagecoach stop and tavern much frequented by Ulysses S. Grant. Today it features old-fashioned home-cooked meals and desserts.

Just west of Kimmswick, the 425-acre Mastodon Historic Site preserves an important archaeological site that contains the bones of American mastodons. The fossil remains of mastodons and other now-extinct animals were first found in the early 1800s in what is now known as the Kimmswick Bone Bed. The area became known as one of the most extensive Pleistocene bone beds in the country, attracting archaeological and paleontological interest from around the world. A museum tells the natural and cultural story of the area, while picnicking and hiking along the Tom Stockwell Wildflower Trail offer chances to explore the land where mastodons and Native American hunters once lived.

Follow Highway 61 south along the Mississippi to Ste. Genevieve, founded in the 1750s as a French village. Ste. Genevieve is one of the oldest European settlements west of the Mississippi and contains an important collection of French Colonial architecture. Now a National Historic District, the entire town gives testament to the lasting quality of French craftsmanship. Nine original structures are open to the public; the Guibourd-Valle House and the Bolduc House are especially noteworthy. Located at 66 South Main, the Interpretive Center has historical displays and shows a movie about the town's past.

Drive south on Highway 66 to Perryville. St. Mary's of the Barrens, a Catholic seminary established in 1818, contains a number of museums and the Tuscan-style Church of the Assumption, begun in 1827. The seminary is the oldest institution of higher learning west of the Mississippi. The French were not the only Europeans to settle this area. South of Perryville to the east of Highway 66 is a cluster of villages settled by Germans: Altenburg, Frohna, and Wittenberg. Altenburg has a collection of original structures from the 1830s and a museum of that commemorates the early Lutheran farming history of the area. Continue south on Highway 66, and follow Highway 177 east to Trail of Tears State Park. This 3,415-acre park is a memorial to the Cherokee Indians who lost their lives during a forced relocation to Oklahoma. The park is located on the site where 9 of 13 groups of Cherokee Indians crossed the Mississippi River in harsh winter conditions in 1838-

1839. Thousands lost their lives on the trail, including dozens on or near the park's grounds. The park's visitor center features exhibits that interpret the forced march, and numerous picnic areas and campsites are scattered throughout the park. The park's many trails offer opportunities for hiking, and the bluffs and cliffs along the river are noted as roosting sites for bald eagles.

Follow Highway 177 to Cape Girardeau, which began its history as a fur-trading fort. The town sweeps up from the Mississippi to a high promontory, with a number of 19th-century buildings along the waterfront, and has the distinction of being the birthplace of Rush Limbaugh.

From Cape Girardeau, follow Highway 61 south to New Madrid. In 1789, this site was selected to be the capital of the colony that Spain hoped to establish in the Louisiana Territory. Not much became of Spain's plans for this colony, and now New Madrid is most famous for the devastating 1811 earthquake that centered on the New Madrid Fault. With an estimated magnitude reaching over eight on the Richter Scale, this earthquake was one of the largest in recent geologic history. **(Approximately 190 miles)**

Arrow Rock (B-3)

See also Columbia

Population 70
Elevation 700 ft
Area Code 660
Zip 65320
Information Historic Site Administrator, PO Box 1; phone 660/837-3330
Web Site www.arrowrock.org

What to See and Do

Arrow Rock State Historic Site. *4th and Van Buren sts, Arrow Rock (65320). In town. Phone 660/837-3330.* A 200-acre plot with many restored buildings and historical landmarks of the Old Santa Fe Trail. Picnicking, concession, camping (dump station; standard fees). Visitors center. (Daily; closed Jan 1, Thanksgiving, Dec 25) Park includes

> **Old Tavern.** *Main St, Arrow Rock (65320). Phone 660/837-3200.* (Circa 1834) Restored; period furnishings, historical exhibits, and general store; restaurant. (May-Oct, Tues-Sun)

Van Meter State Park. *Hwy 122, Miami (65344). 22 miles NW on Hwy 41, then W and N on Hwy 122. Phone 660/886-7537.* More than 900 acres. Remains found at this archaeological site date from 10,000 BC; Old Fort, only known earthworks of its kind west of the Mississippi. Visitor center explains the history of the area. Fishing; picnicking, playground, camping. (Daily)

Walking Tour. *309 Main St, Arrow Rock (65320). Phone 660/837-3231.* Guided tour includes restored log courthouse (1839), gunshop and house (circa 1844), printshop (1868), stone jail (1870), medical museums, and Arrow Rock State Historic Site. Tour begins at Main Street boardwalk. (Memorial Day-Labor Day: daily; spring and fall: weekends; also by appointment) **$$**

Special Event

Arrow Rock Lyceum Theatre. *5 S 9th St, Columbia (65201). Phone 660/837-3311.* Missouri's oldest professional regional theater. June-Oct.

Ballwin (C-5)

Web Site www.ballwin.mo.us

Restaurants

★ ★ ★ **GIOVANNI'S LITTLE PLACE.** *14560 Manchester Rd, Ballwin (63011). Phone 636/227-7230; fax 636/227-9917.* A wedding gift to the owner's son—this casual offspring of Giovanni's boasts a similar yet varied menu and offers much more atmosphere. As at the original, the chef emphasizes fresh ingredients and seafood. Italian menu. Breakfast, dinner. Closed Jan 1, Dec 25. Bar. **$$$**

★ ★ ★ **SEVENTH INN.** *100 Seven Trails Dr, Ballwin (63011). Phone 636/227-6686; fax 636/227-6595.* American menu. Breakfast, dinner, late-night. Closed Mon; Easter. Bar. Children's menu. Valet parking. **$$$**

Blue Springs (B-2)

See also Independence, Kansas City

Population 40,153
Elevation 950 ft
Area Code 816
Information Chamber of Commerce, 1000 Main St, 64015; phone 816/229-8558
Web Site www.bluespringsgov.com

What to See and Do

Civil War Museum of Jackson County. *22807 Woods Chapel Rd, Lone Jack (64070). S on Hwy 7 to Hwy 50, then 7 miles E. Phone 816/697-8833.* Exhibits, historic battlefield and soldiers' cemetery. (Apr-Oct: daily; rest of year: Mon-Fri; closed Jan 1, Thanksgiving, Dec 25) **DONATION**

Fleming Park. *7401 W Park Rd, Blue Springs. S on Hwy 7, then 2 miles W on Hwy 40 to Woods Chapel Rd S. Phone 816/795-8888.* This more than 4,400-acre park includes 970-acre Lake Jacomo and 960-acre Blue Springs Lake. Fishing, boating (rentals, marina); camping. Wildlife exhibit, special activities (fee). Park (daily). **FREE** In the park is

> **Missouri Town 1855.** *8010 E Park Rd, Blue Springs (64014). E side of Lake Jacomo. Phone 816/795-8200.* More than 20 original western Missouri buildings from 1820 to 1860 brought to the site and restored. Mercantile store, blacksmith and cabinetmaker's shop. Furnishings, gardens, livestock and site interpreters in period attire. Special events; candlelight tours (fee). (Mar-mid-Nov: Tues-Sun; rest of year: Sat-Sun; closed Jan 1, Thanksgiving, Dec 25) **$$**

Restaurant

★ ★ ★ **MARINA GROG & GALLEY.** *22 SW Scherer Rd, #A, Lees Summit (64806). Phone 816/578-5511; fax 816/578-5588. www.marinagrogandgalley.com.* Relish in the beautiful lake views from the elegant dining room. A fine dining seafood experience that promises to push the limit on decadence. Seafood menu. Dinner. Closed Jan 1, Thanksgiving, Dec 25. Bar. Children's menu. Outdoor seating. **$$$**

Bonne Terre (D-5)

See also Pilot Knob, Ste. Genevieve

Population 3,871
Elevation 830 ft
Area Code 573
Zip 63628
Information Chamber of Commerce, 11 SW Main St, PO Box 175; phone 573/358-4000

What to See and Do

Bonne Terre Mine Tours. *39 N Allen St, Bonne Terre (63628). On Hwy 47, at Park and Allen sts. Phone 573/358-2148.* One-hour walking tours through lead and silver mines that operated from 1864 to 1962; historic mining tools, ore cars, ore samples, underground lake (boat tour), flower garden; museum exhibits. (May-Sept: daily; rest of year: Fri-Mon)

Mark Twain National Forest. *W via Hwy 47, S via Hwy 21, E via Hwy 8 (65401). Phone 573/438-5427.* (Potosi Ranger District) Swimming beach, boat launching at Council Bluff Recreation Area; nature trails, camping. (Daily) **FREE**

St. Francois State Park. *8920 Hwy 67 N, Bonne Terre (63628). 4 miles N on Hwy 67. Phone 573/358-2173.* A 2,700-acre park with fishing, canoeing; hiking, picnicking, improved camping. Naturalists. (Daily)

Washington State Park. *Hwy 21, DeSoto (63020). 15 miles NW via Hwy 47, 21. Phone 636/586-2995.* A more than 1,400-acre park containing petroglyphs (interpretations available). Swimming pool, fishing, canoeing on Big River; hiking trails, playground, cabins, improved camping. (Daily) **FREE**

Branson/Table Rock Lake Area (E-3)

See also Cassville, Rockaway Beach, Springfield

Population 3,706
Elevation 722 ft
Area Code 417
Zip 65616
Information Branson/Lakes Area Chamber of Commerce, 269 Hwy 248, PO Box 1897; phone 417/334-4084 or toll-free 800/214-3661
Web Site www.bransonchamber.com

The resort town of Branson, situated in the Ozarks, is in the region that provided the setting for Harold Bell Wright's novel *The Shepherd of the Hills*. Both Lake Taneycomo and Table Rock Lake have excellent fishing for trout, bass, and crappie. In recent years, Branson has become a mecca for fans of country music.

What to See and Do

Andy Williams Moon River Theatre. *2500 W Hwy 76, Branson (65616). Phone 417/334-4500. www.andywilliams.com.* Apr-Dec.

Baldknobbers Jamboree. *2845 W Hwy 76, Branson (65616). Phone 417/334-4528. www.baldknobbers.com.* Mar-mid-Apr: Fri-Sat; mid-Apr-mid-Dec: Mon-Sat.

Blackwood Family Music Show. *Hwy 248, Branson (65616). Phone 417/336-5863.* Mar-Dec.

Branson Creek Golf Club. *144 Maple St, Hollister (65672). Phone 417/339-4653; toll-free 888/772-9990. www.bransoncreekgolf.com.* This Tom Fazio-designed par-71 course, completed in 2000, features 18 holes. A second course is being constructed on the site.

Branson Scenic Railway. *206 E Main St, Branson (65616). Phone 417/334-6110; toll-free 800/287-2462.* Forty-mile roundtrip through Ozark Foothills. (Mid-Mar-mid-Dec, schedule varies; closed Easter, Thanksgiving) **$$$$**

Branson's Magical Mansion. *Hwy 248 (Shepherd of the Hills Expy), Branson (65616). Phone 417/336-3986.* Featuring Van Burch and Wellford. Apr-Dec.

College of the Ozarks. *100 Opportunity Ave, Point Lookout (65726). Phone 417/334-6411.* (1906) (1,500 students). Liberal arts college where students work, rather than pay, for their education. On campus is

> **Ralph Foster Museum.** *Hwy 65 and Hwy V, Point Lookout (65726). Phone 417/334-6411.* Ozark-area Native American artifacts, relics; apothecary, cameo, gun, coin collections; mounted game animals; Ozarks Hall of Fame. (Jan-mid-Dec, Mon-Sat; closed Thanksgiving) **$$**

Dutton Family Theatre. *3454 W Hwy 76, Branson (65616). Phone 417/332-2772. www.theduttons.com.* Apr-Dec.

Elvis and the Superstars Show. *205 S Commercial, Branson (65616). Phone 417/336-2112; toll-free 800/358-4795. www.elvisinbranson.com.* Year-round.

⭐ **Grand Country Music Hall.** *1945 W Hwy 76, Branson (65616). Phone 417/335-2484. www.grandcountry.com.*

Grand Palace. *2700 W Hwy 76, Branson. Phone 417/334-7263. www.thegrandpalace.com.* Late Apr-Dec.

Great American Music Festival. *399 Indian Point Rd, Branson (65616). In Silver Dollar City. Phone toll-free 800/475-9370.* More than 200 musicians play rhythm and blues, jazz, gospel, swing, Cajun, and more. Mid-May-early June.

Hughes Brothers Celebrity Theatre. *3425 W Hwy 76, Branson (65616). Phone 417/334-0076.*

Jimmy Osmond's American Jukebox Theatre. *3600 W Hwy 76, Branson (65616). Phone 417/336-6100.* Apr-Dec.

Jim Stafford Theatre. *3440 W Hwy 76, Branson (65616). Phone 417/335-8080.*

Lawrence Welk Show. *Lawrence Welk Champagne Theatre, 1984 Hwy 165, Branson (65616). Phone 417/336-3575.*

Mel Tillis Theater. *2527 N Hwy 248 (Shepherd of the Hills Expy), Branson (65616). Phone 417/335-6635.* Mar-Dec.

Presley's Country Jubilee. *2920 W Hwy 76, Branson (65616). Phone 417/334-4874.* Mar-mid-Dec.

Ride the Ducks. *Branson. 2 1/2 miles W on Hwy 76. Phone 417/334-3825.* Scenic 70-minute land and water tour on amphibious vehicles. (Mar-Nov, daily)

Ripley's Believe It Or Not! Museum. *3326 W Hwy 76, Branson (65616). Phone 417/337-5300.* Hundreds of exhibits in eight galleries. **$$$$**

⭐ **Shepherd of the Hills.** *5586 W Hwy 76, Branson (65616). Phone 417/334-4191.* Jeep-drawn conveyance tours (70 minutes) include authentically furnished Old Matt's Cabin, home of the prominent characters in Harold Bell Wright's Ozark novel *The Shepherd of the Hills;* Old Matt's Mill, an operating steam-powered saw and gristmill; 230-foot Inspiration Tower; craft demonstrations, horseback riding, and music shows. (Late Apr-late Oct, daily) On the grounds is

> **Outdoor Theater.** *Phone 417/334-4191 (ticket information).* Outdoor historical pageant adapted from Harold Bell Wright's best-selling novel. (May-late Oct, nightly)

Shepherd of the Hills Trout Hatchery. *483 Hatchery Rd, Branson (65616). Phone 417/334-4865.* Largest trout hatchery in the state. Visitor center has aquariums, exhibits, video presentation. Guided tours (Memorial Day-Labor Day, Mon-Fri). Hiking trails, picnicking. (Daily; closed Jan 1, Thanksgiving, Dec 25) **FREE**

Shoji Tabuchi Theatre. *3260 Hwy 248 (Shepherd of the Hills Expy), Branson (65616). Phone 417/334-7469. www.shoji.com.* Mar-Dec.

Showboat *Branson Belle*. *Branson. Phone 417/336-7171.* Lunch and dinner cruises depart from Highway 165 near Table Rock Dam. (Apr-Dec, daily) **$$$$**

Silver Dollar City. *399 Indian Point Rd, Branson (65616). Phone 417/338-2611.* **$$$$**

Sons of the Pioneers. *76 Country Music Blvd, Branson (65616).* Early May-Oct.

Stone Hill Winery. *601 Hwy 165, Branson (65616). Phone 417/334-1897.* Guided tours and bottling demonstrations. Gift shop. (Daily; closed Jan 1, Thanksgiving, Dec 25) **FREE**

Table Rock Dam and Lake. *4600 Hwy 165, Branson (65616). Phone 417/334-4101.* This 43,100-acre reservoir, formed by impounding waters of White River, offers swimming, water-skiing, scuba diving, fishing for bass, crappie, and walleye, boating (rentals, commercial docks, marine dump station) hunting for deer, turkey, rabbit, and waterfowl, picnicking, playgrounds, camping (13 parks, fee charged in most areas; showers, trailer dump stations). (Daily)

Table Rock Helicopters. *3309 W Hwy 76, Branson (65616). Phone 417/334-6102.* Scenic tours of lake area. (Mar-Nov, daily) **$$$$**

Table Rock State Park. *5272 State Hwy 165, Branson (65616). Phone 417/334-4704.* More than 350 acres. Fishing, sailing (docks, ramp), boating (marina, launch, rentals), scuba service; picnicking; improved camping (dump station). (Daily) **FREE**

Waltzing Waters. *3617 W Hwy 76, Branson (65616). Phone 417/334-4144.* Colored fountains set to music create a display more than 20 feet high and 60 feet wide. Indoor performances hourly. Stage shows. (Tues-Sun) **$$$**

White Water. *3505 W Hwy 76, Branson (65616). Phone 417/334-7487.* Family water park; streams, slides, flumes, wave pool. (May-mid-Aug, daily) **$$$$**

Will Rogers Theatre. *470 Hwy 248, Branson (65616). Phone 417/336-1333.*

Special Event

Festival of American Music and Craftsmanship. *399 Indian Point Rd, Branson (65616). In Silver Dollar City. Phone toll-free 800/475-9370.* Celebrating arts, crafts, and cooking from across America, with demonstrations, exhibits, and entertainment. Early Sept-late Oct.

Limited-Service Hotels

★ ★ **BEST WESTERN MOUNTAIN OAK LODGE.** *8514 Hwy 76, Branson (65615). Phone 417/338-2141; toll-free 800/868-6625; fax 417/338-8320. www.bestwestern.com.* 150 rooms, 3 story. Complimentary continental breakfast. Check-out noon. Restaurant, bar. Indoor pool. **$**

★ ★ **CLARION HOTEL.** *2820 Hwy 76 W, Branson (65616). Phone 417/334-7666; toll-free 800/725-2236; fax 417/334-7720. www.palaceinn.com.* 166 rooms, 7 story. Complimentary continental breakfast. Check-out 11 am. Restaurant, bar. Indoor pool, whirlpool. **$**

★ ★ **DAYS INN.** *3524 Keeter St, Branson (65616). Phone 417/334-5544; toll-free 800/329-7466; fax 417/334-2935. www.daysinn.com.* 425 rooms, 4 story. Pets accepted; fee. Complimentary continental breakfast. Check-out 11 am. Restaurant. Outdoor pool, children's pool, whirlpool. **$**

★ **HAMPTON INN.** *3695 W Hwy 76, Country Music Blvd, Branson (65616). Phone 417/337-5762; toll-free 800/426-7866; fax 417/337-8733. www.hamptoninn.com.* 110 rooms, 2 story. Complimentary continental breakfast. Check-out noon. Indoor pool, whirlpool. **$**

★ ★ **RADISSON HOTEL BRANSON.** *120 S Wildwood Dr, Branson (65616). Phone 417/335-5767; toll-free 888/566-5290; fax 417/335-7979. www.radisson.com.* Opened in 1994, this hotel overlooks the Ozarks from the theater district of Branson, near shopping, dining, and entertainment. 500 rooms, 10 story. Check-out 11 am. Restaurant, bar. Fitness room. Indoor pool, outdoor pool, whirlpool. **$**

★ **RAMADA INN.** *1700 W Hwy 76, Branson (65616). Phone 417/334-1000; toll-free 800/641-4106; fax 417/339-3046. www.ramada.com.* 296 rooms, 6 story. Check-out 11 am. Outdoor pool. **$**

Full-Service Resorts

★ ★ ★ **BIG CEDAR LODGE.** *612 Devils Pool Rd, Ridgedale (65739). Phone 417/335-2777; fax 417/339-5060. www.bigcedarlodge.com.* There is something for everyone at this resort lodge. Guests can stay in one of three lodges, a cabin, or cottage. Visitors will enjoy boating and swimming on the lake, tennis, golf, horseback riding, a 10,000-acre nature park with hiking trails, and much more. 224 rooms. Check-out 11 am. Restaurant, bar. Children's activity center. Fitness room. Two outdoor pools. Tennis. **$**

★ ★ ★ **CHATEAU ON THE LAKE.** *415 N Hwy 265, Branson (65616). Phone 417/334-1161; toll-free 888/333-5253; fax 417/339-5566. www.jqhhotels.com.* Chateau on the Lake welcomes visitors to a world of serene beauty from its mountaintop location in the Ozarks. Its superior setting overlooking Table Rock Lake might just convince guests that they have left behind the hectic world, yet this superior resort remains only minutes from the thrilling entertainment of Branson. Supremely comfortable, the elegantly appointed guest rooms and suites show off enchanting water and mountain views. The service here is peerless, and thoughtful amenities ensure that guests have a memorable visit. Fitness buffs head for the 24-hour health club, while the spa and salon are magnets for more sybaritic-minded travelers. From an old-fashioned soda fountain café to haute cuisine, dining at the Chateau is always a treat. 300 rooms, 10 story. Check-in 3 pm, check-out 11 am. Restaurant, bar. Fitness room. Indoor pool, outdoor pool, whirlpool. Tennis. Business center. **$$**

★ ★ ★ **LODGE OF THE OZARKS ENTERTAINMENT COMPLEX.** *3431 W Hwy 76, Branson (65616). Phone 417/334-7535; toll-free 877/866-2219; fax 417/334-6861. www.lodgeoftheozarks .com.* This hotel offers large rooms and is walking distance from theaters, shopping, and other attractions. 190 rooms, 4 story. Complimentary continental breakfast. Check-out 11 am. Restaurant, bar. Indoor pool, whirlpool. **$**

Specialty Lodgings

The following lodging establishments are approved by Mobil Travel Guide, but due to their unique and individualized nature have not been given a traditional Mobil Star rating. Included in this listing you may find bed-and-breakfasts, limited-service inns, guest ranches, and other unique hotel properties.

BRANSON HOTEL BED AND BREAKFAST. *214 W Main St, Branson (65616). Phone 417/335-6104; toll-free 800/933-0651; fax 417/339-3324. www.bransonhotelbb.com.* 7 rooms, 2 story. Children of all ages. Complimentary full breakfast. Check-in 3-6 pm, check-out 11 am. Built in 1903 with Victorian décor, antiques. **$**

BRANSON HOUSE BED & BREAKFAST. *120 N 4th St, Branson (78208). Phone 417/334-0959. www.bransonhouseinn.com.* 6 rooms, 2 story. Children over 9 only. Complimentary full breakfast. Check-in 3-6 pm, check-out 11 am. **$**

Restaurants

★ ★ **CANDLESTICK INN.** *127 Taney St, Marvel Cave Park (65616). Phone 417/334-3633; fax 417/336-4348. www.candlestickinn.com.* Seafood, steak menu. Lunch, dinner. Closed Dec 25. Bar. Children's menu. **$$$**

★ **FRIENDSHIP HOUSE.** *College of the Ozarks, Point Lookout (65726). Phone 417/334-6411; fax 417/335-5271.* Breakfast, lunch, dinner, brunch. Student operated. **$**

★ **MR G'S CHICAGO-STYLE PIZZA.** *202-1/2 N Commercial, Marvel Cave Park (65616). Phone 417/335-8156.* Italian menu. Lunch, dinner. Closed holidays. Bar. **$**

★ **UNCLE JOE'S BAR-B-Q.** *2819 Hwy 76 W, Branson (65616). Phone 417/334-4548; fax 417/334-2027.* Barbecue menu. Lunch, dinner. Closed Dec-Jan. Children's menu. **$$**

Camdenton (D-3)

See also Lake of the Ozarks, Lake Ozark, Lebanon, Osage Beach

Population 2,561
Elevation 1,043 ft
Area Code 573
Zip 65020
Information Chamber of Commerce, PO Box 1375; phone 573/346-2227 or toll-free 800/769-1004
Web Site www.camdentonchamber.com

Camdenton is near the Niangua Arm of the Lake of the Ozarks (see).

What to See and Do

Bridal Cave. *Lake Rd 588 and Hwy 5, Camdenton (65020). 2 miles N on Hwy 5, then 1 1/2 miles on Lake Rd 88. Phone 573/346-2676.* Tour (one hour) includes colorful onyx formations, underground lake; temperature constant 60° F; lighted concrete walks. Nature trails, visitor center, picnic area, gift shop. (Daily; closed Thanksgiving, Dec 25) **$$$**

Ha Ha Tonka State Park. *Hwy D and Hwy 54, Camdenton (65020). 5 miles SW via Hwy 54. Phone 573/346-2986.* More than 2,500 acres on the Niangua Arm of the Lake of the Ozarks; classic example of "karst" topography characterized by sinks, caves, underground streams, large springs, and natural bridges, all remnants of an immense ancient cavern system. Features include the Colosseum, a natural theater-like pit; Whispering Dell, a 150-foot sink basin that transmits sound along its entire length; Natural Bridge, 70-feet wide, 100-feet high, and spanning 60-feet; remains of a burned castle (circa 1905). Fishing; hiking, picnicking. (Daily) **FREE**

Pomme de Terre State Park. *Pittsburg. 30 miles W via Hwy 54, then S on County D, near Nemo. Phone 417/852-4291.* On the shore of 7,800-acre Pomme de Terre Reservoir; a favorite for water activities, including muskie fishing. Swimming, beaches, fishing, boating (rentals, marina); hiking trails; picnicking; camping (hook-ups, dump station). (Daily) **FREE**

Special Event

Dogwood Festival. *611 N Hwy 5, Camdenton (65020). Phone 573/346-2227.* Entertainment, crafts, food, carnival, parade. Mid-Apr.

Cameron (B-2)

See also Bethany, Excelsior Springs, St. Joseph

Established 1855
Population 4,831
Elevation 1,036 ft
Area Code 816
Zip 64429
Information Chamber of Commerce, PO Box 252; phone 816/632-2005
Web Site www.cameron-mo.com

Cameron was laid out by Samuel McCorkle, who named the town after his wife, Malinda Cameron. The completion of the railroad in 1858 spurred population and economic growth, making Cameron an agricultural trade center.

What to See and Do

Wallace State Park. *RR 4, Cameron (64429). 7 miles S on Hwy 69, I-35, then E on Hwy 121. Phone 816/632-3745.* More than 500 acres. Swimming, fishing, canoeing; hiking trails, picnicking, playground, improved camping (dump station). (Daily) **FREE**

Limited-Service Hotels

★ **ECONO LODGE CAMERON.** *220 E Grand Ave, Cameron (64429). Phone 816/632-6571; toll-free 800/252-7466; fax 816/632-6571. www.choicehotels.com.* 36 rooms, 2 story. Pets accepted; fee. Complimentary continental breakfast. Check-out 11 am. Outdoor pool. **$**

★ ★ **FAMILY BUDGET INN.** *4014 Miller St, Bethany (64424). Phone 660/425-7915; toll-free 877/283-4388; fax 660/425-3697.* 78 rooms. Pets accepted; fee. Check-out 11 am. **$**

Cape Girardeau (D-6)

See also Sikeston, Ste. Genevieve

Settled 1793
Population 34,438
Elevation 400 ft
Area Code 573
Zip 63701

Information Convention & Visitors Bureau, 100 Broadway, PO Box 617; phone 573/335-1631 or toll-free 800/777-0068
Web Site www.capegirardeaucvb.org

On early maps a rocky promontory on the Mississippi River, 125 miles below St. Louis, was labeled "Cape Girardot" (or "Girardeau"), named for a French ensign believed to have settled there about 1720. In 1792, an agent for the Spanish government, Louis Lorimier, set up a trading post at the site of the present city and encouraged settlement through the Spanish policy of offering tax-exempt land at nominal cost.

Cape Girardeau's location assured flourishing river traffic before the Civil War; sawmills, flour mills, and packing houses contributed to the prosperity. The war, however, ended river trade, and the earliest railroads bypassed the town, triggering further decline. In the late 1880s, the arrival of new railroads and the 1928 completion of a bridge across the Mississippi contributed to industrial growth and the widening of Cape Girardeau's economic base. Southeast Missouri State University (1873), which has a mural in its library depicting the history of the area, is located in the town.

What to See and Do

Bollinger Mill State Historic Site. *113 Bollinger Mill Rd, Cape Girardeau (63755). Phone 573/243-4591.* This day-use park features a historic 19th-century gristmill and the oldest covered bridge in the state (1868). Guided tours are available. (Daily; closed holidays) **$**

Cape River Heritage Museum. *538 Independence, Cape Girardeau (63703). Phone 573/334-0405.* Exhibits on Cape Girardeau's early heritage, 19th-century industry, education, and culture. Gift shop. (Mar-Dec, Fri-Sat; also by appointment; closed Thanksgiving, Dec 25). **$**

Cape Rock Park. *Reached by Cape Rock Dr. Phone 573/335-5421; toll-free 800/777-0068.* Site of the original trading post. Scenic river views.

Court of Common Pleas Building. *Spanish and Themis sts, Cape Girardeau (63703).* Central portion built about 1854 to replace previous log structure. During the Civil War, cells in the basement housed prisoners. Outstanding view of the Mississippi River from the park.

Glenn House. *325 S Spanish St, Cape Girardeau (63703). Phone 573/334-1177.* (Circa 1885) Victorian house with period furnishings, memorabilia of the Mississippi River and steamboat era; tours. (Apr-Dec, Fri-Sun; closed Thanksgiving, Dec 25) **$$**

Old St. Vincent's Church. *Cape Girardeau (63703). Spanish and Main sts.* English Gothic Revival church showing Roman influences. More than 100 medieval-design plaster masks. Hand-carved doors. Tours by appointment (fee).

Rose Display Garden. *Capaha Park, Perry Ave and Parkview Dr, Cape Girardeau (63703).* Test garden (approximately 300 plants) for new roses; blooming season May-Sept. Garden (daily). **FREE**

St. Louis Iron Mountain and Southern Railway. *Jackson. NW via I-55 exit 99, then 4 miles W on Hwy 61 (Hwy 72) at junction Hwy 25. Phone 573/243-1688; toll-free 800/455-7245.* A 1946 steam locomotive pulls vintage 1920s cars through scenic woodlands; trips range from 80 minutes to five hours. (Apr-Oct, Sat-Sun; also by charter) **$$$**

Trail of Tears State Park. *429 Moccasin Spring, Cape Girardeau (63703). Phone 573/334-1711.* A more than 3,000-acre park on limestone bluffs overlooking the Mississippi River. Commemorates the forced migration of the Cherokee Nation over the Trail of Tears from their homeland to Oklahoma. Fishing, boating; hiking and equestrian trails, picnicking, primitive and improved camping (showers, trailer hook-ups, standard fees). Interpretive center (seasonal). (Daily) **FREE**

Special Event

SEMO District Fair. *Arena Park, Cape Girardeau (63703). Phone 573/334-9250.* Agricultural products, crops, animals; entertainment, carnival, food. One week in mid-Sept.

Limited-Service Hotels

★ ★ **DRURY INN.** *104 S Vantage Dr, Cape Girardeau (63701). Phone 573/334-7151; toll-free 800/378-7946; fax 573/334-7151. www.druryinn.com.* 139 rooms, 2 story. Pets accepted. Complimentary full breakfast. Check-out noon. Restaurant, bar. Fitness room. Outdoor pool, children's pool. **$**

★ ★ **HOLIDAY INN.** *3257 William St, Cape Girardeau (63701). Phone 573/334-4491; toll-free 800/*

645-3379; fax 573/334-7459. www.holiday-inn.com. 186 rooms, 2 story. Pets accepted, some restrictions; fee. Check-out 11 am. Restaurant, bar. Fitness room. Indoor pool, outdoor pool, children's pool. **$**
🐾 🏃 🏊

★ **PEAR TREE INN.** 3248 William St, Cape Girardeau (63703). Phone 573/334-3000; fax 573/334-3000. 78 rooms, 3 story. Pets accepted, some restrictions. Complimentary continental breakfast. Check-out noon. Outdoor pool, children's pool. **$**
🐾 🏊

Restaurants

★ **BG'S OLDE TYME DELI & SALOON.** 205 S Plaza Way, Cape Girardeau (63703). Phone 573/335-8860; fax 573/339-1110. American menu. Lunch, dinner, brunch. Closed holidays. Bar. Children's menu. Continuous showings of contemporary movies. **$**
📷

★ **BROUSSARD'S CAJUN CUISINE.** 120 N Main St, Cape Girardeau (63701). Phone 573/334-7235. Cajun/Creole menu. Lunch, dinner. Closed Easter, Thanksgiving, Dec 25. Bar. **$$**

Carthage (D-2)

See also Joplin, Lamar, Mount Vernon

Founded 1842
Population 10,747
Elevation 1,002 ft
Area Code 417
Zip 64836
Information Chamber of Commerce, 107 E 3rd St; phone 417/358-2373
Web Site www.carthagenow.com

Carthage was founded as the seat of Jasper County in 1842. The first major Civil War battle west of the Mississippi River was fought here July 5, 1861. Belle Starr, a Confederate spy and outlaw, lived here as a girl. Annie Baxter, the first woman in the United States to hold elective office, was elected County Clerk here in 1890; and James Scott, ragtime musician and composer began his career here in 1906. Many interesting Victorian houses can still be found in Carthage.

What to See and Do

Battle of Carthage Civil War Museum. 205 E Grant, Carthage (64836). Features artifacts, a wall-sized mural, and a diorama depicting the progress of the battle. (Daily) **FREE**

Jasper County Courthouse. 302 S Main, Carthage (64836). Phone 417/358-0421. (1894) Built of Carthage marble, with mural by Lowell Davis depicting local history. (Mon-Fri; closed holidays)

Powers Museum. 1617 Oak St, Carthage (64836). Phone 417/358-2667. Museum devoted to local history and arts. Rotating exhibits on late 19th-early 20th-century clothing, furniture, holiday celebrations. Research library; gift shop. (Mid-Mar-mid-Dec, Tues-Sun; closed holidays) **FREE**

Precious Moments Chapel. 480 Chapel Rd, Carthage (64836). S on Hwy 71A to Hwy HH, then W to Chapel Rd. Phone 417/358-7599; toll-free 800/543-7975. This structure houses murals by Samuel J. Butcher. Museum; gardens; gift shops; cafés. (Mar-Dec: daily; Jan-Feb: limited hours) **$**

Special Event

Maple Leaf Festival. 107 E 3rd St, Carthage (64836). Phone 417/358-2373. Parade, marching band competition, arts and crafts, house tours. Mid-Oct.

Limited-Service Hotel

★ **DAYS INN.** 2244 Grand Ave, Carthage (64836). Phone 417/358-2499; toll-free 888/454-2499. www.daysinn.com. 40 rooms. Complimentary continental breakfast. Check-out 11 am. **$**

Specialty Lodging

The following lodging establishment is approved by Mobil Travel Guide, but due to its unique and individualized nature has not been given a traditional Mobil Star rating. Included in this listing you may find bed-and-breakfasts, limited-service inns, guest ranches, and other unique hotel properties.

GRAND AVENUE BED AND BREAKFAST. 1615 Grand Ave, Carthage (64836). Phone 417/358-7265. www.grand-avenue.com. 4 rooms, 2 story. Complimentary full breakfast. Check-in 4-6 pm, check-out 11 am. High-speed Internet access. Outdoor pool. Queen Anne-style, Victorian house (1890); antiques. **$**
📷 🏊

Restaurant

★ **BAMBOO GARDEN.** *104 N Garrison Ave, Carthage (64836). Phone 417/358-1611.* Chinese menu. Lunch, dinner. Closed Thanksgiving, Dec 25. **$**

Cassville (E-3)

See also Branson/Table Rock Lake Area

Population 2,371
Elevation 1,324 ft
Area Code 417
Zip 65625
Information Chamber of Commerce, 504 Main St; phone 417/847-2814
Web Site www.cassville.com

What to See and Do

Mark Twain National Forest. *Cassville. E via Hwy 76 or Hwy 86; S via Hwy 112. Phone 417/847-2144.* (Cassville Ranger District) Approximately 70,300 acres. Fishing, boat launching; camping at Big Bay Campground (fee), picnicking at Piney Creek Wilderness Area. (Daily)

Ozark Wonder Cave. *Noel. 45 miles W via Hwy 76, then 5 miles S on Hwy 59. Phone 417/475-3579.* Seven rooms with multicolored onyx, stalactites, and stalagmites; 45-minute tour. (Daily) **$$**

Roaring River State Park. *Hwy 112 S, Cassville (65625). 7 miles S on Hwy 112. Phone 417/847-2539.* Approximately 3,300 acres of spectacular hill country. Trout fishing; hiking, picnicking; dining lodge, general store. Improved camping (dump station), cabins, motel. Naturalist program and nature center; fish hatchery. Standard fees (Mar-Oct, daily). **FREE**

Chillicothe (B-3)

Settled 1837
Population 8,804
Elevation 798 ft
Area Code 660
Zip 64601
Information Chamber of Commerce, 715 Washington St, 2nd Floor, PO Box 407; phone 660/646-4050 or toll-free 877/224-4554
Web Site www.chillicothemo.com

Chillicothe, seat of Livingston County, is a Shawnee word meaning "our big town." Named for Chillicothe, Ohio, the city is located in a rich farming, livestock, and dairy region. Sloan's Liniment was developed here about 1870 by Earl Sloan. An Amish community located approximately 25 miles northwest of town, near Jamesport, has many interesting shops.

What to See and Do

General John J. Pershing Boyhood Home State Historic Site. *1000 Pershing Dr, Laclede. 20 miles E on Hwy 36, then 1 mile N on Hwy 5. Phone 660/963-2525. www.mostateparks.com/pershingsite.htm.* This 11-room house built in 1858 has been restored to and furnished in the 1860s-1880s period; museum; guided tours. Also here is a statue of "Black Jack" Pershing, a Wall of Honor, and the relocated Prairie Mound School, the one-room schoolhouse where Pershing taught before entering West Point. (Daily; closed holidays) **$**

Pershing State Park. *29277 Hwy 130, Chillicothe (64651). 18 miles E on Hwy 36, then S on Hwy 130. Phone 660/963-2299.* This 3,500-acre memorial to General John J. Pershing offers fishing, canoeing, hiking trails, picnicking, improved camping (dump station). North of the park is the Locust Creek covered bridge, the longest of four remaining covered bridges in the state. (Daily) **FREE**

Swan Lake National Wildlife Refuge. *19 miles E on Hwy 36 to Laclede Jct, then 13 miles S on Hwy 139 to Sumner; main entrance 1 mile S. Phone 660/856-3323.* This 10,795-acre resting and feeding area attracts one of the largest concentrations of Canadian geese in North America. Fishing; hunting. Observation tower (daily), visitor center with exhibits, specimens, and wildlife movies (Mon-Fri). Refuge and fishing (Mar-mid-Oct, Mon-Fri). Self-guided interpretive trail. **FREE**

Limited-Service Hotels

★ **BEST WESTERN CHILLICOTHE INN & SUITES.** *1020 S Washington St, Chillicothe (64601). Phone 660/646-0572; toll-free 800/990-9150; fax 660/646-1274. www.bestwestern.com.* 60 rooms, 2 story. Pets accepted; fee. Complimentary continental breakfast. Check-out noon. Outdoor pool. **$**

★ ★ **GRAND RIVER INN.** *606 W Business 36, Chillicothe (64601). Phone 660/646-6590.* 60 rooms,

2 story. Pets accepted. Complimentary continental breakfast. Check-out noon. Restaurant, bar. Outdoor pool, whirlpool. **$**

Clayton (C-5)

See also St. Louis

Settled 1820
Population 13,874
Elevation 550 ft
Area Code 314
Zip 63105
Information Chamber of Commerce, 225 S Meramec, Suite 300; phone 314/726-3033
Web Site www.claytonmochamber.com

Clayton, a central suburb of St. Louis, was first settled by Virginia-born Ralph Clayton, for whom the city is named. In 1877, the budding town became the seat of St. Louis County when Clayton and another early settler, Martin Hanley, donated part of their land for a new courthouse. Today, Clayton is a major suburban St. Louis residential and business center.

What to See and Do

Forest Park. *Clayton. Approximately 2 miles E via Clayton Rd or Forsyth Blvd.*

Special Event

St. Louis Art Fair. *Central Business District, Clayton (63105). Phone 314/863-0278.* One of the top three juried art fairs in the nation. First full weekend in Sept.

Full-Service Hotels

★ ★ ★ **CLAYTON ON THE PARK.** *8025 Bonhomme Ave, Clayton (63105). Phone 314/721-6543; fax 314/721-8588.* 109 rooms, 23 story, all suites. Pets accepted; fee. Complimentary continental breakfast. Check-in 4 pm, check-out 1 pm. High-speed Internet access. Restaurant, bar. Fitness room. **$$**

★ ★ ★ **DANIELE HOTEL.** *216 N Meramec, Clayton (63105). Phone 314/721-0101; toll-free 800/ 325-8302; fax 314/721-2015. www.thedanielehotel.com.* Guests staying at the hotel will enjoy the complimentary limousine service that transports visitors to and from the airport and the local area. A restaurant, outdoor pool, and other facilities are available, and there are plenty of attractions nearby. 77 rooms, 4 story. Pets accepted. Check-in 3 pm, check-out noon. High-speed Internet access, wireless Internet access. Restaurant, bar. Fitness room. Outdoor pool. Airport transportation available. Business center. **$**

★ ★ ★ **SHERATON CLAYTON PLAZA.** *7730 Bonhomme Ave, Clayton (63105). Phone 314/863- 0400; toll-free 800/325-3535; fax 314/863-8513. www.sheraton.com.* 257 rooms, 15 story. Pets accepted, some restrictions. Check-in 3 pm, check-out noon. High-speed Internet access. Two restaurants, bar. Fitness room. Indoor pool, whirlpool. Airport transportation available. Business center. **$$**

Full-Service Inn

★ ★ ★ **SEVEN GABLES INN.** *26 N Meramec Ave, Clayton (63105). Phone 314/863-8400; toll-free 800/ 433-6590; fax 314/863-8846. www.sevengablesinn.com.* Surrounded by upscale shops, galleries, and the finest dining establishments, this inn offers a blend of old-world charm and today's modern conveniences. The inn was inspired by sketches in Nathaniel Hawthorne's novel *The House of Seven Gables.* 32 rooms, 3 story. Complimentary continental breakfast. Check-in 3 pm, check-out noon. Restaurant, bar. Airport transportation available. **$**

Restaurants

★ ★ **ANNIE GUNN'S.** *16806 Chesterfield Airport Rd, Chesterfield (63005). Phone 636/532-7684; fax 636/532-0561.* American menu. Lunch, dinner, late-night. Closed Thanksgiving, Dec 25. Bar. Outdoor seating. Originally built in 1935 as a meat market and smokehouse. **$$$**

★ ★ ★ **BENEDETTO'S.** *10411 Clayton Rd, Frontenac (63131). Phone 314/432-8585; fax 314/ 432-3199.* Despite its suburban location, this cozy restaurant has the feel of an old Italian neighborhood. Bow-tied waiters present elaborate dishes. Italian menu. Lunch, dinner. Closed Easter, Thanksgiving, Dec 25. Bar. **$$**

★ **BRISTOL'S SEAFOOD GRILL.** *11801 Olive Blvd, Creve Coeur (63141). Phone 314/567-0272.*

Seafood menu. Lunch, dinner, Sun brunch. Bar. Children's menu. Stained-glass windows. **$$$**

★ ★ ★ **CAFÉ DE FRANCE.** *7515 Forsyth Blvd, Clayton (63105). Phone 314/678-0200; fax 314/678-0127. www.cafedefrancestlouis.com.* Husband and wife Marcel and Monique Keraval run the kitchen and front-of-house respectively at this formal French restaurant. Specialties of duck, seafood, and game, such as quail escolier stuffed with golden raisins, truffles, and pecans with juniper sauce, can be ordered prix fixe or à la carte and have attracted diners for over 20 years. French menu. Lunch, dinner. Closed Sun; holidays. Bar. Casual attire. **$$$**

★ **CAFE NAPOLI.** *7754 Forsyth, Clayton (63105). Phone 314/863-5731; fax 314/863-2835. www.cafe napoli.com.* Twinkling fairy lights, pink tablecloths, and an intimate mood add to the great people-watching atmosphere (Clayton's big hitters often dine here). The menu is also a treat, with southern Italian specialties and a great wine list. Italian menu. Lunch, dinner. Closed holidays. Bar. Valet parking. **$$$**

★ ★ **CAFE PROVENCAL.** *26 N Mermac, Clayton (63105). Phone 314/725-2755; fax 314/863-8846. www.cafeprovencal.com.* French menu. Lunch, dinner. Closed holidays. Bar. Valet parking. **$$**

★ ★ ★ **CARDWELL'S.** *8100 Maryland, Clayton (63105). Phone 314/726-5055; fax 314/726-1909. www.cardwellsinclayton.com.* This restaurant's celebrity chefs dish up an innovative American-style menu. Chic modern décor is the perfect complement to the trend-setting menu. Seafood menu. Lunch, dinner. Closed Sun; Thanksgiving, Dec 25. Bar. Children's menu. Outdoor seating. **$$**

★ ★ **FRANK PAPA'S.** *2241 S Brentwood Blvd, Brentwood (63144). Phone 314/961-3344; fax 314/961-1490.* Italian menu. Dinner. Closed Sun; holidays. Bar. Storefront restaurant. **$$$**

★ ★ ★ **GP AGOSTINO'S.** *15846 Manchester Rd, Ellisville (63011). Phone 636/391-5480; fax 636/391-3892. www.agostinosstlouis.com.* The owners, Agostino and Rosa, were born and raised in Palermo, Sicily. The cuisine and service of this fine dining Italian restaurant outside of St. Louis reflects their upbringings. Try the land and sea pasta. Italian menu. Lunch, dinner, late-night. Bar. Jacket required (dinner). **$$**

★ ★ ★ **JOHN MINEO'S.** *13490 Clayton Rd, Town and Country (63131). Phone 314/434-5244; fax 314/434-0714.* For decades this Italian-continental restaurant has lured diners with dishes such as Dover sole and veal chop, as well as daily fresh fish specials and house-made pasta. The intimate, white-tablecloth dining room has crystal chandeliers. Italian menu. Dinner. Closed Sun; holidays. Bar. Jacket required. **$$$**

★ ★ **NORMA JEAN.** *216 N Meramec, St. Louis (63105). Phone 314/721-0101; fax 314/721-0609. www.thedanielehotel.com.* American menu. Breakfast, lunch, dinner. Closed Thanksgiving, Dec 25. Bar. Valet parking. **$$**

★ ★ **PORTABELLA.** *15 N Cental Ave, Clayton (63105). Phone 314/725-6588; fax 314/725-6631. www.portabellarestaurant.com.* American menu. Lunch, dinner. Closed Thanksgiving, Dec 25. Bar. **$$$**

★ ★ **REMY'S.** *222 S Bemiston, Clayton (63105). Phone 314/726-5757; fax 314/909-4944. www.grihome.com.* Mediterranean menu. Lunch, dinner, late-night. Closed holidays. Bar. Outdoor seating. **$$**

★ **YACOVELLI'S.** *407 Dunn Rd, Florissant (63031). Phone 314/839-1000; fax 314/839-0469. www.yacovellis.com.* Italian menu. Breakfast, lunch, dinner, brunch. Closed Easter, Thanksgiving, Dec 25. Bar. Children's menu. **$$**

Clinton (C-3)

See also Harrisonville, Sedalia

Population 8,703
Elevation 803 ft
Area Code 660
Zip 64735
Information Chamber of Commerce, 200 S Main St; phone 660/885-8166 or toll-free 800/222-5251
Web Site www.clintonmo.org

Selected as the county seat in 1837, Clinton was called "the model town of the prairies." It has a large and attractive downtown square and is the northern gateway to Harry S. Truman Lake.

What to See and Do

Harry S. Truman State Park. *Hwy UU, Warsaw (65355). Approximately 20 miles E on Hwy 7, then 2 miles N on Hwy UU, on Truman Lake. Phone 660/438-7711.* Swimming, beach, fishing, boating (ramp, rentals, marina); hiking, picnicking, camping (hook-ups, dump station). (Daily)

Henry County Historical Society Museum and Cultural Arts Center.
203 W Franklin St, Clinton (64735). Phone 660/885-8414. Built in 1886 by Anheuser-Busch as a distributing point, this restored structure now houses historical documents, cemetery records, war relics, Native American artifacts, antique dolls, glass, china; Victorian parlor and old-fashioned kitchen; stable. Turn of the Century Village has 1890s store, bank, saddle shop; art gallery. (Apr-Dec, Mon-Sat, limited hours; also by appointment) **$$**

Restaurant

★ **UCHIE'S FINE FOODS.** *127 W Franklin, Clinton (64735). Phone 660/885-3262.* American menu. Breakfast, lunch, dinner. Closed Thanksgiving, Dec 25. **$**

Columbia (B-4)

See also Arrow Rock, Fulton, Hermann, Jefferson City

Settled 1819
Population 69,101
Elevation 758 ft
Area Code 573
Information Convention & Visitors Bureau, 300 S Providence Rd, PO Box N, 65205; phone 573/875-1231 or toll-free 800/652-0987
Web Site www.ci.columbia.mo.us

An educational center from its earliest years, Columbia is the home of Columbia College, Stephens College, and the University of Missouri, the oldest state university west of the Mississippi. Established as Smithton, the town was moved a short distance to ensure a better water supply and renamed Columbia. In 1822, the Boone's Lick Trail was rerouted to pass through the town. The University of Missouri was established in 1839, and the citizens of Boone County raised $117,900—in hard times and often with personal hardship—to secure the designation of a state university. Classes began in 1841, and the town has revolved around the institution ever since. The School of Journalism, founded in 1908, was the first degree-granting journalism school in the world.

What to See and Do

Nifong Park. *3801 Ponderosa Dr, Columbia (65201).* *Nifong Blvd at Ponderosa Dr, off Hwy 63. Phone 573/443-8936.* The park includes a visitor center, restored 1877 Maplewood house (Apr-Oct, Sun, limited hours), Maplewood Barn Theater (summer; fee), Boone County Historical Society Museum; petting zoo, lake, and picnicking. Park (daily). **FREE**

Shelter Gardens. *1817 W Broadway, Columbia (65201). On grounds of Shelter Insurance Co; S at I-70 Stadium Blvd exit. Phone 573/445-8441.* Miniature mid-American environment with a pool and stream, domestic and wild flowers, more than 300 varieties of trees and shrubs, rose garden, garden for the visually impaired; replica of a one-room schoolhouse, and a gazebo. Concerts in summer. (Daily, weather permitting; closed Dec 25) **FREE**

Stephens College. *1200 E Broadway, Columbia (65215). E Broadway and College Ave. Phone 573/442-2211.* (1833) (800 women) On 240-acre campus is the Firestone Baars Chapel on Walnut Street (Mon-Fri), designed in 1956 by Eero Saarinen; art gallery (Sept-May, daily), solar-heated visitors center.

University of Missouri-Columbia. *311 Jesse Hall, Columbia (65201). Phone 573/882-6333. www.missouri.edu.* (1839) (22,140 students) This 1,334-acre campus contains numerous collections, exhibits, galleries, and attractions. Campus tours (Mon-Fri). Campus map/guide at the Visitor Relations office, Reynolds Alumni and Visitor Center, Conley Avenue. Of special interest are

> **Botany Greenhouses and Herbarium.** *Tucker Hall, off Hitt St, E of McKee Gymnasium. Phone 573/882-6888.* Greenhouse has tropical and desert rooms displaying cacti, yucca, orchids, palms, and climbing bougainvillea. (Mon-Fri, by appointment) **FREE**

> **Edison Electric Dynamo.** *E 6th St and Stewart Rd, Columbia. Lobby of Engineering Building.* The recently restored dynamo, given to the university in 1882 by its inventor, Thomas Alva Edison, was used on campus in 1883 for the first demonstration of incandescent lighting west of the Mississippi. (Mon-Fri)

> **Ellis Library.** *Lowry Mall between Memorial Union and Jesse Hall, Ninth St and Conley Ave, Columbia. Phone 573/882-4391.* One of the largest libraries in the Midwest. Exhibits; rare book room contains a page from a Gutenberg Bible. **State Historical Society of Missouri,** east ground wing, has early newspapers and works by Missouri artists (phone

573/882-7083); Western Historical Manuscripts, including holdings from the Great Plains region (phone 573/882-6028 for schedule). Main library (Mon-Sun; closed holidays; schedule varies).

Museum of Anthropology. *Tucker Hall, Columbia (65211). Swallow Hall on Francis Quadrangle. Phone 573/882-3764.* Artifacts from 9000 BC to the present. Gift shop. (Mon-Fri; closed holidays) **FREE**

Museum of Art and Archaeology. *1 Pickard Hall, Columbia (65211). On Francis Quadrangle. Phone 573/882-3591.* Comprehensive collection including more than 13,000 objects from around the world, from the paleolithic period to the present. Cast gallery has casts made from original Greek and Roman sculptures. Gift shop. (Tues-Sun; closed holidays) **FREE**

Research Reactor Facility. *205 Research Reactor, Columbia (65211). S of Memorial Stadium on Providence Rd in University Research Park. Phone 573/882-4211.* Guided tours include displays and a view of the reactor core. (Mon-Fri; appointment required) **FREE**

Special Events

Boone County Fair. *5212 N Oakland Gravel Rd, Columbia (65202). Phone 573/474-9435.* First held in 1835, earliest fair west of the Mississippi; includes exhibits and a horse show. Late July.

Boone County Heritage Festival. *Nifong Park, Columbia. Phone 573/875-1231.* Mid-Sept.

Show-Me State Games. *1105 Carrie Frankie Dr, Columbia. Phone 573/882-2101.* Missouri's largest amateur athletic event with approximately 20,000 participants in 30 different events. May-June.

Limited-Service Hotels

★ ★ **HOLIDAY INN.** *2200 I-70 Dr SW, Columbia (65203). Phone 573/445-8531; toll-free 800/465-4329; fax 573/445-7607. www.holiday-inn.com.* 311 rooms, 6 story. Pets accepted. Check-out 11 am. Restaurant, bar. Fitness room. Indoor pool, outdoor pool, whirlpool. Adjacent to Exposition Center. **$**
🔲 🏃 🌊

★ ★ **QUALITY INN.** *1612 N Providence Rd, Columbia (65202). Phone 573/449-2491; toll-free 800/228-5751; fax 573/874-6720. www.qualityinn.com.*

142 rooms, 2 story. Pets accepted, some restrictions; fee. Check-out noon. Restaurant, bar. Fitness room. Indoor pool, whirlpool. **$**
🔲 🏃 🌊

Restaurants

★ ★ **BOONE TAVERN.** *811 E Walnut St, Columbia (65201). Phone 573/442-5123; fax 573/874-8724. www.boonetavern.com.* Turn-of-the-century memorabilia. American menu. Lunch, dinner. Closed Jan 1, Dec 25. Bar. Children's menu. Outdoor seating. **$$**

★ **FLAT BRANCH PUB & BREWING.** *115 S 5th St, Columbia (65201). Phone 573/499-0400. www.flatbranch.com.* American menu. Lunch, dinner. Closed holidays. Bar. Children's menu. Outdoor seating. **$$**

Excelsior Springs (B-2)

See also Cameron, Independence, Kansas City

Population 10,354
Elevation 900 ft
Area Code 816
Zip 64024
Information Chamber of Commerce, 101 E Broadway; phone 816/630-6161
Web Site www.exsmo.com

Excelsior Springs was established in 1880 when two settlers, Anthony W. Wyman and J. V. D. Flack, discovered various natural springs on Wyman's property. Today the city is a health resort offering visitors bottled water from the springs and medicinal baths in the city-operated bathhouse.

What to See and Do

Excelsior Springs Historical Museum. *101 E Broadway, Excelsior Springs (64024). Phone 816/630-0101.* Includes murals, bank, antiques, antique bedroom, doctor's office, dental equipment. (Tues-Sat) **FREE**

Hall of Waters. *201 E Broadway, Excelsior Springs (64024). Phone 816/630-0753.* Samples of mineral water may be purchased. Mineral baths for both men and women (by appointment). **$$$$**

🔲 **Jesse James's Farm.** *Excelsior Springs. Approximately 12 miles W on Hwy 92 to Kearney, then follow* signs 3 miles on Jesse James Farm Rd. Phone 816/628-6065. House where outlaw James was born and raised with brother Frank; original furnishings; guided tours. Visitor center; 15-minute film, historical museum. (Daily) **$$$**

Watkins Woolen Mill State Park and State Historic Site. *26600 Park Rd N, Lawson (64062). 6 1/2 miles N on Hwy 69, then 1 1/2 miles W on County MM. Phone 816/296-3357 (site).* Woolen factory and gristmill built and equipped in 1860; contains original machinery. Original owner's house, summer kitchen, ice house, smokehouse, fruit dryhouse, family cemetery, church, and school. Guided tours (daily; closed holidays). Recreation area adjoining the site has swimming, fishing; bicycle and hiking trail, camping (dump station). (Daily)

Full-Service Inn

★ ★ ★ **THE INN ON CRESCENT LAKE.** *1261 St. Louis Ave, Excelsior Springs (64024). Phone 816/630-6745. www.crescentinn.com.* This inn can be found in the historic town of Excelsior Springs and is great for a weekend getaway. It was built in 1915 on 22 acres of beautifully landscaped yard, surrounded by two cresent-shaped ponds, and offers guests a romantic setting. 10 rooms. Children over 16 years only. Complimentary full breakfast. Check-in 4-7 pm, check-out 11 am. Restaurant. Fitness room. Outdoor pool. **$**
🕿 🖾

Fulton (C-4)

See also Columbia, Jefferson City

Population 10,033
Elevation 770 ft
Area Code 573
Zip 65251
Information Kingdom of Callaway Chamber of Commerce, 409 Court St; phone 573/642-3055 or toll-free 800/257-3554
Web Site www.callawaychamber.com

Named in honor of Robert Fulton, inventor of the steamboat, this town was home to both architect General M. F. Bell, who designed many of Fulton's historic buildings, and Henry Bellaman, author of the best-selling novel *King's Row,* which depicted life in Fulton at the turn of the century. The town is home to Westminster College (1851), William Woods University (1870), and the Missouri School for the Deaf. A Ranger District office of the Mark Twain National Forest is located here.

What to See and Do

Kingdom Expo and Car Museum. *1920 N Bluff St (Business 54 N), Fulton (65251). Phone 573/642-2080.* Collection of 100 rare automobiles, classic fire trucks, model trains, and restored tractors. Rotating exhibits include more than 300 china doll heads, Kennedy family memorabilia, and ladies' hats. Exhibition hall. Gift shop. (Daily; closed Thanksgiving) **$$$**

Little Dixie Lake Conservation Area. *1821 State Rd RA, Millersburg (65251). 10 miles NW via County F or I-70. Phone 573/592-4080.* More than 600 acres with a 205-acre lake; fishing (permit required), boating (ramp, 10 hp limit), rowboat rentals (Apr-Oct); hiking, picnicking. (Daily) **FREE**

Westminster College. *501 Westminster Ave, Fulton (65251). Phone 573/642-3361.* (1851) (750 students) Winston Churchill delivered his "Iron Curtain" address here on March 5, 1946. On campus is

Breakthrough. *7th St and Westminster Ave, Fulton.* This 32-foot sculpture by Churchill's granddaughter was created to memorialize the Berlin Wall. The piece uses eight concrete sections of the actual wall; two human silhouettes cut through the concrete represent "freedom passing through."

Winston Churchill Memorial and Library. *7th St and Westminster Ave, Fulton (65251). Phone 573/592-5369.* To memorialize Churchill's "Iron Curtain" speech, the bombed ruins of Sir Christopher Wren's 17th-century Church of St. Mary, Aldermanbury, were dismantled, shipped from London to Westminster College, reassembled, and finally restored. The church was rehalloed in 1969 with Lord Mountbatten of Burma and Churchill's daughter, Lady Mary Soames, in attendance. The undercroft of the church houses a museum, gallery, and research library with letters, manuscripts, published works, photos, memorabilia; five original Churchill oil paintings; philatelic collections; antique maps; clerical vestments; slide show. (Daily; closed Jan 1, Thanksgiving, Dec 25) **$$**

George Washington Carver National Monument (E-2)

See also Joplin

2 miles W of Diamond on County V, then 1/2 mile S.

Web Site www.nps.gov/gwca

Born a slave on the farm of Moses Carver, George Washington Carver (1864-1943) rose to become an eminent teacher, humanitarian, botanist, agronomist, and pioneer conservationist. Carver was the first African American to graduate from Iowa State University. He received both a bachelor's and a master's degree in science. He then headed the Department of Agriculture at Booker T. Washington's Tuskegee Institute in Alabama.

Authorized as a national monument in 1943, this memorial to Carver perpetuates a vital part of the American historical heritage. The visitor center contains a museum and audiovisual presentation depicting Carver's life and work. A 3/4-mile, self-guided trail passes the birthplace site, the statue of Carver by Robert Amendola, the restored 1881 Moses Carver house, the family cemetery, and the woods and streams where Carver spent his boyhood. (Daily; closed Jan 1, Thanksgiving, Dec 25) Phone 417/325-4151. **FREE**

Hannibal (B-5)

See also Monroe City

Settled 1818
Population 18,004
Elevation 491 ft
Area Code 573
Zip 63401
Information Visitors & Convention Bureau, 505 N 3rd St; phone 573/221-2477
Web Site www.visithannibal.com

Hannibal is world-famous as the home town of the great novelist Samuel Clemens (Mark Twain) as well as the setting of *The Adventures of Tom Sawyer*, which records many actual events of Clemens's boyhood. Here he served his printer's apprenticeship and gained a fascination for "steamboating" in the days when the river was the source of the town's prosperity.

What to See and Do

Adventures of Tom Sawyer Diorama Museum. *323 N Main St, Hannibal (63401). Phone 573/221-3525. The Adventures of Tom Sawyer* in 3-D miniature scenes carved by Art Sieving. (Daily; closed holidays) **$**

Becky Thatcher House. *209-211 Hill St, Hannibal (63401).* House where Laura Hawkins (Becky Thatcher) lived during Samuel Clemens's boyhood; upstairs rooms have authentic furnishings. (Daily; closed Jan 1, Thanksgiving, Dec 25) **FREE**

Hannibal Trolley. *220 N Main St, Hannibal (63401). Phone 573/221-1161.* Narrated tour aboard trolley. Open-air summer months, enclosed rest of season. (Mid-Apr-Oct: daily; rest of year: by appointment) **$$$$**

Haunted House on Hill Street. *215 Hill St, Hannibal (63401). Phone 573/221-2220.* Life-size wax figures of Mark Twain, his family, and his famous characters; gift shop. (Apr-late Oct, daily) **$$$**

Mark Twain Cave. *7097 Country Rd 453, Hannibal (63401). 1 mile S, off Hwy 79. Phone 573/221-1656.* This is the cave in *The Adventures of Tom Sawyer* in which Tom and Becky Thatcher were lost and where Injun Joe died; 52° F temperature. One-hour guided tours (daily; closed Thanksgiving, Dec 25). Lantern tours to nearby Cameron Cave (Memorial Day-Labor Day, daily). Campground adjacent. **$$$**

⭐ **Mark Twain Museum and Boyhood Home.** *208 Hill St, Hannibal (63401). Phone 573/221-9010.* Museum houses Mark Twain memorabilia, including books, letters, photographs, and family items. Two-story white frame house in which the Clemens family lived in the 1840s and 1850s, restored and furnished with period pieces and relics. Gift shop. (Daily; closed holidays) **$$$** Admission includes

   John M. Clemens Justice of the Peace Office. *Hill St, Hannibal (63401).* Restored courtroom where Twain's father presided as justice of the peace.

   Museum Annex. *415 N Main, Hannibal (63401).* Audiovisual presentations on Mark Twain and Hannibal; displays.

Mark Twain's Hannibal

Start a tour of Hannibal, an old Mississippi riverboat town and hometown to Samuel Longhorn Clemens—better known as Mark Twain—at the Hannibal Convention and Visitors Bureau (505 N 3rd St). Towering above the visitor center is the Mark Twain Lighthouse, located at the crest of Cardiff Hill. It's a hefty climb up to the lighthouse, the largest inland lighthouse in the United States, but the views of Hannibal and the Mississippi are worth it.

A block south of the Visitors Bureau is the Mark Twain Boyhood Home and Museum (208 Hill St), which features the original 1843 Clemens home, restored to look as it did when Twain lived here in the 1840s. Tours are offered. Directly across the street at 215 Hill Street is the Haunted House on Hill Street Wax Museum, which contains 27 lifelike, hand-carved wax figures of Twain, his family, and many characters from his books, plus several "haunted" rooms with ghostly inhabitants. Next door at 211 Hill Street is the period home of Laura Hawkins, Mark Twain's youthful sweetheart, who is represented as Becky Thatcher in Twain's novels. On the corner of Hill and Main streets is the Clemens Law office, where Twain's father, J. M. Clemens, presided as Hannibal's justice of the peace. Attached to the building is a historic courtroom, which served as the model for scenes from *The Adventures of Tom Sawyer*. At the base of Cardiff Hill at Main Street is the Tom and Huck Statue, which commemorates Twain's most famous

characters, Huck Finn and Tom Sawyer. Frederick Hibbard sculpted this bronze statue in 1926.

Stretching along Main Street are a number of historic buildings and interesting shops. Follow Main Street south, passing shops and boutiques in historic storefronts. A worthy stop is Mrs. Clemens Antique Mall (305 N Main), which features two floors of antiques and an ice-cream parlor. At Bird and Main streets, stands the handsome Pilaster House/Grant's Drug Store, dating from the 1830s. The Clemens family lived here briefly in the 1940s, and Judge Clemens died here in 1847. Today, the building is preserved as an 1890s apothecary. An interesting anomaly amidst all this Twain-ania is the Optical Center and Museum (214 N Main), a science center that details how contact lenses and eyeglasses, as well as other optical equipment, are made.

At Main and Center streets is the Mark Twain Museum and Gift Shop, a newly restored structure that contains a collection of original Norman Rockwell paintings that were used for illustrated editions of *The Adventures of Huckleberry Finn.* The museum also serves as a memento of Hannibal's riverboat past. Speaking of riverboats, conclude your visit to Hannibal with a riverboat cruise. At the base of Center Street is Mississippi Riverboat Cruises, which features a one-hour excursion tour on the river, with great views of this historic river town.

Pilaster House and Grant's Drugstore. *Hill and Main sts, Hannibal (63401).* (1846-1847) The Clemens family lived in this Greek Revival house, which contains a restored old-time drugstore, pioneer kitchen, doctor's office, and living quarters where John Clemens, Twain's father, died.

Mark Twain Riverboat Excursions. *Hannibal. Departs from the foot of Center St. Phone 573/221-3222; toll-free 800/621-2322.* One-hour cruises on the Mississippi River; also two-hour dinner cruises. (Early May-Oct, daily)

Molly Brown Birthplace and Museum. *600 Butler St, Hannibal (63401). Phone 573/221-2100.* Antique-filled home has memorabilia of the "unsinkable" Molly

Brown, who survived the *Titanic* disaster. (Apr-May, Sept-Oct: weekends; June-Aug: daily) **$$**

Optical Science Center and Museum. *216 Main St, Hannibal (63401). Phone 573/221-2020.* Hands-on learning stations provide first-hand optical demonstrations. Computerized light show, wraparound theater. (Apr-Oct, daily). **$$**

Riverview Park. *Hannibal. Phone 573/221-0154.* This 400-acre park on bluffs overlooking the Mississippi River contains a statue of Samuel Clemens at Inspiration Point. Nature trails. Picnicking; playground. (Mon-Fri) **FREE**

Rockcliffe Mansion. *Hill St, Hannibal (63401). Phone 573/221-4140.* Restored Beaux Arts mansion overlooking the river; 30 rooms, many original furnishings. Samuel Clemens addressed a gathering here in 1902. Guided tours. (Daily; closed Jan 1, Thanksgiving, Dec 25) **$$$**

Tom and Huck Statue. *Main and North sts, Hannibal (63401). At the foot of the hill that was their playground.* Life-size bronze figures of Huck Finn and Tom Sawyer by F. C. Hibbard.

Twainland Express. *400 N 3rd St, Hannibal (63401). Phone 573/221-5593.* Narrated tours past points of interest in historic Hannibal, some aboard open-air, train-style trams. (Apr-Oct: weekends; May-Sept: daily) **$$$**

Special Events

Autumn Folklife Festival. *1221 Market St, Hannibal (63401). Phone 573/221-6545.* Mid-1800s crafts, food, entertainment. Third weekend in Oct.

Mississippi River Arts Festival. *1221 Market St, Hannibal (63401). Phone 573/221-6545.* Memorial Day weekend.

Tom Sawyer Days. *505 N 3rd St, Hannibal (63401). Phone 573/221-2477.* National fence painting contest, frog jumping, entertainment. Four days early in July.

Limited-Service Hotels

★ **BEST WESTERN HOTEL CLEMENS.** *401 N 3rd St, Hannibal (63401). Phone 573/248-1150; toll-free 800/780-7234; fax 573/248-1155. www.bestwestern.com.* 78 rooms, 3 story. Complimentary continental breakfast. Check-out 11 am. Indoor pool, whirlpool. Airport transportation available. In a historic district near the Mississippi River. **$**

★ ★ **HANNIBAL INN AND CONFERENCE CENTER.** *4141 Market St, Hannibal (63401). Phone 573/221-6610; toll-free 800/325-0777; fax 573/221-3840.* This inn offers a variety of rooms and suites to better accommodate its guests. It also offers a continental breakfast, an indoor pool, game room, tennis courts, a restaurant and lounge, and more. There is plenty to do in the surrounding area as well. 241 rooms, 2 story. Pets accepted. Complimentary continental breakfast. Check-out 11 am. Restaurant, bar. Indoor pool, whirlpool. Tennis. **$**

★ **SUPER 8.** *120 Huckleberry Heights Dr, Hannibal (63401). Phone 572/221-5863; toll-free 800/800-8000; fax 573/221-5478. www.super8.com.* 59 rooms, 3 story. Complimentary continental breakfast. Check-out 11 am. Outdoor pool. A city park is adjacent. **$**

Full-Service Inn

★ ★ ★ **GARTH WOODSIDE MANSION B&B.** *11069 New London Rd, Hannibal (63401). Phone 573/221-2789; toll-free 888/427-8407; fax 573/221-9941. www.garthmansion.com.* With eight guest rooms, each with its own private bath, this is a great bed-and-breakfast for a romantic or weekend getaway. This second-empire/Victorian mansion (1871) where Mark Twain was often a guest is located on 33 acres of grass, woodland, gardens, and ponds. 8 rooms, 3 story. Complimentary full breakfast. Check-in 4 pm, check-out 11 am. High-speed Internet access. **$**

Restaurant

★ **LOGUE'S.** *121 Huckleberry Heights Dr, Hannibal (63401). Phone 573/248-1854; fax 573/248-2244.* American menu. Breakfast, lunch, dinner. Closed holidays. Children's menu. **$**

Harrisonville (C-2)

See also Clinton, Independence, Kansas City

Population 7,683
Elevation 904 ft
Area Code 816
Zip 64701
Information Chamber of Commerce, 400 E Mechanic; phone 816/380-5271
Web Site www.ci.harrisonville.mo.us

Harrisonville, the retail and government center of Cass County, was named for Albert Harrison, a Missouri congressman.

Special Event

Living History Festival. *400 E Mechanic St, Harrisonville (64701). Phone 816/380-4396.* Living historians bring to life the Lewis and Clark expedition in an encampment setting. First weekend in Oct.

Limited-Service Hotel

★ **BEST WESTERN HARRISONVILLE.** *2201 N Rockhaven Rd, Harrisonville (64701). Phone 816/884-3200; toll-free 800/780-7234; fax 816/884-3200. www.bestwestern.com.* 45 rooms. Check-out 11 am. Outdoor pool. **$**

Hermann (C-4)

See also Columbia

Founded 1836
Population 2,754
Elevation 519 ft
Area Code 573
Zip 65041
Information Visitor Information Center, German School Building, PO Box 104; phone 573/486-2744 or toll-free 800/932-8687
Web Site www.hermanmo.com

German immigrants, unhappy with the English atmosphere of Philadelphia, bought this land and founded the town with the purpose of maintaining their German culture. Grape cultivation and wine-making started early and was a thriving business until Prohibition. Today winemaking has been revived in the area, and German culture is still in evidence.

What to See and Do

Deutsche Schule Arts and Crafts. *German School Building, 312 Schiller St, Hermann (65041). Phone 573/486-2744.* Exhibits from more than 100 craftspeople, including handmade quilting, china painting, basket-making, toll painting, woodcutting. Demonstrations by crafters during festival weekends. (Daily; closed Easter, Thanksgiving; also Dec 25-mid-Jan) **FREE**

Deutschheim State Historic Site. *109 W 2nd St, Hermann (65041). Phone 573/486-2200.* Dedicated to Missouri's German immigrants and German-American folk art and material culture, 1830-1920. The site includes the authentically furnished Pommer-Gentner House (1840) on Market Street and Strehly House and Winery (circa 1840-1867) on West 2nd Street. Kitchen, herb, and flower gardens; special events. Tours. (Daily; closed holidays) **$$**

Graham Cave State Park. *217 Hwy TT, Montgomery (63361). 13 miles N on Hwy 19, then 5 miles W, off I-70. Phone 573/564-3476.* Native Americans occupied this cave approximately 10,000 years ago. About 350 acres with fishing; nature trails, playground, improved camping (dump station). Visitor center. (Daily) **FREE**

Hermannhof Winery. *330 E 1st St, Hermann (65041). Phone 573/486-5959.* This 150-year-old winery includes ten wine cellars. Sausage making; cheeses. Sampling. (Daily) **$**

Historic Hermann Museum. *312 Schiller St, Hermann (65041). German School Building. Phone 573/486-2017.* Heritage Museum in 1871 building, with artifacts of early settlers; River Room depicts the history of early river men; children's museum has toys, furniture of 1890s; handmade German bedroom set; 1886 pump organ. Mechanism of town clock may be seen. (Apr-Oct, Tues-Sun) **$**

Stone Hill Winery and Restaurant. *1110 Stone Hill Hwy, Hermann (65041). Phone toll-free 800/909-9463. www.stonehillwinery.com.* Guided tour of wine cellars; wine tasting. Restaurant. Gift shop. (See SPECIAL EVENTS) (Daily) **$**

White House. *232 Wharf St, Hermann (65041). Phone 573/486-3200.* (Late 1860s) Restored hotel; tours; doll collection, mineral collection. (Apr-mid-Nov, schedule varies) **$**

Special Events

Great Stone Hill Grape Stomp. *Stone Hill Winery and Restaurant, 1110 Stone Hill Hwy, Hermann (65041). Phone toll-free 800/909-9463. www.stonehillwinery.com.* Enjoy rompin' and stompin' in a barrel full of juicy grapes to celebrate the beginning of grape harvest. Second Sat in Aug.

KristKindl Markt. *Stone Hill Winery and Restaurant, 1110 Stone Hill Hwy, Hermann (65041). Phone toll-free 800/909-9463. www.stonehillwinery.com.* Traditional German Christmas market; music, food. First weekend in Dec.

Maifest. *Hermann. Phone 573/486-2744.* Dancing, parades; crafts; house tour. Third full weekend in May.

Octoberfest. *Hermann. Phone 573/486-2744.* Area wineries. Wine cellar tours, wine samples; craft demonstrations; German music, food. First four weekends in Oct.

Limited-Service Hotel

★ **HERMANN MOTEL.** *112 E 10th St, Hermann (65041). Phone 573/486-3131; fax 573/486-5244. www. hermannmotel.com.* 24 rooms. Check-out 11 am. **$**
🅿

Restaurant

★ ★ **VINTAGE.** *1110 Stone Hill Hwy, Hermann (65041). Phone 573/486-3479; toll-free 800/909-9463; fax 573/486-3828. www.stonehillwinery.com.* American menu. Lunch, dinner. Closed mid-Dec-mid-Feb; Thanksgiving, Dec 25. Children's menu. Reservations recommended. In former stable and carriage house of working winery. **$$**

Independence (B-2)

See also Blue Springs, Excelsior Springs, Harrisonville, Kansas City, Lexington

Founded 1827
Population 112,301
Elevation 900 ft
Area Code 816
Information Tourism Division, 111 E Maple, 64050; phone 816/325-7111 or toll-free 800/748-7323
Web Site www.ci.independence.mo.us

Independence was an outfitting point for westbound wagon trains from 1830 to 1850. The scene of much of the "Mormon Wars" of the early 1830s, it was ravaged by raiders and occupied by Union and Confederate troops during the Civil War. Today it is best known as the hometown of President Harry S. Truman.

What to See and Do

1859 Marshall's Home and Jail Museum. *217 N Main St, Independence (64050). Phone 816/252-1892.* Restored building contains dungeonlike cells, marshall's living quarters, regional history museum. One-room schoolhouse (1870). (Apr-Oct: daily; Nov-Dec and Mar: Tues-Sun) **$$**

Bingham-Waggoner Estate. *313 W Pacific, Independence (64050). Phone 816/461-3491.* Famous Missouri artist George Caleb Bingham lived here from 1864 to 1870; also the homestead of the Waggoner family, millers of "Queen of the Pantry" flour. (Apr-Oct, daily) **$$**

Community of Christ World Headquarters, Temple and Auditorium. *1001 W Walnut St, Independence (64050). Phone 816/833-1000. www.rlds.org.* Auditorium, museum, and art gallery; 6,300-pipe organ; recitals (June-Aug: daily; rest of year: Sun). Japanese meditation garden. Guided tours (daily; closed Jan 1, Thanksgiving, Dec 25).

Fort Osage. *105 Osage, Sibley (64088). 10 miles E of Hwy 291 on Hwy 24 to Buckner, then 3 miles N to Sibley, and 1 mile N following signs. Phone 816/795-8200.* Restoration of one of the first US outposts in the Louisiana Territory following the purchase from France. Built in 1808 by William Clark of the Lewis and Clark expedition, the fort includes officers' quarters, soldiers' barracks, trading post, factor's house, museum; costumed guides. Visitor center contains dioramas, exhibits, gift shop. Special events; candlelight tours (fee). (Mid-Apr-mid-Nov: Wed-Sun; rest of year: Sat-Sun; closed Jan 1, Thanksgiving, Dec 25) **$$**

Harry S. Truman Courtroom and Office Museum. *Jackson County Courthouse, 112 W Lexington, Independence (64050). Phone 816/795-8200.* Restored office and courtroom where Truman began his political career as presiding county judge; 30-minute audiovisual show on Truman's boyhood and early career. Tours. (Sun-Thurs, by appointment) **$$**

⭐ **Harry S. Truman National Historic Site (Truman House).** *Main and Truman sts, Independence (64050). Phone 816/254-9929. www.nps.gov/hstr.* Truman's residence from the time of his marriage to Bess Wallace in 1919 until his death in 1972. An excellent example of late 19th-century Victorian architecture. The house, built by Bess Truman's grandfather, was the birthplace of Margaret Truman and served as the summer White House from 1945 to 1953. Guided tours. Ticket center at Truman Road and Main Sreet. (Memorial Day-Labor Day: daily; rest of year: Tues-Sun; closed Jan 1, Thanksgiving, Dec 25) **$**

National Frontier Trails Center. *318 W Pacific, Independence (64050). At Osage St. Phone 816/325-7575.* Partially restored flour mill at site of Santa Fe, California, and Oregon trails serves as a museum, interpretive center, library, and archive of westward pioneer expansion; 17-minute film, exhibits. (Daily; closed Jan 1, Thanksgiving, Dec 25). **$$**

Pioneer Spring Cabin. *Truman and Noland rds, Independence (64050). Phone 816/325-7111.* Cabin furnished with items typical of those brought westward by the pioneers; the spring was the meeting place of Native Americans and settlers. (Apr-Oct, Mon-Fri) **FREE**

Truman Farm Home. *12301 Blue Ridge Blvd, Grandview (64030). 19 miles S via I-435 to Hwy 71, S on Hwy 71. Phone 816/254-2720.* Truman lived in this two-story, white frame house in the decade preceding World War I; during these years—"the best years," according to Truman—he farmed the surrounding 600 acres, worked as a mason and postmaster, served as a soldier, and courted Bess Wallace. Interior features period furnishings, including original family pieces; outbuildings including garage, outhouse, chicken coop, and smokehouse. (Mid-May-late Aug, Fri-Sun) **FREE**

Truman Presidential Museum and Library. *500 W Hwy 24, Independence (64050). www.trumanlibrary.org.* Includes presidential papers; mementos of public life; reproduction of President Truman's White House office; Thomas Hart Benton mural; interactive exhibit. Graves of President and Mrs. Truman in courtyard. Museum (daily; closed Jan 1, Thanksgiving, Dec 25). Library (Mon-Fri). **$$**

Vaile Mansion. *1500 N Liberty, Independence (64050). Phone 816/325-7111.* (1881) House designed for local entrepreneur Colonel Harvey Vaile has 30 rooms and is an example of Second Empire architecture; ceiling murals. (Apr-Oct and Dec, daily) **$$**

Special Events

Santa-Cali-Gon. *210 W Truman Rd, Independence (64050). Phone 816/252-4745.* Celebration commemorating the Santa Fe, California, and Oregon trails; melodrama, contests, arts and crafts, square dancing. Labor Day weekend.

Truman Celebration. *Independence. Phone 816/254-2720.* Tribute to President Truman. Early May.

Limited-Service Hotel

★ **COMFORT INN.** *4200 S Noland Rd, Independence (64055). Phone 816/373-8856; fax 816/373-3312.* 171 rooms, 2 story. Pets accepted; fee. Complimentary continental breakfast. Check-out noon. Indoor pool, outdoor pool, whirlpool. **$**
🐾 🏊

Specialty Lodging

The following lodging establishment is approved by Mobil Travel Guide, but due to its unique and individualized nature has not been given a traditional Mobil Star rating. Included in this listing you may find bed-and-breakfasts, limited-service inns, guest ranches, and other unique hotel properties.

WOODSTOCK INN BED & BREAKFAST. *1212 W Lexington Ave, Independence (64050). Phone 816/833-2233; toll-free 800/276-5202; fax 816/461-7226. www.independence-missouri.com.* 11 rooms, 2 story. Complimentary full breakfast. Check-in 4 pm, check-out 11 am. High-speed Internet access. In a historic area of town near the Truman house and library. **$**

Restaurants

★ ★ **RHEINLAND.** *208 N Main St, Independence (64050). Phone 816/461-5383; fax 816/461-9159.* German menu. Breakfast, lunch, dinner, brunch. Closed Thanksgiving, Dec 25. Children's menu. **$$**

★ **SALVATORE'S.** *12801 Hwy 40 E, Independence (64055). Phone 816/737-2400; fax 816/356-6622. salvatores.us.* Italian menu. Lunch, dinner. Closed Thanksgiving, Dec 25. Bar. Children's menu. Outdoor seating. **$$**

★ ★ **V'S ITALIANO.** *10819 Hwy 40 E, Independence (64055). Phone 816/353-1241; fax 816/358-2011. www.vsrestaurant.com.* This place started off as a little café back in 1963, but my, how it's grown. A little off the beaten path, it's worth the drive. American, Italian menu. Lunch, dinner, Sun brunch. Closed Thanksgiving, Dec 25. Bar. Children's menu. Casual attire. **$$**

Jefferson City (C-4)

See also Columbia, Fulton, Sedalia

Settled circa 1825
Population 35,481
Elevation 702 ft
Area Code 573
Information Jefferson City Convention & Visitors Bureau, 213 Adams St, PO Box 2227, 65102; phone 573/634-3616 or toll-free 800/769-4183
Web Site www.visitjeffersoncity.com

Jefferson City was chosen for the state capital in 1826. Near a river landing, it consisted of a foundry, a shop, and a mission. Its growth was not steady and as late as 1895, efforts were made to move the seat of government. Since 1900, however, the city has prospered. The present capitol, completed in 1917, confirmed its status. Named for Thomas Jefferson, it is known locally as "Jeff City."

What to See and Do

Cole County Historical Society Museum. *109 Madison St, Jefferson City (65101). Phone 573/635-1850.* (Circa 1870). One of three four-story row houses built in the Federal style, the museum features Victorian furnishings and household items; inaugural gowns from Missouri's first ladies, dating from 1877; research library. Guided tours (Tues-Sat). **$**

Governor's Mansion. *100 Madison St, Jefferson City (65101). Phone 573/751-4141.* (1871). Renaissance Revival architecture by George Ingham Barnett; period furnishings, stenciled ceilings, period wall coverings, and late 19th-century chandeliers. Tours (Tues and Thurs; closed Aug and Dec). **FREE**

Runge Conservation Nature Center. *303 Commerce, Jefferson City (65101). Phone 573/526-5544.* Hiking trails, aquarium, nature exhibits. (Daily; closed holidays) **FREE**

State Capitol. *High St and Broadway, Jefferson City (65101). Phone 573/751-4127.* (1918). On a bluff overlooking the Missouri River, this building of Carthage stone is the third state capitol in Jefferson City; both predecessors burned. A Thomas Hart Benton mural is in the House Lounge, third floor, west wing; also paintings by N. C. Wyeth and Frank Brangwyn. Tours (35-45 minutes). (Daily; closed holidays) **FREE** Also here are

Jefferson Landing State Historic Site. *Jefferson and Water sts, Jefferson City (65101). Phone 573/751-3475.* Restored mid-1800s riverboat landing. Lohman Building (1839) features exhibits and audiovisual presentation on the history of Jefferson City and the Missouri Capitol. Union Hotel (1855) contains a gallery of exhibits by local artists. (Tues-Sat; closed holidays) **FREE**

Missouri State Museum. *201 W Capitol Ave, Jefferson City (65101). Phone 573/751-4127.* Offers two permanent exhibits; History Hall, with several themes of Missouri history, and Resources Hall. (Daily; closed holidays) **FREE**

Special Events

Cole County Fair. *1445 Fairgrounds Rd, Jefferson City (65101). Phone 573/893-3950.* Rides, shows, arts and crafts. Last week in July.

Cole County Fall Festival. *Jefferson City. Phone 573/634-2824.* Craft fair, jazzfest, parade. Second weekend in Sept.

Limited-Service Hotels

★ ★ **BEST WESTERN CAPITAL INN.** *1937 Christy Dr, Jefferson City (65101). Phone 573/635-4175; toll-free 800/780-7234; fax 573/635-6769. www.bestwestern.com.* 79 rooms, 2 story. Complimentary continental breakfast. Check-out noon. Restaurant, bar. Indoor pool. **$**

★ ★ **HOTEL DEVILLE.** *319 W Miller St, Jefferson City (65101). Phone 573/636-5231; toll-free 800/392-3366; fax 573/636-5260. www.devillehotel.com.* 98 rooms, 3 story. Check-out noon. Restaurant, bar. Outdoor pool. **$**

Full-Service Hotel

★ ★ ★ **CAPITOL PLAZA HOTEL.** *451 W McCarty St, Jefferson City (65101). Phone 573/635-1234; toll-free 800/338-8088; fax 573/635-4565. www.jqhhotels.com.* This full-service hotel offers renovated guest rooms, a pool, whirlpool, and cascading waterfall in the atrium, a restaurant, café and lounge, high-speed Internet connections, and more. It is across from the Truman building and near attractions. 255 rooms, 9 story. Check-out noon. Restaurant, bar. Fitness room. Indoor pool. **$**

Restaurants

★ ★ **MADISON'S CAFE.** *216 Madison St, Jefferson City (65101). Phone 573/634-2988; fax 573/634-3740. www.madisonscafe.com.* Italian menu. Lunch, dinner. Closed Thanksgiving, Dec 25. Children's menu. Casual attire. **$$**

★ **VEIT'S DIAMOND.** *2001 Missouri Blvd, Jefferson City (65109). Phone 573/635-1213.* American menu. Dinner. Bar. Children's menu. **$$**

Joplin (D-2)

See also Carthage, George Washington Carver National Monument, Mount Vernon; also see Pittsburg, KS

Settled 1838
Population 40,961
Elevation 972 ft
Area Code 417
Information Convention & Visitors Bureau, 222 W 3rd St, 64801; phone 417/625-4789 or toll-free 800/657-2534
Web Site www.joplincvb.com

The discovery of lead here convinced an early settler to establish a town and name it after another settler, Rev. Harris G. Joplin. As the mining boom continued, another community, Murphysburg, grew up on the west side of Joplin Creek. The two towns were rivals until 1873 when both agreed to incorporate into one city. Today Joplin, one of Missouri's larger cities, is home to many manufacturing industries.

What to See and Do

Missouri Southern State College. *3950 Newman Rd, Joplin (64801). Phone 417/625-9300.* (1937) (6,000 students) This 332-acre campus includes Taylor Performing Arts Center, Mission Hills estate, and Spiva Art Center (phone 417/625-9563) with changing exhibits (Tues-Sun; closed early Aug, holidays). Tours. **FREE**

Museum Complex. *Joplin (64801). Schifferdecker Park, W edge of city on Hwy 66.* (Tues-Sun; closed holidays.) Here are

> **Dorothea B. Hoover Historical Museum.** *W 7th St and Schifferdecker Ave, Joplin (64801). Phone 417/623-1180.* Period rooms with late 19th-century furnishing; miniatures, including a circus, photographs, musical instruments, Victorian doll house, and playhouse; antique toys; dolls; Native American artifacts; cut glass. Under 12 only with adult. **FREE**

> **Tri-State Mineral Museum.** *Schifferdecker Park, 7th and Schifferdecker Ave, Joplin (64801).* Models of lead- and zinc-mining equipment, mineral and history displays. **FREE**

Post Memorial Art Reference Library. *300 Main St, Joplin (64801). Phone 417/782-7678.* Art research facility resembling 16th-century English hall. Furniture and artwork date to the 13th century. (Mon-Sat; closed holidays) **FREE**

Thomas Hart Benton Exhibit. *303 E 3rd St, Joplin (64801). In Municipal Building.* Includes mural, "Joplin at the Turn of the Century, 1896-1906," as well as photographs, clay models, personal letters, and other paintings by Benton. (Mon-Fri; closed holidays) **FREE**

Limited-Service Hotels

★ **DRURY INN.** *3601 S Range Line Rd, Joplin (64804). Phone 417/781-8000; toll-free 800/378-7946; fax 417/781-8000. www.druryinn.com.* 109 rooms, 4 story. Pets accepted, some restrictions. Complimentary continental breakfast. Check-out noon. Fitness room. Indoor pool, whirlpool. **$**

★ ★ **HOLIDAY INN.** *3615 S Range Line Rd, Joplin (64804). Phone 417/782-1000; toll-free 800/465-4329; fax 417/623-4093. www.holiday-inn.com.* 262 rooms, 5 story. Pets accepted, some restrictions. Check-out noon. Restaurant, bar. Fitness room. Indoor pool, outdoor pool, whirlpool. **$**

Restaurants

★ **KITCHEN PASS.** *1212 S Main St, Joplin (64801). Phone 417/624-9095; fax 417/624-6886. www.kitchenpass.net.* Seafood, steak menu. Breakfast, lunch, dinner. Closed Sun; holidays. Bar. Children's menu. **$$**

★ **WILDER'S.** *1216 Main St, Joplin (64801). Phone 417/623-7230; fax 417/624-6886.* Seafood, steak menu. Dinner. Closed holidays. Bar. **$$$**

Kansas City (B-2)

See also Blue Springs, Excelsior Springs, Harrisonville, Independence, Lexington, St. Joseph, Weston

Settled 1838
Population 435,146
Elevation 800 ft
Area Code 816
Information Kansas City Convention & Visitors Bureau, 1100 Main St, Suite 2550, 64105; phone 816/221-5242 or toll-free 800/767-7700
Web Site www.visitkc.com

Suburbs In Missouri: Blue Springs, Excelsior Springs, Independence. In Kansas: Kansas City, Overland Park. (See individual alphabetical listings.)

Kansas City is the distributing point for a huge agricultural region. It is one of the country's leading grain and livestock markets and is famous for its steak and barbecue. The city is also a great industrial center, with food processing, milling, petroleum refining, and vehicle assembly high in importance. Kansas City, Kansas, across the Missouri River, is politically separate, but the two cities form an economic unit constituting the Greater Kansas City area.

Kansas City, Missouri, was developed as a steamboat landing for the town of Westport, 4 miles south on the Santa Fe Trail, and a competitor with Independence as the trail's eastern terminus and outfitting point. The buildings that sprang up along this landing soon eclipsed Westport, which was eventually incorporated into the new city. Kansas City's roaring overland trade was disturbed by the border warfare of the 1850s and the Civil War, but peace and the railroads brought new growth and prosperity. A network of railway lines following the natural water-level routes that converge at the mouth of the Kansas River made Kansas City a great terminus.

Famous for their "booster" spirit, its citizens were aroused to the need for civic improvement in the 1890s by the crusade of William Rockhill Nelson, *Kansas City Star* publisher. As a result, today's Kansas City boasts 52 boulevards totaling 155 miles, and more fountains than any city except Rome.

Kansas City Fun Fact

Kansas City has more miles of boulevards than Paris and more fountains than any city except Rome.

Public Transportation

Area Transit Authority Phone 816/221-0660

Airport Quad City International Airport; cash machines, Terminals A, B, C.

Information Phone 816/243-5237

Lost and found Phone 816/243-5215

Airlines Air Canada, America West, American Airlines, Continental, Delta/Delta Express, Delta Connection/Comair, Midwest Express, Northwest, Southwest, United, US Airways, US Airways Express, Vanguard

What to See and Do

⭐ *Arabia* **Steamboat Museum.** *400 Grand Blvd, Kansas City (64106). Phone 816/471-4030. www.1856 .com.* Excavated pioneer artifacts from the steamboat *Arabia,* which went down in 1856. The boat, discovered in 1988, carried 200 tons of cargo. Replica of main deck; hands-on displays. (Daily; closed holidays)

Art and Design Center. *4510 State Line Rd, Kansas City (66103).* More than 20 shops and galleries located in a old historic area.

Board of Trade. *4800 Main St, Kansas City (64112). Phone 816/753-7500.* Stock index trading and world's largest hard winter wheat market. Visitors may observe trading from the third floor. (Mon-Fri) **FREE**

City Market. *Kansas City. Main to Grand sts, 3rd to 5th sts.* Outdoor farmers' market since early 1800s (Apr-Sept, daily). Indoor farmers' market (year-round, daily).

Country Club Plaza. *4745 Central St, Kansas City (64112). 47th between Nichols Pkwy and Madison Ave, S of downtown. Phone 816/753-0100.* The nation's first planned shopping center (1922) consists of 55 acres encompassing more than 180 shops and 25 restaurants in and around Spanish/Moorish-style arcaded buildings. The plaza features tree-lined walks, statues, fountains, and murals; re-creations of Spain's Seville light and Giralda tower; horse-drawn carriage rides; free entertainment. Shops (daily).

⭐ **Crown Center.** *2450 Grand, Kansas City (64108). Phone 816/274-8444.* This entertainment complex offers shopping, theaters, restaurants, and hotels around a landscaped central square; exhibits and ice skating (mid-Nov-Mar). Shops (daily). In Crown Center are

Coterie–Kansas City's Family Theatre. *Phone 816/474-6552.* Nonprofit professional theater. (Early Feb-late Dec, Tues-Sun) **$$**

Hallmark Visitors Center. *Phone 816/274-5672.* Exhibit areas focus on history of the greeting card industry. Included are audiovisual and interactive displays; die-making and manufacturing demonstrations; film presentation. (Tues-Sat; closed holidays) **FREE**

Kaleidoscope. *Phone 816/274-8300.* Participatory creative art exhibit for children ages 5-12 only; Discovery Room features hands-on creative area; studio with specially designed art projects. (Mid-June-Aug: Mon-Sat; rest of year: Sat or by appointment). Adults may view activity through one-way mirrors. Three 90-minute sessions per day; tickets available half-hour before each session. **FREE**

Government buildings. *Kansas City. 11th to 13th sts, Holmes to McGee sts.* Includes City Hall with observation roof on 30th floor (Mon-Fri; closed holidays); federal, state and county buildings. **FREE**

Jesse James Bank Museum. *103 N Water St, Liberty (64068). 15 miles N via I-35, on Old Town Sq. Phone 816/781-4458.* (1858). Restored site of the first daylight bank robbery by the James gang (1866). Jesse James memorabilia; hand-scribed bank ledger books and other relics of early banking. (Mon-Sat; closed Jan 1, Thanksgiving, Dec 25) **$$**

John Wornall House Museum. *6115 Wornall Rd, Kansas City (64113). Phone 816/444-1858.* (1858). Restored farmhouse interprets the lives of prosperous Missouri farm families from 1830 to 1865; herb garden; gift shop. (Tues-Sun; closed Jan, holidays). **$$**

Kansas City Art Institute. *4415 Warwick Blvd, Kansas City (64111). Phone 816/472-4852.* (Circa 1885).

Kansas City Blades (IHL). *Kemper Memorial Arena, 1800 Genessee, Kansas City (64102).* Professional hockey team.

Kansas City Chiefs (NFL). *Arrowhead Stadium, One Arrowhead Dr, Kansas City (64129). Phone 816/920-9300; toll-free 800/676-5488.* Professional football team.

Kansas City Museum. *Union Station, 3218 Gladstone Blvd, Kansas City (64108). Phone 816/483-8300. www.kcmuseum.com.* Science, history, and technology exhibits housed in former estate of lumber millionaire Robert A. Long; re-creation of 1821 trading post, 1860 storefront and functioning 1910 drugstore; planetarium; gift shop. (Tues-Sun; closed holidays) **$$**

Kansas City Royals (MLB). *Kauffman Stadium, One Royal Way, Kansas City (64129). Phone 816/921-8000. www.kcroyals.com.* Professional baseball team.

Kansas City Wizards (MLS). *Arrowhead Stadium, One Arrowhead Dr, Kansas City (64129). Phone 816/920-9300. www.kcwizards.com.* Professional soccer team.

Kansas City Zoo. *Swope Park, 6800 Zoo Dr, Kansas City (64132). Off I-435 and Hwy 71. Phone 816/513-5700. www.kansascityzoo.org.* Explore 200 acres landscaped to resemble natural animal habitats. Sea lion and wild bird shows; IMAX theater; miniature train, pony, and camel rides; interpretive programs. (Daily; closed holidays) **$$**

Kemper Museum of Contemporary Art and Design. *4420 Warwick Blvd, Kansas City (64111). Phone 816/561-3737. www.kemperart.org.* (Tues-Sun; closed holidays) **FREE**

Nelson-Atkins Museum of Art. *4525 Oak St, Kansas City (64111). At 47th St. Phone 816/751-1278. www.nelson-atkins.org.* Collections range from Sumerian art of 3000 BC to contemporary paintings and sculpture; period rooms; decorative arts; Kansas City Sculpture Park featuring Henry Moore sculpture garden. Guided tours (free). (Tues-Sun; closed holidays) **FREE**

Oceans of Fun. *4545 NE Worlds of Fun Ave, Kansas City (64161). 10 miles NE via I-435 exit 54, between Parvin Rd and NE 48th St. Phone 816/454-4545. www.worldsoffun.com.* This 60-acre family water park features wave pool, twisting water slides, boats, children's pools, and playgrounds. One- and two-day passports; also combination Worlds of Fun/Oceans of Fun passports. (Late May-late Aug: daily; early Sept: weekends only) **$$$$**

Thomas Hart Benton Home and Studio State Historic Site. *3616 Belleview, Kansas City (64111). Phone 816/931-5722.* (1903-1904) Eclectic-style residence of the artist from 1939 until his death in 1975; the studio contains many of Benton's tools and equipment; changing exhibits. (Daily; closed holidays) **$**

Toy and Miniature Museum of Kansas City. *5235 Oak St, Kansas City (64112). At 52nd St, on University of Missouri-Kansas City campus. Phone 816/333-2055.* Miniatures, antique doll houses, and furnishings from 1840s to mid-20th century. (Wed-Sun; closed holidays, the first two weeks in Sept) **$$**

Union Cemetery. *227 E 28th St Terrace, Kansas City (66108).* (1857). Some notables buried here include artist George Caleb Bingham and Alexander Majors, founder of the Pony Express; graves of more than 1,000 Civil War soldiers. Self-guided walking tours.

University of Missouri-Kansas City. *5100 Rockhill Rd, Kansas City (64110). Phone 816/235-1000.* (1933) (11,500 students) On the campus is the Toy and Miniature Museum of Kansas City, library with

Americana and local historical exhibits, Marr Sound Archives, Jazz Film Archives, Geosciences Museum and Belger Art Center. Performances by Conservatory of Music and Academic Theater.

Westport. *Broadway and Westport Rd, Kansas City (64111).* Renovated 1830s historic district includes specialty shops, galleries, and restaurants; Pioneer Park traces Westport's role in the founding of Kansas City. Shops (daily).

Worlds of Fun. *4545 NE Worlds of Fun Ave, Kansas City (64161). 10 miles NE via I-435 exit 54. Phone 816/454-4545. www.worldsoffun.com.* A 170-acre entertainment complex with amusement rides, live entertainment, children's area, special events, restaurants; includes looping steel and wooden roller coasters and white-water raft, spill water, log flume, and hydroflume rides. (Late May-Aug: daily; Apr and Sept-Oct: weekends) **$$$$**

Special Events

American Royal Barbecue. *American Royal Center, 1701 American Royal Ct, Kansas City (64102). Kemper Arena. Phone 816/221-9800.* First weekend in Oct.

American Royal Livestock, Horse Show, and Rodeo. *American Royal Center, 1701 American Royal Ct, Kansas City (64102). Phone 816/221-9800.* Late Oct-early Nov.

Ethnic Enrichment Festival. *306 E 12th St, Kansas City (64111). Phone 816/842-7530.* Many nationalities celebrate with music, dance, cuisine, and crafts. Three days in Aug.

Kansas City Pro Rodeo. *Benjamin Ranch, 6401 E 87th St, Kansas City (64138). Phone 816/761-1234.* Saddle bronco riding, steer wrestling, barback riding, barrel racing, calf roping, and bull riding are some of the events held at the Benjamin Ranch. Week of July 4.

Kansas City Symphony. *1020 Central St, Kansas City (64105). Phone 816/471-0400.* Concert series of symphonic and pop music. Fri-Sun, some Wed.

Lyric Opera. *1029 Central St, Kansas City (64105). Phone 816/471-7344.* Opera productions in English. Performances on Mon, Wed, Fri-Sat. Apr-May and mid-Sept-mid-Oct; holiday production in Dec.

Missouri Repertory Theatre. *Center for the Performing Arts, 4949 Cherry St, Kansas City (64110). Phone 816/235-2700.* Professional equity theater company; classic and contemporary productions. Annual performance of *A Christmas Carol.* Sept-May, Tues-Sun.

Starlight Theater. *Swope Park, 4600 Starlight Rd, Kansas City (64132). Phone 816/363-7827.* Outdoor amphitheater featuring Broadway musicals and contemporary concerts. Performances nightly. Early June-Aug.

St. Patrick's Day Parade. *Pershing and Grand sts, Kansas City. Downtown. Phone 816/931-7373. www.kcirishparade.com.* One of the nation's largest, this St. Patrick's Day parade is approximately 1 mile in length and features a variety of themed floats, bands, and performers. Mar.

Limited-Service Hotels

★ **BAYMONT INN.** *2214 Taney St, North Kansas City (64116). Phone 816/221-1200; toll-free 800/301-0200; fax 816/471-6207. www.baymontinn.com.* 94 rooms, 3 story. Pets accepted, some restrictions. Complimentary continental breakfast. Check-out noon. **$**

★ ★ **DOUBLETREE HOTEL.** *1301 Wyandotte St, Kansas City (63801). Phone 816/474-6664; toll-free 800/222-8733; fax 816/474-0424. www.doubletree.com.* This hotel, located in the downtown business district near the Kansas City Convention Center, has guest rooms with European charm. 388 rooms, 28 story. Pets accepted, some restrictions; fee. Check-out noon. Restaurant, bar. Fitness room. Outdoor pool. Business center. **$$**

★ ★ **HOTEL SAVOY.** *219 W 9th St, Kansas City (64105). Phone 816/842-3575; toll-free 800/728-6922; fax 816/842-3575. www.bandbonline.com.* This restored 1888 landmark building features original architectural details such as stained and leaded glass, tile floors, and tin ceilings. The Savoy Grille is located on the property, and many attractions are nearby. 22 rooms, 6 story. Complimentary full breakfast. Check-in 3 pm, check-out 1 pm. Restaurant, bar. **$**

★ ★ **QUARTERAGE HOTEL.** *560 Westport Rd, Kansas City (64111). Phone 816/931-0001; toll-free 800/942-4233; fax 816/931-8891. www.quarterage hotel.com.* 123 rooms, 4 story. Complimentary full breakfast. Check-in 3 pm, check-out noon. High-speed Internet access. Airport transportation available. Business center. **$**

Full-Service Hotels

★ ★ ★ THE FAIRMONT KANSAS CITY AT THE PLAZA.
401 Ward Pkwy, Kansas City (64112). Phone 816/756-1500; toll-free 800/441-1414; fax 816/531-1483. www.fairmont.com. The Fairmont is the place to stay in Kansas City. This elegant and contemporary hotel located within the exclusive Plaza shopping and dining area is the perfect choice for business or leisure travelers to this Midwestern metropolis. The guest rooms and suites are stylish and are equipped with modern amenities and luxurious details. A 24-hour business center and a fitness center with outdoor pool and spa treatments are among the additional perks. The Oak Room restaurant celebrates the cuisine of America's heartland with steaks and chops. More than a dozen restaurants await just outside the door at the Plaza, tempting visitors with a variety of menus and atmospheres. 366 rooms, 12 story. Pets accepted; fee. Check-in 3 pm, check-out noon. High-speed Internet access. Restaurant, bar. Fitness room. Outdoor pool, children's pool. Airport transportation available. Business center. **$$**

★ ★ ★ HOTEL PHILLIPS.
106 W 12th St, Kansas City (64105). Phone 816/221-7000; toll-free 800/433-1426; fax 816/221-3477. www.hotelphillips.com. The Hotel Phillips is a stylish home-away-from-home for visitors to Kansas City. Located in the heart of downtown, this intimate boutique hotel is a convenient base for business travelers. Seductive Art Deco furnishings and gracious service make this hotel a standout. While the historic integrity of this 1931 landmark has been preserved, modern amenities have been added to the plush rooms and suites. From oversized bathrooms and pillow choices to state-of-the-art technology, guests are truly catered to at this hotel. Guests relive the 1930s at Phillips Chophouse, where a convivial spirit and a mouthwatering menu attract hotel guests and locals alike. Live music draws patrons to 12 Baltimore Café and Bar, where diners enjoy light meals and cocktails. 217 rooms, 20 story. Check-in 3 pm, check-out noon. High-speed Internet access. Two restaurants, two bars. Fitness room. Airport transportation available. Business center. **$$**

★ ★ ★ HYATT REGENCY CROWN CENTER.
2345 McGee St, Kansas City (64108). Phone 816/421-1234; toll-free 888/591-1234; fax 816/435-4190. www.hyatt.com. Connected to the Crown Center by an elevated walkway and near the Truman Sports Complex, an amusement park, and the international airport, this hotel is convenient and comfortable. 731 rooms, 42 story. Check-in 3 pm, check-out noon. High-speed Internet access, wireless Internet access. Five restaurants, bars. Fitness room. Outdoor pool, whirlpool. Tennis. Airport transportation available. Business center. **$$**

★ ★ ★ MARRIOTT KANSAS CITY AIRPORT.
775 Brasilia Ave, Kansas City (64153). Phone 816/464-2200; toll-free 800/228-9290; fax 816/464-5915. www.marriott.com. This hotel is located on the Kansas City International Airport's grounds and is perfect for business or pleasure. T-Bone Charlie's is found just off the lobby and an indoor pool and health club are available. 378 rooms, 9 story. Check-out noon. Restaurant, bar. Fitness room. Indoor pool, whirlpool. Airport transportation available. Business center. **$**

★ ★ ★ MARRIOTT KANSAS CITY COUNTRY CLUB PLAZA.
4445 Main St, Kansas City (64111). Phone 816/531-3000; toll-free 800/228-9290; fax 816/531-3007. www.marriott.com/mcipl. Located ten minutes from busy downtown, this hotel is near many shops, restaurants, and an active night life. It offers a health club with an indoor pool, whirlpool and weight room, a restaurant, and more. 295 rooms, 19 story. Check-in 3 pm, check-out noon. High-speed Internet access, wireless Internet access. Restaurant, bar. Fitness room. Indoor pool, whirlpool. Airport transportation available. Business center. **$**

★ ★ ★ MARRIOTT KANSAS CITY DOWNTOWN.
200 W 12th St, Kansas City (64105). Phone 816/421-6800; toll-free 800/228-9290; fax 816/855-4418. www.marriott.com. This is a large hotel is located downtown near the city market, casinos, family attractions, and more. 983 rooms, 22 story. Pets accepted; fee. Check-in 3 pm, check-out noon. Wireless Internet access. Two restaurants, two bars. Fitness room (fee). Indoor pool. Airport transportation available. Business center. **$$**

★ ★ ★ THE RAPHAEL HOTEL.
325 Ward Pkwy, Kansas City (64112). Phone 816/756-3800; toll-free 800/695-8284; fax 816/802-2131. www.raphaelkc.com. This hotel is located in the midtown area near shops, restaurants, and other attractions for visitors to the

area. 123 rooms, 9 story. Check-in 4 pm, check-out 1 pm. High-speed Internet access. Restaurant, bar. Airport transportation available. Business center. **$$**
🚶

★ ★ ★ **SHERATON SUITES COUNTRY CLUB PLAZA.** *770 W 47th St, Kansas City (64112). Phone 816/931-4400; toll-free 800/325-3535; fax 816/561-7330. www.sheraton.com.* This is an all-suite hotel offering many facilities including a restaurant, lounge, indoor and outdoor heated pools, whirlpool, weight room, and more. The hotel is located near sports, cultural, and family attractions. 257 rooms, 18 story, all suites. Pets accepted. Check-in 3 pm, check-out noon. High-speed Internet access. Restaurant, bar. Fitness room. Indoor pool, outdoor pool, whirlpool. Airport transportation available. Business center. **$**
🐾 🏋 🛏 🚶

★ ★ ★ **THE WESTIN CROWN CENTER.** *1 Pershing Rd, Kansas City (64108). Phone 816/474-4400; toll-free 800/228-3000; fax 816/391-4438. www.westin.com/crowncenter.* Located in the downtown area within Hallmark's Crown Center where visitors will find shops, restaurants, and theaters. The hotel is also near the Liberty Memorial and the Bartle Convention Center and offers many amenities and facilities. 729 rooms, 13 story. Pets accepted, some restrictions. Check-in 3 pm, check-out noon. High-speed Internet access. Two restaurants, two bars. Children's activity center. Fitness room (fee). Outdoor pool, whirlpool. Tennis. Airport transportation available. Business center. **$$**
🐾 🏋 🛏 🎿 🚶

Specialty Lodging

The following lodging establishment is approved by Mobil Travel Guide, but due to its unique and individualized nature has not been given a traditional Mobil Star rating. Included in this listing you may find bed-and-breakfasts, limited-service inns, guest ranches, and other unique hotel properties.

SOUTHMORELAND ON THE PLAZA. *116 E 46th St, Kansas City (64112). Phone 816/531-7979; fax 816/531-2407. www.southmoreland.com.* Each room in this quiet bed-and-breakfast is uniquely furnished and decorated. Rooms feature either a fireplace, Jacuzzi tub, or a private deck. The property is located near the Country Club Plaza shopping district and other attractions. 13 rooms, 3 story. Children over 13 years only. Complimentary full breakfast. Check-in

4:30 pm, check-out 11 am. High-speed Internet access, wireless Internet access. **$**

Restaurants

★ ★ ★ **AMERICAN.** *200 E 25th St, Ste 400, Kansas City (64108). Phone 816/545-8000; fax 816/545-8020. www.theamericanrestaurantkc.com.* The flagship restaurant of the Crown Center, American, built in 1974, is a tribute to the ingredients and fine cuisine of our native land. The menu was created with the assistance of James Beard, the father of American cooking, and Joe Baum, the legendary restauranteur of the late, great Windows on the World in New York City. Today, the restaurant is still as dreamy and elegant as ever, with spectacular downtown views, polished service, and one of the city's best wine lists. The dining room's signature fan-shaped oak canopies, along with a sweeping staircase, give the restaurant a majestic sense of romance and history. The kitchen's dedication to delicious American fare like poultry, beef, game, fresh fish, and local seasonal produce has not faltered over the years. Indeed, even 30 years later, American remains a Kansas City jewel. American menu. Lunch, dinner. Closed Sun; holidays. Bar. Children's menu. Business casual attire. Reservations recommended. Valet parking. **$$$**

★ **ANDRE'S CONFISERIE SUISSE.** *5018 Main St, Kansas City (64112). Phone 816/561-3440; toll-free 800/892-1234; fax 816/561-2922. www.andreschocolates.com.* Swiss menu. Lunch. Closed Sun-Mon. Business casual attire. **$**

★ **ARTHUR BRYANT'S BARBEQUE.** *1727 Brooklyn Ave, Kansas City (64127). Phone 816/231-1123; fax 816/241-7427. www.arthurbryantsbbq.com.* Barbecue menu. Lunch, dinner. Closed holidays. Casual attire. **$**

★ **BERLINER BEAR.** *7815 Wornall Rd, Kansas City (64114). Phone 816/444-2828.* German menu. Lunch, dinner. Closed Mon; holidays. Bar. Children's menu. Casual attire. **$$**

★ ★ **BUGATTI'S LITTLE ITALY.** *3200 N Ameristar Dr, Kansas City (64161). Phone 816/414-7000. www.ameristarcasinos.com.* Italian menu. Breakfast, lunch, dinner, brunch. Bar. **$$**

★ ★ **CALIFORNOS.** *4124 Pennsylvania, Kansas City (64111). Phone 816/531-7878. www.californos.com.* American menu. Lunch, dinner. Closed Sun; holidays. Bar. Casual attire. Reservations recommended. Valet parking. Outdoor seating. **$$**

★ ★ **CANYON CAFE.** *4626 Broadway, Kansas City (64112). Phone 816/561-6111; fax 816/561-6265. www.canyoncafe.com.* Southwestern menu. Lunch, dinner. Closed Thanksgiving, Dec 25. Bar. Children's menu. Casual attire. Reservations recommended. **$$**

★ ★ **CASCONE'S ITALIAN RESTAURANT.** *3733 N Oak, Kansas City (64116). Phone 816/454-7977; fax 816/454-8041. www.cascones.com.* Italian menu. Lunch, dinner. Closed holidays. Bar. Children's menu. Casual attire. Reservations recommended. Outdoor seating. **$$**

★ ★ **CHAPPELL'S.** *323 Armour Rd, North Kansas City (64116). Phone 816/421-0002; fax 816/472-7141. www.chappellsrestaurant.com.* This place has an enormous collection of sports memorabilia and is a hit with the college kids. You won't feel out of place with your family or your parents. Steak menu. Lunch, dinner. Closed Sun; Jan 1, Thanksgiving, Dec 25. Bar. Children's menu. Casual attire. **$$**

★ ★ **CLASSIC CUP CAFE.** *301 W 47th St, Kansas City (64112). Phone 816/753-1840; fax 816/753-8608. www.classiccup.com.* This casual, European-style bistro and wine cellar is located in downtown's Country Club Plaza. American menu. Breakfast, lunch, dinner, Sun brunch. Closed holidays. Bar. Casual attire. Outdoor seating. **$$**

★ ★ ★ **EBT.** *1310 Carondelet Dr, Kansas City (64114). Phone 816/942-8870; fax 816/941-8532. www.ebtrestaurant.com.* Mid-1900s sandstone columns and two ornate brass elevators provide the setting for this fine dining location, serving dishes such as pistachio-encrusted salmon and pepper steak. Tableside presentations are offered, and there is an extensive wine list. American menu. Lunch, dinner. Closed Sun-Mon; Thanksgiving, Dec 25. Bar. Children's menu. Business casual attire. Reservations recommended. **$$$**

★ ★ **FIGLIO.** *209 W 46th Terrace, Kansas City (64112). Phone 816/561-0505; fax 816/531-2916. www.dineoutinkc.com.* Italian menu. Lunch, dinner, brunch. Closed Dec 25. Bar. Children's menu. Casual attire. Reservations recommended. Valet parking. Outdoor seating. **$$**

★ ★ **FIORELLA'S JACK STACK BARBECUE.** *13441 Holmes St, Kansas City (64145). Phone 816/942-9141; toll-free 877/419-7427; fax 816/942-5166. www.jackstackbbq.com.* Barbecue menu. Lunch, dinner. Closed Thanksgiving, Dec 25. Bar. Children's

menu. Casual attire. Reservations recommended. Outdoor seating. **$$**

★ ★ **GAROZZO'S RISTORANTE.** *526 Harrison, Kansas City (64106). Phone 816/221-2455; fax 816/221-7174. www.garozzos.com.* Italian menu. Lunch, dinner. Closed holidays. Bar. Children's menu. Casual attire. Reservations recommended. **$$**

★ ★ **GOLDEN OX.** *1600 Genessee St, Kansas City (64102). Phone 816/842-2866; fax 816/842-4617. www.goldenox.com.* Another classic, down in the old stockyard area of the West Bottoms. The Ox has been serving steaks to hungry Kansas Citians since 1949—they must be doing something right. Steak menu. Lunch, dinner. Closed Jan 1, Dec 25. Bar. Children's menu. Casual attire. **$$$**

★ ★ ★ **GRAND STREET CAFE.** *4740 Grand St, Kansas City (64112). Phone 816/561-8000; fax 816/561-8350. www.eatpbj.com.* American menu. Lunch, dinner, brunch. Closed holidays. Bar. Children's menu. Business casual attire. Reservations recommended. Outdoor seating. **$$$**

★ ★ **HARDWARE CAFE.** *5 E Kansas Ave, Liberty (64068). Phone 816/792-3500; fax 816/792-5023. www.thehardwarecafe.com.* American menu. Breakfast, lunch, dinner. Closed Sun. Children's menu. Converted hardware store; old-fashioned soda fountain, historical building. No credit cards accepted. **$$**

★ **ILIKI CAFE.** *6431 N Cosby Ave, Kansas City (64151). Phone 816/587-0009; fax 816/587-6011. www.iliki.com.* Mediterranean menu. Lunch, dinner. Closed Sun; holidays. Bar. Casual attire. **$$**

★ ★ **JESS & JIM'S STEAK HOUSE.** *517 E 135th St, Kansas City (64145). Phone 816/941-9499; fax 816/941-6348. www.jessandjims.com.* Steak menu. Lunch, dinner. Closed holidays. Bar. Children's menu. Casual attire. **$$$**

★ ★ ★ **JJ'S.** *910 W 48th St, Kansas City (64112). Phone 816/561-7136; fax 816/561-5490. www.jjs-restaurant.com.* Unique upscale European fare is served at this friendly bistro. American menu. Lunch, dinner. Closed holidays. Bar. Business casual attire. Reservations recommended. Valet parking. **$$$**

★ ★ **K. C. MASTERPIECE.** *4747 Wyandotte St, Kansas City (64112). Phone 816/531-3332; fax 816/531-5505. www.kcmrestaurants.com.* Barbecue menu. Lunch, dinner. Closed Thanksgiving, Dec 25. Bar. Children's menu. Casual attire. Reservations recommended. Valet parking. **$$**

★ **L. C.'S BAR-B-Q.** *5800 Blue Park Way, Kansas City (64129). Phone 816/923-4484; fax 816/923-5386.* Barbecue menu. Lunch, dinner. Closed Sun; holidays. **$$**

★ ★ ★ **LE FOU FROG.** *400 E 5th St, Kansas City (64106). Phone 816/474-6060; fax 816/474-3066. www.lefoufrog.com.* A perfect place to dine when seeing a show at the convention center. Sauces are light and presentation is excellent. Great portions and a large special menu gives diners something to ponder. French menu. Lunch, dinner. Closed Mon; holidays. Bar. Casual attire. Reservations recommended. Valet parking. Outdoor seating. **$$$**

★ ★ ★ **LIDIA'S KANSAS CITY.** *101 W 22nd St, Kansas City (64108). Phone 816/221-3722; fax 816/842-1960. www.lidiasitaly.com.* Created by acclaimed New York restauranteur Lidia Bastianich, this trendy restaurant offers a chic, rustic atmosphere, with rough brick walls and exposed wooden beams. Italian menu. Lunch, dinner. Closed holidays. Bar. Children's menu. Business casual attire. Reservations recommended. Outdoor seating. **$$**

★ ★ **MACALUSO'S ON 39TH.** *1403 W 39th St, Kansas City (64111). Phone 816/561-0100; fax 816/561-0100. www.macalusoson39th.com.* Italian menu. Dinner. Closed Sun; holidays. Bar. Casual attire. Reservations recommended. **$$$**

★ ★ ★ **THE MAJESTIC STEAKHOUSE.** *931 Broadway, Kansas City (64105). Phone 816/471-8484; fax 816/471-8686. www.majesticgroup.com.* The historic Fitzpatrick Saloon building in downtown Kansas City is home to one of the best, most entertaining steakhouses in town. It has a great place to indulge in a cigar. Turn-of-the-century décor with stained-glass windows, ceiling fans, and an ornate tin ceiling. Steak menu. Lunch, dinner. Closed holidays. Bar. Business casual attire. Reservations recommended. **$$$**

★ ★ **MILANO.** *2450 Grand Ave, Kansas City (64108). Phone 816/426-1130; fax 816/426-1177.* Italian menu. Lunch, dinner. Closed holidays. Bar. Children's menu. Business casual attire. Reservations recommended. **$$**

★ ★ ★ **O'DOWD'S LITTLE DUBLIN.** *4742 Pennsylvania Ave, Kansas City (64112). Phone 816/561-2700; fax 816/960-0567. www.odowdslittledublin.com.* This authentic Irish pub, with much of its interior built in Ireland then shipped here, serves the best fish and chips in town. Irish menu. Lunch, dinner, late-night. Closed Memorial Day. Bar. Children's menu. Casual attire. Reservations recommended. Outdoor seating. **$**

★ **PHOENIX PIANO BAR & GRILL.** *302 W 8th St, Kansas City (64105). Phone 816/472-0001; fax 816/472-5705. www.phoenixjazz.net.* American menu. Lunch, dinner, late-night. Closed Sun; holidays. Piano bar; pictures of famous jazz musicians. Casual attire. Outdoor seating. **$$**

★ ★ ★ **PLAZA III STEAKHOUSE.** *4749 Pennsylvania Ave, Kansas City (64112). Phone 816/753-0000; fax 816/753-7118. www.plazaiiisteakhouse.com.* The epitome of the Kansas City steakhouse, with USDA prime aged cuts of Midwestern beef, chops, fresh fish, and lobster. Lunch includes their famous steak soup. Steak menu. Lunch, dinner. Closed holidays. Bar. Children's menu. Business casual attire. Reservations recommended. Valet parking. **$$$**

★ ★ ★ **RAPHAEL DINING ROOM.** *325 Ward Pkwy, Kansas City (64112). Phone 816/756-3800; toll-free 800/821-5343; fax 816/802-2131. www.raphaelkc.com.* The elegant dining room is known for its romantic ambience and discreet service. International/Fusion menu. Breakfast, lunch, dinner. Bar. Business casual attire. Reservations recommended. Valet parking. **$$$**

★ ★ **SHIRAZ.** *320 Southwest Blvd, Kansas City (64108). Phone 816/472-0015; fax 816/472-4439. www.shirazkc.com.* Mediterranean menu. Lunch, dinner. Closed Sun; holidays. Bar. Casual attire. Reservations recommended. Valet parking. Outdoor seating. **$$**

★ **SMUGGLER'S INN.** *1650 Universal Plaza Dr, Kansas City (64120). Phone 816/483-0400; fax 816/483-1109.* American menu. Lunch, dinner. Closed Memorial Day, July 4, Labor Day. Bar. **$$**

★ ★ **STEPHENSON'S APPLE FARM.** *16401 E Hwy 40, Kansas City (64136). Phone 816/373-5405; fax 816/373-3228. www.stephensons.bigstep.com.* From its humble beginnings as a roadside fruit stand in 1900, this family-owned restaurant grew over the years to become a home-style family tradition. Set in an orchard, mazelike dining spaces give way to a brick-floored patio among the trees. American menu. Lunch, dinner. Closed Dec 24-25. Bar. Children's menu. Casual attire. Reservations recommended. Outdoor seating. **$$**

★ ★ **STROUD'S.** *1015 E 85th St, Kansas City (64113). Phone 816/333-2132; fax 816/333-2162. www.stroudsrestaurant.com.* American menu. Lunch, dinner. Closed Thanksgiving, Dec 25. Bar. **$$**

Kirksville (A-4)

See also Macon

Founded 1841
Population 17,152
Area Code 660
Zip 63501
Information Kirksville Area Chamber of Commerce, 304 S Franklin, PO Box 251; phone 660/665-3766
Web Site www.kirksvillechamber.com

Kirksville is a trade center for surrounding communities and the home of Kirksville College of Osteopathic Medicine (1892), the world's first such college. An early pioneer, Jesse Kirk, traded a turkey dinner for the right to name the town after himself.

What to See and Do

Sugar Creek Conservation Area. *Hwys N and 11, Kirksville (63501).* 8 miles SW on Hwy 11. Phone *660/785-2420.* A 2,609-acre forest. Hunting, primitive camping, horseback riding trails. (Daily)

Thousand Hills State Park. *Hwy 6 N, Kirksville (63501).* 4 miles W on Hwy 6, then 2 miles S on Hwy 157. Phone *660/665-6995.* More than 3,000 acres. Swimming, bathhouse, fishing, boating (ramp, marina, rentals), canoeing; hiking trails, picnicking, dining lodge, store, improved camping (dump station), cabins. (Daily) **FREE**

Truman State University. *100 E Normal, Kirksville (63501). Phone 660/785-4016. www.truman.edu.* (1867) (6,000 students) E. M. Violette Museum on campus has a gun collection, Native American artifacts, historical items (by appointment only). Pickler Memorial Library has Schwengel-Lincoln Collection of memorabilia on Abraham Lincoln (Mon-Fri); also historical textiles and related arts (by appointment). Campus tours.

Limited-Service Hotels

★ **SHAMROCK INN.** *2501 S Business 63, Kirksville (63501). Phone 660/665-8352; toll-free 800/301-2772; fax 660/665-0072.* 45 rooms. Pets accepted, some restrictions; fee. Check-out 11 am. Outdoor pool. **$**
🅿 🐾 🌊

★ **SUPER 8.** *1101 Country Club Dr, Kirksville (63501). Phone 660/665-8826; toll-free 800/800-8000; fax 660/665-8826. www.super8.com.* 61 rooms, 3 story. Check-out 11 am. **$**

Ladue (C-5)

Restaurants

★ ★ **BUSCH'S GROVE.** *9160 Clayton Rd, Ladue (63124). Phone 314/993-0011. www.buschsgrove.com.* Seafood, steak menu. Lunch, dinner. Bar. Children's menu. Outdoor seating. Built in 1860. **$$**

★ ★ ★ **KREIS'S.** *535 S Lindbergh Blvd, St Louis (63131). Phone 314/993-0735. www.kreisrestaurant .com.* Pronounced "Chris" or "Krice," this German-influenced steakhouse has been at the same location more than 50 years. In a renovated 1930s brick house with beamed ceilings. Steak menu. Dinner. Closed holidays. Bar. **$$**

★ ★ ★ **SCHNEITHORST'S HOFAMBERG INN.** *1600 S Lindbergh Blvd, Ladue (63131). Phone 314/993-5600; fax 314/993-1069. www.schneithorst.com.* Unusual ethnic influences give traditional German cuisine an unexpected new face on this menu. Atlantic salmon with rainforest fruit relish and seafood strudel Johann Strauss are a few examples. In true German fashion, 33 specialty beers are available on tap. German, American menu. Lunch, dinner, Sun brunch. Bar. Children's menu. Outdoor seating. **$$**

Lake of the Ozarks (C-3)

See also Camdenton, Lake Ozark, Osage Beach

Approximately 42 miles SW of Jefferson City on Hwy 54.

Web Site www.funlake.com

Completed in 1931, the 2,543-foot-long Bagnell Dam impounds the Osage River to form this 54,000-acre recreational lake, which has an irregular 1,150-mile shoreline. Fishing, boating, and swimming are excellent here. Boats may be rented.

What to See and Do

Jacob's Cave. *23114 Hwy TT, Versailles (65084). N on Hwy 5, exit at State Rd TT. Phone 573/378-4374. www.jacobscave.com.* Famous for its depth illusion, reflective pools, prehistoric bones, and the world's largest geode. One-mile tours on concrete, wheelchair-accessible walkways. (Daily; closed Dec 25) **$$$**

Lake of the Ozarks State Park. *403 Hwy 134, Kaiser (65047). SE of Osage Beach on Hwy 42. Phone 573/348-2694.* This more than 17,000-acre park, the largest in the state, has 89 miles of shoreline with two public swimming and boat launching areas. Public Beach #1 is at the end of Highway 134, and Grand Glaize Beach is 1/2 mile from Highway 54, 2 miles south of Grand Glaize Bridge. On the grounds is a large cave with streams of water that continuously pour from stalactites. Fishing, canoeing; hiking, horseback riding, picnicking, improved camping (dump station). Naturalist. (Daily) **FREE**

Paddlewheeler *Tom Sawyer* **Excursion Boat.** *Lake of the Ozarks. W end of Bagnell Dam. Phone 573/365-3300.* 90-minute narrated sightseeing excursions on a sternwheeler (Apr-Oct, daily); charters available. **$$$**

Lake Ozark (C-4)

See also Camdenton, Lake of the Ozarks, Osage Beach

Population 681
Elevation 703 ft
Area Code 573
Zip 65049

What to See and Do

Casino Pier. *1046 Bagnell Dam Blvd, Lake Ozark (65049). 1/2 block S of Bagnell Dam, on Hwy 54 Business. Phone 573/365-2020.* One- and two-hour cruises aboard the *Commander* depart hourly (Apr-Oct, daily); also breakfast, brunch, and dinner and dance cruises. **$$$$**

Limited-Service Hotel

★ ★ **HOLIDAY INN.** *120 Holiday Ln, Lake Ozark (65049). Phone 573/365-2334; toll-free 800/532-3575; fax 573/365-6887. www.holiday-inn.com.* 207 rooms, 3 story. Pets accepted, some restrictions; fee. Complimentary continental breakfast. Check-out 11 am. Restaurant, bar. Fitness room. One indoor pool, two outdoor pools, whirlpool. **$**

Full-Service Resort

★ ★ ★ **LODGE OF FOUR SEASONS.** *Horseshoe Bend Pkwy (Hwy HH), Lake Ozark (65049). Phone 573/365-3000; toll-free 800/843-5253; fax 573/365-8525. www.4seasonsresort.com.* Located in the Ozark Hills, the property overlooks the winding shoreline. Many of the rooms and two- and three-bedroom condominiums have views of the lake or Japanese garden and pool. A golf course and health spa are on the premises. 304 rooms, 4 story. Check-in 4 pm, check-out 11 am. Restaurant, bar. Children's activity center. Fitness room, spa. Outdoor pool, children's pool, whirlpool. Golf. Airport transportation available. **$$**

Restaurants

★ ★ **BENTLEY'S.** *Hwy 54 (Business), Lake Ozark (65049). Phone 573/365-5301; fax 573/365-6438.* Seafood, steak menu. Dinner. Closed Jan 1, Thanksgiving, Dec 25. Bar. Children's menu. **$$**

★ ★ **J. B. HOOK'S GREAT OCEAN FISH & STEAKS.** *2260 Bagnell Dam Blvd, Lake Ozark (65049). Phone 573/365-3255; fax 573/365-4798. www.jbhooks.com.* Steak menu. Lunch, dinner. Closed Dec 25. Bar. Outdoor seating (lunch only). **$$**

★ ★ ★ **TOLEDO'S.** *Horseshoe Bend Pkwy (Hwy HH), Lake Ozark (65049). Phone 573/365-3000; fax 573/365-8525. www.4seasonsresort.com.* Enjoy the view of the Japanese gardens and the lake while listening to live jazz and feasting on the cuisine of Executive Chef Steve Zimmerman. Local ingredients are prepared in a variety of styles. American menu. Breakfast, lunch, dinner. Bar. Children's menu. Valet parking. **$$**

Lamar (D-2)

See also Carthage, Nevada

Population 4,168
Elevation 985 ft
Area Code 417
Zip 64759
Information Barton County Chamber of Commerce,

110 W 10th St, PO Box 577; phone 417/682-3595
Web Site www.bartoncounty.com

What to See and Do

⭐ **Harry S. Truman Birthplace State Historic Site.**
1009 Truman Ave, Lamar (64759). Phone 417/682-2279; toll-free 800/334-6946. www.mostateparks.com/ trumansite.htm. Restored 1 1/2-story house where Truman was born on May 8, 1884, and lived until he was 11 months old; six rooms with period furnishings, outdoor smokehouse, and hand-dug well. Guided tours. (Daily; closed holidays) **FREE**

Prairie State Park. *128 NW 150th Ln, Liberal (64762). 16 miles W on Hwy 160. Phone 417/843-6711.* This nearly 3,500-acre park preserves an example of Missouri's original prairie; onsite are a flock of prairie chickens and a small herd of buffalo. Hiking. Picnicking. Visitor center; wildlife observation. (Tues-Sat) **FREE**

Special Events

Lamar Free Fair. *Lamar Square, Lamar (64759). Phone 417/682-3911.* Livestock exhibits; contests, displays; parade, carnival, entertainment. Third full week in Aug.

Truman Days. *407 E 11th St, Lamar (64759). Phone 417/682-2279.* Celebrates Truman's birthday. Parade, contests, entertainment, Truman drama, and impersonator. Second Sat in May.

Limited-Service Hotel

⭐ **BLUE TOP INN.** *65 SE 1st Ln, Lamar (64759). Phone 417/682-3333; toll-free 800/407-3030; fax 417/682-3336.* 25 rooms. Check-out 11 am. Outdoor pool. **$**
🏊

Lebanon (D-4)

See also Camdenton, Waynesville

Founded 1849
Population 9,983
Elevation 1,266 ft
Area Code 417
Zip 65536
Information Lebanon Area Chamber of Commerce, 500 E Elm St, Cowan Civic Center; phone 417/588-3256

Web Site www.lebanonmissouri.com

Lebanon was founded in the mid-1800s beside an Indian trail that today is Interstate 44. As the seat of the newly-created Laclede County, the town was originally called Wyota; however, the name was changed when a respected minister asked that it be renamed after his hometown of Lebanon, Tennessee.

What to See and Do

Bennett Spring State Park. *26250 Hwy 64A, Lebanon (65536). 12 miles W on Hwy 64. Phone 417/532-4338.* Nearly 3,100 acres. Swimming pool, trout fishing (Mar-Oct); picnicking, store, dining lodge, improved camping (dump station), cabins. Nature center, naturalist. (Daily) (See SPECIAL EVENTS) **FREE**

Special Events

Hillbilly Days. *Bennet Springs State Park, Lebanon (65536). Phone 417/588-3256.* Arts and crafts, contests, country music, antique cars. Father's Day weekend.

Laclede County Fair. *Lebanon (65536). Phone 417/588-9607.* Fairgrounds. One week in mid-July.

Limited-Service Hotel

⭐ ⭐ **BEST WESTERN WYOTA INN.** *I-44 at exit 130, Lebanon (65536). Phone 417/532-6171; toll-free 800/780-7234; fax 417/532-6174. www.bestwestern.com.* 52 rooms, 2 story. Pets accepted, some restrictions; fee. Complimentary continental breakfast. Check-out 11 am. Restaurant. Outdoor pool. **$**
🔲 🔾 🏊

Lexington (B-3)

See also Independence, Kansas City; also see Gothenburg, NE

Settled 1822
Population 4,860
Elevation 849 ft
Area Code 660
Zip 64067
Information Tourism Bureau, 817 Main St, PO Box 132; phone 660/259-4711
Web Site www.historiclexington.com

This historic city with more than 110 antebellum houses was founded by settlers from Lexington,

Kentucky. The site of a three-day battle during the Civil War, many of the Union Army's entrenchments are still visible today. Situated on bluffs overlooking the Missouri River, Lexington was an important river port during the 19th century. Today the area is one of the state's largest producers of apples.

What to See and Do

Battle of Lexington State Historic Site. *Extension Hwy N, Lexington (64067). Phone 660/259-4654.* The site of one of the Civil War's largest western campaign battles (September 18-20, 1861). Anderson House, which stood in the center of the battle and changed hands from North to South three times, has been restored. Visitor center with exhibits and video. Guided tours. (Daily; closed holidays) **$$**

Lafayette County Courthouse. *1001 Main St, Lexington (64067). Phone 660/259-4315.* (1847) Oldest court-house in constant use west of the Mississippi. It has a Civil War cannonball embedded in the east column. (Mon-Fri; closed holidays)

Lexington Historical Museum. *112 S 13th St, Lexington (64067). Phone 660/259-6313.* Built as a Presbyterian church in 1846; contains Pony Express and Battle of Lexington relics, photographs, and other historical Lexington items. (Mid-Apr-mid-Oct, daily) **$**

Log House Museum. *817 Main St, Lexington (64067). Main St at Broadway. Phone 660/259-4711.* Exhibits include candle making, quilting, hearth cooking. (Wed-Sun, also by appointment) **$**

Limited-Service Hotel

★ **LEXINGTON INN.** *1078 N Outer Rd W, Lexington (64067). Phone 660/259-4641; toll-free 800/289-4641; fax 660/259-6604.* 60 rooms, 2 story. Pets accepted, some restrictions; fee. Check-out 11 am. Restaurant, bar. Outdoor pool. **$**
🔁 ➡️ 🏊

Macon (B-4)

See also Kirksville

Population 5,571
Elevation 859 ft
Area Code 660
Zip 63552
Information Macon Area Chamber of Commerce, 218 N Rollins, Suite 102A; phone 660/385-2811

Web Site www.maconmochamber.com

What to See and Do

Long Branch State Park. *28615 Visitor Center Rd, Macon (63552). 2 miles W on Hwy 36. Phone 660/773-5229.* Approximately 1,800-acre park on western shore of Long Branch Lake offers swimming, beach, fishing, boating (ramps, marina), picnicking (shelters), camping (hook-ups, dump station). (Daily) **FREE**

Limited-Service Hotel

★ ★ **BEST WESTERN INN.** *28933 Sunset Dr, Macon (63552). Phone 660/385-2125; toll-free 800/901-2125; fax 660/385-4900. www.bestwestern.com.* 46 rooms, 2 story. Pets accepted, some restrictions; fee. Complimentary continental breakfast. Check-out 11 am. Outdoor pool. **$**
🅿️ ➡️ 🏊

Restaurants

★ ★ **GASLIGHT ROOM.** *203 N Rollins St, Macon (63552). Phone 660/385-4013. www.gaslightroom.com.* American menu. Lunch, dinner. Closed Jan 1, Thanksgiving, Dec 25. Bar. In historic hotel. **$$**

★ **LONG BRANCH.** *28855 Sunset Dr, Macon (63552). Phone 660/385-4600; fax 660/385-4600.* Lunch, dinner. Closed Jan 1, Dec 25. Bar. Children's menu. **$$**

Monroe City (B-4)

See also Hannibal

Founded 1857
Population 2,701
Elevation 749 ft
Area Code 573
Zip 63456
Information Chamber of Commerce, 314 S Main St, in Nutrition Center, Box 22; phone toll-free 800/735-4391

What to See and Do

⭐ **Mark Twain Birthplace and State Park.** *Monroe City. 9 miles SW on Hwy 24 to Hwy 107, then 7 miles S. Phone 573/565-2228.* Almost 2,000 acres of wooded park. The museum has a frame house where Samuel Clemens (Mark Twain) was born on November 30,

1835; exhibits on the author's life; and some personal artifacts; slide show (daily); movies (summer weekends). Swimming, fishing, boating; picnicking, camping (dump station; fee). (Daily; museum closed holidays)

Limited-Service Hotel

★ **RAINBOW.** *308 5th St, Monroe City (63456). Phone 573/735-4526.* 20 rooms. Check-out 11 am. Outdoor pool. **$**

Mound City (A-2)

See also St. Joseph

Population 1,273
Elevation 900 ft
Area Code 660
Zip 64470
Information Chamber of Commerce, PO Box 68; phone 660/442-3262
Web Site www.moundcitychamber.com

What to See and Do

Big Lake State Park. *204 Lake Shore Dr, Craig (64437). 7 miles SW on Hwy 118, then S on Hwy 111.* Located at a 625-acre natural oxbow lake. Swimming pool, fishing, boating, canoeing; picnicking, dining lodge, improved camping (dump station), cabins. (Daily) **FREE**

Squaw Creek National Wildlife Refuge. *Hwy 159 S, Mound City (64470). 5 miles S via I-29, exit 79, then 3 miles W on Hwy 159.* View bald eagles, geese, ducks, pelicans (during migrations), deer, and pheasant along a 10-mile auto tour route; hiking trail; display in office (Mon-Fri). Refuge (daily). For information contact Refuge Manager, PO Box 158. **FREE**

Mount Vernon (D-3)

See also Carthage, Joplin, Springfield

Population 3,726
Elevation 1,176 ft
Area Code 417
Zip 65712
Information Chamber of Commerce, 425 E Mount Vernon Blvd, PO Box 373; phone 417/466-7654

Limited-Service Hotel

★ **BUDGET HOST INN.** *1015 E Mount Vernon Blvd, Mount Vernon (65712). Phone 417/466-2125; toll-free 800/283-4678; fax 417/466-4440. www.budget host.com.* 21 rooms. Pets accepted; fee. Check-out 11 am. Outdoor pool. **$**

Nevada (D-2)

See also Lamar; also see Fort Scott, KS

Founded 1855
Population 8,597
Elevation 880 ft
Area Code 417
Zip 64772
Information Nevada-Vernon Chamber of Commerce, 201 E Cherry, Suite 204; phone 417/667-5300 or toll-free 800/910-4276
Web Site www.nevada-mo.com

Settled by families from Kentucky and Tennessee, Nevada became known as the "bushwhackers capital" due to the Confederate guerrillas headquartered here during the Civil War. The town was burned to the ground in 1863 by Union troops and was not rebuilt until after the war. Today Nevada is a shopping and trading center for the surrounding area.

What to See and Do

Bushwhacker Museum. *231 N Main St, Nevada (64772). At Hunter St, three blocks N of Hwy 54. Phone 417/667-5841.* The museum, operated by Vernon County Historical Society, includes a restored 19th-century jail; exhibits, including an original cell room; Civil War relics; period clothing, tools, medical items; Osage artifacts. (May-Sept: daily; Oct: Sat-Sun) **$**

Schell Osage Conservation Area. *Schell City (64783). 12 miles E on Hwy 54, then 12 miles N on County AA, near Schell City. Phone 417/432-3414.* Winter home to bald eagles and thousands of wild ducks and geese. (Daily; some areas closed during duck-hunting season) **FREE**

Special Event

Bushwhacker Days. *231 N Main St, Nevada (64772). Phone 417/667-5300.* Parade; arts and crafts, antique machine and car shows; street square dance, midway. Mid-June.

Limited-Service Hotels

★ **DAYS INN.** *2345 E Marvel Rd, Nevada (64772). Phone 417/667-6777; toll-free 800/329-7466; fax 417/667-6135. www.daysinn.com.* 46 rooms, 2 story. Pets accepted. Complimentary continental breakfast. Check-out 11 am. Outdoor pool, whirlpool. **$**

★ **SUPER 8.** *2301 E Austin St, Nevada (64772). Phone 417/667-8888; toll-free 800/800-8000; fax 417/667-8883. www.super8.com.* 59 rooms, 2 story. Pets accepted, some restrictions. Complimentary continental breakfast. Check-out 11 am. Indoor pool, whirlpool. **$**

Restaurant

★ **J. T. MALONEY'S.** *2117 E Austin, Nevada (64772). Phone 417/667-7719.* American, seafood menu. Lunch, dinner. Closed Jan 1, Thanksgiving, Dec 25. Bar. Children's menu. **$$$**

Osage Beach (C-4)

See also Camdenton, Lake of the Ozarks, Lake Ozark

Population 2,599
Elevation 895 ft
Area Code 573
Zip 65065
Information Lake Area Chamber of Commerce, 1 Willmore Ln, PO Box 1570, Lake Ozark 65049; phone 573/964-1008 or toll-free 800/451-4117
Web Site www.lakeareachamber.com

A major resort community on the Lake of the Ozarks (see), the town came into existence with the 1931 completion of the lake. Today Osage Beach features some of the lake area's most popular attractions.

What to See and Do

Big Surf Water Park. *Hwys 54 and Y, Linn Creek (65052). 3 miles SW on Hwy 54 to County Y. Phone 573/346-6111.* This 22-acre park features river and tube rides, wave pool, body flumes; volleyball, changing facilities, concession. (Memorial Day-Labor Day, daily) **$$$$** Adjacent is

Big Shot Amusement Park. *Hwys 54 and Y, Linn Creek (65052). Phone 573/346-6111.* Miniature golf, bumper boats, go-carts, and other rides. Gift shop; concession. (Mar-Nov, daily, weather permitting) Admission to the park is free; fees charged at each attraction. **$$$$**

Special Event

Lee Mace's Ozark Opry. *Hwy 54, Osage Beach (65065). Phone 573/348-3383.* Mon-Sat evenings. Late Apr-mid-Oct.

Limited-Service Hotels

★ ★ **BEST WESTERN DOGWOOD HILLS RESORT INN.** *1252 Hwy KK, Osage Beach (65065). Phone 573/348-1735; toll-free 800/780-7234; fax 573/348-0014. www.dogwoodhillsresort.com.* 47 rooms, 3 story. Check-in 4 pm, check-out 11 am. Restaurant (Mar-Oct), bar. Outdoor pool, whirlpool. Golf. **$**

★ ★ **INN AT GRAND GLAIZE.** *5142 Hwy 54, Osage Beach (65065). Phone 573/348-4731; toll-free 800/348-4731; fax 573/348-4694. www.innatgrandglaize.com.* 151 rooms, 5 story. Check-out noon. Restaurant, bar. Fitness room. Outdoor pool, children's pool, whirlpool. **$**

Full-Service Resort

★ ★ ★ **TAN-TAR-A RESORT.** *Hwy KK, Osage Beach (65065). Phone 573/348-3131; fax 573/348-8629. www.tan-tar-a.com.* This property is on the scenic Lake of the Ozarks and offers more than 30 recreational activities, including indoor and outdoor pools, waterskiing, a full spa, jogging, plenty of golf, and more. The hotel is near many area restaurants and attractions. 365 rooms, 8 story. Check-in 4 pm, check-out noon. Restaurant, bar. Children's activity center. Fitness room. One indoor pool, four outdoor pools, two children's pools, whirlpool. Golf. Tennis. **$**

Restaurants

★ ★ **THE BRASS DOOR.** *Hwy 54, Osage Beach (65065). Phone 573/348-9229; fax 573/348-9339. www.the-brass-door.com.* Steak menu. Dinner. Closed Jan 1, Thanksgiving, Dec 25. Children's menu. **$$$**

★ ★ **DOMENICO'S CARRY-OUT PIZZA.** *4737 Hwy 54, Osage Beach (65065). Phone 573/348-2844.* Italian, American menu. Dinner. Closed holidays. Bar. Children's menu. **$$**

★ ★ **HAPPY FISHERMAN.** *Hwy 54, Osage Beach (65065). Phone 573/348-3311; fax 573/348-4595.* American menu. Lunch, dinner. Closed mid-Dec-Jan. Bar. Children's menu. **$$**

★ ★ **POTTED STEER.** *Hwy 54, Osage Beach (65065). Phone 573/348-5053.* Bar. **$$**

★ ★ **VISTA GRANDE.** *Hwy 54, Osage Beach (65065). Phone 573/348-1231; fax 573/348-0158.* American, Mexican menu. Lunch, dinner. Closed Jan 1, Thanksgiving, Dec 25. Bar. Children's menu. **$$**

Pilot Knob (D-5)

See also Bonne Terre

Population 783
Elevation 1,000 ft
Area Code 573
Zip 63663

What to See and Do

Johnson's Shut-Ins State Park. *Hwy N, Middle Brook (63656). 4 miles N on Hwy 21 to Graniteville, then 13 miles SW on County N. Phone 573/546-2450.* This nearly 8,500-acre area, left in its wilderness state, has a spectacular canyonlike defile along the river. The park is at the southern end of the 20-mile-long Ozark backpacking trail, which traverses Missouri's highest mountain, Taum Sauk. Swimming, fishing; hiking, picnicking, playground, improved camping (dump station). (Daily) **FREE**

Sam A. Baker State Park. *Des Arc. 30 miles S on Hwy 21 and Hwy 49 to Des Arc, then 12 miles SE on Hwy 143. Phone 573/856-4411.* The St. François and Big Creek rivers flow through this more than 5,000-acre park. Canoe rentals; hiking trails; picnicking, playground, store, cabins, dining lodge (Apr-Oct), improved camping (dump station). Nature center. (Daily)

Full-Service Resort

★ ★ **WILDERNESS LODGE.** *Peola Rd, Lesterville (63654). Phone 573/637-2295; toll-free 888/969-9129; fax 573/637-2504. www.wildernesslodgeresort.com.* 27

rooms. Check-in 4:30 pm, check-out 1 pm. Restaurant (public by reservation), bar. Outdoor pool. Business center. **$**
🏊 🚶

Poplar Bluff (E-5)

See also Sikeston, Van Buren

Settled 1819
Population 16,996
Area Code 573
Information Chamber of Commerce, 1111 W Pine, PO Box 3986, 63902-3986; phone 573/785-7761
Web Site www.poplarbluffchamber.org

Solomon Kittrell, the first settler here, immediately set up two vital industries—a tannery and a distillery. Poplar Bluff is now an industrial and farm marketing center.

What to See and Do

Lake Wappapello State Park. *Hwy 172, Williamsville (63967). 15 miles N on Hwy 67, then 9 miles E on Hwy 172. Phone 573/297-3232.* Approximately 1,800 acres. Swimming, fishing; hiking, playground, improved camping (dump station), cabins. (Daily) **FREE**

Mark Twain National Forests. *1420 Maude, Poplar Bluff (63901). 7 miles N on Hwy 67. Phone 573/785-1475.* (Poplar Bluff Ranger District). More than 150,000 acres on the rolling hills of Ozark Plateau, with 49 acres of lakes, and 33 miles of horseback riding trails. Fishing, float trips (Black River); hunting, hiking, camping (standard fees).

Limited-Service Hotels

★ **DRURY INN.** *Business 60 and US 67 N, Poplar Bluff (63901). Phone 573/686-2451; toll-free 800/325-8300; fax 573/686-2451. www.druryinn.com.* 78 rooms, 3 story. Pets accepted, some restrictions. Complimentary continental breakfast. Check-out noon. Indoor pool. **$**
🐾 🏊

★ **SUPER 8.** *2831 N Westwood Blvd, Poplar Bluff (63901). Phone 573/785-0176; toll-free 800/800-8000; fax 573/785-2865. www.super8.com.* 63 rooms, 2 story. Complimentary continental breakfast. Check-out 11 am. **$**

Rockaway Beach (E-3)

See also Branson/Table Rock Lake Area

Population 275
Elevation 800 ft
Area Code 417
Zip 65740
Information Bureau of Tourism; PO Box 1004; phone 417/561-4280 or toll-free 800/798-0178
Web Site www.runaway.to/rockawaybeach

This popular resort area is on the shores of Lake Taneycomo, which was created by the impounding of the White River by a 1,700-foot dam near Ozark Beach. Attractions include fishing, boating (rentals), tennis, golf, flea markets, and arcades.

Restaurant

★ **HILLSIDE INN.** *Main St, Rockaway Beach (65740).* Phone 417/561-8252. American menu. Breakfast, lunch, dinner. Children's menu. **$$**

Rolla (D-4)

See also Sullivan, Waynesville

Settled 1855
Population 14,090
Elevation 1,119 ft
Area Code 573
Zip 65401
Information Rolla Area Chamber of Commerce, 1301 Kings Highway; phone 573/364-3577 or toll-free 888/809-3817
Web Site www.rollachamber.org

According to legend, the town was named by a homesick settler from Raleigh, North Carolina, who spelled the name as he pronounced it. Called "the child of the railroad" because it began with the building of the St. Louis-San Francisco Railroad, the town is located in a scenic area with several fishing streams nearby. Mark Twain National Forest maintains its headquarters in Rolla.

What to See and Do

Ed Clark Museum of Missouri Geology. *Buehler Park, 111 Fairgrounds Rd, Rolla (65401). Phone 573/368-2100.* Displays of mineral resources, geological history, and land surveying. (Mon-Fri; closed holidays) **FREE**

Maramec Spring Park and Remains of Old Ironworks. *21880 Maramec Spring Dr, Rolla (65559). 8 miles E on I-44 to St. James, then 7 miles SE on Hwy 8. Phone 573/265-7387.* The spring discharges an average of 96.3 million gallons per day. The ironworks was first established in 1826; the present furnace was built in 1857. Trout fishing (Mar-Oct); trails, scenic road, picnicking, playground, campground (fee). Nature center; observation tower; two museums. (Daily) **$**

Mark Twain National Forests. *401 Fairgrounds Rd, Rolla (65401). SW via I-44, Hwy 63. Phone 573/364-4621.* (Rolla-Houston Ranger Districts) More than 192,000 acres; cradles the headwaters of the Gasconade, Little Piney, and Big Piney rivers. Swimming; fishing; hunting; boating. Picnicking. Camping (standard fees). Paddy Creek Wilderness Area covers about 6,800 acres with 30 miles of hiking and riding trails. Contact the Ranger District office.

Memoryville, USA. *Hwy 44 and 63 N, Rolla (65401). Phone 573/364-1810.* More than 30 antique cars; art gallery, restoration shop; antique, gift shop; lounge, restaurant. (Daily; closed Jan 1, Thanksgiving, Dec 25) **$$**

Montauk State Park. *Hwy 119, Salem (65560). 35 miles S on Hwy 63 to Licking, then 2 miles S on Hwy 137, then 10 miles E on County VV. Phone 573/548-2201.* Approximately 1,300 acres. Trout fishing; hiking trail, picnicking, store, motel, dining lodge, improved camping (dump station), cabins. (Daily) **FREE**

St. James Winery. *Rolla. 10 miles E via I-44, St. James exit, then three blocks E on County B (north access road). Phone 573/265-7912.* Dry and semi-dry wines, sweet champagne, sparkling wines, concord, catawba, and berry wines all produced here. Hourly tours; tasting room; gift shop. (Daily; closed Dec 25)

University of Missouri-Rolla. *1870 Miner Cir, Rolla (65409). Phone 573/341-4328.* (1870) (5,000 students) On campus are

Minerals Museum. *Rolla (65409). First floor, McNutt Hall. Geology Department. Phone 573/341-4616.* Begun in 1904 as part of the Missouri mining exhibit for the St. Louis World's Fair, today the exhibit contains 4,000 specimens from around the world. (Mon-Fri; closed holidays) **FREE**

UMR Nuclear Reactor. *1870 Miner Cir, Rolla (65409). Phone 573/341-4236.* Swimming pool-type reactor contains 32,000 gallons of water. Tours. (Mon-Fri; closed holidays) **FREE**

UM-Rolla Stonehenge. *14th St and Bishop Ave, Rolla (65409). Phone 573/341-4328.* Partial reproduction of Stonehenge, the ancient circle of megaliths on Salisbury Plain in England. Features five trilithons standing 13 feet high. Interpretive guides available. **FREE**

Special Events

Central Missouri Regional Fair. *Fairgrounds, Hwy 63 S, Rolla (65401). Phone 573/341-5789.* Early Aug.

St. Pat's Celebration. *Rolla. Phone 573/341-4328.* University of Missouri celebration of St. Patrick, patron saint of engineers; parade, painting Main Street green, beard judging contests, shillelagh judging, entertainment. Mar.

Limited-Service Hotels

★ **BEST WESTERN COACHLIGHT.** *1403 Martin Springs Dr, Rolla (65401). Phone 573/341-2511; toll-free 800/780-7234; fax 573/368-3055. www.bestwestern.com.* 88 rooms, 2 story. Pets accepted, some restrictions. Complimentary continental breakfast. Check-out noon. **$**
🐾

★ **DRURY INN.** *2006 N Bishop Ave, Rolla (65401). Phone 573/364-4000; toll-free 800/436-3310; fax 573/364-4000. www.druryinn.com.* 86 rooms, 2 story. Pets accepted, some restrictions. Complimentary continental breakfast. Check-out noon. Outdoor pool. **$**
🐾 ⚊

★ ★ **ZENO'S MOTEL AND STEAK HOUSE.** *1621 Martin Springs Dr, Rolla (65401). Phone 573/364-1301.* 51 rooms. Check-out noon. Restaurant, bar. Indoor pool, outdoor pool, whirlpool. **$**
⚊

Restaurant

★ **JOHNNY'S SMOKE STAK.** *201 Hwy 72, Rolla (65401). Phone 573/364-4838; fax 573/368-3681.* Barbecue menu. Lunch, dinner. Closed Jan 1, Thanksgiving, Dec 25. Children's menu. **$**

Sedalia (C-3)

See also Clinton, Jefferson City

Population 19,800
Elevation 919 ft
Area Code 660
Zip 65301
Information Chamber of Commerce, 600 E Third St; phone 660/826-2222 or toll-free 800/827-5295
Web Site www.sedaliachamber.com

Known as the "queen city of the prairies," Sedalia was a prosperous railhead town in the 1800s with great cattle herds arriving for shipment to eastern markets. During the Civil War, the settlement functioned as a military post. A monument at Lamine and Main streets marks the site of the Maple Leaf Club, one of the city's many saloons that catered to railroad men. The monument is dedicated to Scott Joplin, who composed and performed the "Maple Leaf Rag" here, triggering the ragtime craze at the turn of the 20th century. Whiteman Air Force Base is 21 miles west of Sedalia.

What to See and Do

Bothwell Lodge State Historic Site. *19350 Bothwell State Park, Sedalia (65301). 6 miles N on Hwy 65. Phone 660/827-0510.* Approximately 180 acres, including hiking trails and picnic areas. Tours of the stone lodge (daily). (See SPECIAL EVENTS) **$**

Knob Noster State Park. *873 SE 10, Sedalia (65336). 20 miles W on Hwy 50, then S on Hwy 132. Phone 660/563-2463.* Lakes and streams on more than 3,500 acres. Fishing, boating, canoeing; hiking, picnicking, improved camping (dump stations), laundry facilities. Visitor center, naturalist program. (Daily) **FREE**

Pettis County Courthouse. *Downtown, 415 S Ohio, Sedalia (65301). Phone 660/826-4892.* Historic courthouse contains local artifacts and exhibits. (Mon-Fri; closed holidays) **FREE**

Sedalia Ragtime Archives. *State Fair Community College Library, Maple Leaf Room, 3201 W 16th St, Sedalia (65301). Phone 660/530-5800.* Includes original sheet music, piano rolls, tapes of interviews with Eubie Blake. (Mon-Fri; closed school holidays) **FREE**

Special Events

Band concerts. *Liberty Park, 1500 W. 3rd St, Sedalia (65301). Liberty Park band shell.Phone 660/826-2222.* Thurs evenings. Mid-June-late July.

Missouri State Fair. *Fairgrounds, 2503 W 16th St, Sedalia (65301). Phone 660/530-5600.* One of the country's leading state fairs; held here since 1901. Stage shows, rodeo, competitive exhibits, livestock, auto races. Aug.

Scott Joplin Ragtime Festival. *Sedalia. Phone 660/826-2271.* Entertainment by ragtime greats. Early June.

Limited-Service Hotel

★ ★ **BEST WESTERN STATE FAIR MOTOR INN.** *3120 S Limit Ave (Hwy 65 S and 32nd), Sedalia (65301). Phone 660/826-6100; toll-free 800/780-7234; fax 660/827-3850. www.bestwestern.com.* 117 rooms, 2 story. Pets accepted. Check-out 11 am. Restaurant, bar. Fitness room. Indoor pool, children's pool, whirlpool. Airport transportation available. **$**

Sikeston (E-6)

See also Cape Girardeau, Poplar Bluff

Founded 1860
Population 17,641
Elevation 325 ft
Area Code 573
Zip 63801
Information Sikeston-Miner Convention & Visitors Bureau, 1 Industrial Dr, PO Box 1983; phone toll-free 888/309-6591
Web Site www.sikeston.net

Although settlers were in this region before the Louisiana Purchase, John Sikes established the town of Sikeston in 1860 on El Camino Real, the overland route from St. Louis to New Orleans, at the terminus of the Cairo and Fulton Railway (now the Union Pacific).

What to See and Do

Southeast Missouri Agricultural Museum. *Hwy 532 # 461, Bertrand (63823). 4 miles E via Hwy 532. Phone 573/471-3945.* Collection of antique farm machinery; reconstructed log cabins, 1920s service station.

Relocated railroad depot, wooden caboose, one-room schoolhouse. (Apr-Oct, daily) **$$**

Special Events

Bootheel Rodeo. *Rodeo Grounds, Sikeston. Phone toll-free 800/455-2855.* Country music and rodeo events; parade. First full week in Aug.

Cotton Carnival. *Downtown, Sikeston. Phone toll-free 888/309-6591.* Parades, contests. Last full week in Sept.

Limited-Service Hotels

★ ★ **BEST WESTERN COACH HOUSE INN.** *220 S Interstate Dr, Sikeston (63801). Phone 573/471-9700; toll-free 887/471-9700; fax 573/471-4285. www.bestwestern.com.* 63 rooms, 2 story. Pets accepted, some restrictions; fee. Check-out noon. Restaurant, bar. Outdoor pool. **$**

★ **DRURY INN.** *2602 E Malone Ave, Sikeston (63801). Phone 573/471-4100; toll-free 800/325-8300; fax 573/471-4100. www.druryinn.com.* 80 rooms, 4 story. Pets accepted, some restrictions. Complimentary continental breakfast. Check-out noon. Indoor pool, outdoor pool, whirlpool. **$**

Restaurants

★ **FISHERMAN'S NET.** *915 S Kings Hwy, Sikeston (63801). Phone 573/471-8102; fax 573/471-8102. www.fishermansnet.net.* Seafood menu. Lunch, dinner. Closed Sun-Mon; holidays. Children's menu. **$$**

★ **LAMBERT'S.** *2515 E Malone, Sikeston (63801). Phone 573/471-4261; fax 573/471-7563. www.throwedrolls.com.* American menu. Lunch, dinner. Closed Jan 1, Dec 25. Children's menu. No credit cards accepted. **$$**

Springfield (D-3)

See also Branson/Table Rock Lake Area, Mount Vernon

Population 140,494
Elevation 1,316 ft
Area Code 417
Information Convention & Visitors Bureau, 3315 E Battlefield Rd, 65804; phone 417/881-5300 or toll-free 800/678-8767
Web Site www.springfieldmo.org

In the southwest corner of the state and at the northern edge of the Ozark highlands, Springfield, known as Ozark Mountain Country's Big City, is near some of Missouri's most picturesque scenery and recreational areas. A few settlers came here as early as 1821, but settlement was temporarily discouraged when the government made southwestern Missouri a reservation. Later, the tribes were moved west and the town began to develop. Its strategic location made it a military objective in the Civil War. The Confederates took the town in the Battle of Wilson's Creek, August 10, 1861; Union forces recaptured it in 1862. Confederate attempts to regain it were numerous but unsuccessful. "Wild Bill" Hickock, later one of the famous frontier marshals, was a scout and spy for Union forces headquartered in Springfield.

Springfield's growth has been largely due to a healthy economy based on diversified industry; manufacturing and the service industry provide the majority of jobs. Springfield is the home of six major colleges and universities, including Southwest Missouri State University.

What to See and Do

⭐ **Bass Pro Shops Outdoor World Showroom and Fish and Wildlife Museum.** *1935 S Campbell Ave, Springfield (65807). Phone 417/887-7334. www. outdoor-world.com.* This 300,000-square-foot sporting goods store features a four-story waterfall, indoor boat and RV showroom, art gallery, and indoor firing range. The restaurant has a 30,000-gallon saltwater aquarium. (Daily) **$$**

Crystal Cave. *7225 N Crystal Cave Ln, Springfield (65803). 5 miles N of I-44 on Hwy H, exit 80B. Phone 417/833-9599.* Once a Native American habitat; contains a variety of colorful formations; temperature 59° F; guided tours. Gift shop, picnic area. (Daily) **$$$**

Dickerson Park Zoo. *3043 N Fort, Springfield (65803). Phone 417/864-1800. www.dickersonparkzoo.org.* Animals in naturalistic settings; features elephant herd; train rides. Playground; concession, picnic area. Gift shop. (Daily; closed Jan 1, Thanksgiving, Dec 25) **$$**

Discovery Center. *438 St. Louis St, Springfield (65806). Phone 417/862-9910. www.discoverycenter.org.* Interactive hands-on museum; includes "Discovery Town Theatre", where you can be a star on stage, create a

newspaper, run a make-believe TV station, or dig for dinosaur bones. (Tues-Sun) **$$$**

Exotic Animal Paradise. *124 Jungle Dr, Strafford, Springfield (65757). 12 miles E on I-44, exit 88, then E on outer road to entrance. Phone 417/859-2016. www.exoticanimalparadise.com.* Approximately 3,000 wild animals and rare birds may be seen along a 9-mile drive. (Daily; closed Thanksgiving, Dec 25; winter hours vary according to weather) **$$$**

Fantastic Caverns. *4872 N Farm Rd 125, Springfield (65803). 4 miles NW via I-44, then N 1 1/2 miles at Hwy 13. Phone 417/833-2010.* Cave tours (45-minutes) in a jeep-drawn tram. (Daily; closed Thanksgiving, Dec 24-25) **$$$$**

History Museum. *Historic City Hall, 830 Boonville, Springfield (65802). Phone 417/864-1976.* Permanent and rotating exhibits on Springfield, Greene County, and the Ozarks. (Tues-Sat) **$$**

⭐ **Laura Ingalls Wilder-Rose Wilder Lane Museum and Home.** *3068 Highway A, Mansfield (65704). 50 miles E on Hwy 60, at Hwy 5. Phone 417/924-3626.* House where Laura Ingalls Wilder wrote the Little House books; artifacts and memorabilia of Laura, husband Almanzo, and daughter Rose Wilder Lane; four handwritten manuscripts; many items mentioned in Wilder's books, including Pa's fiddle. (Mar-mid-Nov, daily)

Springfield Art Museum. *1111 E Brookside Dr, Springfield (65807). Phone 417/837-5700.* American and European paintings, sculpture, and graphics. (Tues-Sun; closed holidays) (See SPECIAL EVENTS) **DONATION**

Springfield National Cemetery. *1702 E Seminole, Springfield (65804). Phone 417/881-9499.* One of the few national cemeteries where Union and Confederate soldiers from the same state are buried side-by-side. (Daily)

Wilson's Creek National Battlefield. *6424 W Farm Rd 182, Republic (65738). 10 miles SW via I-44, County M and County ZZ. Phone 417/732-2662.* Scene of August 10, 1861, Civil War battle between the Confederate and Union forces for control of Missouri. At the entrance is a visitor center, which has a film, battle map light display, and a museum area. Also here are maps of a self-guided 5-mile road tour featuring waysides, exhibits, and walking trails. Highlights are the Bloody Hill trail, the Ray House, and the headquarters of General Price. Living History program (call for schedule). Battlefield (daily; closed Jan 1, Dec 25). Contact Superintendent, Rte 2, Box 75, Republic 65738. **$$**

Special Events

Ozark Empire Fair. *Ozark Empire Fairgrounds, Norton and Grant sts, Springfield (65802). Phone 417/833-2660.* Late July-early Aug.

Tent Theater. *Southwest Missouri State University campus, 128 Garfield Ave, Springfield (65775). Phone 417/836-5979.* Dramas, comedies, and musicals in repertory in circuslike tent. Late June-early Aug.

Watercolor USA. *Springfield Art Museum, 1111 E Brookside Dr, Springfield (65807). Phone 417/837-5700.* National competitive exhibition of aquamedia painting. Early June-early Aug.

Limited-Service Hotels

★ **BEST WESTERN DEERFIELD INN.** *3343 E Battlefield St, Springfield (65804). Phone 417/887-2323; toll-free 877/822-6560; fax 417/887-1242. www.bestwestern.com.* 103 rooms, 3 story. Complimentary continental breakfast. Check-out noon. Indoor pool. **$**

★ **BEST WESTERN ROUTE 66 RAIL HAVEN.** *203 S Glenstone Ave, Springfield (65802). Phone 417/866-1963; toll-free 800/780-7234; fax 417/866-1963. www.bestwestern.com.* 93 rooms. Pets accepted, some restrictions. Complimentary continental breakfast. Check-out noon. Outdoor pool, whirlpool. **$**

★ ★ **CLARION HOTEL.** *3333 S Glenstone Ave, Springfield (65803). Phone 417/883-6550; toll-free 800/756-7318; fax 417/883-5720. www.clarionhotel.com.* 199 rooms, 2 story. Pets accepted; fee. Check-out noon. Restaurant, bar. Outdoor pool. **$**

★ **HAMPTON INN.** *222 N Ingram Mill Rd, Springfield (65802). Phone 417/863-1440; toll-free 800/426-7866; fax 417/863-2215. www.hamptoninn.com.* 99 rooms, 2 story. Complimentary continental breakfast. Check-out noon. Fitness room. Outdoor pool, whirlpool. **$**

★ ★ **HOLIDAY INN.** *333 John Q Hammons Pkwy, Springfield (65806). Phone 417/864-7333; toll-free 800/465-4329; fax 417/831-5893. www.holiday-*

inn.com. 271 rooms. Pets accepted, some restrictions; fee. Check-out noon. Restaurant, bar. Fitness room. Indoor pool, outdoor pool, whirlpool. Tennis. **$**

Full-Service Hotel

★ ★ ★ **SHERATON HAWTHORN PARK HOTEL.** *2431 N Glenstone Ave, Springfield (65803). Phone 417/831-3131; toll-free 800/223-0092; fax 417/831-9786. www.sheraton.com.* 201 rooms, 10 story. Check-out noon. Restaurant, bar. Fitness room. Indoor pool, outdoor pool, whirlpool. Airport transportation available. **$**

Specialty Lodgings

The following lodging establishments are approved by Mobil Travel Guide, but due to their unique and individualized nature have not been given a traditional Mobil Star rating. Included in this listing you may find bed-and-breakfasts, limited-service inns, guest ranches, and other unique hotel properties.

THE MANSION AT ELFINDALE. *1701 S Fort, Springfield (65807). Phone 417/831-5400; toll-free 800/443-0237; fax 417/831-5415. www.mansionatelfindale.com.* 13 rooms, 3 story. Children over 11 years only. Complimentary full breakfast. Check-in 3 pm, check-out 11 am. **$**

WALNUT STREET INN. *900 E Walnut St, Springfield (65806). Phone 417/864-6346; toll-free 800/593-6346; fax 417/864-6184. www.walnutstreetinn.com.* 14 rooms, 3 story. Complimentary full breakfast. Check-in 2 pm, check-out 11 am. Queen Anne-style Victorian inn built in 1894. **$**

Restaurants

★ ★ **GEE'S EAST WIND.** *2951 E Sunshine, Springfield (65804). Phone 417/883-4567. www.blueheronpottedsteer.com.* Chinese, American menu. Lunch, dinner. Closed Sun; Thanksgiving, Dec 25; last week in June, first week in July. Bar. Children's menu. **$$**

★ **J. PARRIONO'S PASTA HOUSE.** *1550 E Battlefield, Springfield (65804). Phone 417/882-1808; fax 417/882-4522.* Italian menu. Lunch, dinner. Closed holidays. Bar. Children's menu. **$$**

★ ★ ★ **LE MIRABELLE.** *2620 S Glenstone Ave, Springfield (65804). Phone 417/883-2550.* Tucked away on the end of a shopping center, the candlelit, flower-filled dining room of this classic French restaurant is a pleasant surprise. Since 1976, its extensive menu has featured nearly 30 entrées including roast duckling and Dover sole. French menu. Dinner. Closed Sun; holidays. Bar. **$$**

St. Charles (C-5)

See also St. Louis, St. Louis Lambert Airport Area, Wentzville

Settled 1769
Population 54,555
Elevation 536 ft
Area Code 636
Information Convention and Visitors Bureau, 230 S Main, 63301; phone 636/946-7776 or toll-free 800/366-2427
Web Site www.historicstcharles.com

St. Charles, one of the early settlements on the Missouri River, was the first capital of the state (1821-1826). Between 1832 to 1870, a wave of German immigrants settled here and developed the town, but St. Louis, by virtue of its location on the Mississippi, became the state's most important city. St. Charles is the home of Sacred Heart Convent (1818) and Lindenwood University (1827). Frenchtown, a northern ward of old St. Charles, is home to many antique shops.

What to See and Do

Katy Trail State Park. *St. Charles (63301). Trailheads in St. Charles and other towns. Phone 660/882-8196; toll-free 800/334-6946. www.mostateparks.com/katytrail.* A 236-mile bicycling and hiking trail across Missouri, among the longest of its kind in the United States. (Daily)

⭐ **St. Charles Historic District.** *St. Charles.* Nine-block area along South Main Street with restored houses, antique and gift shops, restaurants, the 1836 Newbill-McElhiney House. Also here are

> **First Missouri State Capitol State Historic Site.** *200-216 S Main St, St. Charles (63301). Phone 636/940-3322.* Eleven rooms of the capitol have been restored to their original state; nine rooms have 1820 period furnishings; also restoration of the

Peck Brothers General Store and house. Interpretive center. (Daily; closed holidays) **$**

Lewis and Clark Center. *701 Riverside, St. Charles (63301). Phone 636/947-3199.* Museum depicts the 1804-1806 expedition from St. Charles to the Pacific Ocean. Hands-on exhibits, lifesize models of Sacagawea and the men of the expedition; Mandan and Sioux villages, display of Missouri River; gift shop. (Daily; closed holidays) **$**

Special Events

Christmas Traditions. *St. Charles. Phone toll-free 800/366-2427.* Month-long celebration with carolers, Santas of the Past, living history characters, parade, fife and drum corps. Day after Thanksgiving-Dec 24.

Festival of the Little Hills. *Frontier Park and Main St, St. Charles (63301). Phone toll-free 800/366-2427.* Bluegrass and country music; 19th-century crafts, antiques. Late Aug.

Lewis and Clark Heritage Days. *Frontier Park, Riverside Dr, St. Charles (63301). Phone toll-free 800/366-2427.* Reenactment of the explorers' encampment in 1804 prior to embarking on their exploration of the Louisiana Purchase; parade, fife and drum corps. Mid-May.

Limited-Service Hotels

★ **HAMPTON INN.** *3720 W Clay St, St. Charles (63301). Phone 636/947-6800; toll-free 800/426-7867; fax 636/947-0020. www.hamptoninn.com.* 122 rooms, 4 story. Complimentary continental breakfast. Check-out noon. Fitness room. Indoor pool, whirlpool. **$**
🧖 🏊

★ ★ **HOLIDAY INN.** *4341 Veteran's Memorial Pkwy, St. Peters (63376). Phone 636/928-1500; toll-free 800/767-3837; fax 636/922-1840. www.holiday-inn.com.* 195 rooms, 6 story. Pets accepted; fee. Check-out noon. Restaurant, bar. Fitness room. Indoor pool, outdoor pool, whirlpool. Business center. **$**
🐾 🧖 🏊 🚶

Restaurants

★ **CHINA ROYAL.** *5911 N Lindbergh, Hazelwood (63042). Phone 314/731-1313.* Chinese menu. Lunch, dinner, Sun brunch. Bar. **$**

★ ★ **ST. CHARLES VINTAGE HOUSE.** *1219 S Main St, St. Charles (63301). Phone 636/946-7155;*

fax 636/723-4711. American, German, seafood menu. Dinner. Closed Mon. Bar. Children's menu. Outdoor seating. Former winery (1860). **$$**

St. Joseph (B-2)

See also Cameron, Kansas City, Mound City, Weston; also see Atchison, KS and Hiawatha, KS

Settled 1826
Population 71,852
Elevation 833 ft
Area Code 816
Information Convention & Visitors Bureau, 109 S 4th St, 64501; phone 816/233-6688 or toll-free 800/785-0360
Web Site www.stjomo.com

A historic city with beautiful parks and large industries, St. Joseph retains traces of the frontier settlement of the 1840s in the "original town" near the Missouri River. It was founded and named by Joseph Robidoux III, a French fur trader from St. Louis, who established his post in 1826. St. Joseph, the western terminus of the first railroad to cross the state, became the eastern terminus of the Pony Express, whose riders carried mail to and from Sacramento, California from 1860 to 1861 using relays of fast ponies. The record trip, which carried copies of President Lincoln's inaugural address, was made in seven days and 17 hours. The telegraph ended the need for the Pony Express. The Civil War disrupted the region, largely Southern in sympathy, but postwar railroad building and cattle trade restored the city.

What to See and Do

Albrecht-Kemper Museum of Art. *2818 Frederick Blvd, St. Joseph (64506). Phone 816/233-7003.* Exhibits of 18th-, 19th- and 20th-century American paintings, sculpture, graphic art. Formal gardens. (Tues-Sun; closed holidays) **$$**

Glore Psychiatric Museum. *3406 Frederick Ave, St. Joseph (64506).* Housed in a ward of the original 1874 administration building, the museum displays the evolution of treatment philosophy and techniques over a 400-year period. (Daily) **FREE**

Jesse James Home. *1202 Penn St, St. Joseph (64503). Phone 816/232-8206.* One-story frame cottage where the outlaw had been living quietly as "Mr. Howard"

until he was killed here, April 3, 1882, by an associate, Bob Ford. Some original furnishings. (Daily) **$**

Missouri Theater. *715 Edmond St, St. Joseph (64501). Phone 816/271-4628.* Renovated 1926 movie palace decorated in pre-Persian motif with bas relief on exterior. (Daily by appointment; closed holidays) **$**

Patee House Museum. *1202 Penn St, St. Joseph (64503). Phone 816/232-8206.* Built in 1858 as a hotel; in 1860 it served as headquarters of the Pony Express. Contains pioneer exhibits related to transportation and communication; includes restored 1860 Buffalo Saloon; woodburning engine and the original last mail car from the Hannibal and St. Joseph railroad. Also 1917 Japanese tea house; ice-cream parlor. (Apr-Oct: daily; Jan-Mar and Nov: weekends) **$$**

Pony Express Museum. *914 Penn St, St. Joseph (64503). Phone 816/279-5059; toll-free 800/530-5930.* Museum in old Pikes Peak (Pony Express) Stables, the starting point of the first westward ride. Original stables; displays illustrate the creation, operation, management, and termination of the famed mail service. (Daily; closed holidays) **$$**

Pony Express Region Tourist Information Centers. *502 N Woodvine Rd, St. Joseph (64506). W of I-29 exit 47; also at I-35 and Hwy 36 at Cameron. Phone 816/232-1839.* Housed in historic railroad cabooses, centers provide brochures and information on St. Joseph, northwest Missouri, and northeast Kansas; free maps. (Daily)

Robidoux Row Museum. *3rd and Poulin Sts, St. Joseph (64506). Phone 816/232-5861.* (Circa 1850). Built by the city's founder, French fur trader Joseph Robidoux, as temporary housing for newly arrived settlers who had purchased land from him. Authentically restored; some original furnishings. Tours. (Tues-Sun; closed holidays) **$**

Society of Memories Doll Museum. *1115 S 12th St, St. Joseph (64503). Phone 816/233-1420.* More than 600 antique dolls; miniature rooms and houses, old toys, antique clothing. (Tues-Sun; tour by appointment) **$**

St. Joseph Museum. *1100 Charles St, St. Joseph (64501). Phone 816/232-8471.* Native American collections; natural history; local and Western history exhibits, including Civil War, Pony Express, and Jesse James era. (Daily; closed holidays) Free on Sun.

St. Joseph Park System. *St. Joseph. Phone 816/271-5500.* Of the more than 40 parks and facilities, most are along a 9 1/2-mile drive from Krug Park (W of St.

Joseph Ave in the N end of the city) to Hyde Park (4th and Hyde Park Ave in the S end of the city). Approximately 26 miles of parkway system stretching over 1,500 acres of land. The park system provides a variety of recreational facilities, including 18-hole golf, tennis courts, ballfields, and an indoor ice arena. (Daily)

Special Events

Apple Blossom Festival. *825 Edmond St, St. Joseph (64501). Phone toll-free 800/785-0360.* Originally a celebration of area apple growers. Parade with more than 200 entries; food, music, crafts. First weekend in May.

Southside Fall Festival. *St. Joseph. Phone 816/238-1450.* Crafts, parade, entertainment, rodeo. Mid-Sept.

Trails West. *118 S 8th St, St. Joseph (64501). Phone toll-free 800/216-7080.* Arts festival celebrating cultural heritage. Stage performances, historical reenactments, music, food. Mid-Aug.

Limited-Service Hotels

★ **DAYS INN.** *4312 Frederick Blvd, St. Joseph (64506). Phone 816/279-1671; toll-free 800/329-7466; fax 816/279-6729. www.daysinn.com.* 100 rooms, 2 story. Complimentary continental breakfast. Check-out 11 am. Bar. Outdoor pool. **$**
🔲 🏊

★ **DRURY INN.** *4213 Frederick Blvd, St. Joseph (64506). Phone 816/364-4700; fax 816/364-4700. www.druryinn.com.* 133 rooms, 4 story. Pets accepted. Complimentary continental breakfast. Check-out noon. Fitness room. Indoor pool. **$**
🔲 🏃 🏊

★ ★ **HOLIDAY INN.** *102 S 3rd St, St. Joseph (64501). Phone 816/279-8000; toll-free 800/824-7402; fax 816/279-1484. www.holiday-inn.com.* 170 rooms, 6 story. Pets accepted. Check-out noon. Restaurant, bar. Fitness room. Indoor pool, whirlpool. **$**
🔲 🏃 🏊

Restaurants

★ ★ **36TH STREET FOOD & DRINK COMPANY.** *501 N Belt Hwy, St. Joseph (64506). Phone 816/364-1564; fax 816/364-6006.* American menu. Lunch, dinner. Closed Sun; Dec 25. Bar. **$$**

★ **BARBOSA'S CASTILLO.** *906 Sylvanie St, St. Joseph (64501). Phone 816/233-4970; fax 816/233-6376.* Mexican menu. Lunch, dinner. Closed Sun; holi-

days. Bar. Children's menu. Dining on two levels in a restored Victorian mansion (1891). Valet parking. **$$**
🔲

St. Louis (C-5)

See also Clayton, St. Charles, St. Louis Lambert Airport Area, Ste. Genevieve, Wentzville

Settled 1764
Population 396,685
Elevation 470 ft
Area Code 314
Information Convention & Visitors Commission, 1 Metropolitan Square, Suite 1100, 63102; phone 314/421-1023 or toll-free 800/325-7962
Web Site www.explorestlouis.com
Suburbs Clayton, St. Charles, Wentzville

One of the oldest settlements in the Mississippi Valley, St. Louis was founded by Pierre Laclede as a fur trading post and was named for Louis IX of France. Early French settlers, a large German immigration in the mid-1800s, and a happy mix of other national strains contribute to the city's cosmopolitan flavor. A flourishing French community by the time of the Revolutionary War, St. Louis was attacked by a band of British-led Native Americans, but was successfully defended by its citizens and a French garrison. In 1804, it was the scene of the transfer of Louisiana to the United States, which opened the way to the westward expansion that overran the peaceful town with immigrants and adventurers. The first Mississippi steamboat docked at St. Louis in 1817. Missouri's first constitutional convention was held here in 1820. During the Civil War, though divided in sympathy, the city was a base of Union operations. In 1904, the Louisiana Purchase Exposition, known as the St. Louis World's Fair, brought international fame to the city and added to its cultural resources; its first art museum was established in connection with the fair.

For more than 200 years, St. Louis has been the dominant city in the state. It is the home of St. Louis University (1818), the University of Missouri-St. Louis (1963) and Washington University (1853), which lies at the border of St. Louis and Clayton. Distinguished by wealth, grace, and culture, St. Louis is also a city of solid and diversified industry. It is one of the world's largest markets for wool, lumber, and pharmaceuticals, and a principal grain and hog center. It is also the center for the only industrial area in the country producing six basic metals: iron, lead, zinc, copper, aluminum, and magnesium. St. Louis is an important producer of beer, chemicals, and transportation equipment. Strategically located near the confluence of the Missouri and Mississippi rivers, the city is one of the country's major railroad terminals and trucking centers. Seven bridges span the Mississippi here.

After the steamboat era, St. Louis grew westward, away from the riverfront, which deteriorated into slums. This original center of the city has now been developed as the Jefferson National Expansion Memorial. Municipal and private redevelopment of downtown and riverfront St. Louis also has been outstanding: America's Center, St. Louis's convention complex, is the hub of the 16-square-block Convention Plaza; Busch Stadium brings St. Louis Cardinals fans into the downtown area; and the rehabilitated Union Station offers visitors a unique shopping experience within a restored turn-of-the-century railroad station.

> ### St. Louis Fun Fact
>
> At the St. Louis World's Fair in 1904, Richard Blechyden served tea with ice and invented iced tea.

Additional Visitor Information

The St. Louis Convention & Visitors Commission, 1 Metropolitan Square, Suite 1100, 63102, has brochures on things to see in St. Louis; phone 314/421-1023 or toll-free 800/325-7962. Also obtain brochures at the St. Louis Visitors Center, 7th and Washington. *St. Louis Magazine*, at newsstands, has up-to-date information on cultural events and articles of interest to visitors. For 24-hour tourist information, phone 314/421-2100.

Public Transportation

Buses, trains Bi-State Transit System, phone 314/231-2345

Airport St. Louis Lambert Airport. For additional accommodations, see ST. LOUIS LAMBERT AIRPORT AREA, which follows ST. LOUIS.

What to See and Do

Aloe Plaza. *18th and Market sts, St. Louis (63103).*

Across from Union Station. Contains extensive fountain group by Carl Milles symbolizing the meeting of the Mississippi and Missouri rivers.

Anheuser-Busch Brewery. *12th and Lynch sts, St. Louis (63118). I-55, exit 206C. Phone 314/577-2333. www.budweisertours.com.* Trace the making of Budweiser beer from farm fields to finished product in a tour of the nation's largest brewery. Inside the 150-year-old plant, whose grounds encompass 100 acres, you'll also experience a historic brewhouse, beechwood aging cellars, a packing facility, and Clydesdale stables. Adults can sample Bud products. (Daily, closed holidays) **FREE**

Bass Pro Shops Sportsmans Warehouse. *1365 S Fifth St, St. Charles (63301). Phone 636/688-2500. www.basspro.com.* The Bass Pro Shops Sportsmans Warehouse isn't just for fishermen. This hangar-sized, 70,000-square-foot store northwest of St. Louis is heaven on earth for anyone who loves the great outdoors. It's packed with fishing and boating supplies, of course, but is also loaded with outdoor clothes, footwear, and even outdoors-themed home décor items. Workshops and activities address such themes as fly fishing and camping.

Bigfoot 4x4 Inc. *6311 N Lindbergh Blvd, Hazelwood (63042). At I-270. Phone 314/731-2822. www. bigfoot4x4.com.* Visit the birthplace and home of Bigfoot, where the monster truck phenomenon began. This photo opportunity waiting to happen includes several trucks on display—including Bigfoot 5, the world's largest, widest, and heaviest pickup—along with an extensive souvenir collection and a factory area where monster trucks are built. (Mon-Fri 9 am-6 pm, Sat 9 am-3 pm) **FREE**

Butterfly House and Education Center. *Faust Park, 15193 Olive Blvd, Chesterfield (63017). 20 miles W via Hwy 40, Olive St exit. Phone 636/530-0076. www.butterflyhouse.org.* Three-story crystal palace conservatory with more than 2,000 butterflies in free flight. Educational programs, films, miracle of metamorphosis display. (Memorial Day-Labor Day: daily; rest of year: Tues-Sun) **$$**

Campbell House Museum. *1508 Locust St, St. Louis (63103). Phone 314/421-0325.* Mansion with original 1840-1880 furnishings. (Mar-Dec, Wed-Sun; closed holidays) **$$**

Cathedral of St. Louis. *4431 Lindell Blvd, St. Louis (63108). At Newstead Ave. Phone 314/373-8243.* (1907) The city's cathedral is a fine example of Romanesque architecture with Byzantine details; the interior mosaic work is among the most extensive in the world. Mosaic museum (fee). Tours (by appointment, fee).

Christ Church Cathedral. *1210 Locust St, St. Louis (63103). Phone 314/231-3454.* (1859-1867). The first Episcopal parish west of the Mississippi River, founded in 1819. English Gothic sandstone building; altar carved in England from stone taken from a quarry in Caen, France; Tiffany windows on north wall. Occasional concerts. (Sun-Fri) Tours (by appointment).

Craft Alliance Gallery. *6640 Delmar Blvd, St. Louis (63130). N on Hanley Rd to Delmar Blvd, E. Phone 314/725-1177.* Contemporary ceramic, fiber, metal, glass, and wood exhibits. (Tues-Sat; closed holidays) **FREE**

⭐ **Delta Queen** and **Mississippi Queen**. *St. Louis. Phone toll-free 800/543-1949. www.deltaqueen.com.* Paddlewheelers offer 3-8-night cruises on the Ohio, Cumberland, Mississippi, and Tennessee rivers. Contact Delta Queen Steamboat Co, 30 Robin St Wharf, New Orleans, LA 70130-1890.

DeMenil Mansion and Museum. *3352 DeMenil Pl, St. Louis (63118). Phone 314/771-5828.* Antebellum, Greek Revival house with period furnishings; restaurant (lunch) in carriage house. Mansion on old Arsenal Hill in the colorful brewery district. Gift shop. (Tues-Sat) **$$**

Dr. Edmund A. Babler Memorial. *800 Guy Park Dr, St. Louis (63005). 25 miles W on Hwy 100, then N on Hwy 109. Phone 314/458-3813.* Approximately 2,500 acres. Swimming pool; hiking trail, picnicking, playground, improved camping (dump station). Interpretive center, naturalist. (Daily) **FREE**

Eads Bridge. *St. Louis.* Riverfront area (1874) Designed by engineer James B. Eads, the Eads was the first bridge to span the wide southern section of the Mississippi and the first bridge in which steel and the cantilever were used extensively; approach ramps are carried on enormous Romanesque stone arches.

Edgar M. Queeny Park. *St. Louis. 19 miles W via I-64 (Hwy 40) or Clayton Rd, S on Mason Rd. Phone 636/391-0922.* A 569-acre park. Swimming pool; hiking trail, tennis, ice rink (fee), picnicking, hayrides, horseback riding trails, playground. (Daily)

Eugene Field House and Toy Museum. *634 S Broadway, St. Louis (63102). Phone 314/421-4689.* (1845) Birthplace of famous children's poet; mementos, manuscripts, and many original furnishings; antique toys and dolls. (Wed-Sun; closed holidays) **$$**

⭐ **Forest Park.** *Skinker Blvd, Kingshighway Blvd, and Oakland Ave, St. Louis (63110). W via I-64 (Hwy 40). Phone 314/289-5300.* This 1,200-acre park was the site of most of the 1904 Louisiana Purchase Exposition. Many of the city's major attractions are here. (See SPECIAL EVENTS)

Gateway Riverboat Cruises. *50 N Leonor K Sullivan Blvd, St. Louis (63102). Dock is below Gateway Arch. Phone 314/621-4040; toll-free 800/878-7411. www. gatewaycruises.com.* One-hour narrated cruise of the Mississippi River aboard the *Huck Finn, Tom Sawyer,* and *Becky Thatcher* riverboats, replicas of 19th-century sternwheelers. (Memorial Day-Labor Day, daily) **$$$**

Grant's Farm. *10501 Gravois Rd, St. Louis (63123). SW via I-55. Phone 314/843-1700. www.grantsfarm.com.* This 281-acre wooded tract contains a log cabin (1856) and land once owned by Ulysses S. Grant. Anheuser-Busch Clydesdale barn; carriage house with horse-drawn vehicles, trophy room; deer park where deer, buffalo, longhorn steer, and other animals roam freely in their natural habitat; bird and elephant show, small animal feeding area. Tours by miniature train. (May-Sept: Tues-Sun; mid-Apr-May and Sep-mid-Oct: Wed-Sun) **FREE**

Gray Line bus tours. *312 W Morris, St. Louis (62232). Phone 314/421-4753; toll-free 800/542-4287.*

Hidden Valley Ski Area. *Eureka. 28 miles W on I-44, then 3 miles S on Hwy F to Hidden Valley Dr. Phone 636/938-5373. www.hiddenvalleyski.com.* Two triple chairlifts, four rope tows; patrol, school, rentals, snowmaking; cafeteria, restaurant, concession, bar. Longest run 1,760 feet; vertical drop 282 feet. Night skiing. (Dec-Mar, daily; closed Dec 24-25) **$$$$**

International Bowling Museum and Hall of Fame. *111 Stadium Plz, St. Louis (63102). Across from Busch Stadium. Phone 314/231-6340. www.bowlingmuseum .com.* Bowling is enjoying a resurgence of popularity, and there's no better place to revel in the sport than in this 50,000-square-foot facility. View wacky bowling shirts and the very sublime Hall of Fame, and bowl a few frames. The museum shares the building with the St. Louis Cardinals Museum, which boasts an outstanding collection of Redbirds memorabilia. (Apr-Sept: daily 11 am-5 pm; Oct-Mar: Tues-Sat 11 am-4 pm; closed holidays) **$$**

Jefferson Barracks Historical Park. *533 Grant Rd, St. Louis (63125). S Broadway at Kingston, 10 miles S on I-55, S Broadway exit.* Phone 314/544-5714. Army post established in 1826, used through 1946. St. Louis County now maintains 424 acres of the original tract. Restored buildings include a stable (1851), a laborer's house (1851), two powder magazines (1851 and 1857), ordnance room, and visitor center. Picnicking. Buildings (Wed-Sun; closed holidays). **FREE**

Jefferson National Expansion Memorial. *11 N 4th St, St. Louis (63102). Phone 314/655-1700. www.nps.gov/ jeff.* The Jefferson National Expansion Memorial, located along the Mississippi River, pays tribute to Thomas Jefferson and his influence on freedom and democracy. **$** Here are

Gateway Arch. *The Gateway Arch Riverfront, St. Louis (63102). Phone toll-free 877/982-1410. www.gatewayarch.com.* Eero Saarinen's Gateway Arch is a 630-foot stainless steel arch that symbolizes the starting point of the westward expansion of the United States. Visitor center includes capsule transporter to observation deck (fee). Videotapes for the hearing impaired; tours for the visually impaired. Observation deck inaccessible to wheelchairs. *Note:* there is often a wait for observation deck capsules, which are small and confining. (Memorial Day-Labor Day: daily 8 am-10 pm; rest of year: daily 9 am-6 pm; closed Jan 1, Thanksgiving, Dec 25) **$$**

Museum of Westward Expansion. *11 N 4th St, St. Louis (63102). Phone 314/655-1700. www.nps.gov/ jeff.* The Museum of Westward Expansion offers exhibits on the people and events of 19th-century western America, special exhibits and films (fee) on St. Louis, construction of the arch, and the westward movement. (Daily; closed Jan 1, Thanksgiving, Dec 25)

Old Courthouse. *11 N 4th St, St. Louis (63102). At Market St.* Phone 314/655-1600. Begun in 1837 and completed in 1862, this building houses five museum galleries on St. Louis history, including various displays, dioramas, and films; two restored courtrooms. First two trials of the Dred Scott case were held in this building. Guided tour. (Daily; closed Jan 1, Thanksgiving, Dec 25) **FREE**

Jewel Box Floral Conservatory. *Wells and McKinley drs, St. Louis (63101).* Seventeen-and-a-half acre site with formal lily pools; floral displays; special holiday shows. Free admission Mon-Tues mornings. (Daily) **$**

Laclede's Landing. *720 N 2nd St, St. Louis (63102). N edge of riverfront, between Eads and King bridges.* Phone 314/241-1155. Early St. Louis commercial district (mid-1800s) includes a nine-block area of renovated pre-Civil War and Victorian buildings that house specialty shops, restaurants, and nightclubs.

Laumeier Sculpture Park. *12580 Rott Rd, St. Louis (63127). Geyer and Rott rds.* Phone 314/821-1209. Sculpture by contemporary artists on the grounds of the Laumeier mansion; art gallery (Tues-Sun). Nature trails, picnic area. (Daily) **FREE**

Lone Elk Park. *St. Louis. Hwy 141 and N Outer Rd, 23 miles SW on I-44, adjacent to Castlewood State Park.* Phone 314/615-7275. Approximately 400-acre preserve for bison, elk, deer, and Barbados sheep. Picnicking. (Daily) **FREE**

Magic House, St. Louis Children's Museum. *516 S Kirkwood Rd, Kirkwood (63122). 8 miles W via I-44, Lindbergh exit.* Phone 314/822-8900. Hands-on exhibits include electrostatic generator and a three-story circular slide. (Memorial Day-Labor Day: daily; rest of year: Tues-Sun; closed holidays) **$$$**

Mastodon State Historic Site. *1050 Museum Dr, Imperial, St. Louis (62052). 20 miles S off Hwy 55, near Hwy 67 Imperial exit.* Phone 636/464-2976. Excavation of mastodon remains and Native American artifacts; museum (fee). Hiking, picnicking. (Daily) **FREE**

Missouri Botanical Garden. *4344 Shaw Blvd, St. Louis (63110). Phone 314/577-5141; toll-free 800/642-8842. www.mobot.org.* This 79-acre park includes rose, woodland, and herb gardens; scented garden for the blind; electric tram rides (fee). Restaurant, floral display hall. Sections of the botanical garden are well over a century old. (Daily; closed Dec 25) **$$** Included in admission are

Climatron. *Missouri Botanical Gardens, St. Louis.* Phone 314/577-5141. Seventy-foot high, prize-winning geodesic dome—first of its kind to be used as a conservatory—houses a two-level, half-acre tropical rain forest with canopies, rocky outcrops, waterfalls, and mature tree collection; exhibits explain the many facets of a rain forest. Entrance to Climatron through series of sacred lotus and lily pools.

Japanese Garden. *Missouri Botanical Garden, St. Louis.* Phone toll-free 800/642-8842. Largest traditional Japanese garden in North America, with lake landscaped with many varieties of water irises, waterfalls, bridges, and a teahouse.

Missouri History Museum-Missouri Historical Society. *5700 Lindel Blvd, St. Louis (63112). In the Jefferson Memorial Building Phone 314/746-4599. www.mohistory.org.* Exhibits on St. Louis and the American West; artwork, costumes, and decorative arts; toys, firearms; 19th-century fire-fighting equipment; St. Louis history slide show; ragtime-rock 'n' roll music exhibit; 1904 World's Fair and Charles A. Lindbergh collections. (Daily; closed holidays) **FREE**

Museum of the Dog. *Queeny Park, 1721 S Mason Rd, St. Louis (63131). W via I-64 (Hwy 40). Phone 314/821-3647. www.akc.org/love/museum/aboutmuseum.cfm.* This museum has more than 500 exhibits of dog-related art and houses a reference library and gift shop. (Tues-Sat 10 am-4 pm, Sun 1-5 pm; closed holidays) **$**

Museum of Transportation. *3015 Barrett Station Rd, Kirkwood (63122). 16 miles SW via I-44, N on I-270 to Big Bend and Dougherty Ferry Rd exits. Phone 314/965-7998.* One of the more interesting collections anywhere in the country can be found here. The Museum of Transportation houses an extensive collection of passenger and freight train equipment (ranging from elevated cars from Chicago to the last steam locomotive to operate in Missouri), as well as the riverboats and airplanes that local history has helped support. Visitors can ride on some of the railroad equipment, or take a more leisurely trip on more primitive modes of transport (like horse-drawn carts). (Daily; closed Jan 1, Thanksgiving, Dec 25) **$$**

NASCAR Speedpark. *5555 St. Louis Mills Blvd, Hazelwood (63042). Phone 314/227-5600. www.nascarspeedpark.com.* This mini-amusement park northwest of downtown, and one of five now open across North America, contains everything from an arcade to a rock-climbing wall to a NASCAR merchandise store. But its main draw is its multitude of racetracks. You can even climb into a mock stock car and experience centrifugal forces, turns, and crash impacts as you "drive" a full-motion NASCAR Silicon Motor Speedway simulator. (Mon-Fri 10 am-9:30 pm, Sat 10 am-10 pm, Sun 11 am-7 pm; closed Easter, Thanksgiving, Dec 25) **$$$$**

Old Cathedral. *209 Walnut St, St. Louis (63102). At Memorial Dr, under Gateway Arch. Phone 314/231-3250.* (1831) Basilica of St. Louis, King of France, on the site of the first church built in St. Louis in 1770;

museum on the west side contains the original church bell and other religious artifacts. (Daily) **$**

Powell Symphony Hall. *718 N Grand Blvd, St. Louis (63103). Phone 314/534-1700 (box office).* (1925) Decorated in ivory and 24-karat gold leaf, the hall, built as a movie and vaudeville house, is now home of the St. Louis Symphony Orchestra (mid-Sept-mid-May). After-concert tours available by appointment.

President Casino on the *Admiral*. *Downtown, St. Louis (63102). Docked at Laclede's landing. Phone 314/622-3000.* (Daily)

Purina Farms. *200 Checkerboard Dr, Gray Summit (63039). 35 miles W via I-44, Gray Summit exit, then two blocks N on Hwy 100 and 1 mile W on County MM. Phone 314/982-3232.* Domestic animals, educational graphic displays, videos, hands-on activities. Grain bin theater. Petting areas, animal demonstrations, play area with maze, ponds. Snack bar, gift shop. Self-guided tours. (Mid-Mar-May and Sept-Nov: Wed-Sun; June-Aug: Tues-Sun) Reservations required. **FREE**

Six Flags St. Louis. *I-44 and Six Flags Rd, Eureka (63025). 30 miles SW via I-44, exit 261. Phone 636/938-4800. www.sixflags.com.* This edition of the theme park franchise has rides and attractions for kids and grownups, plus live shows throughout summer. Big among the two dozen or so rides here are the roller coasters, especially Batman the Ride and the Ninja. Parking (fee). (Mid-May-late Aug: daily from 10 am; early-Apr-mid-May and late Aug-Halloween: weekends from 10 am; closing times vary) **$$$$**

Soldiers' Memorial Military Museum. *1315 Chestnut St, St. Louis (63103). Phone 314/622-4550.* Honoring St. Louis's war dead; memorabilia from pre-Civil War, World War I, World War II, Korea, and Vietnam. (Daily; closed Jan 1, Thanksgiving, Dec 25) **FREE**

St. Louis Art Museum. *1 Fine Arts Dr, St. Louis (63110). Phone 314/721-0072.* Built for the 1904 World's Fair as the Palace of Fine Arts. Collections of American and European paintings, prints, drawings, and decorative arts. Also African, Asian, and pre-Columbian art; 47-foot statue in front depicts St. Louis the Crusader astride his horse. Lectures, films, workshops. Restaurant, museum shop. (Tues-Sun; closed Jan 1, Thanksgiving, Dec 25)

St. Louis Blues (NHL). *Savvis Center, 1401 Clark Ave, St. Louis (63103). Phone 314/241-1888.* Professional hockey team.

St. Louis Cardinals (MLB). *Busch Stadium, 250 Stadium Plz, St. Louis (63102). Phone 314/421-3060.* Professional baseball team.

St. Louis Cardinals Hall of Fame Museum. *Busch Stadium, 100 Stadium Plz, St. Louis (63102). Between gates 5 and 6. Phone 314/231-6340.* St. Louis baseball from 1860-present; Stan Musial memorabilia. Gift shop. Also stadium tours (Apr-Dec: daily; rest of year: limited hours). Building (daily). **$$$**

St. Louis Centre. *Locust and 6th sts, St. Louis (63101). Downtown. Phone 314/231-5522.* One of the largest urban shopping malls in the country; features 130 shops and Taste of St. Louis food court with 28 restaurants. (Daily)

St. Louis Rams (NFL). *Edward Jones Dome, 901 N Broadway, St. Louis (63101). Phone 314/425-8830. www.stlouisrams.com.* Professional football team.

St. Louis Science Center. *5050 Oakland Ave, St. Louis (63110). Phone 314/289-4444; toll-free 800/456-7572. www.slsc.org.* Features three buildings with more than 700 exhibits. Also Omnimax theater, planetarium, children's discovery room (various fees). Outdoor science park. Gift shops. Restaurant. (Daily; closed Thanksgiving, Dec 25)

St. Louis Union Station. *1820 Market St, St. Louis (63103). Phone 314/421-6655.* This block-long stone chateauesque railroad station (1894) was the world's busiest passenger terminal from 1905 to the late 1940s. After the last train pulled out on October 31, 1978, the station and train shed were restored and redeveloped as a marketplace with more than 100 specialty shops and restaurants, nightclubs, and a hotel, as well as entertainment areas, plazas, and a 1 1/2-acre lake. The station was designed by a local architect to be modeled after a walled medieval city in southern France; its interior features high Romanesque and Sullivanesque design. "Memories," a collection of photographs, letters, memorabilia, and films, brings the station's history to life.

St. Louis University. *221 N Grand, St. Louis (63103). Phone 314/977-8886; toll-free 800/758-3678. www.slu.edu.* (1818) (10,000 students) Oldest university west of the Mississippi River; includes Pius XII Memorial Library with Vatican Microfilm Library—the only depository for copies of Vatican documents in the Western Hemisphere (academic year, daily; closed holidays). Also here is

Cupples House and Art Gallery. *St. Louis University Campus, 3673 West Mall, St. Louis (63108). On John E Connelly Mall (formerly W Pine Blvd), W of Pius XII Library. Phone 314/977-3025.* Historic Romanesque building (1889) with 42 rooms, 22 fireplaces, original furnishings, period pieces; houses 20th-century graphics collection. (Tues-Sat, hours vary) **$$**

St. Louis Zoo. *Forest Park, 1 Government Dr, St. Louis (63110). Phone 314/781-0900; toll-free 800/966-8877. www.stlzoo.org.* The St. Louis Zoo is widely considered one of the best in the country. Lions, cheetahs, and giraffes roam in natural African settings, while other areas showcase exotic species from the poles to the tropics. At Discovery Corner kids can feed birds, mingle with otters, and more. There are plenty of places to eat and shop, too. Fee ($) for some attractions. (Memorial Day-Labor Day: daily 8 am-7 pm; rest of year: daily 9 am-5 pm; closed Jan 1, Dec 25) **FREE**

Steinberg Memorial Skating Rink. *St. Louis.* Roller skating (June-Sept), ice skating (Nov-Mar); rentals. **$$**

Ulysses S. Grant National Historic Site. *7400 Grant Rd, St. Louis (63123). Off Gravois Rd. Phone 314/842-3298.* Site consists of five historic structures: two-story residence known as White Haven, stone outbuilding, barn, ice house, and chicken house. The White Haven property was a focal point in Ulysses's and wife Julia's lives for four decades. Grounds feature more than 50 species of trees and are a haven for a variety of wildlife. Visitors center includes exhibits and information on the Grants and White Haven. Guided tours. (Daily; closed Jan 1, Thanksgiving, Dec 25)

Washington University. *1 Brookings Dr, St. Louis (63130). E on Forsyth Blvd, hilltop campus entrance at Hoyt Dr. Phone 314/935-5000.* (1853) (11,000 students) On campus are Graham Chapel, Edison Theatre, and Francis Field, site of the first Olympic Games in the United States (1904). Also here is

Washington University Gallery of Art. *Steinberg Hall, Forsyth and Skinker blvds, St. Louis (63130). Phone 314/935-5490.* Established in 1888, this was the first art museum west of the Mississippi River; a branch of the museum later became the St. Louis Art Museum. Collections of 19th- and 20th-century American and European paintings; sculpture and old and modern prints. (Oct-Apr, Tues-Sun; closed holidays) **FREE**

West Port Plaza. *Page and I-270, Maryland Heights (63043). Approximately 15 miles W via I-64 (Hwy 40), N on I-270, E on Page Blvd to W Port Plaza Dr. Phone 314/576-7100.* Alpine-like setting with approximately 30 European-style shops and 20 restaurants. (Daily)

Special Events

Fair St. Louis. *Jefferson National Expansion Memorial Park, St. Louis (63101). Phone 314/434-3434.* Three-day festival with parade, food, air and water shows, entertainment. July 4 weekend.

Great Forest Park Balloon Race. *Forest Park, 5600 Clayton Ave, St. Louis (63110). Phone 314/289-5300.* Food, entertainment, parachute jumps, and other contests. Mid-Sept.

Gypsy Caravan. *8001 Natural Bridge, St. Louis (63101). Phone 314/286-4452.* One of the largest flea markets in the Midwest, with more than 600 vendors; arts and crafts, entertainment, concessions. Memorial Day.

Muny Opera. *Forest Park, St. Louis (63110). Phone 314/361-1900.* 12,000-seat outdoor theater. Light opera and musical comedy. Mid-June-Aug.

St. Louis Symphony Orchestra. *Powell Symphony Hall, 718 N Grand Blvd, St. Louis (63103). Phone 314/534-1700.* Sept-May.

Limited-Service Hotels

★ ★ **COURTYARD BY MARRIOTT.** *2340 Market St, St. Louis (63103). Phone 314/241-9111; toll-free 800/321-2211; fax 314/241-8113. www.courtyard.com.* Visitors to St. Louis hoping to explore the impressively restored Union Station will find ideal accommodations here, down the street from the Station, one of the city's major shopping and dining areas. 151 rooms, 4 story. Check-in 3 pm, check-out noon. Restaurant. Fitness room. Indoor pool, whirlpool. **$**

★ ★ **DRURY INN.** *201 S 20th St, St. Louis (63103). Phone 314/231-3900; fax 314/231-3900. www.druryinn.com.* 176 rooms, 7 story. Pets accepted, some restrictions. Complimentary continental breakfast. Check-out noon. Restaurant, bar. Fitness room. Indoor pool, whirlpool. Restored 1907 railroad hotel. **$**

★ **HAMPTON INN.** *2211 Market St, St. Louis (63103). Phone 314/241-3200; toll-free 800/426-7866; fax 314/241-9351. www.hamptoninn.com.* The

downtown location of this large hotel, close to the Arch, Union Station, and sports arenas, makes it a great choice for those who plan to tackle as many local attractions as possible. 239 rooms, 11 story. Pets accepted, some restrictions. Complimentary continental breakfast. Check-in 3 pm, check-out noon. Bar. Fitness room. Indoor pool, whirlpool. **$**

★ ★ **HOLIDAY INN.** *811 N 9th St, St. Louis (63101). Phone 314/421-4000; toll-free 800/289-8338; fax 314/421-5974. www.holiday-inn.com.* 295 rooms, 4 story. Check-out noon. Restaurant, bar. Fitness room. Indoor pool, whirlpool. Business center. **$**

★ ★ **RADISSON HOTEL & SUITES.** *200 N 4th St, St. Louis (63102). Phone 314/621-8200; toll-free 800/333-3333; fax 314/621-8073. www.radisson.com.* This hotel offers a lobby lounge, a restaurant on the second floor, and a rooftop pool. It is located in the downtown area of St. Louis and is near many shops, restaurants, and entertainment establishments. 454 rooms, 29 story. Check-out noon. Restaurant, bar. Outdoor pool. **$$**

Full-Service Hotels

★ ★ ★ **CHASE PARK PLAZA.** *212 N Kingshighway Blvd, St. Louis (63108). Phone 314/633-3000; fax 314/633-3003.* 250 rooms. Check-in 3 pm, check-out noon. High-speed Internet access. Five restaurants, three bars. Fitness room, spa. Outdoor pool, whirlpool. Business center. **$$$**

★ ★ **CHESHIRE LODGE.** *6300 Clayton Rd, St. Louis (63117). Phone 314/647-7300; toll-free 800/325-7378; fax 314/647-0442. www.cheshirelodge.com.* 106 rooms, 4 story. Complimentary continental breakfast. Check-in 3 pm, check-out 1 pm. High-speed Internet access, wireless Internet access. Restaurant, two bars. Indoor pool, outdoor pool. Airport transportation available. Business center. Elegant Tudor décor. **$**

★ ★ ★ **HILTON ST. LOUIS FRONTENAC.** *1335 S Lindbergh Blvd, St. Louis (63131). Phone 314/993-1100; toll-free 800/325-7800; fax 314/993-8546. www.hilton.com.* Located between downtown St. Louis and Lambert International Airport, this hotel offers guest rooms and suites with European charm. It is near the St. Louis Zoo, the Science Center, Six

Flags Amusement Park, and more. 263 rooms, 3 story. Pets accepted, some restrictions; fee. Check-in 3 pm, check-out noon. High-speed Internet access, wireless Internet access. Two restaurants, bar. Fitness room. Outdoor pool. Airport transportation available. Business center. **$$**

★ ★ ★ HYATT REGENCY ST. LOUIS. *1 St. Louis Union Station, St. Louis (63103). Phone 314/ 231-1234; toll-free 800/633-7313; fax 314/923-3970. www.hyatt.com.* In the renovated Union Station railroad terminal (1894); the main lobby and lounge occupy Grand Hall. With facilities like an outdoor pool, health club, saunas, a pizzeria, and a fine dining restaurant, this hotel is a perfect place for both business and leisure travelers. It is located above a mall where visitors will find many stores. 538 rooms, 6 story. Check-out noon. Restaurant, bar. Fitness room. Outdoor pool. **$$**

★ ★ ★ MARRIOTT ST. LOUIS PAVILION. *1 S Broadway, St. Louis (63102). Phone 314/421- 1776; toll-free 800/228-9290; fax 314/331-9029. www.marriott.com.* With a central location across from Busch Stadium and only two blocks from the Gateway Arch, this hotel is easily acessible from the airport via the city's Metrolink transit system. It offers an indoor pool, health club, and other facilities. 672 rooms, 25 story. Check-out noon. Restaurant, bar. Fitness room. Indoor pool, whirlpool. Business center. **$$**

★ ★ ★ OMNI MAJESTIC HOTEL. *1019 Pine St, St. Louis (63101). Phone 314/436-2355; toll-free 800/843-6664; fax 314/436-0223. www.omnihotels.com.* This European-style hotel (1913) is located in downtown Saint Louis and is listed in the National Register of Historic Buildings. It offers many modern amenities including a full-service fitness center. 91 rooms, 9 story. Check-out noon. Restaurant, bar. Fitness room. Airport transportation available. **$$**

★ ★ ★ THE PARKWAY HOTEL. *4550 Forest Park Blvd, St. Louis (63110). Phone 314/256-7777; toll-free 866/314-7000; fax 314/256-7999. www.theparkwayhotel .com.* 220 rooms. Check-in 4 pm, check-out noon. High-speed Internet access. Restaurant. Airport transportation available. Business Center. **$$**

★ ★ ★ RENAISSANCE GRAND HOTEL. *800 Washington Ave, St. Louis (63101). Phone 314/ 621-9600; toll-free 800/468-3571; fax 314/621-9601. www.renaissancehotels.com.* 918 rooms. Pets accepted. Check-in 4 pm, check-out noon. High-speed Internet access. Four restaurants, bar. Fitness room. Indoor pool, whirlpool. Airport transportation available. Business center. **$**

★ ★ ★ RENAISSANCE ST. LOUIS SUITES. *827 Washington Ave, St. Louis (63101). Phone 314/ 621-9700; toll-free 800/468-3571; fax 314/621-9702. www.renaissancehotels.com.* 165 rooms, 24 story, all suites. Pets accepted, some restrictions; fee. Check-in 4 pm, check-out noon. High-speed Internet access. Restaurant, bar. Fitness room. Whirlpool. Airport transportation available. Business center. **$$**

★ ★ ★ ★ THE RITZ-CARLTON, ST. LOUIS. *100 Carondelet Plz, Clayton (63105). Phone 314/863-6300; toll-free 800/241-3333; fax 314/863-3525. www.ritz-carlton.com.* The Ritz-Carlton is the jewel in the crown of Clayton, an exclusive residential and shopping area just outside St. Louis. This sophisticated hotel shares the best of the city with its privileged guests. The guest rooms are spacious and plush, and all have private balconies with sweeping views of the city skyline. A comprehensive fitness center includes lap and hydrotherapy pools. The restaurants and lounges, characterized by their convivial spirit, fine dining, and seamless service, are popular with locals and hotel guests alike. Cigar aficionados head straight for the Cigar Lounge for its clubby setting and wide selection of premium cigars, while oenophiles delight in the Wine Room's delicious dishes expertly paired with special vintages. 301 rooms, 18 story. Pets accepted, some restrictions; fee. Check-in 3 pm, check-out noon. High-speed Internet access. Two restaurants, two bars. Fitness room. Indoor pool, whirlpool. Airport transportation available. Business center. **$$$**

★ ★ ★ SHERATON ST. LOUIS CITY CENTER HOTEL AND SUITES. *400 S 14th St, St. Joseph (63103). Phone 314/231-5007; toll-free 800/325-3535; fax 314/231-5008. www.sheraton.com.* 288 rooms, 13 story. Check-out noon. Restaurant. Fitness room. Indoor pool. Business center. **$$**

★ **STAYBRIDGE SUITES.** *1855 Craigshire Rd, St. Louis (63121). Phone 314/878-1555; toll-free 800/238-8000; fax 314/878-9203. www.staybridge.com.* This is an all-suite property that offers a choice between one- and two-room suites. Each room features a kitchen and a living area with a TV, VCR, and a pull-out sofa bed. A buffet breakfast is included along with use of the hotel facilities. 106 rooms, 2 story, all suites. Pets accepted, some restrictions. Complimentary continental breakfast. Check-in 3 pm, check-out noon. High-speed Internet access. Fitness room. Outdoor pool, whirlpool. Airport transportation available. Business center. **$**

★ ★ ★ **THE WESTIN ST. LOUIS.** *811 Spruce St, St. Louis (63102). Phone 314/621-2000; toll-free 800/228-3000; fax 314/552-5700. www.westin.com.* 221 rooms, 9 story. Check-out noon. Restaurant. Fitness room. Business center. **$$**

Restaurants

★ **BLUEBERRY HILL.** *6504 Delmar Blvd, St. Louis (63130). Phone 314/727-0880; fax 314/727-0880. www.blueberryhill.com.* American menu, Bar food. Lunch, dinner, late-night. Closed Super Bowl Sun. Bar. Casual attire. Outdoor seating. **$**

★ **BROADWAY OYSTER BAR.** *736 S Broadway, St. Louis (63102). Phone 314/621-8811; fax 314/621-1995. www.broadwayoysterbar.com.* Cajun/Creole menu. Lunch, dinner. Closed holidays. Bar. Outdoor seating. **$$**

★ ★ **CANDICCI'S.** *12513 Olive Street Rd, St. Louis (63141). Phone 314/878-5858; fax 314/878-8702. www.candiccis.com.* Italian menu. Lunch, dinner. Closed holidays. Bar. Children's menu. Outdoor seating. **$$**

★ ★ **CARDWELL'S AT THE PLAZA.** *94 Plaza Frontenac, St. Louis (63131). Phone 314/997-8885; fax 314/872-8835. www.cardwellsattheplaza.com.* American menu. Lunch, dinner. Closed holidays. Bar. Children's menu. Business casual attire. Reservations recommended. Outdoor seating. **$$$**

★ **CHARCOAL HOUSE.** *9855 Manchester Rd, St. Louis (63119). Phone 314/968-4842; fax 314/968-2405.* This place *is* your grandfather's steakhouse. The service is friendly, the food is traditional, and the prices are realistic. Settle in and check out old-school choices

such as porterhouse steaks and hash-brown casserole, and invoke the spirit of the good old days. American menu. Lunch, dinner. Closed Sun; holidays. Bar. Children's menu. Business casual attire. Reservations recommended. **$$**

★ **CHARLIE GITTO'S.** *207 N 6th St, St. Louis (63101). Phone 314/436-2828; fax 314/436-3024. www.saucecafe.com.* American, Italian menu. Lunch, dinner. Closed holidays. Bar. Children's menu. **$$**

★ **CHUY ARZOLA'S.** *6405 Clayton Ave, St. Louis (63139). Phone 314/644-4430; fax 314/644-0495.* Tex-Mex menu. Lunch, dinner. Closed holidays. Bar. Children's menu. Casual attire. Outdoor seating. **$**

★ **CROWN CANDY KITCHEN.** *1401 St. Louis Ave, St. Louis (63106). Phone 314/621-9650. www.crowncandykitchen.com.* For more than 90 years, this local legend has been every ice cream lover's fantasy. Any patron who can consume five ice cream creations—sundaes, shakes, whatever you fancy—in 30 minutes or less gets them all free, but you don't have to eat nearly that much to enjoy the fare. American menu. Lunch, dinner. Closed holidays. **$**

★ ★ **CUNETTO HOUSE OF PASTA.** *5453 Magnolia Ave, St. Louis (63139). Phone 314/781-1135; fax 314/781-5674. www.cunetto.com.* This restaurant is located in an old Italian neighborhood. Italian menu. Lunch, dinner. Closed Sun; holidays. Bar. Casual attire. Outdoor seating. **$$**

★ ★ **DIERDORF & HART'S STEAK HOUSE.** *701 E Market St, St. Louis (63146). Phone 314/878-1801; fax 314/878-8989. www.dierdorfharts.com.* Owned by two local football legends, this steakhouse features a man's-man menu. Here, the steak is done one of four ways—tenderloin filet, New York strip, porterhouse, or ribeye and served with stalwart side dishes. Steak menu. Lunch, dinner. Closed holidays. Bar. Business casual attire. Reservations recommended. **$$$**

★ ★ ★ **DOMINIC'S RESTAURANT.** *5101 Wilson Ave, St. Louis (63110). Phone 314/771-1632; fax 314/771-1695. www.dominicsrestaurant.com.* Italian menu. Dinner. Closed Sun; holidays. Bar. Jacket required. Valet parking. **$$$**

★ **FRAZER'S TRAVELING BROWN BAG.** *1811 Pestalozzi, St. Louis (63118). Phone 314/773-8646; fax*

314/773-8315. *www.frazergoodeats.com*. International/ Fusion menu. Dinner. Closed Sun; holidays. Bar. Outdoor seating. **$$**

★ **GINO'S RISTORANTE.** *4502 Hampton Ave, St. Louis (63109). Phone 314/351-4187; fax 314/351-4235. www.ginosstl.com.* Italian menu. Dinner. Closed Mon; holidays. Bar. Children's menu. Casual attire. Outdoor seating. **$$**

★ ★ **GIOVANNI'S.** *5201 Shaw Ave, St. Louis (63110). Phone 314/772-5958; fax 314/772-0343. www.giovannisonthehill.com.* This restaurant is best described as timeless Italian. The highlight is its focus on fresh seafood, which is flown in daily. The veal and beef dishes are also exceptional. Italian menu. Dinner. Closed Jan 1, Thanksgiving, Dec 25. Valet parking. **$$$**

★ ★ **GIUSEPPE'S.** *4141 S Grand Blvd, St. Louis (63118). Phone 314/832-3779.* Italian menu. Lunch, dinner. Closed Mon; holidays. Bar. **$$**

★ ★ **THE GRILL.** *100 Carondelet Plz, St. Louis (63105). Phone 314/863-6300; toll-free 800/241-3333; fax 314/863-3525. www.ritzcarlton.com.* Located at the elegant Ritz-Carlton hotel (see) near downtown St. Louis, this upscale dining room serves grilled beef, seafood, and fresh pasta, and a seafood buffet on Wednesdays. American menu. Dinner. Bar. Children's menu. Business casual attire. Reservations recommended. Valet parking. **$$$**

★ ★ **HACIENDA.** *9748 Manchester Rd, Rockhill (63119). Phone 314/962-7100; fax 314/918-1441. www.hacienda-stl.com.* Mexican menu. Lunch, dinner. Closed holidays. Bar. (1861) Built as a residence for a steamboat captain. Outdoor seating. **$$**

★ **HAMMERSTONE'S.** *2028 S 9th, St. Louis (63104). Phone 314/773-5565; fax 314/773-6818.* American menu. Breakfast, lunch, dinner. Closed holidays. Bar. Children's menu. Outdoor seating. **$$**

★ **HANNEGAN'S.** *719 N 2nd St, St. Louis (63102). Phone 314/241-8877; fax 314/241-6066. www. hannegansrestaurant.com.* American menu. Lunch, dinner. Closed holidays. Bar. Children's menu. Replica of US Senate dining room; political memorabilia. **$$**

★ ★ **HARRY'S.** *2144 Market St, St. Louis (63103). Phone 314/421-6969; fax 314/421-5114. www.harrys restaurantandbar.com.* American, Caribbean menu.

Lunch, dinner. Closed holidays. Bar. Valet parking. **$$$**

★ ★ **HARVEST.** *1059 S Big Bend Rd, St. Louis (63117). Phone 314/645-3522; fax 314/645-3080. www.harveststlouis.com.* Fusion menu. Dinner. Closed Mon; holidays. Bar. Business casual attire. Reservations recommended. **$$$**

★ **HOUSE OF INDIA.** *8501 Delmar Blvd, St. Louis (63124). Phone 314/567-6850; fax 314/344-1145. www.hoistl.com.* Indian menu. Lunch, dinner. Closed holidays. Casual attire. Reservations recommended. **$$**

★ ★ **J. F. SANFILIPPO'S.** *705 N Broadway, St. Louis (63102). Phone 314/621-7213; fax 314/621-5307. www.sanfilippos.com.* Italian menu. Lunch, dinner. Closed Sun; holidays. Bar. Children's menu. **$$**

★ **JOHN D. MCGURK'S.** *1200 Russell Blvd, St. Louis (63104). Phone 314/776-8309; fax 314/776-6829. www.mcgurks.com.* Irish, American menu. Lunch, dinner. Closed holidays. Bar. Children's menu. Housed in an 1861 building. **$$**

★ ★ **JOSEPH'S ITALIAN CAFE.** *107 N 6th St, St. Louis (63101). Phone 314/421-6366; fax 314/421-1664.* Italian menu. Lunch, dinner. Closed Sun. Outdoor seating. **$$**

★ ★ **K. C. MASTERPIECE.** *16123 Chesterfield Pkwy W, St. Louis (63141). Phone 636/530-0052; fax 636/530-0954. www.kcmrestaurants.com.* The makers of the original barbecue sauce opened the doors of their signature restaurant in 1987. Since then, it's become one of the most popular barbecue restaurants in the Midwest. Barbecue menu. Lunch, dinner. Closed Thanksgiving, Dec 25. Bar. Children's menu. **$$**

★ ★ **KEMOLL'S.** *1 Metropolitan Sq, St. Louis (63102). Phone 314/421-0555; fax 314/436-1692. www.kemolls.com.* Since 1927, this downtown landmark restaurant has served upscale, classic specialties in an elegant atmosphere. The name was originally shortened from the Sicilian name Camuglia, and the restaurant is still run by fourth-generation family members. Italian menu. Lunch, dinner. Closed holidays. Five dining rooms. **$$$**

★ **KING & I.** *3157 S Grand Blvd, St. Louis (63118). Phone 314/771-1777; fax 314/771-1777.* Thai menu. Lunch, dinner. Closed Mon; holidays. Bar. **$$**

★ **LE PETIT BISTRO.** *172 W County Center, Des Peres (63131). Phone 314/965-1777; fax 314/965-1760.*

French, Italian menu. Lunch, dinner. Closed holidays. Casual attire. Outdoor seating. **$$**

★ ★ ★ **LOMBARDO'S TRATTORIA.** *201 S 20th St, St. Louis (63103). Phone 314/621-0666; fax 314/621-1863. www.lombardorestaurants.com.* Family-owned and operated for three generations, this restaurant is located in a converted hotel. The menu boasts coveted family classics as well as creative seasonal entrées. Italian menu. Lunch, dinner. Closed Sun; holidays. Bar. Children's menu. **$$$**

★ ★ **LORUSSO'S CUCINA.** *3121 Watson Rd, St. Louis (63139). Phone 314/647-6222; fax 314/647-2821. www.lorussos.com.* Italian menu. Lunch, dinner. Closed Mon; holidays. Bar. Children's menu. Business casual attire. Reservations recommended. **$$**

★ ★ **LYNCH STREET BISTRO.** *1031 Lynch St, St. Louis (63118). Phone 314/772-5777; fax 314/772-6515. www.lynchstreetbistro.com.* International/Fusion menu. Dinner. Closed Sun; holidays. Bar. Children's menu. **$$**

★ **MAGGIE O'BRIEN'S.** *2000 Market St, St. Louis (63103). Phone 314/421-1388; fax 314/421-6712. www.maggieobriens.com.* Grab a satisfying bite here before a Cardinals or Rams game, then take the restaurant's complimentary shuttle to the event. Maggie's serves time-honored Irish and American pub grub, with choices ranging from nachos and quesadillas to burgers, sandwiches, and even pasta. American, Irish menu. Lunch, dinner. Closed holidays. Children's menu. Valet parking. Outdoor seating. **$$**

★ ★ ★ **MALMAISON AT ST. ALBANS.** *3519 St. Albans Rd, St. Albans (63073). Phone 636/458-0131; fax 636/273-3800. www.fivestarfrench.com.* A rustic replica of a French inn tucked away in the countryside outside of St. Louis, this restaurant offers a small yet fresh seasonal menu that promises to entice the guests' senses. French menu. Lunch, dinner. Bar. Jacket required. Outdoor seating. **$$$**

★ ★ **MAMA CAMPISI'S.** *2132 Edwards St, St. Louis (63110). Phone 314/771-1797.* Italian menu. Lunch, dinner. Closed Mon-Tues. Bar. **$$**

★ **MANDARIN HOUSE.** *9150 Overland Plz, St. Louis (63114). Phone 317/427-8070; fax 314/621-7226.* Chinese menu. Lunch, dinner. Bar. Inside the shopping mall at Union Station. **$$**

★ **MARCIANO'S.** *333 Westport Plz, St. Louis (63146). Phone 314/878-8180; fax 314/878-2108.* Italian menu. Lunch, dinner. Closed holidays. Bar. Children's menu. Business casual attire. Outdoor seating. **$$**

★ ★ **MIKE SHANNON'S.** *100 N 7th St, St. Louis (63101). Phone 314/421-1540; fax 314/241-5642. www.shannonsteak.com.* The most famous sports hangout in town is owned and operated by the popular broadcaster and former Cardinals third baseman—you may see the man himself at the bar after games. Oversized steaks, grilled chicken, and other classic American dishes are the specialties. American menu. Lunch, dinner. Closed holidays. Bar. **$$**

★ ★ **PATRICK'S.** *342 Westport Plz, St. Louis (63146). Phone 314/878-6767; fax 314/878-4980. www.patricksatwestportplaza.com.* Seafood menu. Lunch, dinner, brunch. Closed holidays. Bar. Children's menu. Business casual attire. Reservations recommended. Outdoor seating. **$$$**

★ ★ **PAUL MANNO'S CAFE.** *75 Forum Ctr, Chesterfield (63017). Phone 314/878-1274; fax 314/878-1274.* Italian menu. Dinner. Closed holidays. Bar. **$$**

★ **ROBATA OF JAPAN.** *111 Westport Plz, St. Louis (63146). Phone 314/434-1007; fax 314/434-9735. www.gasho.com.* Japanese menu. Lunch, dinner. Bar. Children's menu. Casual attire. Reservations recommended. **$$**

★ **SALEEM'S LEBANESE CUISINE.** *6501 Delmar Blvd, St. Louis (63130). Phone 314/721-7947; fax 314/721-2295.* Middle Eastern menu. Dinner, late-night. Closed Sun; holidays. **$**

★ ★ **SIDNEY STREET CAFE.** *2000 Sidney St, St. Louis (63104). Phone 314/771-5777; fax 314/454-0807.* American menu. Dinner. Closed Sun-Mon; holidays. Bar. In restored building (circa 1885); antiques. **$$**

★ **SPIRO'S.** *3122 Watson Rd, St. Louis (63139). Phone 314/645-8383; fax 314/781-0968.* American menu. Lunch, dinner. Closed Mon; holidays. Children's menu. Reservations recommended. **$$**

★ ★ **ST. LOUIS BREWERY & TAP ROOM.** *2100 Locust St, St. Louis (63103). Phone 314/241-2337; fax 314/241-8101. www.schlafly.com.* American menu. Lunch, dinner, late-night. Closed holidays. Bar. **$$**

★ **THAI CAFE.** *6170 Delmar Blvd, St. Louis (63112). Phone 314/862-6868; fax 314/862-6868.* Thai menu. Lunch, dinner. Closed Mon; holidays. Valet parking. **$$**

★ ★ ★ ★ **TONY'S.** *410 Market St, St. Louis (63102). Phone 314/231-7007; fax 314/231-4740. www.tonysstlouis.com.* Italian food may bring to mind images of red sauce and mozzarella cheese, but at Tony's, a consistent favorite for the rustic dishes of this Mediterranean country, you'll find a menu of luscious Italian fare prepared with a measured and sophisticated hand. Expect appetizers like smoked salmon with mascarpone cheese and asparagus and Belgian endive; pastas like penne with lobster and shrimp; and entrées like tenderloin of beef with foie gras in a port wine demi-glaze and truffle-sauced veal loin chop. In terms of ambience, Tony's is one of those stylish eateries that works just as well for entertaining a business colleague as for sharing dinner with a more intimate acquaintance. The room has an urban, postmodern style, with sleek low lighting; widely spaced linen-topped tables; and glossy, butter-toned, wood-paneled walls. The chef's tasting menu is a nice choice for gourmands with healthy appetites. Italian menu. Dinner, late-night. Closed holidays. Bar. Jacket required. Valet parking. **$$$$**

★ ★ **TRATTORIA MARCELLA.** *3600 Watson Rd, St. Louis (63109). Phone 314/352-7706; fax 314/352-0848.* Italian menu. Dinner. Closed Sun-Mon; holidays. Bar. Casual attire. Reservations recommended. **$$**

★ ★ **YEMANJA BRASIL.** *2900 Missouri Ave, St. Louis (63118). Phone 314/771-7457; fax 314/771-0296.* Brazilian menu. Dinner. Bar. Outdoor seating. **$$**

★ **ZIA'S.** *5256 Wilson Ave, St. Louis (63110). Phone 314/776-0020; fax 314/776-5778. www.zias.com.* Italian menu. Lunch, dinner. Closed Sun; holidays. Bar. Outdoor seating. Informal, modern corner restaurant. **$$**

St. Louis Lambert Airport Area (C-5)

See also St. Charles, St. Louis

Web Site www.lambert-stlouis.com

Airport Information

Information Phone 314/426-8000

Lost and Found Phone 314/426-8100

Airlines Air Canada Jazz, America West, American Airlines, ComAir, Continental Airlines, Delta Air Lines, Frontier Airlines, Midwest Airlines, Northwest Airlines, KLM Royal Dutch Airlines, Southwest Airlines, United Airlines, US Airways

Limited-Service Hotels

★ **DRURY INN.** *10490 Natural Bridge Rd, St. Louis (63134). Phone 314/423-7700; toll-free 800/378-7946; fax 314/423-7700. www.druryhotels.com.* 173 rooms, 6 story. Pets accepted, some restrictions. Complimentary full breakfast. Check-in 3 pm, check-out noon. High-speed Internet access. Fitness room. Indoor pool, whirlpool. Airport transportation available. **$**
✈ 🐾 🕴 ⌘

★ ★ **EMBASSY SUITES.** *11237 Lone Eagle Dr, Bridgeton (63044). Phone 314/739-8929; toll-free 800/362-2779; fax 314/739-6355. www.embassysuites.com.* Located near Lambert International Airport and the Metro Link Rail. 159 rooms, 6 story, all suites. Complimentary full breakfast. Check-out noon. Restaurant, bar. Fitness room. Indoor pool, whirlpool. **$$**
🕴 ⌘

★ **HAMPTON INN.** *10800 Pear Tree Ln, St. Ann (63074). Phone 314/427-3400; toll-free 800/426-7866; fax 314/423-7765. www.hamptoninn.com.* 155 rooms, 4 story. Pets accepted. Complimentary continental breakfast. Check-out noon. Outdoor pool. Airport transportation available. **$**
🐾 ⌘

★ ★ **HENRY VIII HOTEL.** *4690 N Lindbergh Blvd, Bridgeton (63044). Phone 314/731-3040; toll-free 800/325-1588; fax 314/731-4210.* 386 rooms, 5 story. Check-out 11 am. Restaurant, bar. Fitness room. Indoor pool, outdoor pool, whirlpool. Airport transportation available. Some English Tudor architecture. **$**
🅿 🕴 ⌘

Full-Service Hotels

★ ★ ★ **CROWNE PLAZA.** *11228 Lone Eagle Dr, Bridgeton (63044). Phone 314/291-6700; toll-free 800/227-6963; fax 314/770-1205. www.crowneplaza.com.* Located only five minutes from the Lambert International Airport, this hotel was built in 1991 and offers modern accommodations for travelers. An eight-story glass atrium is a great place to relax, along with the indoor pool or Jacuzzi. 351 rooms, 8 story. Check-out noon. Restaurant, bar. Fitness room. Indoor pool, whirlpool. **$$**
🕴 ⌘

★ ★ ★ **MARRIOTT ST. LOUIS AIRPORT.** *I-70 at Lambert International Airport, St. Louis (63134). Phone 314/423-9700; toll-free 800/228-9290; fax 314/ 423-0213. www.marriott.com.* Located at the Lambert International Airport, this hotel offers full-service amenities including two resturants, a lounge, a health club, both an indoor and outdoor pool, two lighted tennis courts, and more. 601 rooms, 9 story. Check-in 3 pm, check-out noon. High-speed Internet access. Three restaurants, bar. Fitness room. Indoor pool, outdoor pool, whirlpool. Tennis. Airport transportation available. Business center. **$$**

★ ★ ★ **RENAISSANCE ST. LOUIS HOTEL.** *9801 Natural Bridge Rd, St. Louis (63134). Phone 314/ 429-1100; toll-free 888/340-2594; fax 314/429-3625. www.renaissancehotels.com.* Located in the historic district with its own 19th-century charm, this hotel offers great accommodations along with excellent service. The property is adjacent to the Lambert International Airport and offers an old-fashioned riverboat casino. 393 rooms, 12 story. Check-in 3 pm, check-out noon. High-speed Internet access. Restaurant, bar. Fitness room. Indoor pool, outdoor pool, whirlpool. Airport transportation available. Business center. **$$**

Restaurant

★ ★ **LOMBARDO'S.** *10488 Natural Bridge Rd, St. Louis (63134). Phone 314/429-5151; fax 314/423-7700. www.lombardorestaurants.com.* Italian menu. Lunch, dinner. Closed Sun; holidays. Bar. Children's menu. Casual attire. Reservations recommended. **$$**

Ste. Genevieve (D-6)

See also Bonne Terre, Cape Girardeau, St. Louis

Founded 1735
Population 4,411
Elevation 401 ft
Area Code 573
Zip 63670
Information Great River Road Interpretive Center, 66 S Main; phone 573/883-7097 or toll-free 800/373-7007
Web Site www.ste-genevieve.com

Ste. Genevieve, the first permanent settlement in Missouri, developed on the banks of the Mississippi River early in the 18th century when Frenchmen began mining lead in the region. After a great flood in 1785, the village was moved to higher ground. Once St. Louis's chief rival, Ste. Genevieve preserves its French heritage in its festivals, old houses, and massive red brick church. Today the town is an important lime-producing center.

What to See and Do

Bolduc House Museum. *125 S Main St, Ste. Genevieve (63670). Phone 573/883-3105.* (Circa 1770) Restored French house with walls of upright heavy oak logs; period furnishings, orchard, and herb garden. (Apr-Nov, daily) **$**

Felix Valle Home State Historic Site. *198 Merchant St, Ste. Genevieve (63670). Phone 573/883-7102.* (1818) A restored and furnished Federal-style stone house of an early fur trader. Guided tours are available. (Daily; closed holidays) **$**

Guibourd-Valle House. *1 N 4th St, Ste. Genevieve (63670). Phone 573/883-7544.* Late 18th-century restored vertical log house on stone foundation; French heirlooms. Attic with Norman truss and hand-hewn oak beams secured by wooden pegs. Courtyard; rose garden; stone well; costumed guides. (Apr-Oct: daily; Mar and Nov: weekends) **$$**

Ste. Genevieve Museum. *Merchant St and DuBourg Pl, Ste. Genevieve (63670). Phone 573/883-3461.* Display of salt manufacturing, the state's first industry. Scale model of rail car transfer boat, *Ste. Genevieve*, which carried trains across the Mississippi. Native American artifacts; local mementos. (Daily; closed holidays) **$**

Special Event

Jour de Fete a Ste. Genevieve. *Historic Area, Ste. Genevieve. 4 miles E via I-55, Hwy 32.Phone 573/883-7097.* Tours of historic French houses; art show, French market, antiques. Second weekend in Aug.

Specialty Lodging

The following lodging establishment is approved by Mobil Travel Guide, but due to its unique and individualized nature has not been given a traditional Mobil Star rating. Included in this listing you may find bed-and-breakfasts, limited-service inns, guest ranches, and other unique hotel properties.

SOUTHERN HOTEL BED & BREAKFAST. *146 S 3rd St, Ste. Genevieve (63670). Phone 573/883-3493; toll-free 800/275-1412; fax 573/883-9612.*

www.southernhotelbb.com. 8 rooms, 3 story. Children over 12 years only. Complimentary full breakfast. Check-in 4-6 pm, check-out 11 am. Built in 1791. **$**

Restaurants

★ **ANVIL SALOON.** *46 S 3rd St, Ste. Genevieve (63670). Phone 573/883-7323.* German, American menu. Lunch, dinner. Closed holidays. Bar. Oldest commercially operated building in the city (circa 1850); early Western saloon décor. **$$**

★ **OLD BRICK HOUSE.** *90 S 3rd St, Ste. Genevieve (63670). Phone 573/883-2724; fax 573/883-1020.* American menu. Breakfast, lunch, dinner. Closed Memorial Day, Labor Day, Dec 25. Bar. Children's menu. One of the first brick buildings (1785) west of the Mississippi. **$$**

Stockton (D-2)

Population 1,579
Elevation 965 ft
Area Code 417
Zip 65785
Information Chamber of Commerce, PO Box 410; phone 417/276-5213

Stockton is the seat of Cedar County. The Stockton Dam, located 2 miles from the town square, offers many recreational activities.

What to See and Do

Stockton State Park. *Hwy 215, Dadeville (65785). Phone 417/276-4259.* On the shore of 25,000-acre Stockton Lake, impounded by Stockton Dam. Swimming, fishing in stocked lake for bass, crappie, walleye, catfish, and bluegill; boating, canoeing; playground, lodging, restaurant, improved camping, laundry facilities. (Daily) **FREE**

Sullivan (C-5)

See also Rolla

Population 5,661
Elevation 987 ft
Area Code 573

Zip 63080
Information Chamber of Commerce, 2 W Springfield, PO Box 536; phone 573/468-3314
Web Site www.sullivanmo.com

What to See and Do

Jesse James Wax Museum. *I 44, exit 230, Stanton (63079). 5 miles E on I-44 Exit 230, on S Service Rd. Phone 573/927-5233.* Life-size wax figures of the James gang; $100,000 gun collection; personal belongings of notorious raiders of the Old West; antiques; doll collection. Guided tours. (June-Aug: daily; rest of year: weekends; closed Thanksgiving, Dec 25) **$$**

Meramec Caverns. *I-44, exit 230, Stanton (63079). 5 miles E on I-44, exit 230, then 3 miles S through La Jolla Park, follow signs. Phone 573/468-3166.* Cave used for gunpowder manufacture during the Civil War and by Jesse James as a hideout in the 1870s; five levels; lighted; concrete walks; 60° F; guided tours (one hour and 20 minutes). Picnicking. Camping; motel, restaurant, gift shop. Canoe rentals; boat rides. (Daily; closed Thanksgiving, Dec 25) **$$$$**

Meramec State Park. *2800 S Hwy 185, Sullivan (63080). 4 miles SE on Hwy 185, off I-44, exit 226. Phone 573/468-6072.* This is one of the largest and most scenic of the state's parks. In its more than 6,700 acres are 30 caves and many springs. Swimming on the Meramec River, fishing, boating (ramp, rentals), canoeing; hiking trails, picnicking, playground, dining lodge, camping (trailer hook-ups, dump station), cabins, motel, laundry facilities. Nature center, naturalist. Cave tours. (Daily) **$$**

Onondaga Cave State Park. *7556 Hwy H, Sullivan (65535). 10 miles SW on I-44, then 6 miles SE on County H, past Leasburg. Phone 573/245-6600.* Contains historical cave site in a 1,300-acre park. Picnicking, camping (fee). Visitor center. Cave tour (Mar-Oct, daily). Park (daily). **$$$**

Limited-Service Hotel

★ **SUPER 8.** *601 N Service Rd W, Sullivan (63080). Phone 573/468-8076; toll-free 800/800-8000; fax 573/468-8076. www.super8.com.* 60 rooms, 3 story. Pets accepted; fee. Check-out 11 am. **$**

University City (C-5)

Web Site www.ucitymo.org

Restaurants

★ **CICERO'S.** *6691 Delmar Blvd, University City (63130). Phone 314/862-0009; fax 314/862-4222. www.ciseros.com.* Italian menu. Lunch, dinner, late-night. Closed holidays. Bar. Children's menu. Outdoor seating. **$$**

★ **RIDDLE PENULTIMATE.** *6307 Delmar Blvd, University City (63130). Phone 314/725-6985; fax 314/725-1153. www.riddlescafe.com.* International/Fusion menu. Dinner, late-night. Closed Mon; holidays. Bar. Outdoor seating. **$$**

Van Buren (E-5)

See also Poplar Bluff

Population 893
Elevation 475 ft
Area Code 573
Zip 63965
Information Van Buren-Big Spring Area Chamber of Commerce, PO Box 356; phone 800/692-7582
Web Site www.semo.net/vanburen

A Ranger District office of the Mark Twain National Forest is located here.

What to See and Do

Clearwater Lake. *Hwy HH, Piedmont (63957). 12 miles E on Hwy 60, then 6 miles N on Hwy 34, then NE on County HH, near Piedmont. Phone 573/223-7777.* Formed by a dam on the Black River. Five different parks surround the lake. Swimming, water-skiing, fishing, hunting, boating (ramps, dock, rentals); nature and exercise trails, picnicking, camping (spring-fall, fee; electric hook-ups, dump stations). Nature trail paved for wheelchair access. Visitor center (May-Sept, limited hours). Park (daily) **FREE**

✪ **Ozark National Scenic Riverways.** *Van Buren. Off Hwy 60, reached from Hwy 17, 19, 21, or 106. Phone 573/323-4236.* More than 80,000 acres with 134 miles of riverfront along the Current and Jacks Fork rivers, both clear, free-flowing streams that are fed by numerous springs. Big Spring, south of town, is one of the largest single-outlet springs in the United States with a flow of 276 million gallons daily. Swimming, fishing, floating, boat trips (Memorial Day-Labor Day; some fees); picnicking, seven campgrounds (daily; fee). Cave tours (Memorial Day-Labor Day, daily; fee). Cultural demonstrations, including corn milling, at Alley Spring Mill; tours. There is a visitor center at Alley Spring Mill and in Van Buren on Highway 60, 6 miles West of Eminence on Highway 106 (Memorial Day-Labor Day, daily). Contact the Superintendent, Ozark National Scenic Riverways, PO Box 490.

Waynesville (D-4)

See also Lebanon, Rolla

Population 3,207
Elevation 805 ft
Area Code 573
Zip 65583
Information Waynesville/St. Robert Chamber of Commerce, 137 St. Robert Blvd, PO Box 6; phone 573/336-5121

Special Event

Christmas on the Square. *487 Mockingbird Ln, Waynesville (65583). Phone 573/335-5121.* Carolers, vendors, crafts, food. Sleigh rides. First Thurs in Dec.

Limited-Service Hotel

★ **BEST WESTERN MONTIS INN.** *14086 Hwy Z, St. Robert (65584). Phone 573/336-4299; toll-free 800/780-7234; fax 573/336-2872. www.bestwestern.com.* 45 rooms, 2 story. Pets accepted, some restrictions. Complimentary continental breakfast. Check-out noon. Outdoor pool. **$**
🐾 🏊

Webster Groves (C-5)

Restaurants

★ ★ **BIG SKY CAFE.** *47 S Old Orchard, Webster Groves (63119). Phone 314/962-5757; fax 314/962-6478. www.bigskycafe.net.* American menu. Dinner. Closed holidays. Bar. Outdoor seating. **$$**

★ **CRAVINGS.** *8149 Big Bend Blvd, Webster Groves (63119). Phone 314/961-3534; fax 314/961-9595.*

www.cravingsonline.com. American menu. Lunch, dinner. Closed Sun-Mon; holidays. Valet parking. **$$**

★ ★ **ZINNIA.** *7491 Big Bend Blvd, Webster Groves (63119). Phone 314/962-0572. www.ksdk.com.* American menu. Lunch, dinner. Closed Mon; holidays. Bar. Outdoor seating. **$$$**

Wentzville (C-5)

See also St. Charles, St. Louis

Population 5,088
Elevation 603 ft
Area Code 636
Zip 63385
Information Chamber of Commerce, 5 W Pearce, PO Box 11; phone 636/327-6914

Daniel Boone and his family were the first to settle in the area around Wentzville, which was named after Erasmus L. Wentz, principal engineer of the North Missouri Railroad. Between 1850 to 1880 the area was devoted to growing tobacco; the original Liggett and Myers Tobacco Company factory still stands in Wentzville.

What to See and Do

Cuivre River State Park. *678 St Rte 147, Troy (63379). 13 miles N on Hwy 61, then 3 miles E on Hwy 47 to Hwy 147. Phone 636/528-7247.* One of the state's largest and most natural parks, this 6,251-acre area contains rugged, wooded terrain, native prairie, and an 88-acre lake. Swimming, beach, fishing, boating (ramp); 30 miles of hiking and horseback riding trails, picnicking, camping (hook-ups, dump station). (Daily) **FREE**

Daniel Boone Home. *Wentzville. 5 miles SE via County Z, F, near Defiance. Phone 636/987-2221.* (Circa 1803) Built by Boone and his son Nathan, this stone house is where Boone died in 1820; restored and authentically furnished; museum. Guided tours. Picnicking, snack bar. (Mid-Mar-mid-Dec: daily; rest of year: Sat-Sun; closed Thanksgiving, Dec 25) **$$**

Limited-Service Hotel

★ ★ **HOLIDAY INN.** *900 Corporate Pkwy, Wentzville (63385). Phone 636/327-7001; toll-free 800/465-4329; fax 636/327-7019. www.holiday-inn.com.* 138 rooms, 4 story. Pets accepted, some restrictions;

fee. Check-out 1 pm. Restaurant, bar. Outdoor pool. **$**
🐾 ⌕

West Plains (E-4)

Settled 1840
Population 8,913
Elevation 1,007 ft
Area Code 417
Zip 65775
Information Greater West Plains Area Chamber of Commerce, 401 Jefferson Ave; phone 417/256-4433
Web Site www.wpchamber.com

Limited-Service Hotel

★ ★ **RAMADA INN.** *1301 Preacher Roe Blvd, West Plains (65775). Phone 417/256-8191; toll-free 800/272-6232; fax 417/256-8069. www.ramada.com.* 80 rooms, 2 story. Pets accepted; fee. Check-out noon. Restaurant, bar. Outdoor pool. **$**
🐾 ⌕

Weston (B-2)

See also Kansas City, St. Joseph

Settled 1837
Population 1,528
Elevation 800 ft
Area Code 816
Zip 64098
Information Information Center, 502 Main St, PO Box 53; phone 816/640-2909
Web Site www.ci.weston.mo.us

Before the Civil War, Weston was at its peak. Founded on whiskey, hemp, and tobacco, it rivaled St. Louis as a commercial trade center and promised to become a major US city. But disasters—fire, floods, and the Civil War—felled Weston's urban future. Today Weston, the first "district" west of the Mississippi entered into the National Register of Historic Sites, is a quiet town with more than 100 antebellum homes and other buildings.

What to See and Do

Historical Museum. *601 Main St, Weston (64098). Phone 816/640-2977.* On the site of the International Hotel built by stagecoach king and distillery founder

Benjamin Holladay. (Mid-Mar-mid-Dec, Tues-Sun; closed holidays) **FREE**

Lewis and Clark State Park. *801 Lakecrest Blvd, Weston (64484). 17 miles NW on Hwy 45 and Hwy 138. Phone 816/579-5564.* Approximately 120 acres on the southeast shore of Sugar Lake. Swimming, fishing, boating, canoeing; picnicking, playground, improved camping (dump station). (Daily) **FREE**

Snow Creek Ski Area. *1 Snow Creek Dr, Weston (64098). 5 miles N on Hwy 45 at Snow Creek Dr. Phone 816/386-2200. www.skipeaks.com/sc_home.* Two triple, double chairlift, rope tow; nine intermediate trails. Rentals; ski school, snowmaking. Lodge, restaurant. Vertical drop 300 feet. (Mid-Dec-mid-Mar, daily) **$$$$**

Specialty Lodging

The following lodging establishment is approved by Mobil Travel Guide, but due to its unique and individualized nature has not been given a traditional Mobil Star rating. Included in this listing you may find bed-and-breakfasts, limited-service inns, guest ranches, and other unique hotel properties.

INN AT WESTON LANDING. *526 Welt, Weston (64098). Phone 816/640-5788.* 4 rooms, 2 story. Complimentary full breakfast. Check-in 4-6 pm, check-out 11 am. Restaurant. Built atop the cellars of a former brewery (1842). Irish atmosphere; each room individually decorated. **$**

🄳

Restaurant

★ ★ **AMERICA BOWMAN.** *500 Welt St, Weston (64098). Phone 816/640-5235. www.westonmo.com.* Irish menu. Lunch, dinner. Closed Mon; holidays. Bar. Mid-19th-century Irish pub atmosphere. **$$**

Nebraska

In little more than a century, Nebraska—part of what was once called the "great American desert"—has evolved from a vast prairie occupied by Native Americans and buffalo to a farming, ranching, and manufacturing mainstay of America, with an ample variety of recreational and cultural opportunities.

Spaniards visited the region first, but it was on the basis of explorations by Father Marquette and Louis Jolliet in 1673 that French voyageurs, fur traders, and missionaries swept over the land and France claimed it. Nevertheless, it was recognized as Spanish land until 1800, when it became a plaything of European politics and was sold by Napoleon to the United States as part of the Louisiana Purchase in 1803. Famous pathfinders like John C. Frémont, Kit Carson, and the men who trapped for John Jacob Astor thought it a land unfit for cultivation.

Population: 1,578,385
Area: 77,358 square miles
Elevation: 840-5,424 feet
Peak: Near Bushnell (Kimball County)
Entered Union: March 1, 1867 (37th state)
Capital: Lincoln
Motto: Equality Before the Law
Nickname: Cornhusker State
Flower: Goldenrod
Bird: Western Meadowlark
Tree: Cottonwood
Fair: August in Lincoln
Time Zone: Central and Mountain
Web Site: www.visitnebraska.org
Fun Facts:
- Nebraska is the birthplace of the Reuben sandwich.
- Nebraska has more miles of river than any other state.
- The nationwide 911system of emergency communications was developed and first used in Lincoln, Nebraska.

Nebraska was the path for many westward-bound travelers. Native Americans, fur trappers and explorers, pioneers, the Pony Express, the Mormon and Oregon trails, the Overland Freight Company, and the railroads all made their way through the state, following the natural path of the Platte River. In 1854, Nebraska became a US territory along with Kansas. Febold Feboldson, the Paul Bunyan of the Great Plains, is said to be responsible for the perfectly straight southern boundary line with Kansas. According to the legend, he bred bees with eagles for 15 years until he had an eagle-sized bee. He then hitched the critter to a plow and made a beeline between the two states.

Farming is big business in southern and eastern Nebraska. With continually improving crop returns, Nebraska has few equals in total output of farm production. It is a leading producer of wild hay, beans, grain sorghum, sugar beets, wheat, soybeans, rye, corn, and alfalfa. Good grazing land can be found in the north central and northwest parts of the state. America's largest formation of stabilized sand dunes is located in the Sandhills, heart of Nebraska's nearly $5-billion cattle industry. Real cowboy country, the ranches of the Sandhills have given starts to many professional rodeo stars.

Within 13 years after being named a territory, statehood was approved by Congress; the town of Lincoln won the fight for the state capital over Omaha, and the Homestead Act opened the way for settlement. The Pawnee were often friendly with settlers but were devastated by the smallpox, cholera, and tuberculosis the settlers brought with them. Wars with the Native Americans ended by1890; by then

Calendar Highlights

MAY

Willa Cather Spring Conference (*Hastings*). *Willa Cather State Historic Site. Phone 402/746-2653.* Features a different Cather novel each year. Discussion groups, banquet, entertainment. Tour of "Cather Country."

JUNE

Cottonwood Prairie Festival (*Hastings*). *Brickyard Park. Phone toll-free 800/967-2189.* Music, crafts, food.

NCAA College Baseball World Series (*Omaha*). *Rosenblatt Stadium. Phone 402/444-4750.*

"NEBRASKAland DAYS" Celebration (*North Platte*). *Phone 308/532-7939.* Parades, entertainment, food, and the famous PRCA Rodeo.

JULY

Central Nebraska Ethnic Festival (*Grand Island*). *Phone 308/385-5455.* Music, dance, ethnic meals, dramatic presentations.

July Jamm (*Lincoln*). *Phone 402/434-6900.* Art show, music festival.

Oregon Trail Days (*Gering*). *Phone Scotts Bluff-Gering United Chamber of Commerce, 308/632-2133.* Parades, chili cook-off, contests, square dancing, barbecue, music festival.

AUGUST

Nebraska State Fair (*Lincoln*). *State Fair Park. Phone 402/474-5371.*

SEPTEMBER

The Light of the World Christmas Pageant (*Minden*). *Kearney County Courthouse, Town Square. Phone the Chamber of Commerce, 308/832-1811.* A town tradition for many years; highlight of outdoor pageant is illumination of courthouse dome by 10,000 lights.

River City Round-Up (*Omaha*). *Fairgrounds. Phone 402/554-9610.* Celebration of agriculture and western heritage includes parade, barbecues, trail rides.

---

the land was teeming with farms and ranches. Railroads were creating new towns for repairs and supplies, and the twin aids of irrigation and better stock pushed up farm profits.

The fine highway system makes it a pleasure to drive in the state. Several villages and towns settled by Old World immigrants still celebrate their ethnic heritage in folk festivals each year. Native Americans on the Santee, Winnebago, and Omaha reservations also keep their customs at annual powwows. Besides pioneer and Native American history, Nebraska offers a wealth of state parks and recreation areas. The angler has many well-stocked fishing streams and lakes from which to choose. For hunters, game birds, waterfowl, and deer are abundant, and seasons are long.

When to Go/Climate

Nebraska experiences the typically extreme temperatures of the Plains states. Winters are icy cold, summers stifling hot. The state is dry and prone to droughts; tornadoes are a summer reality. Fall and spring are good times to visit.

AVERAGE HIGH/LOW TEMPERATURES (° F)

Omaha

Jan 30/11	**May** 73/52	**Sept** 75/55
Feb 35/17	**June** 82/67	**Oct** 64/43
Mar 48/28	**July** 87/67	**Nov** 48/30
Apr 62/40	**Aug** 84/64	**Dec** 33/16

Scottsbluff

Jan 38/12	**May** 71/42	**Sept** 77/46
Feb 44/17	**June** 82/59	**Oct** 66/34
Mar 50/22	**July** 90/52	**Nov** 50/22
Apr 61/32	**Aug** 87/56	**Dec** 40/13

Parks and Recreation

Water-related activities, hiking, riding, various other sports, picnicking and visitor centers, as well as camping, are available in many areas. The state maintains 87 areas, including state parks, recreation areas, and historical parks; park-user permit required ($2.50/day, $14/year). Seven areas have cabins ($30-$210/night). Camping ($3-$13/site/night, plus $3 for electricity, at some parks), 14-day limit at most sites. Some facilities are open May-Sept only. Pets on leash only; health certificate required for pets of out-of-state owners. All mechanically powered boats must be registered. Cross-country skiing is a popular winter sport in the larger state parks. For detailed information contact Game and Parks Commission, Division of State Parks, PO Box 30370, Lincoln, 68503; or phone 402/471-0641.

FISHING AND HUNTING

Nonresident fishing permit: annual $45; three-day $14; aquatic stamp for all fishing permits $5. Nonresident small game hunting permit: $67; deer permit, $175; antelope permit, $130; wild turkey $65; habitat stamp for game birds, animals, and fur-bearing animals, $13.

Nebraska has 11,000 miles of streams and more than 3,300 lakes with trout, northern pike, walleye, sauger, white bass, striped bass, large and small mouth bass, catfish, bluegill, and crappie. Pheasant, quail, prairie chicken, wild turkey, sharp-tailed grouse, cottontail rabbit, squirrel, ducks, geese, antelope, and deer are available here also.

For details, write the Game and Parks Commission, PO Box 30370, Lincoln, 68503-0370; or phone 402/471-0641.

Driving Information

Safety belts are mandatory for all persons in the front seat of any 1973 or newer vehicle. Children under 5 years must be in approved passenger restraints anywhere in a vehicle: ages 4-5 may use regulation safety belts; under age 4 must use approved safety seats. Phone 402/471-2515.

INTERSTATE HIGHWAY SYSTEM

The following alphabetical listing of Nebraska towns shows that these cities are within 10 miles of the indicated interstate highways. Check a highway map for the nearest exit.

Highway Number	Cities/Towns within 10 Miles
Interstate 80	Cozad, Gothenburg, Grand Island, Kearney, Kimball, Lexington, Lincoln, North Platte, Ogallala, Omaha, Sidney, York.

Additional Visitor Information

The Department of Economic Development, Travel and Tourism Division, PO Box 98907, 7301 Centennial Mall S, Lincoln, 68509, phone 800/228-4307, supplies visitor information about the state; events, parks, hiking, biking, camping, and boating are some of the topics featured. *NEBRASKAland,* published monthly, is available from the Game and Parks Commission, PO Box 30370, Lincoln, 68503.

To aid the traveler, visitor centers are located at Melia Hill, off Interstate 80 between Omaha and Lincoln (daily) and at the Nebraska/Omaha Travel Information Center at 10th Street and Deer Park Boulevard (intersection of Interstate 80 and 13th St) in Omaha (May-Oct, daily). There are also 25 information centers at rest areas along Interstate 80 (June-Aug).

HOMESTEADING ALONG THE MISSOURI RIVER

Wooded river bluffs, historic towns, and Homestead National Monument are among the attractions of this drive through southeast Nebraska. Take Highway 77 from Lincoln south to Beatrice, the first of several charming small towns on this route. A few miles west of town, Homestead National Monument showcases a restored tallgrass prairie and explains the Homestead Act of 1862, which led to widespread settlement in the western United States. From Beatrice, drive east through the farmlands along Highway 136 to Auburn, a town known for its antique stores. Continue on to Brownville, which features a Missouri River History Museum aboard the dry-docked Captain Meriwether Lewis, and riverboat cruises aboard the Spirit of Brownville. From Brownville, backtrack to Auburn and head north on Highway 75 to Nebraska City, the birthplace of Arbor Day. Head west on Highway 34 north of Nebraska City to return to Lincoln. **(Approximately 180 miles)**

NEBRASKA FROM CRAZY HORSE TO CARHENGE

Vast, lightly populated, and filled with raw beauty, the Sandhills country of western Nebraska takes visitors by surprise. Start in North Platte with a visit to Buffalo Bill Ranch State Historical Park, which preserves the Western icon's home on the range. Head north on Highway 83 to the Nebraska National Forest; at 90,000 acres, it's the largest hand-planted forest in the country. Continue north to Valentine, set along the Niobrara River, a favorite for canoeing. Drive west on Highway 20 to Merriman, site of the Sandhills Ranch State Historical Park (still a working ranch despite its name), then on to Chadron to visit the Museum of the Fur Trade. Continue west to Fort Robinson State Park, where Crazy Horse died. The nearby Pine Ridge and Oglala National Grassland are great spots for horseback riding, mountain biking, and hiking. To return to civilization, take Highway 2 south from Crawford to Alliance, home to the famous "Carhenge" spoof on England's Stonehenge. From Alliance, head south on Highway 385 to pick up the Oregon Trail route at Bridgeport, or return to North Platte on Highway 2 east and Highway 83 south. **(Approximately 550 miles)**

Auburn (D-6)

See also Nebraska City

Population 3,443
Elevation 994 ft
Area Code 402
Zip 68305
Information Chamber of Commerce, 1211 J St; phone 402/274-3521
Web Site www.ci.auburn.ne.us

What to See and Do

⭐ **Brownville.** *9 miles E on Hwy 136.* Restored riverboat town of the 1800s. More than 30 buildings, many of which are open to the public.

Brownville State Recreation Area. *RR 1, Brownville (68305). Phone 402/883-2575.* Approximately 20 acres. Fishing; boat ramps. Picnicking. Camping. Entry permit required. **$**

Brownville Village Theater. *PO Box 95, Brownville (68321). Phone 402/825-4121.* Nebraska's oldest repertory theater; plays produced by Nebraska Wesleyan University in a converted church; eight weeks beginning on the last Sat in June. **$$$**

Captain Bailey Museum. *Brownsville.* (June-Aug: daily; May and Sept-Oct: weekends only) **$**

Carson House. Built by Richard Brown, founder of Brownville. Original 1864-1872 furnishings. (Memorial Day-Labor Day: daily; Apr-May and Sept-Oct: weekends) **$**

Depot. Museum. (May-Aug, daily) **FREE**

Land Office. Reproduction of the land office where Daniel Freeman filed for the first homestead in the United States; houses Tourist Center and Brownville Historical Society Headquarters. **FREE**

Missouri River History Museum. *Hwy 136, Auburn. Aboard the Captain Meriwether Lewis, former Corps of Engineers dredge, which has been drydocked and* restored. *Phone 402/825-3341. Contains exhibits on river history. (Memorial Day-Labor Day: daily; rest of year: weekends)* **$**

Old Dental Office. *(May-Aug, daily)* **FREE**

Schoolhouse Art Gallery. *(May-Sept, Sat-Sun)* **FREE**

Spirit of Brownville. *Departs from Brownville State Recreation Area. Phone 402/825-6441. Cruises (2 hours) on the Missouri River. (Mid-June-mid-Aug, Thurs-Sun)*

Indian Cave State Park. *RR 1, Shubert (68437). 9 miles E on Hwy 136, then 14 miles S on Hwy 67, then E on Hwy 64. Phone 402/883-2575.* On approximately 3,400 acres, including oak-covered Missouri River bluffs and the old St. Deroin townsite, which has been partially reconstructed; living history demonstrations. Fishing. Hiking trails (20 miles), horseback riding. Cross-country skiing, sledding. Picnicking. Primitive and improved camping (fee, dump station). Also here are ancient petroglyphs in Indian Cave; scenic overlooks of the river. Redbud trees bloom in profusion during spring. **$$**

Nemaha Valley Museum. *1423 19th St, Auburn (68305). Phone 402/274-3203.* Exhibits trace history of Nemaha County; period rooms; farm equipment. *(Tues-Sun afternoons)* **FREE**

Verdon Lake State Recreation Area. *RR 1, Shubert (68437). 17 miles S via Hwy 73, 75, then E on Hwy 73. Phone 402/883-2575.* Approximately 30 acres on a 33-acre lake. Fishing. Picnicking. Camping. Entry permit required. **$$**

Special Events

Nemaha County Fair. *Auburn fairgrounds. Phone 402/274-3521.* Early Aug.

Spring Festival with Antique Flea Market. *131 Main, Brownville. Phone 402/825-6001.* Memorial Day weekend.

Limited-Service Hotels

★ **AUBURN INN.** *517 J St, Auburn (68305). Phone 402/274-3143; toll-free 800/272-3143; fax 402/274-4404.* 36 rooms. Pets accepted, some restrictions; fee. Check-out 11 am. **$**

★ **PALMER HOUSE.** *1918 J St, Auburn (68305). Phone 402/274-3193; toll-free 800/272-3143; fax 402/274-4165.* 22 rooms. Pets accepted, some restrictions; fee. Check-out 11 am. **$**

Restaurant

★ **WHEELER INN.** *1905 J St, Auburn (68305). Phone 402/274-4931; fax 402/274-2500.* American menu. Dinner. Closed Sun; holidays. Bar. Casual attire. **$$**

Beatrice (D-5)

See also Fairbury, Homestead National Monument, Lincoln

Founded 1857
Population 12,354
Elevation 1,284 ft
Area Code 402
Zip 68310
Information Chamber of Commerce, 226 S 6th St; phone 402/223-2338 or toll-free 800/755-7745
Web Site www.beatricechamber.com

Beatrice (be-AT-riss), a prosperous farm and industrial community, was named for the daughter of Judge John Kinney, a member of the Nebraska Association that founded this settlement on the Blue River. Hollywood stars Harold Lloyd and Robert Taylor grew up in Beatrice.

What to See and Do

Gage County Historical Museum. *101 N 2nd St, Beatrice (68310). Phone 402/228-1679.* Local historical artifacts housed in former Burlington Northern Depot (1906). History and artifacts of all towns in the county are displayed. Artifacts of industry, medicine, agriculture, railroads, and rural life. Special exhibits (fee). Tours by appointment. *(June-Labor Day: Tues-Sun; rest of year: Tues-Fri, also Sun afternoons; closed holidays)* **FREE**

Special Events

Gage County Fair. *Fairgrounds, W Scott St, Beatrice. Phone 402/223-2338.* Late July.

Homestead Days. *Beatrice. Phone 402/223-2338.* Five-day event with pioneer theme. Demonstrations, parade. June.

Blair (C-6)

See also Fremont, Omaha; also see Missouri Valley, IA

Founded 1869
Population 6,860
Elevation 1,075 ft
Area Code 402
Zip 68008
Information Chamber of Commerce, 1526 Washington St; phone 402/533-4455
Web Site www.blairchamber.org

What to See and Do

Dana College. *2848 College Dr, Blair (68008). Phone 402/426-7216.* (1884) (500 students) Liberal arts school founded by Danish pioneers; campus includes Danish immigrant archives, gas lamps from Copenhagen and Hans Christian Andersen beech trees. Heritage and Lauritz Melchior memorial rooms in the library include complete collections of Royal Copenhagen and Bing & Grondahl Christmas plates (After Labor Day-mid-May: daily; early June-early Aug: Mon-Fri; closed holidays). On campus is

> **Tower of the Four Winds.** *Blair. Phone 402/533-4455.* Set on a hill overlooking Blair, the 44-foot tower displays a mosaic interpretation of a vision seen by Black Elk, an Oglala Sioux prophet and medicine man.

Fort Atkinson State Historical Park. *S 7th St and Madison St, Fort Calhoun. 1 mile E of Hwy 75 and Fort Calhoun. Phone 402/468-5611.* Ongoing reconstruction of military post established in 1820 (16 years after Lewis and Clark recommended the site) to protect the fur trade and secure the Louisiana Purchase; museum (late May-early Sept, daily). Park (daily). Visitors can watch the reconstruction of the old barracks. **$$**

Special Events

Gateway to the West Days. *1526 Washington St, Blair (68008). Phone 402/533-4455.* Carnival, parade, street dance. Mid-June.

Sights and Sounds of Christmas. *Dana College, 2848 College Dr, Blair (68008). Phone 402/426-9000.* Danish, German, French, American, and other ethnic Christmas customs, foods, traditions; smorgasbord (reservations required); concert in a setting of hundreds of poinsettias and evergreen trees, dramatic presentations. First weekend in Dec.

Limited-Service Hotel

★ **ECONO LODGE.** *1355 Hwy 30 S, Blair (68008). Phone 402/426-2340; fax 402/426-8703.* 32 rooms, 2 story. Pets accepted; fee. Check-out 11 am. **$**
🅳 🐾

Bridgeport (C-1)

See also Chimney Rock National Historic Site, Scottsbluff

Founded 1900
Population 1,581
Elevation 3,666 ft
Area Code 308
Zip 69336
Information Chamber of Commerce, 428 Main St, PO Box 640; phone 308/262-1825
Web Site www.bridgeport-ne.com

What to See and Do

Bridgeport State Recreation Area. *Bridgeport. W edge of town on Hwy 26.* Approximately 190 acres of sand pit lakes on the North Platte River. Swimming; fishing; boating (ramp). Hiking. Picnicking. Camping (dump station). **$$**

Carhenge. *Hwy 87, Alliance (69301). 38 miles N on Hwy 385. Phone 308/762-1520.* This 10-acre site is a roadside spoof on England's Stonehenge, made of more than 30 discarded cars.(Daily) **FREE**

Oregon Trail Wagon Train. *Bridgeport. 12 miles W via Hwy 26, Hwy 92. Phone 308/586-1850.* Re-creation of an 1840s wagon train, with authentic covered wagons. Chuck wagon cookouts, canoeing, camping, and one- and four-day wagon trips. Fees charged for meals, rentals, and activities; reservations necessary for evening events.

Broken Bow (C-4)

Founded 1882
Population 3,778
Elevation 2,475 ft
Area Code 308

Zip 68822
Information Chamber of Commerce, 444 S 8th Ave; phone 308/872-5691
Web Site www.brokenbow-ne.com

What to See and Do

Victoria Springs State Recreation Area. *Broken Bow. 21 miles NW on Hwy 2, then 7 miles E on Secondary Hwy 21A. Phone 308/749-2235.* Approximately 60 acres; mineral springs. Fishing; nonpower boating (rentals). Hiking. Picnicking. Camping (fee), shelters, rental cabins.

Limited-Service Hotel

★ **SUPER 8.** *840 W Hwy 20, Broken Bow (68822). Phone 308/872-6428; fax 308/872-5031. www.super8.com.* 32 rooms, 2 story. Complimentary continental breakfast. Check-out 11 am. **$**

Chadron (A-1)

See also Crawford

Founded 1885
Population 5,588
Elevation 3,380 ft
Information Chamber of Commerce, 706 W Third St, PO Box 646; phone 308/432-4401 or toll-free 800/603-2937
Web Site www.chadron.com

Starting point of a sensational 1,000-mile horse race to Chicago in 1893, Chadron saw nine men leave in competition for a $1,000 prize. Doc Middleton, former outlaw, was one of the starters, but John Berry beat him to the door of Buffalo Bill's Wild West Show in 13 days and 16 hours. The headquarters and a Ranger District office of the Nebraska National Forest and headquarters of the Oglala National Grasslands are located here.

What to See and Do

Chadron State College. *1000 Main St, Chadron (69337). Phone 308/432-6000.* (1911) (3,600 students) Tours. Planetarium, museum open to public by appointment.

Chadron State Park. *15951 Hwy 385, Chadron (69337). 9 miles S on Hwy 385. Phone 308/432-6167.* Approximately 950 acres; scenic pine ridge, lagoon, creek. Swimming pool (daily; fee); fishing; paddleboats (rentals). Hiking, horseback riding. Cross-country skiing. Picnicking, playground. Camping (dump station, hookups, standard fees), cabins. Scenic drives. **$$**

Museum of the Fur Trade. *6321 Hwy 20, Chadron (69337). 3 1/2 miles E on Hwy 20. Phone 308/432-3843.* Displays depict the history of the North American fur trade from 1500-1900; fine gun collection; Native American exhibits. Restored trading post (1837) and storehouse used by James Bordeaux, a French trader; garden of primitive crops. (Memorial Day-Sept: daily; rest of year: by appointment) **$$**

Nebraska National Forest. *125 N Main St, Chadron (69337). S off Hwy 20. Phone 308/432-0300.* Fishing, hunting. Picnicking. Camping. (See THEDFORD and Samuel R. McKelvie National Forest, VALENTINE).

Walgreen Lake State Recreation Area. *Chadron. 20 miles SE via Hwy 20, then 2 miles S via Hwy 87.* Approximately 80 acres on a 50-acre lake. According to legend, a Loch Ness-type creature inhabits the Sandhills Lake here. Fishing; boating (nonpower or electric). Picnicking. Camping. Standard hours, fees.

Special Events

Dawes County Fair. *Dawes County Fairgrounds, Chadron. Phone 308/432-3373.* Five days in early Aug.

Fur Trade Days. *Main St, Chadron. Phone 308/432-3149.* Three days in early July.

Ride the Ridge. *16524 Hwy 385, Chadron (69337). Phone 308/432-4475.* 12-mile trail ride through scenic Pine Ridge. Catered meal and ranch rodeo at the end of the ride. July.

Limited-Service Hotels

★ **BEST WESTERN WEST HILLS INN.** *1100 W 10th St, Chadron (69337). Phone 308/432-3305; toll-free 877/432-3305; fax 308/432-5990. www.bestwestern.com.* 66 rooms, 2 story. Pets accepted, some restrictions. Complimentary continental breakfast. Check-out 11 am. Fitness room. Indoor pool, whirlpool. **$**

★ **SUPER 8.** *840 W Hwy 20, Chadron (69337). Phone 308/432-4471; fax 308/432-3991. www.super8.com.* 45 rooms, 2 story. Check-out 11 am. Indoor pool, whirlpool. **$**

Chimney Rock National Historic Site (B-1)

See also Bridgeport, Gering, Scottsbluff

13 miles W of Bridgeport off Hwy 26, Hwy 92.

Web Site www.nps.gov/chro

A landmark of the Oregon Trail, Chimney Rock rises almost 500 feet above the south bank of the North Platte River. Starting as a cone-shaped mound, it becomes a narrow 150-foot column towering above the landscape. For early travelers, many of whom sketched and described it in their journals, Chimney Rock marked the end of the prairies. It became a National Historic Site in 1956. Visitor center (fee).

Columbus (C-5)

Founded 1856
Population 19,480
Elevation 1,449 ft
Area Code 402
Information Chamber of Commerce, 764 33rd Ave, PO Box 515, 68601; phone 402/564-2769
Web Site www.ci.columbus.ne.us

Named by its founders for Ohio's capital, Columbus has become a center of industry, agriculture, and statewide electrical power.

What to See and Do

Parks. Pawnee Park. *S on Hwy 30, 81. Phone 402/564-0914.* Swimming pool. Ball fields, tennis. Picnicking facilities, playground on 130 acres along Loup River. Quincentenary bell tower dedicated to Columbus's voyage to the new world. **Lake North and Loup Park.** *4 miles N on Monastery Rd. Phone 402/564-3171.* Swimming, water-skiing; fishing; boating (ramps, docks). Picnicking. Camping. **Wilkinson Wildlife Management Area.** *SE of Platte Center/NW of Columbus. Phone 402/471-0641.* 630 acres of permanent wetland area. Hiking; fishing and hunting. **FREE**

Platte County Historical Society. *2916 16th St, Columbus (68601). 29th Ave and 16th St. Phone 402/564-1856.* Exhibits on local history; period schoolroom, barbershop; research library; cultural center. (Apr-mid-Oct, Fri-Sun) **$**

Special Events

Columbus Days. *Columbus. Phone 402/564-2769.* Mid-Aug.

Horse racing. *Agricultural Park, 822 15th St, Columbus (68601). Phone 402/564-0133.* Pari-mutuel betting. Late July-early Sept.

Platte County Fair. *Agricultural Park, 2610 14th St, Columbus (68601). Phone 402/563-4901.* Mid-July.

Limited-Service Hotels

★ ★ **NEW WORLD INN & CONFERENCE CENTER.** *265 33rd Ave, Columbus (68601). Phone 402/564-1492; toll-free 800/433-1492; fax 402/563-3989. www.newworldinn.com.* 140 rooms, 2 story. Check-out noon. Restaurant, bar. Indoor pool, whirlpool. Airport transportation available. Indoor courtyard. **$**
⚓

★ **SUPER 8.** *3324 20th St, Columbus (68601). Phone 402/563-3456; fax 402/563-3456. www.super8.com.* 63 rooms, 2 story. Check-out 11 am. **$**

Cozad (C-3)

See also Gothenburg, Lexington

Population 3,823
Elevation 2,490 ft
Area Code 308
Zip 69130
Information Chamber of Commerce, 211 W 8th St, PO Box 14; phone 308/784-3930
Web Site www.ci.cozad.ne.us

Cozad is headquarters for a number of industries, as well as a shipping and agricultural center known for the production of alfalfa.

What to See and Do

Gallagher Canyon State Recreation Area. *Hwys 751 and 424, Cozad (69130). 8 miles S on Hwy 21. Phone 308/784-3907.* Approximately 20 acres of park surround 400 acres of water. Fishing; boating (ramp). Hiking. Picnicking. Camping. Standard hours, fees.

Robert Henri Museum and Historical Walkway. *112 E 8th St, Cozad (69130). Phone 308/784-4154.* Museum occupies the childhood home of artist Robert Henri, founder of the Ash Can School, and former hotel built by Henri's father. Other historic buildings along the walkway are an original Pony Express station, a pioneer school and an early 20th-century church. (Memorial Day-Sept, Tues-Sat, also by appointment) **$**

Limited-Service Hotel

★ ★ **CIRCLE S BEST VALUE INN.** *440 S Meridian St, Cozad (69130). Phone 308/784-2290; toll-free 800/237-5852; fax 308/784-3917.* 49 rooms, 2 story. Pets accepted, some restrictions; fee. Check-out 11 am. Restaurant. Outdoor pool. **$**

Restaurant

★ **CROSSROADS.** *128 E 8th, Cozad (69130). Phone 308/784-2080.* Breakfast, lunch, dinner. Closed holidays. **$**

Crawford (B-1)

See also Chadron

Founded 1885
Population 1,115
Elevation 3,673 ft
Area Code 308
Zip 69339
Information Chamber of Commerce, PO Box 145; phone 308/665-1817
Web Site www.crawfordnebraska.com

What to See and Do

⭐ **Fort Robinson State Park.** *3200 Hwy 20, Crawford (69339). 3 miles W on Hwy 20. Phone 308/665-2660.* Approximately 22,000 acres of pine-covered hills; rocky buttes. Fort established in 1874 in the midst of Native American fighting (the Sioux leader, Crazy Horse, was killed here). Swimming pool (fee); fishing. Hiking, horseback riding. Cross-country skiing. Picnicking, restaurant, lodge (see LIMITED-SERVICE HOTEL). Camping (dump station), cabins. Post Playhouse; stagecoach and jeep rides (daily, summer); cookouts. Displays herds of buffalo. Park entry permit required. Also here are

Fort Robinson Museum. *Phone 308/665-2919.* Main museum located in former headquarters building (1905); authentic costumes and weapons of Native Americans and soldiers. Other exhibit buildings include a 1874 guardhouse, 1904 harness repair, 1906 blacksmith and 1900 wheelwright shops, 1887 adobe officer quarters and 1908 veterinary hospital. Site of Red Cloud Indian Agency (1873-1877). Guided tours (Memorial Day-Labor Day). Museum (Memorial Day-Labor Day: daily; rest of the year: Mon-Fri). Maintained by the State Historical Society. **$**

Trailside Museum. *Phone 308/665-2929.* Exhibits of natural history from Fort Robinson area. Museum also offers natural history tours of the area and daily science field trips to Toadstool Park and fossil sites (fee). (Memorial Day-Labor Day: daily; May: Wed-Sun). Operated by University of Nebraska State Museum. **DONATION**

Nebraska National Forest. *125 N Main St, Chadron (69337). 8 miles S on NE 2. Phone 308/432-0300. www.fs.fed.us/r2/nebraska.* (see CHADRON)

Oglala National Grassland. *16524 Hwy 385, Chadron (69337). 10 miles N via Hwy 2, 71. Phone 308/432-4475.* Nearly 95,000 acres of prairie grasses in the badlands of northwestern Nebraska, popular for hunting (in season), hiking, and backpacking.

Limited-Service Hotel

★ ★ **FORT ROBINSON LODGE.** *3200 W Hwy 20, Crawford (69339). Phone 308/665-2900; fax 308/665-2906.* 53 rooms, 2 story. Closed late Nov-mid-Apr. Check-out 11 am. Restaurant. Indoor pool. Tennis. Access to facilities of state park. **$**

Crofton (A-5)

See also Vermillion, Yankton

Population 820
Elevation 1,440 ft
Area Code 402
Zip 68730
Information Chamber of Commerce, PO Box 81; phone 402/388-4385
Web Site www.crofton-ne.com

What to See and Do

Lewis and Clark Lake State Recreation Area. *43349 South Dakota Hwy 52, Crofton (68730). 9 miles N via Hwy 121.* Phone 605/668-2985. Approximately 1,300 acres with a 7,982-acre lake. Six separate recreation areas on Lewis and Clark Trail. Swimming; fishing; boating (ramps). Picnicking. Tent and trailer camping (dump station).

Fairbury (D-5)

See also Beatrice

Population 4,335
Area Code 402
Zip 68352
Information Chamber of Commerce, 515 4th St, PO Box 274; phone 402/729-3000
Web Site www.fairbury.com

What to See and Do

Alexandria Lakes State Recreation Area. *Fairbury. 12 miles W via Hwy 136, then 3 1/2 miles N on Hwy 53.* Phone 402/729-3000. Approximately 50 acres with 46 acres of water. Swimming; fishing; boating (no motors). Picnicking, concession. Camping (dump station).

Rock Creek Station State Historical Park. *57415 710th Rd, Fairbury (68352). 5 1/2 miles E, 1 mile S on marked country roads.* Phone 402/729-5777. Located on the site of the Pony Express station and Oregon Trail ruts. Reconstructed post office and ranch buildings, picnic area and visitors center with interpretive material and slide presentation. Hiking, nature trails. Picnicking, playground. Camping. (Daily) **$$**

Special Event

Fairbury Fest. *518 E St, Fairbury (68352).* Phone 402/729-3000. Parade, crafts, dances. Early Sept.

Limited-Service Hotel

★ **CAPRI MOTEL.** *1100 14th St, Fairbury (68352).* Phone 402/729-3317. 36 rooms. Complimentary continental breakfast. Check-out 11 am. **$**

Fremont (C-6)

See also Blair, Omaha

Founded 1856
Population 23,680
Elevation 1,198 ft
Area Code 402
Information Fremont Area Chamber of Commerce & Dodge County Convention and Visitors Bureau, 605 N Broad St, PO Box 182, 68026-0182; phone 402/753-6414 or toll-free 800/727-8323
Web Site www.visitdodgecountyne.org

This town was named for John C. Frémont, Union general in the Civil War, who ran for president of the United States. In the town's early days, the crops were so bad that lots sold for 75¢ each. Finally, travelers on the Overland Trail brought in enough trade that the town began to prosper and grow. Midland Lutheran College gives a collegiate atmosphere to an otherwise industrial town, chiefly involved in food processing and retail trade.

What to See and Do

Fremont and Elkhorn Valley Railroad. *1835 N Somers Ave, Fremont (68025).* Phone 402/727-0615. Train rides to Nickerson and Hooper aboard vintage rail cars. Reservations recommended. (Schedule varies) **$$$$**

Fremont Dinner Train. *1835 N Somers Ave, Fremont (68025).* Phone 402/727-8321; toll-free 800/942-7245. Two restored 1940s rail cars make 30-mile round trips through Elkhorn Valley. Dinner and varied entertainment. (Sat-Sun, also some holidays) **$$$$**

Fremont State Recreation Area. *2351 County Road 18, Ames (68621). 3 miles W on Hwy 30.* Phone 402/727-3290. Approximately 660 acres with 22 lakes. Swimming; fishing; boating (ramp, rentals). Picnicking, concession. Tent and trailer sites (dump station). (Apr-mid-Oct) **$$**

Louis E. May Historical Museum. *1643 N Nye Ave, Fremont (68025).* Phone 402/721-4515. (1874). The 25-room house of Fremont's first mayor; oak and mahogany paneling, art glass windows, rooms furnished in late 19th-century style. (May-Aug and Dec: Wed-Sun; Apr and Sept-Oct: Wed-Sat; closed Jan 1, Thanksgiving, Dec 25) **$$**

Special Events

Homesteaders Fair. *1643 N Nye, Fremont. Phone 402/ 721-4515.* Festivities include a parade, carnival, and an ice cream social. Early Oct.

John C. Frémont Days. *Downtown, Fremont. Phone 402/727-9428.* Balloon race, train rides, historical reenactments, barbecue. Mid-July.

Limited-Service Hotels

★ **COMFORT INN.** *1649 E 23rd St, Fremont (68025). Phone 402/721-1109; fax 402/721-1109. www.choicehotels.com.* 48 rooms, 2 story. Pets accepted; fee. Complimentary continental breakfast. Check-out 11 am. Indoor pool, whirlpool. **$**

★ ★ **HOLIDAY LODGE.** *1220 E 23rd St, Fremont (68025). Phone 402/727-1110; toll-free 800/743-7666; fax 402/727-4579.* 100 rooms, 2 story. Pets accepted, some restrictions; fee. Check-out noon. Restaurant, bar. Fitness room. Indoor pool, whirlpool. **$**

Gering (B-1)

See also Chimney Rock National Historic Site, Scotts Bluff National Monument, Scottsbluff

Population 7,946
Elevation 3,914 ft
Information Scottsbluff-Gering United Chamber of Commerce, 1517 Broadway, Suite 104, Scottsbluff 69361; phone 308/632-2133 or toll-free 800/788-9475
Web Site www.gering.org

What to See and Do

North Platte Valley Museum. *11th St and J St, Gering (69341). Phone 308/436-5411.* Sod house (1889), log house (1890), items and literature of local historical interest. (May-Sept: daily; rest of year: by appointment) **$**

Special Events

Oregon Trail Days. *Gering. Phone 308/632-2133.* Parades, chili cook-off, contests, square dancing, barbecue, music festival. Four days in mid-July.

Sugar Valley Rally. *Gering. Phone 308/632-2133.* Gathering of antique automobiles; precision driving contest. Early June.

Gothenburg (C-3)

See also Cozad, Lexington, North Platte

Population 3,232
Elevation 2,567 ft
Area Code 308
Zip 69138
Information Chamber of Commerce, 1021 Lake Ave, PO Box 263; phone 308/537-3505 or toll-free 800/ 482-5520
Web Site www.ci.gothenburg.ne.us

What to See and Do

Pony Express Station. *Ehmen Park, 15th St, Gothenburg. Phone 308/537-3505.* (1854). Pony Express station 1860-1861; later a stop for the Overland Stage; memorabilia, artifacts. (May-Sept, daily) Carriage rides (fee). **FREE**

Special Events

Harvest Festival. *1021 Lake St, Gothenburg (69138). Phone 308/537-3505.* Art show, contests, antique farm machinery. Third week of Sept.

Pony Express Rodeo. *Rodeo Grounds, Gothenburg. Phone 308/537-3505.* Carnival, barbeque, "mutton busting." July 4 weekend.

Grand Island (C-4)

See also Hastings, Kearney, York

Founded 1857
Population 39,386
Elevation 1,870 ft
Area Code 308
Information Grand Island/Hall County Convention & Visitors Bureau, 309 W 2nd St, PO Box 1486, 68802; phone 308/382-4400 or toll-free 800/658-3178
Web Site www.visitgrandisland.com

Named by French trappers for a large island in the Platte River, the town was moved 5 miles north in 1869 to its present location on the Union Pacific Railroad, which dominated Grand Island's early existence. Traditionally a trade center for a rich irrigated agriculture and livestock region, the city now has diversified industry, including meat and food processing, agricultural and irrigation equipment, and mobile homes.

What to See and Do

Crane Meadows Nature Center. *9325 S Alda Rd, Wood River (68883). S side of Exit 305 on I-80. Phone 308/382-1820.* Educational center features exhibits and programs about Platte River habitat. Five miles of public nature trails. (Daily; closed holidays) **$$**

Fonner Park. *700 E Stolley Park Rd, Grand Island (68801). Phone 308/382-4515.* Thoroughbred racing. Pari-mutuel betting. **$**

Island Oasis Water Park. *321 Fonner Park Rd, Grand Island (68801). Phone 308/385-5381.* The 6-acre park has four water slides, a wave pool, children's pool, lazy river. Sand volleyball; concessions. (Memorial Day-Labor Day, daily) **$$**

Mormon Island State Recreation Area. *7425 S Hwy 281, Grand Island (68832). 10 miles S via Hwy 34, 281. Phone 308/385-6211.* Approximately 90 acres; 61 water acres on Mormon Trail. Swimming; fishing; boating (nonpower or electric). Picnicking. Tent and trailer sites (dump station).

⭐ **Stuhr Museum of the Prairie Pioneer.** *3133 W Hwy 34, Grand Island (68801). 4 miles N of I-80 at junction Hwy 281 and Hwy 34. Phone 308/385-5316.* Museum, on 200 acres situated on an island surrounded by a man-made lake, was designed by Edward Durell Stone. (Daily; closed Jan 1, Thanksgiving, Dec 25) **$$** Included are

   Antique Auto and Farm Machinery Exhibit. *Hwy 281 and Hwy 34, Grand Island (68801). Phone 308/382-4400.* More than 200 items on display, including many steam tractors. (May-mid-Oct, daily)

   Gus Fonner Memorial Rotunda. *Hwy 281 and Hwy 34, Grand Island (68801). Phone 308/382-4400.* Native American and Old West collections of Gus Fonner. (Daily)

   Railroad Town. *Hwy 281 and Hwy 34, Grand Island (68801). Phone 308/382-4400.* Turn-of-the-century outdoor museum contains 60 original buildings, including three houses; the cottage where Henry Fonda was born; schoolhouse, newspaper office, bank, post office, hotel, country church, depot

and railstock; blacksmith, shoe and barber shops. (May-mid-Oct, daily)

Special Events

Central Nebraska Ethnic Festival. *100 E 1st St, Grand Island (68801). Phone 308/385-5444.* Music, dance, ethnic meals, dramatic presentations. Fourth weekend in July.

Harvest of Harmony Festival & Parade. *Grand Island. Phone 308/382-9210.* Band and queen competitions. First Sat in Oct.

Husker Harvest Days. *Cornhusker Army Ammunition Plant, 309 W 2nd St, Grand Island (68801). Hwy 30 W. Phone 308/382-9210. www.huskerharvestdays.com.* Agricultural exhibits, techniques, and equipment used in irrigation. Mid-Sept.

Limited-Service Hotels

★ **DAYS INN.** *2620 N Diers Ave, Grand Island (68803). Phone 308/384-8624; toll-free 888/384-8624; fax 308/384-1626. www.daysinn.com.* 63 rooms, 2 story. Complimentary continental breakfast. Check-out 11 am. **$**

★ ★ **HOLIDAY INN.** *2503 S Locust St, Grand Island (68801). Phone 308/384-1330; toll-free 800/548-5542; fax 308/382-4615. www.holiday-inn.com.* 199 rooms, 2 story. Check-out noon. Restaurant, bar. Children's pool, whirlpool. **$**
🛋

★ ★ **HOWARD JOHNSON.** *3333 Ramada Rd, Grand Island (68801). Phone 308/384-5150; fax 308/384-6551. www.hojo.com.* 181 rooms, 2 story. Pets accepted; fee. Complimentary continental breakfast. Check-out noon. Restaurant, bar. Indoor pool, whirlpool. **$**
🐾 🛋

Restaurant

★ **HUNAN.** *2249 N Webb Rd, Grand Island (68803). Phone 308/384-6964; fax 308/384-0227. www.hunan.com.* Chinese menu. Lunch, dinner. Closed Dec 25. Bar. **$$**

Hastings (D-4)

See also Grand Island

Founded 1872
Population 22,837
Elevation 1,931 ft
Area Code 402
Information Convention & Visitors Bureau, 100 N Shore Dr, PO Box 941, 68902; phone 402/461-2370 or toll-free 800/967-2189
Web Site www.visithastingsnebraska.com

Hastings came into being almost overnight when two railroad lines crossed. Within eight years of its founding, its population swelled to almost 3,000. After 75 years as a depot and supply center, the town turned out large quantities of ammunition during World War II and the Korean Conflict.

What to See and Do

Crystal Lake State Recreation Area. *Ayr. 10 miles S on Hwy 281. Phone 402/461-2370.* Approximately 30 acres surrounding a 30-acre lake. Swimming; fishing; boating (nonpower or electric). Picnicking. Camping, trailer pads. Standard hours, fees.

Hastings Museum. *1330 N Burlington Ave, Hastings (68901). Phone 402/461-2399.* Includes natural science, pioneer history, Native American lore, bird displays; guns, antique cars, horse-drawn vehicles; sod house, country store, coin room. (Daily; closed Thanksgiving, Dec 24-Dec 25) J. M. McDonald Planetarium, sky shows (daily). Lied Superscreen Theatre (fee). **$$**

Lake Hastings. *Hastings. 1 mile N off Hwy 281.* Waterskiing; fishing; boating. Picnicking. (May-Sept, daily)

Willa Cather State Historic Site. *413 N Webster St, Red Cloud (68970). 38 miles S via Hwy 281 on Webster St (branch museum of Nebraska State Historical Society). Phone 402/746-2653.* Author's letters, first editions, photos; Cather family memorabilia; art gallery; research library; bookstore. (Daily; closed holidays) Other buildings include Cather childhood home, Red Cloud depot, St. Juliana Falconieri Catholic Church, Grace Episcopal Church, and *My Antonia* farmhouse. Tours of properties (four times daily). (See SPECIAL EVENTS) **$$**

Special Events

Cottonwood Festival. *Brickyard Park, Woodland and D St, Hastings (68901). Phone 402/461-2368.* Music, crafts, foods. Mid-June.

Kool-Aid Days. *Downtown, 100 N Shore Dr, Hastings (68902). Phone 402/462-4877.* World's largest Kool-Aid stand. Free games and prizes. Mid-Aug.

Oregon Trail PRCA Rodeo. *947 S Baltimore Ave, Hastings (68901). Phone 402/462-3247.* Labor Day weekend.

Willa Cather Spring Conference. *Willa Cather State Historic Site, 326 N Webster, Red Cloud (68970). Phone 402/746-2653.* Features change each year. Discussion groups, banquet, entertainment. Tour of "Cather Country." First weekend in May.

Limited-Service Hotels

★ ★ **HOLIDAY INN.** *2205 Osborne Dr E, Hastings (68901). Phone 402/463-6721; toll-free 888/905-1200; fax 402/463-6874. www.holiday-inn.com.* 100 rooms, 2 story. Pets accepted. Check-out 11 am. Restaurant, bar. Indoor pool, whirlpool. **$**

★ **SUPER 8.** *2200 N Kansas Ave, Hastings (68901). Phone 402/463-8888; fax 402/463-8899. www.super8.com.* 50 rooms, 2 story. Pets accepted, some restrictions. Check-out 11 am. **$**

Restaurants

★ **BERNARDO'S STEAK HOUSE.** *1109 S Baltimore, Hastings (68901). Phone 402/463-4666.* Steak menu. Lunch, dinner. Closed holidays. Bar. Children's menu. **$**

★ ★ **TAYLOR'S STEAKHOUSE.** *1609 N Kansas, Hastings (68901). Phone 402/462-8000; fax 402/462-8832. www.taylorssteakhouseandcatering.com.* Steak menu. Dinner. Closed Jan 1, Dec 25. Bar. Children's menu. **$$$**

Homestead National Monument (D-5)

See also Beatrice

4 miles NW, just off Hwy 4.

Web Site www.nps.gov/home

This is one of the first sites claimed under the terms of the Homestead Act of 1862. A quarter section, 160 acres, went for a nominal fee to citizens who lived and worked on it for five years; eventually, grants equaling the combined states of Texas and Louisiana were made. Set aside in 1939, the site is a memorial to the pioneer spirit that began cultivation of the West.

At the Brownville Land Office, Daniel Freeman filed Application No. 1 under the act for this land, built a log cabin and, later, a brick house. A surviving homesteader's cabin similar to Freeman's has been moved to the grounds and furnished as an exhibit. Visitors may take a self-guided tour (2 1/2 miles) of the area. Many other historical items are on display in the visitor center museum. Freeman School, 1/4 mile west of the visitor center, is a one-room brick schoolhouse restored to turn-of-the-century appearance; it commemorates the role of education in frontier society. The homestead story is explained in detail. Camping nearby. (Daily; closed Jan 1, Thanksgiving, Dec 25) Phone 402/223-3514.

Kearney (C-4)

See also Grand Island, Lexington, Minden

Founded 1873
Population 24,396
Elevation 2,153 ft
Area Code 308
Zip 68848
Information Visitors Bureau, 1007 2nd Ave; phone 308/237-3101 or toll-free 800/652-9435
Web Site www.kearneycoc.org

Kearney (CAR-nee) is named for the frontier outpost Fort Kearny. It is one of the largest migratory bird flyways in the world, a temporary home for millions of species.

What to See and Do

Fort Kearny State Historical Park. *1020 V Rd, Kearney (68847). 4 miles S on Hwy 10, 3 miles W on link 50A. Phone 308/865-5305.* The first Fort Kearny was erected at Nebraska City in 1846; it was moved here in 1848 to protect the Oregon Trail. In the park are a restored 1864 stockade, sod blacksmith-carpenter shop, museum, and interpretive center (Memorial Day-Labor Day, daily). Swimming; fishing; electric boating. Hiking and bicycling on nature trail (approximately 1 1/2 miles) along the Platte River. Picnicking. Campground (fee, dump station). **$$**

Museum of Nebraska Art. *2401 Central Ave, Kearney (68847). Phone 308/865-8559.* Collection of paintings, sculptures, drawings, and prints created by Nebraskans or with Nebraska as the subject. (Tues-Sat, Sun afternoons; closed holidays) **FREE**

Trails and Rails Museum. *710 W 11th St, Kearney (68847). Phone 308/234-3041.* Restored 1898 depot, 1880s freighters' hotel, 1871 country schoolhouse; displays of pioneer trails and rails, exhibits in baggage room; steam engine, flat car, caboose. (Memorial Day-Labor Day: daily; rest of year: by appointment) **FREE**

University of Nebraska at Kearney. *905 W 25th St, Kearney (68847). Phone 308/865-8441.* (1905) (10,000 students) Offers undergraduate, graduate, and specialist degrees. Two art galleries, planetarium; theater productions, concerts; campus tours. Also here is

> **George W. Frank House.** *W Hwy 30, Kearney. Phone 308/865-8284.* (1889). Three-story mansion with Tiffany window; turn-of-the-century showplace and center of the city's social life. (June-Aug, Tues-Sun)

Limited-Service Hotels

★ ★ **BEST WESTERN INN OF KEARNEY.** *1010 3rd Ave, Kearney (68845). Phone 308/237-5185; toll-free 800/359-1894; fax 308/234-1002. www.best western.com.* 62 rooms, 2 story. Pets accepted; fee. Complimentary full breakfast. Check-out noon. Restaurant. Fitness room. Outdoor pool, children's pool, whirlpool. **$**

★ ★ **HOLIDAY INN.** *110 S 2nd Ave, Kearney (68848). Phone 308/237-5971; fax 308/236-7549. www.holiday-inn.com.* 163 rooms, 2 story. Check-out 11 am. Restaurant, bar. Fitness room. Indoor pool, whirlpool. **$**

★ ★ **RAMADA INN.** *301 2nd Ave, Kearney (68847). Phone 308/237-3141; toll-free 800/652-1909; fax 308/234-4675.* 210 rooms, 2 story. Pets accepted, some restrictions; fee. Complimentary continental breakfast. Check-out 11 am. Restaurant, bar. Indoor pool, children's pool, whirlpool. **$**

Restaurants

★ ★ **ALLEY ROSE.** *2013 Central Ave, Kearney (68847). Phone 308/234-1261; fax 308/237-7468.* Lunch, dinner. Closed Jan 1, Dec 25. Bar. Children's menu. **$$**

★ ★ **GRANDPA'S STEAK HOUSE.** *13 Central Ave, Kearney (68847). Phone 308/237-2882.* Steak menu. Lunch, dinner. Closed holidays. Bar. Children's menu. **$$**

Kimball (C-1)

See also Sidney

Population 2,574
Elevation 4,709 ft
Area Code 308
Zip 69145
Information Chamber of Commerce, 119 E 2nd St; phone 308/235-3782
Web Site www.ci.kimball.ne.us

What to See and Do

Recreation. Oliver Reservoir. *8 miles W on Hwy 30.* Swimming, waterskiing; fishing; boating; picnicking. Camping. **Gotte Park.** *E on Hwy 30.* Swimming pool. Tennis. Picnicking, playground. In the park is a Titan I missile.

Lexington (C-3)

See also Cozad, Gothenburg, Kearney

Founded 1872
Population 6,601
Elevation 2,390 ft
Area Code 308
Zip 68850
Information Lexington Area Chamber of Commerce, 709 E Pacific Ave, PO Box 97; phone 308/324-5504 or toll-free 888/966-0564
Web Site www.ci.lexington.ne.us

Originally a frontier trading post and settlement along the Oregon Trail, Plum Creek was established in 1872. Completion of the Union Pacific Railroad brought more settlers to this farmland; at this time the name was changed to Lexington. The economy of Lexington has been boosted by the addition of agricultural equipment, machine manufacturing, and beef processing to its already prosperous farming and cattle operations. Lexington is also known as the "Antique Center of Nebraska" with its variety of antique and collectible shops.

What to See and Do

Dawson County Historical Museum. *805 N Taft St, Lexington (68850). Phone 308/324-5340.* Exhibits include Dawson County history gallery, furnished rural schoolhouse (1888), 1885 Union Pacific depot, 1903 locomotive, farm equipment, and 1919 experimental biplane. Collection also includes quilts and prehistoric Native American artifacts. Art gallery and archives. (Mon-Sat, closed Jan 1, Thanksgiving, Dec 25) **$**

Heartland Museum of Military Vehicles. *I-80 exit 237, 606 Heartland Rd, Lexington (68850). Phone 308/324-5504.* Collection of restored military vehicles. Includes Bradley fighting vehicle, Airman retriever, troop carriers. (Daily) **DONATION**

Johnson Lake State Recreation Area. *1 E Park Dr #25 A, Elmwood (68937). 7 miles S on Hwy 283. Phone 308/785-2685.* Approximately 80 acres on 2,061-acre lake. Swimming; fishing; boating (ramps). Picnicking. Tent and trailer sites (dump station). **$$**

Special Events

Antique & Craft Extravaganza. *Dawson County Fairgrounds, Lexington. Phone 308/324-5504.* Over 275 antiques, craft and flea market dealers (fee). Labor Day weekend.

Dawson County Fair. *Dawson County Fairgrounds, Lexington. Phone 308/324-5504.* Mid-Aug.

Limited-Service Hotels

★ **FIRST INTERSTATE INN.** *2503 Plum Creek Pkwy, Lexington (68850). Phone 308/324-5601; toll-free 800/462-4667; fax 308/324-4284. www.firstinns.com.* 52 rooms, 2 story. Pets accepted; fee. Complimentary continental breakfast. Check-out noon. Outdoor pool. **$**

★ **SUPER 8.** *104 E River Rd, Lexington (68850).*
Phone 308/324-7434; fax 308/324-4433. www.super8
.com. 47 rooms, 2 story. Check-out 11am. Fitness room.
$
🏃

Lincoln (C-5)

See also Beatrice, Nebraska City, Omaha, York

Settled 1856
Population 191,972
Elevation 1,176 ft
Area Code 402
Information Convention & Visitors Bureau, 1135 M St,
Suite 300, PO Box 83737, 68501; phone 402/434-5335
or toll-free 800/423-8212
Web Site www.lincoln.org

The second-largest city in Nebraska, Lincoln feuded
with Omaha, the territorial seat of government, for
the honor of being capital of the new state. When
the argument was settled in Lincoln's favor in 1867,
books, documents, and office furniture were moved
in covered wagons late one night to escape the armed
band of Omaha boosters. At that time, only 30 people
lived in the new capital but a year later there were
500, and in 1870, 2,500. As a young lawyer in the
1890s, William Jennings Bryan went to Congress from
Lincoln; in 1896, 1900, and 1908 he ran unsuccessfully
for president. General John J. Pershing taught military
science at the University of Nebraska. Business and
many cultural activities revolve around state
government and the university. Lincoln is also a major
grain market, as well as a manufacturing, insurance,
finance, printing, and trade center.

The unicameral form of government in Nebraska,
which was set up by an amendment to the state constitution in 1934 (mostly by the efforts of Nebraska's
famous senator, George W. Norris), is of great interest
to students of political science. It works efficiently and
avoids delays and deadlocks common to two-house
legislatures.

What to See and Do

American Historical Society of Germans from Russia.
631 D St, Lincoln (68502). Phone 402/474-3363.
Located here are the society's headquarters, archives,
library, special displays, and museum; also chapel,

summer kitchen replicas. (Mon-Fri, also Sat mornings; closed holidays) **FREE**

Antelope Park. *33rd and Sheridan sts, 23rd and N sts,
Lincoln.* Nine-hole junior golf course (fee) at Normal
and South Sts. Sunken Garden and Rose Garden at
27th and D sts.

Bluestem Lake State Recreation Area. *SW 56th St and
W Sprague Rd, Lincoln (68503). 13 miles SW via Hwy
77, Hwy 33. Phone 402/471-5566.* Approximately 417
acres on a 325-acre lake. Swimming; fishing; boating.
Picnicking. Camping (dump station).

Branched Oak Lake State Recreation Area. *Agnew. 12
miles NW via Hwy 34, Hwy 79. Phone 402/783-3400.*
Approximately 1,150 acres on a 1,800-acre lake. Swimming; fishing; boating (ramps). Picnicking, concession. Camping (dump station).

Conestoga Lake State Recreation Area. *Lincoln. 6
miles W on Hwy 6, then 3 miles S off Hwy 55A. Phone
402/471-5566.* Approximately 450 acres on 230-acre
lake. Fishing; boating (ramps). Picnicking. Camping
(dump station).

Eugene T. Mahoney State Park. *28500 W Park Hwy,
Ashland (68003). 25 miles NE on I-80, exit 426. Phone
402/944-2523.* More than 690 acres with two lakes.
Swimming pool, waterslide (Memorial Day-Labor
Day, daily); fishing; paddleboats. Hiking, horseback
riding; miniature golf, driving range, tennis courts.
Picnicking, lodging, restaurant. Camping, cabins.
Greenhouse, conservatory. **$$**

Folsom Children's Zoo. *1222 S 27th St, Lincoln (68502).
Phone 402/475-6741.* Exotic animals, contact areas,
botanical gardens. (Apr-mid-Aug, daily) Train and
pony rides (fee). **$$**

Holmes Park. *70th and Van Dorn sts, Lincoln (68502).*
Approximately 550 acres with a large lake. Fishing;
boating (no motors). Golf course (fee), ball fields.
Ice skating. Picnicking, playground. Hyde Memorial
Observatory (Sat evenings). Park (daily). **FREE**

Lincoln Children's Museum. *1420 P St, Lincoln
(68508). Phone 402/477-0128.* A variety of cultural
and scientific exhibits invite exploration and involve
the senses. (Tues-Sun; closed holidays) **$$**

Museum of Nebraska History. *131 Centennial Mall N,
Lincoln (68508). Phone 402/471-4754.* History of
Nebraska summarized in exhibits covering events
from prehistoric times through the 1950s. Native

American Gallery, period rooms. (Tues-Sun; closed holidays) **FREE**

National Museum of Roller Skating. *4730 South St, Lincoln (68506). Phone 402/483-7551.* Skates, costumes, and photographs documenting the sport and industry from 1700 to the present; also archives dealing with world and national competitions since 1910. The only museum in the world devoted solely to roller skating. (Mon-Fri; closed holidays) **FREE**

Nebraska Wesleyan University. *5000 Saint Paul Ave, Lincoln (68504). Phone 402/466-2371.* (1887) (1,500 students) Liberal arts school founded by the United Methodist Church. On campus is the Elder Art Gallery (Late Aug-mid-May, Tues-Sun). Also here are the Old Main Building (1888) and the Nebraska United Methodist Historical Center, containing archives.

Pawnee Lake State Recreaction Area. *Hwy 4, Box 41B, Lincoln (68524). 6 miles W on Hwy 6, then 3 miles N on Hwy 55A. Phone 402/471-5566.* Approximately 1,800 acres on a 740-acre lake. Blue rock area. Swimming; fishing; boating (ramps). Picnicking, concession. Camping (dump station).

Pioneers Park. *3201 S Coddington Ave, Lincoln (68522). 1/2 mile S of junction at Coddington Ave and W Van Dorn St. Phone 402/441-7895.* Hiking, bike trails, bridle path; golf course (fee). Picnicking, playgrounds. Nature preserve and center, outdoor amphitheater. (Daily) **FREE**

State Capitol. *1445 K St, Lincoln (68508). Phone 402/471-0448.* Designed by Bertram Goodhue, the most dominant feature of the building is the central tower, which rises 400 feet. Ground was broken in 1922 for this third capitol building at Lincoln; it was completed ten years later. Sculpture by Lee Lawrie includes reliefs and friezes depicting the history of law and justice, great philosophers, symbols of the state, and a bronze statue of the Sower (32 feet) atop the tower dome. The great hall, rotunda, and legislative chambers are decorated in tile and marble murals, tapestries, and wood-inlaid panels. Half-hour (June-Aug) and hourly guided tours. (Daily; closed holidays). Nearby are

Executive Mansion. *1425 H St, Lincoln (68508). Phone 402/471-3466.* (1957). Georgian Colonial architecture. Guided tours. (Thurs afternoons; closed holidays) **FREE**

Lincoln Monument. *201 N 7th, Lincoln (68508). Phone 402/434-5348.* (1912). This standing figure of Lincoln was designed by sculptor Daniel Chester French, who also produced the seated Lincoln statue for Henry Bacon's Lincoln Memorial in Washington, DC. Architectural setting by Bacon.

Statehood Memorial–Thomas P. Kennard House. *1627 H St, Lincoln (68508). Phone 402/471-4764.* (1869) Restored residence of Nebraska's first secretary of state. (Mon-Fri, by appointment; closed holidays) **$**

Strategic Air & Space Museum. *28210 W Park Hwy, Ashland (68003). Phone 402/944-3100.* Features permanent collection of 33 aircrafts and six missiles relating to the history of SAC and its importance in preservation of world peace. Interactive children's gallery, theater, museum store. (Daily; closed holidays) **$$$**

Union College. *3800 S 48th St, Lincoln (68506). Between Bancroft and Prescott sts. Phone 402/488-2331.* (1891) (600 students) Tours of campus. On campus is

College View Seventh-day Adventist Church. *4015 S 49th St, Lincoln (68506). Phone 402/486-2880.* The church is noted for its stained-glass windows and Rieger pipe organ.

University of Nebraska. *501 N 14th St, Lincoln (68588). Phone 402/472-7211.* (1869) (33,900 students) The university has research-extension divisions throughout the state. On the grounds are

Great Plains Art Collection. *1155 Q St, Lincoln (68588). 13th and R sts. Phone 402/472-6220.* Works by Remington, Russell, and other masters are among the nearly 700 pieces of this collection. Also featured are 4,000 volumes of Great Plains and Western Americana. (Tues-Sun; closed holidays and between exhibits) **FREE**

Sheldon Memorial Art Gallery and Sculpture Garden. *N 12th and R sts, Lincoln (68508). Phone 402/472-2461.* Designed by Philip Johnson. Fine collection of 20th-century American art; changing exhibitions. (Tues-Sun; closed holidays)

University of Nebraska State Museum. *14th and U sts, Lincoln (68588). Phone 402/472-2642 (museum).* Displays of fossils (dinosaurs and mounted elephants), rocks and minerals, ancient life, Nebraska plants and animals. Native American exhibits; changing exhibits. (Daily; closed Jan 1, Thanksgiving, Dec 25) Encounter Center (Tues-Sun). Ralph Mueller Planetarium (Tues-Sun; fee). **$**

Wilderness Park. *Lincoln. First and Van Dorn to 27th and Saltillo Rd.* Approximately 1,450 acres. Hiking, bike, bridle trails. (Daily) **FREE**

Special Events

Camp Creek Threshers. *Waverly. 12 miles NE via Hwy 6. Phone 402/786-3003.* Antique tractor pull; parades of antique farm machinery, cars, and horse-drawn equipment; demonstrations of farm tasks and crafts. Mid-July.

Horse racing. *State Fair Park, 1800 State Fair Park Dr, Lincoln (68508). Phone 402/473-4109.* Thoroughbred racing. Mid-May-mid-July.

July Jamm. *12 and N sts, Lincoln. Downtown. Phone 402/434-6900.* Art show, music festival. Late July.

Nebraska State Fair. *1800 State Fair Park Dr, Lincoln (68508). Phone 402/473-4109.* Contact the State Fair, PO Box 81223, 68501. Late Aug.

Limited-Service Hotels

★ ★ **BEST WESTERN VILLAGER COURTYARD & GARDENS.** *5200 O St, Lincoln (68510). Phone 402/464-9111; fax 402/467-0505. www.bestwestern.com.* 186 rooms, 2 story. Pets accepted. Complimentary continental breakfast. Check-out noon. Restaurant, bar. Fitness room. Outdoor pool, whirlpool. **$**

★ ★ **HOLIDAY INN.** *141 N 9th St, Lincoln (68508). Phone 402/475-4011; toll-free 800/432-0002; fax 402/475-9011. www.holiday-inn.com.* 233 rooms, 16 story. Check-out noon. Restaurant, bar. Indoor pool, whirlpool. **$**

★ **WOODFIN SUITES.** *200 S 68th Pl, Lincoln (68510). Phone 402/483-4900; toll-free 888/433-6183; fax 402/483-4464. www.woodfinsuitehotels.com.* 120 rooms, 2 story. Pets accepted; fee. Complimentary full breakfast. Check-out noon. Fitness room. Outdoor pool, whirlpool. Tennis. **$**

Full-Service Hotel

★ ★ ★ **THE CORNHUSKER.** *333 S 13th St, Lincoln (68508). Phone 402/474-7474; toll-free 800/793-7474; fax 402/474-1847. www.thecornhusker.com.* Continental elan meets Midwestern friendliness at Lincoln's luxurious Cornhusker Hotel. A Nebraska landmark since 1926, today's Cornhusker is a new and improved hotel with sophisticated décor, fine dining, exceptional amenities, and dedicated service. The always-courteous staff makes each guest's visit seamless, from the initial greeting at the door to the efficient check-out. The rooms and suites are elegantly appointed, and for those who require a bit more attention, the tenth-floor Executive Level offers an upgraded experience. Handpainted murals and fiber-optic starlight help make the Terrace Grille a delightful setting for contemporary cuisine, and the Five Reasons Lounge is the perfect place to enjoy a pre- or post-dinner cocktail. 290 rooms, 10 story. Check-out noon. Wireless Internet access. Restaurant, bar. Fitness room. Indoor pool. Airport transportation available. Business center. **$$**

Restaurants

★ ★ **BILLY'S.** *1301 H St, Lincoln (68508). Phone 402/474-0084; fax 420/474-3391.* American menu. Lunch, dinner. Closed Sun; holidays. Bar. In a historic house. Each of three dining rooms pays tribute to a famous Nebraskan. **$$**

★ **YIA YIA.** *1423 O St, Lincoln (68508). Phone 402/477-9166.* Pizza. Lunch, dinner. Closed Sun; holidays. Bar. Outdoor seating. No credit cards accepted. **$**

McCook

Founded 1882
Population 8,112
Elevation 2,576 ft
Area Code 308
Zip 69001
Information Chamber of Commerce, 107 Norris Ave, PO Box 337; phone 308/345-3200 or toll-free 800/657-2179
Web Site www.aboutmccook.com

McCook began as the small settlement of Fairview. The Lincoln Land Company and the Burlington & Missouri Railroad gave the town its name and ensured its growth. It is now a trading center in the middle of a vast reclamation, irrigation, and oil production area.

What to See and Do

Medicine Creek Reservoir State Recreation Area. *McCook. 23 miles NE via Hwy 6, 34, then 7 miles N on an unnumbered road.* Approximately 1,200 acres on a 1,768-acre reservoir. Swimming; fishing; boating (ramps, rentals); biking. Picnicking, concession. Tent and trailer camping (dump station, standard fees).

Museum of the High Plains. *423 Norris Ave, McCook (69001). Phone 308/345-3661.* Pioneer and Native American artifacts; World War II prisoner of war paintings; apothecary shop; fossils; flour mill; oil industry exhibit; special exhibits. (Tues-Sun afternoons; closed holidays) **FREE**

Red Willow Reservoir State Recreation Area. *McCook. 11 miles N on Hwy 83. Phone 308/345-6507.* Approximately 4,500 acres on a 1,628-acre reservoir. Swimming; fishing; boating (ramps). Picnicking, concession. Tent and trailer camping (dump station).

Senator George W. Norris State Historic Site. *706 Norris Ave, McCook (69001). Phone 308/345-8484.* Restored house of former senator (1861-1944); original furnishings; museum depicts events in his life. (Wed-Sat; closed holidays) **$**

Swanson Reservoir State Recreation Area. *Trenton. 23 miles W on Hwy 34.* Approximately 1,100 acres on a 4,973-acre reservoir. Swimming; fishing; boating (ramps). Picnicking, concession. Tent and trailer camping (dump station).

Special Events

Heritage Days. *Norris Park, McCook. Phone 308/345-3200.* Entertainment, parade, arts and crafts fair, carnival. Last full weekend in Sept.

Red Willow County Fair and Rodeo. *Fairgrounds, W 5th and O sts, McCook (69001). Phone 308/345-3200.* Late July.

Limited-Service Hotel

★ ★ **BEST WESTERN CHIEF MOTEL.** *612 W B St, McCook (69001). Phone 308/345-3700; fax 308/345-7182. www.bestwestern.com.* 111 rooms, 2 story. Pets accepted, some restrictions. Complimentary continental breakfast. Check-out 11 am. Restaurant. Fitness room. Indoor pool, whirlpool. **$**

Minden (D-4)

See also Kearney

Founded 1878
Population 2,749
Elevation 2,172 ft
Area Code 308
Zip 68959
Information Chamber of Commerce, 325 N Colorado Ave, PO Box 375; phone 308/832-1811

What to See and Do

✪ **Harold Warp Pioneer Village.** *138 E Hwy 6, Minden (68959). Jct Hwy 6, 34, and Hwy 10. Phone 308/832-1181; toll-free 800/445-4447.* Large collection of Americana that follows man's progress since 1830. Three city blocks and more than 30 buildings, including original sod house, schoolhouse, and pony express station, chronologically represent the country's pioneer heritage. More than 50,000 historic items, including farm implements, 100 vintage tractors, locomotives, 350 antique autos, and 22 historic flying machines. Restaurant; lodging. Camping. (Daily)

Special Event

The Light of the World Christmas Pageant. *Kearney County Courthouse, Town Square, Minden. Phone 308/832-1811.* A town tradition for many years; highlight of the outdoor pageant is the illumination of the courthouse dome by 10,000 lights. Contact the Chamber of Commerce for details. Sat and Sun after Thanksgiving and the first Sun in Dec.

Nebraska City (C-6)

See also Auburn, Lincoln

Founded 1855
Population 6,547
Elevation 1,029 ft
Area Code 402
Zip 68410
Information Chamber of Commerce, 806 First Ave; phone 402/873-3000 or toll-free 800/514-9113
Web Site www.nebraskacity.com

Nebraska City began as a trading post but grew larger and wilder as the Missouri River and overland traffic brought bullwhackers, muleskinners, and riverboat men with bowie knives and pistols in their belts. Located on the Missouri River, Nebraska City ships grain and agricultural products worldwide.

What to See and Do

Arbor Lodge State Historical Park. *2300 2nd Ave, Nebraska City (68410). 1 mile W on 2nd Ave. Phone 402/873-7222.* More than 72 acres of wooded grounds surround the 52-room, neo-colonial mansion of J. Sterling Morton (the originator of Arbor Day and the secretary of agriculture under Grover Cleveland) and summer residence of his son Joy Morton (the founder of Morton Salt Co). Picnicking. Mansion (Apr-Dec, daily). Park grounds (daily). **$$**

Mayhew Cabin and Historic Village Foundation. *2012 4th Corso (Hwy 2), Nebraska City (68410). Phone 402/873-3115. www.johnbrownscave.com.* Original log cabin and cave where slaves were hidden before and after the Civil War. (Apr-Nov, Wed-Sun) **$$**

Old Time Trolleys sightseeing tour. *806 1st Ave, Nebraska City (68410). Phone 402/873-7488.* Historical tour and narrative. (Daily; Apr-Dec weekends only; closed holidays) **$$**

Wildwood Park. *Steinhart Park Rd, Nebraska City. W on 4th Corso, then N. Phone 402/873-3000.* Picnicking, playground. In the park is

Wildwood Historic Home. *420 S Steinhart Park Rd, Nebraska City (68410). Phone 402/873-6340.* (1869). A ten-room house with mid-Victorian furnishings; formal parlor; antique lamps and fixtures. The original brick barn is now an art gallery. (Apr-Nov; Mon-Sat, also Sun afternoons) **$**

Special Events

Applejack Festival. *Phone 402/873-3000.* Celebration of the apple harvest. Parade, antique and craft show, classic car show, football game. Third weekend in Sept.

Arbor Day Celebration. *2300 2nd Ave, Nebraska City (68410). Phone 402/873-3000.* Tree-planting ceremonies in Arbor Lodge State Historical Park; parade, arts festival, fly-in, breakfast. Last weekend in Apr.

Limited-Service Hotel

★ **APPLE INN.** *502 S 11th St, Nebraska City (68410). Phone 402/873-5959; toll-free 800/659-4446; fax*

402/873-6640. www.appleinn.com. 65 rooms, 2 story. Complimentary continental breakfast. Check-out 11 am. Outdoor pool. **$**

⊠

Restaurant

★ ★ **EMBERS STEAKHOUSE.** *1102 4th Corso, Nebraska City (68410). Phone 402/873-6416.* Steak menu. Lunch, dinner. Bar. Children's menu. **$$**

Norfolk (B-5)

See also Wayne

Founded 1866
Population 21,476
Elevation 1,527 ft
Area Code 402
Zip 68701
Information Madison County Convention & Visitors Bureau, PO Box 386, 68702-0386; phone 402/371-2932 or toll-free 888/371-2932
Web Site www.norfolk.ne.us

German families from Wisconsin were the first to till the rich soil around Norfolk. The town's livestock business and expanding industries have brought prosperity, making Norfolk the chief marketplace of northeastern Nebraska.

What to See and Do

Cowboy Trail. *Hwy 81 and Tahazorika Rd, Norfolk (68701). Phone 402/371-4862.* This 321-mile trail follows the former Chicago and North Western railroad line from Norfolk to Chadron, NE. Includes 13,878 feet of handrailed bridges. Trail is suitable for hiking and mountain biking, with horseback riding allowed alongside the trail. Phone the local Chamber of Commerce for more information.

Neligh Mills. *N St and Wylie Dr, Neligh. W off Hwy 275. Phone 402/887-4303.* Complete 19th-century flour mill; milling exhibits. Maintained by the Nebraska State Historical Society. (May-Sept: Tues-Sun; rest of year: by appointment) **$**

Skyview Lake. *Maple Ave and 18th St, Norfolk (68701). 1 mile W on Maple Ave. Phone 403/371-2932.* Fishing; boating (no motors), canoeing. Picnicking.

Special Event

LaVitsef Celebration. *4th St and Norfolk Ave, Norfolk (68701). Phone 402/371-4862.* Fall festival featuring entertainment, parade, softball tournaments. Last weekend in Sept.

Limited-Service Hotels

★ ★ **NORFOLK COUNTRY INN.** *1201 S 13th St, Norfolk (68701). Phone 402/371-4430; toll-free 800/233-0733; fax 402/371-6373. www.norfolkcountryinn .com.* 127 rooms, 2 story. Check-out noon. Restaurant, bar. Outdoor pool. **$**

★ ★ **RAMADA INN.** *1227 Omaha Ave, Norfolk (68701). Phone 402/371-7000; fax 402/371-7000. www.ramada.com.* 98 rooms, 2 story. Check-out 11 am. Restaurant, bar. Indoor pool. **$**

★ **SUPER 8.** *1223 Omaha Ave, Norfolk (68702). Phone 402/379-2220; toll-free 800/800-8000; fax 402/379-3817. www.super8.com.* 66 rooms, 2 story. Complimentary continental breakfast. Check-out 11 am. **$**

Restaurants

★ ★ **BRASS LANTERN.** *1018 S 9th St, Norfolk (68701). Phone 402/371-2500.* Steak menu. Lunch, dinner. Closed Jan 1, Thanksgiving, Dec 25. Bar. Children's menu. **$$**

★ **GRANARY.** *922 S 13th St, Norfolk (68701). Phone 402/371-5334.* American menu. Lunch, dinner. Closed Sun; holidays. Bar. Children's menu. No credit cards accepted. **$**

★ ★ **PRENGER'S.** *116 E Norfolk Ave, Norfolk (68701). Phone 402/379-1900.* American menu. Lunch, dinner. Closed holidays. Bar. Children's menu. **$$**

★ ★ ★ **THE UPTOWN CAFE.** *801 10th St, Norfolk (68779). Phone 402/439-5100; fax 402/439-5300.* Visitors to this restaurant in the middle of the Wild West may be surprised by the refined food and good wine selection. Famed for its support of local artists and musicians, the dining room is filled with paintings and live music. Seafood menu. Lunch, dinner, late-night. Bar. **$$**

North Platte (C-3)

See also Gothenburg

Founded 1866
Population 22,605
Elevation 2,800 ft
Area Code 308
Zip 69103
Information North Platte/Lincoln County Convention & Visitors Bureau, 219 S Dewey, PO Box 1207; phone 308/532-4729 or toll-free 800-955-4528
Web Site www.ci.north-platte.ne.us

North Platte, Buffalo Bill Cody's hometown, is the retail railroad and agricultural hub of west central Nebraska. Cattle, hogs, corn, wheat, alfalfa, and hay are the principal products.

What to See and Do

Arnold Lake. *37 miles NE via Hwy 70, 92 near Arnold. Phone 308/749-2235.* Approximately 15 acres with a 22-acre lake on the upper reaches of the Loup River. Fishing, boating (nonpower or electric). Picnicking. Camping.

Buffalo Bill Ranch State Historical Park. *2921 Scouts Rest Ranch Rd, North Platte (69101). 1 mile N on Buffalo Bill Ave. Phone 308/535-8035.* Remaining of William F. Cody's ranch are the 18-room house, barn, and many outbuildings. Interpretive film; display of buffalo. (Memorial Day-Labor Day: daily; Oct-Apr: Mon-Fri) **$$**

Fort McPherson National Cemetery. *I-80, exit 190, Maxwell. 14 miles E on I-80 to Maxwell, then 3 miles S on county road.* Soldiers and scouts of Native American and later wars are buried here.

Lake Maloney. *6 miles S on Hwy 83. Phone 308/532-4729.* Approximately 1,100 acres on a 1,000-acre lake. Swimming; fishing; boating (ramps). Picnicking. Camping (dump station).

Lincoln County Historical Museum. *2403 N Buffalo Bill Ave, North Platte (69101). Phone 308/534-5640.* Several authentically furnished rooms and exhibits, including a World War II canteen, depict the life and history of Lincoln County. In back is the re-creation of a railroad village with a restored depot, house, church, schoolhouse, log house, and barn. (Memorial Day-Labor Day: daily; rest of year: by appointment) **DONATION**

Special Event

"NEBRASKAland DAYS" Celebration. *509 E 4th St, North Platte (69101). Phone 308/532-7939.* Parades, entertainment, food, and the famous PRCA Rodeo. Mid-late June.

Limited-Service Hotels

★ **BEST WESTERN CHALET LODGE.** *920 N Jeffers St, North Platte (69101). Phone 308/532-2313; fax 308/532-8823. www.bestwestern.com.* 38 rooms, 2 story. Pets accepted; fee. Complimentary continental breakfast. Check-out 11 am. Outdoor pool. **$**

★ **HAMPTON INN.** *200 Platte Oasis Pkwy, North Platte (69101). Phone 308/534-6000; toll-free 800/426-7866; fax 308/534-3415. www.hamptoninn.com.* 111 rooms, 4 story. Complimentary continental breakfast. Check-out noon. Indoor pool, whirlpool. **$**

★ ★ **STOCKMAN INN.** *1402 S Jeffers St, North Platte (69103). Phone 308/534-3630; toll-free 800/624-4643; fax 308/534-0110.* 140 rooms, 2 story. Pets accepted, some restrictions; fee. Complimentary continental breakfast. Check-out noon. Restaurant, bar. Outdoor pool. **$**

★ **SUPER 8.** *220 Eugene Ave, North Platte (69101). Phone 308/532-4224; toll-free 800/800-8000; fax 308/534-4317. www.super8.com.* 113 rooms, 2 story. Complimentary continental breakfast. Check-out 11 am. Fitness room. **$**

Restaurant

★ **GOLDEN DRAGON.** *120 W Leota, North Platte (69101). Phone 308/532-5588; fax 308/532-5588.* Chinese menu. Lunch, dinner. Closed holidays. **$$**

O'Neill (B-4)

Settled 1874
Population 3,852
Elevation 2,000 ft
Area Code 402
Zip 68763
Information Chamber of Commerce, 315 E Douglas; phone 402/336-2355

Web Site www.hearte.com/chamber

General John J. O'Neill founded this Irish colony along the Elkhorn River in the north central portion of the state. His colorful career included fighting as a captain of African American troops for the North in the Civil War and attacking Canada in the armed Fenian invasion of Irish patriots. O'Neill is known as the Irish capital of Nebraska and holds an annual St. Patrick's Day celebration.

What to See and Do

Atkinson Lake State Recreation Area. *O'Neill. 18 miles W on Hwy 20, near Atkinson.* Approximately 53 acres on the Elkhorn River. Fishing; boating (nonpower or electric). Picnicking. Camping.

Pibel Lake State Recreation Area. *O'Neill. 51 miles S on Hwy 281, near Bartlett.* Approximately 40 acres with a 24-acre lake. Fishing; boating (nonpower or electric). Picnicking. Camping.

Limited-Service Hotel

★ **GOLDEN HOTEL.** *406 E Douglas St, O'Neill (68763). Phone 402/336-4436; toll-free 800/658-3148; fax 402/336-3549. www.historicgoldenhotel.com.* 27 rooms, 3 story. Pets accepted. Complimentary continental breakfast. Check-out 11 am. Restored hotel built in 1913. **$**

Ogallala (C-2)

Founded 1868
Population 5,095
Elevation 3,223 ft
Area Code 308
Zip 69153
Information Chamber of Commerce, 204 East A St, PO Box 628; phone 308/284-4066 or toll-free 800/658-4390
Web Site www.ogallala.com

Developed as a shipping point on the Union Pacific Railroad for the great western cattle herds, Ogallala was the goal of the cattle-driving cowboys who rode day and night with their "eyelids pasted open with tobacco." Many of them are buried in a genuine Boot Hill Cemetery, between 11th and 12th streets, on a

100-foot rise above the South Platte River, where there have been no burials since the 1880s.

What to See and Do

Ash Hollow State Historical Park. *Ogallala. 29 miles NW on Hwy 26. Phone 308/778-5651.* Approximately 1,000 acres on the Oregon Trail. The hills, caves, and springs of Ash Hollow have sustained humans from prehistoric times through the pioneer days. Hiking, picnicking. Interpretive center, restored school. **$$**

Crescent Lake National Wildlife Refuge. *10630 Road 181, Oshkosh. 43 miles NW on Hwy 26 to Oshkosh, then 28 miles N on an unnumbered, partially paved road. Phone 308/762-4893.* A nesting and migratory bird refuge comprising more than 45,000 acres with numerous pothole lakes. Birds found in the refuge include Canadian geese, great blue herons, American bitterns, prairie chickens, prairie falcons, and long-billed curlews. Fishing. Nature trail (1 1/2 miles). Refuge office (Mon-Fri). **FREE**

Front Street. *519 E First St (E Hwy 30), Ogallala (69153). Phone 308/284-4066.* Cowboy museum (free), general store, saloon, arcade, restaurant. Shows in Crystal Palace (summer, nightly; fee). (Mon-Sat)

Lake McConaughy State Recreation Area. *1500 Hwy 61 N, Ogallala (69153). 9 miles N on Hwy 61. Phone 308/284-3542.* Approximately 5,500 acres on Nebraska's largest lake (35,700 acres). Swimming; fishing; boating (ramps, rentals). Picnicking, concession. Camping (dump station). **$$**

Lake Ogallala State Recreation Area. *1500 Hwy 61 N, Ogallala (69153). 9 miles N on Hwy 61, below Kingsley Dam. Phone 308/284-3542.* Approximately 300 acres on a 320-acre lake. Fishing; boating (ramps, rentals). Picnicking. Camping (dump station nearby at Martin Bay). **$$**

Mansion on the Hill. *1004 N Spruce St, Ogallala (69153).* This 1890s mansion contains period furniture, pioneer household items. (Memorial Day-Labor Day, daily) Contact the Chamber of Commerce for further information. **FREE**

Special Events

Governor's Cup Sailboat Regatta. *Ogallala. Phone 308/284-4066.* Labor Day weekend.

Keith County Fair and Round-Up Rodeo. *Keith County Fairgrounds, 573 County Rd E H South, Ogallala (69153). Phone 308/726-8217.* Early Aug.

Limited-Service Hotels

★ ★ **BEST WESTERN STAGECOACH INN.** *201 Stagecoach Trail, Ogallala (69153). Phone 308/284-3656; toll-free 800/662-2993; fax 308/284-6734. www.bestwestern.com.* 100 rooms, 2 story. Pets accepted; fee. Complimentary continental breakfast. Check-out noon. Restaurant, bar. Indoor pool, outdoor pool, children's pool, whirlpool. Airport transportation available. **$**

★ **COMFORT INN.** *110 Pony Express Ln, Ogallala (69153). Phone 308/284-4028; fax 308/284-4202. www.choicehotels.com.* 49 rooms, 2 story. Complimentary continental breakfast. Check-out 11 am. Indoor pool, whirlpool. **$**

Restaurant

★ ★ **HILL TOP INN.** *197 Kingsley Dr, Ogallala (69153). Phone 308/284-4534.* Dinner. Closed holidays. Bar. Children's menu. **$$**

Omaha (C-6)

See also Blair, Fremont, Lincoln; also see Council Bluffs, IA

Founded 1854
Population 335,795
Elevation 1,040 ft
Area Code 402
Information Greater Omaha Convention & Visitors Bureau, 6800 Mercy Rd, Suite 202, 68106-2627; phone 402/444-4660 or toll-free 866/937-6624
Web Site www.visitomaha.com

The largest city in Nebraska, Omaha is named for the Native American people who lived here until they signed a treaty with the federal government on June 24, 1854. Opportunists across the Missouri River in Council Bluffs, Iowa, who had been waiting for the new territory to open, then rushed to stake out property, triggering a real estate boom. Omaha also saw the trial of Standing Bear, chief of the Ponca Tribe, which established the precedent that Native Americans were human beings and entitled to constitutional rights and protections.

In and Around the Old Market Area

Begin a walking tour of Omaha in the Old Market Area. One of the few downtown areas that preserves Omaha's original Victorian-era architecture, the Old Market Area is a five-block-square shopping, dining, and gallery district that's the heart and soul of the entire city center. Window shop, stop for coffee, pop into art-filled boutiques—the Old Market Area is made for leisurely strolling. Bounded by Farnam and Jones streets and 10th and 13th Streets, the Old Market Area was originally the food-processing center for the region: Swanson Food, Anheuser Busch, and other stalwarts of the food industry once occupied these buildings. Food is still one of the finest reasons to visit the Old Market Area. Find provisions for a picnic at one of Omaha's best bakeries, Delice European Bakery and Coffee Bar (1206 Howard), and pick up cheese and wine at La Buvette Wine and Grocery (511 S 11th St). On Wednesdays and Saturdays in summer and fall, stop for fresh local produce at the farmers market, held on 11th Street between Jackson and Howard.

Directly south of the Old Market Area on 10th Street is the Durham Western Heritage Museum (801 S 10th St), housed in the architecturally stunning Union Station, an Art Deco gem from Omaha's past. The museum tells the story of Omaha and Nebraska's past, complete with vintage cars and railroad equipment; plus, a period soda fountain is still in operation.

Walk north on 10th Street five blocks to reach Gene Leahy Mall, a 10-acre park with a lake that serves as a reflecting pond for the modern high-rise architecture of Omaha. Trails wind through the park, linking formal flower gardens, a playground for children, a bandstand, and public art displays. To the east, the Leahy Mall connects to Heartland of America Park and Fountain, which is bounded by 8th Street and the Missouri River. The highlight of the park is its lake, with a fountain, that shoots streams of water 300 feet into the air. The *General Marion* tour boat navigates the lake to take visitors closer to the fountain. At night, the water display is accompanied by pulsing lights.

Return to the Leahy Mall along Douglas Street, which leads into the modern city center. At 24th Street, turn north one block to the Joslyn Art Museum (2200 Dodge St), Nebraska's premier center for the visual arts. The museum building is itself a work of art, a fanciful Art Deco structure faced with shimmering pink marble. The permanent collection consists of American and European art from the 19th and 20th centuries. A highlight is the cache of works from Karl Bodmer, a German watercolorist who traveled up the Missouri River in the 1830s, capturing the pristine landscapes, Native Americans, and wildlife before white pioneer settlement.

For a longer walk, continue west on Dodge Street to the Cathedral Neighborhood, which is filled with 19th-century mansions and Victorian homes. The neighborhood is named for St. Cecelia's Cathedral, a massive Spanish Mission-style church at 701 North 40th Street. The Joslyn Castle (3902 Davenport) was built by the family that endowed the city's art museum. A fanciful stone edifice that resembles a Scottish baronial castle, the house stands amid 5 acres of gardens and forest.

During early boom times steamboats docked in Omaha daily, bringing gold-seekers and emigrants to be outfitted for the long journey west. Local merchants further prospered when Omaha was named the eastern terminus for the Union Pacific. The first rail was laid in 1865. Public buildings rose on the prairie; schools, plants, and stockyards flourished in the 1870s and 1880s. Fighting tornadoes, grasshopper plagues, floods, and drought, the people built one of the farm belt's great commercial and industrial cities.

Today, Omaha continues to be a major transportation and agribusiness center, but it is also a recognized leader in telecommunications, insurance, and manufacturing as well as the home of five Fortune 500 companies. Omaha is also the headquarters of STRATCOM, the Strategic Air Command, one of the vital links in the national defense chain.

Visitors are not in Omaha long before hearing the term "Aksarben." It is, in fact, only Nebraska spelled backward and the name of a civic organization.

Public Transportation

Buses (Metro Area Transit), phone 402/341-0800

Airport Omaha Airport (OMA); weather, phone 402/392-1111; cash machines, Terminal Building.

Information Phone 402/422-6817

Lost and found Phone 402/422-6800

What to See and Do

Boys Town. *13628 Flanagan Blvd, Boys Town (68010). 138th and W Dodge Rd. Phone 402/498-1140.* A community for abandoned, abused, neglected, and disabled boys and girls. Founded in 1917 by Father Flanagan, Boys Town now has six direct care programs: a residential care facility for 550 boys and girls on the Boys Town campus; a national diagnostic, treatment, and research institute for children with hearing, speech, and learning disorders; an urban high school for troubled youths who may have difficulty in traditional school settings; Boys Town mini-campuses around the nation; a national training program for other child care facilities; and a family-based program. Boys Town provides services to more than 17,000 youths annually. Tours of Father Flanagan museum and the Hall of History. Visitor center (daily; closed holidays). **FREE**

Durham Western Heritage Museum. *Omaha Union Station, 801 S 10th St, Omaha (68108). Phone 402/444-5071. www.dwhm.org.* Restored Art Deco railroad depot is now a history museum. Exhibits on Omaha history from 1880 to 1954; Byron Reed coin collection; traveling temporary exhibits. (Tues-Sun; closed holidays) **$$**

Fontenelle Forest Nature Center. *1111 N Bellevue Blvd, Bellevue (68005). 7 miles S via Hwy 75. Phone 402/731-3140.* Approximately 1,400 acres of forest; 17 miles of foot trails through forest marsh, lake, prairie, floodplain environments; indoor animal exhibits; guided walks, lectures, films. (Daily; closed Jan 1, Thanksgiving, Dec 25) **$$**

Fun Plex. *7003 Q St, Omaha (68117). I-80, 72nd St exit. Phone 402/331-8436.* Nebraska's largest waterpark includes a water slides, wave-making pool, bumper cars, and go-karts. (Memorial Day-Labor Day, daily) **$$$$**

General Crook House. *5730 N 30th St, Omaha (68111). 30th and Fort sts. Phone 402/455-9990.* Built in 1878 to serve as the residence of the commander of the Department of the Platte. Originally called Quarters I, Fort Omaha, the house soon came to be known by the name of its first occupant, General George Crook. Italianate architecture; many antiques from the Victorian era; Victorian garden in summer. Guided tours (by appointment). (Daily; closed holidays) **$$**

Gerald Ford Birth Site. *32nd and Woolworth Ave, Omaha (68105). Phone 402/444-5955.* Model of the original house, White House memorabilia; park, gardens, Betty Ford Memorial Rose Garden. (Daily) **FREE**

Great Plains Black History Museum. *2213 Lake St, Omaha (68110). Phone 402/345-2212.* Housed in a building designed in 1907 by prominent Nebraska architect Thomas R. Kimball, the museum preserves the history of African Americans and their part in the heritage of Omaha and Nebraska since the territorial period of the 1850s. Included are rare photographs, relics, historical displays; films. (Mon-Fri) **$**

Heartland of America Park. *8th and Douglas sts, Omaha (68102). Phone 402/444-5920.* Bounded by Missouri River on the E, 8th St on the W, and Douglas St on the N. A 31-acre site featuring picnic facilities, arbors, and waterfalls. The park's 15-acre lake has a computer-driven fountain that has a colored light show at night. Excursion boat rides on *The General Marion* (Memorial Day-Labor Day, Wed-Sun; fee). **Gene Leahy Mall,** *bounded by Douglas and Farnam, 10th and 14th sts.* **N. P. Dodge Memorial Park,** *John Pershing Dr, 7 miles N.* Fishing; boating (ramp, marina). Tennis, lighted ball fields. Picnicking, playground. Camping (fee). Inquire about facilities for the disabled. **Elmwood Park,** *Dodge and 60th sts.* Swimming pool. Golf course. Picnicking. **Memorial Park,** *Dodge and 63rd sts, across street from* **Elmwood Park.** World War II memorial, rose garden, walking and jogging paths.

Henry Doorly Zoo. *3701 S 10th St, Omaha (68107). I-80 13th St exit. Phone 402/733-8401 (zoo). www.omahazoo.org.* More than 18,500 animals, many quite rare, are on display in a 110-acre park. Exhibits include an aquarium, indoor rainforest, walk-through aviary, white tigers, and polar bears. Steam train rides (Memorial Day-Labor Day, daily). IMAX 3-D theater (Daily; fee). Restaurant. Picnic areas. (Daily; closed Jan 1, Thanksgiving, Dec 25) **$$$**

Historic Bellevue. *112 W Mission Ave, Bellevue (68005). 9 miles S via Hwy 75. Phone 402/293-3080; toll-free 800/467-2779.* Restored buildings include the first church in the Nebraska territory (1856); old depot (1869), contains period artifacts; settlers' log cabin (circa 1830); and Fontenelle Bank (1856). Sarpy County Historical Museum, 2402 SAC Place, has displays concerning the history of the county and changing exhibits (Tues-Sun; closed Jan 1, Thanksgiving, Dec 25). **$**

Joslyn Art Museum. *24th and Dodge sts, Omaha (68102). Phone 402/342-3300. www.joslyn.org. (1931).* Museum building of Art Deco design with collections of art, ancient through modern, including European and American paintings, sculpture; art of the Western frontier, Native American art; traveling exhibitions. Guided tours, lectures, workshops, films, gallery talks, concerts. A 30,000-volume art reference library; museum shop. (Tues-Sun; closed holidays) **$$$**

Louisville State Recreation Area. *15810 Hwy 50, Louisville (68037). 25 miles SW via I-80, Hwy 50. Phone 402/234-6855.* Approximately 192 acres with 50 acres of water area. Swimming; fishing; boating (no motors). Picnicking, concession. Camping (dump station).

Mormon Trail Center at Winter Quarters. *3215 State St, Omaha (68112). Phone 402/453-9372.* The winter of 1846-1847 took the lives of more than 600 Mormon emigrants who camped near here. A monument commemorates their hardship. Films and pioneer exhibits in visitor center.

Old Market. *Center at 11th and Howard sts, extending E to 10th St and W to 13th. Phone 402/341-1877.* Art galleries, antique shops, restaurants. Revitalization of old warehouse district; some of Omaha's oldest commercial buildings line the market's brick-paved streets.

Omaha Children's Museum. *500 S 20th St, Omaha (68102). Phone 402/342-6163. www.ocm.org.* Self-directed exploration and play for children and families; constantly changing series of hands-on exhibits in science, the arts and humanities, health and creative play. (Tues-Sun; closed holidays)

Platte River State Park. *14421 346th St, Louisville (68037). 17 miles SW on I-80, then 14 miles S on Hwy 50 to Hwy Spur 13E, then W. Phone 402/234-2217.* These 413 acres are located on rolling bluffs overlooking the Platte River. Swimming pool; paddleboats. Hiking, horseback riding; tennis courts, archery range, recreational fields. Cross-country skiing. Picnicking, concession, restaurant. Camper cabins and housekeeping cabins. Arts and crafts building; observation tower; free use of recreational equipment.

Schramm Park State Recreation Area. *21502 W Hwy 31, Gretna (68028). I-80, exit 432, then 6 miles S on Hwy 31. Phone 402/332-3901.* Approximately 330 acres along the north bank of the Platte River. A day-use area offering hiking and nature trails, picnicking and several other activities. In the park are geological displays, fish hatchery ponds, and the Gretna Fish Hatchery Museum, which uses displays and audiovisual presentations to tell the story of fish and fishery management in Nebraska. Museum (Memorial Day-Labor Day: daily; Apr-late May and Labor Day-Nov: Wed-Mon; rest of year: Wed-Sun; closed holidays). Park (daily). **$$** Also located here is

Ak-Sar-Ben Aquarium. *21502 W Hwy 31, Gretna (68028). Phone 402/332-3901.* This modern facility features more than 50 species of fish native to Nebraska, as well as a terrarium, the World Herald Auditorium, a natural history classroom, and orientation and display areas. (Seasons are the same as Gretna Fish Hatchery Museum) **$**

Trolley. *5512 Borman Ave, Omaha (68137). Phone 402/597-3596.* Trackless *Ollie the Trolley* provides transportation along Douglas and Farnam sts to the Old Market, Gene Leahy Mall, and 16th Street Mall. Stops posted along route. (Daily) **$**

Two Rivers State Recreation Area. *27702 F St, Waterloo (68069). 23 miles W off Hwy 275, Hwy 92. Phone 402/359-5165.* More than 600 acres with a water area of 320 acres. Swimming; trout fishing (fee); boating. Picnicking, concession. Camping (dump station), trailer pads (fee), rental cabins (converted Union Pacific Railroad cabooses; late Apr-Oct). **$$**

University of Nebraska at Omaha. *6001 Dodge St, Omaha (68182). Phone 402/554-2393. (1908) (16,000 students)* On campus is

Kountze Planetarium. *68th and Dodge sts, Omaha (68182). On first floor of Durham Science Center. Phone 402/554-3722.* Planetarium shows display galaxies, stars, planets, and other celestial phenomena. Observatory (First Fri, Sat each month). Shows (limited hours; fee). **$$**

Special Events

Christmas at Union Station. *Omaha. Phone 402/444-5071.* For details, contact Durham Western Heritage Museum. Dec.

NCAA College Baseball World Series. *Rosenblatt Stadium, 1202 Bert Murphy Ave, Omaha (68107). Phone 402/444-4750.* Early June.

River City Round-up. *Fairgrounds, 6800 Mercy Rd, Omaha (68106). Phone 402/554-9610.* Celebration of agriculture and western heritage includes parade, barbecues, trail rides. Late Sept.

Summer Arts Festival. *Downtown, Omaha. Phone 402/963-9020.* Last weekend in June.

Limited-Service Hotels

★ ★ **BEST WESTERN REDICK PLAZA HOTEL.** *1504 Harney St, Omaha (68102). Phone 402/342-1500; toll-free 888/342-5339; fax 402/342-2401. www.bestwestern.com.* 89 rooms, 11 story. Complimentary full breakfast. Check-out noon. Restaurant, bar. Fitness room. Airport transportation available. **$**
🏋

★ ★ **DAYS INN.** *1811 Hillcrest Dr, Bellevue (68005). Phone 402/292-3800; toll-free 800/292-7277; fax 402/292-6373. www.the.daysinn.com.* 126 rooms, 2 story. Complimentary full breakfast. Check-out noon. Restaurant, bar. Indoor pool, children's pool, whirlpool. **$**
🏊

★ ★ **DOUBLETREE HOTEL.** *1616 Dodge St, Omaha (68102). Phone 402/346-7600; toll-free 800/222-8733; fax 402/346-5722. www.doubletree.com.* Located in the downtown, business and entertainment district. It is near many attractions including Central Park Mall. 413 rooms, 19 story. Check-out noon. Restaurant, bar. Fitness room. Indoor pool, whirlpool. Airport transportation available. Business center. **$**
🏋 🏊 🏃

★ ★ **DOUBLETREE HOTEL.** *7270 Cedar St, Omaha (68124). Phone 402/397-5141; toll-free 800/222-8733; fax 402/397-3266. www.doubletree.com.* Rooms are spacious and offer a kitchen, separate living area, wet bar, and sofa bed. The hotel is near many of the area's attractions and offers complimentary transportation to guests. 189 rooms, 6 story, all suites. Restaurant. Fitness room. Indoor pool, whirlpool. Airport transportation available. Indoor tropical courtyard. **$**
🏋 🏊

★ ★ **EMBASSY SUITES.** *555 S 10th Street, Omaha (68102). Phone 402/346-9000; toll-free 800/362-2779; fax 402/346-4236. www.embassysuites.com.* 249 rooms, all suites. Pets accepted, some restrictions; fee. Complimentary continental breakfast. Check-in 3 pm, check-out noon. Restaurant, bar. Fitness room. Indoor pool, whirlpool. **$$**
🖥 🐾 🏋 🏊

★ **HAMPTON INN.** *9720 W Dodge Rd, Omaha (68114). Phone 402/391-5300; fax 402/391-8995. www.hamptoninn.com.* 129 rooms, 4 story. Complimentary continental breakfast. Check-out noon. **$**

★ ★ **HILTON GARDEN INN OMAHA DOWNTOWN/OLD MARKET AREA.** *1005 Dodge Street, Omaha (68102). Phone 402/341-4400; fax 402/341-5200.* 178 rooms. Check-in 3 pm, check-out noon. Restaurant. Fitness room. Indoor pool, whirlpool. **$**
🖥 🏋 🏊

★ **LA QUINTA INN.** *3330 N 104th Ave, Omaha (68134). Phone 402/493-1900; fax 402/496-0757. www.laquinta.com.* 130 rooms, 2 story. Pets accepted. Check-out noon. Outdoor pool. **$**
🐾 🏊

Full-Service Hotels

★ ★ ★ **MARRIOTT OMAHA.** *10220 Regency Cir, Omaha (68114). Phone 402/399-9000; fax 402/399-0223. www.marriott.com.* This hotel offers two restaurants, a lounge, an indoor and outdoor pool, health club, and many more amenities for guests to appreciate. It is located near the Joslyn Art Museum, Old Market, golf courses, and tennis facilities. 301 rooms, 6 story. Check-out noon. Restaurant, bar. Fitness room. Indoor pool, outdoor pool, whirlpool. **$**
🏋 🏊

★ ★ ★ **SHERATON OMAHA HOTEL.** *1615 Howard St, Omaha (68102). Phone 402/342-2222; fax 402/342-2569. www.sheraton.com.* 145 rooms, 6 story. Check-out noon. Restaurant. Fitness room. Airport transportation available. Business center. **$$**
🏋 🏃

Restaurants

★ **BOHEMIAN CAFE.** *1406 S 13th St, Omaha (68108). Phone 402/342-9838; fax 402/342-7420.* American, Czech menu. Lunch, dinner. Closed Dec 25. **$$**

★ ★ **BUSTY LE DOUX'S.** *1014 Howard St, Omaha (68102). Phone 402/346-5100; fax 402/345-3789.* Cajun menu. Lunch, dinner. Closed holidays. Bar. Outdoor seating. **$$**

★ ★ ★ **CAFE DE PARIS.** *1228 S 6th St, Omaha (68108). Phone 402/344-0227.* As the name suggests, this is an exceptional French bistro with a menu that does not stray from the classics. Knowledgeable staff, including the sommelier, go to great lengths to make the guest's dining experience one to remember. French menu. Dinner. Closed Sun; holidays. Bar. Jacket required. Reservations recommended. **$$$**

★ **CHU'S CHOP SUEY & STEAKHOUSE.** *6455 Center St, Omaha (68106). Phone 402/553-6454.* Chinese menu. Lunch, dinner. Bar. Children's menu. **$$**

★ ★ ★ **FRENCH CAFE.** *1017 Howard St, Omaha (68102). Phone 402/341-3547; fax 402/341-3561. www.frenchcafe.com.* Elegant French dishes, continually refreshed with contemporary ingredients, have earned this restaurant its unbeatable reputation. Peppersteak is its signature, and the roasted rack of pork is an award winner. Wines from the substantial cellar are suggested with each item. American, French menu. Lunch, dinner. Closed holidays. Bar. **$$$**

★ **GARDEN CAFE.** *1212 Harney St, Omaha (68102). Phone 402/422-1574; fax 402/342-0209.* Breakfast, lunch, dinner. Closed Thanksgiving, Dec 25. Children's menu. Café-style dining. **$**

★ ★ **GORAT'S STEAK HOUSE.** *4917 Center St, Omaha (68106). Phone 402/551-3733; fax 402/551-3735.* Italian menu. Lunch, dinner. Closed Sun; holidays. Bar. Children's menu. Reservations recommended. **$$$**

★ ★ **INDIAN OVEN.** *1010 Howard St, Omaha (68102). Phone 402/342-4856; fax 402/342-4856.* Northern Indian menu. Lunch, dinner. Closed Sun; holidays. Bar. Reservations recommended. Outdoor seating. **$$**

★ **JOHNNY'S CAFE.** *4702 S 27th St, Omaha (68107). Phone 402/731-4774; fax 402/731-6698. www.johnnyscafe.com.* Steak menu. Lunch, dinner. Closed Sun; Jan 1, Dec 25. Bar. Children's menu. **$$**

★ **MC FOSTERS NATURAL KIND CAFE.** *302 S 38th St, Omaha (68131). Phone 402/345-7477; fax 402/345-4585. www.mcfosters.com.* American, seafood menu. Lunch, dinner. Closed holidays. Bar. Children's menu. Casual attire. Outdoor seating. **$$**

★ ★ ★ **SIGNATURE'S.** *1616 Dodge St, Omaha (68102). Phone 402/346-7600; fax 402/346-5722.* Located at the top of the Doubletree Hotel, this restaurant offers a panoramic view of the city's skyline.

A continental concept, the menu highlights influences from all over the world to accommodate the international clientele of the hotel. Seafood menu. Breakfast, lunch, dinner, late-night. Bar. **$$**

★ **TRINI'S.** *1020 Howard St, Omaha (68102). Phone 402/346-8400; fax 402/345-3789.* Mexican, seafood menu. Lunch, dinner. Closed Sun; holidays. **$**

★ ★ ★ **V. MERTZ.** *1022 Howard St, Omaha (68102). Phone 402/345-8980; fax 402/345-6265. www.vmertz.com.* Just off the brick-walled Old Market Passageway, this cozy restaurant offers a quiet, romantic atmosphere. Menu items, consisting of elegant continental dishes, change weekly and complement the extensive wine list. Coat and tie are recommended. American menu. Lunch, dinner. Bar. **$$**

Scotts Bluff National Monument (B-1)

See also Gering, Scottsbluff

3 miles S on Hwy 71 to Gering, then 3 miles W on Hwy 92.

Web Site www.nps.gov/scbl

This 800-foot bluff in western Nebraska was a landmark to pioneers who traveled the California/Oregon Trail by wagon trains. Historians often speak of this natural promontory in the North Platte Valley, which was originally named me-a-pa-te, "hill that is hard to go around," by the Plains Native Americans. Many people, including fur traders, Mormons, and gold seekers, came this way. Westward-bound pioneers, Pony Express riders, and the first transcontinental telegraph all passed through Mitchell Pass (within Monument boundaries) to skirt this pine-studded bluff. The Oregon Trail Museum at the monument's visitor center (daily; closed Dec 25) depicts the story of westward migration along the trail; artwork by the famous pioneer artist and photographer William Henry Jackson is on permanent display. Check with the Oregon Trail Museum for a schedule of special events. A paved road and hiking trail provide access to the summit for a view of the North Platte Valley and other landmarks such as Chimney Rock (see). The summit road is open to traffic daily. Visitors also may walk along the old Oregon Trail, remnants of which still exist within the park. Covering 5 square miles, Scotts Bluff became a national monument in

1919. (Daily) For further information, contact PO Box 27, Gering, 69341-0027; or phone 308/436-4340. Per vehicle **$$**

Scottsbluff (B-1)

See also Bridgeport, Chimney Rock National Historic Site, Gering, Scotts Bluff National Monument

Population 13,711
Elevation 3,885 ft
Area Code 308
Zip 69361
Information Scottsbluff-Gering United Chamber of Commerce, 1517 Broadway, Suite 104; phone 308/632-2133 or toll-free 800/788-9475
Web Site www.scottsbluffgering.net

Scottsbluff is the trading center for a large area of western Nebraska and eastern Wyoming.

What to See and Do

Agate Fossil Beds National Monument. *301 River Rd, Harrison (69346). 9 miles NW on US 26 to Mitchell, then 34 miles N on NE 29. Phone 308/668-2211.* An approximately 2,700-acre area; two self-guided nature trails; visitor center with exhibits of the fossil story of mammals that roamed the area 19-21 million years ago; also exhibits of Plains Native Americans. Visitor center (daily; closed Dec 25). Park (all year). For further info contact the Superintendent, PO Box 27, Gering, 69341. **$$**

Lake Minatare State Recreation Area. *291040 The Point Rd, Minatare (96356). 10 miles E on Hwy 26, then 10 miles N on Stonegate Rd. Phone 308/783-2911.* Approximately 800 acres on a 2,158-acre lake. Swimming; fishing; boating (ramps). Hiking. Picnicking, concession. Camping (dump station). (Mid-Jan-Sept)

Rebecca Winters Grave. *Hwy 26, Scottsbluff. E on S Beltline Rd. Phone 308/632-2133.* A pioneer on the Mormon Trail in 1852, Winters died of cholera and was buried near Scottsbluff. Her grave, marked with a wagon wheel, is one of the most accessible along the old emigrant routes. (Daily) **FREE**

Riverside Zoo. *1600 S Beltline W, Scottsbluff (69361). W of Hwy 71. Phone 308/630-6236.* More than 97 species of both native and exotic animals in a lush park setting. Walk-through aviary, white tiger, moose woods. (Daily, weather permitting). **$$**

West Nebraska Arts Center. *106 E 18th St, Scottsbluff (69361). Phone 308/632-2226.* Changing gallery shows in all media throughout the year showcasing the finest artists in the region. (Daily; closed holidays) **DONATION**

Limited-Service Hotels

★ **CANDLELIGHT INN.** *1822 E 20th Pl, Scottsbluff (69361). Phone 308/635-3751; toll-free 800/424-2305; fax 308/635-1105.* 60 rooms, 2 story. Complimentary continental breakfast. Check-out 11 am. Bar. Fitness room. Airport transportation available. **$**
🏃 ⛱

★ **COMFORT INN.** *2018 Delta Dr, Scottsbluff (69361). Phone 308/632-7510; fax 308/632-8495. www.comfortinn.com.* 46 rooms, 2 story. Complimentary continental breakfast. Check-out 11 am. Fitness room. Indoor pool, whirlpool. **$**
🏃 ⛱

Sidney (C-1)

See also Kimball

Founded 1867
Population 5,959
Elevation 4,085 ft
Area Code 308
Zip 69162
Information Cheyenne County Chamber of Commerce, 740 Illinois St; phone 308/254-5851 or toll-free 800/421-4769.
Web Site www.sidney-nebraska.com

In 1867, Sidney was established as a division point on the Union Pacific Railroad. Fort Sidney was established shortly thereafter, providing military protection for railroad workers and immigrants. Many relics of the Fort Sidney era remain and have been restored. Sidney, the seat of Cheyenne County, is also a peaceful farm, trading, and industrial center.

What to See and Do

Cabela's. *115 Cabela Dr, Sidney (69160). I-80, exit 59. Phone 308/254-5505.* Corporate headquarters for one of the world's largest outdoor gear outfitters. The 73,000-square-foot building displays more than 60,000 products; also over 500 wildlife mounts. Other attractions in the showroom are an 8,000-gallon aquarium; art gallery; gun library; restaurant; and

"Royal Challenge," a twice-life-size bronze sculpture of two battling elk. (Daily)

Fort Sidney Post Commander's Home. *1108 Sixth Ave, Sidney (69162). Phone 308/254-2150.* (1871). One of the original buildings of old Fort Sidney; used in the 19th century to protect railroad workers during the Native American wars; authentically restored. (Memorial Day-Labor Day, daily) **FREE** Other restored buildings in the Fort Sidney complex include

> **Double Set Officer's Quarters Museum.** *6th and Jackson sts, Sidney (69162). Phone 308/254-2150.* Built in 1884 as quarters for married officers. (Daily, afternoons) **FREE**

> **Powder House.** *1033 Fifth Ave, Sidney (69162).* Can be viewed only from the outside.

Special Events

County Fair and NSRA Rodeo. *Fairgrounds, Sidney. Phone toll-free 800/421-4769.* Aug.

Oktoberfest. *Sidney. Phone toll-free 800/421-4769.* First weekend in Oct.

Limited-Service Hotels

★ **COMFORT INN.** *730 E Jennifer Ln, Sidney (69162). Phone 308/254-5011; fax 308/254-5122. www.choicehotels.com.* 55 rooms, 2 story. Complimentary continental breakfast. Check-out 11 am. **$**

★ **DAYS INN.** *3042 Silverberg Dr, Sidney (69162). Phone 308/254-2121; fax 308/254-2121. www.daysinn.com.* 47 rooms, 2 story. Complimentary continental breakfast. Check-out 11 am. Indoor pool, whirlpool. **$**

South Sioux City (B-6)

See also Sioux City, IA

Population 9,677
Elevation 1,096 ft
Area Code 402
Zip 68776
Information Visitors Bureau, 2700 Dakota Ave; phone 402/494-1307 or toll-free 800/793-6327

What to See and Do

Ponca State Park. *RR 2, Ponca. 18 miles NW off NE 12,* on Missouri River. Phone 402/755-2284. Approximately 1,400 acres. Panoramic views of the Missouri River Valley. Swimming pool (fee); fishing; boating (ramps). Hiking, horseback riding. Cross-country skiing. Picnicking. Camping (14-day maximum, fee; dump station, trailer pads), cabins (Mid-Apr-mid-Nov), primitive camping during off-season.

Limited-Service Hotel

★ ★ **MARINA INN CONFERENCE CENTER.** *4th and B sts, South Sioux City (68776). Phone 402/494-4000; toll-free 800/798-7980; fax 402/494-2550.* This hotel is located on the river near a city park, the downtown center, and other attractions. 182 rooms, 5 story. Pets accepted, some restrictions; fee. Check-out 11 am. Restaurant, bar. Indoor pool, whirlpool. Airport transportation available. **$**

Thedford (A-1)

Population 243
Elevation 2,848 ft
Area Code 308
Zip 69166
Web Site www.thedford.org

What to See and Do

Nebraska National Forest. *125 N Main St, Chadron (69337). 15 miles E on Hwy 2. Bessey Ranger District office is 2 miles W of Halsey. Phone 308/533-2257.* Site of the Bessey Nursery (1902), oldest Forest Service tree nursery in the United States. Swimming pool (fee). Hiking; tennis. Picnicking. Camping (some fees). (Also see CHADRON and Samuel R. McKelvie National Forest, VALENTINE.)

Valentine (A-3)

Settled 1882
Population 2,826
Elevation 2,579 ft
Area Code 402
Zip 69201
Information Chamber of Commerce, 239 S Main, PO Box 201; phone 402/376-2969 or toll-free 800/658-4024
Web Site www.valentine-ne.com

Valentine, the seat of Cherry County, depends on cattle raising for its economy.

What to See and Do

Cherry County Historical Museum. *510 N Green St, Valentine (69201). Phone 402/376-2015.* Items and exhibits related to the history of Cherry County; 1882 log cabin; newspapers dating back to 1883; genealogy library. (May-Sept, Thurs-Sat) **DONATION**

Fishing. *Valentine.* Bass, crappie, perch, northern pike in numerous lakes south of town. Lakes include

Big Alkali Lake Wildlife Area. *Valentine. 17 miles S on Hwy 83, then 3 miles W on Hwy 16B.* Swimming; hunting; boating. Picnicking. Camping.

Valentine National Wildlife Refuge. *Valentine. 17 miles S on Hwy 83, then 13 miles W on Hwy 16B. Phone 402/376-3789.* Eight fishing lakes, waterfowl, upland game bird and deer hunting. Nature study, bird watching. (Daily, daylight hours) **FREE**

Fort Niobrara National Wildlife Refuge. *Valentine. 5 miles E on Hwy 12. Phone 402/376-3789.* Visitor center with exhibits. Nature study, canoeing, wildlife observation, picnicking. Also here are Fort Falls Nature Trail; Fort Niobrara Wilderness Area; a prairie dog town; and herds of buffalo, Texas longhorns, and elk. (Memorial Day-Labor Day: daily; rest of year: Mon-Fri) **FREE**

Samuel R. McKelvie National Forest. *HC 74, PO Box 10 and Nenzel, Valentine. 30 miles W on Hwy 20, then 19 miles S on Hwy 97. For information contact PO Box 38, Halsey 69142. Phone 308/533-2257.* Hunting. Hiking. Picnicking. Camping. Part of the Bessey Ranger District of the Nebraska National Forest (see CHADRON and THEDFORD). In the forest on Merritt Reservoir is

Merritt Reservoir State Recreation Area. *Valentine. 25 miles SW on Hwy 97.* Approximately 6,000 acres with a 2,906-acre reservoir in sandhill area. Swimming; fishing; boating (ramps). Picnicking, concession. Camping (dump station). Wildlife refuges nearby. Standard hours, fees.

Sawyer's Sandhills Museum. *440 Valentine St, Valentine (69201). On Hwy 20, four blocks W of Hwy 83. Phone 402/376-3293.* Pioneer and Native American artifacts, antique autos. (Memorial Day-Labor Day, daily by appointment) **$**

Special Events

Cherry County Fair. *County Fairgrounds, Valentine. Phone 402/376-2969.* Cherry County Fairgrounds. Midway, rodeo, agricultural, and crafts exhibits; races; concessions. Mid-Aug.

Old West Days & Poetry Gathering. *Valentine. Phone 402/376-2969.* Music and fun celebrating Old West heritage. Oct.

Wayne (B-5)

See also Norfolk

Founded 1881
Population 5,142
Elevation 1,500 ft
Area Code 402
Zip 68787
Information Wayne Area Chamber of Commerce, 108 W 3rd St; phone 402/375-2240
Web Site www.waynene.com

Laid out when the railroad connecting St. Paul to Sioux City was being built, the town was named after General "Mad Anthony" Wayne.

What to See and Do

Wayne State College. *1111 Main St, Wayne (68787). Phone 402/375-7000.* (1910) (4,000 students) Liberal arts, business, and teacher education. Tours. On campus is

Fred G. Dale Planetarium. *1111 Main St, Wayne (68787). Phone 402/375-7329.* Features dome-shaped screen, dozens of auxiliary and special effects projectors, and unique sound system. (Oct-Apr, by appointment; closed holidays) **FREE**

Special Events

Chicken Show. *Wayne State College, Wayne. Phone 402/375-2240.* Music contests, parade, omelet feed, chicken dinner feed, egg games, craft show, antique show and sale. Second Sat in July.

Wayne County Fair. *Wayne County Fairgrounds, Wayne. Phone 402/375-2240.* 1/2 miles W on Hwy 35. 4-H exhibits, agricultural displays, carnival, nightly entertainment, free barbecue. Aug.

West Point (B-5)

Founded 1857
Population 3,250
Area Code 402
Zip 68788
Web Site www.ci.west-point.ne.us

Named by early settlers who considered it the western extremity of settlement, West Point was originally a mill town.

What to See and Do

John G. Neihardt Center. *306 W Elm St, Bancroft (68004). 11 miles N on Hwy 9, then 8 miles E on Hwy 51, at Elm and Washington sts. Phone 402/648-3388.* Contains memorabilia of Nebraska's late poet laureate; restored one-room study; Sioux Prayer Garden symbolizes Sioux Hoop of the World. (Daily; closed Jan 1, Thanksgiving, Dec 25) **FREE**

York (C-5)

See also Grand Island, Lincoln

Founded 1869
Population 7,884
Elevation 1,609 ft
Area Code 402
Zip 68467
Information York County Visitors Center, 116 S Lincoln Ave, Suite 1; phone 402/362-5531 or toll-free 888/733-9675
Web Site www.yorkchamber.org

What to See and Do

Anna Bemis Palmer Museum. *211 E 7th St, York (68467). Phone 402/363-2630.* Items and displays relating to the history of the city, York County, and the state of Nebraska. (Mon-Fri; closed holidays) **FREE**

Limited-Service Hotels

★ **BEST WESTERN PALMER INN.** *2426 S Lincoln Ave, York (68467). Phone 402/362-5585; toll-free 800/452-3185; fax 402/362-6053. www.best western.com.* 41 rooms. Check-out 11 am. **$**
🅑

★ **DAYS INN.** *3710 S Lincoln Ave, York (68467). Phone 402/362-6355; fax 402/362-2827. www.daysinn .com.* 39 rooms, 2 story. Complimentary continental breakfast. Check-out noon. Indoor pool, whirlpool. **$**
🏊

Restaurant

★ ★ **CHANCES R.** *124 W 5th, York (68467). Phone 402/362-7755; fax 402/362-3929.* American menu. Breakfast, lunch, dinner, late-night, Sun brunch. Closed Dec 25. Bar. Children's menu. Turn-of-the-century décor; many antiques. Valet parking. **$$$**

From the farmland of Nebraska, there are two national parks that you should consider traveling to despite the distance: Badlands National Park and Wind Cave National Park, both in southwestern South Dakota. The dramatic scenery of these national parks is well worth the distance and time it will take you to get there.

Badlands National Park, SD

2 hours, 40 minutes, 110 miles from Chadron, NE

75 miles E of Rapid City via I-90, Hwy 240.

Web Site www.nps.gov/badl

This fantastic, painted landscape of steep canyons, spires, and razor-edged ridges was made a national monument by President Franklin D. Roosevelt in 1939 and became a national park in 1978. Its stark and simple demonstration of geologic processes has an unusual beauty. Soft clays and sandstones deposited as sediments 26 to 37 million years ago by streams from the Black Hills created vast plains, which were inhabited by the saber-toothed cat, the rhinoceros-like brontothere, and ancestors of the present-day camel and horse. Their fossilized bones make the area an enormous prehistoric graveyard. Herds of bison, gone for many years, roam the area again. Pronghorn antelope, mule deer, prairie dogs, and Rocky Mountain bighorn sheep can also be seen.

More than 600 feet of volcanic ash and other sediments were laid down. About 500,000 years ago, streams began carving the present structures, leaving gullies and multicolored canyons.

The Ben Reifel Visitor Center, with exhibits and an audiovisual program, is open all year at Cedar Pass (daily; closed Jan 1, Thanksgiving, Dec 25). The Touch Room is open to children of all ages. Evening programs and activities conducted by ranger-naturalists are offered during the summer. Camping is available at Cedar Pass (fee) and Sage Creek (free). The White River Visitor Center, 60 miles southwest of the Ben Reifel Visitor Center, features colorful displays on the history and culture of the Oglala Sioux. Per-vehicle fee; Golden Eagle, Golden Age, and Golden Access Passports are accepted. For further information, contact PO Box 6, Interior 57750; phone 605/433-5361.

Wind Cave National Park, SD

1 hour 45 minutes, 68 miles from Chadron, NE

11 miles N of Hot Springs on Hwy 385.

Wind Cave, one of many caves in the ring of limestone surrounding the Black Hills, is a maze of subterranean passages known to extend more than 79 miles. It is named for the strong currents of wind that blow in or out of its entrance according to atmospheric pressure. When the pressure decreases, the wind blows outward; when it increases, the wind blows in. It was the rushing sound of air coming out of the entrance that led to its discovery in 1881. The cave and surrounding area became a national park in 1903; today, it comprises 44 square miles.

Wind Cave is a constant 53° F. Various one- to two-hour guided tours (daily; no tours Thanksgiving, Dec 25) and four-hour tours (June-mid-Aug, daily). Tours are moderately strenuous. A sweater or jacket is advised; shoes must have low heels and nonslip soles.

On the surface are prairie grasslands, forests, and a wildlife preserve—the home of bison, pronghorn elk, deer, prairie dogs, and other animals. The Centennial Trail, a 111-mile, multi-use trail, takes visitors from one end of the Black Hills to the other. The trail begins here and ends at Bear Butte State Park. In addition, there is hiking, bicycling, picnicking, and camping at Elk Mountain near headquarters. Visitor center (daily; closed Thanksgiving, Dec 25). Hours may vary throughout the year. Park (daily). Phone 605/745-4600. Tours **$$-$$$$**

Oklahoma

Populated by Native Americans, the area that was to become the state of Oklahoma was practically unknown to Americans at the time of the Louisiana Purchase of 1803. Believing those unsettled lands to be of little value, the government set them aside as "Indian Territory" in 1830, assigning a portion to each of the Five Civilized Tribes. Between 1830-1846, 20,000 Creeks of Georgia and Alabama, 5,000 Choctaws of Mississippi and Louisiana, 4,000 Chickasaws of Mississippi, and 3,000 Seminoles of Florida were forced to move to Oklahoma. In 1838, some 16,000 Cherokees were marched west from their lands in North Carolina, Tennessee, and Georgia by troops under the command of General Winfield Scott. Many hid out in the hills and swamps of their homeland, where their descendants still remain. About one-fourth of those forced west over this "Trail of Tears" died en route of hunger, disease, cold, and exhaustion. But those who reached the Indian Territory were soon running their own affairs with skill and determination. By 1890, 67 different tribal groups resided in Oklahoma. Today Oklahoma has the largest Native American population in the United States.

As the nation moved west, settlers squatted in the Indian Territory, wanting the land for their own. On April 22, 1889, portions of the land were opened for settlement. In the next few years all unassigned Oklahoma land was opened by a series of six "runs." People who jumped the gun were called "Sooners," hence Oklahoma's nickname, the "Sooner State." Close to 17 million acres of land in the state were settled in this way; the last "lottery," a form of run, took place on August 16, 1901. Previously unsettled tracts became cities within eight hours.

Population: 3,145,585
Area: 69,919 square miles
Elevation: 287-4,973 feet
Peak: Black Mesa (Cimarron County)
Entered Union: November 16, 1907 (46th state)
Capital: Oklahoma City
Motto: Labor Conquers All Things
Nickname: Sooner State
Flower: Mistletoe
Bird: Scissor-tailed Flycatcher
Tree: Redbud
Fair: September in Oklahoma City
Time Zone: Central
Web Site: www.travelok.com
Fun Facts:
- Oklahoma has more man-made lakes than any other state.
- Oklahoma has produced more astronauts than any other state.

Oklahoma produces many millions of barrels of oil a year and great quantities of natural gas. It is a leader in coal production and also produces gypsum limestone, tripoli, granite, and other minerals. The state's three largest industries are agriculture, tourism, and petroleum. The McClellan-Kerr Arkansas River Navigation System has given Oklahoma a direct water route to the Mississippi River and to the Gulf of Mexico. The ports of Muskogee, on the Arkansas River, and Catoosa, on the Verdigris River, connect Oklahoma to the inland waterway system and to major US markets.

Oklahoma is developing its recreational resources at a rapid rate. Every year millions of tourists and vacationers visit the growing number of lakes, built mostly for electric power, and the state park system, one of the best in the country.

Calendar Highlights

JANUARY

International Finals Rodeo *(Oklahoma City).* *Myriad Convention Center. Phone 405/235-6540 or 405/948-6800.* International Pro Rodeo Association's top 15 cowboys and cowgirls compete in seven events to determine world championships.

APRIL

Festival of the Arts *(Oklahoma City). Phone 405/ 297-8912 or toll-free 800/225-5652.* International foods, entertainment, children's learning and play area; craft market; artists from many states display their work. Contact Convention & Visitors Bureau.

Medieval Fair *(Norman). University of Oklahoma, Brandt Park. Phone 405/288-2536.* Living history fair depicting life in the Middle Ages; strolling minstrels, jugglers, jesters; knights in armor joust; storytellers.

MAY

Antique Car Swap Meet *(Chickasha). Phone 405/ 224-6552.*

Tri-State Music Festival *(Enid). Phone 580/237-4964.*

AUGUST

American Indian Exposition *(Anadarko). Phone 405/247-6651.* Parade, dance contests, horse races, arts and crafts.

SEPTEMBER

Cherokee National Holiday *(Tahlequah). Phone 918/456-0671 ext. 2610 or toll-free 800/850-0348.* Celebration of the signing of the first Cherokee Constitution in September 1839. Championship cornstalk bow and arrow shoot, powwow, rodeo, tournaments, and other events.

Chili Cookoff & Bluegrass Festival *(Tulsa). Phone 918/583-2617.* The best in bluegrass and country music and the International Chili Society Mid-America Regional Chili Cookoff.

State Fair of Oklahoma *(Oklahoma City). Phone 405/948-6700.* Livestock, crafts, art exhibits; ice show, circus, rodeo; truck pull contests; auto races; concerts; international show, flower and garden show; Native American ceremonial dances; carriage collection; monorail, space tower, carnival, parades. Arena and grandstand attractions.

World Championship Quarter Horse Show *(Oklahoma City). Phone 405/297-8912 or toll-free 800/225-5652.* More than 1,800 horses compete on the state fairgrounds. Contact Convention & Visitors Bureau.

When to Go/Climate

Oklahoma is a state of extremes. Located in the heart of Tornado Alley, temperatures can change dramatically in minutes. An unusual number of sunny days and entire months of mild temperatures help compensate for the often-sweltering summer heat.

AVERAGE HIGH/LOW TEMPERATURES (° F)

Oklahoma City

Jan 47/25	May 79/58	Sept 84/62
Feb 52/30	June 87/66	Oct 74/50
Mar 62/39	July 93/71	Nov 60/39
Apr 72/49	Aug 93/70	Dec 50/29

Tulsa

Jan 45/25	May 80/59	Sept 84/63
Feb 51/30	June 88/68	Oct 74/51
Mar 62/39	July 94/73	Nov 60/40
Apr 73/50	Aug 93/71	Dec 49/29

Parks and Recreation

For further information write Oklahoma Tourism & Recreation Dept, Literature Distribution Center, PO Box 60789, Oklahoma City, 73146.

Water-related activities, hiking, riding, various other sports, picnicking and visitor centers, as well as camping, are available in many areas. Many of the state parks have lodges and cabins as well as campsites and trailer parks. Camping fee ($12-$25) required for assigned campgrounds and trailer hook-ups; tent camping ($7-$9); camping fee ($11-$17) in unassigned areas. For state park reservations, phone the park directly. Pets on leash only. For further information, contact the Division of State Parks, 15 N Robinson, PO Box 52002, Oklahoma City, 73152-2002. Phone 405/521-3411, toll-free 800/652-6552, or 800/654-8240 (reservations).

FISHING AND HUNTING

Nonresident fishing license: five-day, $10; 14-day, $20; annual, $28.50; nonresident hunting license: small game, five-day, $35 (except pheasant, turkey, or deer), annual, $85; deer, $201. Trout fishing license: $7.75.

Many species of fish are found statewide: large-mouth bass, white bass, catfish, crappie, and blue-gill. Rainbow trout can be found throughout the year in the Illinois River, Mountain Fork River, Lake Pawhuska, and Broken Bow Lake; during the winter at Lake Watonga, Blue River, Lake Carl Etling, and below Altus-Lugert dam; striped bass in Lake Keystone, Lake Texoma, and the Arkansas River Navigation System; and smallmouth bass in several eastern streams as well as in Broken Bow, Murray, and Texoma lakes.

For information about fishing and hunting regulations and changes in fees, contact the Oklahoma Department of Wildlife Conservation, 1801 N Lincoln Blvd, Oklahoma City, 73105; phone 405/521-3851. For boating regulations contact Lake Patrol Division, Department of Public Safety, 3600 N Martin Luther King Ave, Oklahoma City, 73136. Phone 405/425-2143.

Driving Information

Safety belts are mandatory for all persons in the front seat of a vehicle. Children under 6 years must be in approved passenger restraints anywhere in a vehicle: ages 4 and 5 may use regulation safety belts; age 3 and under may use regulation safety belts in the back seat, however, in the front seat children must use approved safety seats. Phone 405/523-1570.

INTERSTATE HIGHWAY SYSTEM

The following alphabetical listing of Oklahoma towns in this book shows that these cities are within 10 miles of the indicated Interstate highways. Check a highway map for the nearest exit.

Highway Number	Cities/Towns within 10 Miles
Interstate 35	Ardmore, Guthrie, Marietta, Norman, Oklahoma City, Pauls Valley, Perry.
Interstate 40	Clinton, Elk City, El Reno, Henryetta, Oklahoma City, Sallisaw, Shawnee, Wheatherford.
Interstate 44	Chickasaw, Lawton, Miami, Oklahoma City, Tulsa.

Additional Visitor Information

Free information on the state may be obtained from the Oklahoma Tourism & Recreation Department, Literature Distribution Center, PO Box 52002, Oklahoma City, 73152-2002; phone 405/521-3831 or toll-free 800/652-6552. Also available from the Tourism Dept,

There are 10 traveler information centers in Oklahoma; visitors who stop will find information and brochures. Their locations are as follows: from the N, 10 miles S of OK-KS border on I-35; from the E, 14 miles W of OK-AR border on I-40; from the S, 2 miles N of OK-TX border on Hwy 69/75, or 4 miles N of OK-TX border on I-35; from the SW, on I-44 at the Walters exit; from the W, 9 miles E of OK-TX border on I-40. (Daily, summer, 7 am-7 pm; winter, 8:30 am-5 pm) Also: from the NE, on Will Rogers Tpke E of Miami, Catoosa-intersection of Will Rogers Tpke & US 66; at intersection of I-35 and NE 50th in Oklahoma City; and at the State Capitol Building, NE 23rd and Lincoln Blvd; all centers are closed Dec 25.

EXPLORING OKLAHOMA'S STATE PARKS

Begin your tour of southeastern and eastern Oklahoma at the small town of Broken Bow, located at the edge of the Ouachita National Forest. This is a good place to stock up on picnic supplies for lunch or dinner at one of the gorgeous state parks that lie ahead on this two-day driving route. About 6 miles east of town on Highway 70, history buffs will enjoy exploring the 1880s home of Choctaw Chief Jefferson Gardner. If you would prefer to investigate nature's offerings, head 7 miles north of town along Highway 259 to Beavers Bend State Park, one of the most gorgeous places in this part of the country. Lake Broken Bow, at 14,200 acres, offers park visitors 180 miles of pretty, wooded shoreline, as well as bass fishing, paddleboating, canoeing, and swimming. The park is also adjacent to Mountain Fork River, popular for its trout fishing and canoe trips; on land, you'll get a kick out of horseback riding, miniature golf, and golf on Cedar Creek Golf Course. Stay overnight here, or continue on for an overnight at Lake Wister.

Continue north on scenic Highway 259 through the tree-covered Kiamichi Mountains and you'll enter the Ouachita National Forest. If you turn west on Oklahoma Highway 1, you'll be on the spectacular Talimena Scenic Drive, which makes a 54-mile reach between Talihina, Oklahoma, and Mena, Arkansas. Take plenty of film to capture the vistas from various look-out spots on the sides of the road; look to the north to see the beautiful Winding Stair Mountains. Once you're in Talihina, go 4 miles southwest on Highway 271 to Talimena State Park, a wonderful place for picnicking. Back on Highway 259, continue north and pick up Highway 59 north to Lake Wister State Park, a pretty, wooded spread of 33,428 acres that showcase 4,000-acre Lake Wister and a 2,000-acre waterfowl refuge. You could spend time here hiking, mountain biking (if you bring your own wheels), horseback riding, fishing, and swimming. This is a good overnight spot, and some of the park's 15 cabins have fireplaces. Less than 3 miles northeast of Highway 59 and Highway 270, Heavener Runestone State Park is the place to go to see gigantic stone tablets carved with runic alphabet characters. Nobody seems to understand it, but the markings are thought to be made by Vikings around 1012.

Stay north on Highway 59 about 50 miles to Sallisaw, on the eastern edge of Oklahoma's Green Country. Eleven miles northeast of town via Oklahoma Highway 101, you'll find the Sequoyah's Home Site, with exhibits about the leader who created the Cherokee alphabet. Drive west from Sallisaw via Highway 64 about 10 miles, then follow Oklahoma Highway 82 north to wonderful Tenkiller State Park, hugging the southern end of magnificent Lake Tenkiller. There's great scuba diving here, as well as cabins for taking a break from the world. Follow Highway 82 along the lake's eastern edge, and you'll find scenic park areas called Snake Creek Cove, Sixshooter Camp, Cookson Bend, and Standing Rock Landing. Lodges and resorts surround the lake too. Follow scenic Highway 82 north about 10 miles from the lake's northern end and you'll finish your driving tour at Tallequah, capital city of the Cherokee Nation. Destinations here include the Cherokee Heritage Center, with a good museum, outdoor theater, and authentic Indian village; the Murrell Home, a restored antebellum home that belonged to a prominent early citizen; and the restored 1889 Cherokee National Female Seminary, at Northeastern State University. **(Approximately 90 miles)**

OKLAHOMA'S NATIVE AMERICAN HERITAGE

Drive west from Oklahoma City on Highway 270 to Highway 81 south, a designated scenic route. Cross the Canadian River and head west on Highway 37/152 and south on Highway 281 to Anadarko, a center of Native American heritage, with an American Indian Hall of Fame, Southern Plains Indian Museum, art galleries, tribal museums, and overnight stays in tepees. Continue south on Highway 281 to Medicine Park, a funky old resort town with cobblestone buildings and access to Mount Scott, a remarkable viewpoint for the region, which includes the Wichita Mountains Wildlife Refuge. Immediately south is Lawton/Fort Sill, with a sensational history museum showcasing Geronimo, buffalo soldiers, and tribes, as well as historic cemeteries and granite cliff scenery. Head east on Highway 7 to Duncan to see the marvelous Chisholm Trail Statue and Museum, then go north on Highway 81 back to Oklahoma City. **(Approximately 160 miles)**

Ada (C-4)

See also Pauls Valley, Sulphur

Founded 1890
Population 15,820
Area Code 580
Zip 74820
Information Chamber of Commerce, 300 W Main, PO Box 248, 74821; phone 580/332-2506
Web Site www.adaok.com

Ada is one of the principal cities of southeastern Oklahoma. Important manufactured products here are automotive parts, farm implements, furniture, feed, denim clothing, and biomedical supplies. South of the city are fine silica sand and limestone quarries that provide the raw material for cement. Cattle operations are still important, and oil is produced throughout the county.

What to See and Do

East Central University. *1100 E 14th St, Ada (74820). Main St and Francis Ave. Phone 580/332-8000.* (1909) (4,000 students.) At the entrance to the campus is the fossilized stump of a rare giant Callixylon tree of the Devonian Age.

Wintersmith Park. *1700 Wintersmith, Ada (74820). 18th St at Scenic Dr. Phone 580/436-6300.* Covering approximately 140 acres, the park has an arboretum, restored one-room schoolhouse (1907), small zoo, carousel, 1/2-mile miniature train ride, concerts. Swimming pool, stocked fishing lake; miniature golf, picnic area. Fee for some activities. (Daily) **FREE**

Altus (C-2)

See also Quartz Mountain State Park

Founded 1891
Population 21,910
Elevation 1,398 ft
Area Code 580
Information Chamber of Commerce, 123 Commerce, PO Box 518, 73522; phone 580/482-0210
Web Site www.cityofaltus.org

In the spring of 1891, a flood on Bitter Creek forced a group of settlers to flee to higher ground, taking with them what possessions they could. Gathered together to escape destruction, they founded a town and called it Altus because one of them said the word meant "high ground."

On the border between the high plains and the southland, Altus lies between winter wheat on the north and cotton on the south. The Lugert-Altus irrigation district, using water from Lake Altus on the North Fork of the Red River, feeds 70,000 acres of prosperous farmland growing cotton, wheat, alfalfa seed, and cattle. Nearby Altus Air Force Base is the home of the 97th Air Mobility Wing.

What to See and Do

Museum of the Western Prairie. *1100 Memorial Dr, Altus (73521). Phone 580/482-1044.* Exhibits depict all aspects of pioneer living in southwestern Oklahoma. Also, building featuring displays of early farm implements, coaches, wagons; original reconstructed half-dugout house. Reference library. (Tues-Sat; closed holidays) **DONATION**

Special Events

Great Plains Stampede Rodeo. *Altus. Phone 580/482-0210.* PRCA-sanctioned rodeo; special events. Late Aug.

Jackson County Fair. *1224 Driving Park Rd, Wellston (45692). Phone 740/384-6587.* Livestock, carnival, games, food. Mid-July.

Limited-Service Hotels

★ **BEST WESTERN ALTUS.** *2804 N Main St, Altus (73521). Phone 580/482-9300; fax 580/482-2245. www.bestwestern.com.* 100 rooms, 2 story. Pets accepted, some restrictions; fee. Complimentary continental breakfast. Check-out noon. Fitness room. Indoor pool, outdoor pool. Business center. **$**

★ ★ **RAMADA INN.** *2515 E Broadway St, Altus (73521). Phone 580/477-3000; fax 580/477-0078. www.ramada.com.* 12 rooms, 2 story. Pets accepted; fee. Check-out noon. Restaurant, bar. Indoor pool. **$**

Alva (A-3)

Population 5,495

Elevation 1,350 ft
Area Code 580
Zip 73717
Information Chamber of Commerce, 410 College Ave; phone 580/327-1647 or toll-free 888/854-2262
Web Site www.alvaok.net

What to See and Do

Alabaster Caverns. *50A, Freedom. 25 miles W on Hwy 64, then 7 miles S via Hwy 50, 50A. Phone 580/621-3381.* On approximately 200 acres, Alabaster is said to be the largest known natural gypsum cavern in the world; tours (daily); Cedar Canyon. Bathhouse; picnicking, playground, camping area, trailer sites. (Daily) **$$$**

Cherokee Strip Museum. *901 14th St, Alva (73717). Phone 580/327-2030.* Historical display of Cherokee Strip; Lincoln pictures; collection of flags, soldiers' uniforms; antiques, dolls, toys, furniture; general store, kitchen; miniature trains; authentic covered wagon; adjacent annex houses small farm machinery. Old schoolhouse. (Sat-Sun; summer hours vary; closed holidays) **FREE**

Great Salt Plains. *Hwy 38, Jet. 16 miles E on Hwy 64, then 11 miles E on Hwy 11, then S on Hwy 38. Phone 580/626-4731.* Approximately 840 acres with 9,300-acre lake. Swimming, fishing, boating (ramps); nature trails, picnic area, playground, camping areas, trailer hook-ups (fee), cabins. (Daily)

Little Sahara. *Hwy 281, Alva. 28 miles S and W on Hwy 281. Phone 580/824-1471.* Approximately 1,600 acres. Sand dunes. Picnicking, playground. Trailer hook-ups (fee). (Daily)

Limited-Service Hotel

★ **RANGER INN.** *420 E Oklahoma Blvd, Alva (73717). Phone 580/327-1981; fax 580/327-1981.* 41 rooms. Pets accepted, some restrictions. Check-out 11 am. **$**
🔁

Anadarko (C-3)

See also Chickasha

Founded 1901
Population 6,586
Area Code 405
Zip 73005

Information Chamber of Commerce, 516 W Kentucky, PO Box 366; phone 405/247-6651
Web Site www.anadarko.org

Anadarko, along with the Wichita Indian Agency, were formed in 1859 after eastern tribes were relocated here. The Bureau of Indian Affairs area office is located here.

What to See and Do

Anadarko Philomathic Museum. *Rock Island Depot, 311 E Main St, Anadarko (73005). Phone 405/247-3240.* Train memorabilia displayed in an old ticket office; Native American doll collection; paintings, costumes, and artifacts; military equipment and uniforms; excellent photographic collection; early physician's office; country store. (Tues-Sun; closed holidays) **FREE**

Fort Cobb State Park. *N of city, Fort Cobb. 8 miles W on Hwy 62, then 12 miles NW off Hwy 9. Phone 405/643-2249.* A 2,850-acre park; 4,100-acre lake. Swimming, waterskiing, fishing, boating (ramps, marina); hunting, 18-hole golf, picnic facilities, camping, trailer hook-ups (fee). (Daily) **FREE**

Indian City USA. *Hwy 8, Anadarko. 2 1/2 miles SE on Hwy 8. Phone 405/247-5661 (in Oklahoma); toll-free 800/433-5661. www.indiancityusa.com.* Authentic reconstruction of seven Plains tribes' villages (Pawnee, Wichita, Caddo, Kiowa, Navajo, Pueblo, and Apache) with Native American guides (45-minute tours) and a dance program. Arts and crafts shop. Swimming. Concession. Camping. (Daily; closed Jan 1, Thanksgiving, Dec 25) (See SPECIAL EVENTS) **$$$**

National Hall of Fame for Famous American Indians. *10010 E Central Blvd, Anadarko (73005). E on Hwy 62E. Phone 405/247-5555.* Outdoor museum with sculptured bronze busts of famous Native Americans (daily). Visitor center (daily; closed Thanksgiving, Dec 25). **FREE**

Southern Plains Indian Museum and Crafts Center. *715 E Central Blvd, Anadarko (73005). E on Hwy 62 E. Phone 405/247-6221.* Exhibits of historic and contemporary Native American arts from the southern plains region. (Tues-Sat; closed Jan 1, Thanksgiving, Dec 25) **$$**

Special Events

American Indian Exposition. *Caddo County Fairground, Anadarko.* Phone 405/247-6651. Parade, dances, horse races; arts and crafts. Mid-Aug.

Caddo County Free Fair. *7th St and Broadway, Anadarko (73005).* Phone 405/247-6651. Early Sept.

Holiday Celebration. *Randlett Park, 516 W Kentucky Ave, Anadarko (73005).* Phone 405/247-6651. Hand-built lighted Christmas displays. Late Nov-Dec.

Kiowa Veterans Black Leggins Ceremonial. *Indian City, Anadarko.* Phone 405/247-6651. Early Oct.

Ardmore (D-4)

See also Marietta, Sulphur

Founded 1887
Population 23,079
Elevation 881 ft
Area Code 580
Zip 73401
Information Chamber of Commerce, 410 W Main, PO Box 1585; phone 580/223-7765
Web Site www.ardmore.org

This is an oil and cattle town and a good center for recreation. The Arbuckle Mountains are a few miles north of town.

What to See and Do

Charles B. Goddard Center. *401 1st Ave SW, Ardmore (73401).* Phone 580/226-0909. Contemporary Western graphics, painting, and sculpture. National touring exhibits. Community theater, dance, concerts. (Tues-Sat; closed holidays)

Eliza Cruce Hall Doll Museum. *320 E Street NW, Ardmore (73401). In the public library.* Phone 580/223-8290. Collection of more than 300 antique dolls, some dating to 1728; display includes porcelain, bisque, leather, wood, and wax dolls. (Daily; closed holidays) **FREE**

Greater Southwest Historical Museum. *35 Sunset Dr, Ardmore (73401).* Phone 580/226-3857. "Living" exhibits; oil and agricultural machinery; military memorabilia; re-creation of a pioneer community. (Tues-Sat, Sun afternoon) **DONATION**

Lake Murray State Park. *3310 S Lake Murray Dr, Ardmore (73401). 7 miles SE, off I-35 exit 24 or 29.* Phone 580/223-4044. (see)

Special Event

Carter County Free Fair. *Hardy Murphy Coliseum, 600 Lake Murray Dr S, Ardmore (73401).* Phone 580/223-7765. Various festivities. Early Sept.

Limited-Service Hotels

★ **DAYS INN.** *2614 W Broadway St, Ardmore (73401).* Phone 580/226-1761; fax 580/223-3131. www.daysinn.com. 47 rooms, 2 story. Pets accepted; fee. Complimentary continental breakfast. Check-out 11 am. **$**
🐾

★ ★ **HOLIDAY INN.** *2705 W Holiday Dr, Ardmore (73401).* Phone 580/223-7130; toll-free 800/465-4329; fax 580/223-7130. www.holiday-inn.com. 169 rooms, 2 story. Pets accepted, some restrictions; fee. Check-out 11 am. Restaurant. Fitness room. Outdoor pool, children's pool. Airport transportation available. Tea maker. **$**
🐾 🏋 🌊

Atoka (D-5)

Founded 1867
Population 3,298
Elevation 583 ft
Area Code 580
Zip 74525
Information Chamber of Commerce, PO Box 778; phone 580/889-2410
Web Site www.atokacity.org

What to See and Do

Boggy Depot State Park. *Atoka. 11 miles W on Hwy 7, then 4 miles S on Park Ln.* Phone 580/889-5625. Approximately 420 acres. Picnicking, playgrounds. Camping areas, trailer hook-ups (fee). Historical area. (Daily) **FREE**

Confederate Memorial Museum and Cemetary. *Atoka. 1/2 mile N on Hwy 69.* Phone 580/889-7912. Site reserved as an outpost throughout the Civil War. Museum features artifacts and memorabilia. Cemetery contains the remains of Confederate soldiers. (Mon-Sat; closed holidays) **FREE**

Limited-Service Hotel

★ ★ **BEST WESTERN ATOKA INN.** *2101 S Mississippi Ave, Atoka (74525). Phone 580/889-7381; toll-free 800/780-7234; fax 580/889-6695. www.bestwestern.com.* 54 rooms, 2 story. Pets accepted; fee. Check-out noon. Restaurant. Outdoor pool. Airport transportation available. **$**

🅳 🐾 🏊

Bartlesville (A-5)

See also Pawhuska

Founded 1875
Population 34,256
Elevation 715 ft
Area Code 918
Information Bartlesville Area Chamber of Commerce, 201 S Keeler, PO Box 2366, 74005; phone 918/336-8708 or toll-free 800/364-8708
Web Site www.bartlesville.com

The Bartlesville area is proud of its Western and Native American heritage, which involves three tribes—the Cherokee, Delaware, and Osage. Oklahoma's first electricity was produced here in 1876 when Jacob Bartles, an early settler, hitched a dynamo to the Caney River. Oil, first tapped in the area in 1897, is the economic base of the city, which is the headquarters of the Phillips Petroleum Company.

Bartlesville has become internationally known for its distinguished, modern architecture, a building trend initiated by the H. C. Price family. The town boasts a number of both public and private buildings by Frank Lloyd Wright and Bruce Goff.

What to See and Do

Frank Phillips Mansion. *1107 S Cherokee Ave, Bartlesville (74003). Phone 918/336-2491.* Built in 1909 by the founder of the Phillips Petroleum Company. This Neoclassical house has been restored to the 1930s period; interior includes imported woods, marble, Oriental rugs, and original furnishings. Listed on the National Register of Historic Places. (Wed-Sun; closed holidays). **DONATION**

Nellie Johnstone Oil Well. *In Johnstone Park, 300 N Cherokee, Bartlesville (74003).* Replica of the original rig, the first commercial oil well in the state. An 83-acre park with a low water dam on the Caney River. Fishing; picnicking, playgrounds, children's rides (late May-Labor Day, daily; closed July 4). Park (daily). **FREE**

Price Tower. *510 Dewey Ave, Bartlesville (74003). Phone 918/336-4949.* Designed by Frank Lloyd Wright, this 221-foot office building was built by pipeline construction pioneer H. C. Price as headquarters for his company. The building design is based on a diamond module of 30/60-degree triangles. Although Wright designed many skyscrapers, Price Tower was the only tall building of his to be completed. Guided tours (45 minutes). (Tues-Sat)

Tom Mix Museum. *721 N Delaware, Dewey (74029). Phone 918/534-1555.* Exhibits and memorabilia of silent movie star Tom Mix, the first "King of the Cowboys"; displays of his cowboy gear; stills from his films. (Tues-Sun; closed holidays) **DONATION**

⭐ **Woolaroc.** *Hwy 23, Bartlesville. 12 miles SW on Hwy 123. Phone 918/336-0307.* Complex covering 3,600 acres with wildlife preserve for herds of American bison, longhorn cattle, Scottish Highland cattle, elk, deer, and other native wildlife. These are wild animals and may be dangerous; it is mandatory to stay in your car. Paintings by Russell, Remington, and other great Western artists are at the museum; exhibits on the development of America; artifacts of several Native American tribes, pioneers, and cowboys; also one of finest collections of Colt firearms in country. The Woolaroc Lodge (1925), once a private dwelling, has paintings, bark-covered furnishings, and blankets. The Native American Heritage Center has multimedia shows, authentic Native American crafts, art displays, and a nature trail (1 1/2 miles). Picnic area. (Late May-early Sept: Tues-Sun; rest of year: Wed-Sun; closed Thanksgiving, Dec 25). **$$**

Limited-Service Hotels

★ ★ **BEST WESTERN WESTON INN.** *222 SE Washington Blvd, Bartlesville (74006). Phone 918/335-7755; toll-free 800/780-7234; fax 918/335-7763. www.bestwestern.com.* 109 rooms, 2 story. Pets accepted; fee. Complimentary continental breakfast. Check-out 11 am. Restaurant. Outdoor pool. **$**

🐾 🏊

★ ★ **HOLIDAY INN.** *1410 SE Washington Blvd, Bartlesville (74006). Phone 918/333-8320; toll-free 877/371-5920; fax 918/333-8979. www.holiday-inn.com.* 105 rooms, 3 story. Check-out noon. Restaurant, bar. Fitness room. Indoor pool. **$**

🧍 🏊

Full-Service Inn

★ ★ ★ **INN AT PRICE TOWER.** *510 Dewey Ave, Bartlesville (74005). Phone 918/336-1000.* 21 rooms. Complimentary continental breakfast. Check-in 3 pm, check-out noon. Restaurant, bar. Business center. **$$$**
🏃

Restaurants

★ **MURPHY'S ORIGINAL STEAK HOUSE.** *1625 SW Frank Phillips Blvd, Bartlesville (74003). Phone 918/336-4789; fax 918/362-3929. www. murphys.com.* Steak menu. Breakfast, lunch, dinner, late-night, brunch. Closed holidays. **$$**

★ ★ **STERLING'S GRILLE.** *2905 E Frank Phillips Blvd, Bartlesville (74006). Phone 918/335-0707.* Seafood, steak menu. Lunch, dinner. Bar. Children's menu. Outdoor seating. Three separate rooms with different motifs. **$$**

Boise City (E-1)

See also Dalhart

Population 1,509
Elevation 4,165 ft
Area Code 580
Zip 73933
Information Cimarron County Chamber of Commerce, 6 NE Square, in the red caboose, PO Box 1027; phone 580/544-3344
Web Site www.ccccok.org

What to See and Do

Black Mesa State Park. *Boise City. 19 miles NW on Hwy 325, then 9 miles W on unnumbered roads. Phone 580/426-2222.* Lake Carl Etling (260 acres) offers fishing facilities; boating (ramps). Picnic area, playground. Camping, trailer hook-ups (fee). (Daily) **FREE**

Special Event

Santa Fe Trail Daze Celebration. *6 NE Square, Boise City (73933). Phone 580/544-3344.* Guided tour of Santa Fe Trail crossing, autograph rock, dinosaur tracks, and excavation site. First weekend in June.

Broken Bow (D-6)

See also Idabel

Population 3,961
Elevation 467 ft
Area Code 580
Zip 74728
Information Chamber of Commerce, 113 W Martin Luther King; phone 580/584-3393 or toll-free 800/ 528-7337

What to See and Do

Beavers Bend Resort State Park. *Broken Bow. 6 miles N on Hwy 259, then 3 miles E on Hwy 259A. Phone 580/494-6300.* This 3,522-acre mountainous area is crossed by the Mountain Fork River and includes the Broken Bow Reservoir. Swimming, bathhouse, fishing, boating (no motors); nature trail, picnic areas, playground, grocery, restaurant, camping, trailer hook-ups (fee), cabins. Nature center. (Daily) (See SPECIAL EVENT) **FREE**

Hochatown State Park. *Broken Bow. 10 miles N on Hwy 259. Phone 580/494-6452.* Covers 1,713 acres on 14,220-acre Broken Bow Lake. Swimming, waterskiing, fishing, bait and tackle shop, boating (ramps, marina, rentals, gas dock, boathouses); hiking trails, 18-hole golf course, picnicking, playground, snack bar, trailer hook-ups (fee), dump station, restrooms. (Daily) **FREE**

Special Event

Kiamichi Owa Chito Festival. *Beavers Bend Resort State Park, Broken Bow. Phone 580/494-6509.* Contests, entertainment, food. Third weekend in June.

Limited-Service Hotel

★ ★ **THE CHARLES WESLEY MOTOR LODGE.** *302 N Park Dr, Broken Bow (74728). Phone 580/584-3303; fax 580/584-3433.* 50 rooms, 2 story. Check-out 11 am. Restaurant. Outdoor pool. **$**
🅳 ⛱

Checotah (B-5)

Restaurant

★ ★ **COLOURS.** *Hwy 60, Checotah (74426). Phone 918/689-9173; fax 918/689-9493.* Breakfast, lunch, dinner. Bar. Children's menu. **$$**

Chickasha (C-3)

See also Anadarko

Founded 1892
Population 14,988
Elevation 1,095 ft
Area Code 405
Information Chamber of Commerce, 221 W Chickasha Ave, PO Box 1717, 73023; phone 405/224-0787
Web Site www.chickasha-cc.com

Established to serve as a passenger and freight division point for the Rock Island and Pacific Railroad in 1892, this town site was on land originally given to the Choctaw in 1820. It became part of the Chickasaw Nation in 1834. In 1907, when the Oklahoma and Indian territories were joined to form the 46th state, Chickasha became the seat of Grady County. Today agriculture, livestock, dairy production, manufacturing, and energy-related industries play an important part in the economy of the city and surrounding area.

What to See and Do

Lake Burtschi. *Chickasha. 11 miles SW on Hwy 92.* Fishing. Picnic areas. Camping.

Lake Chickasha. *Chickasha. 15 miles NW off Hwy 62.* Swimming, waterskiing; fishing, hunting. Picnic areas. Camping.

Special Events

Antique Car Swap Meet. *Grady County Fairgrounds, Chickasha. Phone 405/224-0787.* Mid-Oct.

Festival of Light. *9th St, Chickasha. Phone 405/224-0787.* Lighted displays; 16-story Christmas tree; crystal bridge; shopping. Thanksgiving-Dec 31.

Grady County Fair. *Grady County Fairgrounds, Chickasha. Phone 405/224-2216.* Third week in Aug.

Limited-Service Hotel

★ ★ **BEST WESTERN INN.** *2101 S 4th St, Chickasha (73023). Phone 405/224-4890; toll-free 877/489-0647; fax 405/224-3411. www.bestwestern.com.* 148 rooms, 2 story. Pets accepted, some restrictions; fee. Check-out noon. Restaurant, bar. Indoor pool, whirlpool. **$**

Claremore (A-5)

See also Pryor, Tulsa

Population 13,280
Elevation 602 ft
Area Code 918
Zip 74017
Information Claremore Area Chamber of Commerce, 419 W Will Rogers Blvd; phone 918/341-2818
Web Site www.claremore.org

Claremore is most famous as the birthplace of Will Rogers. He was actually born about halfway between this city and Oologah but used to talk more of Claremore because, he said, "nobody but an Indian could pronounce Oologah." Rogers County, of which Claremore is the seat, was named not for Will Rogers but for his father, Clem.

What to See and Do

J.M. Davis Arms & Historical Museum. *333 N Lynn Riggs Blvd, Claremore (74017). Phone 918/341-5707.* Houses 20,000 firearms, steins, arrowheads, saddles, posters, other historical and Native American artifacts, collection of "John Rogers Group" statuaries. (Mon-Sat, also Sun afternoons; closed Thanksgiving, Dec 25). **DONATION**

Lynn Riggs Memorial. *121 N Chickasaw Ave, Claremore (74017). Rogers County Historical Society, 4th and Weenonah.* Houses the author's personal belongings, sculpture of Riggs, original manuscripts, and the original "surrey with the fringe on top" from *Oklahoma!* (Mon-Fri; closed holidays) **FREE**

Will Rogers Birthplace and Dog Iron Ranch. *9501 E 380 Rd, Oologah (74053). 12 miles NW on Hwy 88, then 2 miles N. Phone 918/275-4201.* Home where "Oklahoma's favorite son" was born November 4, 1879. (Daily) **DONATION**

⭐ **Will Rogers Memorial.** *(Hwy 88), 1720 W Will Rogers Blvd, Claremore (74017). Phone 918/341-0719.* Mementos; murals; saddle collection; dioramas; theater, films, tapes, research library. Jo Davidson's statue of Rogers stands in the foyer. The memorial is on 20 acres once owned by the humorist. Garden with Rogers' tomb. (Daily).

Special Events

Rogers County Free Fair. *Claremore Expo Center, Claremore. Phone 918/341-2736.* Mid-Sept.

Will Rogers Days Arts and Crafts Show. *Claremore. Phone 918/341-2818.* Early Nov.

Will Rogers Stampede PRCA Rodeo. *Will Rogers Stampede Arena, Claremore. Phone 918/640-1603.* Late June.

Limited-Service Hotel

★ ★ **BEST WESTERN WILL ROGERS INN.** *940 S Lynn Riggs Blvd, Claremore (74017). Phone 918/341-4410; toll-free 800/644-9455; fax 918/341-6045. www.bestwestern.com.* 52 rooms. Pets accepted. Check-out noon. Restaurant, bar. Outdoor pool. **$**
🐾 🏊

Restaurant

★ ★ **HAMMETT HOUSE.** *1616 W Will Rogers Blvd, Claremore (74017). Phone 918/341-7333. www. hammetthouse.com.* Lunch, dinner. Closed Mon; Thanksgiving, Dec 25. Children's menu. **$$**

Clinton (B-3)

See also Elk City, Weatherford

Founded 1903
Population 9,298
Elevation 1,592 ft
Area Code 580
Zip 73601
Information Chamber of Commerce, 600 Avant; phone 580/323-2222
Web Site www.clintonok.org

This is a cattle, farming, manufacturing, and shipping center founded when Congress approved the purchase of acreage owned by Native Americans at the junction of two railroads. Oil and gas drilling and production take place here.

What to See and Do

Foss State Park. *Hwys 44 and 73, Foss (73647). 14 miles W on I-40, exit 53, then 7 miles N on Hwy 44. Phone 580/592-4433.* An 8,800-acre lake created by a dam on the Washita River. Water-skiing, fishing, boating (ramps, docks, marina); picnic facilities, playgrounds, camping, trailer hook-ups (fee). (Daily) **FREE**

Special Event

Art in the Park Festival. *McLain-Rogers Park, Clinton. Phone 580/323-2222.* Features art from Oklahoma and surrounding states. Early June.

Duncan (C-3)

See also Lawton, Waurika

Founded 1893
Population 21,732
Elevation 1,126 ft
Area Code 580
Information Chamber of Commerce, 911 Walnut Ave, PO Box 699, 73534; phone 580/255-3644
Web Site www.duncanchamber.com

Once a cattle town on the old Chisholm Trail, Duncan has become an oil services and agricultural center. It was here that Erle P. Halliburton developed his oil well cementing business, which now operates all over the world.

What to See and Do

Chisholm Trail Museum. *1000 Chisolm Trail Parkway, Duncan (73533). Phone 580/252-6692.* Interactive displays demonstrating the history of the Chisholm Trail. Historical movies; gift shop. (Daily) **FREE** Also here is

> **On the Chisholm Trail.** *Duncan.* Large bronze statue depicts life-size cowboys, horses, cattle, and chuckwagon. (Daily) **FREE**

Stephens County Historical Museum. *Fuqua Park, Hwy 81 and Beech Ave, Duncan. Phone 580/252-0717.* Houses pioneer and Native American artifacts, antique toys, gem and lapidary display; Plains Indian exhibit. Also log cabin, old schoolhouse, pioneer kitchen (circa 1892), blacksmith shop, dentist's office, law office. (Tues, Thurs-Sat; closed holidays) **FREE**

Limited-Service Hotel

★ ★ **HOLIDAY INN.** *1015 N Hwy 81, Duncan (73534). Phone 580/252-1500; fax 580/255-1851. www.holiday-inn.com.* 138 rooms, 2 story. Pets accepted, some restrictions. Restaurant, bar. Indoor pool, children's pool. **$**

Durant (D-5)

See also Lake Texoma

Settled 1832
Population 12,823
Elevation 647 ft
Area Code 580
Zip 74701
Information Chamber of Commerce, 215 N 4th St; phone 580/924-0848
Web Site www.durant.org

Long a farm and livestock-producing town in Oklahoma's Red River Valley, Durant has become a recreation center since the completion of Lake Texoma. Oil and industry have also stimulated the city's economy. Durant, home of Southeastern Oklahoma State University (1909), has many mansions, magnolia trees, and gardens.

What to See and Do

Fort Washita. *Hwy 199, Durant. 16 miles NW via Hwy 78, 199, on N shore of Lake Texoma. Phone 580/924-6502.* Originally built in 1842 to protect the Five Civilized Tribes from the Plains Indians; used during the Civil War as a Confederate supply depot; remains of 48 buildings are visible. Picnicking. Special events (fee). (Daily; closed holidays) **FREE**

Three Valley Museum. *Main St, Durant (74701). Phone 580/920-1907.* Museum housed in the Choctaw Nation Headquarters building; contains turn-of-the-century artifacts, antique dolls, art, and beadwork. (Mon-Sat, also by appointment; closed Thanksgiving, Dec 25) **FREE**

Special Events

Magnolia Festival. *Downtown, Durant. Phone 580/924-0848.* Crafts, rides, art show, entertainment. First weekend in June.

The Oklahoma Shakespearean Festival. *Southeastern Oklahoma State University, Durant. Phone 580/924-0121, ext 2442.* Musicals; children's show, teen cabaret; dinner theater. Late June-July.

Limited-Service Hotels

★ ★ **BEST WESTERN MARKITA INN.** *2401 W Main St, Durant (74701). Phone 580/924-7676; toll-free 800/780-7234; fax 580/924-3060. www.bestwestern.com.* 62 rooms, 2 story. Check-out noon. Restaurant. Outdoor pool, whirlpool. Airport transportation available. **$**

★ **COMFORT INN.** *2112 W Main St, Durant (74701). Phone 580/924-8881; fax 580/924-0955.* 62 rooms, 2 story. Complimentary continental breakfast. Check-out noon. **$**

El Reno (B-3)

Founded 1889
Population 15,414
Elevation 1,365 ft
Area Code 405
Zip 73036
Information Chamber of Commerce, 206 N Bickford, PO Box 67; phone 405/262-1188
Web Site www.elreno.org

Established in 1889, El Reno was named for Civil War General Jesse L. Reno, who was killed during the Battle of Antietam in 1862. The city lies in the heart of the Canadian River valley. Farming, livestock, and cotton are its principal agricultural pursuits.

Limited-Service Hotel

★ **BEST WESTERN HENSLEY'S.** *I-40 and Country Club Rd, El Reno (73036). Phone 405/262-6490; toll-free 800/780-7234; fax 405/262-7642. www.bestwestern.com.* 60 rooms, 2 story. Pets accepted, fee. Complimentary full breakfast. Check-out 11 am. **$**

Elk City (B-2)

See also Clinton

Population 10,428
Elevation 1,928 ft
Area Code 580
Information Chamber of Commerce, 1016 Airport Industrial Rd, PO Box 972, 73648; phone 580/225-0207 or toll-free 800/280-0207
Web Site www.elkcitychamber.com

This was once a stopping point for cattlemen driving herds from Texas to railheads in Kansas. It was known as the "Great Western" or "Dodge City Cattle Trail." Elk City, centrally located on historic Route 66, lies near the center of the Anadarko Basin, where extensive natural gas exploration takes place.

What to See and Do

Old Town Museum. *2717 W 3rd St, Elk City (73644). Pioneer Rd and Hwy 66. Phone 580/225-2207.* Turn-of-the-century house has Victorian furnishings, Native American artifacts, Beutler Brothers Rodeo memorabilia; Memorial Chapel; early one-room school; wagon yard; gristmill; depot and caboose. (Tues-Sun; closed Jan 1, Easter, Thanksgiving, Dec 25) **$$**

Special Events

Fall Festival of the Arts. *Civic Center, Elk City. Phone 580/225-0207.* Exhibits, children's show, performing arts, and music. Third weekend in Sept.

Rodeo of Champions. *Butler Brothers Arena, Elk City. Phone 580/225-0207. Rodeo grounds, A Ave at W edge of town.* PRCA sanctioned. Labor Day weekend.

Limited-Service Hotel

★ ★ **HOLIDAY INN.** *101 Meadow Ridge, Elk City (73644). Phone 580/225-6637; fax 580/225-6637. www.holiday-inn.com.* 151 rooms, 2 story. Pets accepted, some restrictions. Complimentary full breakfast. Check-out noon. Restaurant, bar. Fitness room. Indoor pool, whirlpool. **$**

Restaurants

★ **COUNTRY DOVE.** *610 W 3rd, Elk City (73644). Phone 580/225-7028; fax 580/225-7045.* Lunch. Closed Sun; holidays. **$**

★ **LUPE'S.** *905 N Main St, Elk City (73644). Phone 580/225-7109; fax 580/225-7102.* American, Mexican menu. Lunch, dinner. Closed holidays. Bar. Children's menu. **$$**

Enid (A-3)

Founded 1893
Population 45,309
Elevation 1,246 ft
Area Code 580
Information Chamber of Commerce, 210 Kenwood Blvd, PO Box 907, 73702; phone 580/237-2494 or toll-free 800/299-2443
Web Site www.enidchamber.com

Like many Oklahoma cities, Enid was born of a land rush. When the Cherokee Outlet (more popularly known as the Cherokee Strip) was opened to settlement on September 16, 1893, a tent city sprang up. It is now a prosperous community, a center for farm marketing and oil processing. Just south of town is Vance Air Force Base, a training base for jet aircraft pilots.

What to See and Do

Homesteader's Sod House. *Enid. 30 miles W on Hwy 60, then 5 1/2 miles N of Cleo Springs on Hwy 8. Phone 580/463-2441.* A two-room sod house built by Marshall McCully in 1894; said to be the only original example of this type of structure still standing in Oklahoma. Period furnishings; farm machinery. (Tues-Sun; closed holidays) **FREE**

Museum of the Cherokee Strip. *507 S 4th St, Enid (73701). Phone 580/237-1907.* Artifacts covering Oklahoma history of the Plains Indians, the Land Run of 1893, and events from 1900-present. (Tues-Sat; closed holidays) **FREE**

Special Events

Cherokee Strip Celebration. *111 W Purdue Ave, Enid (73701). Phone 580/237-1907.* City-wide festival commemorates the opening of the Cherokee Strip to settlers. Includes entertainment, parade, rodeo, arts and crafts, food. Mid-Sept.

Tri-State Music Festival. *Enid (73702). Phone 580/237-4964.* Early May.

Limited-Service Hotels

★ ★ **BEST WESTERN INN.** *2818 S Van Buren St, Enid (73703). Phone 580/242-7110; toll-free 800/378-6308; fax 580/242-6202. www.bestwestern.com.* 99 rooms, 2 story. Pets accepted; fee. Check-out noon. Restaurant, bar. Fitness room. Indoor pool, whirlpool. **$**
🔊 🕅 ⊞

★ ★ **DAYS INN.** *2901 S Van Buren St, Enid (73703). Phone 580/237-6000; fax 580/237-6370. www.daysinn .com.* 100 rooms, 2 story. Check-out noon. Restaurant, bar. Fitness room. **$**
🕅

Restaurant

★ ★ **SAGE ROOM.** *1927 S Van Buren St, Enid (73703). Phone 580/233-1212; fax 580/242-2502.* Seafood menu. Dinner. Closed Sun. Children's menu. **$$$**

Eufaula (C-5)

See also McAlester

Settled 1836
Population 2,652
Elevation 617 ft
Area Code 918
Zip 74432
Information Greater Eufaula Area Chamber of Commerce, 109 S Main, PO Box 738; phone 918/689-2791

Eufaula was first a Native American settlement and later a trading post. The town is still the home of the Eufaula Boarding School for Indian Girls (1849), which was renamed the Eufaula Dormitory after becoming co-educational. Eufaula is also the home of the state's oldest continuously published newspaper, *The Indian Journal.*

What to See and Do

Arrowhead State Park. *Hwy 69, Canadian. 4 miles E of city. Phone 918/339-2204.* Approximately 2,450 acres

located on the south shore of 102,500-acre Lake Eufaula. Beach, bathhouse, waterskiing, fishing, boating (ramps, marina); golf, nature walk, hiking, picnicking, playground, camping, trailer hook-ups (fee). Airstrip. (Daily) **FREE**

Eufaula Dam. *Hwys 9 and 71, Porum (74455). 18 miles NE via Hwy 9, 71. Phone 918/484-5135.* Camping at Dam site East (early Apr-Oct; fee). Swimming beach; nature trail.

Fountainhead State Park. *Fountainhead Rd, Eufaula. 6 miles N on Hwy 69, then 2 miles NW on Hwy 150. Phone 918/689-5311.* Approximately 3,400 acres on the shore of Lake Eufaula. Beach, bathhouse, waterskiing, fishing, boating (ramps, marina); golf, tennis, nature walk, hiking and bridle paths, picnicking, playground, camping, trailer hook-ups (fee). Airstrip. Gift shop. (Daily) **FREE**

Limited-Service Hotel

★ **LAKE EUFAULA INN.** *I-40 and Hwy 150, Checotah (74426). Phone 918/473-2376; toll-free 877/325-5346; fax 918/473-5774.* 48 rooms. Check-out noon. Outdoor pool. **$**
⊞

Grand Lake (A-6)

See also Miami, Pryor, Vinita

What to See and Do

Cherokee Queen I & II boat cruises. *11350 Hwy 59 N, Grand Lake. Sailboat Bridge on Hwy 59. Phone 918/786-4272.* Narrated cruise (two hours) on Grand Lake O' The Cherokees; entertainment, refreshments. **$$$**

Har-Ber Village. *4404 W 20th St, Grove (74344). Phone 918/786-6446.* Reconstructed old-time village with 90 buildings and shops typical of a pioneer town; also a variety of memorabilia collections. Picnicking. (Mar-Nov, daily) **FREE**

Lendonwood Gardens. *1308 W 13th St (Har-Ber Rd), Grove (74344). Phone 918/786-2938.* Houses one of the largest collections of chamaecyparis in the US, plus rhododendrons, day lilies, and azaleas. Gardens include the Display Garden, English Terrace Garden, and Japanese Garden. (Daily) **$$**

Special Events

Pelican Festival. *6807 Hwy 59 N, Grove (74344). Phone 918/786-2289.* Viewing of white pelicans on their southward migration; tours and cruises to view pelicans; events; parade. Last weekend in Sept.

Picture in Scripture Amphitheater. *Disney. 6 miles S via Hwy 85 and Hwy 82, 3 miles E via Hwy 28. Phone 918/435-8207.* Biblical drama of "Jonah and the Whale." June-Aug.

Full-Service Resort

★ ★ **SHANGRI-LA RESORT & CONFERENCE CENTER.** *57401 E Hwy 125 S, Afton (74331). Phone 918/257-4204; toll-free 800/331-4060; fax 918/257-8406. www.shangrilaok.com.* This resort is located on an island in the middle of the lake. It offers several restaurants to choose from, live entertainment on weekends, boat rentals, a pool, tennis facilities, and much more. 101 rooms. Check-in 4 pm, check-out 11 am. Restaurant, bar. Fitness room. Indoor pool, whirlpool. Tennis. **$**

Guthrie (B-4)

See also Oklahoma City

Founded 1889
Population 10,518
Elevation 946 ft
Area Code 405
Zip 73044
Information Chamber of Commerce, 212 W Oklahoma, PO Box 995; phone 405/282-1947
Web Site www.guthrieok.com

Guthrie was founded in just a few hours during the great land rush. Prior to the "run," only a small-frame railroad station and a partially completed land registration office stood on the site. A few hours later, perhaps 20,000 inhabited the tent city on the prairie.

Oklahoma's territorial and first state capital, Guthrie now has the most complete collection of restored Victorian architecture in the United States, with 1,400 acres of the city listed on the National Historic Register. Included are 160 buildings in the central business district and the center of town and numerous Victorian mansions. The town is being restored to the 1907-1910 era, including the expansive Guthrie

Railroad Hotel and the former opera house, the Pollard Theatre. Some who have called Guthrie home at one time or another are Tom Mix, Lon Chaney, Will Rogers, Carry Nation, and O. Henry.

What to See and Do

Oklahoma Territorial Museum. *406 E Oklahoma Ave, Guthrie (73044). Phone 405/282-1889.* Exhibits and displays of life in territorial Oklahoma during the turn of the century. Adjacent is the Carnegie Library (1902-1903), site of inaugurations of the last territorial and the first state governor. (Tues-Sat; closed holidays) **DONATION**

Scottish Rite Masonic Temple. *900 E Oklahoma Ave, Guthrie (73044). Phone 405/282-1281.* A multimillion-dollar Classical Revival building, said to be the largest structure used for Masonic purposes. The building contains the original state capitol, 13 artistic rooms, and 200 stained-glass windows. Surrounding it is a 10-acre park. Visitors welcome; children must be accompanied by an adult. (Mon-Fri; closed holidays) **$$**

State Capital Publishing Museum. *301 W Harrison, Guthrie (73044). Phone 405/282-4123.* Located in the four-story State Capital Publishing Company Building (1902). Houses a collection of original furnishings, vintage letterpress equipment; exhibits featuring the history of the first newspaper in the Oklahoma Territory and period printing technology. (Thurs-Sat; closed holidays) **FREE**

Special Events

Eighty-niner Celebration. *Guthrie. Phone 405/282-2589.* PRCA rodeo, "chuck wagon feed," parade, carnival, races. Apr.

Oklahoma International Bluegrass Festival. *212 W Oklahoma Ave, Guthrie (73044). Phone 405/282-4446.* Performances by top bluegrass bands and musicians. Children's activities, music workshops, concessions; celebrity golf tournament. Late Sept-early Oct.

Territorial Christmas. *Guthrie. Phone 405/282-1947.* Seven miles of lights outline architecture in the Historic District; streets are filled with persons clad in turn-of-the-century style clothes, horse drawn vehicles; window displays echo 1890-1920 era. Fri after Thanksgiving-late Dec.

Limited-Service Hotel

★ ★ **BEST WESTERN TERRITORIAL INN.**

2323 Territorial Trail, Guthrie (73044). Phone 405/ 282-8831; toll-free 800/780-7234; fax 405/282-8831. www.bestwestern.com. 84 rooms, 2 story. Pets accepted. Check-out 11 am. Restaurant, bar. Outdoor pool. **$**

Specialty Lodging

The following lodging establishment is approved by Mobil Travel Guide, but due to its unique and individualized nature has not been given a traditional Mobil Star rating. Included in this listing you may find bed-and-breakfasts, limited-service inns, guest ranches, and other unique hotel properties.

HARRISON HOUSE BED & BREAKFAST INN. *124 W Harrison, Guthrie (73044). Phone 405/ 260-0094; toll-free 800/375-1001.* 34 rooms, 3 story. Complimentary full breakfast. Check-in after 3 pm, check-out 11 am. Pollard Theatre is adjacent. **$**

Restaurant

★ **STABLES CAFE.** *223 N Division, Guthrie (73044). Phone 405/282-0893; fax 405/282-0452.* American menu. Lunch, dinner. Closed holidays. Children's menu. **$$**

Guymon (E-2)

Founded 1890
Population 7,803
Elevation 3,121 ft
Area Code 580
Zip 73942
Information Chamber of Commerce, 711 SE Hwy 3, Rte 5 Box 120; phone 580/338-3376

Located approximately at the center of Oklahoma's panhandle, Guymon owes its growth to oil, natural gas, irrigation, manufacturing, commercial feed lots, and swine production.

What to See and Do

Oklahoma Panhandle State University. *323 Eagle Blvd, Goodwell (73939). 10 miles SW on Hwy 54. Phone 580/349-2611.* (1909) (1,200 students) Agricultural research station; golf course (fee). Campus tours. On campus is

No Man's Land Museum. *207 W Sewell St, Goodwell (73939). Phone 580/349-2670.* (1932) Exhibit divi-

sions relating to the panhandle region including archives, anthropology, biology, geology, pioneer history, and art gallery; changing exhibits; notable archaeological collection and alabaster carvings. (Tues-Fri; closed holidays) **FREE**

Sunset Lake. *Thompson Park, 323 S Crumley St, Guymon (73942). Phone 580/338-2178.* Fishing, paddle boats; picnicking, playground, miniature train rides. Fee for activities. Adjacent game preserve has buffalo, llamas, aoudad sheep, longhorn cattle, and elk. (Daily) **FREE**

Special Events

Panhandle Exposition. *Texas County Fairgrounds, 5th and Sunset Ln, Guymon (73942). Phone 580/338-5446.* Livestock, field, and garden crop displays; grandstand attractions; midway. Late Aug.

Pioneer Days. *Guymon. Phone 580/338-3376.* Chuck wagon breakfast, parade, PRCA rodeo, dancing, entertainment. First weekend in May.

Limited-Service Hotel

★ **ECONO LODGE.** *923 E Hwy 54 E, Guymon (73942). Phone 580/338-5431; fax 580/338-0554. www.econolodge.com.* 40 rooms. Pets accepted; fee. Check-out 11 am. **$**

Hugo (D-5)

Population 5,978
Area Code 580
Zip 74743
Information Chamber of Commerce, 200 S Broadway; phone 580/326-7511
Web Site www.hugochamber.com

What to See and Do

Hugo Lake. *Hugo. 8 miles E on Hwy 70. Phone 580/326-3345.* Nine recreation areas. Swimming, beaches (fee); boat ramps (fee); picnicking, tent and trailer sites (fee). Electrical, water hook-ups in some areas. (Daily) **FREE**

Raymond Gary State Park. *Hwy 209, Fort Towson. 16 miles E on Hwy 70; 2 miles S of Fort Towson on Hwy 209. Phone 580/873-2307.* Approximately 46 acres with a 295-acre lake. Swimming beach, fishing, boating;

picnicking, playgrounds, camping (showers, dump station). (Daily) **FREE**

Limited-Service Hotel

★ **VILLAGE INN MOTEL.** *610 W Jackson St, Hugo (74743). Phone 580/326-3333; fax 580/326-2670.* 50 rooms. Check-out 11 am. Outdoor pool. **$**
🅓 ⌷

Idabel (D-6)

See also Broken Bow

Population 6,957
Area Code 580
Zip 74745
Information Chamber of Commerce, 13 N Central; phone 580/286-3305

The western portion of the Ouachita National Forest is located to the east of Idabel. Although predominantly evergreen, the deciduous growth—a mixture of oak, gum, maple, sycamore, dogwood, and persimmon—makes the forest notable for its magnificent fall color. For information contact Supervisor, PO Box 1270, Federal Building, Hot Springs National Park, AR, 71902; phone 501/321-5202. A Ranger District office of the forest is also located in Idabel; phone 580/286-6564.

What to See and Do

Museum of the Red River. *812 Lincoln Rd, Idabel (74745). S of city on Hwy 70/259 bypass. Phone 580/286-3616.* Interpretive exhibits of historic and prehistoric Native Americans; local archaeology; changing exhibits. (Tues-Sun; closed holidays) **DONATION**

Special Event

Kiamichi Owa Chito Festival of the Forest. *Idabel. Phone 580/286-3305.* Third weekend in June.

Limited-Service Hotel

★ ★ **HOLIDAY INN.** *Hwy 70 W, Idabel (74745). Phone 580/286-6501; fax 580/286-7482. www.holiday-inn.com.* 99 rooms, 2 story. Check-out noon. Restaurant. **$**

Krebs (C-5)

Restaurants

★ ★ **ISLE OF CAPRI.** *150 SW 7th, Krebs (74554). Phone 918/423-3062; fax 918/423-1008.* American, Italian menu. Breakfast, lunch, dinner, brunch. Closed Sun; holidays. Bar. Children's menu. **$$**

★ ★ **PETE'S PLACE.** *120 SW 8th St, Krebs (74554). Phone 918/423-2042; fax 918/423-7859. www.petes.org.* Italian, steak menu. Dinner. Closed Thanksgiving, Dec 25. Children's menu. **$$**

Lake Murray State Park (D-4)

7 miles SE of Ardmore, off I-35, exit 24 or 29.

This 12,496-acre state park, which includes a 5,728-acre man-made lake, can be reached from either Marietta or Ardmore. The museum in Tucker Tower (Feb-Nov, Wed-Sun; fee) has historical and mineral exhibits, including a large, rare meteorite. The park is hilly and wooded with beach, bathhouse, swimming pool, waterskiing, two fishing piers, heated fishing dock, boating (rentals, ramps, marina); horseback riding, 18-hole golf, tennis, two hiking trails, picnic facilities, playground, miniature golf, grocery, lodge, club, camping areas, trailer hook-ups (fee). Airstrip. (Daily) Phone 580/223-4044.

Restaurant

★ ★ **FIRESIDE DINING.** *Hwy 77, Lake Murray State Park (73401). Phone 580/226-4070.* American menu. Dinner. Closed Sun-Mon; holidays. Children's menu. **$$**

Lake Texoma (D-4)

See also Durant, Marietta

14 miles W on Hwy 70.

Area Code 580
Information Project Office, Lake Texoma, Hwy 3, Box 493, Denison TX 75020; phone 903/465-4990

This lake is so named because it is impounded behind Denison Dam on the Red River, the boundary between Oklahoma and Texas. With shores in both states, this is one of the finest and most popular of the lakes in either.

Approximately two-thirds of the lake's 89,000 acres are in Oklahoma. The total shoreline is 580 miles. About 105,000 acres surrounding the lake are federally owned, but the state of Oklahoma has leased 1,600 acres between Madill and Durant for Lake Texoma State Park. The remainder of the lake is under control of the US Army Corp of Engineers, which built the dam. Project office (Mon-Fri; closed holidays).

Fishing boats and outboard motors may be rented at several locations on the lake. Guides are available. Duck and goose hunting is good. Swimming beaches have been developed at many points on the lake. Picnicking, camping, and trailer hook-ups (fee), cabins and supplies at many points, some privately operated and some state-owned. Also here are beach, swimming pool, bathhouse, water skiing, fishing dock, boat dock, storage, and marina; horseback riding, 18-hole golf course, driving range, putting range, tennis courts, shuffleboard; three playgrounds, restaurant, grocery, lodging (see FULL-SERVICE RESORT), cabins, and a 2,500-foot airstrip at Lake Texoma State Park.

At the northern end of the lake, on the courthouse grounds in Tishomingo, is the Chickasaw Council House, the log cabin used as the first seat of government of the Chickasaw Nation in the Indian Territory. Enclosed in a larger building, it has displays on Native American history (Tues-Sun; closed holidays; free).

Fees may be charged at federal recreation sites.

Full-Service Resort

★ ★ **LAKE TEXOMA RESORT.** *E Hwy 70, Kingston (73439). Phone 580/564-2311; fax 580/564-9322. www.oklahomaresorts.com.* 187 rooms. Checkout noon. Restaurant. Children's activity center. Fitness room. Outdoor pool, children's pool. Tennis. Airstrip in park. State-owned, operated. **$**

🚶 ⛴ 🎿

Restaurant

★ **SANFORD'S.** *Hwy 70 E, Kingston (73439). Phone 580/564-3764.* Steak menu. Dinner. Closed Sun-Mon; Thanksgiving, Dec 25. **$$**

Lawton (C-3)

See also Duncan

Founded 1901
Population 80,561
Elevation 1,109 ft
Area Code 580
Information Chamber of Commerce, 629 SW C Ave, PO Box 1376, 73502; phone 580/355-3541
Web Site www.lawtonfortsillchamber.com

Last of the many Oklahoma cities that sprang up overnight, Lawton had its land rush on August 6, 1901. It is now the state's third-largest city and serves as a prominent shopping, recreational, medical, and educational center for the area. Much of the city's prosperity is due to Fort Sill, established in 1869, and to the world's largest Goodyear Tire plant. The Wichita Mountains provide a dramatic backdrop to the city.

What to See and Do

Fort Sill Military Reservation. *Fort Sill and Sheridian Rd, Lawton (73503). 4 miles N on Hwy 277. Phone 580/442-2521.* A 94,268-acre army installation, US Army Field Artillery Center and School. Geronimo, war leader of the Apaches, spent his final years here and is buried in the post's Apache cemetery. (Daily) **FREE** Also here are

Fort Sill National Historic Landmark and Museum. *437 Quanah Rd, Fort Sill (73503). Phone 580/442-5123.* Forty-three buildings built of native stone during the 1870s, many of which are still being used for their original purpose. (Mon-Sat 8:30 am-4:30 pm; closed Jan 1-2, Thanksgiving, Dec 25-26) **FREE**

Old Guardhouse. *Lawton. Phone 580/442-2521.* Commissary Storehouse, Quartermaster Warehouse, School of Fire, Quartermaster Corral, visitor venter, and Cannon Walk. Depicts the history of field artillery and missiles. Cavalry, Native American relics. Film presentation of Fort Sill history, 25 minutes (upon request). Self-guided tour map. (Mon-Sat; closed holidays) **FREE**

Old Post Chapel. *Lawton. Phone 580/442-5123.* One of the oldest houses of worship still in use in the state. (Mon-Sat; services on Sun)

Old Post Headquarters. *Lawton.* From which Generals Grierson and Mackenzie conducted

Native American campaigns. Not open to the public.

Sherman House. *Lawton.* Commandant's home. In 1871, General William Tecumseh Sherman was almost killed by the Kiowa on the front porch. Not open to the public.

Museum of the Great Plains. *Elmer Thomas Park, 601 Ferris Blvd, Lawton (73507). Phone 580/581-3460.* Displays on Native Americans, fur trade, exploration, cattle industry and settlement of the area; period rooms depict Main St of frontier town; outdoor exhibits of a 300-ton Baldwin steam locomotive, depot, and wooden threshers; fortified trading post with a 100-square-foot log stockade, two-story blockhouses and furnished trader's cabin representing such a post in the 1830s-1840s. Trading post (Wed-Sun) has living history programs. (Daily; closed Jan 1, Thanksgiving, Dec 25) **$$**

Percussive Arts Society Museum. *701 Ferris, Lawton (73507). Phone 580/353-1455.* Displays of percussion instruments from around the world. Visitors can try several different instruments. Tours by appointment. (Daily) **$**

Wichita Mountains Wildlife Refuge. *Cache. Headquarters are 13 miles W on Hwy 62 to Cache, then 12 miles N on Hwy 115.* This 59,060-acre refuge has 12 man-made lakes. Nonmotorized boating permitted on four lakes, trolling motors on three lakes; picnicking, camping only at Doris Campground; limited backcountry camping by reservation only (camping fee). Quanah Parker Visitor Center (Mar-Nov, Fri-Sun); self-guided trails. Longhorn cattle, herds of buffalo, elk, deer, and other wildlife can be viewed from several wildlife/scenic viewing areas. (Daily) (See SPECIAL EVENTS) **FREE**

Special Events

Arts For All. *Shelper Park, Lawton. Phone 580/248-5384.* Features visual arts and entertainment by local artists; food; street dance. Mid-May.

Easter Sunday Pageant. *Holy City of the Wichitas, Wichita Mountains National Wildlife Refuge, Lawton. Phone 580/429-3361.* Sat evening before Easter.

International Festival. *Library Plaza, Lawton. Phone 580/581-3470.* Celebrates various cultures of the area; arts and crafts, entertainment, food. Late Sept.

Lawton Birthday and Rodeo Celebration. *LO Ranch Arena, Lawton. Phone 580/355-3541.* Street dancing, rodeo, races, parade. Three days in early Aug.

Limited-Service Hotels

★ **DAYS INN.** *3110 Cache Rd, Lawton (73505). Phone 580/353-3104; fax 580/353-0992. www.days inn.com.* 95 rooms, 2 story. Pets accepted; fee. Complimentary continental breakfast. Check-out noon. Indoor pool, outdoor pool, whirlpool. **$**
🐾 🏊

★ ★ **RAMADA INN.** *601 N 2nd St, Lawton (73507). Phone 580/355-7155; toll-free 888/298-2054; fax 580/353-6162. www.ramada.com.* 98 rooms, 2 story. Pets accepted; fee. Check-out noon. Restaurant, bar. **$**
🐾

Restaurants

★ ★ **FISHERMEN'S COVE.** *6 Wildwood Rd, Lawton (73501). Phone 580/529-2672; fax 580/529-2692.* Seafood menu. Lunch, dinner. Closed Thanksgiving, Dec 25. Children's menu. **$$**

★ ★ **SALAS.** *111 W Lee Blvd (Hwy 7), Lawton (73501). Phone 580/357-1600.* Mexican, American menu. Lunch, dinner. Closed Mon-Tues; Jan 1, Thanksgiving, Dec 25. **$$**

Marietta (D-4)

See also Ardmore, Lake Texoma

Population 2,306
Elevation 841 ft
Area Code 580
Zip 73448
Information Love County Chamber of Commerce, 112 W Main, Box 422; phone 580/276-3102

What to See and Do

Lake Murray State Park. *Marietta. 11 miles NE, off I-35 or Hwy 77.* (see)

Restaurant

★ **MCGEHEE CATFISH.** *RR 2, Marietta (73448). Phone 580/276-2751.* Dinner. Closed Wed; Thanksgiving, Dec 24-26. Children's menu. Limited menu. **$$**

McAlester (C-5)

See also Eufaula

Founded 1870
Population 16,370
Area Code 918
Information McAlester Area Chamber of Commerce & Agriculture, 10 S 3rd St, PO Box 759, 74501; phone 918/423-2550
Web Site www.mcalester.org

James J. McAlester came to the Indian Territory in 1870 armed with a geologist's notebook describing some coal deposits and a fine sense of commercial strategy. He set up a tent store where the heavily traveled Texas Road crossed the California Trail and later married a Native American woman, which made him a member of the Choctaw Nation with full rights. When the railroad came through, he started mining coal. After a dispute with the Choctaw Nation over royalties, McAlester came to terms with them and in 1911 became lieutenant governor of the state.

Cattle raising, peanut farming, women's sportswear and lingerie, aircraft, electronics, and boat and oil field equipment give diversity to the town's economy.

What to See and Do

Lake McAlester. *McAlester. NW of town. Phone 918/423-2550.* Fishing, boating. Stocked by the city. Supplies are available on the road to the lake. (Daily) **FREE**

McAlester Scottish Rite Temple. *305 N 2nd St, McAlester (74501). Phone 918/423-6360.* Unusual copper dome containing multicolored lenses makes this a landmark when lighted. One of its most illustrious members was Will Rogers, taking degrees in 1908. Tours (Mon-Fri, by appointment; closed holidays). **FREE**

Robber's Cave State Park. *2450 SE Regional Ln, McAlester (75478). 35 miles E to Wilburton on Hwy 270, then 5 miles N on Hwy 2. Phone 918/465-2565.* Approximately 8,200 acres including lakes, alpine forests, and an "outlaw cave." Swimming, bathhouse, fishing, boating; hiking and horseback riding trails, picnicking, playground, restaurant, grocery, camping, trailer hook-ups (fee), cabins. Amphitheater. (Daily) **FREE**

Special Event

Sanders Family Bluegrass Festival. *McAlester. 5 miles W via Hwy 270. Phone 918/423-4891.* Bluegrass performances, entertainment. Early June.

Limited-Service Hotels

★ ★ **BEST WESTERN INN OF MCALESTER.** *1215 George Nigh Expy, McAlester (74502). Phone 918/426-0115; toll-free 800/780-7234; fax 918/426-3634. www.bestwestern.com.* 61 rooms, 2 story. Pets accepted. Complimentary continental breakfast. Check-out noon. Restaurant. Outdoor pool. **$**
🔲 🐾 ≋

★ ★ **DAYS INN.** *1217 S George Nigh Expy, McAlester (74502). Phone 918/426-5050; toll-free 800/329-7466; fax 918/426-5055. www.daysinn.com.* 100 rooms, 2 story. Pets accepted, some restrictions; fee. Check-out noon. Restaurant, bar. Indoor pool, whirlpool. Near Municipal Airport. **$**
🐾 ≋

Restaurants

★ **GIACOMO'S.** *501 S George Nigh Expy, McAlester (74501). Phone 918/423-2662.* American, Italian menu. Lunch, dinner. Closed Sat-Sun; holidays. Children's menu. **$$**

★ ★ **TROLLEY'S.** *21 E Monroe St, McAlester (74501). Phone 918/423-2446; fax 918/423-2446.* Dinner. Closed holidays. Service bar. Children's menu. Located in restored house (1886) with former streetcar (1908) addition; décor from early movie theaters. **$$**

Miami (A-6)

See also Grand Lake, Pryor, Vinita

Founded 1891
Population 13,142
Elevation 798 ft
Area Code 918
Zip 74354
Information Chamber of Commerce, 111 N Main, PO Box 760; phone 918/542-4481; or Traveler Information Center, E on Will Rogers Turnpike; phone 918/542-9303
Web Site www.miamiok.org

Situated on the headwaters of Grand Lake, Miami boasts many recreational facilities. Agriculture is diversified and a number of outstanding foundation breeding herds are raised in the area. In recent years, many industries have been attracted to Miami by the low-cost electricity generated by the Grand River Dam Authority.

What to See and Do

Coleman Theatre Beautiful. *103 N Main St, Miami (74354). Phone 918/540-2425.* Built as a vaudeville theater and movie palace in 1929, the theater features a Spanish Mission Revival exterior and Louis XV interior with gold-leaf trim and carved mahogany staircases. Original pipe organ, the "Mighty Wurlitzer," is restored and reinstalled. Tours (Tues-Sat, also by appointment). **FREE**

Grand Lake. *Miami. S on Hwy 59.* (see)

Riverview Park. *Miami. On Neosho River, end of S Main St.* Swimming, fishing, boating; picnicking, camping.

Limited-Service Hotel

★ ★ **BEST WESTERN INN OF MIAMI.** *2225 E Steve Owens Blvd, Miami (74354). Phone 918/542-6681; toll-free 877/884-5422; fax 918/542-3777. www.bestwestern.com.* 80 rooms. Pets accepted. Check-out noon. Restaurant, bar. Outdoor pool. Airport transportation available. **$**

🅳 🐾 🏊

Muskogee (B-5)

See also Tenkiller Ferry Lake

Founded 1872
Population 37,708
Elevation 602 ft
Area Code 918
Information Convention & Tourism, 425 Boston Ave, PO Box 2361, 74403; phone 918/684-6464 or toll-free 888/687-6137
Web Site www.muskogee.org

Located near the confluence of the Verdigris, Grand, and Arkansas rivers, Muskogee was a logical site for a trading center, especially since it was in Cherokee and Creek country. Southward on the old Texas Road, over which families moved to Texas, and northward, over which cattle were driven to market, the town's location was commercially ideal. The railroad superseded the rivers in transportation importance, however, almost before the town was settled.

Today Muskogee is a diversified agricultural and industrial center where glass, paper products and paper containers, rare metals, structural steel and iron, optical machinery, and many other products are manufactured. It is an attractive town dotted with 32 small parks and is the gateway to the eastern lakes area. The port of Muskogee is part of the McClellan-Kerr Arkansas River Navigation System, handling barges that go through the inland waterway system from Pittsburgh and Minneapolis to Houston and New Orleans.

The area's surroundings made it a logical location for the US Union Agency for the Five Civilized Tribes (Cherokee, Chickasaw, Choctaw, Creek, and Seminole). The agency is in the Old Union Building, Honor Heights Drive.

What to See and Do

Five Civilized Tribes Museum. *Agency Hill in Honor Heights Park, 1101 Honor Heights Dr, Muskogee (74401). Phone 918/683-1701.* (1875) Art and artifacts of the Cherokees, Chickasaws, Choctaws, Creeks, and Seminoles; displays relating to their history and culture. (Mar-Dec: daily; rest of year: Tues-Sat; closed Jan 1, Thanksgiving, Dec 25). **$**

Fort Gibson Historic Site. *907 N Garrison, Fort Gibson (74434). 7 miles E on Hwy 62 to Fort Gibson, then 1 mile N on Hwy 80. Phone 918/478-4088.* Established as the state's first military post in 1824, the park includes 12 reconstructed or restored buildings on a 55-acre site; period rooms depict army life in the 1830s and 1870s. Fort Gibson National Cemetery is 1 1/2 miles east. (Mid-Apr-mid-Oct: Tues-Sun 10 am-5 pm; rest of year: Thurs-Sun 10 am-5 pm) **$**

Greenleaf Lake State Park. *Hwy 10, Braggs. 20 miles SE on Hwy 10. Phone 918/487-5196.* On a 930-acre lake stocked with crappie, channel catfish, and black bass. Beach, swimming pool, bathhouse, enclosed fishing dock, boating (boat and equipment rentals, marina, boathouse); hiking, picnicking, playground, camping trailer hook-ups (fee), cabins. (Daily) **FREE**

Honor Heights Park. *Muskogee (74403). Phone 918/684-6302.* A 120-acre park with azalea (mid-Apr), rose (May-Oct), and chrysanthemum gardens (Sept-Nov);

nature walks, lakes, waterfall. Picnicking. (Daily) **FREE**

Tenkiller State Park. *Aqua Park. 30 miles SE on Hwy 64, N on Hwy 10, 10A. Phone 918/489-5641.* (see TENKILLER FERRY LAKE)

USS *Batfish*. *3500 Batfish Rd, Muskogee (74402). Phone 918/682-6294.* World War II submarine. Also military museum; Teddy Roosevelt Historical Monument. (Mid-Mar-mid-Oct, Wed-Mon).

Special Event

Azalea Festival. *Honor Heights Park, Muskogee. Phone toll-free 888/687-6137.* Parade, art shows, garden tours, entertainment. Mid-Apr.

Limited-Service Hotels

★ **DAYS INN.** *900 S 32nd St, Muskogee (74401). Phone 918/683-3911; toll-free 800/329-7466; fax 918/683-5744. www.daysinn.com.* 43 rooms, 2 story. Complimentary continental breakfast. Check-out noon. Outdoor pool. **$**
⊠

★ ★ **RAMADA INN.** *800 S 32nd St, Muskogee (74401). Phone 918/682-4341; fax 918/682-7400. www.ramada.com.* 142 rooms, 2 story. Pets accepted; fee. Check-out noon. Restaurant, bar. Fitness room. Indoor pool, whirlpool. **$**
🐾 👤 ⊠

Restaurant

★ **OKIES.** *219 S 32nd St (Hwy 69), Muskogee (74401). Phone 918/683-1056; fax 918/683-1056.* Lunch, dinner. Closed holidays. Bar. Children's menu. **$$**

Norman (C-4)

Founded 1889
Population 80,071
Elevation 1,104 ft
Area Code 405
Information Convention & Visitors Bureau, 224 W Gray St, Suite 104, 73069; phone 405/366-8095 or toll-free 800/767-7260
Web Site www.ncvb.org

Norman was founded on April 22, 1889, in the famous land rush known as the "Oklahoma land run." The run opened what was once the Indian Territory to modern-day settlement. A year later the University of Oklahoma was founded. The city now offers numerous restaurants, museums, shopping areas, parks, and lodgings, as well as convention, conference, and symposium sites. The city of Norman has a well-balanced economy with education, oil, industry, tourism, high technology, research and development, and agriculture.

What to See and Do

Hunting preserves. *Lexington. 9 miles S, off Hwy 77.* **Lake Thunderbird,** *Little River Arm and Hog Creek Arm, NE of town.*

Lake Thunderbird State Park. *13101 Alamedia Dr, Norman (73026). 12 miles E on Hwy 9. Phone 405/360-3572.* A 4,010-acre park on 6,070-acre Thunderbird Lake. Swimming, bathhouse, fishing, boating (ramp, rentals, marina); hiking, riding, archery, picnicking, playground, café, camping, trailer hook-ups (fee). (Daily) **FREE**

Sooner Theatre. *Norman's Performing Arts Center, 101 E Main, Norman (73069). Phone 405/321-9600.* (1929) Seasonal concerts, ballet and theater productions. **$$$**

University of Oklahoma. *1000 Asp Ave, Room 105, Norman (73019). Phone 405/325-1188; toll-free 800/234-6868.* (1890) (25,000 students) An approximately 3,100-acre campus with more than 225 buildings. The University of Oklahoma Press is a distinguished publishing house. On campus are the Fred Jones Jr. Museum of Art (Tues-Sun; phone 405/325-3272); Oklahoma Museum of Natural History (phone 405/325-4712); Rupel Jones Theater (phone 405/325-4101); University Research Park. (Museums closed holidays) Contact OU Visitor Center, Jacobson Hall, 550 Parrington Oval, 73019.

Special Events

89er Day. *508 N Peters Ave, Norman (73069). Phone 405/701-2061.* Parade, contests, wagon train river crossing. Third week in Apr.

Little River Zoo. *3405 120th St, Norman (73072). Phone 405/366-7229.* Educational zoo with more than 400 species of wild and domesticated animals. Petting zoo. (Daily; closed holidays)**$$**

Medieval Fair. *660 Parrington Oval, Norman (73019). Phone 405/288-2536.* Brandt Park duck pond at the University of Oklahoma. Living history fair depicting life in the Middle Ages; strolling minstrels, jugglers, jesters; knights in armor joust; storytellers. First weekend in Apr.

Specialty Lodgings

The following lodging establishments are approved by Mobil Travel Guide, but due to their unique and individualized nature have not been given a traditional Mobil Star rating. Included in this listing you may find bed-and-breakfasts, limited-service inns, guest ranches, and other unique hotel properties.

HOLMBERG HOUSE BED AND BREAKFAST.
766 Debarr Ave, Norman (73069). Phone 405/321-6221; toll-free 877/621-6221. www.holmberghouse.com. 4 rooms, 3 story. Complimentary full breakfast. Check-in 3 pm, check-out noon. Built in 1914 by the first dean of the University of Oklahoma's College of Fine Arts. **$**
🗐

MONTFORD INN BED & BREAKFAST. *322 W Tonhawa St, Norman (73069). Phone 405/321-2200; toll-free 800/321-8969; fax 405/321-8347. www.montfordinn.com.* Surrounded by lovely gardens, this hotel is also near the local college campus, the YMCA and many restaurants. 16 rooms. Complimentary full breakfast. Check-in 4-10 pm, check-out noon. **$**

Restaurants

★ ★ **CAFE PLAID.** *333 W Boyd St, Norman (73069). Phone 405/360-2233. www.cafeplaid.com.* Breakfast, lunch. Closed holidays. Children's menu. **$**

★ ★ ★ **LEGEND'S.** *1313 W Lindsey St, Norman (73069). Phone 405/329-8888; fax 405/329-8891. www.legendsrestaurant.com.* Owner Joe Sparks has presided over this American-continental restaurant for over 30 years. The intimate dining room is filled with original artwork and features a broad menu of pastas, steaks and daily seafood specials. American menu. Lunch, dinner, late-night. Closed holidays. Bar. Outdoor seating. **$$**

★ **VISTA SPORTS GRILL.** *111 N Peters, Norman (73069). Phone 405/447-0909; fax 405/447-2659. www. vistasportsgrill.com.* Lunch, dinner, late-night. Closed Dec 25. Bar. Children's menu. Sports memorabilia. **$**

Oklahoma City (B-4)

See also Guthrie

Founded 1889
Population 444,719
Elevation 1,207 ft
Area Code 405
Information Convention & Visitors Bureau, 189 W Sheridan, 73102; phone 405/297-8912 or toll-free 800/225-5652
Web Site www.okccvb.org

What is now the site of Oklahoma's capital was barren prairie on the morning of April 22, 1889. Unassigned land was opened to settlement that day, and by nightfall the population numbered 10,000. No city was ever settled faster than during this famous run.

The city sits atop one of the nation's largest oil fields, with wells even on the lawn of the Capitol. First discovered in 1928, the field was rapidly developed throughout the city. It still produces large quantities of high-gravity oil. Oil well equipment manufacture became one of the city's major industries.

Oklahoma City's stockyards and meat packing plants are the largest in the state. The city is also a grain milling and cotton processing center. Iron and steel, furniture, tire manufacturing, electrical equipment, electronics, and aircraft and automobile assembly are other industries. Tinker Air Force Base is southeast of the city.

Additional Visitor Information

The following organizations can provide travelers with assistance and additional information: Oklahoma City Convention & Visitors Bureau, 189 W Sheridan, 73102, phone 405/297-8912 or toll-free 800/225-5652; Oklahoma City Chamber of Commerce, 123 Park Ave, 73102, phone 405/297-8900; Oklahoma Tourism and Recreation Department, 15 N Robinson, 73102, phone 405/521-2406.

Public Transportation

Buses (Central Oklahoma Transportation and Parking Authority), phone 405/235-7433. Information phone 405/680-3200.

The Oklahoma City Experience

Single-day events have shaped both the past and present of this settlement in the American heartland. Oklahoma City was born on April 22, 1889, when the area known as the Unassigned Lands in Oklahoma Territory was opened for settlement; a cannon was fired at noon that day, signaling a rush of thousands of settlers who raced into the two million acres of land to make their claims on the plains.

Just over a century later, the city's spirited energy was put to a horrific challenge with the April 19, 1995 bombing of the Alfred P. Murrah Federal Building. Today, the strength, unity, and hope generated between the city and its nation can be experienced at the new Oklahoma City National Memorial. You'll want to allow ample time to explore and appreciate this breathtaking site.

Begin at the Gates of Time, twin monuments that frame the moment of destruction: 9:02 am. The east gate represents 9:01 a.m. and the west gate 9:03 a.m. The Field of Empty Chairs consists of 168 bronze-and-stone chairs arranged in nine rows, representing the lives lost and the floor each victim was on at the time of the blast. The smaller chairs memorialize the 19 children killed. The glass seats of the chairs are etched with the names of the victims and are lit up at night. Also at the site are an American elm called the Survivors Tree; fruit and flower trees in the Rescuers Orchard; the peaceful Reflection Pool; and the Children's Area, with a wall of hand-painted tiles sent to Oklahoma City in 1995 by children across the nation.

After this sobering start, you'll walk four blocks south of Robinson to a cheerful place called the International Gymnastics Hall of Fame. Located in the First National Center, the Hall of Fame honors such Oklahoma and Olympic gymnastic greats as Shannon Miller, Bart Connor, and Nadia Comenici. Hundreds of photos, medals, uniforms, videos, and memorabilia are on display here.

Walk just another block south of Robinson to its intersection with Reno to find the beautiful Myriad Botanical Gardens, a 17-acre sanctuary in the center of downtown with lovely hills surrounding a sunken lake. At the center is the seven-story Crystal Bridge Tropical Conservatory, featuring an intriguing collection of palm trees, flowers, and exotic plants from across the globe. Along the Adventure Walk, you'll wind beneath a 35-foot-high waterfall, and you can gaze at the tropics from a skywalk. Check out the Crystal Bridge Gift Shop, featuring an outstanding collection of botanical and garden-related items.

Backtrack on Robinson just two blocks to Sheridan, turning right (east) on Sheridan. Continue walking two blocks and you'll reach Bricktown, a hot new entertainment and dining district. The old warehouse district just east of the Santa Fe railroad tracks saw its birth just before World War I, but the latest boom came in the last 15 years. Roam around the old brick streets, poke around in the shops, then take a load off at one of the restaurants, such as Crabtown, the Varsity Sports Grill, Windy City Pizza, or Bricktown Brewery (Oklahoma's first brew pub and microbrewery). Be sure to get tickets for a game at the new Bricktown Ballpark, home of the popular AAA baseball club called the Oklahoma RedHawks. Feet worn out from walking? In Bricktown, you can hop on the new rubber-wheeled trolleys, the Oklahoma Spirit, to tour downtown, or catch a ride on the *Water Taxi*, a narrated tour boat that cruises the Bricktown Canal.

Airport **Will Rogers World Airport**; weather phone 405/478-3377; cash machines, located at upper level Main Terminal.

Information Phone 405/680-3200

Lost and found Phone 405/680-3233

Airlines American, American Eagle, Champion Air, Continental, Delta, Delta Connection/Comair/ASA, Frontier, Great Plains, Northwest, Southwest, United

What to See and Do

45th Infantry Division Museum. *2145 NE 36th St, Oklahoma City (73111). Phone 405/424-5313.* Exhibits include state military history from its beginnings in the early Oklahoma Territory through World War II and Korea to the present National Guard; Desert Storm exhibit; uniforms, vehicles, aircraft, artillery, and an extensive military firearms collection with pieces dating from the American Revolution; memorabilia and original cartoons by Bill Mauldin. (Tues-Sun; closed Jan 1 and Dec 25) **FREE**

Civic Center Music Hall. *201 N Walker, Oklahoma City (73102). Phone 405/297-2584.* Home of the Oklahoma City Philharmonic, Canterbury Choral Society, Ballet Oklahoma, BLAC, and Lyric Theatre of Oklahoma. A variety of entertainment is provided, including Broadway shows and popular concerts.

Frontier City. *11501 NE Expy, Oklahoma City (73131). Phone 405/478-2412.* A 65-acre Western theme park; including more than 75 rides, shows, and attractions; entertainment; shops, restaurants. (Memorial Day-late Aug: daily; Easter-Memorial Day and late Aug-Oct: weekends only) **$$$$**

Garden Exhibition Building and Horticulture Gardens. *3400 NW 36th St, Oklahoma City (73112). Phone 405/943-0827.* Azalea trails; butterfly garden; rose, peony, and iris gardens; arboretum; the conservatory has one of the country's largest cactus and succulent collections (daily). Exhibition Building (Mon-Fri; closed holidays; open Sat-Sun during flower shows). **FREE**

Harn Homestead and 1889er Museum. *313 NE 16th St, Oklahoma City (73104). Phone 405/235-4058. www.harnhomestead.com.* Historic homestead claimed in Land Run of 1889; 1904 farmhouse furnished with pre-statehood objects dating from period of the run. Three-story stone and cedar barn; one-room schoolhouse; working farm. Ten acres of picnic area, shade trees. (Mon-Fri; closed holidays) **$$**

Metro Concourse. *Oklahoma City.* A downtown "city beneath the city," the underground tunnel system connects nearly all the downtown buildings in a 20-square-block area. It is one of the most extensive all-enclosed pedestrian systems in the country. Offices, shops, and restaurants line the concourse system. (Mon-Fri)

Myriad Botanical Gardens. *301 W Reno, Oklahoma City (73102). Phone 405/297-3995.* A 17-acre botanical garden in the heart of the city's redeveloping central business district. Features lake, amphitheater, botanical gardens, and seven-story Crystal Bridge Tropical Conservatory. **$$**

★ **National Cowboy Hall of Fame & Western Heritage Center.** *1700 NE 63rd St, Oklahoma City (73111). Off I-44 W near I-35, between M. L. King, Jr. and Kelley aves. Phone 405/478-2250. www.nationalcowboymuseum.org.* Major art collections depict America's Western heritage; Rodeo Hall of Fame; sculpture, including *End of the Trail, Buffalo Bill,* and *Coming Through the Rye;* portrait gallery of Western film stars; landscaped gardens. (Daily 9 am-5 pm; closed Jan 1, Thanksgiving, Dec 25) **$$**

National Softball Hall of Fame and Museum. *2801 NE 50th St, Oklahoma City (73111). Just W of I-35. Phone 405/424-5266.* Displays of equipment and memorabilia trace the history of the sport; Hall of Fame; stadium complex. (May-Oct: daily; rest of year: Mon-Fri) **$$**

Oklahoma City Museum of Art. *415 Coach Dr, Oklahoma City (73102). Phone 405/236-3100.* Permanent collection of 16th-20th-century European and American paintings, prints, drawings, photographs, sculpture, and decorative arts. Changing exhibitions of regional, national, and international artists. (Tues-Sun) **$$$**

Oklahoma City National Memorial. *NW 5th St and N Robinson Ave, Oklahoma City (73102). Phone 405/235-3313. www.oklahomacitynationalmemorial.org.* A series of monuments in honor of the men, women, and children killed by a bomb at the Murrah Federal Building on April 19, 1995. The Gates of Time memorial represents the moment of the blast, forever frozen in time. The Field of Empty Chairs pays tribute to the 168 lives lost in the bombing. The Survivor Tree is an American elm tree that withstood the blast. Museum (Mon-Sat; Sun afternoon, fee). Also a reflecting pool, orchard, and children's area. (Daily) **FREE**

Oklahoma City Zoo. *2101 NE 50th, Oklahoma City (73111). Exit 50th St off I-35, 1 mile W to zoo entrance. Phone 405/424-3344.* Covers 110 acres with more than 2,000 animals representing 500 species; expansive hoofstock collection; naturalistic island life exhibit; walk-through aviaries; herpetarium; pachyderm building; big cat exhibit; primate and gorilla exhibit; children's zoo with discovery area; Safari Tram. (Daily; closed Jan 1, Dec 25) **$$$** On the zoo grounds is

Aquaticus. *2101 NE 50th, Oklahoma City (73111). Phone 405/424-3344.* A unique marine-life science facility contains a comprehensive collection of aquatic life; shark tank; adaptations and habitat exhibits; underwater viewing. (Daily; closed Jan 1, Dec 25) **$**

Oklahoma Firefighters Museum. *2716 NE 50th St, Oklahoma City (73111). Phone 405/424-3440.* Antique fire equipment dating back to 1736; also first fire station (1869) in Oklahoma reassembled here. (Daily; closed holidays) **$$**

Oklahoma Heritage Center. *201 NW 14th St, Oklahoma City (73103). Phone 405/235-4458.* Restored Hefner family mansion (1917) maintained as a museum; antique furnishings; collection of bells, art; Oklahoma Hall of Fame galleries (third floor) feature work by Oklahoma artists; memorial chapel and gardens. (Mon-Fri; closed holidays) **$$**

Oklahoma National Stockyards. *2501 Exhange Ave, Oklahoma City (73108). Phone 405/235-8675.* One of world's largest cattle markets; auction of cattle, hogs, and sheep; Livestock Exchange Building. (Mon-Tues; closed holidays) **FREE**

⭐ **Omniplex.** *2100 NE 52nd St, Oklahoma City (73111). Phone 405/602-6664.* Houses several museums and attractions within a 10-acre facility. (Daily; closed holidays). **$$$** Includes

International Photography Hall of Fame and Museum. *2100 NE 52nd St, Oklahoma City (73111). Phone 405/424-4055.* Permanent and traveling exhibits; one of world's largest photographic murals. (Daily; closed Thanksgiving, Dec 25)

Kirkpatrick Science and Air Space Museum. *2100 NE 52nd St, Oklahoma City (73111). Phone 405/602-6664.* Includes a hands-on science museum, Air Space Museum, Kirkpatrick Galleries, gardens/greenhouse; Kirkpatrick Planetarium (shows change quarterly). (Daily; closed Thanksgiving, Dec 25)

Red Earth Indian Center. *2100 NE 52nd St, Oklahoma City (73111). Phone 405/427-5228.* Exhibits and educational programs encourage appreciation of Native American cultures. (Daily; closed Thanksgiving, Dec 25)

Remington Park. *One Remington Pl, Oklahoma City (73111). At jct I-35 and I-44. Phone 405/424-1000.* Thoroughbred racing with a four-level grandstand and more than 300 video monitors. Restaurants. (Apr-June and Aug-Dec, Fri-Sun) **$$**

State Capitol. *2300 N Lincoln Blvd, Oklahoma City (73105). Phone 405/521-3356.* Greco-Roman, neoclassical building designed by S. A. Layton and Wemyss Smith. Oil well beneath Capitol building reaches 1 1/4 miles underground. After pumping oil from 1941 to 1986, it is now preserved as a monument. Legislature meets annually for 78 days beginning on the first Mon in Feb. Tours (daily; closed Dec 25). **FREE** Opposite is

State Museum of History. *2100 N Lincoln, Oklahoma City (73105). Phone 405/521-2491.* Exhibits on the history of Oklahoma; extensive collection of Native American artifacts. (Mon-Sat; closed holidays) **FREE**

White Water Bay. *3908 W Reno, Oklahoma City. Via I-40, Meridian exit. Phone 405/478-2412.* Outdoor water park with body surfing, water chutes, slides, rapids, and swimming pool; special playland for tots. (June-Aug: daily; late May and early Sept: weekends) **$$$$**

Special Events

Ballet Oklahoma. *7421 N Classen, Oklahoma City (73106). Phone 405/843-9898.* Oct-Apr.

Festival of the Arts. *Downtown, Hudson Ave, Oklahoma City. Phone 405/270-4848.* International foods, entertainment, children's learning and play area; craft market; artists from many states display their work. Six days in late Apr.

International Finals Rodeo. *333 Gordon Cooper Blvd, Oklahoma City (73107). Phone 405/948-6700.* International Pro Rodeo Association's top 15 cowboys and cowgirls compete in seven events to determine world championships.

Lyric Theatre. *201 N Walker, Oklahoma City (73106). Phone 405/524-9312.*

Oklahoma City Philharmonic Orchestra. *Civic Center Music Hall, 201 N Walker, Oklahoma City (73102). Phone 405/297-2584.* Mid-Sept-May.

State Fair of Oklahoma. *333 Gorden Cooper Blvd, Oklahoma City (73107). Phone 405/948-6700.* Livestock, crafts, art exhibits; ice show, circus, rodeo; truck pull contests; auto races; concerts; international show, flower and garden show; Native American ceremonial dances; carriage collection; monorail, space tower, carnival, parades. Arena and grandstand attractions. Sept.

World Championship Quarter Horse Show. *State Fairgrounds, 3313 Pershing Blvd, Oklahoma City (73107). Phone 405/948-6700.* More than 1,800 horses compete. Early-mid-Nov.

Limited-Service Hotels

★★ BEST WESTERN SADDLEBACK INN.
4300 SW 3rd St, Oklahoma City (73108). Phone 405/947-7000; toll-free 800/228-3903; fax 405/948-7636. www.bestwestern.com. 220 rooms, 3 story. Pets accepted, some restrictions; fee. Check-out noon. Restaurant, bar. Fitness room. Outdoor pool, whirlpool. Airport transportation available. Southwestern décor. **$**

★★ COURTYARD BY MARRIOTT.
4301 Highline Blvd, Oklahoma City (73108). Phone 405/946-6500; toll-free 800/321-2211; fax 405/946-7368. www.courtyard.com. 149 rooms, 3 story. Check-out noon. Restaurant, bar. Fitness room. Outdoor pool, whirlpool. Airport transportation available. **$**

★ DAYS INN.
12013 N I-35 Service Rd, Oklahoma City (73131). Phone 405/478-2554; toll-free 800/329-7466; fax 405/478-5033. www.daysinn.com. 47 rooms, 2 story. Pets accepted; fee. Complimentary continental breakfast. Check-out 11 am. Indoor pool. **$**

★★ EMBASSY SUITES.
1815 S Meridian Ave, Oklahoma City (73108). Phone 405/682-6000; toll-free 800/362-2779; fax 405/682-9835. www.embassysuites .com. This is an airport, all-suite hotel that is near the Meridian strips and more than 30 restaurants and clubs. It offers live entertainment and a dance club of its own along with exercise facilities, a pool and a Jacuzzi. 236 rooms, 6 story, all suites. Pets accepted, some restrictions; fee. Complimentary full breakfast. Check-out noon. Restaurant, bar. Fitness room. Indoor pool, whirlpool. Airport transportation available. Business center. **$**

★ GOVERNORS SUITES INN.
2308 S Meridian Ave, Oklahoma City (73108). Phone 405/682-5299; toll-free 888/819-7575; fax 405/682-3047. 50 rooms, 3 story. Complimentary full breakfast. Check-out 11 am. Fitness room. Outdoor pool, whirlpool. Airport transportation available. **$**

★★ HOLIDAY INN.
6200 N Robinson Ave, Oklahoma City (73118). Phone 405/843-5558; toll-free 800/682-0049; fax 405/840-3410. www.holiday-inn .com. 200 rooms, 3 story. Pets accepted, some restrictions; fee. Check-out noon. Restaurant, bar. Fitness room. Indoor pool, whirlpool. **$**

★ LA QUINTA INN.
8315 S I-35 Service Rd, Oklahoma City (73149). Phone 405/631-8661; toll-free 800/531-5900; fax 405/631-1892. www.laquinta.com. 121 rooms, 2 story. Pets accepted. Complimentary continental breakfast. Check-out noon. Outdoor pool. **$**

Full-Service Hotels

★★★ HILTON OKLAHOMA CITY NORTHWEST.
2945 NW Expy, Oklahoma City (73112). Phone 405/848-4811; toll-free 800/774-1500; fax 405/843-4829. www.hilton.com. Found in the business district and only 20 minutes from downtown and the Will Rogers Airport, this hotel offers guest rooms, four suites and nine poolside cabanas. The Honeymoon suite features a private swimming pool and Jacuzzi. 218 rooms, 9 story. Check-out noon. Restaurant, bar. Fitness room. Outdoor pool, whirlpool. Airport transportation available. **$**

★★★ MARRIOTT WATERFORD.
6300 Waterford Blvd, Oklahoma City (73118). Phone 405/848-4782; toll-free 800/992-2009; fax 405/843-9161. www.marriott.com. Located in the city's premier suburb, this hotel is only 15 minutes from downtown and the airport. Guests can enjoy a drink in the waterfront lounge or take a swim in the outdoor pool. Volleyball and squash facilities are also available. 197 rooms, 9 story. Pets accepted, some restrictions; fee. Check-out noon. Restaurant, bar. Fitness room. Outdoor pool, whirlpool. Tennis. Business center. **$$**

★★★ RENAISSANCE OKLAHOMA CITY CONVENTION CENTER HOTEL.
10 N Broadway, Oklahoma City (73102). Phone 405/228-8000; toll-free 800/468-3571; fax 405/228-8080. www.renaissance hotels.com. 311 rooms, 15 story. Check-out 11 am. Restaurant. Fitness room. Indoor pool, whirlpool. Business center. **$$**

★★★ THE WESTIN OKLAHOMA CITY.
1 N Broadway Ave, Oklahoma City (73102). Phone 405/235-2780; toll-free 800/285-2780; fax 405/232-8752. www.westin.com. This hotel is connected to the Myriad Convention Center and many shops and businesses in the area by an underground concourse.

It is newly renovated and offers oversized guest rooms, outdoor pool, sundeck, and fitness center. 395 rooms, 15 story. Check-out noon. Restaurant, bar. Fitness room. Outdoor pool. Business center. **$$**

Restaurants

★ ★ **ARIA GRILL.** *1 N Broadway, Oklahoma City (73102). Phone 405/815-6063; fax 408/815-6052. www.westinokc.com.* American menu. Breakfast, lunch, dinner, late-night, brunch. Closed holidays. Bar. Children's menu. Valet parking. **$$**

★ ★ ★ **BELLINI'S.** *6305 Waterford Blvd #1, Oklahoma City (73118). Phone 405/848-1065; fax 405/848-5946. www.bellinis.net.* Overlooking a charming duck pond, this casual restaurant has the ambience of an Italian piazza. Be sure to catch the lakeside sunset. American, Italian menu. Lunch, dinner, Sun brunch. Bar. Outdoor seating. Open brick pizza oven. **$$**

★ ★ **BRICKTOWN BREWERY.** *1 N Oklahoma Ave, Oklahoma City (73104). Phone 405/232-2739; fax 405/232-0531. www.bricktownbrewery.com.* American menu. Lunch, dinner, late-night. Closed holidays. Bar. Children's menu. Renovated building in the warehouse district. **$$**

★ ★ **CAFE 501.** *501 S Boulevard St, Edmond (73034). Phone 405/359-1501; fax 405/341-3896. www.cafe501.com.* Eclectic menu. Lunch, dinner. Closed holidays. Children's menu. **$$**

★ ★ **CATTLEMAN'S STEAKHOUSE.** *1309 S Agnew St, Oklahoma City (73108). Phone 405/236-0416; fax 405/235-1969. www.cattlemensrestaurant .com.* Steak menu. Breakfast, lunch, dinner, late-night, brunch. Closed Thanksgiving, Dec 25. In historic Stockyards City district, opened in 1910. **$$**

★ **CLASSEN GRILL.** *5124 N Classen Blvd, Oklahoma City (73118). Phone 405/842-0428.* Seafood, steak menu. Breakfast, lunch. Closed Jan 1, Thanksgiving, Dec 25. Bar. Children's menu. **$**

★ ★ ★ **COACH HOUSE.** *6437 Avondale Dr, Oklahoma City (73116). Phone 405/842-1000; fax 405/843-9777. www.coach-house-restaurant.com.* This intimate French restaurant highlights contemporary interpretations of classic dishes. The 50-seat restaurant also features a bar with an extensive wine list. American, French menu. Lunch, dinner. Closed Sun. Children's menu. **$$$**

★ **COUNTY LINE.** *1226 NE 63rd St, Oklahoma City (73111). Phone 405/478-4955; fax 405/478-5238. www.countyline.com.* Barbecue menu. Lunch, dinner. Closed Thanksgiving, Dec 25. Bar. Children's menu. **$$**

★ ★ **DEEP FORK GRILL.** *5418 N Western Ave, Oklahoma City (73118). Phone 405/848-7678; fax 405/840-0624. www.deepforkgrill.com.* Breakfast, lunch, lunch, dinner, late-night, brunch. Closed Thanksgiving, Dec 25. Bar. Valet parking. **$$**

★ ★ **EDDY'S OF OKLAHOMA CITY.** *4227 N Meridian Ave, Oklahoma City (73112). Phone 405/787-2944. www.eddys-steakhouse.com.* Dinner. Closed Sun. Children's menu. Display of crystal, collectibles. **$$**

★ **GOPURAM TASTE OF INDIA.** *4559 NW 23rd St, Oklahoma City (73127). Phone 405/948-7373; fax 405/948-7388.* Indian menu. Breakfast, lunch, dinner, brunch. Bar. Children's menu. **$**

★ ★ ★ **JW'S STEAKHOUSE.** *3233 NW Expy, Oklahoma City (73112). Phone 405/842-6633; fax 405/842-3152.* The warm, earth-toned dining room has an intimate feel. Seafood menu. Breakfast, lunch, dinner, late-night, brunch. Children's menu. Valet parking. **$$$**

★ ★ ★ **KELLER IN THE KASTLE GERMAN RESTAURANT.** *820 N MacArthur, Oklahoma City (73127). Phone 405/942-6133; fax 405/962-6202. www.kellerinthekastle.com.* Causal hometown service in a fun and interesting atmosphere. German menu. Dinner. Closed Sun-Mon. Bar. Outdoor seating. Building design based on a castle in Normandy (France). **$$$**

★ ★ **KONA RANCH STEAKHOUSE.** *2037 S Meridian, Oklahoma City (73108). Phone 405/681-1000; fax 405/681-0265.* Hawaiian menu. Lunch, dinner. Closed Thanksgiving, Dec 25. Bar. Children's menu. **$$**

★ **LA BAGUETTE BISTRO.** *7408 N May Ave, Oklahoma City (73116). Phone 405/840-3047; fax 405/840-5104. www.labaguettebistro.com.* French menu. Breakfast, lunch, dinner, Sun brunch. Bar. Valet parking. **$$$**

★ ★ **LAS PALOMAS.** *2329 N Meridian, Oklahoma City (73107). Phone 405/949-9988; fax 405/949-9988.* Mexican menu. Lunch, dinner. Children's menu. **$$$**

★ ★ **SLEEPY HOLLOW.** *1101 NE 50th St, Oklahoma City (73111). Phone 405/424-1614; fax 405/427-1936.* Steak menu. Lunch, dinner. Bar. **$$**

★ ★ **SUSHI NEKO.** *4318 N Western Ave, Oklahoma City (73118). Phone 405/528-8862; fax 405/ 521-9877. www.sushineko.com.* Japanese menu. Lunch, dinner, late-night. Closed Sun. Bar. Children's menu. Valet parking. **$$**

Okmulgee (B-5)

See also Henryetta

Founded circa 1900
Population 13,441
Elevation 670 ft
Area Code 918
Zip 74447
Information Chamber of Commerce, 112 N Morton, PO Box 609; phone 918/756-6172.
Web Site www.tourokmulgee.com

The capital of the Creek Nation was established in 1868 and operates at the Creek Indian Complex. The Creeks gave the town its name, which means "bubbling water." Within Okmulgee County nearly 5 million pounds of wild pecans are harvested annually. The city is the home of Oklahoma State University/ Okmulgee, one of the country's largest residential-vocational training schools and a branch of Oklahoma State University.

What to See and Do

Creek Council House Museum. *106 W 6th St, Okmulgee (74447). Phone 918/756-2324.* Museum houses a display of Creek tribal history. (Tues-Sat; closed holidays) **FREE**

Okmulgee State Park. *16830 Dripping Springs Rd, Okmulgee (74447). 5 miles W on Hwy 56. Phone 918/ 756-5971.* Covers 575 acres; 678-acre lake. Fishing, boating (ramps); picnicking, playground, camping, trailer hook-ups (fee). (Daily) **FREE**

Special Events

Creek Nation Rodeo and Festival. *Wood Dr and Hwy 56, Okmulgee (74447). Phone 918/756-6172.* June.

Pecan Festival. *6th and Morton, Okmulgee. Phone 918/756-6172; toll-free 800/355-5552.* If you're looking for a fun festival to attend and like out-of-the-way places, the Pecan Festival in Okmulgee is for you. This festival holds the Guinness World Record for biggest pecan pie ever baked, and a pie approximately 40

feet in diameter is baked every year for the festival's patrons. A carnival, arts and crafts, and various forms of entertainment round out the offerings and create a festive atmosphere. If you've eaten too much pie, join the 8K run. First weekend in June.

Limited-Service Hotels

★ ★ **BEST WESTERN OKMULGEE.** *3499 N Wood Dr, Okmulgee (74447). Phone 918/756-9200; toll-free 800/552-9201; fax 918/752-0022. www.best western.com.* 50 rooms, 2 story. Pets accepted; fee. Complimentary continental breakfast. Check-out 11 am. Restaurant, bar. Outdoor pool. **$**
🐾 ⊠

★ ★ **HENRYETTA INN AND DOME.** *810 E Trudgeon St, Henryetta (74437). Phone 918/652-2581; toll-free 800/515-3663; fax 918/652-2581.* 85 rooms, 2 story. Pets accepted, some restrictions. Check-out noon. Restaurant, bar. Fitness room. Indoor pool. **$**
🐾 🧍 ⊠

Pauls Valley (C-4)

See also Ada

Settled 1847
Population 6,150
Elevation 876 ft
Area Code 405
Zip 73075
Information Chamber of Commerce, 112 E Paul St, Box 638; phone 405/238-6491
Web Site www.paulsvalley.com

What to See and Do

Murray-Lindsay Mansion. *Hwys 405 and 79, Erin Springs (73075). 21 miles W on Hwy 19, 2 miles S on Hwy 76. Phone 405/756-2121.* (1880) A three-story Classic Revival mansion built by Frank Murray, an Irish immigrant who married a woman of Choctaw descent. Starting small, Murray eventually controlled more than 20,000 acres of land within the Chickasaw Nation. The mansion, a showplace within the Nation, contains original period furnishings. (Tues-Sun afternoons; closed holidays) **FREE**

Pauls Valley City Lake. *Pauls Valley. 2 miles E on Hwy 19, then 1 mile N. Phone 405/238-5134.* Fishing, boating (ramps, dock); hiking, picnicking, camping. Fee for some activities. (Daily)

Washita Valley Museum. *1100 N Ash St, Pauls Valley (73075). Phone 405/238-3048.* Artifact collection of the Washita River Culture People (AD 600-800) with paintings by a local artist; a collection of antique medical and surgical instruments; pioneer clothing, photos, and other memorabilia from the early 1900s. (Tues-Fri; closed Thanksgiving, Dec 25) **FREE**

Special Events

Garvin County Free Fair. *Fairgrounds, Willow St and Grant Ave, Pauls Valley (73075). Phone 405/238-6681.* Early Sept.

International Rodeo Association Competition. *Pauls Valley. Phone 405/238-6491.* Last weekend in June.

Limited-Service Hotel

★ **DAYS INN.** *3203 W Grant Ave, Pauls Valley (73075). Phone 405/238-7548; toll-free 800/329-7466; fax 405/238-1262. www.daysinn.com.* 54 rooms, 2 story. Pets accepted, some restrictions. Complimentary continental breakfast. Check-out 11 am. **$**
🐾

Pawhuska (A-5)

See also Bartlesville

Population 3,825
Elevation 818 ft
Area Code 918
Zip 74056
Information Chamber of Commerce, 222 W Main St; phone 918/287-1208
Web Site www.pawhuskachamber.com

This is the county seat of Oklahoma's largest county and is the Osage capital (county boundaries are the same as those of the Osage Nation). This is a good fishing and hunting area with approximately 5,000 private lakes and five major lakes nearby.

The first Boy Scout troop in America was organized here in May 1909 by the Reverend John Mitchell.

What to See and Do

Drummond Home. *305 N Price Ave, Hominy (74035). 21 miles S on Hwy 99. Phone 918/885-2374.* (1905) Restored three-story Victorian house of merchant/cattleman Fred Drummond. Native sandstone, central

square tower, second-floor balcony, and false dormers; original furnishings. (Fri-Sun afternoons; closed holidays) **FREE**

Osage County Historical Society Museum. *700 N Lynn Ave, Pawhuska (74056). Phone 918/287-9924.* Old Santa Fe depot; chuck wagon display; saddles, Western, Native American, pioneer, and oil exhibits. Monument to the first Boy Scout troop in America (1909); correspondence and pictures about the beginning of the Boy Scouts. (Mon-Sat; closed Thanksgiving, Dec 25) **FREE**

Osage Hills State Park. *Pawhuska. 11 miles NE on Hwy 60. Phone 918/336-4141.* A 1,005-acre park with an 18-acre lake. Swimming pool, fishing; picnic facilities, playgrounds, camping areas, trailer hook-ups (fee). (Daily) **FREE**

Tallgrass Prairie Preserve. *Hwy 60 and Kihekah, Pawhuska (74056). 17 miles N on County Rd. Phone 918/287-1208.* Forty thousand acres with buffalo herd. **FREE**

Special Events

Ben Johnson Memorial Steer-Roping Contest. *Pawhuska. Phone 918/287-1208.* Father's Day weekend.

International Roundup Clubs Cavalcade. *Pawhuska. Phone 918/287-1208.* State's largest amateur rodeo. Third weekend in July.

Pawnee (A-4)

See also Perry

Population 2,197
Elevation 900 ft
Area Code 918
Zip 74058
Information Chamber of Commerce, 608 Harrison St; phone 918/762-2108

What to See and Do

Pawnee Bill Ranch Site. *Hwy 64, Pawnee. Phone 918/762-2513.* House of Pawnee Bill, completed in 1910; 14 rooms with original furnishings; Wild West show mementos. Buffalo, longhorn cattle pasture. (Daily, hours vary; closed holidays) **FREE**

Special Events

Pawnee Bill Memorial Rodeo. *Pawnee. Phone 918/762-*

2108. Cattle drive, wagon trains, cowboy poet gathering. Mid-Aug.

Steam Show and Threshing Bee. *Fairgrounds, Pawnee. Phone 918/438-6788*. Steam engine races; exhibits. First full weekend in May.

World's Largest Free Powwow. *Pawnee*. Tribal dances, contests. First weekend in July.

Perry (A-4)

See also Pawnee, Stillwater

Population 4,978
Elevation 1,002 ft
Area Code 580
Zip 73077
Information Chamber of Commerce, 300 6th St; PO Box 426; phone 580/336-4684
Web Site www.perrychamber.fullnet.net

What to See and Do

Cherokee Strip Museum. *2617 W Fir, Perry (73077). Phone 580/336-2405*. Schoolhouse (circa 1895), implement building, pioneer artifacts, and documents depict the era of the 1893 land run; picnic area. (Tues-Sat; closed holidays) **FREE**

Special Event

Cherokee Strip Celebration. *Courthouse Lawn, Perry. Phone 580/336-4684*. Commemorates the opening of the Cherokee Strip to settlers. Parade, entertainment, rodeo, contests, Noble County Fair. Mid-Sept.

Limited-Service Hotel

★★ **BEST WESTERN CHEROKEE STRIP MOTEL.** *Hwy 64, 77 and I-35, Perry (73077). Phone 580/336-2218; fax 580/336-9753. www.bestwestern.com*. 88 rooms. Pets accepted. Check-out noon. Restaurant, bar. Indoor pool. **$**

Ponca City (A-4)

See also Arkansas City, KS

Founded 1893
Population 26,359
Elevation 1,019 ft
Area Code 580

Information Ponca City Tourism, PO Box 1450, 74602; phone 580/763-8092 or toll-free 866/763-8092
Web Site www.poncacitynews.com

Ponca City was founded in a single day in the traditional Oklahoma land rush manner. Although in the Cherokee Strip, the town was named for the Ponca tribe. Ponca City is a modern industrial town surrounded by cattle and wheat country.

What to See and Do

Kaw Lake. *Hwy 2, Ponca City. 8 miles E on Lake Rd. Phone 580/762-5611*. On the Arkansas River; the shoreline covers 168 miles. Water sports, fishing, boating; hunting. Recreation and camping areas (fee) located 1 mile off Hwy 60. (Daily) **FREE**

Lake Ponca. *Ponca City. 4 miles NE*. Water-skiing (license required), fishing, boating; camp and trailer park (fee).

Marland's Grand Home. *Marland-Paris Historic House, 1000 E Grand Ave, Ponca City (74601). Phone 580/767-0427*. Indian Museum, 101 Ranch Room, and D.A.R. Memorial Museum. (Tues-Sat; closed Jan 1, Thanksgiving, Dec 25) **$$**

Marland Mansion Estate. *901 Monument Rd, Ponca City (74604). Phone 580/767-0420*. A 55-room mansion built in 1928 by E. W. Marland, oil baron, governor, and philanthropist. Modeled after the Davanzati Palace in Florence, Italy; features elaborate artwork and hand-painted ceilings. Tours. (Daily; closed Jan 1, Thanksgiving, Dec 25) **$$**

Limited-Service Hotels

★ **DAYS INN.** *1415 E Bradley Ave, Ponca City (74604). Phone 580/767-1406; fax 580/762-9589. www.daysinn.com*. 59 rooms, 3 story. Pets accepted, some restrictions; fee. Complimentary continental breakfast. Check-out 11 am. **$**

★★ **HOLIDAY INN.** *2215 N 14 St, Ponca City (74601). Phone 580/762-8311; toll-free 800/465-4329; fax 580/765-0014. www.holiday-inn.com*. 138 rooms, 2 story. Check-out noon. Restaurant, bar. Fitness room. Outdoor pool. **$**

Poteau (C-6)

See also Fort Smith, AR

Founded 1898
Population 7,210
Elevation 480 ft
Area Code 918
Zip 74953
Information Chamber of Commerce, 201 S Broadway St; phone 918/647-9178

Rich in ancient history and pioneer heritage, Poteau is located in an area of timber and high hills. Just off Hwy 271, a 4 1/2-mile paved road winds to the peak of Cavanal Hill for a spectacular view of the entire Poteau River Valley. Poteau lies approximately 15 miles north of Ouachita National Forest.

What to See and Do

Heavener Runestone. *Poteau. NE of Heavener off Hwy 59. Phone 918/653-2241.* Scandinavian cryptograph in eight runes that scholars believe were inscribed by Vikings in AD 800. Other runes from the Scandinavian alphabet of the 3rd-10th centuries have been found engraved on several stones in the area. (Daily) **FREE**

Kerr Museum. *1507 S McKenna St, Poteau (74953). 6 miles SW. Phone 918/647-8221.* Home of former Senator Robert S. Kerr contains material detailing the history and development of eastern Oklahoma; including natural history, pioneer, Choctaw, and special exhibits. (Tues-Sun afternoons; also by appointment; closed Jan 1, Thanksgiving, Dec 25) **DONATION**

Lake Wister State Park. *Poteau. 9 miles SW on Hwy 271, then 2 miles SE on Hwy 270. Phone 918/655-7756.* On a 4,000-acre lake, facilities include swimming pool, waterskiing, fishing, boating (ramps); hiking trails, picnic facilities, playground, miniature golf, grocery, camping, trailer hook-ups (fee), cabins. (Daily) **FREE**

Spiro Mound Archeological State Park. *Spiro. 17 miles N on Hwy 59, 6 miles E on Hwy 9, then 4 miles N on Spiro Mounds Rd. Phone 918/962-2062.* A 138-acre site with 12 earthen mounds dating from AD 600 to AD 1450. Reconstructed Native American house; excavated items on display in the interpretive center (summer: Tues-Sun; winter: Wed-Sun). Hiking trails, picnicking. **FREE**

Pryor (A-5)

See also Claremore, Grand Lake, Miami, Vinita

Population 8,327
Elevation 626 ft
Area Code 918
Zip 74361
Information Chamber of Commerce, PO Box 367, 74362; phone 918/825-0157
Web Site www.pryorok.com

Pryor was named in honor of Nathaniel Pryor, a scout with Lewis and Clark who built a trading post near the town to do business with the Osage. For years a farming community, Pryor now has a 9,000-acre industrial park with plants producing cement, fertilizers and chemicals, castings, and wallboard.

What to See and Do

Coo-Y-Yah Country Museum. *8th St and Hwy 69S, Pryor (74361). Phone 918/825-2222.* Artifacts from Mayes County representing several cultures including clothing, artwork, Native American and pioneer items; also temporary exhibits. The museum is housed in an old train depot. (Apr-Dec: Tues-Sun afternoons; rest of year: by appointment) **FREE**

Lake Hudson. *Pryor. 10 miles E on Hwy 20.* Robert S. Kerr Dam impounds the waters of the Grand River. Swimming, water-skiing, fishing, boating; camping. **FREE**

Limited-Service Hotel

★ **PRYOR HOUSE MOTOR INN.** *123 S Mill St, Pryor (74361). Phone 918/825-6677; fax 918/825-6678.* 35 rooms, 2 story. Pets accepted; fee. Complimentary continental breakfast. Check-out 11 am. Outdoor pool. **$**

Quartz Mountain State Park (C-2)

See also Altus

---

18 miles N of Altus via Hwy 283, Hwy 44, 44A.

This 4,284-acre scenic preserve is on Lake Altus-Lugert, a 6,260-acre lake with excellent fishing for bass, catfish, and crappie. The wild rock-strewn park has 29 varieties of trees and 140 species of wildflowers. Recreational facilities include a beach, swimming pool, bathhouse, water-skiing, fishing, boating (ramps); hiking, golf, tennis, picnic facilities, playground, café, grocery, lodge, camping, trailer hook-ups (fee), and cabins. Amphitheater. For camping reservations and additional information, phone toll-free 800/654-8240 or contact the Oklahoma Tourism and Recreation Department, 15 N Robinson, Oklahoma City 73105; phone 405/521-2406.

Roman Nose State Park (B-3)

---

7 miles N of Watonga via Hwy 8, 8A.

Named after Chief Henry Roman Nose of the Cheyenne, this is a 750-acre area with a 55-acre man-made lake stocked with bass, crappie, bluegill, rainbow trout, and catfish. Its many recreational facilities include a swimming pool, bathhouse, fishing, boating, paddleboats on Lake Boecher; golf, tennis, picnicking (grills), playgrounds, concession, and lodge. Campsites, trailer hook-ups (fee). For more information, contact the Park Manager, Hwy 1, Box 2-2, Watonga, 73772.

Full-Service Resort

★ ★ **ROMAN NOSE RESORT.** *Hwy 1, Watonga (73772). Phone 580/623-7281; toll-free 800/654-8240; fax 580/623-2538. www.oklahomaresorts.com.* 57 rooms, 3 story. Check-in 3 pm, check-out noon. Restaurant. Children's activity center. Outdoor pool. Tennis. **$**

Sallisaw (B-6)

See also Fort Smith, AR

Population 7,122
Elevation 533 ft
Area Code 918
Zip 74955
Information Chamber of Commerce, 111 N Elm, PO Box 251; phone 918/775-2558

What to See and Do

Blue Ribbon Downs. *Hwy 64 W, Sallisaw. Phone 918/775-7771.* Thoroughbred, quarter horse, appaloosa, and paint horse racing. Pari-mutuel betting. (Schedule varies) **$**

Robert S. Kerr Lake. *Sallisaw. 8 miles S on Hwy 59. Phone 918/775-4474.* Approximately 42,000 acres with 250 miles of shoreline, Kerr Lake was formed with the creation of the inland waterway along the Arkansas River. Swimming, fishing, boating (fee); hunting (in season), picnicking, camping (fee). (Daily) **FREE**

Sallisaw State Park at Brushy Lake. *RR 3, Box 36, Sallisaw. 8 miles N on Marble City Rd, then 1 mile W on County Rd. Phone 918/775-6507.* Fishing, boating (ramp); picnicking, camping (fee). (Daily) **FREE**

✪ **Sequoyah's Cabin.** *Hwy 101, Sallisaw. 11 miles NE on Hwy 101. Phone 918/775-2413.* (Circa 1829) Historic one-room log cabin built by Sequoyah, famous Cherokee who created an 86-character alphabet for the Cherokee language. Historic landmark includes visitor center, mini-museum, artifacts; picnicking. (Tues-Sun; closed holidays) **FREE**

Limited-Service Hotels

★ **BEST WESTERN BLUE RIBBON INN.** *706 S Kerr Blvd, Sallisaw (74955). Phone 918/775-6294; fax 918/775-5151.* 81 rooms, 2 story. Check-out 11 am. Fitness room. Indoor pool, whirlpool. **$**

★ **DAYS INN.** *RR 2, Box 13, Sallisaw (74955). Phone 918/775-4406; fax 918/775-4440. www.daysinn.com.* 33 rooms, 2 story. Pets accepted; fee. Complimentary continental breakfast. Check-out 11 am. **$**

Sequoyah State Park (B-6)

See also Tahlequah

8 miles E of Wagoner on Hwy 51.

These approximately 2,800 acres in Oklahoma's Cookson Hills, once a bandits' hideout, offer many attractions to vacationers. The park is on Fort Gibson Reservoir, created by the dam of the same name. This 19,100-acre reservoir shifts its level less than most hydroelectric power lakes in Oklahoma and is stocked with bass, catfish, and crappie. Fees may be charged at federal recreation sites at the reservoir. The park has many features: a beach, swimming pool, bathhouse, water sports, fishing, boating (ramps, docks, marina, rentals); hiking trail, mountain biking trail, horseback riding, 18-hole golf, tennis, picnic facilities, playgrounds, games, grocery, lodge, camping area, trailer hook-ups (fee), and cabins. For more information, contact the Park Manager, Hwy 1, Box 198-3, Hulbert, 74441.

Limited-Service Hotels

★ **INDIAN LODGE.** *RR 2, Wagoner (74467). Phone 918/485-3184; fax 918/485-3706. www.indianlodge.net.* Shaded grounds, near Fort Gibson Reservoir. 25 rooms. Closed Nov-Mar. Check-out noon. Outdoor pool. **$**

★ ★ **WESTERN HILLS GUEST RANCH.** *19808 Park #10, Wagoner (74447). Phone 918/772-2545; toll-free 800/368-1486; fax 918/772-2030. www.oklahomaresorts.com.* 18 rooms. Check-in 3 pm, check-out noon. Restaurant, bar. Children's activity center. Outdoor pool, children's pool. Tennis. On Fort Gibson Reservoir. **$**

Shawnee (C-4)

Founded 1895
Population 26,017
Elevation 1,055 ft
Area Code 405
Zip 74801

Information Chamber of Commerce, 131 N Bell, PO Box 1613; phone 405/273-6092
Web Site www.shawneenet.com

The history of Shawnee is that of Oklahoma in miniature. In the center of the state, it stands on what was originally Sac and Fox land, which was also claimed at various times by Spain, France, and England; and was opened by a land rush on September 22, 1891. Oil was struck in 1926. Now it has diversified industries in addition to the processing of fruits, vegetables, poultry, and dairy products.

Shawnee is the home of Oklahoma Baptist University (1910). Jim Thorpe, the great Native American athlete, and Dr. Brewster Higley, the physician who wrote "Home on the Range," lived here. Astronaut Gordon Cooper was born and raised in Shawnee.

What to See and Do

Mabee-Gerrer Museum of Art. *1900 W MacArthur Dr, Shawnee (74804). St. Gregory's College. Phone 405/878-5300.* Art gallery features works by 19th- and 20th-century European and American artists as well as works from the Middle Ages and the Renaissance. Museum features artifacts of Egyptian, Babylonian, Grecian, Roman, Persian, Chinese, African, and Polynesian civilizations as well as North, Central, and South American native civilizations. (Tues-Sun; closed holidays) **DONATION**

Seminole Nation Museum. *524 S Wewoka Ave, Wewoka (74884). 30 miles SE via Hwy 177, Hwy 9, Hwy 270. Phone 405/257-5580.* The museum traces the Seminole's history from their removal from Florida over the "Trail of Tears" to the establishment of the capital. Displays include a collection of Native American peace medals; replicas of a Chické (Florida Seminole house), dioramas of the stickball game, the Whipping tree, the Old Wewoka Trading Post; artifacts from the pioneer through the oil boom days of the 1920s. Art gallery with Native American paintings and sculpture. (Tues-Sun; closed holidays) **FREE**

Shawnee Twin Lakes. *Shawnee. 8 miles W.* Fishing, boating, swimming; hunting. Fee for activities.

Special Event

Pott County Fair. *Expo Center, Shawnee. Phone 405/273-6092.* Early Sept.

Limited-Service Hotels

★ ★ **BEST WESTERN CINDERELLA MOTOR INN.** *623 Kickapoo Spur St, Shawnee (74801). Phone 405/273-7010; toll-free 800/480-5111; fax 405/273-7010. www.bestwestern.com.* 90 rooms, 2 story. Pets accepted, some restrictions; fee. Check-out noon. Restaurant, bar. Indoor pool, whirlpool. **$**

★ ★ **RAMADA INN.** *4900 N Harrison Blvd, Shawnee (74801). Phone 405/275-4404; toll-free 800/298-2054; fax 405/275-4998. www.ramada.com.* 106 rooms, 2 story. Pets accepted; fee. Restaurant, bar. Indoor pool. **$**

Stillwater (B-4)

See also Perry

Founded 1889
Population 36,676
Elevation 900 ft
Area Code 405
Information Convention & Visitors Bureau, 409 S Main St, PO Box 1687, 74076; phone 405/743-3697 or toll-free 800/991-6717
Web Site www.come2stillwater.com

Stillwater was born overnight in the great land run of 1889. The settlement was less than a year old when, on Christmas Day 1890, the territorial legislature established Oklahoma State University (formerly Oklahoma A & M). At the time, the settlement had a mayor but no real town government. Yet less than four months later, the new settlers voted to incorporate as a city and to issue $10,000 in bonds to help build the college.

What to See and Do

Lake Carl Blackwell. *11000 W Hwy 51C, Stillwater (74075). 9 miles W on Hwy 51. Phone 405/372-5157.* A 19,364-acre recreation area operated by Oklahoma State University. Swimming, water-skiing, fishing, boating, sailing; hunting, picnic areas, campgrounds, cabins. Fees for various activities.

National Wrestling Hall of Fame. *405 W Hall of Fame Ave, Stillwater (74075). Phone 405/377-5243.* Houses Museum of Wrestling History and Honors Court.

(Mon-Fri; also Sat during university sports events; closed holidays) **FREE**

Oklahoma State University. *Stillwater (74078). Washington St and University Ave, junction Hwy 177 and Hwy 51. Phone 405/744-9341.* (1890) (22,000 students) On a campus of 840 acres with an additional 4,774 acres of experimental university farms statewide. On campus is the Noble Research Center for Agriculture and Renewable Natural Resources, an education/research complex with emphasis on the biological sciences. Buildings vary in style from "Old Central," the oldest collegiate building in the state, built in 1894 of pink brick, to attractive modified Georgian buildings of red brick with slate roofs. Of special interest are the Museum of Higher Education in Oklahoma (Tues-Sat; phone 405/624-3220); Bartlett Center for Studio Arts (Mon-Fri; phone 405/744-6016); and Gardiner Art Gallery (daily; phone 405/744-6016). Relief maps for the visually impaired.

Sheerar Museum. *702 S Duncan St, Stillwater (74074). Phone 405/377-0359.* Historical building houses local history museum, including a 4,000-specimen button collection; also changing exhibits. (Tues-Sun; closed holidays) **FREE**

Special Events

Payne County Free Fair. *Payne County Expo Center, 2814 Expo Circle E, Stillwater. Phone 405/377-1275.* Livestock shows, commercial booths, carnival, children's barnyard, antique farm equipment, tractor pull. Aug.

Run for the Arts. *Stillwater. Phone 405/372-5573.* Fine arts and jazz festival. Fiddle, banjo, and guitar contests; antique auto show. Apr.

Limited-Service Hotels

★ ★ **BEST WESTERN STILLWATER.** *600 E McElroy Rd, Stillwater (74075). Phone 405/377-7010; toll-free 800/353-6894; fax 405/743-1686. www.bestwestern.com.* 122 rooms, 4 story. Pets accepted. Check-out noon. Restaurant, bar. Fitness room. Indoor pool, whirlpool. Business center. **$**

★ ★ **HOLIDAY INN.** *2515 W 6th Ave, Stillwater (74074). Phone 405/372-0800; fax 405/377-8212. www.holiday-inn.com.* 141 rooms, 2 story. Pets accepted. Check-out noon. Restaurant, bar. Indoor pool, whirlpool. Business center. **$**

Restaurant

★ ★ **STILLWATER BAY.** *623 1/2 S Husband St, Stillwater (74074). Phone 405/743-2780. www.stillwater bay.com.* Lunch, dinner. Bar. Children's menu. **$$**

Sulphur (C-4)

See also Ada, Ardmore

Population 4,824
Area Code 580
Zip 73086
Information Chamber of Commerce, 717 W Broadway; phone 580/622-2824
Web Site www.sulphurokla.com

What to See and Do

Arbuckle Wilderness. *I-35, exit 51, Davis. Approximately 9 miles W via Hwy 7, 3 miles S of Davis near jct I-35, Hwy 77; exit 51. Phone 580/369-3383. www.arbucklewilderness.com.* A 6-mile scenic drive-through an animal park; exotic, free-roaming animals; aviaries, zoo, hayrides, camel rides; petting park, catfish feeding; paddle and bumper boats; go-karts; playground; snack bar; gifts. (Daily, weather permitting; closed Dec 25) **$$$$**

Chickasaw National Recreation Area. *Hwy 7 and Hwy 177, Sulphur. S off Hwy 7. Phone 580/622-3165.* **Travertine District** (912 acres), near Sulphur, has mineral and freshwater springs which contain sulphur, iron, bromide, and other minerals. There are streams for wading and swimming, and 20 miles of hiking trails. Travertine Nature Center (daily; closed holidays) has exhibits of the natural history of the area. Guided tours (summer and weekends; rest of year, by appointment). **Veterans Lake** has a fishing dock with access for the disabled. **Lake of the Arbuckles** offers fishing for catfish, largemouth bass, sunfish, crappie, and walleyed pike. There is also swimming, water-skiing, boating (launching at three designated ramps only; fee); picnicking, camping (fee), first-come, first-served basis. (Daily) Contact Superintendent, PO Box 201. **FREE**

Limited-Service Hotel

★ **CHICKASAW LODGE.** *W First and Muskogee, Sulphur (73086). Phone 580/622-2156; fax 580/622-3094.* 69 rooms, 2 story. Check-out 11 am. Outdoor pool, children's pool. **$**

Restaurant

★ **BRICKS.** *2112 W Broadway (Hwy 7), Sulphur (73086). Phone 580/622-3125; fax 580/622-5976.* Barbecue menu. Lunch, dinner. Children's menu. **$**

Tahlequah (B-6)

See also Sequoyah State Park, Tenkiller Ferry Lake

Founded 1845
Population 10,398
Elevation 800 ft
Area Code 918
Zip 74464
Information Tahlequah Area Chamber of Commerce, 123 E Delaware St; phone 918/456-3742 or toll-free 800/456-4860
Web Site www.tahlequahok.com

Tribal branches of the Cherokee met here in 1839 to sign a new constitution forming the Cherokee Nation. They had been driven by the US Army from North Carolina, Alabama, Tennessee, and Georgia over the "Trail of Tears." Many died during the long forced march; a new life then began for the survivors, whose influence has since permeated the history and life of Tahlequah.

The Cherokee were the only tribe with a constitution and a body of law written in their own language, using a written alphabet which had been created by Sequoyah. These talented people published the first newspaper in Indian Territory (Oklahoma) and in 1885 established the first commercial telephone line in Oklahoma. The Southwestern Bell Telephone Company, to which it was later sold, established a monument to this remarkable enterprise on the Old Courthouse Square.

The scene of these historic events is now rapidly growing as a vacation area with lakes and a river offering fishing and water sports of all types.

What to See and Do

⭐ **Cherokee Heritage Center.** *21192 S Keeler Dr, Tahlequah (74464). 3 1/2 miles S on Hwy 62, then 1 mile E on Willis Rd. Phone 918/456-6007.* National Museum of Cherokee artifacts; also reconstructed 1890 rural village (weather permitting). Guided tours of 1650 ancient village (May-late Aug, Mon-Sat). **$$**

Float trips on the Illinois River. *Tahlequah.* Contact the Chamber of Commerce.

Murrell Home. *Murrell Home Rd, Park Hill. 3 miles S on Hwy 82, then 1 mile E on Murrell Rd. Phone 918/456-2751.* Pre-Civil War mansion; many original furnishings. (Wed-Sun; closed Jan 1, Thanksgiving, Dec 25) **FREE** Also park and

> **Murrell Home Nature Trail.** *Tahlequah.* Three-quarter-mile trail with special features for those in wheelchairs. Train ties line edges as guides; bird sanctuary, flower beds. **FREE**

Northeastern State University. *600 N Grand Ave, Tahlequah (74464). On Hwy 82. Phone 918/458-2088.* (1909) (9,500 students) Founded on site of the National Cherokee Female Seminary (1889), now Seminary Hall; John Vaughan Library; arboretum; theater productions. Tours of campus and Tahlequah historic places.

Special Events

Cherokee County Fair. *908 South College, Tahlequah. Phone 918/456-6163.* Mid-Sept.

Cherokee National Holiday. *Tahlequah. Phone 918/456-6007.* Celebration of Constitutional Convention. Championship cornstalk bow and arrow shoot, pow wow. Labor Day weekend.

Illinois River Balloon Fest. *Airport, Tahlequah. Phone 918/456-3742.* Balloon race, balloon glow, arts and crafts, carnival, skydiving exhibition, food. Mid-Aug.

Trail of Tears. *Tsa-La-Gi Amphitheater, Tahlequah. Phone 918/456-6007.* Professional cast presents a musical drama depicting the history of the Cherokee Tribe. Mon-Sat evenings. Mid-June-Labor Day.

Limited-Service Hotel

★ ★ **TAHLEQUAH MOTOR LODGE.** *2501 S Muskogee Ave, Tahlequah (74464). Phone 918/456-2350; toll-free 800/480-8705; fax 918/456-4580.* 53 rooms, 2 story. Complimentary full breakfast. Check-out 11 am. Restaurant. Indoor pool, whirlpool. **$**
🖼️

Tenkiller Ferry Lake (B-6)

See also Muskogee, Tahlequah

40 miles SE of Muskogee, off Hwy 64.

This is one of Oklahoma's most beautiful lakes. Its shores consist of recreation areas, cliffs, rock bluffs, and wooded slopes. The Tenkiller Ferry Dam on the Illinois River is 197 feet high and backs up the stream for 34 miles, creating more than 130 miles of shoreline. There are 12,900 acres of water surface. Tenkiller State Park is on Hwy 100, 9 miles north of Gore. There are four recreation areas on its 1,180 acres, with a nature center; pool, bathhouse, water-skiing, fishing, boating (rentals, ramps, marina); picnic facilities, playground, restaurant, gift shop, camping areas, trailer hook-ups (fee), plus cabins. Like other Oklahoma lakes, Tenkiller is lined with marinas, lodges, and boat docks; and the lower Illinois River is famous for its striped bass fishing. It is stocked with 96,000 trout annually. Black bass and channel catfish are also plentiful, but the fish causing the most excitement among anglers are white bass and crappie. Twelve federal recreational areas provide camping for the public. Six of them have electrical hook-ups, showers, and other facilities.

Full-Service Resort

★ ★ **FIN & FEATHER RESORT.** *RR 1, Box 194, Gore (74435). Phone 918/487-5148; fax 918/487-5025. www.finandfeatherresort.com.* The resort is located on beautiful Lake Tenkiller. 83 rooms. Closed Oct-Easter. Pets accepted, some restrictions; fee. Check-in 4 pm, check-out noon. Restaurant. Indoor pool with retractable roof, children's pool, whirlpool. **$**
🐾 🖼️

Tulsa (B-5)

See also Claremore

Founded 1879
Population 367,302
Elevation 750 ft

Area Code 918
Information Convention & Visitors Bureau, 616 S Boston Ave, Suite 100, 74119-1298; phone 918/585-1201 or toll-free 800/558-3311
Web Site www.visittulsa.com

Not an oil derrick is visible to the casual tourist, yet Tulsa is an important energy city. Oil and gas fields surround it, and offices of energy companies are prevalent: more than 600 energy and energy-oriented firms employ 30,000 people. It is the second largest city in Oklahoma, and its atmosphere is cosmopolitan.

The first well came in across the river in 1901. Tulsa invited oilmen to "come and make your homes in a beautiful little city that is high and dry, peaceful and orderly, where there are good churches, stores, schools, and banks, and where our ordinances prevent the desolation of our homes and property by oil wells."

Oil discoveries came in 1905 and 1912, but Tulsa maintained its aloof attitude. Although most of the town owned oil, worked in oil, or supplied the oil fields, culture remained important. Concerts, theater, museums, and activities at three universities, including the University of Tulsa (1894) and Oral Roberts University (1963), give the city a sophisticated quality.

Tulsa has a well-balanced economy. Aviation and aerospace is the city's second largest industry, including Rockwell International and the American Airlines maintenance base, engineering center, reservations center, and revenue and finance division.

With the completion of the Arkansas River Navigation System, Tulsa gained a water route to the Great Lakes and the Gulf of Mexico. The Port of Catoosa, 3 miles from the city and located on the Verdigris River, is at the headwaters of the waterway and is now America's westernmost inland water port.

Public Transportation

Buses (Tulsa Transit), phone 918/585-1195

Airport Tulsa International Airport; weather phone 918/743-3311; cash machines, Main Terminal, upper level.

Information Phone 918/838-5000

Lost and found Phone 918/838-5090

What to See and Do

Arkansas River Historical Society Museum. *Tulsa Port of Catoosa, 5350 Cimarron Rd, Catoosa (74015). 17 miles E on I-44. Phone 918/266-2291.* Located in the Port Authority Building; pictorial displays and operating models trace the history of the 1,450-mile Arkansas River and McClellan-Kerr Navigation System. (Mon-Fri; closed holidays) **FREE**

Bell's Amusement Park. *3901 E 21st, Tulsa (74114). Phone 918/744-1991. www.bellsfamilyfun.com.* Rides include a large wooden roller coaster, log ride, skyride, and bumper boats, plus two miniature golf courses and an arcade. (June-Aug: daily; Apr-May and Sept: weekends) **$$$$**

Big Splash Water Park. *4707 E 21st, Tulsa. Phone 918/749-7385.* Park with two speed slides (75 feet), three flume rides, wave pool, tube ride; children's pool. (May-Labor Day) **$$$$**

Boston Avenue United Methodist Church. *1301 S Boston Ave, Tulsa (74119). Phone 918/583-5181.* (1929) Designed by Adah Robinson, the church facade was executed in Art Deco, the first large-scale use of the style in sacred architecture, and features a main 225-foot tower and many lesser towers decorated with bas-relief pioneer figures. The sanctuary is ornamented with Italian mosaic reredos. (Mon-Fri; closed holidays)

Creek Council Oak Tree. *18th and Cheyenne, Tulsa.* Landscaped plot housing the "Council Oak," which stands as a memorial to the Lochapokas Creek tribe. In 1834, this tribe brought law and order to a near wilderness.

★ **Gilcrease Museum.** *1400 Gilcrease Museum Rd, Tulsa (74127). Phone 918/596-2700.* Founded by Thomas Gilcrease, oil man of Creek descent. Collection of art concerning westward movement, North American development, and Native Americans. Works by Frederic Remington, Thomas Moran, Charles Russell, George Catlin, and others, including colonial artists such as Thomas Sully; Native American artifacts from 12,000 years ago-present. Library houses some 90,000 items, including the earliest known letter sent to Europe from the New World. Beautiful grounds with historic theme gardens. (Daily; closed Dec 25). **DONATION**

Lake Keystone. *1926 S State Hwy 151, Mannford (74127). 20 miles W on Hwy 64, then S on Hwy 151. Phone 918/865-4991.* Covers 715 acres on the south shore of 26,300-acre Keystone Lake. Swimming, water-skiing, fishing, boating (marina, boathouse); hiking trails, picnicking, playground, grocery, snack bar (seasonal), camping (14-day limit; fee), trailer hook-ups, cabins. Fees may be charged at federal recreation sites on Keystone Lake. (Daily) **FREE**

Mohawk Park. *E 36th St N, Tulsa. Phone 918/669-6272.* Fishing; golf course (fee), picnicking, restaurant. Nature center by appointment. Park entrance fee. Within the park is

> **The Tulsa Zoo.** *5701 E 36th St, Tulsa (74135). Phone 918/669-6200.* More than 200 varieties of animals set within 68 acres of landscaped grounds. Zoo features Native American artifacts, geological specimens, dinosaur replica, live plants and animals; train ride (fee). (Daily; closed Dec 25). **$$$**

Oxley Nature Center. *6700 Mohawk Blvd, Tulsa (74115). Phone 918/669-6644.* An 800-acre wildlife sanctuary with numerous nature trails. Visitor center has exhibits and displays. Guided tours by appointment. (Daily; closed holidays) **FREE**

Philbrook Museum of Art. *2727 S Rockford Rd, Tulsa (74114). Phone 918/749-7941; toll-free 800/324-7941.* Exhibits include Italian Renaissance, 19th-century English, American, and Native American paintings; Native American baskets and pottery; Chinese jades and decorative material; Southeast Asian tradeware; African sculpture. Housed in an Italian Renaissance-revival villa on 23 acres; formal and sculpture gardens. Many national touring exhibitions. A 75,000-square-foot addition houses an auditorium, museum school, and restaurant. (Tues-Sun; closed holidays). **$$**

Sherwin Miller Museum of Jewish Art. *2021 E 71st St, Tulsa (74136). Phone 918/294-1366.* Southwest's largest collection of Judaica contains objects representative of Jewish history, art, ceremonial events, and daily life from around the world. (Mon-Fri, also Sun afternoons; closed Jewish holidays) **FREE**

Tulsa Garden Center. *2435 S Peoria Ave, Tulsa (74114). Phone 918/746-5125.* Library, arboretum; extensive dogwood and azalea plantings. Directly north are rose and iris display gardens (late Apr-early May). East of the Center is the Tulsa Park Department Conservatory, with five seasonal displays each year. Garden Center (Mon-Fri; also weekends during some events; closed holidays and Dec 25-Jan 1). **FREE**

Utica Square. *21st and Utica Sts, Tulsa (74114). Phone 918/742-5531. www.uticasquare.com.* Not only does Utica Square offer some of the finest shopping in Tulsa—stores here include Saks Fifth Avenue, Coach, the Bombay Company, and Williams-Sonoma—it offers a setting that is simply breathtaking. The mall is set in a peaceful landscape that features exquisitely manicured gardens, lush trees, a bronze fountain, and charming, old-time clocks—truly not the typical mall. With a setting like this, you may be able to shop all day! But, when you've finally had enough, you can relax at one of Utica Square's many cafés or fine restaurants. Or, take a break and enjoy one of the many free events that take place here throughout the year: Art in the Square showcases the works of hundreds of local artists; Summer's 5th Night features live music every Thursday in summer; and Lights On! gets everyone in the holiday spirit, with holiday carols, a visit with Santa, and the lighting of 175 trees with more than 300,000 lights.

Walnut Creek. *19 miles W on Hwy 64, then NW on 209 W Ave. Phone 918/242-3362.* Covers 1,429 acres on north side of Keystone Lake. Beach, swimming, bathhouse, waterskiing, fishing, boating (ramps); picnicking, playground, equestrian trails, camping, trailer hook-ups. (Daily) **FREE**

Special Events

Chili Cookoff & Bluegrass Festival. *Tulsa. Phone 918/342-5357.* Early Sept.

Discoveryland! Outdoor Theater. *19501 W 41st St, Tulsa (74105). 10 miles W via W 41st St. Phone 918/742-5255.* Presents Rodgers and Hammerstein's *Oklahoma!* in a 2,000-seat outdoor theater complex with a western theme. Authentic Native American dancing. Western musical revue, and barbecue dinner prior to performance. Mon-Sat. Mid-June-late Aug.

Gilcrease Rendezvous. *1400 N Gilcrease Museum, Tulsa (74127). Phone 918/596-2700.* Patterned after fur traders' engagements of days gone by. Late Apr.

Tulsa Powwow. *Expo Square, 4145 E 21st St, Tulsa (74114). Phone 918/744-1113.* Aug.

Tulsa State Fair. *Expo Square, 4145 E 21st St, Tulsa (74114). Phone 918/744-1113.* Late Sept-early Oct.

Limited-Service Hotels

★ ★ **BEST WESTERN TRADE WINDS CENTRAL INN.** *3141 E Skelly Dr, Tulsa (74105). Phone 918/749-5561; toll-free 800/780-7234; fax 918/749-6312. www.bestwestern.com.* 164 rooms, 2 story. Pets accepted; fee. Complimentary continental breakfast. Check-out noon. Restaurant, bar. Fitness room. Outdoor pool, whirlpool. Airport transportation available. **$**

★ **COMFORT SUITES TULSA.** *8338 E 61st S, Tulsa (74133). Phone 918/254-0088; fax 918/254-6820. www.comfortsuites.com.* 49 rooms, 3 story. Complimentary full breakfast. Check-out 11 am. Fitness room. Outdoor pool. **$**

★ ★ **CROWNE PLAZA.** *100 E 2nd St, Tulsa (74103). Phone 918/582-9000; toll-free 800/227-6963; fax 918/560-2261. www.crowneplaza.com.* 462 rooms, 15 story. Check-in 3 pm, check-out noon. High-speed Internet access. Restaurant, bar. Fitness room. Indoor pool, outdoor pool. Airport transportation available. Business center. **$**

★ ★ **DOUBLETREE HOTEL.** *616 W 7th St, Tulsa (74127). Phone 918/587-8000; toll-free 800/222-8733; fax 918/587-1642. www.doubletree.com.* This hotel is only 9 miles from the Tulsa International Airport and offers all amenities and services expected from a large hotel. 417 rooms, 17 story. Pets accepted; fee. Check-out noon. Restaurant, bar. Fitness room. Indoor pool, whirlpool. Business center. **$**

★ ★ **EMBASSY SUITES.** *3332 S 79th E Ave, Tulsa (74145). Phone 918/622-4000; toll-free 800/362-2779; fax 918/665-2347. www.embassysuites.com.* This hotel offers large suites with a full living area and a galley kitchen. Visitors will enjoy the view of the nine-story atrium while having a drink or appetizer. The property is near a large mall, Woodland Hills, restaurants, and more. 240 rooms, 9 story, all suites. Complimentary full breakfast. Check-out noon. Restaurant, bar. Fitness room. Indoor pool, whirlpool. Airport transportation available. **$**

★ **HAMPTON INN.** *3209 S 79th E Ave, Tulsa (74145). Phone 918/663-1000; toll-free 800/426-7866; fax 918/663-0587. www.hamptoninn.com.* 148 rooms, 4 story. Complimentary continental breakfast. Check-out noon. Outdoor pool. **$**

★ **LA QUINTA INN.** *6030 E Skelly Dr, Tulsa (74135). Phone 918/665-2630; toll-free 800/447-0600; fax* 918/858-9744. www.laquinta.com. 130 rooms, 4 story. Complimentary continental breakfast. Check-out 11 am. Outdoor pool. **$**

★ ★ **RADISSON INN AIRPORT TULSA.** *2201 N 77th E Ave, Tulsa (74115). Phone 918/835-9911; toll-free 800/333-3333; fax 918/838-2452. www.radisson.com.* Located near the Thomas Gilcrease Museum, the Tulsa Zoo, and the University of Tulsa along with other attractions, shopping, and restaurants, this hotel offers great rooms, fitness facilities, and friendly service. 172 rooms, 2 story. Check-out 1 pm. Restaurant, bar. Fitness room. Airport transportation available. Business center. **$**

Full-Service Hotels

★ ★ ★ **HILTON TULSA SOUTHERN HILLS.** *7902 S Lewis St, Tulsa (74136). Phone 918/492-5000; toll-free 800/774-1500; fax 918/492-7256. www.hilton.com.* 293 rooms, 11 story. Check-out noon. Restaurant, bar. Fitness room. Outdoor pool. Business center. **$$**

★ ★ ★ **MARRIOTT TULSA SOUTHERN HILLS.** *1902 E 71st St, Tulsa (74136). Phone 918/493-7000; toll-free 800/228-9290; fax 918/523-0950. www.marriott.com.* Offering well-appointed guest rooms with full amenities, this hotel also has an indoor pool and health club available. It is located near golf courses, tennis facilities, the Tulsa Zoo and other area attractions. 383 rooms, 11 story. Check-out noon. Restaurant, bar. Fitness room. Indoor pool. Airport transportation available. Business center. **$$**

★ ★ ★ **SHERATON TULSA HOTEL.** *10918 E 41st St, Tulsa (74146). Phone 918/627-5000; toll-free 800/325-3535; fax 918/627-4003. www.sheraton.com.* This hotel offers a restaurant, lounge, indoor and outdoor pools and more. It is near the Tulsa International Airport, the Philbrook Museum, and the Big Splash Water Park. 325 rooms, 11 story. Pets accepted, some restrictions. Check-out 11 am. Restaurant, bar. Fitness room. Indoor pool, outdoor pool, whirlpool. Airport transportation available. Business center. **$**

Full-Service Inn

★ ★ ★ THE INN AT JARRETT FARM. *38009 Hwy 75 N, Ramona (74061). Phone 918/371-1200; toll-free 877/371-1200; fax 918/371-1300. www.jarrettfarm.com.* Perched on a hilltop 20 miles north of Tulsa, this 115-acre countryside bed-and-breakfast offers plenty of relaxation space and beautifully serene views. One 1,100-square-foot master suite is located in the ranch-style main house while the other ten suites are in charming yellow cottages dotting the property. Fine American-continental cuisine is served at the inn's dining room. 11 rooms. Complimentary full breakfast. Check-in 4 pm, check-out noon. Restaurant. Outdoor pool, whirlpool. **$$**

Restaurants

★ ★ ★ ATLANTIC SEA GRILL. *8321-A E 61st St, Tulsa (74133). Phone 918/252-7966.* This is a well presented seafood restaurant that prides itself on personalized service and good food. The owner's attention to detail is evident in both the décor and the waitstaff's knowledge of the menu. Perfect for a romantic evening. American menu. Lunch, dinner. Bar. Outdoor seating. **$$**

★ BAXTER'S INTERURBAN GRILL. *717 S Houston, Tulsa (74127). Phone 918/585-3134; fax 918/585-3913. www.baxtersgrill.com.* Mexican menu. Lunch, dinner. Closed Sun. Bar. Children's menu. **$**

★ ★ ★ BODEAN SEAFOOD. *3323 E 51st St, Tulsa (74135). Phone 918/743-3861; fax 918/743-3861. www.bodean.net.* Serving creative seafood dishes and boasting a wine list of 200 labels, this restaurant affords a unique dining experience. Seafood menu. Lunch, dinner. Bar. Valet parking. **$$$**

★ ★ CAMMERELLI'S. *1536 E 15th St, Tulsa (74120). Phone 918/582-8900; fax 918/582-8910.* Italian menu. Breakfast, lunch, dinner, late-night, brunch. Bar. **$$**

★ CASA BONITA. *2120 S Sheridan Rd, Tulsa (74129). Phone 918/836-6464.* American, Mexican menu. Lunch, dinner. Children's menu. Game room. **$**

★ ★ ★ FOUNTAINS. *6540 S Lewis Ave, Tulsa (74136). Phone 918/749-9916; fax 918/749-9917. www.fountainsrestaurant.com.* For more than 25 years, this restaurant has been serving its cusine to a loyal following. Old-fashioned, tableside preparations of Bananas Foster add some entertainment to the comfortable dining room. Breakfast, lunch, dinner, Sun brunch. Bar. Children's menu. **$$**

★ ★ GRADY'S AMERICAN GRILL. *7007 S Memorial Dr, Tulsa (74133). Phone 918/254-7733; fax 918/254-2290.* Lunch, dinner, late-night. Bar. **$$**

★ JAMIL'S. *2833 E 51st, Tulsa (74170). Phone 918/742-9097; fax 918/747-7557.* Steak menu. Dinner, late-night. Children's menu. **$$$**

★ METRO DINER. *3001 E 11th, Tulsa (74104). Phone 918/592-2616; fax 918/583-4638.* Breakfast, lunch, dinner, brunch. Closed Easter, Thanksgiving, Dec 25. Bar. Children's menu. **$**

★ ★ ★ POLO GRILL. *2038 Utica Sq, Tulsa (74114). Phone 918/744-4280; fax 918/749-7082. www.pologrill.com.* Traditional favorites such as pasta, veal, pork, and beef tenderloin are served in this fine dining restaurant in Tulsa. Catering both on and off premises is available. American menu. Lunch, dinner. Closed Sun. Bar. **$$$**

★ RICARDOS. *5629 E 41st, Tulsa (74135). Phone 918/622-2668; fax 918/622-2669. www.ricardostulsa.com.* Mexican menu. Lunch, dinner. Closed Sun. Children's menu. **$$**

★ ★ ROSIE'S RIB JOINT. *8125 E 49th, Tulsa (74145). Phone 918/663-2610; fax 918/663-4675. www.rosiesribjoint.com.* Ribs, seafood menu. Dinner. Closed holidays. Bar. **$$**

★ ★ TIAMO. *6024A S Sheridan, Tulsa (74145). Phone 918/499-1919; fax 918/499-1934.* Italian menu. Lunch, dinner. Bar. **$$**

★ ★ ★ WARREN DUCK CLUB. *6110 S Yale, Tulsa (74136). Phone 918/495-1000; fax 918/495-1944. www.doubletree.com.* Don't fill up on cookies at the Doubletree Hotel in Tulsa, or you will miss out on this fine dining restaurant offering views of the lawn and a spectacular appetizer and dessert buffet. American menu. Dinner, late-night. Bar. Children's menu. Valet parking. **$$$**

Vinita (A-6)

See also Grand Lake, Miami, Pryor

Population 5,804
Elevation 700 ft
Area Code 918
Zip 74301
Information Vinita Area Chamber of Commerce, 125 S

Scraper, PO Box 882; phone 918/256-7133
Web Site www.vinita.com

Among the oldest towns in the state, Vinita was established in 1871 within the Cherokee Nation. Many stately homes attest to the town's cultural significance during the late 1800s. Vinita is also home to one of the world's largest McDonald's restaurants.

What to See and Do

Eastern Trails Museum. *215 W Illinois, Vinita (74301). Phone 918/256-2115.* Historic displays, articles belonging to Vinnie Ream, Native American artifacts. (Mon-Sat afternoons; closed holidays) **FREE**

Special Event

Will Rogers Memorial Rodeo and Parade. *American Legion Rodeo Grounds, Vinita. Phone 918/256-7133.* Late Aug.

Waurika (D-3)

See also Duncan

Population 2,088
Elevation 881 ft
Area Code 580
Zip 73573
Web Site www.waurika.net

Waurika is the site of Monument Rocks, a high point of the Chisholm Trail in southern Oklahoma. Early drovers made two piles of sandstone boulders, each about 12 feet high, on a flat-topped mesa, enabling the viewer to see 10-15 miles in either direction.

What to See and Do

Chisholm Trail Historical Museum. *Hwys 70 and 81, Waurika. 1 mile E via Hwy 70. Phone 580/228-2166.* Chisholm Trail Gallery depicts history and artifacts from 1867; Pioneer Gallery shows development of local history; slide presentation. (Tues-Sun; closed holidays) **FREE**

Waurika Lake. *Hastings. 6 miles NW via Hwy 5. Phone 580/963-2111.* Dam on Beaver Creek, a tributary of the Red River. Swimming, water-skiing, fishing, boating; hunting, picnicking, camping (fee; many sites have electrical hook-ups). Information center (Mon-Fri). (Daily) **FREE**

Weatherford (B-3)

See also Clinton

Settled 1898
Population 10,124
Elevation 1,647 ft
Area Code 580
Zip 73096
Information Chamber of Commerce, 522 W Rainey, PO Box 857; phone 580/772-7744 or toll-free 800/725-7744
Web Site www.weatherfordchamber.com

Weatherford is a progressive, growing city with a diversified economy and is the home of Southwestern Oklahoma State University (1901) as well as *Gemini* and *Apollo* astronaut Thomas P. Stafford.

What to See and Do

Crowder Lake. *Weatherford. 9 miles S on Hwy 54, then 3/4 mile E.* Swimming, fishing, boating.

Red Rock Canyon State Park. *20 miles E on I-40, then 4 1/2 miles S on Hwy 281, near Hinton. Phone 405/542-6344.* Covers 310 acres. Swimming pool, bathhouse; hiking, picnicking, playground, camping, trailer hook-ups (fee). (Daily) **FREE**

Thomas P. Stafford Air and Space Museum. *Stafford Field, 3000 E Logan Rd, Weatherford (73096). Phone 580/772-5871.* Houses memorabilia of the former astronaut. (Daily) **FREE**

Special Event

Southwest Festival of the Arts. *Weatherford. Phone 580/772-7744.* Crafts, performing arts, concerts. Second Sat in Sept.

Limited-Service Hotel

★ **BEST WESTERN MARK MOTOR HOTEL.**
525 E Main St, Weatherford (73096). Phone 580/772-3325; toll-free 800/780-7234; fax 580/772-8950. www.bestwestern.com. 63 rooms, 2 story. Pets accepted, some restrictions. Complimentary full breakfast. Check-out noon. Outdoor pool. **$**

Restaurant

★ ★ **T-BONE STEAK HOUSE.** *1805 E Main St, Weatherford (73096). Phone 580/772-6329; fax 580/772-3897. www.tbonesteakhouse.com.* Lunch, dinner. Bar. Children's menu. **$$**

Woodward (A-2)

Population 12,340
Elevation 1,905 ft
Area Code 580
Information Chamber of Commerce, 1006 Oklahoma Ave, PO Box 1026, 73802; phone 580/256-7411 or toll-free 800/364-5352
Web Site www.woodwardok.com

What to See and Do

Boiling Springs State Park. *Hwy 54, Woodward. 1 mile N on Hwy 34, then 5 miles E on Hwy 34C. Phone 580/256-7664.* Covers 820 acres and has a 7-acre lake. Swimming pool, bathhouse; fishing; hiking, picnicking, playground, concession, camping, trailer hookups (fee), cabins. (Daily) **FREE**

Fort Supply Lake. *Woodward. 15 miles NW via Hwy 270; 1 mile S of Fort Supply. Phone 580/766-2701.* Swimming, fishing; hunting, camping (hook-ups; fees). (Daily) **FREE**

Glass Mountains. *Woodward. E on Hwy 15, just E of jct Hwy 281, Hwy 15, W of Orienta.* Name derived from the mountains' surface, which is made up of sparkling selenite crystals. Roadside rest area.

Historic Fort Supply. *Woodward. 15 miles NW via Hwy 270. Phone 580/766-3767.* Established as a temporary cavalry supply camp in the late 1800s, the fort endured as a trail stop between Kansas, Texas, and Oklahoma. Restored original buildings include the Powder Monkey's House and Teamsters Cabin (circa 1870), the Commanding Officer's Quarters (1878), and the Officer's Quarters (circa mid-1880s). The Guard House (1892) is now a museum. Tours. (Mon-Fri, closed holidays) **FREE**

Plains Indians & Pioneers Museum. *2009 Williams Ave (Hwy 270), Woodward (73801). Phone 580/256-6136.* Changing and permanent displays depict Native American culture and early life on the plains. Pioneer, cowboy, and Native American artifacts and clothing; collection of personal belongings of Temple Houston, son of Sam Houston; exhibits from early-day banks;

original building from historic Fort Supply; agriculture building; art center with changing exhibits. (Tues-Sat; closed holidays) **FREE**

Limited-Service Hotel

★ ★ **NORTHWEST INN.** *Hwy 270 S and 1st St, Woodward (73802). Phone 580/256-7600; toll-free 800/727-7606; fax 580/254-2274.* 124 rooms, 2 story. Pets accepted; fee. Check-out noon. Restaurant, bar. Indoor pool. **$**

Looking for some rejuvenation? An excursion to Hot Springs, Arkansas, just might do the trick. From the Oklahoma-Arkansas border, the restorative powers of the Hot Springs' bathhouses are less than three hours away. After an exhaustive tour around dusty Oklahoma, a little stress-relieving soak will do the soul and body good.

Hot Springs and Hot Springs National Park, AR

Settled Town of Hot Springs: 1807
Population 35,750
Elevation 632 ft
Area Code 501
Information Convention & Visitors Bureau, 134 Convention Blvd, PO Box K, 71902; phone 501/321-2277 or toll-free 800/772-2489
Web Site www.nps.gov/hosp and www.hotsprings.org

One of the most popular spas and resorts in the United States, the colorful city of Hot Springs surrounds portions of the nearly 4,700-acre Hot Springs National Park. Approximately 1 million gallons of thermal water flow daily from the 47 springs within the park. The springs have been administered by the federal government since 1832.

At an average temperature of 143° F, the water flows to a reservoir under the headquarters building; here it is distributed to bathhouses through insulated pipes. Some of it is cooled to 90° F without being exposed to air or mixed with other water. Bathhouses mix cooled and hot thermal water to regulate bath temperatures. The only differences among bathhouses are in the appointments and service.

The Libbey Memorial Physical Medicine Center specializes in hydrotherapy treatments given under the supervision of a registered physical therapist. Patients may be referred to this center by registered physicians or may get a standard bath without a referral.

Hot Springs, however, is more than a spa. It is a cosmopolitan city visited by travelers from all over the world; it is also a delightful vacation spot in the midst of beautiful wooded hills, valleys, and lakes of the Ouachita region. Swimming, boating, and water sports are available at nearby Catherine, Hamilton, and Ouachita lakes. All three offer good year-round fishing for bream, crappie, bass, and rainbow trout. The 42nd President of the United States, William Jefferson Clinton, grew up here. A Ranger District office of the Ouachita National Forests is located in Hot Springs.

What to See and Do

Arkansas Alligator Farm & Petting Zoo. *847 Whittington Ave, Hot Springs (71901). Phone 501/623-6172. www.hotspringsusa.com/gatorfarm.* Houses alligators, rhesus monkeys, mountain lions, llamas, pygmy goats, ducks, and other animals. (Daily) **$$**

Auto tours. *Fountain St and Hot Springs Mountain Dr, Hot Springs. Phone 501/321-2277.* Just north of Bathhouse Row, drive from the end of Fountain Street up Hot Springs Mountain Drive to scenic overlooks at Hot Springs Mountain Tower and a picnic area on the mountaintop. West Mountain Dr, starting from either Prospect Avenue (on the south) or from Whittington Avenue (on the north) also provides excellent vistas of the city and surrounding countryside.

Bath House Show. *701 Central Ave, Hot Springs (71901). Phone 501/623-1415. www.thebathhouseshow .com.* Two-hour show of music and comedy acts derivative of 1930s-present; musical anthologies, re-enactments of radio shows. (Feb-Dec, schedule varies; closed Jan) **$$$$**

Belle of Hot Springs. *5200 Central Ave (Hwy 7 S), Hot Springs (71913). Phone 501/525-4438. www.belleriverboat.com.* Sightseeing, lunch, and dinner cruises along Lake Hamilton on the 400-passenger vessel (Feb-Nov, daily). Charter cruises available.

Coleman's Crystal Mine. *5386 N Hwy 7, Jesseville (71909). 16 miles N on Hwy 7 N. Phone 501/984-5328.* Visitors may dig for quartz crystals; tools supplied. Shop. (Daily; closed Dec 25) **$$$**

Dryden Potteries. *341 Whittington Ave, Hot Springs (71901).* Phone 501/623-4201. www.drydenpottery.com. Pottery-making demonstrations. (Mon-Fri 9 am-3:30 pm, Sat from 9:30 am; closed Jan 1, Thanksgiving, Dec 25) **FREE**

Hot Springs Mountain Tower. *401 Hot Springs Mountain Dr, Hot Springs (71902).* Phone 501/623-6035. Tower rises 216 feet above Hot Springs National Park; glass-enclosed elevator rides 1,256 feet above sea level for spectacular view of Ouachita Mountains; fully enclosed viewing area and higher up, there's an open-air deck. (Daily; closed Jan 1, Thanksgiving, Dec 24-25) **$$$**

Josephine Tussaud Wax Museum. *250 Central Ave, Hot Springs (71901).* Phone 501/623-5836. www.rideaduck.com. Set in the former Southern Club, which was the city's largest casino and supper club until the late 1960s, this museum displays more than 100 wax figures. (Summer: Sun-Thurs 9 am-8 pm, Fri-Sat 9 am-9 pm; winter: Sun-Thurs 9:30 am-5 pm, Fri-Sat 9:30 am-8 pm; closed Jan 1, Thanksgiving, Dec 25) **$$**

Lake Catherine State Park. *5386 N Hwy 7, Hot Springs Village (71909).* S and E via Hwy 128, 171. Phone 501/984-5396. www.arkansasstateparks.com.

Mid-America Science Museum. *500 Mid-America Blvd, Hot Springs (71913).* Phone 501/767-3461. www.midamericamuseum.com. Exhibits focus on life, energy, matter, perception, state of Arkansas. Museum features 35,000-gallon freshwater aquarium; erosion table; laser theater. Snack bar (seasonal), gift shop. (Memorial Day-Labor Day: daily 9:30 am-6 pm; rest of year: Tues-Sun 10 am-5 pm; closed Jan 1, Thanksgiving, Dec 24-25) **$$$**

National Park & Hot Springs Duck Tours. *406 Central Ave, Hot Springs (71901).* Phone 501/321-2911; toll-free 800/682-7044. www.rideaduck.com. The "Amphibious Duck" travels on both land and water. Board in the heart of Hot Springs and proceed onto Lake Hamilton around St. John's Island. (Mar-Oct: daily; Nov-Feb: weather-permitting) **$$$**

Ouachita National Forest. *100 Reserve St, Hot Springs (71902).* 12 miles W on Hwy 270 or 20 miles N on Hwy 7. Phone 501/321-5202. www.fs.fed.us.oonf/ouachita.htm. The Ouachita (WASH-i-taw), located in 15 counties in west-central Arkansas and southeast Oklahoma, covers approximately 1.7 million acres and includes 7 wilderness areas, 35 developed recreation areas, 7 equestrian trails, 9 navigable rivers, and 8 lakes suitable for boating. Some recreation areas charge fees. For more information, contact the Forest Supervisor, PO Box 1270, 71902. (Daily) On Lake Ouachita is

Lake Ouachita State Park. *5451 Mountain Pine Rd, Mountain Pine (71956).* 3 miles W on Hwy 270, 12 miles N on Hwy 227. Phone 501/767-9366. www.lakeouachita.com. Approximately 400 acres. Swimming, fishing, boating (rentals, marina); hiking trails, picnicking, camping (hookups, dump station), cabins. Interpretive programs, exhibits. (Daily)

Tiny Town. *374 Whittington Ave, Hot Springs (71901).* Phone 501/624-4742. Indoor train town with trains across America; mechanical display; handmade miniatures. (Apr-Nov, Mon-Sat) **$$**

⭐ **Walking tour.** Start at

Park Headquarters and Visitor Center. *101 Reserve St, Hot Springs (71901).* Phone 501/624-3383. Exhibit on workings and origin of the hot springs. A self-guided nature trail starts here and follows the Grand Promenade. Visitor center is located in the Hill Wheatley Plaza at the park entrance (daily; closed Jan 1, Dec 25). Gulpha Gorge Campground is available for stays limited to 14 days April-October, and to 30 days in a calendar year (fee). Inquire at National Park Fordyce Visitor Center on Bathhouse Row.

Grand Promenade. *Grand Promenade and Fountain sts, Hot Springs (71902).* Phone 501/624-3383. Leads through a landscaped park above and behind Bathhouse Row, offering pleasant vistas of the city.

Bathhouse Row. *Central Ave, Hot Springs (71902).* Phone 501/624-3383. Self-guided tours of the Fordyce Bathhouse are offered. (Daily; closed July 4, Thanksgiving, Dec 25)

Two Open Hot Springs. *Hot Springs. At the S end of Bathouse Row.* Phone 501/623-6172.

Special Event

Thoroughbred racing. *Oaklawn Jockey Club, 2705 Central Ave, Hot Springs (71902).* Phone 501/623-4411; toll-free 800/625-5296. www.oaklawn.com. While watching and wagering on live races at Oaklawn, fans can also follow simulcast races or dine on a variety of tasty treats. Daily, Jan-Apr.

Limited-Service Hotels

★ **DAYS INN.** *106 Lookout Pt, Hot Springs (71913). Phone 501/525-5666; toll-free 800/995-9559; fax 501/525-5666. www.daysinn.com.* 58 rooms, 2 story. Check-out 11 am. Outdoor pool, whirlpool. **$**
🏊

★ **HAMPTON INN.** *151 Temperance Hill Rd, Hot Springs (71913). Phone 501/525-7000; toll-free 800/426-7866; fax 501/525-7626. www.hamptoninn.com.* 82 rooms, 4 story. Complimentary continental breakfast. Check-out 11 am. Outdoor pool. **$**
🏊

Full-Service Hotels

★ ★ ★ **ARLINGTON RESORT HOTEL AND SPA.** *239 Central Ave, Hot Springs (71901). Phone 501/623-7771; toll-free 800/643-1502; fax 501/623-2243. www.arlingtonhotel.com.* Guests will find total relaxation and enjoyment at this resort in the beautiful Ouachita Mountains of the Hot Springs National Park. Guests can unwind in twin cascading pools or in the refreshing outdoor mountainside hot tub. 484 rooms, 11 story. Check-out 11 am. Restaurant, bar. Fitness room. Two outdoor pools, whirlpool. Tennis. Grand old hotel (circa 1925); overlooks park. **$**
🏋 🏊 🎾

★ ★ ★ **THE AUSTIN HOTEL & CONVENTION CENTER.** *305 Malvern Ave, Hot Springs (71901). Phone 501/623-6600; toll-free 877/623-6697; fax 501/624-7160. www.theaustinhotel.com.* This wonderful getaway is located in the Hot Springs Park with a spectacular view of the Ouachita Mountains. It is a unique setting for guests to rejuvenate themselves with a visit to the famous spa in the park. Art galleries and music shows are just a few miles away. 200 rooms, 14 story. Check-out 11 am. Restaurant, bar. Spa. Indoor, outdoor pool; whirlpool. **$$**
🏊

Restaurants

★ ★ **BOHEMIA.** *517 Park Ave, Hot Springs (71901). Phone 501/623-9661; fax 501/623-9661.* Czech, German menu. Lunch, dinner. Closed Sun; holidays; also part of Dec, Jan. Children's menu. **$**

★ **CAJUN BOILERS.** *2806 Albert Pike Hwy, Hot Springs (71913). Phone 501/767-5695; fax 501/767-0952.* Cajun menu. Dinner. Closed Sun-Mon; Thanksgiving, Dec 25. Children's menu. Dock for boat dining. **$$**

★ ★ **COY'S STEAK HOUSE.** *300 Coy St, Hot Springs (71901). Phone 501/321-1414; fax 501/321-1497.* Seafood, steak menu. Dinner. Closed Thanksgiving, Dec 24-25, 31. Bar. Children's menu. Valet parking. **$$$**

★ **FADED ROSE.** *210 Central Ave, Hot Springs (71901). Phone 501/624-3200; fax 501/624-5380.* Seafood, steak menu. Lunch, dinner. Closed Thanksgiving, Dec 25. In former hotel (1889). **$$**

★ ★ ★ **HAMILTON HOUSE.** *130 Van Lyell Trail, Hot Springs (71913). Phone 501/525-2727; fax 501/525-1717.* This is the most appropriate choice in town for a dress-up, fine-dining occasion. The restaurant occupies four stories of an old estate home with seating in several cozy dining rooms. The quiet, peninsula setting is on beautiful Lake Hamilton. American menu. Dinner. Closed holidays. Bar. Children's menu. Valet parking. Outdoor seating. **$$$**

★ ★ **HOT SPRINGS BRAU-HOUSE.** *801 Central Ave, Hot Springs (71901). Phone 501/624-7866.* German menu. Dinner. Closed Mon; holidays. Bar. Children's menu. Outdoor seating. In cellar of 110-year-old building. **$**

★ **MCCLARD'S BAR-B-Q.** *505 Albert Pike, Hot Springs (71913). Phone 501/624-9586.* Lunch, dinner. Closed Sun-Mon; Thanksgiving, Dec 25. Children's menu. Casual attire. **$**

★ **MILLER'S CHICKEN AND STEAK HOUSE.** *4723 Central Ave, Hot Springs (71913). Phone 501/525-8861.* Dinner. Closed Mon; also Dec-mid-Jan. Bar. Children's menu. **$$**

★ **MOLLIE'S.** *538 W Grand Ave, Hot Springs (71901). Phone 501/623-6582.* Kosher menu. Lunch, dinner. Closed Sun; Jan 1, Thanksgiving, Dec 25. Bar. Children's menu. Outdoor seating. **$$**

Index

Notes

Notes

Notes

Notes